Pioneers, Reformers, & Millionaires

Elizabeth A. Homer 3/2/15

ELIZABETH A. HOMER

Attention colleges and universities, corporations, and history organizations: Quantity discounts are available on bulk purchases of this book for educational purposes, fund-raising, or gift giving. Special books or book excerpts can also be created to fit your specific needs.

Find Elizabeth Homer on Facebook at www.facebook.com/liz.homer.book

Visit the *Pioneers, Reformers, & Millionaires* website at www.elizabethhomer.com for book information, sales, and contact information.

ISBN-13: 978-0-9915530-0-6

ISBN-13: 978-0-9915530-1-3 (pbk)

ISBN-13: 978-0-9915530-2-0 (e-bk)

Edited by: Janet M. Homer

Design and Production by: Judy Seling, Seling Design LLC
Cover art by: Mark Hahn
Printed by: McNaughton and Gunn, Inc., Saline, Michigan, USA

This book is dedicated to my mother,
Mary Ann Homer, who gave me her Michigan
history book collection when I became a curator
and listened to many drafts of this book but did
not learn how it all turned out.

Contents

Part I Pioneers 1834-1870

List of Illustrations

The Capital Area District Library has gratuitously provided many of the photos, designated as CADL.

Other contributors are The Michigan Women's Historical Center and The Turner-Dodge House.

Foreword

Elizabeth Homer's *Pioneers, Reformers, and Millionaires* is a welcome addition to the literature on early Lansing history. Homer tells the story of nineteenth century Lansing from the perspective of a number of the founding families, but these are not the only stories in the book. These individuals, generations of Turners, Dodges, Longyears and others, grew up in and with Lansing. The men, women, and children of these families witnessed and shaped local, state, and national historical events. And historical events there were---from the settling of Lansing in a thicket of forest and swamps to the establishment of industry and a state capital, to the emergence of progressive organizations and cultural institutions.

There are many satisfying features of this book. Homer tells both fascinating personal and crucial national stories. We learn of the day-to-day survival on the frontier, courtship and marriage, and family struggles as well as political divisions, electoral contests, and institution building in the growing city. And women were involved in almost all of these stories. Women founded the settlement, participated in the creation of the first institutions, and weighed in on the important issues of their day such as suffrage and prohibition. This book provides a unique perspective on all of the major historical developments in the nineteenth century, settlement and migration, commerce and industry, the Civil War, Progressivism, and many more, as experienced in Lansing, Michigan.

Lisa Fine, PhD., Michigan State University
Center for Gender in Global Context,
Co-Director and Professor of History
Author of *The Story of Reo Joe. Work, Kin,
and Community in Autotown, U.S.A*

The time will come when our names will be lost and our places know us no more. Yet we shall survive in the memories of our friends as long as the remembrance will serve any good purpose, and then our work and thought and influence will mingle with the great ocean of human achievement, and the sum total of that will be something more, and something different from what it would have been without us.

Augusta Chapin, 1885
Michigan Pioneer Historical Society

Introduction

In the beginning, I would not have guessed this book would evolve into an epic narrative history of two generations of Michigan pioneers and reformers. When I decided to write this book, I had three goals in mind. I wanted to tell the story of the Turners and the Dodges who once lived in the newly restored Turner-Dodge House in Lansing, Michigan's capital city. I wanted to use primary source material because I love to hear the unfiltered voices of the past tell their own story. I also wanted to include women's history, though I wasn't sure how I was going to do that. I was thinking along the lines of a local story, not a story of state or national interest. That is because I did not know what the story was going to be. I would have to research all of that.

I was the curator of the Turner-Dodge House from 1997 through 2008, after 10 years of working at the Michigan Women's Historical Center and Hall of Fame. When I arrived, the City of Lansing had just completed a wonderful restoration of the exterior of the house and some basic work toward restoration of the interior. The house was empty, but arts and cultural activities were offered through the Lansing Parks and Recreation Department. I immediately began to work toward restoration of the interior, but my curiosity drove me to researching the family who lived there in my spare time in the evenings and on weekends. I soon found that this was not a story about a single extended family but of a group of outstanding individuals who came to Ingham County before statehood. They were from western New York. What happened to them is a story composed of many stories, so that is the shape this book took.

Part I tells the story of how these pioneers came to central Michigan during a depression, the founding of the capitol city in seven months, how abolitionist values led to formation of the Republican Party, their efforts to gain rights for women, and the work of these pioneers to found educational institutions, including the Michigan Female College and the founding of the State Agricultural College. The rise of corporations, particularly railroad corporations, and local development of business and transportation after the war are also important themes in the lives of this circle of friends.

When I completed Part I, I thought to myself, "the second generation of pioneers can hardly have been so interesting or so fine. I will just tell a little about the Dodges and the women's history that I know will be there and that will be it." Then I found that the second generation James Turner, James Munroe Turner, was like his father. He was also six feet, four inches tall, kind, honest, and generous. He was a folk hero to much of the state, yet until now I had never heard of him, and no one else knew of him either. The second generation pioneers were reformers as were their parents who were the founders of the Republican Party. Their impact spanned the political, economic, social, and educational development of the state, including the Upper Peninsula. They were grappling with monumental societal problems, ones that dog us today. This section includes tumultuous stories of politics, corruption, and reform. There are heroes and heroines, and some true villains.

In over twenty years as a curator of public history I have talked with many visitors. I know people love history, especially the story aspect of history. They often express the hope that if we study history we will not keep making the same mistakes. That is why I think this story is particularly important. These people were grappling with the issues of their times: cyclical financial disasters; slavery and reconstruction; the rise of corporations, trusts, and monopolies; women's rights; worker's rights; the inherent difficulties facing public education, corruption and greed; and the concentration of wealth in the hands of a few. This is why I linger a bit on some of the lessons reformers were trying to impart to ordinary people during the 1890s, a period the present-day situation is often compared with. Perhaps we can learn those lessons and better understand the present.

I wanted to show my subjects' ideas and how they viewed things. If we really want to learn from history, we must study ideas. Their stories are from original materials of the time, unfiltered by interpretation or evaluation. Thanks to Google and to the University of Michigan that made its library collections available online, Michigan material is much more accessible than an earlier research effort could have known. The Bentley Library at the University of Michigan preserved many important materials and I am fortunate to live within blocks of the State Library and Archive and the Capital Area District Library.

The best resource for determining the course of the book was the two scrapbooks that belonged to Marian Munroe Turner, given to the Turner-Dodge House by a son of Abby and Frank Dodge, also named Franklin Dodge. The scrapbooks were made for preserving newspaper articles, a practice that was popular. The articles were about family and friends but also reflected her interests and often dealt with causes and ideas. The difficulty was that the dates and names of the publications were not noted on the clippings. They weren't in any order, as though they had been saved for a long while and then put into the scrapbooks. Nonetheless, they provided a roadmap to Marian's life and times.

Ingham County, the home to state government, was fortunate in having several good early histories, including one sponsored by the Ingham County Pioneer Society, edited by Franc Adams, and one by a Turner family member, Frank Turner, which was especially useful for his insights about Lansing. Both are by Ingham County pioneers. Another help was the Michigan Pioneer History Society, to which many of the key figures in this book belonged. The organization compiled many original documents and collected memories of those early days for a total of forty volumes, now searchable online. Lansing was also fortunate to have an excellent newspaper throughout most of the nineteenth century, written by talented journalists and editors, and known by various versions of the name *State Republican*.

Some of the concerns that come up when using primary source material are spelling, punctuation, and grammar that are different from present day usage. Sometimes they are matters of antiquated practices, sometimes they are errors. I just left them as they were written with only an occasional small change for readability when necessary. I did not use [sic] to mark errors because I found it distracting and unnecessary. My word processing program objected to terms such as chairman and businessman and offered alternatives. I was glad for the advice but I ignored it and left the gender-biased terms when quoting primary source material. I even used them myself sometimes because modern usage seemed to be disruptive. Sometimes people said things that we find rude or offensive; I left those in, too, assuming the reader will recognize them for what they are.

History books have concentrated on men's history, though this is beginning to change somewhat. It is still rare to be able to read about women's history mainstreamed in its full context. I am sure that future efforts will improve on this attempt. With my experience as the first curator of the Michigan Women's Historical Center, I certainly wanted to find out about the women in this group of friends. I knew from experience that there was more to learn than what is currently known about the women of Lansing and how they participated in political, social, and religious institutions and movements, and how they engaged in community building.

It is not simply because of a lack of sources that women's history has been so long unreported. Sources are available. Some groups wrote their own histories which were preserved at the city library or by the organization. Women who were members of the Michigan Women's Press Association were often activists, such as suffragist Belle Perry of the *Charlotte Tribune*, and gave above-average attention to women. However, I found that the Turner and Munroe women, especially Abby, were active in musical efforts, and this aspect of culture was not as well preserved except for brief announcements of performances. Some women used only their husband's name or initials, so I searched out their given names where I could. Some historians never mentioned the wives of men pioneers in their stories, but I sought out their names, which gave a different dimension to their stories. Women's individual accomplishments were sometimes hard to discern, but many of the stories about what they and their groups did are seeing the light of day for the first time in well over one hundred years, thanks to women's efforts to preserve their own history.

The journey in pursuit of primary source materials that reveal the story of these courageous women and men was a long one, seven years. I made a trip to Western New York, to Cazenovia, Rochester, and Cheektowaga near Buffalo. I traveled to Marquette, Negaunee, the Keweenaw, and through the Ottawa National Forest to Crystal Falls. I was driven by curiosity and by the inspiring character of many of our pioneers. I hope their names survive a little longer in our memories so that their work and thought and influence can serve as a model, and in some cases a warning, and so our own accomplishments can contribute to the great ocean of human achievement in the most beneficial and public-spirited way.

Elizabeth A. Homer

Acknowledgements

Many times an author says of her editor, I couldn't have done it without her. But when you have an editor who is willing to get as deeply involved as you are and give it her intellectual skills and abilities right along with you, that is an invaluable gift. My sister Janet Homer is a poet, writer, and taught writing at the college level. For the last five years she has guided this project through several phases of editing, providing hours of service and valuable advice. This book is much better than it might have been because of her work. Others who have given me help and advice over the years are Nancy Homer, Phil Kline, Camilla Dean Liebold, Karen Petersmark, and Joan C. Smith. Bill Ballenger, Bill Castanier, and Lisa Fine gave it a final read and prepared comments for the book. I am so very grateful to them all.

After the City of Lansing purchased the Turner-Dodge House in 1974, many people were involved with the preservation of the house, and still are through the Friends of Turner-Dodge House. I would like to acknowledge their help in basic research about the first generation of Turners. They included Sue Cantlon, first City of Lansing staff, and early Friends of Turner-Dodge House who produced a brochure: Rick Cantwell, Linda Peckham, Jacquie Sewell, and Jack Thompson and Geneva Wiskeman who provided background for use in the City of Lansing's 1993 Master Plan for the building. After I came to the house in November of 1997, Ron Turner (a descendant of James Turner's brother, Richard) helped by transcribing some of the newspaper clippings from the family scrapbooks and making genealogical charts, and Jerry Lawler generously shared his research on the early history of Lansing. Now both of these good friends are deceased. Marc Levitt researched the Saginaw Mill strike court case, and Rita LaMoreaux researched Chief Okemos. Both were Turner-Dodge House staff. I was also very fortunate to be able to talk with Patty Pemberton, granddaughter of Abby and Frank Dodge, with their grandson Robert McLean and great grandson John Pemberton.

This book is made possible through the efforts of the people of the State of Michigan who have preserved our history through our many libraries and archives and through many national efforts as well. I am so glad we do. We are also fortunate to have the Michigan Women's Historical Center and Hall of Fame in our state, which is a privately funded effort to discover women's history and the John M. Longyear Research Library, Marquette Regional History Center.

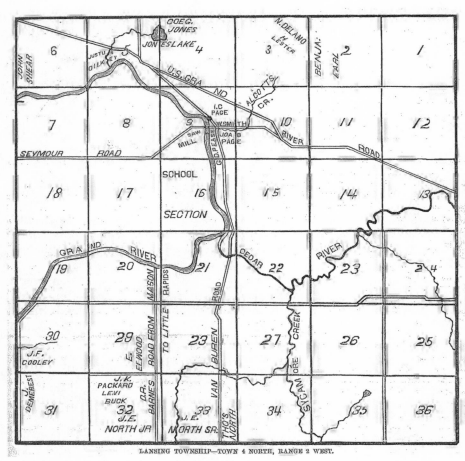

LANSING TOWNSHIP—TOWN 4 NORTH, RANGE 2 WEST.

Plat showing the location of all the actual settlers in the township in August, 1845. Made by James Turner, land-agent. Also showing the wagon roads then laid out or in use. Durant, p. 191. CADL photo.

Main Characters

Marian Munroe was the oldest of nine children. She grew up in Cheektowaga (Amherst) near Buffalo, New York. Her parents were Jesse and Harriet (Parker) Munroe who settled in Eagle, in Clinton County, in 1834.

Hiram and Charity Parker, Marian's uncle and aunt, came to Michigan at the same time and settled near Mason in Ingham County, south of Eagle.

Marian Munroe married James Turner.

Harriet Munroe married John W. Longyear.

Adella Munroe married Daniel Case.

Betsy Munroe married Charles Turner, James' brother.

James Turner lived in Cazenovia, New York. He had nine siblings. He also had step-siblings who were the children of his father Francis Stiles Turner and Lydia Bushnell, but they stayed in New York. James' mother was Deborah Morton Turner. Deborah and Francis Turner and their youngest children settled in Leoni, Michigan between Ann Arbor and Jackson, in 1836. They were Whigs.

They came at a time when other Cazenovians moved to Central Michigan, including Austin Blair, the future governor of Michigan, and William Jackson, James' first employer. Both Blair and Jackson had attended the Cazenovia Seminary of the Genesee Conference of the Methodist Church in New York.

Frank Turner was the son of James' uncle, Richard Turner. Frank became an Ingham County historian.

Daniel L. Case was originally from near Three Rivers, Canada, coming to Michigan in 1830. He was a lifelong friend and business partner of James in many enterprises. Originally a Democrat.

John W. Longyear was from Sandakan, Ulster County, New York. He joined his family already settled in Ingham County in 1844. His brothers were Ephraim, Howard, and Stephen. He studied law with Daniel Case. Originally a Whig.

Abigail Rogers was from Avon, New York. She founded the Michigan Female College in Lansing. Her sister was Delia Rogers. Both Abigail and John W. Longyear had been connected with the Lima Seminary, before coming to Michigan. The Lima Seminary was part of the Genesee Conference of the Methodist Church. Her nephew and niece, Mary and Schuyler F Seager, joined their aunt to teach at the Female College. Abby Turner Dodge was named after her. Schuyler became John W. Longyear's law partner.

Hiram H. Smith came to Michigan in 1835. He grew up in Vermont and took up merchandising in Granville, New York. He was a friend of James Turner, Daniel Case, and John W. Longyear and a business partner in many of their enterprises. Originally a Democrat. His daughter Francis Dennison Smith married Ephraim Longyear.

Part I

Pioneers
1834–1869

Chapter 1

To Be A Pioneer

In 1834, the *Niles Register* reported from Detroit that the arrivals had reached 960 in one day, up from 175 per day the previous year. "The streets of Detroit were full of wagons loading and departing for the West, principally for the region about the Grand river. The character of these emigrants is in every respect a subject of felicitation. They will give Michigan a capital stock of wealth and moral worth unequaled by any of the newly-formed States, and scarcely approximated by Ohio."[1] More than half the new settlers coming into central Michigan were from western New York and among them was a remarkable and influential group destined to be close friends all of their lives and into the next generation. At the heart of this group were Marian Munroe and James Turner. Our story begins with the arrival of the Munroe family in Michigan.

Journey to Michigan Territory

At the outset, Marian's father and mother had come with a wave of Vermonters recruited by the Holland Land Development Company to settle in the wilderness of western New York in 1816. Her father, Jesse, was 25 at the time and her mother, Harriet Parker Munroe, was just 17. Marian wrote of her mother, "No small change was this from the house of comfort, culture and refinement she had left. But these pioneers brought with them brave hearts, full of courage and hope; and a few years of hardy toil saw their hopes changed to fruition and the wilderness blossomed as the rose."[2]

While some pioneers came to the Northwest Territory of the Great Lakes with little money or material belongings, the Munroes were not poor. Their home to the east of the village of Buffalo soon became a stopping place for travelers, an inn known as a half-way house. The numerous outbuildings gave the place the appearance of a lively little village with spacious barns brimming with the fruits of their labor. The large, commodious farmhouse that replaced the original log house was neither empty nor silent, for children soon filled it with the music of merry voices.[3]

Twenty years passed and the forest gave way to cultivated farms. The Munroes (they also sometimes spelled it Munro or Monroe) found themselves surrounded by neighbors, and they felt it no longer a desirable place to bring up their five daughters and one son. So Jesse and Harriet once more turned their faces to the setting sun and sought a new home in the "Far West."[4]

At the time the Munroe family moved, the government was selling federal land for $1.25 an acre to attract settlers to the Northwest Territory. Ohio, Indiana, and Illinois were already sufficiently populated to reach statehood although the boundary between Michigan and Ohio known as the Toledo strip, was vehemently disputed. Jesse and Harriet decided to go to this new frontier and see what it had to offer. Marian, who was 18, stayed home with the five younger children: Betsey, age 15; Josiah, 13; Harriet, 10; Adella, 5; and Eliza, 3. Marian's responsibility was made a little less daunting because many family friends were nearby, and the Bennets, her father's cousin's family, lived on the next farm.[5]

Harriet's brother, Hiram Parker, joined Jesse and Harriet as they scouted through the territory of Illinois, Indiana, and Wisconsin, probably on horseback. They did not find anything that pleased them. Marian writes:

> Then they decided to look through Michigan, the one State they had no idea of settling in when they left home. They had seen "Michiganders," as they were called, returning to the state of New York. Their sallow complexion and the tales they told of shaking with the fever and ague [malaria] made my father think that Michigan was no place for him. Nevertheless, they decided to see for themselves, and give Michigan a look. Much to their surprise, they found the state satisfactory. They liked the beautiful forests with their magnificent trees. My father was captivated at first sight, arguing that land which supported such a growth of trees would raise anything planted. So he located land in Clinton County. There were the black-walnut, butternut, hickory, black cherry, birds-eye-maple, curled-maple, sugar-maple, silver-leaf maple, beech, basswood, sycamore, ironwood, white, black and burr oaks—many being three and four feet in diameter—and the tulip tree, with its beautiful foliage and lovely blossoms. They were absent three months. Still undaunted by toil and hardship, as in youth, Father had purchased a farm in the heart of the Michigan forest. The site selected for the house was an elevation sloping gently down to the brook which wound its way through all the farm, and whose clear, pure waters should supply not only the needs of the family, but to the adjoining lands[6]

When Harriet, Jesse, and Hiram came to mid-Michigan looking for a homestead, it was probably from the south, through Jacksonburgh, Ingham County. Jacksonburg was located at the crossroads of many leading trails in the Lower Peninsula. Named after President Andrew Jackson, it was founded seven years earlier and came to be known simply as Jackson. Hiram discovered land he liked on an old Indian planting ground on the banks of the Red Cedar River, not far from Jacksonburgh.[7] At the time, settlers were avoiding the dense silent forests along the Grand River in northwest Ingham County and Clinton County.[8] Nevertheless, Jesse and Harriet found a beautiful spot on the Looking Glass River in Clinton County, four miles from any other human inhabitants.[9] After locating their land, the three returned to New York to settle their affairs.

Hiram returned to Michigan about five months before Harriet and Jesse. The Munroes were delayed due to the birth of their seventh child at the end of September. They sold their 125-acre farm for the considerable sum of $10,000 [approximately $226,000 in 2012[10]] and arranged to travel from Buffalo to Detroit on the steamer "Robert Fulton," crossing Lake Erie in October of 1836. One hired man went with them and two were sent with the stock through Ohio.[11]

The return route the Munroes traveled from Detroit to their homestead was most likely "The Grand River Trail," an old Indian path. "It ran from the settlement of Pontiac through Indian villages in Oakland, Genesee, and Shiawassee Counties, entering Clinton County from the site of Laingsburg and continuing across the county on the north side of the Looking Glass River until that river entered the Grand at Ionia County."[12] Marian and her sisters left behind some of the best pioneer accounts of what it was like to travel to mid-Michigan and settle in. Years later Harriet Munroe Longyear wrote the passage quoted below for The Pioneer Society, telling the story of those first years when the pioneers settled near where the Michigan state capital of Lansing eventually would be located. (She followed the convention of the time, capitalizing only the given name of a place.)

> The family landed at little, old, black Detroit, with which they were thoroughly disgusted, as they compared it to Buffalo. Here they were obliged to remain a week, waiting the arrival of the little caravan, and searching for a large box of clothing which by some mistake had been separated from the household goods and sent to another warehouse. After a week the search was abandoned and they resumed their journey. The eldest son and four of the daughters (of whom the writer was one) were seated in the light buffalo wagon, one of the elder sisters carrying in her arms the little one of 3 years, while the mother, with her infant boy and one little girl were provided for in one of the large wagons. The heavy fall rains had rendered the roads nearly impassable, the wagons often sinking in mud over the hubs.
>
> There were no bridges and we had to ford the swollen streams. The night of the first day found us but nine miles from the point we had left at an early hour of the morning. But nature gave some compensation for even such trials, for the autumn days were beautifully bright, the skies were the softest blue, with flecks of fleecy clouds. The trees were gorgeous with scarlet, crimson, and gold, while the earth was carpeted with mossy green and the russet of fallen leaves. We had many hardships before we reached the end of that long journey. But while we have not

time or space to recount many of these, we cannot fail to mention the kindness and hospitality of the people all along the way. No matter how small or how poor the accommodations, they counted it no sacrifice to share their very best with the stranger who called at their door.

One night we were entertained at a log house where we witnessed a novel method of building a fire. A stone fireplace extended nearly across the end of the building; large stones were placed against the jambs and served as andirons. Great logs of wood were drawn up to the door. A yoke of oxen were then driven to the other side of the house; the doors being opposite, a log chain was fastened to the neck yoke between the oxen, then passing through the house was attached to one of the logs; the oxen were driven a short distance and the log thus drawn into the house. It was then rolled to the fireplace with iron crowbars. This process was continued until the back-log, fore-log and back-stick were in position; then the smaller material was filled in, and soon the great fire was leaping, blazing, and roaring up through the wide mouth of the stick chimney. The house was filled with a ruddy glow which the brightest coal stoves of the present day cannot equal for light and good cheer.

To those who have not known pioneer life, the stick chimney may seem almost impossibility. Brick and lime were not to be had in a new country, but man's ingenuity never fails him, and in this instance all needed material was ready at his hand. Selecting small branches of suitable length, the ends were crossed so as to form square corners as in laying logs for the house. Our tough heavy clay that has made farming so hard in many parts of Michigan here found a sphere of usefulness. The sticks were laid up with this clay as we now lay bricks with mortar. Sometimes the chimney rested on the ground and sometimes the stone fireplace protruded beyond the other wall of the house and the chimney rested on this. When all was completed a heavy coat of clay was spread over the inside, making it fireproof.

At the close of the day of travel we reached the log cabin of Mr. Laing on the present site of Laingsburg. The house had no floor but the beaten ground. A new house was in process of building and the men and boys of both families took possession of this for the night, while beds were spread on earth floor of the first for the women and children. Mrs. Laing, fearing the mother with her baby could not rest, with typical pioneer hospitality, gave up her own bed, climbed the ladder and laid down under the low roof. The men and boys, having no beds, were unable to sleep and amused themselves by howling like a pack of hungry wolves. The next morning Mr. Laing apologized, saying, with a twinkle in his eyes, "You must excuse my men; I have fed them wolf meat so long they can't help howling."

Our next stop was with Captain Scott, who had built a large double log house in which to entertain travelers, where now stands the hotel of DeWitt. Here we passed the night, and the next morning removed to Mr. Ferguson's, one mile distant, where arrangements were made for women and children to remain till suitable arrangements could be made in the new home.[13]

Jesse and the three hired men went on to Eagle Township, Section 7. They were obliged to cut a road through seven miles of forest before reaching there with the teams. About a mile from the Ferguson family residence, the four came to the home of Mr. and Mrs. Anthony Niles who had lived in Eagle Township since 1834,[14] long enough to be widely known and always ready to help new settlers. Jesse stopped with them and procured provisions. He and his men then made a road from the Niles settlement to the Munroe land. Harriet wrote: "After three weeks' time father came for us. The rains had raised the Looking-glass river so that it could not be forded. We were all taken across the river in an Indian canoe. A pole was used instead of a paddle. We enjoyed the drive through the woods. It was night when we arrived at the Niles settlement, but there was a large living room and a blazing wood fire which gave brightness to the scene and a welcome for the new-comers such as only known to those who settle in a new country."[15] "The journey which could now be accomplished in a few hours had occupied four weeks, and when at last we reached home we were weary enough to desire rest. But the time to rest had not yet come," said Harriet. "There was work for all our busy hands to make things comfortable for the winter which was fast approaching."[16]

The four men had already begun work on the Munroe cabin. There were many obstacles to overcome, both large and small. Sometimes the small things are most apt to stick in one's memory. Harriet recalled: "One day when the men were building the house, they neglected to replenish the fire after their midday meal. When they stopped work for the night and came to prepare their supper the fire was out. Numerous efforts to kindle it were made with flint and steel without results; there were no dry kindlings; everything was fresh and damp. The only alternative was to go to Mr. Niles' for supper and breakfast—six miles. Returning in the morning, one man carried by hand a firebrand, swinging it to keep it burning. There were no matches at that time."[17]

With fall coming to an end, it was essential that the cabin be built quickly but snugly against the approaching winter weather. Settlers everywhere were working against time in order to prepare. Marian held vivid memories of the process:

> They went to work with a will and felled the trees and trimmed them ready to put together for a habitation. They soon had the logs put in place and a cover over them. The roofing consisted of logs hollowed out like a trough, laid side by side, edges close together, rough side up. Then another row, reversed, covered the edges of the first. This made a rain-and-snow-proof roof. The lumber used in making the doors and window casing was from the boxing of the furniture.

There were no saw mills in the country. Floors were made of the logs split into slabs and adzed off. Smooth boulders were used in making the back and jambs to an ample fireplace… The sound of the ax and falling timbers drew the attention of the nearest neighbor, Mr. Shoff, (whose home was one mile to the west) who was out looking for his cattle seeking food in the forest. He came at once to see what it could mean and was surprised and pleased to find a house going up so nearby; then noticing the unusual dimensions, 18x22 feet, he exclaimed, "Why, man, are you going to keep a tavern?" The answer was "Wait till you see my family, and you will not think this is too large." In eight days, the house was enclosed, covered, and a floor laid.[18]

The First Year

Life on the Munroes' 160 acre farm-to-be was underway.

We were home. Each one found something interesting. The little brook that ran near the house gave us great pleasure … The new house was warm and comfortable. It was now November; a light snow fell soon after we arrived…There was no fruit except dried fruits. Portland, five miles west, was a small village. There was one store that kept a few groceries and a stock of domestic goods, Indian maple sugar, etc.

The inhabitants were eastern people delightful to know. Two young men called, and came in a 'new country' sleigh. It was made of ironwood poles, the bark taken off only from the underside of the runners. This was the first sleigh of its kind I had ever seen. I was greatly amused. Lyons, ten miles from Portland, was a larger and more flourishing town. We joined in the festivities of both places. All were neighbors.[19]

As the white population in the area slowly grew, they soon found they were not the only people that made up the community. Many settlers got to know the Native Americans in the region and hosted visits from Chief Okemos and members of his band of Chippewa, Ottawa and Potawatomi. Indian women had many little patches of garden in the area where they planted corn and other vegetables. Captain David Scott told about how he and his explorer friends were invited by the Indians to live in a bark-covered house called a wigwam for several weeks when they first arrived in the area in 1833. During that time, Scott built the log cabin for his wife Eunice, their two sons, and himself in what became DeWitt.[20]

Okemos was a popular figure in the Clinton County area and often camped along the Looking Glass River. According to one Clinton County resident, "Two hundred years earlier Chippewa Indians had a village called Wabwahnahsupu (village green) one mile east of DeWitt on the north bank of the river. These Indians called the river 'Wahwasin' (also spelled Wobwaysin). They were friendly Indians who grew corn and other grains. They also hunted, trapped, and fished. The production of maple syrup was very important to them. Wabwahnahsupu was a village until about 1831 when it became an interim camp used by Indians traveling through the area."[21]

Marian and Harriet put a positive face on their isolation. They never conveyed any sense of danger from the natives in the area. Nor did they fear the weather or wild animals this first winter. Harriet tells of their toils and pleasures and relief when the family's lost trunk was discovered:

> Only a few weeks had passed when the road commissioners came through blazing the trees for the State Road from Detroit, passing in front of our house. This was a great joy to us all, as it seemed to open the way out into the busy world beyond. At Portland, Mr. Bogue kept a small variety store, but there was not a mill nearer than Dexter, and Ann Arbor for supplies. Potatoes, $1.50 per bushel; flour, $9 per barrel; port, $20 per barrel; and we paid $20 for two quarters of beef.

> Friendly Indians often visited us and we were always glad to exchange venison and wild game for anything we had to give them. Father spent nearly the whole winter in journeys to Detroit, Dexter, and Ann Arbor, to procure supplies. Our family consisted that year of 12 people, and grain for the horses had to be brought from a distance. The journey to Detroit and return occupied two weeks and by the time he reached home the last load was exhausted and next morning found him on the road again. It was now midwinter, and the clothing in the lost box was greatly needed, when to the glad surprise of all, father returned from Detroit, bringing it with him. He had found it in a warehouse he had before failed to examine.

> The wood choppers were busy clearing the land, and timber of great value today, was rolled upon the log-heaps and burned to get it out of the way. Birdseye maple, walnut, butternut, curly maple, cherry and many another trees of a century's growth, having no market value where there were no saw mills, were sacrificed in the flames, and the ashes served only to enrich the earth. By early spring, sufficient land was cleared to begin planting and sowing grain and the hope of the coming harvest brightened the prospect for the future years.

> Those were the days of toil in the home as well as in the fields, but they were not without their pleasures, which were enjoyed with a zest unappreciated by those who know not the blessings of labor. There were singing schools, sleigh rides, and parties to which young people were invited. These young people for the most part came from the east, bringing with them the culture, refinement and education which made their society agreeable to all. There were few musical instruments, but nearly all were good singers, and were not afraid to hear their own voices but shared happily in songs and chorus. There were no churches, but Sabbath afternoon was usually spent in musical entertainment.

> The first school in this neighborhood was in the home of Mr. Shoff, and taught by his son Savillian. The next summer a small log school-

house was built half way between Mr. Shoff's and our house, and my sister Marian, now Mrs. Turner, taught the summer school.[22]

The State Road Commissioners came through surveying the State road, which passed by our door. That was most cheering to us. Father with his men built a bridge at his own expense across the Looking-glass river, one mile east from us. This bridge remained there many years for the good of the public.

The winters were severe, deep snow, and feed for the stock very scarce. In the spring the soft-maple trees were chopped down for the animals when the buds were full and red. They would trim out a large treetop in a short time and run to the next one when that fell. They subsisted on buds until vegetation became plentiful. Then they were free to roam where they please, baring the swamps where vegetation was alluring. Our new milch cow ventured too far and was lost in the mire. That was a real tragedy; so much was depending upon the milk for the family. Bravery and self-control had to be called into action. Each one bearing his or her share of sympathy for our mother who knew better than we younger ones what it cost to go without milk.

The sugar maple trees were tapped and maple syrup and sugar was plentiful. Several hundred pounds of sugar were made, which relieved one of the wants of a new country. Fish were plentiful, the men catching with dip-nets hundreds of a night. All surplus was put into half barrels and salted for future use. Wild onions grew along the banks of our brook. In the fall wild-plums, crab-apples and frost-grapes were plentiful. Honey was found in the trees. In the beautiful forests of Michigan there was not only honey but also bees wax, which furnished us with wax candles.

Our discomforts and deprivations were many but all were overcome by cheerfulness and heroic perseverance. Mother was always cheerful. Reptiles and insects there were, but I will leave them to your imagination to picture. Indians were friendly and always hungry. Their liking for white man's bread was simply appalling. We bought venison of them whenever they brought it to us. We had no reason to fear them. They were always sober and peaceful.[23]

It was not long before Jesse hired Anthony Niles and his son Ezekiel to build a barn with lumber brought from the new Portland mill. It was the first frame building in Eagle Township.[24] In about 1837, Jesse became one of the first, if not the first, in the county to plant an orchard.[25] The Munroe clan was soon settled in and, particularly through the marriages of the Munroe daughters, would have a wide influence on the area. Marian recalled, "My father was once asked why he left a good home in the east for the forests of the west, with so much of hardship and toil as must come into a pioneer's life. He replied: 'I wanted to keep my children together, and there was no room for so many there. I have accomplished what I undertook. My four sons are all settled here adjoining the old farm, and my five daughters are not more than 17 miles away.' Few of us can lay down the burden of life feeling that we have reached the goal at which we aimed."[26]

Hiram Parker, Harriet Munroe's brother, had settled in Vevay Township in Ingham County in June after their initial trip to Michigan. He built the body of a log house, returned to his old home in Vermont, married, and came back with his wife Charity[27] and settled in November. The Parker's house was located on a hill, but the forest was so dense it was 20 years before they could see through the timber to a neighbor's house. Hiram said later that had he known a tenth part of what their experience was to be in the wilderness he never would have asked anybody to come with him. However, the loneliness was broken when the Parkers chanced to meet two men in those early months who were already settled there, Hinman Hurd and Hiram H. Smith. It would not be long before he would meet James Turner as well.

These three men and the Munroe sisters were all pioneers scattered around the area who would become founders of Lansing in the decade to come, but they may not have met the Munroes so early had it not been for the Parkers. Local historian of this period, Samuel Durant, gave this account: "The Parkers coincidentally met Hinman Hurd in Troy, New York. Hurd had been out looking for land and had also found a spot in Vevay Township, the future home of the County Seat. When the Parkers returned, they again made an acquaintance with the Hurds and met H. H. Smith."[28] The Hurds were from Erie County, the home county of the Munroes.

Hiram Smith was born in Massachusetts, grew up in Vermont and, after training in a mercantile house, took up merchandising in Granville, New York. He married Frances Dean Dennison of Woodstock, Vermont, and came to Michigan in April of 1835. After a few months, they settled in Summit, Jackson County, and farmed for two years. The Smiths' experience on this farm was a trying one. It was during one of the hardest of winters, one the Parkers and Munroes were fortunate to have missed. Hiram broke up some land and put it to wheat, spending his last dollar for the seed. He husked corn, dug potatoes for a neighbor for fifty cents a day, and took his pay in potatoes and pumpkins which he and Frances lived on during that winter. It was such a severe winter that both of his oxen perished, and he skinned them and used the hide for shoes to protect their feet from freezing. The two of them picked the bones of meat to keep from starving.[29] That spring he engaged Hiram Parker to go with him after some flour, paying him in the commodity he had the most of—corn. Samuel Durant recounted, "Mr. Parker thinks he was then the richest man of the two, for he had a pair of boots and Smith wore rags on his feet. Mr. Smith became the first treasurer of Ingham County, and after his election removed to Mason, subsequently going to Lansing."[30]

The financial difficulties of the Smiths, who could not afford a pair of store-bought shoes, were not unique. The national financial panic and depression that followed was reaching Michigan. The lack of regulation of the money supply added further to the confusion and hardship that affected everyone. Samuel Durant wrote of the sort of situations that came up:

In June 1837, Mr. Parker started for Dexter after flour. On the way he met a couple of men who informed him there was none for sale, as they had tried to purchase some and failed. A speculator at Ann Arbor had purchased it all. Mr. Parker learned there was some at Scio, and to that place he at once repaired. He found that the supply there had also been bought for speculative purposes, but he finally purchased two barrels of it of the miller, who was not particularly friendly to the speculator. The money paid for it was that of the bank of which the speculator was president, and was of the nature known as "wildcat." The miller had specified that the flour must be paid for in "good Eastern money;" but while Mr. Parker was looking his roll of bills over to see if he had the necessary amount (twenty-five dollars) of the article required, the miller espied the "wildcat," and thought that was good enough for the man, as it was his own money. It was paid and Mr. Parker left with the flour. He had not reached home before he learned that the bank had failed and the money was of no account, and, as he had borrowed part of it, he considered he had procured his two barrels of flour at a very fair bargain. Very soon after making the purchase he learned that the price of flour had been raised to seventeen dollars per barrel.[31]

John Munro Longyear, whose family of pioneer farmers lived near Mason, wrote about another tale of the wildcat banking days in northwest Ingham County. He called it "The Gang of Counterfeiters," and, yes, there really were counterfeiters found at a hideout named Bogus Swamp:

Just west of the city is a tract known as the "Bogus Swamp." The cause of this euphonious cognomen being bestowed upon a genuine swamp was by reason of its having been, before the Capital was located, the rendezvous of a gang of counterfeiters and horse thieves. At that time the swamp presented, to the eye of the uninitiated, the appearance of an impenetrable morass, being covered with a rank growth of swampy vegetation that appeared to be as impregnable to the passage of anybody, but that of a snake or other reptile, as it was to the vision. Subsequent events demonstrated that there was a passage through the slime and mire, and that there were men who knew how to use that passage which led to the island or spot of hard ground in the center of the swamp. For a long time people were continually being "taken in" by taking "bogus" coin, and all the efforts of detectives were in vain to stop the nuisance, which became very annoying, as innocent people do not relish being accused of wantonly passing counterfeit money. Subsequent revelations led to the discovery that the swamp was in the line of a gang of horse thieves that extended from central New York to the center of Iowa, which fact accounted for the number of fine horses that were occasionally observed passing through this section of the country.

Finally, a party of government surveyors came to the "Bogus Swamp," and, following their "line," went directly through it, which is said to be a way surveyors have of doing. The party, when they reached the island, in the center, came upon a shanty, out of which rushed several men, who plunged directly into the swamp, leaving everything; but the surveyors having no curiosity, under the circumstances, followed their "line" and passed on through the swamp. It was soon known, however, what had been seen by the surveyors, and the place visited. Nothing, however, was found except some unmistakable indications that this was the source of the counterfeit money. This discovery effectually broke up the gang, and several persons who were known to have belonged to the organization were living in, or near this city, a few years since. The organization had its agents in every town in the State, and a number outside. A few years since as some workmen were engaged in working the road that had been constructed upon the "line" that had been instrumental in the discovery of the counterfeiters, a man who was evidently trying to carry more antiquated corn juice than he had strength for, came staggering along just as the men had finished their dinners, which they had brought with them, and had eaten on the site of the counterfeiter's den. As he came up to where they were sitting, he looked about, and with a drunken leer, remarked: "Boys you (hic) don't dare to dig (hic) under the top of that (hic) bent willow, nor you don't dare (hic) to look in the top of that 'are stub.'" Saying which, he went on his "winding way," while the men immediately refuted the imputation upon their courage by digging at the buried top of the designated tree, and cutting down the stub that had been pointed out. Under the tree were found the dies and the other more bulky implements that had been used by the manufacturers of bogus money. In the top of the stub were found the smaller tools, all of which discoveries were brought to the city and the cast iron articles melted and remolded into plough points. The present aspect of the country known as the "Bogus Swamp," is far different from the appearance it had when this gang were first discovered. The road running through it, together with the thorough ditching, has transformed the once almost impervious jungle to fine and productive farming lands.[32]

The lack of trust in both the coin and paper money supply stayed with the pioneers throughout the century as they were hit repeatedly by panics, depression, financial corruption, and dishonesty. Nevertheless, Vevay Township continued to be settled and the "thrifty village of Mason" sprang up and became the county seat in 1840.[33]

Marian, Log Cabin Teacher

Marian Munroe had not been in the area long when she made a trip to the Parkers that would reach near-legendary status in early Lansing folklore because of the bearing it would have on the settlement of the Turners in Lansing. It was passed down by Durant:

About 1838, Mrs. Turner made a visit to friends residing in Mason, going on horseback, accompanied by a relative. She went via Okemos, [called Hamilton] in Meridian Township, fording the Cedar River at that point, which was so swollen that Mrs. Turner—then Miss Munroe—was obliged to hold her feet upon the horse's back to keep them out of the water. On their return to Clinton County they followed the Indian trail along Grand River, and stopped for lunch on the ground, or very near, where the Turner mansion now stands. Miss Munroe was greatly pleased with the location and the fine view it afforded, and remarked that she would not wonder if, when she was married, she might someday make her home there. The prophecy has long since been fulfilled, and certainly there is no more pleasant site for a home in Ingham County, overlooking as it does, the long sweep of the beautiful river and a broad scope of cultivated country in all directions. At the time of this first visit the whole region was wilderness. The high bluff bank of the river at this point is clothed with a majestic growth of forest-trees, then open and unobstructed by undergrowth, with cold, pure springs gushing from the slopes, and dashing to the river below. This is today the most romantic spot in the vicinity of Lansing, and with a small outlay could be transformed into a picturesque park.[34]

Besides visiting the Parkers and other friends in Vevay Township, Marian was also teaching there. When teachers were needed, it was quite natural that an intelligent young woman with a love of learning such as Marian's would seek a position. Indeed, there were few other employment opportunities available to her in the early 1800s—needlework and household services were the only other likely choices, though women back home in Buffalo might take work in the cotton mills or bookbinderies to do typesetting or, if they had a house, take in boarders.[35] Marian was nineteen and just five feet tall, scarcely as tall as some of the students in her school. She was described as possessed of an appealing character of delightful sweetness and goodness, kindness, and gentleness, which endeared her to all who knew her.[36] Her sister Betsey remembers Marian's early days as a teacher:

I think in the year 1837 or 1838, my oldest sister, Marian Munroe, now Mrs. Turner, was teaching school in our own district, as there were three or four families to supply children, which were seven or eight in all. The names of these families were Jesse Munroe, Abijah Shoff, Daniel Nusome, Adophus Skinner. The teacher's services were gratuitous--also the board; as were those of Mr. Shoff the following winter.

I remember very well Mrs. Jane Starks and myself went to visit Miss Munroe's school, and soon after arriving there, we looked out of the place where a window should have been—as there were places for a door and windows, but neither was in the log house in which the school was kept. To our great surprise, we saw a large number of Indians coming down the hill from the west, which cut us off from the Shoff family; and as they passed the school-house, they cut us off from Jesse Munroe's, and there we were, hemmed in on either side by Indians, and no chance to escape, if we wished to. But we quieted the children by telling them that they were friendly Indians—as they had their ponies and squaws and papooses with them. Many of them came up to the door and windows and asked for scota, or fire in our language, to light their pauguns, or pipes. They also called for quashagun, or bread, which we did not have to give them; and they passed on and on—it seemed to us such a long time for them all to get by. We afterwards learned that there were five or six hundreds of them fleeing to Canada to escape Gen. Brady, as he was gathering them to take to the Black Hills, and they were not willing to go and leave their beautiful hunting grounds to which they were so much attached. They then encamped about one mile from my father's for a few days, and then passed along without molesting any one. On returning from another visit to the school, a huge bear lay in the road before us, who being frightened at our approach, gave a ferocious sound and made a hasty retreat, leaving us to our own company, which we much preferred to that of the bear.[37]

Marian taught school in both Ingham and Clinton Counties. There were two terms taught in a year, summer and winter, and wages were necessarily low because people did not have much money. The first district north of Mason paid seventy-five cents per week. Teachers taught six days a week for four months and boarded around the area, sometimes sleeping with the children three at the head and one across the foot of the bed. Spelling schools, or bees, were one of the few evening entertainments, and children studied their elementary spelling books in the hopes of winning. They would choose sides, the captains for each side choosing the spellers for their team. The contest closed by spelling everyone down. "This was considered to be a much more profitable use of time than playing cards," said local historian Franc L. Adams.[38]

The log schoolhouses in the area had fireplaces, four-legged benches to sit on, and desks for writing made by boring holes in the logs, then driving in two long pegs and laying a board across them. The children faced the desk when they wrote, but when studying they sat the other way on the benches and used the writing board for the back of the seat. The children had separate recess periods—first the boys and then the girls (sometimes there was no outhouse), and the writing lesson usually coincided with it. Pens were made of goose quills, and one of the requirements in the examination of teachers was the ability to make good pens. Marian was expected to have a sharp penknife in order to make and mend pens as needed. The young scholars' examinations were all oral, and certificates were granted. Some teachers taught in every district for twenty miles around, several times over. Bears, wildcats, and wolves had become scarce in the area of Mason and Vevay Township and were rarely a threat to schools or students. Most of the teachers enjoyed their lives as teachers in the wilderness.[39]

Marian and James

It was as a teacher that Marian first met James Turner in about 1840.[40] He was an energetic young merchant of Mason, handsome and impressive at six feet, four inches. It was said he had a genial, kindly smile, which spread over a serene, honest, manly face, radiant with large, luminous eyes.[41] Some said he looked like pictures of the nineteenth century author Washington Irving. He was serving as a school magistrate in Mason, and it was his job. to hire the district's teacher. When Marian applied for the job, he hired her.

James was born in Cazenovia, New York, April 1, 1820, and was a lineal descendant of Humphrey Turner, who emigrated from Devonshire, England, and was among the Pilgrims who settled in Plymouth, Connecticut, in 1628. His father, Francis Stiles Turner, and his mother, Deborah Morton, were married at Middlebury, Vermont, in 1799.[42]

Although James' family on his mother's side and Marian's mother and father were from Vermont, influences and ties with western New York were even stronger for the young couple. Cazenovia was located east of the tips of New York's Finger Lakes about 65 miles from Seneca Falls. It was a hotbed of liberal thinking and noted as an organizing site for the anti-slavery movement from the early 1830s. Many leaders of progressive causes were born or raised there or at one time made Cazenovia their home, including figures in the abolitionists' movement and the campaign for women's rights. The liberal congregations that were evolving in Cazenovia became public forums where many renowned speakers were featured, including Lucretia Mott, Frederick Douglass, and Gerrit Smith. It was at this time that the Turners moved to the Michigan territory, taking with them this early experience that most likely had a continuing influence on James, as he maintained business and family contacts in Cazenovia throughout his life.

There were nine Turner siblings when James' family came to Michigan, seven boys and two girls: Elisha, John, Marshall, and Mary Ann, ranged in age from 32 to 20 at the time. The younger five children, Richard, age 17; James, 15; Charles, 11; Esther, 9; and George, 5, moved with Francis and Deborah to 40 acres near Lima. The three oldest sons bought a combined total of 704 acres of government land between 1837 and 1840 in Washtenaw, Jackson, and Ingham Counties.[43]

It is not surprising that one of the best accounts of James Turner's arrival in Michigan is by his nephew, Frank N. Turner, M.D., who wrote *Historic Michigan, Vol. III, Ingham County* in 1924, an invaluable description of the early days of Lansing. Frank was the son of James' older brother, Richard.

The earliest merchants in Mason were Hiram H. Smith and James Turner. Mr. Smith was senior partner in the firm of Smith & Turner. Mr. Smith was born in the State of New York. He started in business in his native state but failed. Discouraged by this failure he came to Michigan about 1840 [Note: 1836]. He called on his friend of the east named William Jackson, who lived in Jackson, Michigan. He, Jackson, was a merchant and was starting a branch store at Mason, so to encourage his friend, he sent him to Mason with a younger clerk in his employ, James Turner. This venture proved so successful that in a short time the clerks bought the store and stock of their employer... James Turner came to Michigan with his father, Francis Stiles Turner, in 1835. He was ten [Note: he was fifteen] years old, but young as he was, helped his father and brothers clear a few acres and erect a log house on a farm near Lima, Michigan. In 1836 his father died and left his mother with their five youngest children on a new farm. Mrs. Turner had to separate her family. The oldest of the four boys [Richard]

James Turner painting, CADL photo.

returned to the old home, Cazenovia, New York. Richard gained some experience with building railroads in 1837 until he returned to Lansing to help support his mother and the younger children. The youngest was sent to the home of an uncle in Erie, Pennsylvania, and James went with his mother to visit Mr. William Jackson at Leoni, Jackson county. Mr. Jackson, who had been a neighbor in Cazenovia, was pleased when shown some of James' penmanship and ability to handle problems in arithmetic and gave the boy a clerkship in his store. Mr. Jackson had at that time a large store and distillery in the village. He gave the boy a home, paid his tuition in the village school, and let him clerk in the store to pay for it. He advanced so rapidly that in a few months he was sent out with a horse and wagon to sell farmers' wives groceries, dress goods, and Yankee notions. He was a good salesman, always polite and ready to gossip or do some errand for the girls. Another trait was his honesty. He would always point out a defect in quality or quantity of his goods before he sold them, but he always sold. He was nicknamed "Honest Jim."

He was only sixteen years old when he was sent to Mason with Hiram H. Smith, who was nine years his elder. We find him in the social and political life of the village, and acting as agent to land holders in the east, administrator for James Seymour in the Burchard estate before he was twenty-one years old.[44]

James' own early educational advantages were limited to the schooling he received in Jacksonburgh with the help of William Jackson after his father died, but it was said he had a great love for books and an ardent desire to obtain self-education that would fit him for the active duties of business life. He took every opportunity that came his way.[45]

It should also be noted that among the transplanted Cazenovians was Michigan's future governor, Austin Blair. Blair was the same age as James and had many Blair family relatives living at Cazenovia. He was born in a log cabin on his family's farm to the south in Tompkins County. He attended the Cazenovia Seminary, as did William Jackson, and studied law in nearby Oswego. Both Jackson and Blair were well remembered at the seminary and maintained their ties there, attending anniversary gatherings of its graduates, and so forth.[46] After admittance to the bar in 1841, he moved to Michigan, residing first in Jackson and then moving to nearby Eaton Rapids. The three, Turner, Jackson, and Blair, held similar political views and became friends in Michigan, if not before. Other good friends in Mason in those early years were John W. Longyear, a teacher who became an attorney and judge; his brother, Ephraim, a teacher who became an attorney, gold prospector, attorney again, and later a banker; John Burchard, an attorney who became a land developer; Daniel Lampson Case, an attorney and merchant who became a developer and banker; and Hiram H. Smith, mentioned earlier, who was a merchant who became a railroad man and banker. All were entrepreneurs and political leaders and held elected office at one time or another.

It was not long before James and Hiram were known as "the Merchant Princes" of Mason.[47] James's accomplishments were many for such a young man, but at times he still gave his elders cause for amusement. There were chuckles around Mason for several years over the memory of a gristmill raising in 1840 which was followed by dinner for all the workers at the end of the day. It seems James played a prominent role in a fracas involving pumpkin pies used as missiles.[48]

Nearly fifty years later James' son recalled the life of the pioneer shop-keepers to a group of salesmen called The Knights of the Grip (a grip is a small suitcase):

> The local merchants of that day made their semi-annual pilgrimages to the great marts of trade and made their purchases direct from the gentlemen whose names were written over the door. The canal boat, lake schooner and ox team then delivered the purchases at the country store. The relationship of the country merchant in that day with the jobber in the city was the most cordial and confidential nature, while today a personal acquaintance between the two is unusual...

> I believe my father had the distinguished honor of being among the first commercial travelers in central Michigan, beginning his career as such in the year 1839. The western terminus of our civilization and the Michigan Central railroad at the time was at Leoni in Jackson county, and the Knight of the Grip of that day found limited accommodation both for himself and the team that transported him and his wares... The nocturnal stopping places for the man and beast were at the little openings in the primeval forests where night overtook them, and glad they were to find even such. The log cabin in the wilderness was generally guarded by from three to five hungry-looking deer hounds, that vigorously announced the stranger's approach. In front of the house was

a wood pile, consisting only of a big log resting on an accumulation of chips and an ax resting against the log. If the proprietor had taken sufficient time from the chase to provide a half dozen sticks of wood, then the genius that presided on the inside of the cabin was supremely happy.

The stable consisted of a log pen covered over and about with ancient straw which, if the call occurred near the close of a long winter, was well eaten away by the hungry animals sheltered on the inside. At this season, rations of elm and soft maple boughs took the place of marsh hay. Hog and hominy was the staple food for those who found shelter at the house. After supper and prayers, the stranger was given a rush light to climb the ladder to his bed... In the morning he brushes from the coverlet the snow that has drifted in between the logs, and descends, rubbing his eyes, to prepare for pancakes. The landlady meets him with a smile, hands him at the back door a peck measure half filled with soft soap, and tells him to follow the path down to the creek, where he will find a sap trough for a washbasin and plenty of water.

The legal tenders of that date were coon skins, pearl ash, black salts, beeswax, and the pioneer drummer [a salesman beat his drum to alert the customer to his presence] found his load on the return trip quite as burdensome to his team as when he started out.[49]

James and Marian were married in Eagle on October 1, 1843. As young adults already widely respected in the pioneer community, their shared background, outgoing personalities, intelligence, and progressive social conscience inspired all who gathered that day with the Turners and Munroes. There was no doubt that theirs would be a successful and productive union.

They were putting down roots in the frontier town of Mason and, in December of 1844, Marian and James helped found the Presbyterian Society.[50] However, despite their contributions to the growth of the town and their many friendships there, the Turners did not plan to continue to live in Mason. Although not anticipating the auspicious future of the site, Marian and James had already selected a spot for a home in the still unorganized Township of Lansing at the northern edge of Michigan's longest river, the Grand, as it turns west to begin its journey to Lake Michigan. James had secured the site before their marriage and plans were in the works for a new settlement.[51] This was the very spot Marian had fallen in love with several years earlier when she and her sister had passed by one day following the river home to Eagle. However, Marian was not the only one to have taken an interest in this location.

Chapter 2

Discovering Lansing

A t the same time the settlers were moving into the Michigan territory, land speculators were engaging in a very different kind of development and their story is very different. Wealthy Eastern investors saw an opportunity to buy up large tracts of land at the bargain government price to sell soon after for huge profits. Among these were the officers of The Bank of Rochester in western New York between Cazenovia and Buffalo. The bank was headed by a man whose name would become well known in Michigan because of his role in determining the site of the state's permanent capital. This man was James Seymour.

James Seymour was born in Litchfield, Connecticut, on April 20, 1791, and was older and more experienced than many of the pioneers entering Michigan when James and Marian did. As a young man, he worked as a clerk for his cousin, Henry Seymour, the canal commissioner of Pompey, New York. Henry was the original surveyor for the town of Cazenovia and Henry's family lived there several years. Henry was the father of Horatio Seymour who became the governor of New York and in due course an investor with James in Ingham County.[52] James Seymour followed the line of emigration to western New York and helped found the towns of Holly, Clarkson, and Brockport in Monroe County.[53] In 1821 he persuaded the Erie Canal Commission to re-route the canal closer to Clarkson Corners and designate Brockport, one mile to the south, as the terminus rather than Rochester. At once Seymour and developer/speculator Heil Brockway began purchasing land along the proposed canal route near Brockport. Both moved from Clarkson to Brockport and concentrated their commercial activities there. Seymour went into business with his brother William, who became an inventor of farm equipment, and his brother Charles who also moved to the new town.[54] James was active in temperance society work, was an Alderman of the Presbyterian Church, became well known in commercial circles, and attained political prominence.[55] He was known as a polished gentleman of culture and refined manners.[56]

The Bank of Rochester

In 1824 Rochester's first bank charter was granted to the Bank of Rochester with capital assets of $250,000, and James Seymour was named to the Board of Directors. He moved to Rochester in 1829 and became cashier of the bank (treasurer) in 1830 and then president of the bank in 1838.[57] The bank served the business community in Rochester and Monroe County, fostered investment in land, provided mortgages for land purchases, and enjoyed an excellent reputation.

The bank had several contacts in Michigan, including James' brother, Charles Seymour. According to Franklin Ellis, an early historian of Genesee County, Michigan, Charles came to Michigan in 1835, purchased land on the Flint River, and proceeded to build a dam, with a partner, at what became Flushing village. The frame of the mill was completed in 1837. "At this time the circular was issued by President Jackson authorizing land-agents to receive nothing but specie [gold or silver coin] for government lands, owing to the extensive circulation of 'wild-cat' money, and Mr. Seymour returned to the East in the winter of 1837-38, bringing with him when he came back a quantity of good money."[58] Most likely, this was Bank of Rochester money. He bought forty-two lots of pineland, all on shares— meaning each investor owned a percentage of the undivided total purchase. Altogether, he purchased over 18,000 acres. Charles made Flushing his permanent home in February of 1843. He built a sawmill and ran it until he sold it to his brother James later that year. James and Charles continued to develop the area over a fifteen-year period.[59] To this day Seymour Road runs from Miller Road north along the Flint River, passing Flushing on the west side .

James Seymour also began to buy up large tracts of land in Michigan for the Bank of Rochester officers through the bank's Michigan land agent in Marshall, the county seat of Calhoun County. The land agent was Sidney S. Allcott who had been a cotton manufacturer in Rochester, of scrupulously honest reputation, and the first mayor of Marshall, Michigan. Allcott represented several Eastern investors and had a brother William whose family lived in Brockport and Rochester. Allcott identified land and purchasers, handled purchases for the bank and the mortgages that the bank established with purchasers, paid the Michigan taxes, and in general did the work of the absent owners as the situation required. As Charles Seymour did, he received a share of the purchases he made. He also borrowed money from the bank to make his own investments, sometimes against his pay and sometimes as separate loans. All business was conducted by correspondence. Allcott's surviving letters from 1835 until 1841 are a valuable part of the record of how the site for the city of Lansing came to be. The family of Sidney Allcott preserved these letters. Each is folded down to about 3 x 4 inches with a small blob of red sealing wax and addressed in three lines: S. S. Allcott, Marshall, Calhoun Co. There were no stamps at this time and when Allcott received the letter, he paid for it.[60]

At first, Seymour wrote as bank treasurer in consultation with bank president Frederic Bushnell and Charles W. Lee, bank attorney. In December of 1836, Seymour wrote to Allcott about purchases near the county seat of Eaton County (Charlotte) and the feasibility of establishing a mill. Financial conditions had been booming but he knew the business climate was changing. James was concerned about the partners becoming dangerously over-extended, and he said he did not want to be put in the same category with reckless land grabbers. "It is a very difficult time to [invest] money now and for myself, and so says Mr. Lee, we are about out of breath and want to hold up from taking more than our share of 5,000 or 6,000 [acres] more lands... We must not try to <u>make all the money</u>; we could not if we would."[61]

While the economy was still booming, the three partners, Seymour, Bushnell, and Lee, all bought lands together on shares in northwest Ingham County in 1836, just months before Michigan became the 26th state in January of 1837. Three brothers who were wealthy New York City merchant jobbers and investors (all worth over $100,000) had already bought land nearby totaling 1,280 acres in 1835.[62] The three, Robert C., Isaac, and William H. Townsend, held tracts under William's name to the north and south of the site of the Rochester partners.

Fred Bushnell was a seasoned developer and promoter, and according to Frank Turner, Bushnell was the land explorer in the bank partnership. There was a Turner-Bushnell connection since James' father, Francis Stiles Turner, was the stepson of Lydia Bushnell, his father's second wife. The Bushnell wing of the family remained in the East. It was Fred who located the land and waterpower on the Grand River in 1836.[63] The purchases looked promising, but in just a short time the sale and/or development of these lands met with many troubles and delays.

With the economy worsening, James Seymour had to pull back from some of the group's investments, which were also in Genesee, Saint Clair, Allegan, Calhoun and Eaton Counties. He wrote on January 21, 1837: "Our opinion is that it is desirable to sell our land at $5 [Note: a 400 percent profit] and any of the 1800 acres of other farming land." He told Allcott to use the proceeds from lands sold elsewhere for improvements of the land holdings in Ingham County. They planned to build a dam for waterpower and a mill on the Grand River to attract settlers, but Allcott was experiencing financial problems of his own as well as having trouble moving land for others in the atmosphere of panic developing in the state. Just as Michigan was enjoying its first year of statehood, the window of opportunity seemed to be closing. The next month Seymour inquired about the viability of the river site for providing waterpower: "I am very anxious to know how much fall we have at Ingham and hope you will let me know accurately and give us an estimate of improvements in detail and plans of them." When no engineer's report about the incline of the river arrived, Seymour's next letter to Allcott proposed a delay in the Ingham County development until he could get the report and expressed his regrets and misgivings:

Rochester April 5 1837

Dear Sir

I have received yours of 22 Mar and of 15 —There has never been in this country any thing like such a pinch for money, and for this reason, if for no other, we could not now go on with improvements on western lands, or authorize any drafts on us at present—But we have other objections. When we commenced the land business, we had no expectations of doing any thing else, and did not contemplate building mills and going into the lumber business, and although we have since given encouragement of making some such improvements at the Ingham purchase, it was on your representations—that there was a great water power there, of which we expected to have some examination by a competent engineer as to the fall and the quantity of water, both in Grand river and the small stream, and ever since the purchase we have been urging you to have this done. When you made the purchase you estimated the fall across the bend at 25 feet and on Lot 9 at 12 ft., (flooding Sec 16 a little).

Last winter you estimated it only 9 ft., and by your last letter at only 6 feet—Now with such uncertain information we cannot go on expending money and if your engineer would not find out the descent of the river because of the snow I should have but small opinion of him. Mr. Elisha Johnson has recently returned from surveying out a rail road from Hamilton to Lake Huron through the snow although not so very accurate as might be in summer…

In making a dam and building a mill too, we had not any intention of going largely into the lumber business expecting to make a profit by carrying it on, but what we did was to give the place a start and sell it off as soon as an opportunity offered, preferring to confine our operations to buying and selling land and only doing as much as would benefit the sales. As the county of Ingham is still a wilderness, we think a few months delay in building a mill is not very material and one of us will probably be out there in May or June and in the meantime this fall of the stream can be ascertained—If it appears that there is a good water power we will make some improvements—but till then we do not wish to do it.

Yours—J. Seymour[64]
Hon. Horace Seymour

There was ample reason for Seymour to bring things to a halt on the Grand River site because banking and land development was becoming a risky business. Many blamed the banking crises on the federal government under the leadership of President Andrew Jackson, who, with the support of Congress, destroyed the Federal Bank in order to distribute the national surplus funds from all the land sales money, acquired as the West expanded, to state banks, which some detractors referred to as his "pet banks." (Michigan's Governor Stevens T. Mason supported Jackson and said the Federal

Bank was a monopoly. Mason said having more banks would be more democratic.)[65] This redistribution led to the printing of money by the state banks
and the paper currency printing phenomenon grew unchecked nationwide.
So much credit was available from state banks that it had led to wild speculation, bad investments and worthless mortgages, an unfavorable balance of
trade, and inflation. Because the currency from these state banks was used
to pay the government for its public lands, the gold and silver in the national
treasury evolved into a supply of paper money of dubious worth. As mentioned, the situation caused President Jackson to issue his famous "Specie
Circular" in July of 1836 demanding only gold or silver in payment for public
lands[66] and sending Charles Seymour back to New York to get specie and
reliable money that was printed by a trusted bank, the Bank of Rochester.

Demands for gold and silver in exchange for paper that people did not
trust meant more banks struggled, called in their loans, and entered bankruptcy. Three banks went down in Rochester alone. Public confidence was
shattered and the worst depression in American history thus far set in.[67]
The panic of 1837 was long lasting and haunting to those who lived through
it. Dishonesty, corruption, and greed overcame many banks, but not the
Bank of Rochester. It remained free of scandal, never guilty of the illegal and
improper practices of several nearby banks. The Bank Commissioners of
Monroe County reported it conducted business in "a manner most conducive
to the interests of the community in which they are situated."[68]

To make matters worse, Seymour's partner, Frederic Bushnell, was dying,
and Seymour worked patiently to steer a steady course without him. The
partners wanted to sell their Michigan land, but they did not want to sell
at "wholesale prices" or without a good down payment because Seymour
believed "there will be better times within a year." He authorized Allcott to
sell if he could get a suitable deal and reminded him not to sell any Bushnell
land at this time unless he had a power of attorney.[69]

Frederic Bushnell died November 7, 1837, at his parents' home in New
Orleans, and Seymour became president of the bank. Bushnell's "exposure
ague" contracted as a landlooker was blamed for his death.[70] Bushnell, Seymour, and Lee by then jointly owned 3,100 acres in the northwest corner
of Ingham and now it was necessary to partition the land in order to settle
with Bushnell's heirs.

The next year Charles Lee wanted to deliver money to Allcott and hoped
to send it by a Mr. Bush, but Lee wrote on July 15, 1839, "The times here are
very hard and what we shall do for money I know not." Seymour and Lee
would have gladly sold their interest in the land, but there were no buyers. It
was not until September of 1839 that the legal partition of the partners' joint
land was finally accomplished. After the split, Seymour bought out Bushnell's
heirs and took possession of those lands.[71] On January 30, 1840, Seymour's
letter reveals that he is making contact with settlers in Ingham County and
that has alerted him to a problem with his taxes in Michigan. He received
a letter from John Burchard of Mason, an acquaintance from Brockport,

offering his services as a land agent. Therefore, he tells Allcott: "I have seen a letter from a Mr. Burchard of Ingham, an attorney proposing to take the agency of my land in Ingham County which he has seen on the map not knowing probably that you had anything to do with them.—He states that the taxes for the last year were unpaid and returned to the auditor and this year's taxes to Dec 14 were not paid. I hope you will keep up the taxes... I wrote to you last fall and have not heard from you and suppose your mill has engrossed your whole attention but I hope you can find time and purchasers to take all my lands off [my hands] for cash or on credit."[72]

More than a year later, March 20, 1841, Seymour wrote to Allcott to say he has decided to sell his lands in the spring, saying, "As you once suggested my employing another agent I have concluded to empower J. Woolsey Burchard, Treasurer of Ingham County, to sell the Ingham land if he can."[73] He also requested help from Allcott to get lands in other counties sold. However, his letter to Allcott the next month on April 3 indicated land in general was still not moving and he no longer hoped for a profit, so he advised Allcott on strategies for selling the land without a loss through loans to the buyer arranged on a variety of mortgage terms. Seymour closed saying, "Of all the property that has passed through my hands I have never had a tenth part of the trouble as with western lands and I am heartily sick of it."[74] However, Allcott was deeply in debt and unable to be of assistance to Seymour. There were no more letters from Seymour to Allcott.

Marian saved an article, most likely from a Detroit newspaper, in her family scrapbook. Marian must have saved this article because of its explanation of the ordeal the pioneers experienced as a result of the wild cat banking law and the real estate bubble and depression that followed:

> Between August, 1837, and May, 1838, no fewer than 49 banks were started under the new law, with an aggregate nominal capital of between $9,400,000 and $4,000,000... In 1844 the supreme-court declared the banking law unconstitutional and the last hope for the redemption of the notes had departed. It is estimated that $2,000,000 of this wildcat paper was put afloat within the 18 months. At the highest point the nominal banking capital of the state is said to have been $11,000,000, while the real paid-up capital was but about $1,600,000. Often the same parties would be connected with several banks. Michigan bank notes would be sent to other states for circulation and the wildcat issues of Kentucky, Ohio and Indiana would be put in circulation here. Great numbers of counterfeits, as well as bills of broken banks, and some which had never been legally organized at all were in common use as money...
>
> Under the reign of the plethora of money of course the prices of real estate and everything went up. When, one after another, the banks failed and banknotes became worthless, there was a sudden decline in prices of 80 to 90 percent, [the real-estate bubble burst] and a condition of ruin fell upon the state from which it scarcely recovered in 20 years. J. E. B.[75]

John Burchard Settles on the Grand

A civil engineer and surveyor named Cyrus Hewitt recalled coming to Marshall in 1836 to work on laying out and platting several of the towns along the Michigan Central Railroad and north and south of it. Hewitt remembered coming to Eaton Rapids in about 1837, but it was most likely 1839. He went with John Burchard and another man in a "dug out" canoe down the river to the Seymour mill property where he took the levels for the dam that was to be built there.[76]

John had studied law in Rochester, New York, and came to Mason to live in 1839. According to Frank Turner, it was when Seymour learned of John's interest in moving west, he offered his mill site to John, but since it was part of Bushnell's land, he could not sell it to Burchard immediately.[77]

John was quickly recruited as the Justice of the Peace, being the first attorney to reside in the township. He soon became the county prosecuting attorney, appointed on April 26, 1839, by Democratic Governor Stevens T. Mason, thanks to a petition headed by the county judge, Ephraim B. Danforth, and signed by ten other local residents. However, John was not reappointed when William Woodbridge, a Whig, became governor on January 7, 1840. Fortunately John had anticipated the defeat of the unpopular first Governor and had run the previous fall and been elected county treasurer, serving during 1841. At Judge Danforth's request, John was once again appointed prosecuting attorney when Woodbridge stepped down to become a U.S. Senator and John S. Berry, a Democrat, became governor. It was a position that brought a salary of $150 per year, which was helpful because legal work was sparse. (The folly of the politicization of the process of selecting prosecuting attorneys by the governor was repaired in the 1850 State Constitution.)[78] In 1841 John married Frances Haynes and by then he and James Turner were well acquainted—John and James were two of a kind, though John was six years older.

John Burchard had a quick and perceptive mind, and he projected plans and devised many measures to improve the facilities and advance the improvements of the village of Mason and the county.[79] He intended to develop the new site on the Grand River as soon as he could purchase it. It was in 1841 that James Seymour sold the 109.63 acres of land at $5 per acre and loaned John the money to build the dam and sawmill. Frank Turner said Seymour offered the sale for $548 on time as an inducement to John. When the arrangements were complete, Burchard owed on a mortgage of $1,398.[80] Seymour had at last found a way to sell this property at a profit and have money coming in from the interest on the loan, while not having to develop the site himself. John soon had the first log cabin in the area built on the east side of the Grand River. It was quite large, roomy and comfortable,[81] intended to accommodate his family and the workers for his enterprise. The Legislature authorized John's request to build the dam on March 9, 1843.[82]

In November of 1843 James Turner and twelve other men in Vevay Township voted for Democrat John W. Burchard for township supervisor at the annual township meeting.[83] By November, a substantial dam was built from nearby timber and the boulders, clay, and gravel taken from the banks. The footings were in place for the mill when on April 7 of the following year a portion of the dam broke during a spring flood that brought torrents of water down the river. John was killed in a boat accident while attempting to inspect the dam for repairs. He was 29 years old. His loss was deeply mourned by his friends and all of the community at Mason and in Lansing Township, where he had just been elected township supervisor.[84] Frances saved the obituary with the headline, "Fatal Accident." It said, in part:

> Among the first who settled in this place, he was entrusted with many offices by the people, all of which he discharged with credit to himself and to the satisfaction of his constituents… although cut down in the midst of life and usefulness, he lived to see the inhospitable wilderness dotted with fruitful and cultivated fields, and this very spot, [Mason] shaded with the thick foliage of a dense forest,—the lair of the wolf and the deer,—converted into a populous village, the mart of business and wealth, and a county placed in a condition truly enviable… As a politician he was liberal and consistent, ever willing to award the meed and merit to whom it was due, of whatever political party or creed.
>
> By the above decease a wife is bereft of a fond and affectionate friend and bosom companion, and two interesting little children are deprived of a kind father's watchfulness and protection, all, too, in one sad and unexpected moment.[85]

To add to the tragedy, John's body was not recovered immediately. Joseph Kilbourne and some other men made a search in the waters of the Grand. It wasn't until 10 days later that it was found because it had been swept downriver until it came to rest on an island or bar near the Ingersoll property in Delhi Township. At the time of his death, John had made one $10 payment on the mortgage.[86] They had been married only three years and now his widow, Frances, named his friend James Turner the executor of the estate and moved away from the site with her children, Louisa and John. Frances settled in Jackson and eventually married Lane L. Newman of Onondaga Township in 1848. Seymour regained the property and shouldered the development of the dam and mill site from afar.

Any prospects for the Turners of settling near the Burchards were dashed. Marian planted locust trees the following spring along what would someday be the lane of lots 10 and 11 leading to their first house.[87] (This property was not transferred to James Turner until July 5, 1847; however, it was most likely secured earlier by James through John Burchard, acting as land agent for Seymour.) Over time, the Turners acquired more of the land on the north side of the river's bend. It became known as "Turner's Woods." It had been visited and camped on for years by the band of Saginaw Valley Native

Americans led by Chief Okemos who often followed a trail along the river there. The land with a wide variety of hardwoods—oak, maple, walnut, beech, and many others—with little undergrowth and the clear, cool springs that flowed from the bank to the river below were first owned by Fred Bushnell.[88]

James Seymour sought out a contractor to take up where John Burchard had left off and was referred to Joab Page, a man of many talents, a carpenter and builder by trade in New York and his home state of Vermont; he was also an excellent mechanic. His wife, Abigail Olds Page, was also from Vermont. According to his daughter, Cornelia Smith, in 1829-30 he built the first church building ever erected in Vermont "without the use of liquor." He was known for having built the first iron works in Peru, Clinton County, New York. The Page family arrived in Jacksonburgh in 1832 when Abigail and Joab were both 44 years old, and the family was soon well known in the area. Joab built the first sawmill there and another sawmill on the outlet of Grass Lake, which ran through his land. Next he sold his land, and built and kept a tavern called the Grass Lake House on the old Territorial Road, later building a brick hotel there.[89] The Pages once counted sixty covered wagons passing by in one day, carrying families westward with all of their possessions.[90]

The Page family purchased a 160-acre farm in Vevay Township in the fall of 1840. In the autumn of 1844 they moved to the Burchard dam property at the bidding of Seymour, who needed his skills and the skills of his son and sons-in-law as mechanics to complete the sawmill. One son-in-law, Alvin Rolfe, recalled in 1873, it took two days to move from Vevay. "We got there at sundown and found an old log house that had been used for a stable, which we had to clean out before we could find a shelter for the night. My father-in-law took the job of finishing the mill dam and putting up a saw mill." At first, they lived in the Burchards' cabin, but soon a sizeable two-story addition was added to better accommodate the family and anticipated travelers coming to the area. When that happened, Rolfe recalled, "My wife and Louisa, the wife of Chauncy Page, did the cooking for forty or fifty hands. They did the cooking in a five-pail kettle and a tin baker, before a fire in a fireplace." Uncle Joab, as he was called, was elected Justice of the Peace in April 1845 and elected to the office of Lansing Township Supervisor in 1845, 1846, and 1847.[91]

By the mid to late 1840s, land, whether cleared or uncleared, was still in abundance and people knew growth in the new state was all but guaranteed. James Turner decided to take on the role of land agent for James Seymour. (Frank Turner said James Turner was in the land agency business before the age of 21, which would be before April 1841.)[92] Competent land agents were greatly valued because there were those who took the opportunity to mislead non-resident land buyers by creating phony or, at best, poorly conceived, developments to draw investors. One early example in the area of a development plan that did not make it was Biddle City, a mostly on-paper-only town that was platted in the southern part of Lansing Township and probably named for Major John Biddle, head of the Detroit Land Office in the territorial period.[93] The site included the swampy floodplain of the confluence of the Red Cedar River and the Grand River. The panic at the time of statehood led to few buyers.[94] The land was heavily mortgaged by the two sorry speculator/owners, Jerry and William Ford, and eventually sold for taxes.[95]

The advertisement for James' agency in the Whig newspaper, the *Ingham County Herald*,[96] shows he used both New York and local Michigan contacts as references. Considering that so many settlers in the area were from New York, this made good sense.

Dec 12, 1844 Michigan Tax and Land Agency

The subscriber has established an agency for the payment of taxes, sale of lands, investigation of titles, &c., Business entrusted to his care will be promptly attended to.
Particular attention will be paid to the payment of taxes in the townships where they are assigned, if situated within the counties of Ingham, Clinton, Livingston and Jackson, by which a saving of 10 percent will be effected. Address James Turner, Mason, Ingham county, Michigan.
Reference
Wm. Jackson, Leoni, Jackson county, Michigan
Coman, Hopkins & Co., 60 Front St. and John M'Comb, 63 2d Avenue, New York
H. S. Beeche & Co., Buffalo, New York
A. Champion, Rochester, NY
Henry, Hitchcock & Co., Cazenovia, NY
R. Johnson & Co, Cazenovia, NY
Gen. Charles Fay, Cazenovia, NY
L. W. Tinker, Detroit, Michigan

Ingham County Herald, January 9, 1845

Still only in his mid-twenties, James was making extensive business contacts. A few weeks after the above advertisement was published, James added Eaton County to his service area, and James Seymour was added as a reference. James also included a testimonial from all the county public officials saying, "We the undersigned, from our long acquaintance with Mr. James Turner, take pleasure in recommending him to non-resident land owners as a land and tax agent, being satisfied that the business of the land owner and tax payer will at all times meet prompt attention at his hands."[97] The signers included Daniel Case who had taken over as prosecuting attorney and would soon join the Turner circle of family and close friends. Daniel was one of the earliest pioneers in the region and had recently returned from adventures in the southwestern United States. The two met when Daniel was 32 and James was 23.

With cash in short supply, the Turner and Jackson mercantile store accepted maple sugar, grass seed, bees wax, and grain in payment. The store

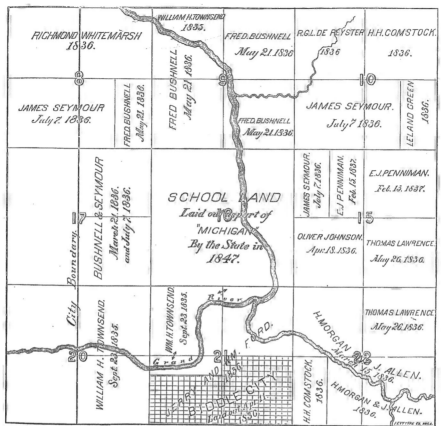

PLAT OF SECTIONS IN THE CITY OF LANSING, SHOWING ORIGINAL LAND ENTRIES.

Durant, p. 123, CADL photo.

carried all sorts of commodities, and in 1846 James and William added new services for wool processing: "wool, in any quantities, can be left with the subscriber at Mason, and it will be promptly forwarded to the machines and the rolls returned to Mason, at five cents per pound." The store also sold dry goods, groceries, crockery, leather, salt, nails and glass.[98]

An advertisement a year later in the *Ingham County Herald* showed the partners' bent for advertising in tough economic times. Since proof of payment by county and town orders (vouchers) could be used to pay taxes, the store offered to accept this paper for merchandise. James and William could then turn around and use it to pay taxes for the absentee landowners they represented as land agents. They offered "the largest stock of GROCERIES ever offered in this market; and any quantity of Crockery, of the hot and latest patterns--which with Leather, Salt, Nails and Glass, makes up the best stock of Goods, Wares and Merchandise ever offered in Mason."[99]

Since the death of John Burchard, progress had been slow at the new development in the furthest northwest corner of Ingham County while Mason had continued to grow. However, things were about to change. In 1846 the Bank of Rochester wound up its affairs and went out of business when its charter expired, and James Seymour moved to Flushing with his wife Mira and three children, Louisa, Hattie and Charles. Genesee County Historian Franklin Ellis said James Seymour was one of the ablest men of his time in the state.[100] Soon James Seymour and the settlers at Mason would be working together to grow Ingham County.

Mr. Seymour Tips the Scale for Lansing

James Turner was credited with playing a very prominent role in the founding of the new capital city. The constitution provided that the Capital was to be moved inland from Detroit in time for the 1848 session of the Legislature and the competition between cities for this prize was furious. According to one early settler, Daniel S. Mevis, who in 1911 wrote his memories of the early days in Lansing in his little book, *Pioneer Recollections*: "Among the people of the early forties, there was one man a little more prominent in the development of the infant city than many of the old worthies of the time. In fact, it is undoubtedly true that James Turner, with the assistance of James and Horatio Seymour, was entitled to the credit of inducing the commissioners to locate the new capitol where it now is."[101]

According to historian Samuel Durant, James himself "was wont to say that the Seymours and the Townsends, of New York, threw a very heavy weight into the scale in favor of Lansing. They had employed a gentleman of Kalamazoo County, [This should read Calhoun County because James Turner was referring to Sidney Allcott.] a good judge of land, to examine the unsold lands in the State and make investments for them. They were paying him for his services and giving him a certain share in the investments. Previous to the agitation in reference to the removal of the Capitol he had located lands for the Townsends to the south of section 16, in Lansing township, and to the north of the same for the Seymours. In 1846 Allcott wrote these parties that he believed the capital would be removed to the vicinity of their lands, and said he would not sell his interest in them for $20,000. They immediately came to Detroit, where the Legislature was then holding its sessions, and exerted all the influences which they could safely bring to bear upon the subject. Mr. Turner always believed that but for their influence the capital would have been located at some other point."[102] Horatio Seymour was also likely involved because his cousin (actually his second cousin) had deeded him half of his property, although they held it jointly and undivided.[103]

James also worked with the county's state representative, Joseph Kilbourne, a Democrat who lived near the farm of James' brother Marshall at Hamilton, and they tried to build alliances with other communities as they lobbied for the Ingham site.[104] The biggest drawback was that there was no railroad, but he found Seymour and Townsend could bring many incentives to the bargaining table to try to encourage the state legislators to choose Michigan, Michigan, (as the site in Lansing Township was first called) over all others who pursued this prize in the hopes of ensuring their own community's successful development. Many towns were offering free land to the government as inducement. In January 1847 Seymour wrote a letter to the legislators saying if the seat of government were moved to his lands, he would give twenty acres and erect the capitol and buildings in the same size and quality as their current buildings for use of the state without charge until permanent buildings could be constructed. He even put up $15,000 in bonds to ensure that the buildings would be ready on time.[105] It was a very generous offer, but he was not taken up on it.

The Townsends' mercantile firm of Townsend and Brothers in New York City offered land, the right for the state to take framing timber and stone from any of their land for use in construction of the state buildings and to build a bridge over the Grand River in Section 21 at their own expense. They offered a bond of $10,000.[106] Their proposal was not accepted either. However, another strategy was very successful. It was said the map that James Seymour provided to each legislator showing the distance in miles from all the major cities to Michigan, Michigan. Showing the capitol site as the hub was very persuasive.[107] When Marian and Adella attended the Pioneer Society meeting on June 5, 1884, Adella addressed the meeting about how Lansing was chosen as the capitol:

> In the year 1836, in the constitution of Michigan, there was a provision that "the seat of Government for the State shall be at Detroit, or at such other place or places as may be prescribed by law, until the year eighteen hundred and forty-seven, when it shall be permanently located by the Legislature."
>
> On the 6th day of January 1847, Mr. Thorp, chairman of the committee in the House on State affairs, introduced a bill to locate the Capitol, pursuant to Section nine of Article twelve of the Constitution of the State. In the bill introduced by Mr. Thorp, the place of location was left blank, which was first filled by the name of Grand Blanc, Genesee County. By a vote of a majority of the committee of the whole, the name of a place would be inserted, but when it came to the passage of the bill, it was sure to be defeated, till almost every city, town and village in the State had been spoken of, or voted for as a site for the Capitol. The bill had many amendments, and the amendments were amended; the Legislature thus playing at legislation. On the 15th day of February, after all these days of voting for and against each place mentioned, a bill passed the House locating the Capitol in the town of Lansing. At that time, the township of Lansing had only eight voters.
>
> The vote on the passage of the bill was forty-four in favor and seventeen against. I have been told that the members of the Legislature had

no idea that the matter was permanently settled; members only voted on the much voted bill in order to get it off their hands so that they might give their precious time to the election of a United States Senator. The bill was sent to the Senate, and every device that was possible was resorted to to amend the bill and send it back to the House, where they intended to kill it. After nearly a month's work on the question of the location of the Capitol, the bill passed the Senate on the 9th day of March by a vote of twelve in favor to eight against it. During the time the question was before the Legislature every effort was made to keep the Capitol in Detroit, or as near it as possible. On reading over the records it can readily be seen that whenever the site mentioned was near Detroit it was looked on with less favor, by the diminished number of votes. The general opinion seemed to be that the Capitol should be near the center of the State as possible; "in this they builded better than they knew." To do this the Capitol was located in a dense wilderness.[108]

The Land Commissioners Arrive

After the act was passed to locate the capital in Lansing Township, a commission to choose the precise location was appointed consisting of three representatives of the state's land commissioner office and James Seymour and William Townsend. The commission selected a spot on which to erect a capitol building, one mile from the Burchard dam, on the School Section, section 16. In May, the commission united in laying out a town plat, two and one fourth miles long, and one wide, encompassing both sides of the river. The Pages were the only people on the tract, and their nearest neighbors were four and a half miles away. Amy and Justus Gilkey and their six grown children were a mile and a half to the northwest. One settler recalled, "Within a few weeks after the town was laid out, one thousand persons moved into the place."[109]

A young itinerant Methodist minister, Rev. Frank A. Blades, happened into the area and by chance met up with the first commissioner to arrive. Blades' family had come from western New York to Detroit, which he characterized as a large village, in 1835, and then settled in Grand Blanc, Genesee County. He was following his new circuit, which included an appointment in Ingham County and one or two in Eaton County. Blades told how the beautiful spot for the capitol was selected in a report to the Michigan Pioneer Society in 1903:

> News in those days did not travel as fast as it does now, but it got around that the capitol of the State was to be located in the wilderness, somewhere in Ingham County, so in the early parts of April, 1847, when I went up to see the eastern part of my circuit, I thought I would go and see if I could find the ground that had been selected. I came up to the place that was afterwards known as "the lower town" of Lansing, but at that time known as Page's saw mill. It was a saw mill on the property

that belonged to the Seymours. I stopped there, near to the supposed location of the capitol, and went in and found an old gentleman by the name of Page, and a very pleasant family. I told him what my mission was, and he gave me certain directions following certain lines of marked trees by which I might find myself upon the school section indicated as the ground selected. At that time most of us were as ready to follow our way through the woods by the old marked trees and witness trees for the section corner or quarter section corner as we are now by the roads. After following the directions given by the old gentleman, I reached a spot that was clearly in my mind within the lines that were designated as the place upon which the capitol would be located. It was on a beautiful knoll in a dense wilderness. The outlook was grand and lovely beyond description; I never saw such a piece of timber before or since.

I sat down on a log and was taking in the scenery, and remember well the thought that passed through my mind: "It is too bad to destroy such scenery as this; too bad to build a babbling town and break this silence and mar this scene so beautiful and grand." While sitting there I heard a noise; it sounded as though it might be a bear or a deer, but a deer hardly made such a noise as that. I waited, and in a few minutes a man emerged from the shadow of the trees into the light; as I remember him he was about six feet high and well proportioned. He saw me nearly as quickly as I saw him, and he was the first to break the silence by saying, "I think this is probably a mutual surprise; it is on my part;" and I assured him that it was none the less so on mine. He asked me who I was, and I told him I was a Methodist minister looking for a congregation. I asked whom I had the honor of meeting in this wild place. He said, "My name is Glen [James Glenn[110]]; I am one of the Commissioners looking for a place to locate the State Capitol." I said to him: "Mr. Glen do you take in this scene? Look how grand and how stately are those trees, and how they sway their branches to the wind. Look upon this scene, how beautiful it is; it is too bad to bring a babbling town into this sacred place." He looked at me and said; "Mr. Blades, I want to make a bargain with you. If you will help me find a place to locate the capitol, I will try to help you find a congregation."

I accepted his proposition. We proceeded to locate the capitol on that beautiful spot by driving into the ground a stake cut with my pocket knife, and marking some small trees to identify the spot, and I learned afterwards that the place we agreed upon was the identical spot select-ed where the capitol should stand, and where it now stands, both the temporary and permanent buildings. The Commissioners met the next day and after a careful examination of the grounds located the place for the capitol.

Mr. Glen expressed the wish that we could get something to eat, and I told him that I left my horse down at the saw-mill, and he remarked that where there is a saw-mill there is always men, and usually there was something to eat. Following the lines back he went down with me, and we got there just before the horn blew for dinner. I introduced him to Mr. Page, and he was very cordially received. I remember we had pork and beans for dinner, and what else we had I don't know, but the "cheek" of Mr. Glen disclosed itself just as the dinner was over. He related to Mr. Page the incident of our meeting in the wilderness, and his proposition to "help me find a congregation;" he said he had already found what we thought to be a good place for the capitol, and he thought right here was a good place for a congregation. "and (addressing Mr. Page), with your approval, I move that Mr. Blades give us a sermon right here and now." The motion was carried unanimously, and as it was always a motto of my life to obey orders when it is possible, I arose, gave out a hymn, which was sung from memory, and after a short prayer, I proceeded to speak and preach to them the best I knew how for about twenty minutes, and this, so far as I know, was the first sermon preached in Lansing. Subsequently I was there in May. I had been invited to preach there Sunday morning, and a place had been selected in the woods under a big beech tree in the vicinity of the place where the capitol now stands.

The ground chosen was soon cleared, the woods disappeared as if by magic, and it was not long before streets were being laid out and buildings began to rise preparatory to the convening of the first Legislature to meet in Lansing for the session of 1848.[111]

The party of the other commissioners and the surveyors took three days to make the forty-mile trip from Jackson with ox teams, finding the last twelve miles from Mason nearly impassable because of the spring's overflowing streams. They remained in the area for several weeks, staying at the home and boarding house of Abigail and Joab Page. They made trips down river to visit Justus Gilkey who sold them his homemade whiskey whenever required. William Townsend had a space of about an acre cleared where the capitol would be built and a game of baseball was played there.[112] The completed town plat included some of the land near section 16 that had been platted by Townsend and, to the north, the land platted by Seymour.[113] The work of building the new state capital was about to begin.

Chapter 3

The Capital "Comes In"

The people in the surrounding area were very enthusiastic about the coming of the capital city. Alvin Rolfe, the son-in-law of Abigail and Joab Page, recalled, "In the winter of 1846-47 the Capitol was located at Lansing and it caused much excitement. People came from a great distance in sleighs to see the Capital and all they could see was a solitary log house that we were living in. When the news came that the Capital had been located in Lansing the people in Delhi and the south part of Lansing Township cut a large log some forty or fifty feet long, and with a great many yoke drew it to the mill. When they got in sight of where we lived they got up on the log and gave three cheers, swung their hats and cried, 'The Capitol has come.' They gave us the log and told us to saw it up for the Capitol, and my impression is that some of it went into the state building."

Marian and her sixteen-year-old sister Adella never forgot the day in early March that they all piled into sleds and made the trip through the forest from Mason to Michigan, Michigan. Just as people might travel to see a ship come into harbor or a circus arrive and set up, they journeyed the fourteen miles to see where the workers would arrive and start construction. Adella described the beginning for the Pioneer Society Annual Meeting on June 5, 1884: "At what is now called North Lansing there were a few acres cleared, and a saw-mill and a log house erected; also at the west side of the river, where the west end of the Franklin Street bridge now stands, there were five acres 'slashed.' At the time the news reached Mason of the location of the Capitol at Lansing, I was there visiting my sister, Mrs. James Turner. A sleigh load of young people, Wilbur F. Storey of Jackson being among the number, came out to 'view the landscape o'er,' as he termed it, and to see the Capitol come in. The log house, saw-mill and the few acres of clearing did not look very imposing, but we thought of the old saying, 'great oaks from little acorns grow,' and we were comforted." [114] In a matter of weeks the transformation that Adella's expedition anticipated was underway, with only months before the legislators would arrive.

From Forest to Capital in Seven Months

The story of the settlement of Michigan's capital is indeed unique although other states' capitals, such as Ohio's, were also located in wilderness. It was not a county seat to begin with, as other capitals were. It did not begin as a town or even a village. It was built "from scratch" in a grueling seven months after it was platted, working against the deadline of the arrival of the state Legislature to begin its first session in January of 1848 as required by the state constitution. The terrain was not only very dense hardwood forest, but swampy, and the nearest railroad was in Jacksonburgh. Yet the goal was to build a prosperous industrialized capital city in the long run and a town ready for legislators, lobbyists, and government business immediately.

Frank Turner, James and Marian's nephew, wrote: "The removal of the state capital from Detroit to the woods of Lansing township, and the clearing out for and building of an embryo city and capitol building in the dense forest in seven months, shows as vast an amount of daring and courage as was ever recorded in any state history." [115] Although this event took place in a period of financial panic and "wildcat" money, some of the old settlers said that hard work, kindly co-operation, and great hopes for the future were better than money and had a wider and freer circulation. "Time has shown they told the truth," said Turner.[116]

Samuel L. Kilbourne of Hamilton, whose father Joseph had been helpful as a legislator from Ingham when the site for the capital was chosen, said in 1909, "At the time the state Legislature selected the site of Lansing for the state capital they appropriated $10,000 for erecting the buildings and $1,000 for removing the archives, records and furniture from Detroit, which until that time, had been the state capital. It may appear that $11,000 was a small amount for the work to be done, but it may have been the principle of the joke about George Washington, who was credited with throwing a silver dollar across the Potomac river in his day while not many could do it now, the explanation being that in those days a dollar would go further than it would now." [117] Local residents traveling to the new settlement site came from cabins and temporary shelters scattered around the mid-Michigan region; many came from the forests and the two county seats of DeWitt in Clinton County and Mason in Ingham. Adella recalled the tremendous effort to prepare for the arrival of the legislators:

> A few weeks brought a great change in this part of the town;—"lower town," as it was then called. The woodsman's ax was heard in all quarters felling the trees of the heavy timbered land. Board shanties and tents were the order of the day, and they sprang up like mushrooms. The place bore a striking resemblance to some of our western and mining cities of the past years as well as the present day. On talking with Mrs. J. N. Bush a few days since about those early days, she said her family and Mr. Powell's family found lodgings that night in one of the board shanties, where

a field bed was spread, and thirty persons lodged there. They thought themselves fortunate to find a place where they could lay their heads.

D. L. Case and Hiram Smith came from Mason; they had the material all prepared for a store at Jefferson, a small village three miles from Mason; it was brought to North Lansing and set up. It was the first building erected for a store; it still stands on the corner of Franklin and Center streets, east of the Franklin House. The work was done by Capt. Cowles, who is still living in Lansing. The store is yet in good condition, showing that the work was faithfully done. It is used at the present time by S. P. Buck as an agricultural implement store.[118]

North Lansing, or Lower Town, grew up along the Grand River north of the capital where Burchard had placed the dam. This area was down river from the capitol, or *lower* on the river, and grew up along the east-west street, then called Franklin Street and now called Grand River Avenue. This was where James Seymour owned much of the land and had it platted for settlement. The story of the founding of Lansing can be traced among the north-end streets named for its founders Burchard, Kilbourne, Seymour, Townsend, and Turner. At the time there was also a little stream named Allcott Creek flowing from the east side into the river. It was common for pioneers to use names from where they had lived before, and in Seymour's hometown of Rochester there was a Franklin Street running along the Genesee River.

Seymour and William Townsend were great promoters and enthusiastic speculators. Frank Turner said that they and the others they had interested in their plans "told their neighbors and business associates in Rochester, New York, that the sylvan forests in town 4, north of range 2 west in Ingham county were ideal hunting grounds and abounded in wild game and wild honey; that fortunes could be made in lumbering; that the land when cleared would produce like the garden of Eden; and the new state capitol, set in one of these beautiful groves, would be an architectural dream."[119]

The logical place for the new settlement was the site of Seymour's dam, but the capitol buildings' site developed along the Grand River about a mile further south of the settlement, as Rev. Blades described. This area became Middle Town and was separated by woods from Lower Town, more woods, and then Upper Town further up the river along Main Street. The less-than-compact development occurred this way because the government wanted to use government lands. Governor Alpheus Felch secured the 16th section, designated as the school section in each county, for the placement of the capitol. The result was a considerable savings to the citizens because by so doing, Felch protected the site of the capital from sale to land speculators at what would have been giveaway prices and saved the state from having to buy land for the state building sites. The move also contributed substantially to the state's educational fund from the proceeds for unneeded land when the government sold it. Ultimately, the school section of 640 acres brought $250,000.[120] Therefore, Kilbourne could say Felch really did make a dollar go further.

There was such a deep forest wilderness that James' brother Richard recalled that, while looking for a stake that marked the ground where the capitol building was to be erected, he became bewildered and was lost in the woods.[121] The state officers overseeing the building of the capitol lent their assistance and would enter into competitive chopping matches.[122] There was so much chopping going on that the clerk at the general store of Bush, Thomas and Lee said it was not uncommon to sell three or four boxes of axes a day, each box containing a dozen axes. The state officers overseeing the building of the capitol lent their assistance and would enter into competitive chopping matches.[123] They all knew they had a deadline to meet. Everybody was invited to take part in the raising of the capitol: "In fact the day was made a holiday for everybody within reach of the Capitol City... Many a gallon of good Kentucky whiskey was used on that state occasion," one participant recalled.[124]

The House on Turner Street

In the midst of the hubbub, James began to clear a place to erect the Turner's home, the first frame house in the settlement, about forty rods (220 yards) from where the Lower Town bridge would be built.[125] The street in front of the house, which was the major north-south street of Lower Town, was named Turner Street. In the spring of 1847 the Turner family moved from Mason to Lansing and were all day on the road because of the mud.[126] Marian was not the first woman to settle there but never could remember the exact date she arrived.[127] The family lived in a tent on the bluff of the outside bend of the meandering river, where the current Turner-Dodge House is located, while waiting for the new house to be finished. At that time, they had two little girls, Harriet, aged three, and baby Marian, not yet two months old. Their first baby had died at birth while they were living in Mason.

All the wood for the house came from Mason. Windows and framework were also made in Mason and transported the thirteen miles. According to Frank Turner:

> The sound of the hammer and the busy workmen added new interest to the scene in Lower Town... The sills and other parts of the frame were hewn out of hardwood; the siding, flooring and cornice were dressed by hand, and the first shingles were riven with an old-fashioned hand frow by workmen in Mason, then hauled by ox team over the hogback road through the almost unbroken wilderness to the few months old Capital City.
>
> While the workmen were erecting this building they had to fight deer flies, mosquitoes, snakes and other pests of the wilderness. I re-member one of them told about killing two moccasin snakes that came

out and sunned themselves on a log in a cat hold just north of the house. He said they were real snakes as the men had nothing to drink but spring water.[128]

When the house was ready, the family must have been very happy to leave tent living behind. The house was small at first, one-and-a-half-stories, with several additions added later to accommodate the Turners' growing family. It was built quickly, and they moved into it in July, before it was finished. There was an outhouse behind the house. Not too long after that, a barn was built.

Stoves were not in use in those early days, but back-to-back brick fireplaces were common, one in the kitchen and one in the parlor with one chimney for both. An iron crane hung in the kitchen's open fireplace suspending the kettles over the fire. A row of pots could hang from hooks along the whole length of the crane. The "spider" was of iron with three legs and set over coals placed on the brick hearth. Marian baked in a tin oven set in front of the fire or in an iron bake kettle with coals under and on top of it. Primitive though they might be, these kitchen furnishings produced many memorable meals.[129]

The table of the Turner family benefited from food items that James received from bartering at his store. Towards the end of the season, Marian harvested corn and potatoes she had planted and cut up her pumpkins in circles to dry on poles in the kitchen. Canning was not yet perfected so the settlers relied on drying many food items. On the south side of the house there was an entrance to the cellar where food could be stored. Marian also searched the brush piles for eggs from the chickens that ran free. The cow provided milk and butter. Potatoes were roasted in the ashes, and johnnycake baked before the fire. Though working hard, she enjoyed her days. "Neighbors would converse like this, 'Mrs. B., how are you getting along with your flax spinning?' or, 'Mrs. M., how much wool are you working up this year, and how soon will your girls have their new woolen dresses done?' The topics discussed by the men might be, 'How do your cattle

The Turner house in Lower Town, CADL photo.

get along on browse?' and, 'Have you got mink skins and ashes enough saved to get your tax money?'"[130]

Because the Turners' was the first wood frame house in the quickly rising town, it was one of the "sights" of the settlement and was soon considered a landmark. Perhaps the residents were a bit homesick for their towns and villages in the East. [131] There is just one account of the life at the Turners' house on Turner Street, published on September 30, 1916, by Frank Turner, who spent many pleasant hours visiting there as a little boy:

> If the walls of this old house could speak they could tell of many remarkable events that took place in the early pioneer days. This house was the meeting place for all the Turner families. Brother James kept open house. The Methodist ministers, when they came on circuit, never neglected to call as they were always sure of good cheer and good beds at the class leader's home. Sometimes the preacher brought the whole family and the more there were the heartier the welcome. The bashful youth brought his blushing sweetheart there to be married and to meet Brother James, who always had a word of good cheer to give them. The good wife always had a wedding cake baked, or in the oven.
>
> Chief Okemos and his band always got hungry when they arrived at "Big Chief James'" house. The Quakers from Albany, New York who were investing money in Michigan lands, always stopped with James because he was their agent as well as the agent of the Seymours, Wadsworths, Danforths, and other New York financiers. What a tale those old walls could tell of the conferences between these men and their agent about the future growth and development of this city in the woods and the prosperous farms that were to surround it. We can imagine a grave Quaker listening to the agent's glowing description of the future growth of the capital city, and finally saying, 'We will leave the matter with thee, James, and trust in thy good judgment.' In those days the agent thought more of the trust and confidence bestowed than the percentage he was to receive.[132]

From the start, James was a leader in the education of children in his church. It was said that, "He was a warm friend of the temperance cause, and an earnest, consistent Christian. He was an active member and supporter of the Methodist Episcopal Church, and, for nineteen years, was Superintendent of the Sabbath-school." The Methodists used James Seymour's building on lot 6, block 14, as a church. It was originally built as a warehouse and later used as a barn—thus it was sometimes called "God's Barn." All denominations joined in buying it and fitting it up for a proper meeting place. The women furnished it and were proud of it. Frank Turner, wrote, "I (Dr. F. N. Turner) went to Sunday school in this building and the older James Turner was our superintendent. Members of this church used to boast of his length of service and no absent or tardy marks against his record. He was a great lover of children and never a youngster walked the streets of North Lansing but he formed his acquaintance and invited him to come to Sunday school."[133]

The Seymour Hotel

During the rush to build the capital in the woods, all of the Turners' closest friends and business partners, Hiram Smith and future brothers-in-law Daniel Case and John W. Longyear, along with James' brother Richard and John's brother Ephraim, soon relocated from Mason. James Seymour was there, though he continued to live with his family in Flushing. Hotels, stables, mercantile stores, a bakery, a tin smith's shop, two bridges, mills, a post office, and more were needed to get the town going.[134] That first year James opened a general store similar to his store in Mason. It was on the first floor of the Seymour Hotel, the first hotel to be built. James continued his work as a land agent and put his brother John's son, Amos, to work in his store. Over time, James helped develop Amos' business skills until Amos was able to go off on his own in the produce and grocery business. Amos became highly respected for the wool and wheat business he later developed for the region and for the two blocks of brick commercial buildings he developed on Michigan Avenue.[135]

Adeline, 19, and Amos, 15, came to James and Marian's home when James' brother John died in June of 1848 in Mason at the age of forty-seven, just six months after the death of his wife Rebecca, very likely in childbirth. The couple was buried in White Oak Township's Mount Pleasant Cemetery near Dansville.[136] They left nine minor children, the youngest about six months of age. After the Turner family moved to Washtenaw County, John had come to Michigan in 1838 or 1839 with Rebecca, their children, and Rebecca's family, the Hayners. John purchased 400 acres of Land Grant land in Washtenaw, Jackson, and southern Ingham Counties[137] They lived on their farm in White Oak Township. John was serving as White Oak Township Supervisor[138] the year he died. Under probate, James assumed responsibility as executive and guardian with Rebecca's brother, Abraham Hayner of White Oak.[139] The younger children were found homes among the other Turner families in Ingham County.[140]

James' brother Richard cleared forest for his own farm on the west side of the Grand River and engaged in business with James. Richard worked as a carpenter on the Seymour Hotel and on the new temporary state capitol building.[141] Daniel Buck, another of the builders, remembered working through Christmas on the plasterwork for the Seymour Hotel to make the deadline for the arrival of the Legislature.[142]

By summer, there were several stores started up in addition to the one belonging to Hiram and Daniel, the Turner store in the Seymour Hotel, and one owned by Crossman and Walker of Flint. These stores provided goods and supplies to those who came to help build the state capitol, the aforementioned Bush, Thomas and Lee store in Upper Town being the largest such enterprise. James' store in the Seymour Hotel exchanged such commodities as wheat, corn, oats, grass seed, flaxseed, pork, lard, tallow and beeswax for candle making, butter, cheese, furs, deerskins, hides, and ashes or black salts made from the ashes.[143] Black salts were impure potash made from wood ashes.[144]

Richard's son, Frank, wrote about the Seymour Hotel based upon his own memories and the recollections of his father:

> The building originally was 48x128 feet, with cellar, and two stories high. Lumber and interior finish for the new hostelry was hauled from the Seymour mills at Flushing by oxen over mere trails. Some of the hardware, hinges for doors, etc., was brought from Eaton Rapids by boat as much of the traffic then was on the Grand river. The hotel was built on the city's first clearing… For miles upon miles west was unbroken timber.
>
> Lansing's first hotel had few conveniences, but was shelter and served good meals. It had one convenience not known to modernity however, and that was a bar. Its lighting system was candles. If guests were sick in the night or wanted anything they "hollered." If the landlord was awake he heard them and responded. If asleep, the guest "hollered until tired."[145]

In February the first year, while the Legislature was still in session, the first musical troupe performed at the Seymour House. It was one of the finest shows of its class and the first of its kind that Lansing had ever seen. One resident remembered: "Wood & Gillam's Minstrels was the first show staged here and the dining room was packed with state officials, legislators, townspeople and visitors from Dewitt and other places." There were two mulattoes who were the owners and twelve members of the company, "all colored men and they gave a regular old fashion minstrel show. It was there I first heard the song 'The Camptown Races,' with the chorus which became famous, 'I'll bet my money on the bob-tailed mare; who'll bet on the grey?'"[146]

James Seymour as a long-time prohibitionist was opposed to having a bar in his hotel but at the time the capital was being built, not enough public sentiment was aligned with the temperance position against unregulated drinking, public or private. Seymour eventually disassociated himself from the hotel because of his views opposing liquor.[147] Frank Turner recalls, "One of the early pioneers relates how a saloon was started in a small tent with a rough board for the bar and a barrel of whisky for stock in trade. This saloonist did not do much business because Mr. Seymour had his stock destroyed and the man banished. Mr. Seymour, when he finished his hotel, found he would have to put in a bar, but refusing to do this, he sold or leased the building."[148]

James Seymour was not the only one in Lower Town who was tough on saloonists. Adella Munroe Case remembered how Joab Page handled things when he was a member of the Town Board to grant liquor licenses for selling intoxicating liquors. "A man wanted a license to sell liquor; he refused, and said the law required a man to have a good moral character, and this man was notoriously bad; he could not grant the license. The man applied who bore a very good character; he was to get the license and the bad man before mentioned was to sell the whisky. Although Mr. Page knew nothing of the bargain he still refused to grant a license; when pressed for a reason for his refusal, he said he held that a man of good moral character would not sell intoxicating liquors; he would do good to his neighbor, not evil."[149]

Joel Warner, a circus promoter and proprietor in the early 1870s and the city's mayor in 1878, remembered the Seymour Hotel this way:

> Business at that time was very much condensed and clustered about the corners of Franklin and Center sts. James Seymour and his copartners owned nearly all of the land in this immediate vicinity, and to boom their property erected a fine hotel, which they call the Seymour House. This was the attractive feature of the village, and, for several years the leading hotel in Lansing. This hotel was headquarters for the law makers of the state, who were at the time in session in the new capitol, located on the block bordered by Washington and Capitol aves. on the east and west and by Allegan and Washtenaw sts. on the north and south. As an aggregation of law makers and fun makers, this general assembly here out-Webstered Daniel the Great and put to shame the favorite Sons of Momus.
>
> Social events were limited for the lack of convenient places to meet. There were no theaters, no clubs, and no special attractions, and when the men and boys wanted an evening of good social enjoyment they would gather in the spacious bar room of the hotel and listen to the jokes and yarns of the others.
>
> A two-plank walk extended from the hotel to the capitol over which the distinguished sojourners were wont to tramp to and from every day during their stay in the city of the woods. One member, an old hunter, always carried his gun and one night he came home with a large turkey strung over his shoulder that he had killed near the hill where Bailey M. Buck now lives. Fresh meat, other than wild game, was a scarce article. Partridges and quail were plenty, and the hotel table was always well supplied with these dainty and palatable meats, and when the warm spring days brought the chattering squirrel from his winter hiding place, the landlord would go or send a man out with a shotgun, who would return in an hour or so with a dozen black squirrels that would provide a delicious potpie for dinner.
>
> Quite frequently deer were killed within what is now the corporate limits of the city, and one day I remember a large black bear came into the village. Just west of the bridge two Indians took the trail and captured the animal about where the School for the Blind is located.
>
> Indians were very plenty here in those days. Old Okemos, a noted chief, with his tribe made frequent visits to the village. They would go into camp in what was known as the Turner woods, now occupied by the spacious residence of Hon. F. L. Dodge. They would remain several days, exchanging furs, dried venison, roots, herbs, etc., for such articles as their tastes desired and of what the two merchants kept a good sup-

ply, especially for the Indian trade. A small quantity of "fire water" was usually sandwiched in with other purchases.

It was an interesting sight to see the Indians coming to town. They came on their ponies, Indian file, or to make it plain for the uninitiated, single file. Old Okemos always in the lead. The squaws, like the males, rode astride and carried their camp equipage strapped on behind the rider. The train always reached from Center st. out beyond the Camp farm, nearly a mile in length. It was always a half holiday when this grand caravan was headed for camping ground in the Turner woods, and on one occasion the attraction proved so great that the Legislature adjourned and loaned their august presence as spectators to this wild and weird pageant illustrated by our original American citizens.

Another incentive for the assembling of the people was the arrival of the stage from Detroit. The Seymour House was the landing place for the stage and at its arrival daily about 6 p.m., the sound of the driver's horn for which the inhabitants were listening, would cause a stampede of the whole population for the corners, and about the hotel. The stage driver was a bigger man than Jackson. The interest and excitement that occurs about our railroad stations of the present day on arrival of trains are not to be compared with the interest taken in the arrival of the old Concord coach, drawn by four foaming steeds and the crack and flourish of the Jehu's whip.

North Lansing was about the whole thing in those days. It was the principal part of what is now our beautiful city. We were one happy family. No jealousies, no social distinction—all seemed united in the one great object of building a city, people with fathers and mothers, of who our children in after years might with pride turn back the pages for the book of progress and say "they were my ancestors."[150]

Besides the Page family's Grand River House near the Seymour Hotel, six other hotels in Upper Town and Middle Town and a small eating-place were soon completed, but not until after the legislators and lobbyists began arriving in December of 1847 for the January session.[151] In 1853, the Seymour Hotel was sold, became the Franklin House and changed hands many times over during the rest of the century. Frank Turner said it was popular as a stopping place for stages that plied between Lansing and Detroit and Lansing and northern points, "Horses were changed at the old hotel, which had a barn of huge proportions in the rear. With the coming of the railroads, the stage business became a dead issue. From that period the hotel's patronage began to decline."[152]

The Manufactories

Limited accommodations for the Legislature was not the only problem the Ingham pioneers faced. Manufacturing and industry were slow to develop. Lack of hard money in the area and the losses many had suffered during the real-estate bubble of 1837 were still inhibiting growth. People continued to favor payment in silver or gold coin over paper currency and feared deflation caused by bankers who loaned out too much money and did not hold enough in reserve. Understanding this issue was very important to every settler who wanted to help Lansing grow and continued to be for the rest of the century, as long as adequate bank regulation and enforcement eluded them.

The untrustworthiness of paper money, the scarcity of coin, and the demand for astute appraisal of goods brought in for trade in his store were the everyday challenges that James Turner faced as a merchant in early Lansing. The scarcity of reliable money was one challenge he decided to face head-on by bringing good money from trustworthy sources into the community through the export of pearl ash to the East.

Potash factories, producers of potassium carbonate from wood ash, were an established part of manufacturing in the East. Because of the financial panic, banking problems, and slow economic recovery, the trading of commodities such as ash and black salts was very important to the Michigan settlers as well. However, because there was no processing factory near Lansing,[153] James established a pearl ash factory, or ashery, on the riverbank across from the mill on Franklin Street to meet the need (pearl ash was a more refined product than potash). When the pioneer farmers first arrived, they might simply mix ash from the trees they burned during the clearing of the land with the soil of their newly cleared land as the Munroes did or leach rain through ashes for lye to mix with animal fat to make soap. A pearl ash factory provided the means to trade ash for merchandise they could not produce on the farm and to obtain cash. Even though annual taxes for a 160-acre farm were less than $5.00 a year for most of the settlers, it was often a huge effort to raise this amount in cash.[154]

There was no shortage of customers for the Turner Pearl Ash Factory. Some backwoodsmen made a living by burning off the hardwood trees for ash and processing them into pure black salts during the winter. They made maple syrup in the early spring and brought their products into town. Dressed in raccoon skin hats and big fur coats, they stopped at James' ashery and his general store, and then were off to a saloon on the south end for liquid refreshment and the news.

The process of making potash was somewhat like boiling maple syrup down to sugar. Water was poured over dry ashes in a wooden vat and liquid ashes drained off the bottom and boiled down in a five-gallon iron kettle, or pot, over an open fire until all the moisture was gone. The resulting block of cooked "pot-ash," containing particles of carbon, was called "black salts." James' ash factory could start the process from either the ashes or the black salts to burn off the carbon and create "pearl ash." Pearl ash was produced by maintaining a hardwood fire under a potash kettle until the black salts first liquefied and then the moisture was removed. This refined potash could be sold for a variety of purposes and was needed for saleratus (a naturally occurring sodium or potassium bicarbonate) used as baking soda, for glass and soap making, dyeing, and scouring wool fleece.

As one settler explained: "The black-salts were sold to merchants in Charlotte or Lansing, who had them made into potash, then drawn to Marshall and shipped to Buffalo, where they were made into saleratus, ready to be shipped back to the merchants and sold to the same families who had cut the timber and burned the logs that made the ashes they had raked up to make the black-salts that made the saleratus that raised our pancakes."[155]

The establishment of the Turner foundry and machine works in 1848 was another important event marking the advance of the town. As Frank Cowles, a Lansing pioneer recalled, it was "James Turner's foundry, where plow points and small castings were manufactured, and where the writer, in big-eyed wonder, first saw molten iron run from the stack into vessels and form them into the molds."[156] James set up this business with his brothers, Richard and George, at Race Street and Franklin Avenue, just two blocks south of his home.

The three Turner brothers purchased the property along Grand River from James Seymour in order to expand the millrace (the fast moving channel of water leading from the millpond to the foundry furnace) so that they could deliver water for their foundry and their machine shop, which were powered by waterwheels. They paid $200 and entered into a contract to conserve water so that all of the businesses along the river might prosper, a stipulation James Seymour always required. Though the supply of water might seem inexhaustible, it was feared overuse by one factory might lead to problems for others. Under the agreement, they were not to use more than their fair share and to take from the millrace only the water necessary to operate water wheels.[157]

Disputes were dealt with democratically. The partners anticipated growth and agreed that in the future if half or more of the water power of the dam were in the hands of one owner or owners, he/they could appoint a committee to decide whether or what repairs and improvements were necessary. All of the owners would pay expenses in proportion to the amount of their interests. "In its early days it [the foundry] did a general jobbing business, made plows, agricultural and similar implements. Some of the old castings found in the homes and other buildings in the city were made there."[158]

The brothers employed highly skilled workmen. The patternmakers were respected for their painstaking accuracy and interest in their work. Richard was known to take a boy from the streets, bring him into the machine shop, and nurture his development.[159] The brothers operated the foundry until George's death in 1863 at the age of thirty-five. He had been the business head of the enterprise.[160] In addition to this foundry, in about 1850 under the name of Turner & Coatsworth, the Turners also established a foundry and machine shop in Mason, which they held until February 1856 when it was sold.[161]

As for the Seymour enterprises, it was not until 1848 that the Burchard property was re-deeded to James Seymour to pay back the loans Seymour had extended to Burchard with the county to establish the Lower Town dam and mill, and the deed was recorded on March 10, 1850. Between 1848 and 1850, the framework for the walls was built and the foundry started.[162] In 1849 Seymour called on Joseph H. Kilbourne to come to Lansing from Meridian Township to take charge of the Seymour property, build a large sawmill and attend to its operation. Kilbourn also sold some large tracts of land he owned and built the first woolen mills in this part of the state. In Meridian, on ceded land once occupied by Chief Okemos and three hundred tribe members, Kilbourn and his brother-in-law had already built a sawmill and a large double log house in the early 1840s, opened a store and cleared land for a farm. As a legislator, he had helped Seymour, Townsend, and James Turner push for the location of the capitol in Lansing Township.[163] Kilbourn was again elected to serve the first year the Legislature met in Lansing and helped organize the Methodist Church there along with the Turners, serving as a trustee for several years. In those early days, his big log house was used as headquarters for services. In 1862, his son Samuel married Louisa Burchard, daughter of John and Frances.[164]

These little mills, foundries, and factories along the river were a natural part of the industrialization taking place in Michigan at the time. Manufactories, as they were sometimes called, were patterned after the well-established industrialization in the Eastern states where work depended less and less on manual power and more on mechanized power. Looking back, Adella Munroe Case recalled the gristmill that Daniel Case established. (A gristmill grinds corn and wheat; the more mill stones, the finer the meal or flour.) "It was a large mill for those days, having three run of French burr stones, not a primitive affair, as has been stated in the 'History of the City of Lansing,' [by John M. Longyear] which says 'the stones were made of the native boulders.' Case and Smith, the other members of the firm not having removed to Lansing, built the mill. The mill that now occupies the site is the third one, the other two having been burned."[165]

Everything was fresh and new. To pioneers the sense of triumph when a difficulty was overcome, such as the lack of safe currency problem being resolved with the introduction of the pearl ash factory, was an intense pleasure that does not come at all under easier circumstances.[166] The founding of a seat of government in the forest in the space of seven months required the brave hearts, strong arms, and tireless work of all those who came first. Their accomplishment and faith in their own strength and creativity is a testament to the Michigan pioneer spirit and set these men and women apart from the settlers who would soon flood into the community. As Betsey Munroe put it, "none but pioneers could have held out."[167] For the builders of both families and the Capital City, these beginnings fostered deep feelings of kinship among the pioneers that helped them face the challenges to come and endured from one generation to the next.

Looking back on this time, Reverend Augusta Chapin, an Ingham pioneer who also pioneered as a woman minister of the Unitarian church, spoke to a Pioneer Society meeting about the spirit of these industrious women and men: "They carried forward these improvements regardless of cost in time and strength, labor and money; our villages and cities they helped build; our railroads also they encouraged with gifts of land and money. They never ceased to foster to the extent of their ability our schools, churches, and all measures for social culture and every public benefit. They planted the orchards the fruit of which we eat, and the shade trees under which we enjoy the leisure they in a large measure earned for us. It is impossible that we should overestimate the importance of their work, or do too much to honor them."[168]

Chapter 4

Lansing at Midcentury

L ansing was still under construction. The legislators' arrival was not without its own hardships, and the residents of the town sought to make them
as comfortable as possible, lest they should vote to leave. According to Frank
Turner, "There are ample data to show that members of this Legislature
(1848) met many difficulties in the way of transportation, board and lodging
in the new capital. Members from eastern and southern parts of the state
came by rail to Jackson, then by stage or private conveyance over corduroy
and dirt roads forty miles to Lansing. Members from the west and north
came by Indian trail or new-made highways, which at the beginning of the
session were muddy and full of roots and stumps. The rate of travel was three
or four miles an hour, and the fare to Jackson, without much baggage, $3
to $4. While in the city, most of the members had to board and lodge at the
Seymour hotel one mile away from the capitol."[169]

To make the daily trip from the capitol to his hotel less taxing, James
Seymour had the plank sidewalk built at his own expense. "When there was
a night session and the men had to travel Washington avenue by light of
old-fashioned tin lanterns on a sidewalk of two planks laid on a foundation
of mud and roots—what remarks they made about the streets, hotel accommodations and central location of the capitol were not very complimentary
to the members who placed it there. In a number of the first sessions a bill
was introduced to change it to some other place, but it never passed." New
activity was offered as "the people cut off or isolated in the wilderness tried
to entertain the members by suppers (game suppers), socials, card parties,
dances, singing schools, writing schools, lectures, and debates."[170]

The legislative sessions, which drew the twenty-two senators and sixty-six representatives, were also of great interest. From far and near the
settlers drove in to see the capitol and to listen to the deliberations of the
young state's lawmakers.[171] Harriet Longyear, then Miss Harriet Munroe,
came to Lansing in the winter of 1848 to visit her sister Marian and to see
and hear a session of the Legislature. Rev. Blades came to see the session
because his father, a Whig, was there representing Genesee County in the
Legislature. Blades said, "The Legislature of 1848 was not a phenomenal but

rather a typical one. From the amount of plank-road charters granted it might have been called the 'plank-road Legislature.'"[172] Blades witnessed a debate over a piece of railway legislation that caught some lobbyists' gift-giving gold pens to get its passage:

> There was a great deal of opposition to the legislation pending, and there was some very hard work being done in favor of it. It was then I saw for the first time a gold pen, and they were very prominent on the desks of some of the members of both House and Senate. It so happened that my father, William Blades, was one of the members who was decidedly and bitterly opposed to the measure, whatever it was, and after he had made as good a speech as he knew how to against the measure, a prominent member of the bar from Southern Michigan arose to answer him, and after a very lengthy argument in which he severely called down the gentleman from Genesee for his opposition, he turned to the speaker and in a very vehement manner said: "Mr. speaker, I want something from the gentleman from Genesee beside rhetoric; I want facts, I want some tangible evidence in support of his position, and reason for his opposition to this measure."
>
> It was at this moment that the gentleman from Genesee arose in his place and said: "Mr. Speaker, will the gentleman permit me to interrupt him just for a moment? He demands some facts, some tangible evidence. Permit me to say in reply, sir, that there is no gold pen on my desk." And in less than one minute there was not a gold pen to be seen on any desk in either the upper or lower house, nor could you find anybody who had seen one! My recollection is that the measure did not prevail. In this I may be mistaken as this was fifty-five years ago. Of course no such thing could possibly happen in a Legislature in Michigan in this year of grace 1903.[173]

The constitutionally mandated first session of the Legislature in its permanent home lasted for ninety-two days and adjourned on April 3.[174] It enacted a record number of 295 laws and passed fifty-two resolutions. After the session, most left the area that some had dubbed "the hole in the woods" for the older, more settled towns they called home. When Marian and Harriet stood on the north bank of the river near the Turner home that winter and looked south through the leafless trees down Washington Street, the main street leading to the capitol, they saw a street with few people and many trees cut down but not logged up. Only by winding around the logs and stumps could a team get through. To get to the post office in the Bush and Thomas store in Upper Town, they took the towpath on the bank of the river.[175] That spring the settlers used every available root and log to keep back the water from the streets. The worst place was north of the capitol at Washington and Ottawa where the water completely submerged the road. Logs and planks were thrown into the street to keep it passable.[176]

Politics

However much more work there was to do to create the town, the town was political from the beginning. Political talk was routinely in the air. According to Frank Turner: "There were many subjects to talk about, at that period from 1837-1857, as there was a great upheaval in the political, social and religious world going on. In politics, slavery, state sovereignty, state rights, and constitutional authority was debated in all political parties; Emerson, Thoreau and the Concord school were introducing transcendentalism and higher intellectual thought; Hawthorne and his coterie were introducing communism on an agricultural basis at Brook Farm. The religious world was stirred by the advent of Milleritism, Mormonism and Spiritualism. This was a strenuous time. All classes, all conditions of society had to work hard with their hands to gain a livelihood, and equally hard with their brains to defend the principles of democracy, the rules of society, and the faith of our fathers."

In the evenings, the desire for social interaction led to the organization of Lansing's first of many clubs, a debating society of fifteen or twenty members. Here the great questions of the times were discussed, and acquaintances grew into friends.[177] It was impossible for any state or territory to exist untouched by politics, and this was particularly true of the city taking its place as a center of Michigan's political affairs. Residents had brought with them the progressive political views and interests of their western New York communities.

Even though the Northwest Ordinance established by Congress in 1787 prohibited slavery in the Great Lakes territory, anti-slavery sentiment had been smoldering for some time in Michigan, particularly in the southern counties that had been settled the longest. The first meeting of the Anti-slavery Society in Michigan was held in 1836 in Ann Arbor, about fourteen miles east of Lima where the Turners originally settled. The Quakers who settled along the Michigan border were passionate about ending slavery and assisting escaping slaves to safety in Canada. Sometimes a route was used that went through Marshall or Jackson and then through Lansing to Port Huron. James often acted as a land agent for the Quakers of New York who were investing in Michigan land, but we do not know the extent of his dealings with the Quakers beyond his land agent business or whether the Turners ever directly aided the Underground Railroad. We do know that a distant relative of Marian's, George C. Munro, was active with the Quakers and the Underground Railroad in Jonesville, Hillsdale County.[178]

James was involved in politics in the course of his merchandizing business. He had the opportunity to talk with customers and meet people in the business such as Zachariah Chandler, a New Englander and abolitionist who, like James, was only marginally active in politics in his early years. Chandler traveled throughout the state for his own merchandizing business in Detroit, visiting the small stores in the small towns and villages scattered around the state and acting as their supplier. Chandler loved to talk politics and the state of things in Detroit. Like James, he took part in Whig party activities. When partisan feeling was bitter and a strong ruffian element (the Democrats) was likely to show up at the polls, Chandler joined the men of strong frame and pugnacity of spirit who furnished the Whig bodyguard to force a way though the dense mobs that sometimes gathered about the voting places. The ruffians sought by jostling and occasional assaults to keep the more timid of the Whigs away from the ballot boxes.[179]

Though politics could be rowdy, as time went by, James became increasingly active in the anti-slavery political affairs in Ingham and Jackson Counties along with friends from the town of his birth. He attended the September 9, 1847, Whig convention held at the courthouse in Mason, and he was appointed to the standing corresponding committee in Lansing Township. Alongside James were William Jackson, who had helped James when James first came to Jacksonburgh as a boy, and Austin Blair. Blair was a free thinker in religion and favored the doctrines of the Unitarian Church.[180] He was emerging as an anti-slavery leader and was a Whig member of the House of Representatives from Jackson County from 1846 to 1849. Blair served on the Judiciary Committee and was the leading proponent of the successful 1846 effort to abolish capital punishment in Michigan. He was ahead of his times when he introduced legislation that would have allowed black citizens the right to vote.

Blair left the Whig party because they did not take a strong enough anti-slavery stance and became a delegate to the founding convention of the Free Soil party in Buffalo, New York, in 1848, which nominated Martin Van Buren for President. The party was called the Free Soilers because they took an independent stand on neither the soil of the Democrats nor Whigs and wanted new states to be free soil—meaning free of slavery. James and William stayed with the Whigs, as did another Mason friend and abolitionist, John W. Longyear. However, like Blair, they were not satisfied with things as they stood. According to political historian Floyd Benjamin Streeter, "In both the Democratic and Whig parties the prominent men from New England and eastern New York tended to collect about a leader from their section and form a conservative faction in their respective parties while those from western New York and other sections recently reclaimed from the wilderness usually grouped about a radical leader from home. Of course there were exceptions, due mainly to early training, personal interests, or demands of constituents."[181] This factionalism within parties made it possible to form new parties.

In Michigan, the Whig party had formed to oppose the policies of President Andrew Jackson and the Democratic party for their "experiments" with the currency and banking. In particular, the Whigs supported the power of Congress over the Executive Branch and in 1837 had "urged the people to oust from office those irresponsible office holders who … lacked the 'common characteristic of sobriety,' and to elect in their place a more intelligent and capable set of men." [182] The name was chosen in reference to the American Whigs of the 1770s who fought for independence from Great Britain.

The Whig party counted among its members such national political figures as Daniel Webster from Massachusetts and Henry Clay of Kentucky. In Michigan in the 1830s, William Woodbridge opposed the government of Governor Stevens T. Mason and led the Whigs. But it was Zachariah Chandler, coming from Bedford, New Hampshire, to Detroit in 1833 and serving as mayor of Detroit in 1851-52, who was instrumental in leading Michigan Whigs toward the formation of a new party of the abolitionists' cause.

In the year prior to moving to Lansing, the Legislature in Detroit had many serious issues to contend with besides its relocation. Among the most serious was Michigan's continuing and escalating opposition to slavery. Fearing war with the South but adamantly opposed to the further extension of slavery, they wanted the provision of the Northwest Ordinance of 1787 prohibiting slavery in the new territory to prevail for the whole country. Every vote involved maneuvers among the factions within both the Democratic and Whig parties.[183] During Austin Blair's first term of office, the 1847 session took the following position to prohibit slavery by a vote of 18 to 4 in the Senate and unanimously in the House: "Resolved, That in the acquisition of any new territory, whether by purchase, conquest, or otherwise, we deem it the duty of the General Government to extend over the same the Ordinance of 1787, with all its rights, privileges, liberties and immunities." [184] The state Legislature's resolution supported the position of Michigan's anti-slavery advocate Congressman Kingsley Bingham, a western New Yorker, and attempted to rein in Senator Lewis Cass, a New Englander whom they found too willing to compromise with the Southern Democrats because he promoted the idea of popular sovereignty—letting the new territories decide their status as slave or free states. Bingham and Cass were both Democrats.

A similar resolution passed in Lansing in 1848. In 1849, as the national argument focused on whether the Congress had the power to prohibit slavery, the Michigan Legislature added to the resolution that they believed Congress has the power to prohibit the introduction or existence of slavery within any of the territories. This resolution ended with: "Resolved, That our Senators in Congress be instructed, and our Representatives requested, to use all honorable means to accomplish the objects expressed in the foregoing resolution." This time the vote was 14-7 in the Senate and 46-17 in the House.[185] When Senator Cass threatened to resign over it, the resolution was revoked. Now Kingsley Bingham was on the outs, so when he did not heed the directive, the Michigan Democratic party booted him out and things were quiet for a while.

Abolition was not the only issue of human rights that was gaining adherents during this period. Women's rights were beginning to be considered by a few of the abolitionists as a logical extension of the current liberal thinking. Marian was named as an owner of the property along with James because in Michigan women were extended the right to own property beginning in 1844. The year 1846 marked the beginning of the agitation for women's right to vote in Michigan. Ernestine L. Rose, a reformer from New York, spoke

twice in the legislative hall in Detroit—two years before the first Women's
Rights Convention was held at Seneca Falls, New York—once on the "Science of Government" and once on "Antagonisms in Society." Representative
Austin Blair was one of the few who offered support. A resolution was passed
by the House of Representatives expressing a "high sense of her ability, eloquence and grace of delivery," but the legislators did not heed her calls for
action.[186] Her work in Detroit, Ann Arbor, and other places was three or four
years prior to the first attempt to revise the 1850 Michigan constitution, and
it would be nine years before the House Committee's report on elections in
response to women's petitions, and twelve years before the favorable "report
of the Senate upon the memorial of ladies, praying for the privilege of the
elective franchise."[187]

The idea of women's rights was not yet accepted, so when one path failed
to lead to progress, another path was taken up. Such an opportunity would
soon come to Lansing to improve the status of women. The Turners and their
family and friends would lend their support for women's rights as they did
for the cause of abolition.

Expanding the Family Circle

During this hectic time of great enterprise, the families of the settlers also
grew and new families of the next generation were begun. When Marian
arrived in Eagle in 1836 she was the oldest of seven children. Her mother
miscarried in 1837 but two more brothers were born in Eagle: Horace in
1839 and James Turner Munroe in 1843, named in honor of their greatly
admired new son-in-law. The Munroe family had grown to nine children
but two, Betsey and Marian, were no longer at home. In 1849 two more of
Marian's sisters married, strengthening the ties of friendship and kinship and
as it happened, the leadership in the Lansing community as well. Of the five
sisters, only 16 year old Eliza remained at home in Eagle.

Adella's marriage to Daniel Case in March was undoubtedly looked upon
as a good match. As one of the Munroe girls, Adella, age 18, had already
acquired a reputation as a highly cultured and refined young woman with
exceptional musical ability.[188] Daniel was 38 and a widower with three children. He had come to the Michigan territory twenty years before and when
he came to Jacksonburgh in 1830 there was but one cabin and nothing else for
thirty miles. He was no stranger to the Turner circle and, like the Munroes,
Smiths, Turners, and Longyears, he was liberal-spirited and conscientious,
a friend to humanity. He was appointed prosecuting attorney of Ingham
County following Burchard, and in 1846 he engaged in the mercantile business with Hiram Smith first at Mason and then Lansing but continued in
office until 1848.[189] It was said, "for keen observation, quick decision, fluent,
incisive and forcible utterance he probably had no superior in the band of
able pioneers who founded Lansing."[190]

Adella had been teaching in Delhi Township to the south of Lansing but now she and Daniel moved to Portland in Ionia County, twenty-five miles northwest of Lansing but only eight miles from the Munroes in Eagle. In 1850, the firm of Case and Smith was dissolved and the flourmill sold to Alvin N. Hart, a Lapeer Senator in the 1849 session who was frequently involved in the group's enterprises. Daniel purchased the goods from the store and opened a similar business in Portland. While he ran the business during the three years they lived there, Adella honed her interest in the scientific study of horticulture and plant cultivation. Daniel was honored by election to the Legislature from Ionia County on the Democratic ticket and served in the session of 1851.[191]

In June of 1849 Harriet, age 23, married a teacher colleague of Adella's. He was a former law student of Daniel's and a friend of James and Marian's from their Mason days—John Wesley Longyear. John was as interested in politics as his brothers-in-law and Hiram and, like them, he was an active member of the fraternal order of Masons. In keeping with the ideals of the Masons, he subscribed to the principles of honorable civic-mindedness and high regard for learning and progress.

The Longyears were Germans from Sandakan, Ulster County, New York, where John was born October 22, 1820. He graduated from the co-educational Lima Seminary of the Genesee Wesleyan Conference of the Methodist Church, just south of Rochester, about 100 miles west of their Cazenovian seminary. He began the study of law soon after. In 1844 he removed to Mason where his family and his relatives, the Dubois family, had settled nearby several years earlier. He helped on his father's farm and completed his legal education with Daniel Case, teaching a district school during the winter while pursuing his law studies. He was admitted to the bar in 1846 and came to the capital town site in the spring of 1847 with his brother Ephraim, who was six years younger. In turn, Ephraim, who had also been teaching schools in the Alaiedon area, taught at the first school in Middle Town while studying law with John and was admitted to the bar the same year they arrived in Lansing.[192]

While John was practicing law and taking an interest in Whig party politics, Harriet was involved with the cultural life of the town. A singing school was well patronized and all singers were in great demand for concerts and church choirs. Instrumental music was performed, mostly by stringed bands. Some families whose members were good players were always busy, especially during winter months.[193] Harriet remembered the first concert that was held in the young city; it was given in the old State Houses' Representative Hall. "A blind pianist, named Hoyt, came one day to her house, saying that he understood she had the only piano in Lansing, and asking if he could use it for a concert in the evening. She told him that she would be willing, were it not that the instrument was out of order. Every note was accompanied by a rattling noise, and there was no one in town who knew enough about pianos to repair it. The musician asked to see the piano, and despite his total blindness took the instrument to pieces, found a loose screw which was the cause of the rattling, remedied the problem and put the many parts back in place again. That night he gave his concert to a large audience and returned a greatly improved piano to its owner."[194]

The Plank Road

The state was experiencing a boom period after a decline in the early fifties, but Lansing was not fully benefiting. Getting to Lansing was still a difficult, expensive, and time-consuming journey for legislators and settlers alike. Farm production was significantly limited to what the local markets could bear since there was no way to get produce to greater markets in more populated areas. The current plank road from Detroit came only as far as Howell, thirty-four miles from Lansing. Developers and speculators might fail to predict or simply overlook the difficulties of gaining access to the site, but with the presence of the legislators and the growing production of farms, the time for a solution had come. "The garden of Eden would not pay for raising articles which could not be marketed and the completest mill or factory that ever was built could not flourish without customers," wrote Michigan historian James Campbell in 1876.[195]

The difficulty was that no state or county department or public utility company existed to take on the role of road building. After several years of talk, the community looked to James to get things going. His business ability and unimpeachable honor and integrity gave him the power to carry forward great public works that few men in the state possessed. Though still a young man, he was regularly turned to for public works guidance, and he carried through on the building of the Lansing and Howell Plank road, overcoming many obstacles.[196]

In 1870, John Munro Longyear, son of John W. and Harriet, described the coming of the plank road this way:

> At an early day rumors began to float about the streets of Lansing to the effect that a plank road was coming from Detroit to this place. The end of the road between Howell and Lansing was taken charge of by Hon. James Turner, of Lansing, and under his superintendence it was rapidly pushed forward to completion. When it was finally finished, great joy took possession of the inhabitants of the little "Bergh" located in the interior of the State, and it was proclaimed that "Lansing, the Capital of Michigan, was accessible to the world;" that is, it could be reached from Detroit in a day or two by means of stages, or private conveyances, which means of easy accessibility would at the present day indicate almost inaccessibility, but at that time people were content to plod along without sighing for the dust, smoke, cinders, deafening roar and dangers immeasurable of the more modern railway travel. They were content to

sit quietly and safely within the rocking stage coach, which, to them, was a rapid conveyance, when, by numerous changes of horses, it managed to rumble over eighty miles a day, and for a person to go to bed at a distance of one hundred miles from the place in which he awaked in the morning, was unknown.[197]

Beginning in 1840 the federal government allowed states that were custodians of government lands to use ten percent of the net proceeds of land sales to build highways and allowed 500,000 acres to be sold to contractors who built them. The contractor was granted the right-of-way for a road through all state and government-owned lands and a bonus of every alternate section of wild land within six miles of each side of the road for each mile constructed. The catch was that they did not get it until the road was completed. It was not until the law was changed to allow the builder to have twenty sections of land to sell and pay for labor after finishing just a ten-mile stretch at a time that the arrangement became feasible for Lansing.[198]

Thus, James' career in the construction of plank roads began under the firm name of Smith, Turner and Seymour. Frank Turner describes the grueling work and the immense task that was involved in building a plank road:

PRELIMINARY WORK

The best highway, or trunk line, built in the period from 1840 to 1865 was the plank road. Oak timber was cheap and easy to prepare and for five to ten years made a solid, smooth roadbed. Legislatures of 1848-49-50 were flooded with bills for "plank road charters." Most of them were worthless as the companies could not furnish the security required. The city needed a highway to Detroit and needed it badly. The thirty-five miles would cost, with cheap materials and labor, nearly $100,000.

H.H. Smith and James Turner, pioneer merchants in Lansing, with the help of James Seymour and others who were large land holders in Lansing and the northern part of Ingham county, formed a company to build a plank road to Detroit. A bill was presented to the Legislature and a charter was granted in 1851.

Some provisions in the charter were that the roadbed must be wide enough for two tracks, i.e., plank eight feet wide with dirt or gravel track of same width to be used when one track was being repaired and the teams to pass.

The right-of-way must be cleared one hundred feet wide. From Howell to Lansing this right-of-way was cleared only to sixty-six feet. The farmers later cleared the balance, or thirty-four feet, and used it for crops and shade trees until 1923, when the present highway department ordered the farmers to vacate seventeen feet on each side of the road. The old ninety-nine-year charter had not been repealed, but had until 1949 to run before land could be leased to them.

Another provision of the charter was the privilege to charge toll of certain rate per mile to the public. For aid in collecting this, gates were placed every five miles with a house for the gate keeper.

The greatest privilege was in carrying the United State mail. People in Williamston, Fowlerville, Okemos [Hamilton], Howell and Brighton could hear from friends and relatives cheaper and oftener. Congress in 1847 passed an act establishing post offices to collect and distribute mails; also introducing stamps to show that carriage was paid. This was the first appearance of postage stamps. The outer wrapper of letters or envelope came later.

FINANCING THE ROAD

Detroit financiers and wealthy men in the state of New York who owned lands in Michigan saw they would be increased in value by this road. The men who built and financed the road from Howell to Lansing—James Turner and H.H. Smith—were helped by donations of work and money from merchants and other business men in Howell, Fowlerville, Williamston and Okemos. The farmers along the line gave work and helped in delivering materials for the road. James Seymour gave land and money and helped Smith and Turner raise money in Rochester, New York—Mr. Seymour's home—by selling to wealthy men some of the wild lands which they possessed after a few miles of road were built. The record or land sales in the fifties will show that Lampson Bros. of Leroy, New York, Ellis Bros., and others in the East bought these lands. This firm of financiers and contractors, Turner, Smith & Co., by completing this road in two years established a name and reputation so that Quakers in Albany and bankers in New York City and Boston sent them money to be invested in lands, rail and other roads that led to our capital city in the woods. It would be difficult to estimate the amount of money this firm and its associates handled as agents for Eastern capitalists in Ingham and adjoining counties and at Lansing. They had the foresight, ability, integrity and honesty that made them good agents.

COST OF TIMBER

There was twenty-one miles of this road in Ingham County. Four houses were built for gate keepers. Five bridges had to be constructed to span Pine Lake outlet, Cedar River, and Deer, Doan, and Kalamink Creeks.

Scores of culverts were built. Hundreds of rods of corduroy [Note: a log road bed with sand over it] were used in wet and swampy places. All the above was built of timber. Oak was used for strength and durability. This oak was cut on the right-of-way and sections of state land granted to the company for building the road.

How much oak was used in this twenty-one miles? Each plank laid was three inches thick, eight feet long and from eight inches to twenty inches wide, so every linear foot took twenty-four feet of best oak plank.

Then in twenty-one miles there was used 2,661,120 feet of oak. In bridges, culverts, gate houses and corduroy structure there was enough oak
used to increase the total to five million feet. In lumbering there is a waste
of 50 percent in manufacture, so we can double the amount and find
that ten million feet of standing oak timber went into this twenty-one
miles of road. This ten million feet of oak at five cents a foot would make
a cost item of five hundred thousand dollars. The grading would cost
today [1924] five thousand dollars a mile or $105,000. Building bridges
and gate houses would run to $50,000 so the aggregate cost of this road
today would, at lowest estimate be $655,000.

PIONEER FINANCIERS
    These three men were young. Mr. Turner was twenty-seven years
old and Mr. Smith thirty or thirty-five. [Note: at the end of 1853, James
was 33 and Hiram was 43.] Charles Seymour, the son of James Seymour,
was also a partner in the road construction firm. Lansing at that time
was full of young men who formed partnerships in trade, manufacturing, contracting, etc. These firms and companies were optimistic, full
of enthusiasm and not afraid of work with their hands when necessary
to accomplish objects.[199]

During that time, Hiram became acquainted with Miss Mary Jane Waldo
in Williamston and married her during the time the company was building
the road. It was his second marriage. James stayed in Fowlerville while overseeing the work.[200] When the road was completed, James established a store
on the plank road, locating it part of the time at Leroy and afterwards at Fowlerville.[201] William Dryer, who was a long-time friend and Cazenovian, was
put in charge of the store and a sawmill where the planks for the road were
manufactured.[202] There were seven tollhouses on the road as collection stops
between Lansing and Howell; Number One was one mile east of Lansing.[203]
    One pioneer remembered the completion of the plank road (which hap-
pened in 1853, not 1850 as stated below) when he attended its opening at 15
years of age, "When the old plank road was finished to Detroit, there was a
great celebration. It was in 1850 and I remember distinctly the great throngs,
or at least they seemed great to me then, gathered on the plank road and
paraded up and down on the new boards. The people were so proud of that
road they did not know what to do. Up until that time, the road to Detroit
was a very poor one indeed, and during the wet seasons it was almost impossible to travel in some places. So you can imagine what a great thing it was to
have a half way decent means of travel to Detroit, at that time our source of
goods and wares." He said people rejoiced over the completion of the plank
road more than over any later improvements though they might surpass it
in excellence and comfort.[204]
    From then on there was a constant stream of travel and traffic that
passed over the plank road, but when the Detroit and Milwaukee Railway
was completed, it attracted a large portion of the plank road's business. The

road was well maintained and eventually the bad places were filled in with gravel. Byl around 1870 the whole Detroit to Lansing road had become a solid turnpike.[205]

Growing a Capital City in Hard Times

By midcentury, the census of 1850 showed the state population was almost 400,000.[206] The rate of growth was slowed during the 1840s and wasn't stimulated until the gold strikes in California and Australia increased the supply of gold. People blamed the disorganization of the national currency system and a shortage of trustworthy money in the state. After the panic of 1837 the hard times lasted for more than ten years.[207] The honor of being the state capital did not make the economic struggles for the people of the secluded little town much easier. Hard work, borrowing for the future, and helping one another seemed to be the remedy that most of the Turner circle chose.

The first years in their new little house were crowded. Their family had grown considerably. In 1850, James' mother Deborah, sixty-nine, was staying with them and the two older children of his late brother John,: Adeline and Amos. All in all, there were eight living in James and Marian's house including their own small children, Harriet, 5, Marian, 4, and James Munroe Turner (called Jimmy or Jim), who was just two months old at the time.[208]

There was much hard work for both Marian and James to keep this household of eight in food and clothing, firewood and candlelight. Even though James had the mercantile business, land agency, and pearl ash factory on Franklin Street, and his other enterprises as well, they were struggling just as everyone else was struggling. Marian's role was mostly confined to the time-consuming and demanding responsibilities of homemaker and caregiver, providing for the food, clothing, and wellbeing of the family. This work made homes self-sufficient and cushioned frontier families against the impact of the depression. Frank Turner described the contribution of the pioneer woman this way:

> The wives of the early settlers were noted for their morality, intellectuality and spirituality. They met all dangers of woods life with courage and fortitude, worked hard to make home life amid rude surroundings attractive and cheerful. They were the cooks, tailors, dressmakers, spinners, weavers, truck gardeners, poultry raisers, cheese and butter makers, teachers, moral and religious instructors, nurses and midwives of the scattered settlements.
>
> The first church societies were formed by them and buildings erected from their household funds. When their husbands prepared the wool for clothing they carded, spun on a big wheel spinner, wove, and made it into garments, hosiery and mittens. The fiber of flax was gathered by their help, sorted into tow [short, coarse fibers used for coarse linen] and flax, spun on small wheel spinner and woven in their own rude hand looms. They taught these arts to their daughters.[209]

Although Ephraim (Eph, for short) had planned to partner with his brother John in his law office, there wasn't enough legal work in Lansing and the county to keep them both busy. Like so many looking for an opportunity in hard times, Ephraim joined the California Gold Rush in 1852 and at the age of twenty-five headed west to seek his fortune along with other young men from Michigan who found financial opportunities lacking. He settled at the Yankee Jim mining camp, about seventy miles northeast of Sacramento, at a time when gold mining meant panning for gold on the earth's surface. According to historian and pioneer, Stephen D. Bingham, "He was among the early California pioneers, and was one of the first miners in the famous mine on the American river, where he also engaged, with success, in practice of law, and took part in many often exciting scenes that transpired there." [210]

When writing to Harriet, Ephraim asked for her assistance in helping "F" (the girl he left behind) understand why he could not come home. Reading between the lines, it appears that Ephraim hoped to make enough money in Califor-

nia to pay off some money he owed, to marry when he returned, and to engage in investing in his own state. His letters, preserved by John, shared his insight into the life in the gold fields, which drew quite a few young men from Lansing and would have drawn many more if they could *The Franklin Street bridge. CADL photo.* have afforded to go.

On November 28, 1852, he wrote he had been prospecting on a new claim when a rather laughable incident occurred. "I am a member of a Co. of 9 prospectors. Last evening some of the Co. learned that new diggings had been struck about dark on a hill a short distance from town, we immediately wrote out notices, Sharpened our stakes, went on the hill & staked off 9 claims by moon light, this morning I went up again & found people laying of claims all around ours & now the whole hill is taken up. There is so much fuss about the claims here that it is hard to tell whether the claims are good or not, that is yet to be found out, I like the excitement anyway."

Charles Turner was talking about coming and a few weeks later in January, Ephraim was conflicted about whether it would be a good idea for his brother Stevens to come out to California, too. The plan was for Stevens to come out and make about $300, enough to start in business at home, but Eph said business had been very poor where he was and the winter very hard. He didn't think everyone was suited to the hard work of a dig, which included digging ditches and wells, and shoveling dirt into a sluice day after day, "but if a man has a rich claim he can stand most anything." Eph believed it was one's individual power that would "make the victory." However, "no place I imagine is better calculated for acquiring bad habits than Cal—especially the mines, nothing to refine or elevate, little chance for intellectual improvement, 'a red shirt & a rich claim make the aristocracy'—Liquor, Tobacco & cards are always on hand & ahead of everything else, besides the public gambling houses, every store, tavern & cafe has its table & packs of cards... You may well imagine any one so inclined would be soon initiated."[211] Ephraim survived all the temptations and hard knocks and one year later he was home and happily married to "F"—Frances (Franc) Dennison Smith, the charming and intellectual oldest daughter of Hiram by his first wife. The ties of kinship between the friends from Mason grew stronger. Ephraim entered the firm of his brother on a path to wealth as an investor, corporate lawyer, and banker.

By 1854 Hiram, Daniel, and James were called the "triumvirate of Lower Town." They were not wealthy, but they had accomplished a great deal. Working constantly, bringing the plank road to the area and having the advantage of being an integral part of a capital city helped ensure their eventual financial success. But there were still serious setbacks. James became so worn down from years of hard work that after the plank road was completed, at age 34, he was required to spend the winter in Florida where he went for his health after being diagnosed with a pulmonary difficulty. While he was gone, Daniel handled the Turner businesses.[212] Marian had the care of the family and the farm.

Another of James' circle, his business partner of a decade, was facing difficulties: James Seymour found his borrowing got ahead of his ability to gain profit from land sales. Feeling depressed and hopeless, Seymour wrote this telling letter to his cousin, Horatio Seymour, the Governor of New York in 1853-1854 (and later, 1863-1864.) It shows how quickly the fortunes of pioneers and land speculators could change. The letter, which was written the day after Christmas, also reveals one way James and Daniel were able to borrow money and invest. It meant they might be wealthy in property and enterprises but low on ready cash because of the debt they were carrying.

Flushing Dec 26, 1854

Dr Sir

I have sent out about two months ago a full statement of accounts relating to the Lansing property made up to 20th October. In Mr. Turner's account he has left out his charge for commissions for the present intending to apply the amount on his debt to you. He started in October for the south for the benefit of his health

I have for some time past been entirely destitute of means to support my family, except as I charge a commission for selling and collecting as other agents do and I shall run behind some at that. It was impossible for me to do anything about the land until I had some pay, and I hope this year I could close it up here by sales, but I cannot accomplish it. For a while I had some loose means not in any trust from which I collected slowly partly sufficient to support my family and the remnants which were mainly the last end of my sawmill business at Flushing including some doubtful tracts I assigned to the bank and am working them up in refitting the old mill there (which was mainly decayed) and almost worthless, except some of the machinery on water power. They offered if I would do this to discharge me from personal liability and have done so. Situated as I am, I must devote my whole time and energy to the support of my family having a wife and six children dependent on me

My son Charles is now in a mercantile business at Flushing, has only $4000 capitol which is available and $2000 plank road stock & has a wife to support and cannot aid me much. I am with him nominally as a partner but in reality as a clerk as I have no interest in the concern and he does not like to have me considered his [partner] nor is he able to do more than allow me a small portion of his profits equal to a clerks wages, which with boarding him and his wife will give me but a scanty support. My two eldest daughters aid some by teaching but in this country employment is uncertain & it does not amount to much.

I hope in a year or two my brother William can aid me some. For some years he has had trouble with a patent suit [over the invention of an agricultural machine] in the U.S. Court, and a judgment against him at one time of $17,000 and costs on which a new trial was granted last winter and it has been reduced to $7,500 which he will probably pay.

I am in my 64th year, discouraged by my past misfortune and future prospects for life, feeling the infirmities of age coming on me fast, and having no hope of being able to do anything more towards the payment of my debts. I hope you will be willing to release me from setting up the concern at Lansing and discharge me from further personal liability if there should not be enough from the property to pay you. If the plank road stock was equal to cash there would be about sufficient I think.

Mr. Turner's health becoming poor in consequence of intense application to business, he has sold out his furnace and intends hereafter if his health is restored to devote his whole time to land agencies and has formed a partnership with Daniel L. Case his brother-in-law who attends to the business during his absence. Mr. Turner considers himself worth ten or twelve thousand dollars, Mr. Case has probably $15,000 or $20,000. Both or either are perfectly trustworthy and good businessmen. They wish to sell off and collect for you here.

If I can get free from my old embarrassment, I should look round and see if I could find some business which would support me without relying on my son for I fear I may embarrass him. I do not know any chance; if I did I could do nothing in my present situation. As I am now situated I have no reason to hope that for the future I can earn any more than a support for my family

When I contrast my former prospects with my present situation I am sometimes almost overcome, yet I trust in a kind Providence that I shall not be wholly destitute. I have ever felt the most sincere gratitude for your kindness in assisting me with advances, when made I have not the least doubt they were perfectly secure and that I could make it greatly advantages to you, but have been disappointed in this as in other matters and while there was any hope left I have been unwilling to ask you to release me. Whatever may be your decision, I trust my feelings of gratitude for your liberality will not be changed and I hope the same kind Providence, which has in his wisdom suffered me to be deprived of my earthly good, will continue you in prosperity and bless you in his favor in this and a better world.

ever yours truly
J. Seymour
Hon. Horatio Seymour

In the fall of 1855, after James returned from Florida, the Turners prepared for two family weddings. One would further strengthen the "ties that bind" between the Munroes and Turners when James' brother Charles married Marian's youngest sister. The ties of friendship were strengthened when James' sister Esther married Charles' friend, Noah Phelps. Charles married Eliza Munroe on October 16, 1855. At 31, he was four years younger than his brother James was and Eliza, now 22, was the toddler who arrived in Eagle nineteen years earlier. Charles had become a medical doctor by studying with Dr. Phelps in Mason and two years in Europe. Dr. Phelps' brother, Noah Phelps, married Esther the day before the marriage of Eliza and Charles. Noah and Esther moved east of Lansing to Meridian Township, improved a large farm near Hamilton, and Noah became a successful and progressive farmer.[213] Charles and Eliza settled in nearby Grand Ledge

James Turner hired instructors to teach school each year for the sum of $600 and Miss Hattie Seymour was one of the assistant teachers. While these were small wages, her income was important to the Seymours and was considered a "princely sum" by the town folks.[214] Less than three years later the country was once again moving into a depression, a downturn James Seymour had to face in his financially weakened position. James Seymour died about a decade after the above letter was written at the home of his daughter Louise who was by then living in Lansing and married to the town's Presbyterian minister, Rev. Chester S. Armstrong. Seymour left his Michigan business interests in the hands of Horatio Seymour and his son Charles, with the assistance of James Turner.[215] Over 100 years later, in 1969, the State University of New York at Brockport named the new student union The Seymour Union after James Seymour as a co-founder of Brockport, and his brother

William Seymour as a well-known inventor of agricultural machinery and an early member of its Board of Trustees.

The Turners' son, Jim, remembered what it was like at the house on Turner Street in the late 1850s. The house was crowded and their financial circumstances were humble, he said. His memory of his early childhood seemed unaware of his father's many business enterprises and saw his life more akin to that of a farm family. He warmly recalled his younger days for a newspaper interviewer who wrote:

> James M., Jimmy, would remember with a characteristic smile that he "came into the world without a cent in his pocket." The settlement had attained sufficient magnitude to warrant the erection of a small country schoolhouse. Here he gained the rudiments of an education during the winter months and did what little his budding strength would allow to help his father in the summer. He grubbed and hoed, burned brush, guided the plow and directed the stubborn course of the wayward and unsatisfactory "drag." As James grew older, he was entrusted with the care of a wisely selected assortment of farm stock, thus acquiring the taste for stock breeding which turned to such excellent advantage during his later years. At 10 years of age he bought a few sheep with money earned by his own small hands, selling the wool there at the encouraging war-time price of one dollar a pound.[216]

Jim also remembered the less affluent years when he was four and his father was taken ill, and when he was seven and the national depression that began with the panic of 1857 had set in. "In those days most of the present site of this city was a wilderness, and James M. was born in the midst of it. Fortunately, for him, he inherited the rugged courage and iron will which makes the pioneer. Looking back forty years, James M., who was born in 1850, remembered the family as 'wretchedly poor in those days… Our clothing was strictly confined to the limits of what our financial circumstances would warrant. Such things as shoes and stockings in summer were unknown. I never had a suit of flannels in the winter at that time and I never owned an overcoat until I was old enough to work and earn one.'"[217] The standard of living then was considerably different for Jim and the town from what it would be in the decades to come.

Mary Jane and Hiram were in similar financial circumstance. Hiram "was engaged in business with James, and cleared himself a farm. As he had no capital he had to work with his men to cut timber, brush and logs before it could be sewn to wheat, etc. He kept his own cows and used to drive them from his home in North Lansing near Maple street up to the woods to pasture—work all day and drive them home." [218] One funny story about Hiram was remembered by Frank Turner: Hiram "maintained some of his pride for he always wore good clothes to his work and then back when he returned home. One day when it rained he placed his good clothes in a hollow log to keep them dry and a fire got into the log some way and burned them up. That night he went home after dark for he did not want his neighbors to see him looking like a coal heaver or charcoal burner in his working clothes. Mrs. Smith waited for him until sun-down to milk the cows as her baby and the small children were hungry, and she was forced to borrow some milk from the neighbors. She told the neighbors she could not milk. She had never learned but remarked that all her children would have to learn and she made her word good, for that part of domestic training was not neglected in her home." [219]

The Turners' nephew, John Munro Longyear, wrote about this period. He recalled the press for land in early Lansing that he said forced the expansion of the city's land area. He attributed it to the fact that land speculators had bought such large tracts of land that those who were not wealthy had to buy on the outskirts of these large tracts. He liked to get at his point by telling this story about "a certain Mr. Smith:"

> Some of the difficulties experienced in the purchase of lots by the early settlers may be understood by a perusal of the following anecdote, which is told by the first settlers, and some of the later inhabitants claim that it would apply very well to the present time: Mr. Smith, who is generally well known in this country, came to this place in 1851 with the intention of becoming a resident of the Capital. Picking out the lot he desired, he hunted up the agent, or owner—no great task in those days accompanied him to the desired location, and asked his price. "Well," said the speculator, "this is a central location, the ground is high, and within five years it will be in the center of a large town, and will double in value in that time." To all of which Mr. Smith assented, and again asked his price. "I don't care to sell the land," was the reply, "but as I should like to encourage immigration to this place, I will sell this lot to you. The timber on it is alone worth the price of the land, and in the future the capitalists of the State will come here to reside, building elegant residences, making this lot worth thousands of dollars." Mr. Smith, thinking that the value of the timber was the value of the land, began to anticipate a reasonable bargain, and confidently asked the price. "Well, as I said before, I should like to encourage immigration, and if you will keep 'mum' about it, I will let you have this lot for $450 per foot." Mr. Smith drew a long breath; his face assumed a lengthy shape, and, after a long pause, he smiled faintly, and sarcastically remarked, "I will take six inches." [220]

Tough times were not entirely grim. Longyear recalled a little boys' prank:

> One of my exploits was an attempt to scare Uncle Ephraim's wife, 'Aunt Frank.' (She was a morphine victim but we didn't know it at the time.) We boys thought she was 'persnickety' and we thought to scare some of it out of her. We made a pumpkin Jack-o-lantern, put a lighted candle inside it, placed it on the front porch, rang the door-bell and hid to see the fun. Jim Turner laid on the ground beside the iron fence. Howard and I laid on the ground outside the front fence.

We had expected Aunt Frank to open the door and be properly frightened by the apparition of the lantern. But Uncle Ephraim opened the door. A kick scattered the pumpkin over the front yard and then he came down the steps and found Jim. He made Jim tell who he was, but Jim did not implicate Howard or me, for which we were duly grateful.

Jim got a lecture of disturbing houses where there were sick people, was led to the gate, within ten feet of Howard and me, and allowed to go home. After Uncle had re-entered his house we re-joined Jim, who had received what should have come to me, but we did not discuss the exploit. It had not been a success and we ignored it.[221]

Horatio Seymour did come to visit his cousin in Lansing after the letter. George Sanford noted his arrival for one such trip in September of 1856. Sanford said his stagecoach from Jackson was forced to stop about ten miles from Lansing when the travelers were confronted by a dense smoke from burning in the nearby terrain that became impenetrable as the darkness came on. Sanford recalled, "A man [was sent] with a lantern in the road ahead to pilot the way, and two others beside the leaders, enabled the driver to pick his way only with difficulty. All of the passengers walked, including two ladies. A little girl of one of the ladies not being old enough to walk, a gentleman of the party took her in his arms and carried her. I noticed the gentleman closely. Tall, erect, with a benign and intelligent face, a deep, rich, cultured voice, he was a man to be noticed in any place. We shared with him the labor of carrying the little girl. Arriving in town, we stopped at the Lansing House, a frame building standing across the avenue, east of the present Lansing House… We registered next to the kind gentleman who had carried the child. He registered, 'H. Seymour, Utica, N. Y.'" [222]

The pioneers called the autumn of 1856 the 'smoky fall'. "All fall the marshes and woods in Ingham county and central Michigan were burning. There had been a severe drought the preceding summer, farmers and others clearing land improved the opportunity to burn brush and logs but had carelessly allowed the fire to spread until it was beyond their control. During this smoky period people got lost, cows that were allowed to pasture on unfenced lands entered enclosed gardens and foraged upon cabbages and late vegetables without being seen or driven out. This pall of smoke lasted until fall rains came and quenched the fires," wrote Frank Turner.[223]

Despite Seymour's comment to Horatio that James was going to limit his work to his land agency, James was not home long before he was once again taking up all of his many business and civic activities, including manager of the plank road business. The times did not allow for much rest. Michigan continued to suffer from a lack of sound currency, and many small businesses such as his were failing because they could not afford to keep up their stores' supplies. James seemed able to secure loans through his many contacts, but others could not. Zachariah Chandler supplied his customers with the goods they required and was credited with averting countless bankruptcies.

On top of everything else, there were still weather worries. The toll road was doing important business for the region, but some felt it wasn't doing enough. In December of 1855, James analyzed a period of 90 days, not counting five days when the bridges were out because of the November flooding. According to the gatekeeper's freight statistics, business was slow on the road. James told those who were concerned about the slowdown, "I think it is hardly a fair average for one-fourth of the year, as no flour of consequence has left yet the high water precluding flouring, and the roads so near impassable that much less than one-fourth of the wheat has come to town for shipment. I think freights may be safely set down as 12,000 tons. I have procured the above from the Gate as a road statistic."[224]

The end of the decade marked the passing of the well-known and well-liked chief of the Indians living in the area. There were many stories about Chief Okemos' visits to the homes of the local settlers during this period, including the house on Turner Street. Because the Turner home was located on the Indian trail along the river, Chief Okemos stopped there frequently. He traveled from his land in Ionia County (bought with annuity payments from the Indian Land Cession of 1819) along the Grand River west of Lansing to the community of Hamilton to the east almost until his death, at about age 83.[225] Marian, born in Mason in 1844, wrote of an early memory of hers from the years in the Turner Street house entitled "When I Was a Young Girl, by Marian Turner Reasoner," which was published in the *Lansing State Republican* on November 30, 1899:

> When I was a young girl Old Okemos, the chief of the Saginaw Chippewa, was a frequent visitor at our house. I remember that we looked upon him as a great chief and we were much interested in hearing him talk of the terrible battles he had fought. We gazed upon the scars on his head and face with awe and decided he must have been one of the greatest warriors
>
> He always wore an immense knife in his belt that was of unceasing interest to the children. If we had pennies they always went for tobacco for the hero, and we were made happy by seeing the big knife taken out to cut off a slice. My father fearlessly corrected him for using "fire water" and the old chief would give a grunt of disapproval which would frighten us all.
>
> As he grew older his visits became less frequent and he was almost blind. He came to us one night quite late in summer, he put his pony in a field near the house and mother prepared a bed for him on the floor by the kitchen fire. He was astir very early in the morning. A cousin (who was visiting me) and I hastily dressed and after filling our pockets with doughnuts, followed him out. We soon discovered that his pony was missing and as he was too blind to follow it, we took compassion on his helplessness and tracked the pony west on the plank road, then north, then east, finding it near Jones Lake. The old veteran seemed delighted

with our success, kissed us both, then mounted and rode away, leaving us alone.

We were badly frightened, not knowing the way home. We wandered about for some time and at last came to William Jones' house, where we were given a bowl of mush and milk. After a time William yoked his oxen and took us home. We had been gone since 5 in the morning and such a welcome as we received - tears, shakings and caresses (not to mention what happened the next morning), all of which fixed the memory of Old Okemos indelibly upon my mind.

Chief Okemos, a great friend of the white man, died at this camp near the Looking Glass River on December 4, 1858. "His body was placed in a canoe coffin and floated down the river by canoe to the Grand River, then up the Grand, to the Indian burial grounds in Ionia County."[226] In 1859 the Legislature changed the name of the village of Hamilton to Okemos in his honor. In 1988, The Nokomis Learning Center was founded in the city of Okemos to preserve the Native American history, arts and culture of Chief Okemos' people—the Ojibwa (Chippewa), Odawa (Ottawa), and the Potawatomi nations.

Chief Okemos painting. CADL photo.

While the area outside the community was still wilderness, the mid-century advancements of the settlement were significant. In the time that the Turners lived in their house on Turner Street (about eleven years) their family had grown, the community had grown, the Legislature had held sessions regularly in the new capitol, the business, political, and social life took hold, the educational system of the city was established, and transportation was greatly improved. The Turners and their circle had been among the leadership through it all, contributing in every way they could.

Chapter 5

Education for All

The growth of educational opportunities was a sure sign that Lansing was moving away from its frontier status. In their Mason years Marian, Adella, Daniel, John, and Ephraim had all been log cabin teachers, and James was a school magistrate while only in his early twenties, but times and needs were changing from those early days of pioneer life. The Turners, Cases, Longyears, and Smiths gave much care in support of the education of the town's children, including juvenile offenders, and they sought higher education opportunities for women. New to the area and to the state was a first-of-its-kind school for farming education. There were a few nay-sayers who grumbled that they shouldn't undertake the education of the youth, just leave it up to the parents and their children, but the Lansing leaders were squarely for free public education for the public good.[227]

Updating Local Schools

In April 1847, while surveyors were still staking out the capitol grounds, a school was started in a small shanty located in North Lansing. This was the only cleared ground in the woods, and the area had the largest number of inhabitants with children of school age. Miss Ann E. Powell was the first teacher, starting with ten pupils, but soon there were more. A new building was built for the winter term that served for about four years before it, too, was outgrown.[228] Ann Powell was an exceptional woman of education and culture. She was educated at Olivet College, having acquired her early education in Oneida County, New York. She lived near Olivet when there was but one log house in the village. The little school in Lansing was her first teaching assignment.[229] She earned $2.00 a week and provided her own board.[230] Uncle Joab Page was school director.[231]

A new log cabin school was built in October for C. P. Spragee and his wife, who started a private school. "Two of the ox teams were sent to Flushing, 40 miles away for fine lumber for the floor of the school building, as it was the nearest fine mill. The building was finished in about two weeks. It was two stories high, with school rooms above and below, and there is no doubt but that Mr. Spragee started the first graded school that was ever taught in this city, he and his wife being the teachers." [232] A public school at Middle Town was soon to follow, with Ephraim Longyear as teacher.[233]

When the Lansing Board of Education was organized in 1851, James was elected a member and held the position throughout his life, however toilsome and thankless the job might have been at times. Daniel also served on the board, and Adella recalled at a meeting of the Pioneer Society, "The school board decided that the town had outgrown the small frame school house of the first year of settlement, so they thought it best to build a brick schoolhouse. They had but two hundred dollars in the treasury, just enough to buy the lime, so they issued orders for the labor. James Turner, J. R. Price, and D. L. Case were the officers of the School Board at the time. Mr. Price was sent to the south part of the State to see the best schoolhouses and get a plan. As they had no money, they decided to issue school orders in lieu of money. They paid their men every two weeks. A few hours previous to the time of paying the men, these three men would meet and make out orders enough to pay all the men. Orders were issued as low as ten cents in value. Their orders passed as freely as the money would have done." [234] The new brick schoolhouse was a source of community pride; no jackknife carvings or pencil marks would mar these walls or furniture. The new school was planned under an innovative model to unite schools.

The brick building was designed to accommodate a new kind of school with many more pupils and larger classrooms. In 1852 it became one of the first of the school districts, or common schools, to become a union school. The complaints about schools in general were numerous—absenteeism, disorder, promoting from one school to the next whether the student was prepared to move on or not, lack of parental involvement, poorly prepared teachers, inadequate curricula, and bad spelling. The idea was that by bringing the pupils together, creating a union of the primary, intermediate, and high schools, there could be improved attendance and less disorder, and by assigning students to specific grade levels, there would be greater incentive for them to study and progress. They hoped by consolidating the pupils in larger buildings and larger classrooms, the unity of effort (coordination) would better prepare the primary grade students for the work of the intermediate and high school levels and that the resulting efficiencies would allow students to be prepared more quickly and by a younger age.

For those with foresight, the pressure to change was urgent. Over the next few years, the State Board of Education observed the union schools with great interest as a way to reform the schools and update the program of study with an eye toward adopting the model through legislation. The Superintendent of Public Instruction, John M. Gregory, urged communities not to look at education as a costless gift of one generation to the next. They needed to make changes because of the tremendous changes that were occurring in the workforce in agriculture, manufacturing, and commerce.

> No former age has ever made such a demand for educated men, or offered such a field for educated labor... The farmer no longer follows

blindly, as of old, the footsteps of his fathers, as if the light of their experience were the only lamp for his path. He asks of science what are the elements of his soils; what the laws of vegetable growth; what the powers of fertilizers; what is the true condition of a successful culture. He has learned that "brains are the best manure for his soil."

The mechanic does not now, as formerly, count his trade well learned when he can copy without mistake the motions of the master workman. He studies books as well as models, and asks after the principles which underlie his processes. Analyzing the movements of his art, he cunningly harnesses the powers of machinery to do what his ancestors did by hard hand labor… the workmanship of the shops grows at once less costly and more beautiful…

Processes of the most difficult chemistry are daily wrought in the shops and manufactories, requiring more knowledge for their success than was possessed by the professors of that science twenty years ago.

In commerce, a still more urgent demand has arisen for education in its factors [salespeople] and merchants. The steamship, the railroad, and the electric telegraph, have so enlarged the fields of trade, and extended the relations of commerce, that the most trained and practiced intellects find full employment in managing the combinations and contingences of the great commercial enterprises. The numerous failures in mercantile life are proofs, sad but strong, of the demands which modern trade and commerce make for better educated minds to meet their great problems, and overmaster their difficulties… and the State that fails to educate the child, may find itself compelled to support or punish the man.[235]

Local school boards were told that if the young were not educated to keep up, there would be serious consequences for them and for their communities, and an increased burden on the state. However, they knew there are limits to a teacher's capabilities, even in a well-organized and orderly union school with a graded path of study and good attendance. "Six hours only out of the twenty-four are spent by pupils under the care of the teacher; the remaining eighteen all belong to the parent, besides all holidays and Sabbaths. Without the parents' aid, punctual and regular attendance cannot be enforced, nor a steady and unflagging interest in study maintained," said Gregory. "Let the multitude of ruined characters and blighted hopes, found throughout the land, furnish the proof of the sad truthfulness of this picture."

The Boys Reform School

James became involved in the education and reform of juvenile offenders about two years after his return from Florida. James was always kindly towards children and had compassion for the wayward youth who might be a terror at home and a scourge in the community but struggles for an education and once incarcerated must be reclaimed. Perhaps his interest in the incarcerated was engendered by his experience as a prison guard in

Jacksonburgh during the fall and winter of 1840.[236] James was ready to help when the first steps were taken by the State in 1855 to establish a separate place of detention for young boys under the age of fifteen, later raised to age sixteen. The House of Corrections for Juvenile Offenders, as it was first called, was located on the east side of Lansing on a farm of twenty-one acres near a shallow grassy lake and marsh that was a happy home for muskrats but was soon filled in for the school's garden. It was established by the Legislature at a cost of $25,000 to instruct and reform the errant inmates. James accepted a six-year term appointment by Governor Bingham to the first three-person Board of Control. They set the course for the facility aimed at managing it humanely and with a desire to bring good from the system.[237]

However, in order to do so they would have to make changes in the original premise of the institution, including a change in its name in 1859 to The State Reform School, indicating the more progressive notion of reform versus correction. They believed the ability of the school to carry out its reforming influence was dependent upon what power of personal kindness and control could be exercised by the officers and teachers in charge.[238]

Theodore Foster, who had served as one of its building commissioners before it opened, was chosen to become The House of Correction's first superintendent. In 1856, Foster and his wife Francis moved their family from Scio, where he had been a leading abolitionist and influential editor of their organ *The Signal of Liberty* newspaper at Ann Arbor from 1841 to 1847 and then editor of *The Free Democrat* of Detroit.

On August 16, 1857, Foster wrote to his sister Lydia Comstock in Hudson, Wisconsin, "We are filling up here from time to time, the population of our House being nearly sixty souls. We have now 36 boys committed here, and 2 girls, and we expect eight more boys tomorrow. Our boys, except two, are all thieves, and our girls are both prostitutes, altho the youngest is but eleven years of age. The Board tells me that I must consider myself a father to them all. Is not this a hard task? Especially when I am required to make them all into good boys and girls. We are greatly cramped up for want of room, especially when the character of our girls is taken into account." Since the age of consent at this time was ten years of age, these little girls were considered to have chosen prostitution purposefully and were commonly not considered as victims of a crime but the perpetrators.[239]

Foster confided in his sister that he found the work of the reform school unexpectedly politicized; "The Democrats here publish in their papers and circulate through the country the most abominable lies about the government and officers of the institution. They call us hardhearted, cruel, unfeeling, etc., and the Institution is denounced as a 'Young State Prison,' the 'Boys Bastille.' So that if you should come to see us, you may hear some hard stories about your brother before you arrive. The object of the papers is to make political capital out of it for the next election. The things annoyed me some at first, but in this country a man cannot hold any public post if it be no more than constable, without being maligned and lied about for political purposes.

We have a full set of officers here now, and the enterprise, according to my view is in a favorable condition. We seem to use every means for reformation or improvement that can possibly be devised."[240]

Historian Franc Adams said that the first board saw a firm but kind mode of conducting the school was a means of saving many boys from the consequence of vicious training. Foster served as superintendent for four years and then became a member of the Board of Control.[241] Foster went on to serve as editor of the *Lansing State Republican* in 1864, with his daughter serving as his editorial assistant, but became too ill to continue and died of consumption in December of the next year. It was said there could be found no man in Michigan who had done more for the success of the Republican party.[242]

By 1862 the school had reached its capacity with 160 students. They spent five hours on schoolwork and six hours in the vocational training of tailoring, shoemaking, chair making, and the necessary work about the premises. Recreation and religious services were provided, and the facility had a reading room and a bathing room.[243] In a report by James and the other two board members in 1859, they said, "The inmates are not only acquiring an education to fit them for future usefulness, but they are at the same time acquiring habits of self-control, self-respect and obedience." One innovation aimed at fostering upright conduct was to choose a doorkeeper from among the inmates, choosing only from the "star" inmates who were always boys who were candidates for discharge. A small salary was paid upon their dismissal.[244]

Early on the board studied the possibility of removing all prison-like restraints on their young inmates and visited an institution in a neighboring state that had no fence, locks on the doors, or gates. At first they thought it couldn't work: "The Board are satisfied that restraints sufficient for the *safe keeping* of its inmates is a necessity of our Institution and will remain a necessity so long as the bulk of its inmates are nursed in jails, and are unaccustomed to any disciplinary restraints from early childhood." [245] However, eventually these restraints were removed.[246]

Between September 1856 and September 1879, there were 2,135 commitments of which 1,972 were white boys, 152 were black boys, three were Native Americans, and eight were girls. It was said no distinction was made because of differences of birth or color and that all were on an equal footing, with good behavior being the only password that allowed an inmate to go free.[247] The board continually pushed for additional small facilities located around the state, rather than making the present institution any larger, so that inmates would continue to be assured of individual attention. They wanted a separate facility for girls which "could be put on the grounds of our Institution and would only need an additional Matron and Teacher... and they could at once be put at the sewing, cooking and washing of the Institution, or at manufacturing cane and flag seats for chairs, or other employment suitable for their age and ability."[248] Nevertheless, it was twenty years before Girls Reform School legislation was pushed through the Legislature by the

Michigan Women's Christian Temperance Union, and the facility was not opened in Adrian until May 31, 1879.[249]

It was the duty of the board to study each case and determine when an inmate was so far reformed that they would not commit any more crimes and might be honorably discharged. In the first three years, twenty-four inmates were discharged. Theodore Foster kept a record of the grounds for dismissal and how far the hopes and expectations for each youth had been realized:

#7 This girl, twelve years old, was not an orphan, but she might as well have been, for all the good she derived from the example of her parents. Both father and mother were so very intemperate that the girl preferred roaming the streets to a residence at home. After nine months she was apprenticed, and has sustained a good character.

#10 This boy was unfortunate in having both father and mother very intemperate. But he soon won the confidence of the officers, and during the greater part of the fourteen months he stayed with us, he was sent to all parts of the city and vicinity with the team, and was trusty in every respect. He has energy and ability enough to make a very useful man.

#12 This boy was eighteen years old when discharged. He was a resident with us twenty-six months. He had been in jail considerably, and had an appetite for intoxicating liquors, but he was quiet and orderly, apparently well disposed, and was generally liked and trusted. Soon after his discharge he hung around the saloons, and having stolen a sum of money, he was sent to the State Prison for two years.

#15 Was a colored boy of sixteen. He remained with us twenty-five months. He was a hard boy when received but when dismissed he had become one of the most exemplary inmates of the Institution. He returned to his parents in Canada, but owing to his color and the hardness of the times, he has had much difficulty in getting employment. He writes, under date of Sept. 10, 1859: "I am sorry to hear that J. C., my once companion, has acted as he has. I thought a great deal of C., but I certainly cannot think a great deal of his actions now. I can say for myself that I am able to resist all such temptations. On Sundays, the church welcomes me; and there are prayer meetings on Tuesday evenings – I am welcomed and desired there to be. I have been working out the last three weeks, cooking on the cars for men laying the railroad, for ten shillings a week, but I have got through."

#17. This boy was eighteen when discharged, having been an inmate with us thirty-one months. He is an only son, and his mother is said to be a very good woman. He was peaceable, industrious and a good workman with tools. After his return home, he wrote as follows: "It is with pleasure I now write to you to let you know how I am getting along. I am now at work in a chair shop at six shillings a day; and after a week or two I will get a dollar a day. I am striving to become a good boy, although temptations are stronger than they used to be with me... Tell Mrs. Hibbard that I thank her from the bottom of my heart for what she did for me. I would like if you would get some boy to write to me; for I wish to hear from you very much."

#20 Was of French descent, and aged sixteen. He was a very hard, resolute, and unflinching criminal. He stayed thirty-one months, and his conduct constantly improved. When last heard from, he was attending School, and studying the French and Latin.

#24 Was a homeless, friendless orphan boy of fifteen, who grew up to fight his way through the world, and became such an annoyance in all the places in which he lived that he was sent to this Institution for six years. During the last two months he was with us he occupied the post of doorkeeper, and carried the keys of the Institution. After a residence of two months he was dismissed, and now has a situation at ten dollars per month.[250]

The Reform School had many interesting visitors in 1857, including the governor and legislators, the State Superintendent of Instruction, all of the delegates attending the Baptist Convention held in Lansing including Reverend Dr. Stone of Kalamazoo College who addressed the school, and a delegation of six blind students from the School for the Blind who joined the inmates in an afternoon of singing. Over 100 visitors came for National Independence Day and celebrated with firecrackers and lemonade. Inmates and guests celebrated Christmas with a bountiful dinner of six turkeys and the proper accompaniments prepared by Mrs. Hibbard. The usual period of six hours of labor was devoted to recreation and sport. Teachers came from the town to teach ten Sabbath Day classes and gave "cheerful and unwearied assistance" to this program, which was considered one of the most successful elements of the reform work. "I have taken especial pains to procure female teachers, as our scholars are nearly deprived of the influence of woman's society and instruction; and we believe this course is productive of a great amount of good to the boys," said the staff teacher, Mr. Crosby. [251]

The Superintendent of Public Instruction said in 1859 that he could vouch for "the faithfulness with which the officers and teachers are discharging their delicate and important trust. It will be well if these poor boys always find friends so wisely and warmly devoted to their improvement."[252]

The Female College

Before the Reform School was established there were two colleges starting up in the Lansing area, the Female College, a private institution to advance the education of women, and an agricultural college, a public institution to foster scientific farming. Both were very innovative and controversial, but their growth and path to success followed very different lines of development. The first to form was the Female College, bringing together a highly esteemed board of liberal-spirited politicians, businessmen, and educators to aid in its development.

Abigail and Delia Rogers were two sisters who were already prominent as educators when they opened the Female College with their own money in 1855, holding daily sessions in the state capitol building for two years until a permanent building was obtained. Opening the school in the state capital was part of their deliberate strategy to attain equal educational opportunity for women either by getting women admitted to the University of Michigan or by creating an equally good school for women with state support or both.

Abigail Rogers, Michigan Women's Hall of Fame photo.

The Rogers were born in Avon, New York. Abigail attended the nearby seminary at Lima, south of Rochester, where she completed a more advanced course than was common for young women. (This seminary was part of the Methodist Genesee Conference that included Cazenovia Seminary.) She began her career at the age of 19 as an educator at a seminary for girls in Coburg, Canada. She returned to New York as a preceptress of a seminary in White Plains and for several years as preceptress of the female department at the Lima Seminary, which was considered the largest and most important institution for advanced education for women in the country.

At the age of 29, she and Delia, 27, came to Michigan where she briefly taught at the new Methodist College at Albion and the high school at Ypsilanti. Frank Turner said they traveled from New York to Michigan on horseback. When the teacher training school opened at Albion in 1853, she was appointed preceptress. It was acknowledged with pride that it was "the work of Miss Rogers, as first Preceptress of the Normal School [teachers college], that set the high standard which has always continued to mark this position. The exalted aims and large success which so many young women have shown, who have trained here, had their beginnings in the foundation which she laid in the first years of the school." [253] She was sought after as a speaker on education and was a founder of the State Education Association. She was elected Vice President at its first annual meeting on October 12, 1852.[254] Not finding the female department model up to her high ideal, she came to Lansing to establish a new college for women.[255] There she found the support and friendship of those of her native state ready to champion the cause and help raise the funds. John Longyear had attended the Lima Seminary and Marian had lived near Avon, where Abigail grew up.

The Turners were immediately involved, and consequently, the older Turner children attended the Female College a few blocks away from their home. By 1858 Michigan children were, on the average, in school for about six months a year, but the Female College offered longer sessions. The school quickly became known for its college preparatory department and very rigorous college curriculum. Abigail was the head of this school and Delia was her capable assistant. Not long after they arrived, their young niece and nephew,

Mary and Schuyler F. Seager, came from the Seminary at Lima, where their father was a professor, to be instructors at the school.

Abigail was the same age as Marian. When their youngest child was born in 1861, James and Marian named her Abigail Rogers Turner after their friend who was by then one of the State's most prominent feminists (had there been such a word in those days) and educators. Abigail was an imposing and charismatic role model for any young girl. According to Frank Turner, she was tall and endowed with lots of vitality and energy. She was a great worker in both mind and body and an inspiration to those who met her. She was a good disciplinarian who taught morals and spirituality by example as well as by instruction.

Many schools of higher education were popping up around the state that admitted women, but Michigan's two state-supported schools, the University of Michigan and the Agricultural College did not. At Kalamazoo College, a coeducational Baptist college, Lucinda Hinsdale Stone headed the female department.[256] Olivet College in neighboring Eaton County, started by the founder of Oberlin, was also coeducational. The trouble with the female departments and the colleges for women was that they were often not as rigorous as the studies provided at a university and that when enrolled in the female department, women were often denied admission to courses in such departments as medicine, science, or engineering. There were some exceptions, such as the female department at Kalamazoo College, but overall Abigail said that at the private academies and seminaries "the Course of Instruction is necessarily limited, and too often extremely superficial."[257]

The University of Michigan in Ann Arbor was established in 1817, twenty years before Michigan became a state. The originating statute said that the school would be "open to all persons who possess the requisite literary and moral qualifications." The charter provided for a female department to look after the education of women. It seemed obvious that women were included within the ordinary definition of the word "persons." However, opponents argued that "no University had ever attempted to do that work, and that a mixed School, or a School for the co-education of the sexes has never been understood as constituting any part of the definition of the word 'University,' and that it would be a misapplication of the funds of the University to appropriate them to the education of women."[258] In opposition to prevailing opinion, Abigail intended to build a school of university caliber under the nose of the Legislature.

By its incorporation in 1858, the Female College assembled a remarkable Board of Trustees using Abigail's education connections and the help of the political and business friends of James, Daniel, Hiram, and John. It was composed of twenty liberal and influential luminaries of the state and five similar men from New York. Wirt Dexter, the son of a co-founder of the University of Michigan, lived in Chicago. Of the five from New York state, Horatio Seymour, Moses H. Grinnell and Colonel L. D. Coman were from New York City, T. S. Weddle and W. H. Rogers were from Rochester. From

Detroit came Eber B. Ward, Shubael Conant, John Owen, Zachariah Chandler, former governor Robert McClelland, and soon-to-be governor Henry P. Baldwin. From around the state came James Seymour, Alvin N. Hart who was involved in Lansing development but from Lapeer, Minos McRoberts M. D. of Mason, J. E. Beebe of Jackson, C. Joslin and B. Follett of Ypsilanti, and C. N. Beecher of Flint.[259]

These board members had many ties in politics, business, finance, and social life. The seven from Lansing were James Turner, John W. Longyear, Daniel L. Case, Hiram Smith, Whitney Jones, J. C. Bailey, and F. LaRue. Seymour, Coman, Hart, Owen, and Chandler were already connected as stockholders in the Howell-Lansing Plank Road and James was its treasurer.[260] Ward, Owen, and Conant had worked together to help found a "Classical and High School" for boys in 1855 in Detroit, and Conant was the founder of an anti-slavery society in Detroit in 1837. Three, Chandler, Baldwin, and Ward, were connected through the Second National Bank in Detroit, which built support and ties to other Detroit financiers and Republican party founders such as Christian H. Buhl, James F. Joy, and Russell Alger. All remained life-long friends.

The board raised money and contributed their own money to the college to build the five-story school building just a few blocks from the Turner home at 106 North Street (later renumbered as 100 East North Street) and the Case home at 514 Seymour Street. Hiram owned property in the northwest part of town at the foot of Franklin Avenue, and he, along with J. W. Collins and James, donated twenty acres to the project.[261] A large initial subscription of $20,000 was also donated despite the depression. In addition, Abigail Rogers obtained contributions from the Detroit area and many in-kind contributions and services so that the center part and north wing of the building were completed in 1858.

Eliza Seager Smith remembered when townswomen joined in helping to complete the furnishings for the building in a generous spirit and manner that she said all but disappeared, at least in its outward manifestations, after the inhabitants experienced an increase of wealth and comfort in later years. Broadloom carpeting was not yet available and so carpeting had to be ordered in narrow strips and sewn to suit the room size. "With that spirit of friendly cordiality and helpfulness so characteristic of new communities… the ladies of Lansing came together, and by the pleasant lightening of labor made by many hands, fitted and sewed the carpets for all the rooms in the building."[262]

The school soon had twenty-five boarders and perhaps twice that number of day pupils. The Turners' children, including their son Jim, participated in its rigorous academic curriculum and preparatory course. Music, drawing, and painting were also offered in the Ornamental Department for any student who wished to take them and to give encouragement to those students with promise in the arts. Some twenty years later, one student recalled the unique character of Abigail Rogers:

There are those living today who will remember the kind and sympathetic interest with which she met their timid and self-distrusting beginnings, as scholars in the "Old Seminary:" the tact and firmness with which she encouraged the eager learners and repressed any over-confident zeal; and above all, the lofty standard of honor, and truth, and conscientious sincerity, which in everything, was impressed upon all who were ever under her instruction. In every sense, her thorough education, her courtesy, her refinement, made their mark upon her pupils. She was a lady of "the old school" and the ceremonious courtesies of old-time forms had their last exponent in her.

I well remember how, at the close of the session each day, in the "Old Seminary," as the young ladies passed, in a long, decorous line from the school room, each one turned at the door and 'made a courtesy' which was so graciously and kindly returned by her stately figure standing at the desk. In all this there was no assumption of her personal sense, either in the teacher or pupil. It was that reciprocal consideration which honors both the giver and the recipient. A History of the Michigan State Normal School.[38]

The philosophy of the college was evident at the end of the 1857-58 school year in a report by trustees Ezra Jones and Daniel. They reported to the State Superintendent: "The young ladies of the Institution had been instructed that they were not to receive ideas and theories advanced by their teachers and the authors that they studied merely because they were advanced, but that they should examine for themselves and see if the things they learned were true; thus fitting them, in their future studies and observations, to select from the mixed literature and conflicting theories of the day, only such principles in morals and science as are well based."[263] The students were encouraged in the highest habits of the mind: curiosity, objectivity, open-mindedness, respect for evidence. They were being taught to think for themselves. The Michigan Female College, sometimes called Seminary, was on its way to becoming a recognized social and educational power in Lansing whose far-reaching influence was not easy to estimate.[264]

The Agricultural College

The Agricultural College of the State of Michigan (its name was shortened to the State Agricultural College in 1861) was an even more fledgling venture than the Female College when it opened its doors to male students in May of 1857. The farm was located on both sides of the Red Cedar River, three and one-half miles east of Lansing. It faced the challenge of being the first of its kind in the nation, and in the beginning its farm was more of a promise than an actual farm. A major advantage it had for facilitating its success was that, though an agricultural curriculum was a new idea in education, it had the funding of the state Legislature. Nevertheless, even the backing of the Legislature and the law does not always insure that things will go smoothly.

The Female College had an advantage over the Agricultural College because it was located in a settled area of Lower Town. The Agricultural College was located on a 676.57-acre tract[265] of primeval forest without an acre fully cleared. Only a few acres had been slashed down and the logs and brush cleared, except for dead trees and trees blackened by fire that dotted the desolate scene. College Hall, a dormitory where the boys slept four to a room, and a small brick barn constituted the campus, which was surrounded by logs, stumps, carpenters' and masons' leavings, and rubbish. From the hotels in Middle Town, it was a trip east on Michigan Avenue filled with mud holes and lined with deep woods broken only by an occasional small opening for new settlers.[266] The plan was for students to do work to help them with the cost of attending college, and the first group of students found their principle work was chopping.[267]

In 1858 the agricultural students were ravaged by fever and ague, later called malaria. The relationship between swamps, marshes, and disease was recognized. However, it was believed at the time that the plowing and the stirring of 100 acres or more on the south side of the Red Cedar River, with all its decaying vegetation, turned loose an immense amount of miasma, and that is what caused the illness. One student recalled, "In the latter part of August and for part of September, there were 70 out of the 100 students unable to attend classes, at least they could come every other day, as the fever was mainly intermittent. That is, one day the patient felt as well as ever, and the next, never felt worse. The main consolation the sufferers got was the frequent assurances that it was the ague and nobody ever died from it. Classes were greatly interrupted and in some cases suspended for a short time."[268] As one settler explained, the effects could be long lasting, "After the fever, you felt as if you had come within the influence of some wandering planet—not killed outright, but so demoralized that life seemed a burden… Your back was out of fix, your appetite was crazy, your head ached and your eyes glared. You did not care a straw for yourself or other people, or even the dogs, which looked on sympathetically."[269]

According to William J. Beal, a professor of botany, the boys were "meeting all winter in the chapel at 5:30 in the morning for prayers; reciting in company in the few classes that at first were formed; swinging the ax side by side… laughing with unquenchable jollity of youth at the grime and blackness that transformed their boyish faces into something strange… as they hauled together the blackened logs after the first burning; working in gangs with the stump machines. They took long walks together through the woods to study the flora, where the ghostly beech-drops and the showy orchids grew; and to the not distant swamps, where the feet sink out of sight in the deep sphagnum; and the delicate gold thread, and the mysterious sun dew, and the flaunting blooms of the pitcher plant, and the softer beauty of the splendid lady's slipper soon filled their botany boxes with richest treasurer."[270]

The college found "violent opposition and prejudice existed in the minds of many people, especially the farming population." Some who found no fault with the leadership of the first president, Joseph R. Williams, said that since he had previously been involved in political life, the college was the object of bitter party feeling.[271] Williams, who was originally from Massachusetts, a graduate of Harvard, and a gentleman farmer with an astute understanding of the school's line of study, was pressured to resign and went on to become a Republican State Senator. He lobbied in Washington, D. C., for the Morrill Land-Grant Act, which passed in 1862, the culmination of a fifteen-year national political movement to establish agricultural colleges. He was part of the Blair Administration for a short period before his untimely death. A boy's dormitory on the Michigan State University campus was named for him, but it eventually burned and in 1933 Williams Hall, a women's dormitory, was named for his wife Sarah Langdon Williams, a suffragist and reformer.

Over the first two and a half years of its existence, complaints escalated about the lack of progress at the school and were loudly heard from some in the Legislature and public who were against the whole idea of an agricultural college in the first place. The college's supporters argued that the Legislature should never have stipulated that the college must be within ten miles of Lansing. They said the Agricultural Society should have solicited an improved farm, which, they believed, would have been donated by someone or some community just to get the college located in their area, saving the college time and expense.[272] In addition, while funding was to be provided by the Legislature, that did not work out very well either. The school ended the term in debt and with low credit. The state appropriation was slow to arrive, and then was only a portion of what was expected. Frosts in both the spring and fall of 1859 damaged the wheat and corn crops and caused a loss of $2000 of farm income. When President Williams resigned in the spring of 1859, he was not replaced until 1863 to save money. However, by the fall of 1859, the debt was reduced and the work was well underway.[273] The Board of the College, John R. Kellogg, George Willard and Witter Baxter, urged critics to be patient: "Our state University, now so magnificent in growth [there were 550 students at Ann Arbor],[274] was not a success from the outset. Years of trial and almost of entire defeat passed, before rising above the region of party and sectarian strifes and personal ambitions, it breathed free in the purer atmosphere of true learning and universal education."[275]

Of great interest to both Lansing colleges, but particularly to the agriculturalists in the Department of Civil and Rural Engineering, was the experiment going on next to the Agricultural College, north of the campus. If the Agricultural College was too young and its lands too unimproved to conduct the sort of study and experiment envisioned, it was greatly advantaged by the grand experiment of its neighbor Zachariah Chandler. Chandler lived in Detroit but purchased 3,160 acres of land about three miles north of the State Agricultural College that included marsh meadow, a tamarack swamp, and 800 acres of oak-opening uplands. He told his friends, "If this tract can be reclaimed, others can be, and I propose to give the experiment of reclamation a thorough trial. I have the money, and I believe I have the pluck. If I succeed, it will be a good thing for the State, for it will show how to add millions of dollars' worth of land to its farms. If I fail, it will also be a good thing, for it will settle an open question, and no man need repeat my attempt." He was in the area frequently, implementing his theories and pushing his experiment. He spent tens of thousands of dollars restructuring a creek bed into a channel with lateral ditches. Throughout his career, he brought state and national visitors to the farm to observe his progress. By his death, he had created a four-mile drainage ditch from Park Lake to the Looking Glass River and drained about 1,000 acres in the western area of the marsh.[276] The home of a myriad of wildlife and stopover for migratory birds gave way to more useable land, fewer mosquitoes, and less malaria. The drained swamp became a working farm where the students could study muck farming. Chandler Road was eventually built across Chandler's Marsh to Abbot Road on the campus of the Agricultural College. (After East Lansing was established in 1907, the name for the section from the campus to the town limit was changed to Abbott Road. In 2007 the spelling was corrected to Abbot Road.)

The Female College and the Agricultural College were on friendly terms. The latter was shut off by location from almost all association except within the college itself; hence, there was visiting back and forth, possibly encouraged by a mathematics professor, Calvin Tracy, who was in charge of the boys. He was said to have "an indefinable something that we call tact, aptness, faculty" that was an inspiration to even the least likely geometry student. He was a good friend of Harriet A. Sessions, a teacher of similar character at the Female College. They were subsequently married in March of 1859.[277] One of the students recalled, "The mutual interest and visiting between the two colleges were greatly increased in October 1858, when the M. A. C. boys [the name Michigan Agricultural College was not official until 1909] were invited to a husking bee at the 'Fem. Sem.' A field of several acres of corn, as I remember, was standing in the shock just east of the buildings, now used for the School for the Blind. The night was lighted by one of those brilliant harvest moons and also by the smiling faces of the 'Fem Sem.' students who acted as partners in the husking… When the corn was all husked and picked up, and the stalks bound and set up, we were treated to a bountiful lunch and then to a jolly social time, not soon to be forgotten." [278]

What was said of the Agricultural College was that "there grew up among the boys a warm fellowship with each other and with honored professors, and a strong and loving appreciation of the school that, in the very limitations of its first beginnings, offered to them better conditions for the acquirement of culture and character than mere lectures, libraries and laboratories can give." [279] This could also be said for the pioneering Female College and the unique environment for learning it provided for its students.

The Lansing pioneers believed that because they lived in a participatory democracy the citizens must be given an education in order to participate well, not just for themselves but also for the welfare of the country. The State

Superintendent, John M. Gregory, put it this way: "A government in which the great questions of public policy are argued and settled at the bar of public opinion, and the perils and prosperity of the State are the private cares of the people,—in a government thus thoroughly popular in its forms and forces, the Educational System, by which the minds and hearts of the people are to be informed, and the public sentiment is to be molded, assumes an importance which can never belong to it in a State less popular in its structure." Only the "cultivated intellect and hearts of an educated people can defend… against the surging tides of party strife, with its blinding appeals to passion and prejudice, against all those insidious tendencies to public and private corruption engendered."[280] In the perilous years ahead, the work of these champions of education would be put to the test.

Chapter 6

From City to Civil War

From the beginning, Michigan had a strong system of township government. Until Lansing was incorporated as a city, it was a part of the Township of Lansing. The male voters in the villages and township elected the township officers who served both the villages and the township in general. This system ceased when the three interconnected villages, Lower Town to the north, Middle Town where the capitol was located, and Upper Town to the south (which was pretty much on the wane by then), were incorporated as one city by an act of the Legislature on February 15, 1859. It was at that time divided into three wards.[281] The electorate had been 643 voters in the entire township in 1858 and was now 613 in just the city of Lansing.[282]

Hiram H. Smith, who had been an Ingham County Commissioner and State Representative, was elected the first mayor, and the new council elected James the first city auditor.[283] According to Frank Turner, Hiram "was a pioneer who had executive ability, and was not afraid to use or exercise his powers, when occasion required, to gain respect and dignity for the office. It was rather difficult to change from the old township government, which had been used twelve years, 1847 to 1859, and inaugurate the municipal form the citizens were not acquainted with, or knew nothing about. Mr. Smith worked hard to get the various departments of the new government working in a legal manner and various offices filled by businessmen who were permanent residents, so improvements would be made, homes built, and the city's general appearance changed from three scattered villages in the woods into a small, compact city."[284] Education maintained its place of prominence and James, Ephraim, and Charles W. Butler served on the school board.

The incorporation created a new community of individuals whose collective rights, privileges, and responsibilities were to be determined by rules and regulations they adopted. Among the early actions of the council was city beautification. "When the land was cleared all of the forest trees were cut down and for years the streets were devoid of shade of any kind. The common council passed an ordinance requiring owners of lots to set shade trees in the streets on which their lots abutted, and provided that if they neglected to do so within a certain time, the city would cause it to be done and assess the expense to the abutting real estate, and the result is that Lansing streets are as well and beautifully shaded as those of any city in the State."[285] Once on this path, the city went on to become a national model for urban tree management and has produced many prominent municipal arborists and forestry leaders in the state and nationally.

John M. Longyear wrote a humorous promotional piece in 1870 hoping to attract business and manufacturing to the city. The title of the booklet signals his gift for exaggeration by presuming to write a history that went fifty-two years into the future: "A History of the City of Lansing, 1850-1922." This tale might explain why he wrote it under the for-fun pseudonym M. Dash (after the printer's character—"one-em dash.")[286] He describes the incorporation this way:

> In the year 1859 a charter was given to the city of Lansing, and straightway commenced the organization of a city government. Intrigues of politicians aspiring to the exalted honor of becoming mayor, or at least clerk or alderman, were rife everywhere. The inducements offered by the new city to persons desirous of becoming mayor were a salary of $1 per annum, with but little to do, and the salaries of other officers were proportionately large. But notwithstanding the salaries, good and efficient men were elected to the positions, Hon. H. H. Smith being elected to the responsible position of mayor.
>
> The city began to assume metropolitan airs; a pound was established, and a force of men was set at work upon Washington avenue with plows, scrapers, shovels, and wagons, and straightway the irregularities of that thoroughfare began to assume a different aspect; hills were moved into hollows, and the street generally presented a marked contrast to its appearance a short time before. By this change some residences were left so high above the street that it became necessary to construct flights of stairs from the sidewalks to the houses above, while others were left so far below the level of the street that in order to be able to look out upon persons passing by, the inmates were obliged to gaze from the second story, and in some cases, from the attic windows, the windows of the lower story being confronted by a blank mound of bare clay.
>
> For a number of years the advantages of this change were evident; the roadway was continually in such a soft and pliable condition that the hoofs of the horses were never damaged by concussion, and painted vehicles were unnecessary as they all looked alike after once passing through this street. Fast driving was unknown, consequently no one was run over and killed. Taken altogether, the benefits were so great and manifold that other streets have been graded every succeeding year, the most noted of which grades were those of Michigan avenue and Cedar street. The troubles arising from these grades were particularly edifying to lawyers and civil engineers, as they were litigated and surveyed several times over, for it seems the dwellers upon the streets, not appreciating the benefits (mentioned above) accruing from 'heavy grades,' incontinently

refused to pay the tax demanded therefore, but after two or three years of controversy the final assessment has been made.

To the juvenile portion of the community, at least, the opening of the pound was the most interesting proceedings relative to the establishment of the city government. On the day when the proclamation declared that it would be opened, all persons were admonished to shut up their live stock, with the exception of cows, who, on account of their peaceful disposition, were to be allowed the range of the streets of the city, but all hogs or horses found loose upon the streets were to be incarcerated in the pound, the person bringing such animals to be liberally rewarded. On the designated day the desks at the school-houses, generally occupied by boys, were notably vacant, while at an early hour extensive droves of hogs were seen wending their way towards the place provided for all vagrant swine or horses, followed by one or more boys, who saw almost unlimited wealth before them, as each hog represented to them five cents, and each horse was worth fifty cents. By noon the street leading to the pound was thronged with hogs, horses, boys, and irate owners of live stock, who generally arrived just in time to see their animals enter the enclosure called the pound, and the boys dodge around the corner in search of more stray live stock. Before night the stock of vagrant animals was exhausted, whereupon several enterprising youths commenced to let down enclosures wherein the prohibited animals were shut up, and the inmates driven to swell the crowd at the pound. A number of youths transferred the horses from the barns of their fathers to the pound, thus enriching themselves, and occasioning the parents to wish that the city pound could be subjected to the same operation that Mr. Page had subjected the river to several years before, which damaging reflection was of no practical benefit to any one, for it took ready money to recover live stock from the poundmaster. Such were some of the benefits accruing to the citizens of Lansing immediately after the granting of the city charter.[287]

The House of Kind Hearts

By 1858, the Turner family finances were improved and they were able to build a new burnt orange brick house on North Street. It was set back from the road among the hardwood trees near the river. The house was in the popular flat-roofed Greek revival style with two stories in the middle and one-story wings to the east and west. They built their home on the high north bank where Marian had once said she would like to live. It was the spot where they had pitched their tent while their first home was being built on Turner Street, but now many trees had been removed on the south side of the river and year around it offered a splendid view directly down Washington Street to the wood frame capitol building. Their new house became known to friends as "The House of Kind Hearts."[288]

The year they moved in, there were six Turner children: Harriet, 14; Marian, 12; Jim 8; Adda, 6; Jenny, 3; and Eva, 1. Two years later, another baby was born but died its first year. The 1860 census listed May Makepeace, age 22, as a domestic living with them.

The new house had six bedrooms, two upstairs and two in each wing of the main floor. There was a dining room and parlor in the central portion of the first floor. There were potbelly stoves in each of the four first floor bedrooms and convection heating rose to the two upper bedchambers through registers. The basement kitchen had a hearth with a modest slate mantel and a new cast iron cooking stove instead of the traditional fireplace. Between the kitchen and the pantry was a pass-through cupboard. Even the basement walls were plastered and had eight-inch baseboards and nice hardwood woodwork and cupboards. There was room in the basement for bedchambers and workrooms for hired help and a cellar door and stairs on the east side that allowed produce to be brought through the laundry room into the kitchen.

In recent times, some have thought the house was used as part of the Underground Railroad, but there is no evidence of it. Nevertheless, some association with the Underground Railroad abolitionists is not out of the question in as much as the family was supportive of ending slavery and had connections with known participants in the Underground Railroad such as the Quakers and New Lebanon Shakers of New York. A clipping found in Marian's scrapbook indicates that they knew Martha Clarke, a well-known participant in the Underground Railroad in Detroit who was born the same year as Marian and came to Detroit at age 26. This is Clarke's (as originally spelled) obituary:

"Mother Clark" Helped Many Slaves to Freedom

Mrs. Martha Clark, colored, who came to Detroit in 1844 and who for more than a generation in a humble manner helped poor people of her race, died on Sunday at her home, 104 East Larned street, and was buried Wednesday afternoon. She was 84 years. Her husband, Cyrus Clark, a brother of Lewis Clark, the original of George Harris in Harriet Beecher Stowe's novel "Uncle Tom's Cabin," died 18 years ago.

Mrs. Clark was born in Kentucky of free parents. Her husband was born a slave. When they came to Detroit in the early '40s they had a home on the site of the present Wayne county jail. Up to the breaking out of the civil war they were very active in assisting runaway slaves into Canada.

One fugitive captured in their house whose case was somewhat celebrated in his day was known as Charles Rose. The owner of Rose secured a decree from the United States court authorizing him to take Rose back to the south. Rose was in jail and the colored people of the town armed themselves and declared that he would never be returned to slavery. Fearing an attempt to rescue by the colored people, extra guards were placed around the jail. The colored force placed pickets in the streets on all sides of the jail. Mrs. Clark herself personally supplied the pickets with food. The authorities of the town, anticipating a riot, raised $300 and gave it to the slave owner as the price for Rose. The latter was then released.

Mrs. Clark's husband worked for many years at the old Ladue & Eldridge tannery. She had two children and both were educated at Oberlin college, Ohio. Only one is now living, Walter Y. Clark, who, back in the '80s was at different times coroner of Wayne county, deputy county clerk and deputy sheriff. Since 1887 he has been employed in the bureau of printing and engraving at Washington. Nearly all her life she was an active member of the Baptist church.[289]

It seems likely the Turner's had a direct connection with Martha Clarke, but we do not know what it was. From the writings of Lewis Clarke, Martha Clarke's brother-in-law, we know that either the newspaper misspelled the family name or the "e" was dropped after they moved to Detroit. Lewis Clarke was later a speaker at the formation of the Republican party in Jackson. We also

The Turner Hose built in 1858. CADL photo.

know that Lewis Clarke said he was just one of several people that Harriett Beecher Stowe interviewed for development of *Uncle Tom's Cabin's* character, George Harris.[290] Knowledge about slavery was being disseminated by books such as Stowe's, the writings and speeches of the Clarkes, and by African-Americans who had gained freedom and moved to mid-Michigan. One such person was James Little, a freed slave who came to the area in 1847 from eastern New York. He lived on his farmland just west of Lansing in neighboring Eaton County and attended the Methodist Church with the Turners. The area's black population was small; the census of 1850 identified only thirteen black people living in Lansing, seven women and six men.[291]

The leading Methodists in Michigan, following the national leadership that hoped to avoid a rift with their southern churches, urged member churches to refrain from agitating, forming abolition societies, and attending Methodist abolition conventions. This only led to the greater vigor of the movement within the denomination. In 1841, when the leadership refused to ordain two abolitionists as elders, more members left the church. The seceders joined the Wesleyan Methodist Church of Michigan, which had formed that year. The opponents of slavery increased very rapidly in the

Methodist Episcopal Church. By the 1850s the annual conferences adopted resolutions demanding the eradication of slavery.[292]

The Republican Party Forms to Fight Slavery

Many others throughout mid-Michigan shared the Turners' abolitionist sentiments. In 1840 a convention was held in Jackson, where an Anti-Slavery Society was organized that established a state political party affiliated with the Liberty Party, an anti-slavery party formed in Albany, New York, that year.[293] Frank Turner wrote of Williamston Township, east of Lansing: "The older inhabitants always told me that during the Civil war most of the inhabitants of the district were strong abolitionists and strong anti-slavery men, so they named it the district of the African sympathizers, or Africa. It was located on the north bank of the Red Cedar river on a road running east and about one and a half miles northeast of Red Bridge."[294]

James was in the vanguard of a moral uprising that would eventually envelop the state. He was a Whig along with John W. Longyear and fellow Cazenovians William Jackson and Austin Blair. They supported the founding of the Republican party to further the political fight against slavery, and it was probably because of the strength of support in the central Michigan area, including the Jackson newspaper editor Charles DeLand, that the first public meeting was held in Jackson on July 6, 1854. Lansing was too small at the time to host such a meeting. The groundwork leading up to the first meeting led to between 1,500 and 2,000 people attending the meeting held at the Jackson City Hall.[295] The hall proved entirely inadequate for the size of the crowd. They adjourned and moved to an oak grove on the outskirts of the village where a platform had been erected. "The scene, as the crowd moved toward the grove was an inspiring one. As far back as the eye could reach was a procession of men, with many women also. The grove itself was a beautiful piece of woods, situated on what was known as 'Morgan's Forty,' situated between the village and the race course. The scene there was an animated one, suggesting a huge picnic, the Jackson brass band enlivening the occasion with patriotic airs."[296] Among the speakers were Reverend Mr. Alanson of St. Clair, Reverend Mr. Cook of Oakland, and Prof. Erastus O. Haven of the University of Michigan (Haven later became its president).

According to one account, Martha Clarke's brother-in-law was a highlight of the abolitionist reformers' convention: "One of the pleasantest incidents in the convention was the appearance of Lewis Clark, a fugitive slave, upon the stand. He is a man white as most [white] men, and has an honest, open countenance, but is of slight mental cultivation. His earnest, plain, unlettered statements had a telling effect upon the company. He was loudly and frequently applauded."[297]

Below is the resolution passed by the first convention, a resolution that was among the political actions setting in motion events that would eventually lead to the Civil War:

RESOLVED, That the repeal of the "Missouri Compromise," contained in the recent act of Congress for the creation of the territories Nebraska and Kansas, thus admitting slavery into a region till then sealed against it by law, equal in extent to the 13 old states, is an act unprecedented in the history of the country, and one which must engage the earnest and serious attention of every Northern man. And as Northern freemen, independent of all former party ties, we here hold this measure up to the public execration for the following reasons:

That it actually admits and was intended to admit slavery into said Territories, and thus (to use the words applied by Judge Tucker, of Virginia, to the fathers of the commonwealth) "sews the seed of an evil which like leprosy has descended upon their posterity with accumulated rancor, visiting the sins of the fathers upon succeeding generation." That it was sprung upon the country stealthily and by surprise, without necessity, without petition and without previous discussion, thus violating the cardinal principle of Republican Government, which requires all legislation to accord with the opinions and sentiments of the people.

That on the part of the South it is an open an undisguised breach of faith, as contracted between the North and South in the settlement of the Missouri question in 1820, by which the tranquility of the two sections was restored, a Compromise binding upon all honorable men.

That it is also an open violation of the Compromise of 1850, by which, for the sake of peace, and to calm the distempered impulse of certain enemies of the Union and at the South, the North accepted and acquiesced in the odious "fugitive Slave Law" of that year.

That it is greatly injurious to the free states, and to the territories themselves, tending to retard the settlement and to prevent the improvement of the country by means of free labor, and to discourage foreign immigrants resorting thither for their homes.

That one of its principal aims is to give to the Slave States such a decided and practical preponderance in all the measures of government as shall reduce the North, with all her industry, wealth and enterprise, to be the mere province of a few slave holding oligarchs of the South—to a condition too shameful to be contemplated.

Because, as openly avowed by its Southern friends, it is intended as an entering wedge to the still further augmentation of the slave power by the acquisition of the other territories, cursed with the same "leprosy."

RESOLVED, That the obnoxious measure to which we have alluded ought to be repealed, and a provision substituted for it, prohibiting slavery in said territories, and each of them.

RESOLVED, That after this gross breach of faith and wanton affront to us as Northern men, we hold ourselves absolved from all "compromises," except those expressed in the Constitution, for the protection of slavery and slave-owners: that we now demand measures of protection and immunity for ourselves, and among them we demand the REPEAL

OF THE FUGITIVE SLAVE LAW, and an act to abolish slavery in the District of Columbia.

RESOLVED, That we notice without dismay certain popular indications by slaveholders on the frontier of said territories of a purpose on their part to prevent, by violence, the settlement of the country by non-slaveholding men. To the latter we say: Be of good cheer, preserve in the right, remember the Republican motto, "THE NORTH WILL DEFEND YOU."

RESOLVED, That postponing and suspending all differences with regard to political economy or administrative policy, in view of the imminent danger that Kansas and Nebraska will be grasped by slavery, and a thousand miles of slave soil be thus interposed between the free states of the Atlantic and those of the Pacific, we will act cordially and faithfully in unison to avert and repeal this gigantic wrong and shame.

RESOLVED, That in view of the necessity of battling for the first principle of republican government and against the schemes of aristocracy the most revolting and oppressive with which the earth was ever cursed, or man debased, we will co-operate and be known as REPUBLICANS until the contest is terminated.

RESOLVED, That we earnestly recommend the calling of a general convention of the Free States, and such of the Slaveholding States, or portions thereof, as may desire to be there represented, with a view to the adoption of other more extended and effectual measures in resistance to the encroachments of slavery: and that a committee of five persons be appointed to correspond and co-operate with our friends in the other states on the subject.[298]

Not all of the planks of the resolution were about slavery. The time-honored issues of accountability, debt retirement, taxation, and education funding were also important. Since the power over corporations was held by individual states, these new Republicans, from the day they were formed, wanted more state control over corporations to guard the rights of the public and individuals through better regulation of the sale of state lands and the regulation of railroads. "Commercial wants require the enactment of a general railroad law, which, while it shall secure the investment and encourage the enterprise of stockholders, shall also guard and protect the rights of the public and of individuals, and that the preparation of such a measure requires the first talents of the State." [299] James Turner believed in all the issues and would be guided by them.

The electors from each district selected delegates from their districts to serve on the nominating committee for state offices, a committee of eighty-eight. James, J. B. Tompkins, and Hinman G. Hurd were selected from the Lansing district. It was the nominating committee's charge to design a balanced ticket that would appeal to Free Soilers, Whigs holding a variety of views, and Anti-Nebraska Democrats (opposed to the Kansas-Nebraska Act), as well as the temperance men. They succeeded in this and the ticket was approved with Kingsley S. Bingham, a farmer from Livingston County and former Democratic Senator, at the head of the ticket.[300]

James was involved in many political activities and continued to work toward the success of the new party with a group of leaders that included Daniel, whose departure from the Democratic party gained statewide attention. Daniel began with a public speaking campaign protesting the Democratic Convention's change in position on slavery. According to a news clipping in Marian's scrapbook:

Local Democrats Leave the Party

Mr. Case had always been an active Democrat until the bitter and bloody contest in Kansas between pro slavery and free state parties. The conduct of President Pierce toward the slave power forced Mr. Case to sever his relations with his party, and in 1856 he fully identified himself with the Republican party and canvassed the state for Fremont and Dayton. During that exciting campaign, Mr. Case delivered an address to the democracy of Ingham county, giving the reason for his political change, which was considered one of its most powerful and convincing political arguments of the time. It was signed by Mr. Case and 23 of his fellow Democrats, among who were ... H. H. Smith, B. E. Hart, John R. Price, C. A. Jenison and John Tooker. The powerful appeal of these gentlemen to their late political associates attracted attention throughout the state and was an important factor in the campaign of that year.[301]

Behind this newspaper article is a story of moral outrage on the part of the Lansing Democrats. Still boiling mad about the actions of the National Party, Daniel and his like-minded friends were furious when the Ingham County Democrats at the convention in Mason did not approve their resolution refuting the National Party position. They called upon their fellow Democrats not to support their party's candidates or their claims that Congress did not have the constitutional power to prohibit slavery in the territories. Stump speaking had been raised to an art form, and Daniel was an excellent speaker whose persuasive powers had been refined before many a courtroom jury. He wrote and delivered a fifteen-page speech in Ingham County and throughout the state that outlined what had led to his decision to leave the party. Here are some of the highlights:

This same Democratic Convention deliberately endorsed and approved of all the acts of the present Administration: in its violation of solemn pledges in repealing the Missouri Compromise, in oppressing freemen in Kansas, in sustaining Slavery there even with the United States army, in forcing upon an unwilling people barbarous and inhuman laws, passed by a Legislature chosen by the Slave power of the State of Missouri. This same Administration, so applauded and approved by this Democratic Convention, sustains judges in packing juries to indict freemen for daring to denounce these laws passed by a foreign people. It sustains Slavery officers in burning cities and robbing the free inhabitants of the Territory, shooting and indiscriminately murdering freemen for the love of freedom, sustaining an armed mob furnished with United States arms and munitions of war on the banks of the Missouri river, to rob and plunder emigrants bound to Kansas, thus stopping free citizens from entering the Territory, and claiming a part in the inheritance of our common country. And all this is done in the name of Squatter Sovereignty. And in all these acts the Administration is sustained by the Democratic Convention of Cincinnati... Shall these things continue, and with our approbation and support? Shall the voice of the Democracy of Michigan be heard for Slavery and against Freedom? It was not so in days past, and so far as our influence can go, it shall not be so in days to come. Look back, fellow Democrats, only a few years, and see where we all stood. No man could then say that by word or deed we favored the extension of Slavery.[302]

Of the failure of the Ingham County Democratic party to approve his group's resolutions, Daniel said,

> In this act, a few leaders and placemen have attempted to commit the freemen of the Democratic party in favor of the extension of an institution we had been taught to consider as antagonistic to the free principles which we cherish as our birthright. Notwithstanding their admission that the resolutions express the feeling of the rank and file of the Democracy, yet, with a hankering for victory which outweighs their love of freedom and their country's weal, *they surrender themselves to the dictation of their Southern masters, and humbly receive the chains which are to bind them and their posterity to the power of Slavery for all time to come.*
>
> Fellow Democrats—the acts of the present Administration in repealing the Missouri Compromise; in admitting and sustaining Slavery in the Territory of Kansas; in forcing laws upon the people thereof which are inhuman and barbarous... the action of the Convention of the National Democracy, so called, convened at Cincinnati, in approving all the acts of this Administration; and, finally, the rejection of those truly Democratic resolutions by our Democratic County Convention, all speak too plainly the condition of the party and its complete abandonment of the pure and holy doctrines of the Jeffersonian Democracy.[303]

For most, leaving the Democratic party was not an easy thing to do. For Hiram and Daniel it was complicated even more because they were former Democratic State Legislators. The Democrats were the advocates for equal rights, equal privileges, and the same laws for all. They were for economy in government, gradual elimination of the debt, and against establishing a central bank. The members had supported strong leaders and officials who represented the masses against the aristocratic elite, particularly represented by the business wealth centered on Jefferson Avenue in Detroit. The Democrats had dominated Michigan territorial politics.[304] Although still believing in these principles, many now felt their party had failed them. It was in the hands of the Southern Democrats.

In 1858, the Republican party elected Daniel Case Auditor General for a two-year term and he discharged the duties of the office with marked ability. He was one of the earliest and most helpful supporters of Zachariah Chandler. Chandler always freely acknowledged his great obligation to Daniel, who aided him materially to attain his position of unquestioned political leadership in the state.[305] John N. Bush, a Lansing pioneer, long remembered:

> A notable mass meeting held in Lansing before that war which turned the north against the south at which a stirring speech was delivered by Auditor General Daniel Case against the south, and well do I remember how that crowd was wrought up. At the close of the meeting a sheet was spread for signatures of those who would pledge themselves to oppose the south. It was signed, I remember, by more than a hundred. This was but the preparation for the great struggle to come two years after.
>
> I remember that during that time the Hon. Cassius M. Clay, who was making speeches over the country for abolition, spoke in Mason. In the midst of the audience as he was about to speak appeared three of four men with a rebel flag, held aloft in defiance. The blood of the northern sympathizers in the gathering rose and men declared that they would tear down the colors, but the speaker interceded and begged the crowd not to interfere. He began to speak at once and turning the guns of his sarcasm loose on those men drove them from the crowd, glad to get away from his stinging rebukes.[306]

The North Will Defend You

As early as 1859 steps were taken in Michigan to make the state military system more effective by organizing camps of instruction and increasing the number of uniformed companies. Various men with military experience devoted time to making addresses and visiting the principle towns to rouse military spirit. In 1860, when the signs of trouble ahead were plainer and the public feeling was strongly aroused, Austin Blair, who was on the same ticket with Abraham Lincoln, obtained a majority of just 2,500 votes for governor over Governor Barry, his only opponent. Blair did not find the state prepared for the challenges ahead.

When the strongly Republican Legislature met in 1861, they were confronted with a dire fiscal situation. John McKinney, the outgoing state treasurer, had embezzled the public funds and left the treasury empty and liable for large outstanding and pressing debts.[307] Because of the constitutional restraints on borrowing by the state, there was no way for the state to raise funds by issuing bonds. John Owen, the incoming treasure, who was well-known in Lansing due to his politics and connection with the Female College board, at once made arrangements to use his personal credit to keep the treasury in funds until the ordinary sources could provide revenue in the due course of government business. Owen's patriotic course saved Michigan's credit standing and enabled Michigan to borrow under fair terms when a war-loan was soon needed.[308] John McKinney went to jail after a trial brought by Stephen D. Bingham, the Prosecuting Attorney for Ingham County, and argued in the Michigan Supreme Court by the Attorney General Charles Upson and John W. Longyear for the State. O. M. Barnes, a longtime resident of Mason, defended McKinney.[309]

Because Michigan had played a strong political role in support of abolition, despite the financial situation, Blair now took a leading role during the war. Historian James V. Campbell wrote in 1876:

> In his first inaugural address in January 1861, Blair recommended that the state offer its entire military resources to Lincoln for maintaining the supremacy of the U.S. Constitution. Within days of the outbreak of the American Civil War in April, Blair responded by calling for ten companies of volunteers. The Legislature later retroactively authorized the Governor's quick actions, authorized a war loan of $1,000,000, and passed the Soldiers' Relief Law, requiring counties to provide relief to the families of soldiers. By mid-May, the first regiment of Michigan soldiers, under the command of Colonel O. B. Wilcox left to engage in the field of combat, and was the first western force to arrive at the seat of combat. The second regiment, under the command of Colonel Israel B. Richardson, soon followed.[310]

The national government was also in financial difficulty during the war and having trouble with credit. Michigan's Senator Zachariah Chandler, like Blair and Owen, turned to his personal wealth to help solve the problem in an act made even more wondrous given his aversion to speculation of any kind. According to his biographer, Arthur Tappan Pierson, at one point during the war the credit of the United States reached an alarmingly low ebb as measured by the price of its bonds. Chandler then went to New York with Representative Rowland E. Trowbridge of Michigan, feeling depressed because there seemed to be no remedy that the government could undertake. Chandler's biographer wrote, "The next day there was a decided improvement in the rates for 'governments' on Wall street, and the firmer feeling it created never wholly disappeared but was followed by a gradual appreciation in this class of securities. Mr. Trowbridge called his attention to the advance on the day following, and the Senator answered, 'I know all about it. I gave my broker orders to buy heavily and the street, finding that out, said 'Chandler is just over from Washington and knows something," and so they followed my lead, and there was a rush which sent the market up."[311]

Not only were there problems of financing, there was the problem of disbelief that the South would really go to war. Chandler recalled:

> The battle of Bull Run seems to have been the culminating point of the rebellion. Up to that time the North hardly seemed to appreciate the fact that we were in the midst of war; that a gigantic and wicked rebellion

was shaking the very foundation-stones of our political institutions; that the rebel meant a bloody, fratricidal war. The firing upon Sumter was considered rather the action of a frenzied mob than the fixed, determined intent to break up and destroy the best Government the world had ever seen. That battle left the enemies of the country masters of the field and virtually besiegers of the capital.

From the 21st day of July, 1861, the nations of the earth considered the experiment of republicans institutions a failure, or at least an untried experiment. Rebellion had triumphed, and the nations believed the Republic was tottering to its fall. Our securities became valueless outside our borders, and our armies to be raised were considered men in buckram [Meaning non-existent people, a phrase from Shakespeare's Henry IV.][312]

But the North did not see the results of Bull Run as a win for either side, said Chandler, "and forthwith began to put forth their mighty energies. Up to this time the earnestness of this rebellion had not been appreciated by the North."

According to the *State Republican*, "When the first call for volunteers rang through the north and men from every village and hamlet joined the movement toward the front, Lansing was not last or least. There was smallness in population but largeness in enthusiasm and on the first call went Charles Foster, William Green, E. F. Sibert and a dozen in all, who never came back. Many others sickened and died on the field."[313]

Historian and Michigan pioneer Samuel B. McCracken wrote in 1900, "As showing the sentiment that prevailed with the people of the north during the war, and their determination to prosecute it to a finish, the following song, inspired by one of the early calls for troops, is worthy of reproduction:"

THREE HUNDRED THOUSAND MORE
Music composed by P.S. Gilmore

We are coming, Father Abraham, three hundred thousand more,
From Mississippi's winding stream and from New England's shore;
We leave our plows and workshops, our wives and children dear,
With hearts too full for utterance, with but a silent tear;
We dare not look behind us, but steadfastly before,
We are coming, Father Abraham, three hundred thousand more

> Chorus [Four part harmony]
> We are coming, we are coming, our Union to restore;
> We are coming Father Abraham, with three hundred thousand
> more...
> If you look all up our valleys, where the growing harvests shine,
> You may see our sturdy farmer-boys fast forming into line;

And children from their mothers' knees are pulling at the weeds,
And learning how to reap and sow, against their country's needs;

And a farewell group stands weeping at every cottage door,
We are coming, Father Abraham, three hundred thousand more.[314]

At first, many hoped that the war would be short, that a show of force would be all that was necessary, but Blair prepared for a longer effort. While the third and fourth regiments were being raised, Blair received directions from the Secretary of War limiting the number of regiments from Michigan to four and asking Blair not to raise more than that number. Blair decided to disregard these instructions and continued to establish the fifth, sixth, and seventh regiments, all of which were deployed by mid-September of 1861. A Jackson citizen recalled about Blair: "In the dark days of the rebellion he was a tower of strength to President Lincoln. Through the indefatigable efforts of the governor, Michigan placed the first soldiers on rebel soil. He was a great and good man, an orator of renown." Under Blair's guidance, Michigan continued to supply troops for the Union forces throughout the war. One notable unit was a black unit, known as the 102nd United States Colored Troops. At the outset of the war, Michigan had a total population of approximately 800,000 and an estimated 110,000 able-bodied men capable of bearing arms. By the end of the war, 90,747 Michigan men had joined the fight. Of these, 13,405 died in service.

Blair personally helped raise about $100,000 from private citizens to organize and equip the initial muster of troops. When Blair left office in 1864, he was almost destitute, having expended much of his personal wealth in support of the war effort. During this time of conflict, he ran the state government from his hometown of Jackson, making that community a hub of Michigan's war effort. Blair was known for uncompromising honesty and the Jackson citizenry told the story of how he was frequently approached by agents of the railroads during the war: "The agents made tempting offers of reward providing Michigan troops were sent over their respective roads. Each of these agents were denounced in emphatic language by the governor, who would send no troops over the roads in question, neither would he travel over them in his journeys to and from the front, which were frequently made during the entire war."[315]

He was called "The War Governor" throughout the country and was revered for his Herculean efforts in leading the state. "He was confident of the success of the Union cause, never lost heart or faltered, and kept up the spirits of the people at home and of the soldiers in the field," according to Michigan Act 59, honoring Blair. Michigan citizens were very proud of Blair and the fact that their soldiers were considered among the best trained and best equipped. In 1895 the Michigan Legislature appropriated $10,000 for a statue in Blair's memory. It stands in front of the capitol, the first and only time that an actual person has been honored with a statue on the capitol's grounds.[316]

John Longyear's voice was often heard in state and local conventions, and he was one of the leaders at the bar in Lansing. By the beginning of the war, his practice extended into all the State and Federal Courts and into many of the circuits. For three years he practiced with Schuyler F. Seager, nephew of Abigail Rogers, and the firm was one of the best known and most successful in the state.[317] In 1862 he was elected to Congress to represent the views of the Radical Republicans (the most anti-slavery faction of the Republican party) of the Third District, and he was re-elected in 1864.

At first Harriett and the four Longyear children, John Munro, Howard, Ida, and their youngest, James Turner Longyear were together. Their home was about three miles from the Longyear sheep farm east of Lansing. The farm was located not far from Tollhouse Number One on the plank road that extended from Franklin Street in North Lansing. When John was home, he could be seen on the farm with its large sheep barn, tending to his sheep, building fences, and looking after his crops.[318] All the cousins and Munroe sisters were now living in Lansing and could easily get together at each other's homes to exchange news and read letters from friends and relatives serving in the war while their own husbands were gone on government business. John Munro recalled when he was 12, "In 1862 I was away at school. My mother was an invalid, my father was elected to Congress and the home was broken up for the winter. Three of my mother's sisters took my two younger brothers and sister to live with them and I was sent to school at Olivet, Michigan."[319] In 1865 at the end of the war, James Turner Longyear died at eight years of age. Horace and Jennie Munroe came from Eagle to manage the Longyear farm in 1866.[320]

It was said: "He studied the relations of the States to the Nation from the standpoint of the Constitutional lawyer, and not from that of the politician. He never took the time of the House, except upon important matters, and then only when he had studied the subject with great care, so that he was always listened to with marked attention. His argument on the first Reconstruction Bill in Congress in 1864, was recognized as one of the most logical discussions of the whole subject that was made during that session." [321] He said the governments of seceding states had been overthrown and consequently the United States government had full authority. He argued that meant that Congress had the right to make the end of slavery and involuntary servitude a condition of reconstruction. The speech became part of the national discussion about the proper status of a state that had seceded and led to the adoption of the thirteenth amendment.[322]

Soon after the war began, the women of Lansing formed the Lansing Military Aid Society. The state librarian, Harriett Tenney, was elected president and headed the organization until the close of the war. The society headquarters were several rooms in the old capitol where they looked after the welfare of soldiers, providing aid in the field and in the hospitals. The society was also involved in raising funds for relief. Abigail Rogers also gave untiring leadership to the work.[323] There were similar soldiers relief societies and ladies' soldier relief societies organized throughout the county and state. In November of 1861, Frank Siberd wrote to the *Republican* from the Third

Infantry encamped south of Alexander, "The Ladies Military Aid Society will accept our thanks for the following hospital stores: five pairs of pillow cases, eight hospital shirts, four sheets, five pair socks, two paper pins, seven pair slippers, three rolls bandages, fifteen towels, four bags of dried fruit, one can jell, ten jars jell, four dressing gowns, eleven bottles currant wine, one bottle strawberries. Several jars and one bottle was broken; besides the above there was one bottle of pure currant wine, with Stanley Briggs' trade mark on it, marked for Steven [Stephen] Longyear, our efficient Quartermaster Sergeant." The organization pursued these activities for four years.

The war touched many Lansing families in many ways. John Longyear's partner Schuyler Seager left his law practice and enlisted in the 20th Michigan Infantry as a private but was soon promoted to Second Lieutenant of the Sixth Calvary company. H. F. Dubois, a nephew of the Longyears' from Ingham County, was wounded in the side and kidney. While still sick he wrote to his Congressman uncle on January 2, 1864, from St. Mary's Hospital in Detroit. He feared that he would not be able to go back to his regiment because he would never again be able to carry his knapsack. "I have not a wish to get out of the army until the rebellion is put down," he told his uncle and said he sought a commission in the African-American First Regiment that needed officers. "Half a dozen boys went down to Cincinnati to be commissioned in black regiments. They say it is ten times as hard work to get commissioned in black as white regs and that it is almost necessary to have gone through a college course to answer all the questions independent of military. So you see, instead of being anything disgraceful about it, it will rather be an honor to which only the best can aspire. On this account the 1st Colored here at this City is but half officered." Of Detroit, DuBois reported, "The river has been frozen over solid so sleigh ferries run in place of boats. It's plenty of excitement here with skating carnivals and the different skating parks, Theaters, Operas, lectures, fires, returning of veteran soldiers, sending off of new recruits, the Free Press lies and faultfinding with everything in general and the 'nigger regiment' in particular, concerts, and a murder now and then thrown in."[324] (Today's *Detroit Free Press* is as far different from the newspaper it was as the Democratic party is from its former self.)

The largest army hospital in Michigan was Harper Hospital, established in 1863 in Detroit to serve the wounded. Howard Longyear came as a student to assist Dr. David O. Farrand, the hospital's superintendent. There were eight one-story buildings with a capacity to serve 800 patients. Howard later became a noted physician at Harper when it became a civilian hospital. John and Howard's brother, Stephen, was promoted to sergeant in Virginia. He was a Third Infantry volunteer,[325] and several Turner nephews were serving.

The Civil War Years

John Longyear discovered the Munroe's cousins Charles and Jesse Parker at the Parole Camp near Annapolis in May of 1864. They were among the thousands of Union prisoners of the Confederacy who had been sent back behind the Federal lines to the camp. They were given parole providing they would not rejoin their units until they had been regularly exchanged for Confederate soldiers. The Confederate Army could keep these soldiers from fighting and not have to feed them. Their sister, Hattie Parker Guest, was at one of the hospitals occupying the United States Naval Academy buildings. Her husband had been killed early in the war in the battle of Pittsburg Landing.[326]

In 1864 President Lincoln appointed Daniel paymaster of the army at the rank of major. He entered upon the duties of the position with his usual zeal and energy, but he resigned the office as soon as he could when his health failed, after the capture of Atlanta by General Sherman.[327] The pressures on Daniel and Adella were enormous. Daniel's son, Daniel (Adella's stepson), was a student at West Point when the Civil War broke out. He enlisted in the 78th New York infantry and was later confined to rebel prisons. In February of 1865, John Longyear received a letter from Daniel in his beautiful and highly legible hand thanking him for obtaining a Special Order for the Exchange of his son Daniel, "The poor boy if alive is still a prisoner and I fear he will never be released until death releases him from the suffering caused by the cruelties by the fiends who are systematically murdering our poor boys." He told his brother-in-law, "This anxiety for his safety and suffering is intolerable... If Mr. Lincoln will put the Rebel officers in our hands on the same amount and quality of rations that our men receive at their hands, and house and clothe them in the same manner, and have them guarded and cared for by our returned prisoners, within thirty days our men will be exchanged or so many as could be delivered in that time and the balance would be treated humanely." He angrily wrote he wished Lincoln would be taken prisoner because he thought if Andrew Johnson would take over as president, he would bring the rebels to terms. He closed saying Mrs. Longyear, Harriett, had started to Washington, D.C. that morning and that although he had long wished to come down, "funds are too short."[328] Daniel's son was imprisoned for ten months and died soon after the war from exposure suffered during his incarceration, thus meeting the same fate as Daniel's father had endured after being taken prisoner and then released after the war of 1812.[329]

Hiram's son Dwight S. Smith, at age 14, was appointed a midshipman in the naval service of President Lincoln. After four years, he made it home safely.[330] There was hardly a Michigan family anywhere not touched by the war. John N. Bush said of the period, "I have heard the boys tell how they have poured over letters from home or replied to a missive from wife or sweetheart while out on the field, coming to the conclusion that they would drop the terrible business of war and go home to the ones most dear to them, yet they have told me that when the call of battle sounded the resolution was forgotten and the fray welcomed. These are the evidences that these men with silver brows fought with the greatest good and the peace and prosperity of our homes attest to their valor. Now there comes a day when an appeal to reason rather than cold steel and leaden bullets brings about the greatest good, and I anticipate that no such tragedy as the Civil War will ever again cast a cloud over this fair land."[331] Allen S. Shattuck recalled to a meeting of Lansing pioneers:

> May 13, 1861, the Lansing company was enrolled in the Third Michigan, June 13 they left going through Washington, Georgetown and other cities on their way to the front. On July 16 the Lansing men were preparing to take part in the first battle of Bull Run and the Lansing company may lay just claim to having fired the first shots of the battle. Later came the retreat to Washington. Williamsburg, Fair Oaks, in the latter the Lansing men being in the foremost. Eight fell dead and fifteen were wounded so severely that only three of them ever reported for duty again. Sure as a courier should be described approaching, you could put it down that "Third Michigan to the front" would be in the text of the order from headquarters. There were Fredericksburg, Chancellorsville, Gettysburg—few were the great battles not participated in by the Third Michigan until there were not enough left in the regiment to go into action. The Third Michigan never lost a gun in supporting a battery, and the boys always went as far as orders sent them. At the close of the war 28 of the Lansing company lay dead and 48 were wounded, only a few of whom were ever able to make a living afterward. Here the magnificence of the government who fought for it comes in. We get better pensions than any nation on the earth.[332]

Though James remained in Michigan as a civilian, he was working each day to enable Michigan to give its all. Throughout the war James lent his business and financial skills in support of the Blair administration, particularly in dealing with the aftermath of the scandalous McKinney tenure as treasurer. He was close to John Owen, a prominent Methodist leader as well as educational and financial leader who had invested in the plank road and served on the Female College board of trustees with James since 1860. After Owen was elected State Treasurer, he asked James to be Deputy State Treasurer and to help. For the next six years the two worked together to repair Michigan's financial standing.[333] It was said his financial skills, reputation for honesty, and executive capacity paved the way for the governor and the state to undertake the Michigan war effort. Owen had the same characteristics. At the end of the war, *The State Republican* said of James, "It is but just to say that to his efforts, as well as those of Mr. Owen, much credit is due for the favorable condition of the State Finances."[334]

As deputy state treasurer, James was paid $855 in 1863. Office hours for the Treasurer Department were 8 a.m. to noon and 1:30 to 4:00 p.m.[335] James also pursued other state needs such as overseeing the building of a new administrative building and working on expanding the railroad service south to Jackson. The new building was urgently needed because there were so many clerks in the state capitol building handling the business of war that more room was vital. On September 16, 1863, James was appointed the Agent of the Board of State Auditors to superintend the erection and completion of the new structure for the state Treasury Department.[336] However, there were other pressing problems as well. Most pressing for Lansing was that stage lines and private conveyances afforded the only means of transportation—even for the Civil War troops. One reason Governor Blair found it necessary to conduct business from Jackson or Detroit was because of the lack of railroad transportation and a telegraph from Lansing to the outside world.[337] James would not be able to accomplish this work until the war was over and reconstruction was under way.

Chapter 7

The Years After the War

Michigan had some advantages during the recovery because it had been far from the actual battlefields. However, Frank Turner wrote after the war: "Can the pages of any history be searched for any good effects from the shedding of the blood of our fellow men?" He also wrote of the great political, social and economic upheaval that followed: "Ingham county never had a military camp or rendezvous during the Civil war, so we were not troubled by camp parasites and camp followers or drifts. The only gain in this war was the improvements in rural districts and the introduction of labor-saving machinery on the farm and in the workshops. The changes in our social relations, our civic and industrial activities after the Civil war were so marked that volumes could be written about the same. Our schools and the improvement in their service have been noticed and commented upon … as have also the going out of the seminary form of instruction and the coming of the broader high school system."[338]

Coming Home

Even as the residents began to pick up the pieces after the war, the memories of perplexing anxiety, many petty annoyances, great sacrifices of time to the war effort, and the fear of the continual drafts which threatened each community with conscription of their ablest men, stayed with them. These factors together with the large expenditures of money by the state, counties, and townships, and by individuals, had all combined to render the burdens and cares of the people at times so heavy as to be almost unbearable. Michigan raised $14,500,000 for war purposes, and although understood through silent numbers, this achievement was considered astonishing.[339] This sacrifice left almost every institution on every government level suffering from neglect.

Governor Henry H. Crapo's emotional welcome to the first returning troops on June 14, 1865, expressed gratitude to the soldiers, but his words also conveyed the Civil War's human legacy of pain and loss in the state. He said to the Michigan soldiers, in part: "Although you return to us bearing honorable marks of years of toil, of hardship, of privation, and of suffering—many of you with bodies mutilated, maimed and scarred—mourning the loss of brave comrades ruthlessly slain on the field of battle, tortured to death by inches, or foully murdered in cold blood, not with the weapon of a soldier, but by the lingering pangs of starvation and exposure—yet you will in the future enjoy the proud satisfaction of having aided in achieving for your country her second independence—in vindicating the National honor and dignity— in overthrowing that despotic and unholy power which has dared to raise its hideous head on this continent for the purpose of trampling upon and destroying that inalienable right to life, liberty and the pursuit of happiness, which is the birth right of all—and finally, in placing the Union, established by the blood of our fathers, upon an imperishable foundation."[340]

Michigan troops were the first to receive "homing orders." The first regiment to arrive in Michigan was the Twelfth regiment. The last, the Third and Fourth regiments, arrived a year later on June 10, 1866.[341] Though the troops were of course relieved that the war was over and glad to be on Michigan soil once more, they nevertheless came with heavy hearts after the death of the great leader whom so many had trusted would take the country through the coming repercussions of the war.

In the midst of recovery from the Civil War, the great shock of President Lincoln's assassination threw the country into turmoil and despair. Marian clipped the first report of the death of President Lincoln from a newspaper she had obtained. It gave the full account as it came into the *New York Tribune* from Washington in dispatch after dispatch as more facts were learned. The story began with the headline that read: "Special Dispatch to the N.Y. Tribune." It concluded with the eleventh dispatch:

Washington, Friday, April 14, 1865—1¼ a.m.

The President is slowly dying. The brain is slowly oozing through the ball-hole in his forehead. He is of course insensible. There is an occasional lifting of his hand, and heavy stertorous breathing; that's all.

Mrs. Lincoln and her two sons are in a room of the house opposite to Ford's Theater, where the President was taken, and adjoining that where he is lying. Mr. Sumner is seated at the head of the bed. Secretary Stanton, Welles, Dennison, Usher and McCullock, and Mr. Speed are in the room. A large number of surgeons, generals, and personal family friends of Mr. Lincoln fill the house. All are in tears. Andy Johnson is here. He was in bed in his room at the Kirkwood when the assassination was committed. He was immediately apprised of the event, and got up. The precaution was taken to provide a guard of soldiers for him, and these were at his door before the news was well through the city…

We give the above dispatches in the order in which they reached us, the first having been received a little before midnight, for we know that every line, every letter will be read with the intensest interest. In the sudden shock of a calamity so appalling we can do little else than give such details of the murder of the President as have reached us. Sudden death is always overwhelming; assassination of the humblest of men is always frightfully startling; when the head of thirty millions of people is hurried into eternity by the hand of a murderer—that head a man so good, so wise, so noble as ABRAHAM LINCOLN, the Chief Magistrate of a nation in the condition of ours at this moment, – the sorrow and the shock are too great for many words. There are none in all this broad land today who love their country, who wish well to their race, that will not bow down in profound grief at the event it has brought upon us. For once all party rancor will be forgotten, and no right-thinking man can hear of Mr. Lincoln's death without accepting it as a national calamity. We can give in these its first moments, no thought of the future. God, in his inscrutable Providence, has thus visited the Nation; the future we must leave to Him.

Later.—The accounts are confused and contradictory. One dispatch announces that the President died at 12 ½ p.m. Another, an hour later, states that he is still living, but dying slowly. We go to press without knowing the exact truth, but presume there is not the slightest ground for hope. Mr. Seward and his son are both seriously wounded, but were not killed. But there can be little hope that the Secretary can rally with this additional and frightful wound [however, he survived].[342]

The death of Lincoln was a terrible setback for the nation. Now a country torn with pain and hard feelings would have to go about healing and rebuilding without the steady hand of one of its greatest presidents.

In September of 1866 Horatio Seymour, then the Democratic Governor of New York and candidate for President, came to Lansing for several days to take care of his business affairs and to do some politicking. When he met with James, who was a Senatorial candidate in District 21 on the Republican ticket, Seymour told James he supported Negro suffrage and that he had advised former rebel officers of high rank to go home and secure the right of suffrage for Negroes in the Southern States. These sentiments were supported by the Radical Republicans and were a powerful message to the state Democrats. Consequently, James reported Seymour's position to *The Lansing State Republican* for publication. When Seymour returned a few weeks later, the Republican newspaper lamented that he did not meet with Democrats and make a speech on his position.[343]

In 1866 John W. Longyear was a delegate to the Loyalists Convention in Philadelphia. The purpose of the convention was to raise public opinion against President Andrew Johnson's lenient reconstruction policy toward Southern Democrats and states that seceded. John stepped down as Congressional Representative in deference to Austin Blair whom those in the inner circle of the Republican party of the Third Congressional District thought should go to Washington since he was the nationally known and revered War Governor. Blair would have preferred to be chosen by the Michigan Legislature for U.S. Senator, a seat also sought by Zachariah Chandler.

In a "smoke-filled room" discussion in Jackson, the supporters of the two men could not reach agreement but Chandler prevailed. At the Republican Convention, John Longyear's name was removed from consideration for Congress and a resolution was passed commending him for the course he had pursued in the last four years upon the great question of reconstruction, the legal status of states that seceded, and "the admitting to Congress of those whose hands were red with the blood of our fellow men."[344]

In the fall of 1866 Zachariah Chandler and Daniel Case stumped the district with Blair, who won handily so that all six Congressional Representatives from Michigan were Republicans. Blair told a crowd in October, "In coming to this hall this evening, I noticed a transparency bearing the words of the lamented Lincoln, 'with malice towards none, charity for all.' I believe this motto controls the action of the Republican party in the present campaign. We are in the midst of a revolution, which is peaceful now, although marked with blood and carnage for four years."[345]

For several years after his assassination, *The Lansing State Republican* regularly carried reminders of Lincoln as the nation mourned. There were periodic anecdotes from Lincoln's friends, a reprint of his Gettysburg Address, and memories of the Lincoln family members. Although the fighting was over, the reconstruction battle continued in Washington and was reported on in nearly every edition of *The Lansing State Republican*. In 1867, George Sanford took over the editorship from N. B. Jones, and party rhetoric was stepped up. Marian and James read a blow-by-blow account of the Andrew Johnson impeachment process, about the thoughts and deeds of Liberal Republican Horace Greely who angered many Northerners by supporting a general amnesty for Confederate officials and signing a bail bond for Jefferson Davis. They read reports of Lucy Stone voting in New Jersey and the progress of women as it was being debated in other states. They read about the atrocities happening in the south against blacks, the formation of the Klu Klux Klan in Michigan, and the regular exploits of a fictitious character named Nasby in a satiric anti-slavery nationally syndicated column. The new editor expressed many passionate opinions on state and national politics. *The Lansing State Republican* was the voice of the Radical Republicans and boasted the largest circulation in the state. According to Sanford's estimation, the Republican party stood for "universal education, religious toleration and the same civil and political rights for all classes, without regard to color or race," and he did not want people to forget it.[346]

In February of 1867 Frederick Douglass was invited to speak in Lansing on national issues, mostly dealing with the controversies related to the Johnson impeachment proceedings. Douglass was a former slave and an internationally recognized anti-slavery leader, writer, editor and orator. *The Lansing State Republican* reported: "Fred Douglas's lecture at Capital Hall on Wednesday evening last, was a truly able and eloquent one, and was listened to by a very large audience, notwithstanding the rainy night. 'Dangers to the Republic' was the theme and it was handled in a manner worthy of a great intellect. The immense patronage of the President, with its corrupting power; his irresponsible power of removal from office; his pardoning power; secret diplomacy; the Vice Presidency and the Veto power, were the special dangers which experience had taught us should be eliminated from our Republican system. The lecture was the work of a great mind, the result of deep and patient thought, of careful elaboration, and possessed power and eloquence in a rare degree." [347]

May 30, 1868, was the first Memorial Day people marked the graves of soldiers who served in "The Great Rebellion." It was an idea initiated by John A. Logan, Commander-in-Chief of the Grand Army of the Republic, a newly formed veteran's organization. His wife, Mary Logan, who had served at his side during the war, mustering supplies and recruiting nurses for field hospitals, had suggested that a day be set aside to decorate the graves of the soldiers after seeing it done in the South.[348] Logan had been an Illinois Democratic legislator and U.S. Congressman who joined the war in 1861. He fought as an unattached volunteer with the Michigan regiment at the Battle of Bull Run. Logan was called "Black Jack" Logan by his men (for his dark eyes and hair) and was widely admired as a hard fighter. Logan rose from the ranks of the volunteers to serve as one of Lincoln's most able Generals. After the war, he returned to Congress as a Republican, serving with Austin Blair, and later as a Senator. Logan managed the process for the impeachment trial of Johnson.[349] A school in Detroit was named for him in 1867, rebuilt in 1926 after a fire, it exists today. A John A. Logan Camp of the Sons of the Union Veterans meets in Grand Rapids to this day. When he died on December 26, 1886, he was mourned almost as much as President Grant, and it was said that Logan had been one of the most conspicuous figures in the military and political history of the country for a quarter century. Logan Circle in Washington D.C. has a twenty-five foot statue honoring him. In 1894, a street was named for Logan in Lansing and similar honors were made in other communities in and outside of Michigan. In 1994 the street was renamed Martin Luther King Boulevard by the Lansing City Council and a memorial to Logan was placed at the entrance to Mount Hope Cemetery instead.

The wounds of the war were slow to heal and from time to time were inflamed anew. In March of 1879 John Rich, the speaker of the Michigan House of Representatives, saved an article for his scrapbook containing a speech by Senator Chandler. The speech was published in many newspapers throughout the country and became known as Chandler's "Jeff Davis Speech." When the U.S. Senate took up the issue of soldier's pensions and attempts were made to obtain pensions for confederate soldiers, even to provide a pension to Jefferson Davis, the leader of the rebellion and convicted of treason, Chandler rose and said:

> Mr. President, twenty-two years ago tomorrow, in the old Hall of the Senate, now occupied by the Supreme Court of the United States, I, in company with Mr. Jefferson Davis, stood up and swore before Al-

mighty God that I would support the Constitution of the United States. Mr. Jefferson Davis came from the cabinet of Franklin Pierce into the Senate of the United States and took the oath with me to be faithful to the government. During four years I sat in this body with Mr. Jefferson Davis and saw the preparations going on from day to day for the overthrow of this government. With treason in his heart and perjury on his lips he took the oath to sustain the government that he meant to overthrow.

Sir, there was a method in his madness. He, in cooperation with other men from his section and in the Cabinet of Mr. Buchanan, made careful preparations for the event that was to follow. Your armies were scattered all over this broad land where they could not be used in an emergency; your fleets were scattered wherever the winds blew and water was found to float them, where they could not be used to put down rebellion; your Treasury was depleted. Preparations were carefully made. Your arms were sold under an apparently innocent clause in an army bill providing that the Secretary of War might, at his discretion, sell such arms as he deemed it for the interest of the government to sell.

Sirs, eighteen years ago last month I sat in these halls and listened to Jefferson Davis delivering his farewell address, informing us what our constitutional duties to this government were, and then he left and entered into a rebellion to overthrow the government he had sworn to support! I remained here, sir, during the whole of that terrible rebellion. I saw our brave soldiers by thousands and hundreds of thousands, aye, I might say millions, pass through to the theater of war, and I saw their shattered ranks return; I saw steamboat after steamboat and railroad train after railroad train arrive with the maimed and the wounded; I was with my friend from Rhode Island (Mr. Burnside) when he commanded the Army of the Potomac, and saw piles of legs and arms that made humanity shudder; I saw the widow and the orphan in their homes, and heard the weeping and the wailing of those who had lost their dearest and their best. Mr. President, I little thought at that time that I should live to hear in the Senate of the United States eulogies upon Jefferson Davis, living—a living rebel eulogized on the floor of the Senate of the United States! Sir, I am amazed to hear it; and I can tell the gentlemen on the other side that they little know the spirit of the North when they come here at this day, and, with bravado on their lips, utter eulogies upon a man whom every man, woman, and child in the North believes to have been a double-dyed traitor to his government. (Applause in the galleries.)[350]

"Old Zach," as he was affectionately called in Michigan, died November 1, the same year as this speech. As a national figure, his death was widely mourned. As one of Michigan's most respected leaders, his statue was placed in the U.S. Capitol Statuary Hall along with territorial governor, Lewis Cass. In 2011 it was replaced with a statue of President Gerald Ford. Chandler's statue is now in the Michigan capitol.

Railroads and the Telegraph

During the first two years of the war when Blair made his headquarters in Detroit, there were calls for moving the state capitol because of the lack of railroad transportation and telegraph. The railroads built in Michigan prior to the Civil War bypassed the capital city to the northeast and south. With no railroads entering Lansing, there was no telegraph because the railroads needed to open a path through the wilderness that the telegraph wires could follow.

Messengers carried important news from Lansing to Jackson on horse-back; from there it was telegraphed to Detroit and the East. "Proceedings of the legislature were sent every day at 4 p.m. via messenger on horseback to Jackson. From there the same was telegraphed to Detroit papers to be published at 11 a.m. the following day. The newspaper reporter sometimes had to make these trips. When snow drifts or deep mud prevented the mes-senger from getting to Jackson or Owosso, the newspaper would print in its legislative column, 'Delays in Transmission.'"[351] When the transcontinental telegraph opened at the end of 1861, pressure for the telegraph and a railroad in Lansing became even greater; however, only a telegraph line to Jackson was put in.

Although it would be several years before the goal was reached, as early as 1856 James was working to get railroads built through Lansing. However, first he had to show need. The *Lansing Republican* reported:

James Turner, Esq., the indefatigable Secretary of the Saginaw and Lan-sing Railroad Company, is making every possible effort to place this subject before capitalists in its true light. The following note from him gives one item of the statistics which he has collected; Statement of Wheat, flour, mer-chandise, Household goods and other Freights that have passed Gate No. 1, of the Lansing & Howell Plank road, from Sep. 10th to Dec. 15th inclusive.

> Wheat, 29,302 busls, at 60 lbs per bushels is 879,000 Tons
> Merchandise, Coal and Iron, &c. 952,325 Tons
> Household goods 565,075 Tons
> Freight other than above 348,900 Tons
> Total 2,745,300 Tons
> Add 138000 bbls. flour at 9 bbls, per ton, say 15,000 Tons
> Total 2,760,300 Tons[352]

In 1857, Daniel and Hiram attended the opening of the southeasterly Jackson Palmyra Railroad, a celebration involving business and commu-nity-spirited men in Jackson. Because Daniel and Hiram had first come to Jackson when it was a frontier town, they were well known there. Each gave a speech in support of the Jackson-Lansing connection to the Amboy line. It was reported that O. M. Barnes, one of their friends going back to their days in Mason, lamented, "Lansing—the Seat of Government—A Beautiful and thriving town yet still without Railroad Communications. Although that magnificent enterprise, the 'Amboy, Lansing, and Grand Traverse Bay'

Railroad, via Saginaw and the rest of the World may possibly fail of success, we trust that 'branch' may double its length so that we may yet reach the political center of the state by 'riding a rail.'" The mayor told Hiram, "the Jackson and Lansing Railroad—push it along." [353] The Amboy, Lansing, and Traverse Bay Railroad was successful five years later, reaching Lansing from the north fifteen years after the city's founding. Frank Turner wrote of this event:

> This was built by a corporation that had its offices in Owosso. Judge Amos Gould of Owosso was president, George C. Monroe [Monroe was active in the Underground Railroad and a shirttail relative of Marian's.] of Jonesville and Alvin N. Hart of Lansing were stockholders and directors. The road was thirty miles long and when built was nicknamed 'Almighty Long and Tremendous Bad.' From its sharp curves it received another name, i.e., "Ramshorn Railroad." It was commenced in 1857 and was built from Owosso to Bath at the close of 1860. From Bath to Lansing, a distance of seven miles, the builders met with obstacles, a bad sink hole on Big Marsh (Chandler's) and a high hill to cut through on Gunnisonville road. A high bridge now spans this cut.

> From Bath to Lansing a stage was run to accommodate passengers coming to Lansing. This stage road was noted for its mud. Some fastidious passengers walked the seven miles rather than ride a mud-covered stage or have their clothing covered with mud. When it was built to Lansing the company erected a depot, freight house and small roundhouse on East Franklin avenue. The ground around these buildings was always muddy and wet after a rain. This was the first railroad depot built in the capital.[354]

Now the road connected with Owosso and from there people could go by train either east through Fenton and Pontiac to Detroit on the shores of Lake Erie or west through St. Johns, Ionia, and Grand Rapids to the shores of Lake Michigan at Grand Haven. It was a great accomplishment that had been long delayed. Frank Turner said there were several reasons, "the first of which was poverty. The state was poor. When it was admitted into the Union in 1837 we had a financial panic. The free banking, or wildcat money, made it worse; also the five million loan [borrowed by the state for the public improvement plan under Governor Mason] did not relieve or clear up financial matters. When we moved the capital in 1847 we had another financial panic." After the financial loan fiasco, the state would not build or finance railroads for the inhabitants.

Delay also resulted because the benefits of 5,838,775 acres of government-owned swamps and overflow lands designated by Congress in 1850 was so slow in coming. The act said that when these lands were sold proceeds had to be used in draining or reclaiming them, which facilitated railroad building. By act of the state Legislature of 1851, the state fixed a minimum price per acre of 75 cents on the lands received. The state was custodian of this fund of nearly five million dollars and paid interest on it that went into the Primary School Fund. Railroad building accelerated in 1859 when the Legislature authorized the sale of 400,000 acres and raised money used for draining and reclaiming the land.[355]

Many once again feared that the legislators might move the capital, which also slowed progress in getting a railroad. One settler who arrived in Lansing in 1847, O. A. Jenison, recalled to the Pioneer Society in 1878, "I might tell you of the many 'pull-backs' Lansing has had in struggling for an existence, the greatest of which was the fact that, at the expiration of its first twenty years, there was a chance of the capital being again removed. This club constantly hung over our heads like the sword of Damocles, and undoubtedly deterred many from investing in our city." [356]

In 1863, after years of discussion, three days before Christmas, a meeting for potential investors was held in the courthouse to organize the Jackson and Lansing Railroad Company. The Legislature had just passed the first act empowering a municipality to use public credit for grants to a railroad, but because of the lack of public funding, subscription financing was called for and $28,000 was pledged for shares of stock.[357] More organizing was needed, but those present knew they would succeed because they were sure they could sustain the railroad commercially. In terms of economic activity and diversity, Lansing was among the states' most functionally complex cities, on a par with the older pre-statehood cities of Kalamazoo and Port Huron. Only Pontiac, Saginaw/East Saginaw, Grand Rapids and the port city of Detroit ranked higher in diverse commerce and activity.[358] The farmers, business people, and the general public wanted to hook up with the lines that could take them to Chicago and Detroit.

In February of 1865 a new company, the Jackson, Lansing and Saginaw Railroad Company, was finally incorporated with James Turner as treasurer and land commissioner. James originated this effort and devoted the greater portion of his time to the successful completion of this work.[359] Daniel gave $1,000 to aid in securing the Jackson, Lansing and Saginaw railroad and the depot grounds at North Lansing, as he did for so many public-spirited projects.[360] Businessmen contributed goods from their stores, such as flour and quinine (for malaria) for the workers.[361] Adella recalled, "When the first railroad came into Lansing money and labor were freely given; the work not progressing fast enough to satisfy our active businessmen, they left their places of business and worked with their own hands to carry forward the laying of the track which they had before paid for by their liberal subscriptions." [362] James' spirited leadership was the epitome of the saying, "Where there is a will, there is a way." The length of the new Jackson, Lansing and Saginaw Railroad was 116 miles, all open by 1868.[363]

A New Constitution is Proposed for Michigan

James had never sought legislative office and when the legislative district tried to nominate him for State Representative several years earlier, he cheerfully removed his name in favor of Peter Lindeman of Mason.[364] None the less, he ran for the Legislature at the end of the war and won easily. In 1867, the year James served as a Senator, a state Constitutional Convention was held. John Longyear was a delegate and was soon recognized as one of the convention's most influential members.[365] The State Constitution had not been revised since 1850. People wanted changes in regulations governing many fields such as railroads and the banking rules, and complained that Michiganians were too dependent upon the currency of the East, Canada, Ohio and Indiana. In Lansing, they complained that officials' salaries were too low and that state officers could not afford to make their homes in Lansing. Some figured that if the salaries were in line with other states they would be more inclined to stay in the capital city.[366] Some of the burning issues of the convention were Negro suffrage, the legal status of intoxicating liquor (the 1850 constitution prohibited its sale), and women's rights. Groups all over the state peppered the delegates with petitions on the liquor question and woman's suffrage. Changes in federal law also had an impact on the convention.

On January 16, 1867, James had the honor of being in the Michigan Legislature when Michigan became the twelfth state to ratify the Fourteenth Amendment to ensure civil rights and safety for blacks and to extend to all citizens the protections of the Constitution against unjust state laws. It included the Due Process and Equal Protection Clauses, although this amendment was also the first to define "citizens" and "voters" as male. This definition was a deliberate legal and political setback for women.

Supporters of women's rights hoped to undo the negative impact through the new state constitution and made a push to get the inclusion of woman's suffrage before the convention. The issue was brought to the public's attention whenever possible. In Mason that January, the Mason Literary Society discussion was based on the following: "Resolved, that women should be allowed the elective franchise." The program was open to the public and debated with four members on the affirmative side and four on the negative side.[367]

John Longyear submitted two petitions from his area to the convention urging woman's suffrage be included in the new constitution. *The Journal of the Constitutional Convention of 1867* read: "June 26th, 1867, By Mr. Longyear: petition of Marvin Salter and 45 other men, and Meoriah J. Norton and 17 other ladies, citizens of the State, praying for equal suffrage to men and women. Referred to the Committee on Elections." [368] Another Journal entry read, "July 18, 1867, By Mr. Longyear: petition of S. D. Fobes and 82 other men; Mrs. S. S. Coryell and 137 other women, citizens of Lansing and vicinity, asking for equal suffrage for men and women. Referred to the Committee on Elections."[369]

It seemed that this would be an opportune time to achieve suffrage for women because the issue of voting rights for blacks was being addressed across the country. Pressure from women suffrage supporters got the issue before the convention so that the issue of winning woman's voting rights was debated and came very close to winning. It was voted down by just three votes, 31 to 34. Stephen D. Bingham was a supporter of women's rights and editorialized in the *State Republican* that too few women petitioned and that if 40,000 of the state's 230,000 women had petitioned, the right to the franchise would have been granted. He said, "'No taxation without representation' was the war cry that gave us a republican government, the same unanswerable appeal will give to woman the elective franchise." [370]

The Constitutional Convention succeeded in putting forward a measure to remove state obstacles to Negro males voting. The delegates accepted it, but the provision was cited as one of several reasons that contributed to the rejection of the proposed constitution by the voters of Michigan. Many moderate abolitionists were for ending slavery but little else. They did not give thought to the more advanced views of radical abolitionists, as they were called, who were concerned with how to achieve the status of blacks as full citizens. For the radicals the issue of voting rights for black men was a difficult sell and representatives from the Blair administration worked hard to get the support of their own party. Charles May served as Blair's Lieutenant Governor during the war from 1863 to 1865 and continued his activism in Republican politics. He was one of the administration's best public speakers and, on March 4, 1868, spoke to local Republican party members at the Grant Club, laying out the political situation and arguing eloquently for the votes of his audience in favor of the new constitution. In his speech, he tried to address objections to a variety of aspects of the proposed constitution and to allay the fears of his listeners about the weakening of their own power and self-interest if a new group were allowed to join the electorate. This speech laid out the politics of the day and was considered so significant it was circulated in the form of a handbill prior to the vote on the new constitution. Here are some of its key points:

Fellow-Republicans of Jackson:

I am here by your invitation, to discuss the issues of the spring campaign, and to advocate the adoption of the new Constitution. On the first Monday of April next, the electors of Michigan will have questions of the highest gravity and importance submitted to them for their decision. In addition to the responsibility of the yearly election of local officers, will be decided the great question of our fundamental law for many years to come…

A WORD TO REPUBLICANS—UNION AND HARMONY

In discussing this question I wish to address myself especially to Republicans. We are the dominant party of the state. We had a large and controlling majority in the Constitutional Convention. We must meet the responsibility of this proposed political change, and we have the power in our hands to effect it. If a full Republican vote is polled for the new Constitution, it will be adopted. What we need, therefore, in order to secure this result is union and harmony in the party. It is unnecessary; it is useless for us to go to our political opponents. Following its time honored instincts and prejudice the Democratic party will cast its whole vote against the new Constitution. When did that party ever fail to vote against human rights and especially against the negro? ... This is why I wish to address myself especially to Republicans tonight.

TOLERATION ON THE QUESTION OF PROHIBITION

One great cause of difference in the party is removed by the separate submission of the question of prohibition in connection with that of annual or biannual sessions of the Legislature. Of the first of these questions, the question of prohibition ... I wish to say that we must tolerate each other's opinions on this question, and not let them stand in the way of a hearty and united support of the main instrument. Following my own long cherished convictions of duty, I shall vote for prohibition. My neighbor, who is as good a Republican as I am, is in favor of license. Is there anything in this to prevent us both voting for equal Suffrage and the new Constitution? I repeat it, we must tolerate each other. Let the temperance question be fought out on its own merits. It is not an issue between the two political parties today. We should have in the Republican party no intolerance and no ostracism on account of it.

THE MAIN QUESTION

Turning to the main question, we find that all are agreed that we have outgrown the old Constitution; that it is inadequate to the present condition and wants of the State and that we should have a new one. Both parties were agreed that we should have a Constitutional Convention. The new Constitution indeed, is the joint work of both parties. Except as to one question no party issue was made in the Convention upon any of its articles or provisions. All were sustained and opposed indifferently by delegates of both parties on other than party grounds. On the question of suffrage itself the ablest and most influential Democrat in the body, Hon. G. V. N. Lothrop, spoke in favor of the principle of impartial suffrage...

EQUAL SUFFRAGE FUNDAMENTAL TO THE PARTY

First, we are bound to sustain it because it is FUNDAMENTAL to the party. We are committed to it by the origin and history of the party.

The Republican party was organized on the Anti-Slavery idea, it was organized to prevent the spread of slavery; to keep it out of the new territories, and to stay its encroachments in the Government. It triumphed on this idea in 1860 when slavery rebelled, and the war followed. To put down the rebellion and to bring the war to a successful issue, it became necessary to destroy slavery. Hence the immortal proclamation of Lincoln.

All this was done by the Republican party. Every step in this great contest; from opposition to the spread of slavery to its final destruction, was taken by the Republican party; was under Republican rule... Just in proportion as we have been bold and outspoken on the side of liberty we have been successful. Whenever we have lowered the standard a single inch for expediency we have lost by it. This should teach us a great lesson.

PARTY CONSISTENCY

Again we are committed to this doctrine of equal suffrage by party consistency. I know this is not the highest ground but there is great force in it. The coming Presidential campaign must be fought out on the Congressional plan of reconstruction… Again, if the National Republican Convention to meet at Chicago shall incorporate this principle of equal suffrage in their platform; as I sincerely trust they will; what then will be the position we shall occupy in Michigan if we oppose it at the coming election? …

HIGHER GROUNDS

But rising out of mere party considerations and reasons there are broad and solid principles upon which to rest this doctrine of equal suffrage. Whether we look at it on grounds of political economy, of public policy, or of absolute political right, we find equal warrant for giving all men the ballot.[371]

The Lansing State Republican claimed of the Democrats, "It is not that they are opposed to the suffrage clause, or the Constitution; the question is to defeat it, and acquire future capital for the Democratic party not only in Michigan, but throughout the Union. What Republican will aid them in this selfish purpose."[372] Despite arguments by the Republican state leaders such as May and the charges against the Democrats for playing party politics to defeat the Republican's Constitution as stated in *The Lansing State Republican,* the Constitution failed to gain approval. However, two years later the Fifteenth Amendment was approved by Congress giving black men the franchise at last and ratified by both houses of the Michigan Legislature on March 8, 1869. It was a victory for a goal long sought by the Radical Republicans.

Education After the War

Following the war the Lansing progressives renewed their work to improve the local public schools, the Female College and education for women, the Boys Reform School, and the college for agricultural education after a period of neglect during the war. In 1864 Daniel Case was appointed by Governor Luce as a member of the Board of Control for the Michigan School for the Deaf and Blind in Flint and served as treasurer of the board for several years.[373]

The session of 1867 was extremely busy. James was a member of the Finance Committee, where he was in a position to help the Reform School in Lansing and the Asylum for the Insane in Kalamazoo, the latter of special interest to him as Chairman of the Committee on the Asylum for the Insane.[374] The asylum was facing pent-up needs after the war, citing overcrowding and the inability to reach out to all those who needed help. The asylum superintendent told the senators the asylum staff had identified 129 deaths by suicide in Michigan in the past year and that many of them might be living had they received prompt treatment. The superintendent argued: "Let the Legislature first provide for the wants of the Insane Asylum, for the Reform School, the Asylum for the Deaf, Dumb and Blind and for the safety of the criminals in the State Prison. Levy a 1-20th mill tax to aid the University, he said, but the needs of the University are by no means imperative. Let us meet the calls of necessity and mercy, and then, if there is anything to spare, extend the liberal hand to other institutions which require aid. In other words the true principle is, 'to be just before you are generous.'"[375]

The committee on the reform school submitted a lengthy report on its condition and introduced three bills making appropriations for the amount of $125,000. Building up the free public school system of the state was a continuing challenge among many facing the young state after the war. Stable funding for education had always been a concern. Lansing was moving forward, but not all the schools in the area were. "The Report to the Superintendent of Schools for Ingham County" in 1868 gave a bleak picture of the conditions of the county schools and raised issues concerning facilities, equipment, and teacher preparation. In the previous year, there were 7,011 children in the county between the ages of five and twenty and 6,612 were attending school.[376]

Because of the years of neglect, many of the county's school facilities were in particularly poor shape. The report found that of the 131 schoolhouses in the district, 104 were frame, sixteen were brick, and eleven were log. Many were placed on lots considered unfit for school purposes. Twenty-three school buildings were deemed unfit; forty-two had no privy. Only thirty-four had suitable furniture, 104 had insufficient furniture and ninety-eight had damaged furniture. With the exception of the Lansing Schools, there was a universal lack of furniture of graduated sizes to fit students of different ages, a lack of recitation seats or benches, and almost an entire lack of educational apparatus. There were no outline maps in fifty-seven, no blackboards in ninety-five and many of the blackboards available were described as "not worth the name." Of the 131 schools, only four were graded, only twenty-three had a good system of classification, and only thirty-two had uniform books because most schools boards had failed to specify books. Lack of uniform books meant each child had to be helped individually, taking a toll on the teacher's time. School libraries were described as deplorable, and the superintendent asked forlornly, "What can be done to make them what the law intended they should be—sources of instruction and mental profit?" By the end of the war, many teachers were sadly lacking in proper preparation. Just five had attended a Normal School for teachers. The state offered institutes to provide training on new teaching methods and support. Many teachers welcomed the state institutes and attended the one in Mason. All but three of the teachers were women.[377]

In Congress, John Longyear had worked on land issues for Michigan and had acquired a reputation for his effective work in committee.[378] During the Constitutional Convention John was chair of the Committee on Public

Lands. He managed to interject into the committee some political moves in tandem with the state Legislature's efforts on behalf of the Female College, which were aimed at stabilizing funding by urging the sale of more swamplands. He proposed setting up a drainage fund and using a portion of the proceeds for the endowment of a college for the education of females, similar to the

The Female College, with one wing. CADL photo.

Primary School Fund that was set up earlier from the sale of swamp lands. A resolution to that effect was referred to his committee. John also offered this resolution as another line of approach: "Resolved, That the committee on education be instructed to inquire into the expediency of providing for the establishment and endowment of a college for the education of females." The resolution was referred to the Committee on Education.[379] Abigail Rogers and the Board wanted permanent state funding because they knew of several schools, after much usefulness for a time, had either on the death or withdrawal of their originators, greatly declined in character or altogether passed out of existence. They hoped that if their efforts at the capitol were successful, permanence would be insured by ultimate acceptance and adoption once the State recognized and acted upon its obligations to girls and women, the neglected half of its children. Abigail made the case for higher educational institutions for women and for pushing for progress on both the state and national level. She also argued that state support would assure young women of all income levels could have access to higher education, not just the well-to-do.[380] Nevertheless, efforts for an appropriation did not succeed.

The state's thirty-first annual *Superintendent's Report* provided an assessment of all of the state's school educational achievements, including Abigail Roger's 1868 report to the superintendent. It showed how the supporters of higher education for women gained wider public support and were able to pass various measures to advance the cause of women—particularly when James was a state Senator—only to have them killed by a small number of men who wished to maintain the status quo. The report by Oramel Hosford, Superintendent of Public Instruction, stated: "The one great object which they proposed to themselves was to keep before the public mind as constantly as they could, *the duty of the State to provide for the education of its daughters as it had already provided for the education of its sons,* and they thought that a location at the Capital, though at that time subject to many disadvantages, would give them vantage-ground for this purpose; since besides the representatives of the people regularly assembled here, many other persons were constantly coming from all parts, drawn by various interests, either public or private, and they judged that the circle of influence, could they succeed in reaching its sources, must, of necessity, become far wider from here than from any other place in the State."[381]

The Female College had gained the sympathy of the state superintendent of schools. Three times the Legislature passed joint resolutions asking Congress to grant federal lands in each state to endow a female college. The state house passed a resolution urging regents of the University of Michigan to admit women, and the senate asked for funds to endow the Female College. In Abigail's report to the state superintendent, she said, in part:

> As a school, the enterprise may be justly regarded as a success, since, besides over a thousand young ladies from Michigan, pupils have been received from nine other States… The first graduate received her diploma in 1860, and the Alumnae of the Institution now number forty.
>
> Additional room is greatly needed, and the last Legislature, on the petition of the Corporation and influential citizens, passed an act enabling the city to raise fifty thousand dollars to complete the buildings. Lansing will prove how well she understands the value, educational and pecuniary, of literary institutions, in voting this tax, and thus doing all in her power towards securing what is of such vital importance to her own welfare…
>
> And the many rich women of our State have here a noble field to aid with liberal hands in bestowing permanent benefits upon their own sex, by founding scholarships and instituting various other aids for those noble spirits who aspire to education in spite of all opposing circumstances. And if endowments something after the manner of "Fellowships" in the English Universities could be made, enabling women who desired it to continue their studies and prolong the period of culture instead of being forced back to labor for bread, some problems, long in dispute, might be solved by actual experiment…
>
> Your late circular, calling attention to the joint resolutions of our Legislature, and inviting cooperation "until public aid for female education shall be proportionate to that provided for men," partly suggested this statement of the subject with which the history and interests of the Michigan Female College have been and are so intimately involved, instead of the ordinary statistical report. All of which, in the cause of Female Education, is respectfully submitted.
> A. C. Rogers
>   Lansing, March 31st, 1868[382]

Besides lobbying the legislators, supporters still hoped to make a breakthrough at the University of Michigan despite the opposition of its president.

When President Henry Tappan stepped down because of strife at the University, E. O. (Erastus Otis) Haven, a minister of the Methodist Church and activist in the Republican party's formation, became president. Haven at first opposed the admission of women but not with quite the level of prejudice as his predecessor. His two main objections were the lack of women's residential facilities and concerns about the behavior of the young women and men if they were allowed to be together away from their families. He was afraid he would have a revolution on his hands. Therefore, although he said he believed in the equal status of women and men, he opposed admitting women to the university.[383] However, as events unfolded, Haven would soon gracefully bow to the weight of public opinion.

Support continued to brew in the Legislature. With the encouragement of Senator James Turner, it adopted a concurrent resolution to tell the University there was an unfairness they needed to correct: "Resolved, that it is the deliberate opinion of this Legislature that the high objects for which the University of Michigan was organized, will never be fully attained until women are admitted to all its rights and privileges."[384] Haven responded, adding some additional thoughtful arguments of his own for admitting women, including drawing on the principles of his faith: "I have come to this conclusion slowly. A few objections have sometimes seemed to me strong, but the most of what is urged against it is fanciful, and partakes of the nature of thoughtless opposition made to what is new. The standard of education would not be changed. The habits of study would not be affected. The honor of the University would be rather increased than diminished. It does not injure the young men at the Sorbonne in Paris that ladies also can listen to the lectures. The demand that women should enjoy the same advantages as men grows out of Christian civilization, and if difficulties arise, we must not shrink from them, but overcome them. Responsibility makes strength." [385]

Many young women of prominent families attended the Female College. Among them was the previously mentioned Augusta Chapin of Lansing, who became the first woman minister ordained in Michigan in 1863. Anna Ballard, also of Lansing, became Lansing's first female medical doctor in 1879 and was a Women's Christian Temperance Union leader. Gertrude Howe became an educator and missionary to China. Fanny Foster, whose father was the superintendent of the Reform School, attended the Female College and later became president of the Lansing Woman's Suffrage Association. In 1869 she went as a delegate to the National Woman's Suffrage Convention at Chicago.[386] Several nurtured their intellectual life and abilities by becoming members of the Lansing Women's Club when it was formed and by taking the leadership of new civic organizations as they formed in the years to come. Madelon Stockwell, whom Abigail had likely known since her days at Albion College where Stockwell's father was a professor, was eventually admitted as the first woman to attend the University of Michigan with the help of Lucinda Stone, a colleague of Abigail's from Kalamazoo College. A women's dormitory was named for Stockwell at the University of Michigan in

1940. Many women who looked back to this time acknowledged the positive influence Abigail Rogers had on their lives.[387]

Abbie Turner was seven when the Female College closed so unexpectedly. It was most likely in the music program at the Female College that Abbie's talents as a pianist were first recognized and developed. Although Abigail had been sick the year before and taken time to go to Arkansas to recover, her death in 1869 came as a shock. In the fourteenth year of the Female College, Abigail died of "congestion of the brain." In memorializing her loss, the *Lansing Republican* said, "She was the acknowledged and leading champion of the higher education of women in Michigan." [388]

She did not live to see this but her death may have speeded up the admission of women at the Agricultural College as the college's students sought a place to finish out their studies. Frank Turner later wrote of his cousin Abbie's namesake: "Her great work, the work on which she spent her whole life was the admission of women into the University of Michigan and the Michigan Agricultural College on an equal basis with men. All women who have been admitted to The University of Michigan and Michigan Agricultural College since her death must remember that Miss Rogers' lifelong efforts opened the doors of higher education to them."[389] However, when those who knew her died away, Abigail Rogers was forgotten and lost from history. It was not until 2007 when she was inducted into the Michigan Women's Hall of Fame that people became aware of her contributions once again.

Without public funding, upon her death the Female College closed, much as Abigail had feared. The Agricultural College (now Michigan State University) was immediately approached by women applicants. The college president said the college received more applicants than they could accept because of housing considerations. "Applications for admission of ladies have been and still are frequent and urgent. The Faculty admitted a few, who occupy rooms on the floor of the Steward's family, or in private houses. They studied chemistry, botany, horticulture, floriculture, trigonometry, surveying, entomology, bookkeeping and other branches. Their progress in study was rapid, and their improvement marked," said President Theophilus Capen Abbot in his report on the 1870 term.[390] The ten women who were admitted followed the work requirements for helping to pay for their education by doing whatever the college required. They prepared seed for the ground, cut potatoes, transplanted tomatoes and flowering plants, pruned shrubbery, gathered fruit, worked in the greenhouse, and many other tasks. Abbot thought it would be quite feasible to build another building to accommodate more women students. The college was beginning to receive annual payments from the perpetual fund set up by the U.S. Congress, yielding seven percent interest from the sale of public land and had recently built a new facility with state funds, anticipating growth. Only a relatively inexpensive dormitory would be needed.[391]

Abbot said, "Women are turning their attention more and more to studies such as are taught here. Some would like the out-of-door labor, some the aid which the compensation for their labor would afford them in acquiring an education, and it is to be regretted that they cannot avail themselves of the same privilege here that is offered to young men." Whether a young woman had an agricultural background or not, Abbot had a vision for how things would work:

> Many ladies would find our course of study agreeable and useful. They would find a knowledge of scientific principles conferring as much additional interest and delight upon them in the practice of floriculture, the care of gardens, ornamental shrubs, and orchards, in the operations of the kitchen, and in their general reading, as it does upon men. Women are frequently left in circumstances where they would highly prize some knowledge of agriculture.
>
> The applications of chemistry to women's work are so many that a half year's course of daily lectures would not be too long a one. Among the applications are, cooking, preserving of fruits, utilization of materials usually wasted, cleansing by acids and soaps, dyeing, bleaching, manufacture of soaps of different kinds, disinfection, fermentation, and neutralization of poisons. A course of lecture on dairying is now given every year.[392]

There were 132 students at the Agricultural College; twelve graduated that year, for a total of fifty-six graduates since inception. Working mainly on Saturdays, the students put down more than two train carloads of tile drain during the year for drainage of portions of the college farm. There was just enough opposition in the Legislature and on the State Board of Education to the plan to provide housing and a home economics curriculum for women to block progress until 1895, but the building that was finally chosen for the women's program was Abbot Hall.[393] (Although at first it seemed like a good idea, women's departments were developed that steered many women away from the curricula offered to men, and quotas kept down the number of women admitted to many programs for more than 100 years until passage of Title IX of the Education Amendments of 1972 stopped sex segregation in classes and programs and the use of quotas against women's enrollment.)

The new president at the University of Michigan, James Angell, was soon reporting success with admitting women and said of the 84 young ladies admitted during 1872, "The young women have addressed themselves to their work with great zeal… Their work so far does not evince less aptitude or less power of grappling even with the higher mathematics than we find in the young men. They are subjected precisely to the same tests as the men… They receive no favors and they desire none… Nor does this work seem to put a dangerous strain upon their powers… Their presence has not called for the enactment of a single new law, or for the slightest change in our methods of government or grade of work. The numerous inquiries which are sent to me from various parts of the country … show that a profound and widespread interest in the subject has been awakened." [394]

While the older Turner girls advanced through the rigorous education of the Female College, the Turners and Longyears decided to send their fifteen-year-old sons back east for education at the Cazenovia Seminary. Both sons, James Turner and John Longyear, had Munroe as a middle name, but John's middle name was spelled Munro. John was called Munro by the family. Methodists founded the college as a nonsectarian Seminary of the Genesee Conference in 1824. As at the Lima Seminary, they admitted women as well as men. John attended Georgetown College, a Jesuit institution, in Washington D.C. while his father served in Congress. John Munro said, "My uncle, James Turner, was anxious to send his son away to school and wanted me to go with him, but Uncle James being a strong Methodist, would not consider a Catholic school at all. As a result Jim and I were sent to Cazenovia Seminary, a Methodist Institution and one favorably known to Uncle James. It was a most excellent institution and had a large attendance. However I was not physically able to keep up the work and at Thanksgiving vacation we were sent to visit my aunt Miss Case [Adella], and my cousin Marian Turner, Jim's sister." John was looked after by a doctor there all winter long, receiving four baths a day. (This may have been at the Clifton Spring Sanitarium, since it was located near Rochester and known to the family.) No diet seemed to help him recover from severe weight loss. He went home to Lansing and spent the next four or five years there in semi-invalid condition.[395]

Young Jim's two years of schooling at the Seminary at Cazenovia was the only formal education he obtained outside of the Female College and district school in Lansing. Upon returning to Lansing, Jim acquired his business education under the tutelage of his Uncle Daniel at his uncle's general store while employed as a clerk. Young James' father would soon be calling upon him to take on other work where he was needed. After two years of employment as a clerk and learning business from his uncle, Jim went to work in the land office of the Jackson, Lansing and Saginaw Railway Company.

Chapter 8

Well-directed Efforts

In championing his Senate nomination from the 21st district embracing Ingham and Clinton counties, *The Lansing State Republican* pointed to the issues it regarded as most affecting Lansing that James was likely to have before him: the building of a new capitol, the enlargement of the Reform School, and the great interests connected with the railroads affecting the region: the Lansing, Jackson and Saginaw Railroad, the Ionia and Lansing Railroad, the Peninsular Railroad, the extension of the Howell and Detroit Railroad, and the Grand Trunk Railroad.[396] As predicted, James was prominently identified with railroad legislation.

Evading the Railroad Monopolies

During James' term in the Legislature, many communities were asking the state to authorize their requests for public grants of $20,000 to $50,000 to build railroads. This practice was a form of community economic development, they argued. The policy was not without its critics. Some, such as Governor Henry Crapo, the first lumber baron to be elected Governor, were very opposed to using public monies to fund private corporations and warned of the time when "the freemen of the state shall become the bondmen of corporations."[397] Nonetheless, some saw it as a way to evade the grasp of the railroad barons and their monopolies.

Among the latter group were a few citizens in Portland who had begun to push the idea of a railroad in the summer of 1866. Hervey Bartow of Portland was chosen to confer with James Turner before James took office about the possibility of procuring a railroad through Portland on a line from Lansing to Ionia. A Portland company was formed, and in November the Portland voters agreed to tax themselves five percent, 254 for the tax to 24 against, despite agitation against it from the representatives of the Detroit and Marquette Railroad. The possibility of a Lansing railroad that could reach the Lake Michigan shore was getting closer with each step. "Our friends at Portland are confident that the day of deliverance from exorbitant freights is close at hand," reported the *Lansing State Republican* in October of 1866.[398] Bartow eventually obtained throughway with little cost to the railroad, but then there seemed to be a peculiar falling off of zeal at Lansing and Ionia.[399] The project inched forward.

By April of 1868, *The Lansing State Republican* reported:

Lansing and Ionia Railroad—This project is again attracting the attention of the citizens of Ionia and of the region northwest of that place. In 1866 nearly $7,000 to the mile was raised in municipal aid and good subscriptions along the line. Hampton Rich, of Ionia, was elected President and James Turner, of this city, is one of the Directors. Now that 300 men are at work on the grade of the Detroit and Howell Railroad with the prospect of a speedy extension of that road to Lansing, there comes an offer on the part of the Michigan Central to guarantee the bonds of the Lansing and Ionia road. The Greenville Independent alludes to the question as follows:

"There now seems to be a good prospect that the Ionia and Lansing Railroad may be pushed forward to immediate completion. It is understood the Michigan Central has become interested in the project and will assist the company. We have no definite details, but Mr. Turner of Lansing, one of the I. & L. R. R. Directors, is in town and with others held an informal meeting last night."

A Michigan Central representative attended the meeting in Greenville and said that the company was willing to encourage the building of the Ionia and Lansing Railroad and would probably soon make definite offers of aid. Carrying through fell to James whose "influence with the Jackson, Lansing and Saginaw, and the Michigan Central Company was largely instrumental in the early construction of the railroad," according to Frank Turner. In December 1868 James wrote to James F. Joy, owner of the Michigan Central Railroad, giving in a condensed form statistics of the population, resources, and business of the region through which the new railroad projected to go from Lansing to Howard City, and thence eventually to Pentwater, in Oceana County, on Lake Michigan.[400] In addition, as agent for non-resident landholders, James loaned money from the New Lebanon Shakers, who had trusted his advice on investments for many years.[401] The Mount Lebanon Shaker Society in New Lebanon, New York, was the largest of the Shaker communal societies and was involved in ever-expanding commercial and industrial activity. It was mainly through James' influence that Eastern investors were persuaded to invest the additional money needed for the Ionia and Lansing Railroad.[402]

Even while work led by James continued to develop the railway system for Lansing, there was still apprehension. The community needed and welcomed the help of the Michigan Central Railroad, yet they felt threatened by the monopolies that were developing in railroading nationally. They saw what was happening with the Vanderbilt monopoly, the escalating power of corporations, and the concentration of wealth and power in the country in the hands of a few. With Stephen D. Bingham as editor, the *Lansing State*

Republican reported maneuvers of various railroad tycoons as they tried to fight off each other's takeovers and mounted rate wars that affected the pocketbooks of the nation. In April of 1868 the paper reported that Cornelius Vanderbilt was to issue orders to the superintendent of his New York Central Railroad not to ship goods brought into Albany on the Hudson River steamers. If he forces western merchants to ship their products by his railroad instead of steamers, "what will prevent him, if his plans are consummated, from laying down the same rule in relation to produce sent to Buffalo by the lake marine! ... Such things as competitive through rates, now beneficial to everybody, will be abolished. Even now, the cost of sending the commodities of the West to sea ports is twenty percent of their value, and this will probably be increased to fifty."[403]

There were calls by the *Lansing State Republican* for railroad regulation reform on a national level instead of leaving it to the fractured power of the individual states. Reform meant to regulate the passenger and freight rates for the benefit of the public rather than private individuals and their corporations. "The nation, under railroad oppression is being rapidly educated in this direction, and ten years will bring about a great change from that now existing between railroad directors and the public. A single house in Chicago now pays $300,000 a year for the freight on its merchandise from New York. Every dollar comes out of the consumer, and every dollar increase paid upon the rates now demanded for freight increases this burden of direct taxation, mostly upon the necessaries of everyday life."[404] The paper called for a thorough investigation of monopolies and railroad rates. Bingham conjectured that if Lansing could get a through railroad with the Canadian Grand Trunk to Port Huron, shippers could reach eastern ports at Boston or Portland and bring the region's grains nearer to European markets without paying inflated rates on Vanderbilt's railroads. "Chicago and the valley of the Mississippi need this additional outlet, and the interests of the whole State of Michigan imperatively demand it. Once accomplished, the power of the Vanderbilt monopoly over the State of Michigan, under any circumstances of the future, cannot endanger her prosperity."[405] At issue was whether the towns of Michigan could stand up to the power of Vanderbilt.

Locally, the development of the railroad network continued. From 1868 to 1870 Hiram Smith expanded his career in railroading. He superintended the building of the Detroit, Lansing, and Northern Railroad and the Detroit and Bay City Railroad. In 1869, stockholders of the Jackson, Lansing and Saginaw Railroad Company received land grants and notes. James and Daniel contracted to buy 960 acres at the rate of $4.16 per acre, with $1,000 to be paid on contract.[406] They did this through the Turner and Case Land and Tax Agency, which purchased land all over mid-Michigan. James still held the position of treasurer of the Jackson, Lansing and Saginaw Railroad, and superintendent and treasurer of the Ionia and Lansing Railroad.[407] It was at this point the elder Turner turned to his son Jim whose considerable hands-on experience in business practices and railroading prepared him to be given charge of the construction of the Ionia and Lansing Railroad.[408] The long-sought dream of making Lansing a central transportation hub was finally being realized.

Material Wealth

After the war, both a commercial and residential building boom began in Lansing. Between 1866 and 1868 it was estimated that $945,000 was spent on building and grading streets.[409] The well-to-do began to build bigger houses than the capital had seen in the past. In about this period, class-consciousness seemed to be growing in the Lansing community and across the nation. Lest there be any doubt, *The Lansing State Republican* reported a list of 164 men in the county with incomes over $1,000 (roughly $15,450 today[410]) as taken from the tax rolls. Ephraim Longyear ($3,024), John W. Longyear ($2,033), and James Turner ($2,591) were among the nineteen earning over $2,000, and Daniel Case was listed as earning $1,887 that year.[411] Only five Lansing residents had incomes of $3,000, or more. Hiram Smith was not listed but would have been had he not moved to Jackson to re-marry and take on banking, more business enterprises with his son Dwight and his brother Henry, and more railroading.[412] These relatively high incomes would be considered moderate by today's standards.

Even the incomes of the most well to do in Lansing were a far cry from the fortunes amassed after the war by the tycoons or "robber barons" as they were sometimes called. In contrast to the most well-to-do of Lansing, Vanderbilt was said to have $134,000,000. Mark Twain unfurled his satire against Vanderbilt, who lived in New York City. Twain's press coverage in an "Open Letter to Com. Vanderbilt." (The Commodore had earned his first fortune in shipping before turning to railroading.) raised the matter of the Erie Railroad because Vanderbilt had been involved in an all-too-public ongoing battle with Daniel Drew, treasurer of the Erie Railroad. Their tactics included insider trading and stock market manipulation. The letter was carried in many newspapers, including the *Lansing State Republican*: "How my heart goes out in sympathy to you, Commodore Vanderbilt! Most men have at least a few friends, whose devotion is a comfort and a solace to them, but you seem to be the idol of only a small swarm of small souls, who love to glorify your most flagrant unworthiness in print … friends who applaud your superhuman stinginess with the same gusto that they do your most magnificent displays of commercial genius and daring, and likewise your most lawless violations of commercial honor. One day one of your subjects comes out with a column or two detailing your rise from penury to affluence, and praising you as if you were the last and noblest work of God, but unconsciously telling how exquisitely mean a man has to be in order to achieve what you have achieved. Next, a subject of yours prints a long article to show how, in some shrewd, underhanded way, you have 'come it' over the public with some Erie dodge or other, and added another million or so to your greasy greenbacks; and behold! *he* praises you, and never hints that immoral practices, in so prominent a place as you occupy, are a damming example to the rising commercial generation—more, a damming thing to the whole nation." [413] Only time would tell how long the provincial railroads of Michigan could hold out against the pressure of such men as Vanderbilt and the other monopolists.

In campaigning for defeat of the Democrats in the election of 1868, *The Lansing State Republican* argued, "Unable to control the government against the will of the Republican voters of the Northern States, they hope to accomplish their object by again surrendering the nation to the very men, who, as Democrats and secessionists, brought on war, and created the debt which they ultimately seek to repudiate. This idea of a government for favored classes is but carrying out the existing idea of caste in the old world, and is natural to all men who by means of wealth or position have a controlling influence in organizing and governing society. Its adoption would give us a repetition of the feudal system of Europe in the middle ages." [414]

However, the chances of Democrats taking over appeared slim. A straw poll indicating how the presidential election was going was taken on the train cars between Mason and Lansing on a Friday in August of 1868 and was reported in the newspaper: "Gentlemen, 24 for Grant and 10 for Seymour. Ladies, 19 for Grant and 6 for Seymour. On Tuesday night, a vote on the train from Jackson to Lansing resulted for Grant 54; Seymour 19." [415] The straw poll foreshadowed the fall results, which were most acceptable at the Turner house. Fall soon turned to winter and the joyous season of Christmas settled down upon the community.

Christmas at the Turners' in 1868 was filled with music. The family had a tradition of singing carols in the parlor at Christmastime when Turners and Munroes came to visit. Little Abbie, already an accomplished pianist, played the piano for them all. When Marian and James and the children attended the Christmas Eve celebration at church together, the church was "rich and beautiful," and the distribution of presents was enjoyed by all. "The oddity of many of the presents, though valuable, excited a pleasing effect upon the audience. A novel feature of the program that year was the personification of Santa Clause by Alfred Bixby. Who represented that imaginary god of the children in a manner highly pleasing and laughable." In the meantime, a "whiskey ring, though of lesser proportions than its celebrated namesake, was out and about under the following circumstances: Some ten or a dozen young men invested in jew's harps and mouthorgans—costing from two to ten cents each—and proceeded to serenade the various saloons, thus securing quite a number of drinks for the price of each instrument." It was considered a good joke, until the saloon-keepers caught on and closed their doors to the sham minstrels. [416]

A disgraceful row occurred on Christmas Eve at a saloon on Franklin, which resulted in several men being severely pummeled. No arrests were made. Elsewhere a most disgusting scene of helpless intoxication was witnessed on the street. The victim fell into the gutter, where he would undoubtedly have frozen, but for the timely assistance of some acquaintances that happened to be passing by. Christmas day in North Lansing was one of comparative dullness and inactivity. However, the coming year brought excitement to the Turners as Grant approached his inauguration.[417]

General Grant was immensely popular in Michigan. The Turner family hands down the story that Abbie played piano for President Grant in Washington D.C. in 1869, when she was eight years old.[418] From the time Abbie was a little girl she was considered a gifted pianist, and the city must have been excited by the prospect. Perhaps it was at Christmas that her parents gave her a large, beautiful, ornate, "square" piano custom-made for her with "Abbie Turner" inscribed on an inside panel. For this special occasion, they had it shipped by train to Washington. Years later, in 2008, a musket ball was found inside the piano during restoration work for her great grandson John Pemberton, but no one knows the circumstances by which it arrived there.

Undoubtedly, the Turners looked forward to the administration of President Grant after the turbulent post-war years of the Johnson presidency, and his inaugural address was probably far more to their liking for the change it represented from the previous administration. Abbie's uncle John W. Longyear had played an important role in Congress during the Civil War years, and the family closely followed the battles over reconstruction. They were outraged by Johnson's single-minded efforts opposing Negro rights and his lack of efforts at Reconstruction as set forth by the Radical Republicans in Congress. He had escaped impeachment by only one vote. As Radicals, they wanted much more for the newly freed African Americans. However, there was one drawback to the election: the Turners had been placed in the position of opposing Grant's Democratic opponent, their long-time friend and James' business associate, Horatio Seymour. Grant promised peace and the end to political turmoil. The Turners and friends were undoubtedly looking to the future with optimism.

In his inaugural speech, Grant sounded the important themes of the day, many as relevant today as that afternoon, including enforcement of the laws and setting the economy right by paying off the country's debt. He pledged to get back to specie payment—being able to receive gold or silver coins by holders of paper money—a measure needed to restore trust in paper for transactions and thus, for credit. In order for people to confidently loan and borrow, they had to know that money would retain its value over time, which had been a big problem. He pleaded for tolerance, patience, and the end to regional pride. The hope that reconstruction would go more positively, smoothly, and free of corruption under Grant was soon dashed, but James did not live to see the Grant administration play out.

A Great Loss

When James died at home on October 10, 1869, he was only 49. It was a great loss for his family and for the state of Michigan. Typhoid was common in a day when water or food contamination was known, but not understood. *The Ingham County News* reported, "Hon. James Turner died at his residence, in North Lansing, on Sunday morning, at eight o'clock, after a short illness with the typhoid fever. His funeral occurred on Tuesday, at his residence, and was attended by a large number of relatives, friends and acquaintances. Special trains ran from Jackson and the North, to accommodate those who wished to be present on that occasion. The sermon was preached by Rev. Mr. Spencer, of Jackson, a former friend and pastor of the family. Mr. Turner was an old citizen of Michigan and enjoyed the confidence and friendship of a large portion of the State."[419]

There were many tributes and expressions of loss from near and far. The Board of Directors of the Jackson, Lansing and Saginaw Railroad expressed their regret at his death: "As one of the originators and managers of the public improvements placed under the charge of this Board of Directors, this company, and the communities benefited by the construction of the Jackson, Lansing and Saginaw Railroad, owe the deceased a debt of lasting gratitude for his early, earnest, unyielding, and well-directed efforts in behalf of this enterprise; for his persevering industry and sterling integrity; for the wisdom of his counsels and the vigor of his execution. James Turner was a man of commanding personal appearance, being six feet four inches in height, and well proportioned, weighing two hundred and forty-five pounds. He possessed great strength, and remarkable powers of endurance. He was kind-hearted and benevolent; liberal to a fault; a real friend and helper to the poor." [420]

Marian was fifty-one years old and had been married for twenty-six years to the day to this exceptional human being. Now she would don black clothing and veil and continue on alone at her home on North Street with her six children. Marian, age 23; Jim, 19; Adda, 17; Eva 12; Abbie, 9 and little Jesse at 5 ½ made up the Turner family now. All were intelligent, capable, and healthy children, except Adda, who suffered over the years from an unknown and painful illness, an ongoing concern for Marian and the family.

Marian's mother, Harriet Munroe, died on August 24, 1870. She had been the joyous and warm-hearted matriarch of the Munroe family. For the fifty-four years of her marriage to Jesse, they had endured the hard struggles and the incessant labor of pioneer farming life together. Custom dictated that for several years the family would wear the traditional black mourning clothes, an outward sign of their inner losses.

The Pioneering Spirit

The death of James marked the passing of an era. Marian and Jim attended the Ingham County Pioneers Annual Meeting at Mason some twenty-five years later, on June 4, 1895. Jim spoke eloquently before the gathering, summing up for all the achievements and spirit of that unique moment in the passage of Michigan into statehood and "Auld Lang Syne," days gone by. The following extraordinary speech, sharing memories now somewhat colored and filtered by the passage of time, showed not only the depth and breadth of the pioneer character but of the speaker as well.

Brave Hearts and Strong Arms Hewed a Capital from a Forest

Mr. President, Ladies and Gentlemen: we would be more than human if we could fitly express the sentiments that naturally animate us on this occasion... As I came down with the delegation from Lansing today, I was impressed with the peculiar appropriateness of calling the meeting at Mason, for we can hardly contemplate the early days of Ingham county without at once associating the name Mason most prominently in our minds. It would be impossible to have founded our town of Lansing first. It had to be nurtured and transplanted from here, and the trials and struggles of opening up the wilderness here afforded the means of development which gave the necessary courage, hope and determination to Judge Danforth, Daniel L. Case, John W. Longyear, Hiram H. Smith, James Turner, Joab Page, John W. Burchard, Whitney Smith, Mr. Pease, Rolfe, U. P. and F. M. Cowles, and the others of that resolute band to go forth from here and hew out the new homes for themselves and their families and aid in the building up of the capital city. To the citizens of Mason, we can say you sent us a stout hearted band. They were never dismayed by obstacles, no matter how formidable they at the time appeared. Their training here had been too effective for that, and it is thus that the later generations are being permitted to enjoy so much that their minds conceived and their hands developed.

It took brave men to subdue Ingham county from the dark, overhanging forest that was on every side of the early settler, and much we today owe to their perseverance, indomitable will and industry, and we wonder now what unseen force it was that impelled them to the Herculean efforts "which has made the wilderness blossom as the rose." Did you ever contemplate what to us would have been the result if in the place of those strong limbed, brawny armed, brave hearted men there had come here the same number of modern young men, with the peaked toed, patent leather shoes, creased pants, part your hair in the middle, la de da fin de siècle young dudes? Imagine for the moment such babes in the woods, and how soon they would have been eaten up by the mosquitoes and carried away by the humming birds, leaving this country the wilderness that it was. At that early date no use had been found for this "What is it' of the present period; men were then estimated by what they could do in relation to their development of the new country, and not by the kind of a house they lived in or the size of their bank account.

Here the sound of rural labor in the sweetest, gentlest trains,
Filled the breezes with their music where no jar or discord reigns,
Where no sound of selfish traffic could be heard within the mart,
And disasters born of commerce brought no anguish to the heart.
Here were no conflicting dogmas, here no quarrels of the press,

Here the wealthy were not worried by pale poverty's distress,
Here the poor were free from envy of a neighbor's greater wealth,
For the man was counted richest who enjoyed the finest health.
Politics were uninvented, office seekers all unknown.
Non-producers, lean and stinted, lived on what they earned alone.
Women knew no height of fashion wore no ribbons, pearls or lace,
Decked their forms with simple vesture, with a modest native
    grace;
Ignorant of all around them, save their duty is it queer
They enjoyed the rights God gave them, each in her respective
    sphere?
    [From "A Fragment," Homer D. L. Sweet, Pompey, N. Y.]

In those good old days of Ingham county, questions of the currency, international agreements, and parity of the metals had little in them to disturb the settler. The coin of the realm was coon skins, beeswax and black salts, so that then we had three standards, each readily maintained at parity with the other, without even the moral support of Grover Cleveland or the Rothschild-Belmont syndicate.

A time there was ere England's griefs began,
When every rood of land maintained its man,
For him light labor spread her wholesome store,
Just gave what life required but gave no more:
His best companions, innocence and health!
And his best riches, ignorance of wealth.
    [From "The Deserted Village," by Oliver Goldsmith, 1710]

Educational matters in that early day were not overlooked, and it is quite evident that the pioneers understood that the common school was, as now, the bulwark of our liberties. My father about the year 1840 was one of the school moderators, and candidates to teach the district school were asked to present themselves. Two young ladies appeared, my mother, then, Miss Marian Monroe, and a girl who, fortunately for me, was less attractive (being cross eyed). The former was quickly chosen, and thus the fate of your orator was sealed, as the marriage of my father to this same schoolmaam is able to be with us today, and with us join in all the pleasant reminiscences of the earlier period. I am sure that my mother readily adapted herself to the pioneer surroundings, as she began life in 1818 in Erie county, N. Y., which must have been quite as primitive at that early date as was Ingham county in 1840.

At the outset here social conditions were rude, but I am sure they were devoid of shams and hypocrisy; and friendships of that early period were of a most cordial and genuine character. Classes had not then arisen. They were 'Brothers all,' and each, I am sure, was considerate and helpful to his neighbor. I had related to me a few years ago an incident denoting what was probably the first flutter in Ingham county society—a quilting or husking bee was the event of the season—at the house of a gentleman who is still living, and was Lansing's first mayor, but soon after the neighborhood was agog at the airs assumed by this family in the service of the feast, and the fact was soon whispered about that the Smiths had actually served their guest with store sugar on the occasion.

Most of the early settlers of Ingham county were natives of York state, as they called it, and in coming here they pushed their way to what was then the western frontier. We are now looked upon by our friends in Washington and Oregon as pretty well east, but in the day they came this was no doubt counted the very ragged edge of civilization, and wild beasts, wild men and wild forests had to be driven back and subdued as much here as in the present west. Since the advent of some of you to this county has come the development of the railroad, telegraph, steamboat, telephone, modern printing press and the thousands of wonderful things that only a visit to the late world's fair could properly impress upon us.

Sometimes I wonder if all these marvelous things have really added to the sum of human happiness, if the millionaire in his home provided with all the modern conveniences, with wealth without limit at his command, is really as happy and contented as the dwellers in our original log houses, warmed and cheered by the blaze and glow of the cavernous old fireplace, surrounded in the evening by perhaps the good neighbors fresh from the chase, or who had been present during the day at a logging bee or a raising, and now at night come in with keen appetites to enjoy the steaming supper that the good wife had prepared. Why, friends, the good cheer of one of those old time homes was really an inspiration, and the kindly effect of its influence could never be measured in dollars and cents.

> There is no friend like the old friend,
> That has shared our morning days!
> No greeting like his welcome,
> No homage like his praise.
> There are no times like the old times;
> They shall never be forgot;
> There is no place like the old place;
> Keep green the dear old spot.
> [Oliver Wendell Holmes]

Fortunate it is for the present generation that our country was settled by those who preceded us, for the boys of today would not be equal to the task. It has been said that the true explanation of the wonderful work done by those who first cleared the farms here was that they were fed on potash. This point should be investigated, and if potash put all the fire and life and energy into those early settlers we should begin feeding it to the babies now, with the hope that it might have its impress upon the generation that is to so soon take our places. Possibly it would be found that a little lime for the upbuilding of the backbone, and a little sand to make grit, should be added to this prescription if we expect to produce a generation that could be at any time utilized for pioneers to a new country. I am sure that we all feel that it is good to be here today, and I want to join you in thanking our Mason friends for doing so much to make this occasion a memorable one. Surely this home coming of so many will not soon be forgotten.

> Breathes there the man with soul so dead,
> Who never to himself hath said,
> This is my own, my native land!
> Whose heart hath ne'er within him burned,
> As home his footsteps he hath turned,
> From wandering on a foreign strand?
> If such there breathe go mark him well;
> For him no minstrel raptures swell;
> High though his titles, proud his name,
> Boundless his wealth as wish can claim;
> Despite those titles, power and pelf,
> The wretch, concentrated all in self,
> Living shall forfeit fair renown,
> And doubly dying shall go down
> To the vile dust from whence he sprung,
> Unwept, unhonored and unsung.
> *[From "The Lay of the Last Minstrel," Sir Walter Scott]*

The lands constituting the present county of Ingham were doubtless embraced in the treaty of November 17, 1807, between Gov. Hull of the territory of Michigan and the Ottawa, Chippewa, Wyandot and Pottawatomie Indians, and by what was known as the treaty of Saginaw, signed by the chiefs of the Chippewa and Ottawa nations, which was concluded in September, 1819. I have a distinct recollection of the old chief Okemos, who was one of the subscribers to the treaty of Saginaw, which was negotiated, I believe, by Gen. Cass, and I have a vivid recollection of a visit paid to my father by Okemos, about the year 1858, when some of the young men of his tribe disputed his authority as chief, and he drew from inside his shirt a roll of dirty buckskin. He unrolled a beautiful silken flag, which he insisted constituted his proper credentials, it having been handed him by what he was pleased to call the gents of the Great Father at Washington when he attached his mark to the treaty of Saginaw. I wish that this little souvenir might have been preserved and handed down to this pioneer society...

At the time my parents settled at Lansing there was no cleared land in the vicinity, but three acres had been slashed and was soon cleared off after their arrival. The files in the clerk's office show that after the first courthouse was built there was a claim allowed to my father, James

Turner, of $100 for painting the building, and $42 for furnishing the stoves and pipe and expense of putting them up. At the same time, Hiram H. Smith, now a resident of Jackson, was allowed $3.75 for painting the fence about the court house. The present court house was not built until after my parents' removal from Mason, being completed in the spring of 1858, having been erected by gallant Matthew Elder, who in the war of the rebellion gave his life with others that his country might live... There is a sweet fragrance to the history, and I trust that the annual meeting of the society will forever keep green the memory of the sturdy pioneer, and let us trust that they and their descendants may.

> So live, that when the summons comes to join
> The innumerable caravan which moves
> To that mysterious realm, where each shall take
> His chamber in the silent halls of death,
> They go not, like the quarry-slave at night,
> Scourged to his dungeons, but, sustained and soothed
> By an unfaltering trust, approach his grave
> Like one who wraps the drapery of his couch
> About him and lies down to pleasant dreams.
> *[From "Thanatopsis," William Cullen Bryant]*

Part II

Reformers &
Millionaires
1870-1912

Chapter 9

A Meaningful Life

Marian did not have to worry about her material circumstances. The Turner real estate in Ingham County was valued at $7,682 and there was additional property in Gratiot County, other items and animals, and just $20 in railroad stock. After paying expenses to settle accounts, there was a total value of $16,642.[421] She and John W. Longyear were the administrators of the estate. Jim managed the Turner businesses with the help of his uncles.

For Marian, a meaningful life could not be only about the memories we have but about the memories we create. After a period of about two and a half years of public mourning, Marian began to resume her normal activities. She observed that gradually she and her sisters and the younger women of the next generation of the family seemed to have more time. With the adoption of the latest technological advances in their homes, they, and many other women they knew, were also slowly gaining some measure of freedom from the essential daily chores of homemaking and caregiving. Many women had more time to attend to matters outside the home and to build into their lives another layer of meaning in a wider sphere. Marian joined these women to support the work of new organizations formed after the war to help the growing number of poor in the city, preserve pioneer history, and regulate alcohol to curb its use. She was a leader in her church during a period when Methodists and other denominations were slowly beginning to support improving the status of women members. Other women in her family joined new literary and cultural groups.

On April 20, 1868, the Lansing Ladies Aid Society of the Methodist Church was founded, and Marian became President. The Society raised funds for church improvements and increasingly worked with charities to aid the needy as the plight of the poor became particularly acute in the face of economic downturn. By 1870, the number of manufacturing employees in Michigan had grown from 9,344 to 64,000 in just twenty years and there were nearly 9,500 manufacturing establishments in the state. Nevertheless, growth slowed with the nationwide prolonged depression which began in 1873, and many were thrown out of work.[422] Employment possibilities for women were very limited and poverty grew among women and children.

Marian's devotion to the reform causes of helping the poor and temperance was an inspiration to all.[423]

Helping the Poor

Most counties had poor farms where poor people, indigent soldiers, and those who were considered incompetent or crazy could live. The first institution to help the poor in Ingham County was a poor farm of 200 acres, established in 1843 in Alaiedon Township with Hiram Smith in charge. A superintendent of the farm organized the residents to work the farm and a board of supervisors administered a small budget of county funds that supplemented the proceeds of the farm in order to provide medical attention and relief.[424]

As urban communities grew, this agrarian model for care of the disadvantaged no longer seemed to meet their needs. Since the situation was not unique, there was a national movement building to create new institutions to aid the poor. In Michigan, the stirring poems of Will Carleton from Lenawee County created awareness, and he became a household name across the country. He focused the attention on the poor and needy, whatever the reason for their plight, and bolstered the work of reformers who were establishing organizations and poor houses in urban settings. His poems were published in *Harper's Weekly,* and he became known as Michigan's "People's Poet." Michigan schools celebrated Will Carleton Day, and every schoolchild knew his poems. "Over the Hill to the Poor House" was particularly well known, and many people could recite it by heart. In July of 1871 Carleton visited Lansing and gave a two and a half hour performance to "the most critical and appreciative audience ever assembled here," said *The Lansing Republican.*[425] He read this famous poem:

OVER THE HILL TO THE POOR HOUSE
Over the hill to the poor-house I'm trudgin' my weary way—
I, a woman of seventy, and only a trifle gray—
I, who am smart an' chipper, for all the years I'm told,
As many another woman that's only half as old.

Over the hill to the poor-house—I can't quite make it clear!
Over the hill to the poor-house—it seems so horrid queer!
Many a step I've taken a-toilin' to and fro,
But this is a sort of journey I never thought to go.

What is the use of heapin' on me a pauper's shame?
Am I lazy or crazy? Am I blind or lame?
True, I am not so supple, nor yet so awful stout:
But charity ain't no favor, if one can live without.

I am willin' and anxious an' ready any day
To work for a decent livin', an' pay my honest way;
For I can earn my victuals, an' more too, I'll be bound,

If any body only is willin' to have me round.
Once I was young an' han'some—I was, upon my soul—

Once my cheeks was roses, my eyes as black as coal;
An I can't remember, in them days, of hearin' people say,
For any kind of reason, that I was in their way.

'Tain't no use of boastin', or talkin' over free,
But many a house an' home was open then to me
Many a han'some offer I had from likely men,
And nobody ever hinted that I was a burden then.

An when to John I was married, sure he was good and smart,
But he and all the neighbors would own I done my part;
For life was all before me, an' I was young an' strong,
And I worked the best that I could in tryin' to get along.

An so we worked together; and life was hard, but gay,
With now and then a baby for to cheer us on our way;
Till we had half a dozen, an' all growed clean an' neat,
An' went to school like others, an' had enough to eat.

So we worked for the child'rn, and raised 'em every one;
Worked for 'em summer and winter, just as we ought to 've done;
Only perhaps we humored 'em, which some good folks condemn.
But every couple's child'rn's a heap the best to them.

Strange how much we think of our blessed little ones!—
I'd have died for my daughters, I'd have died for my sons;
And God he made that rule of love; but when we're old and gray,
I've noticed it sometimes somehow fails to work the other way.

Strange, another thing: when our boys an' girls was grown,
An when, exceptin' Charley, they'd left us there alone;
When John he nearer an' nearer come, an' dearer seemed to be,
The Lord of Hosts he come one day an' took him away from me.

Still I was bound to struggle, an' never to cringe or fall—
Still I worked for Charley, for Charley was now my all;
And Charley was pretty good to me, with scarce a word or frown,
Till at last he went a-courtin', and brought a wife from town.

She was somewhat dressy, an' hadn't a pleasant smile—
She was quite conceity, and carried a heap o' style;
But if ever I tried to be friends, I did with her, I know;
But she was hard and proud, an' I couldn't make it go.

She had an edication, an' that was good for her;
But when she twitted me on mine, 'twas carryin' things too fur;
An' I told her once, 'fore company (an'it almost made her sick),
That I never swallowed a grammar, or 'et 'rithmetic.

So 'twas only a few days before the thing was done—
They was a family of themselves, and I another one;
And a very little cottage one family will do,
But I never have seen a house that was big enough for two.

An' I never could speak to suit her, never could please her eye,
An' it made me independent, and then I didn't try;
But I was terribly staggered, an' felt it like a blow,
When Charley turned ag'in me, an' told me I could go.

I went to live with Susan, but Susan's house was small,
And she was always a-hintin' how snug it was for us all;
And what with her husband's sister, and what with child'rn three,
'Twas easy to discover that there wasn't room for me.

An' then I went to Thomas, the oldest son I've got,
For Thomas's buildings'd cover the half of an acre lot;
But all the child'rn was on me—I couldn't stand their sauce—
And Thomas said I needn't think I was comin' there to boss.

An' then I wrote to Rebecca, my girl who lives out West,
And to Isaac, not far from her—some twenty miles at best;
And one of'em said 'twas too warm there for any one so old,
And t'other had an opinion the climate was too cold.

So they have shirked and slighted me, an' shifted me about-
So they have well-nigh soured me, an' wore my old heart out;
But still I've borne up pretty well, an' wasn't much put down,
Till Charley went to the poor-master, an' put me on the town.

Over the hill to the poor-house—my chil'rn dear, good-by!
Many a night I've watched you when only God was nigh;
And God 'll judge between us; but I will al'ays pray
That you shall never suffer the half I do to-day.

Other visits by Carleton to the capital were sponsored by the Lansing Library and Literary Society and for years "Over the Hill to the Poor House" was recited on Mother's Day and made people cry. Most importantly, it moved many people to show more understanding of the poor and to give more meaning and happiness to their own lives by helping others. In 1919, the Michigan Legislature passed a law making it the duty of teachers to teach at least one of his poems to their class, and October 21 was officially declared Will Carleton Day in Michigan.

The same month as Carleton's visit, Sojourner Truth came to Mead's Hall to speak about the condition of the freed slaves now living in dire circumstances in the Washington D. C. area and the failure of Reconstruction to help. The lecture was attended *en masse* by the people of Lansing. She was in her seventies and renowned as an abolitionist and outspoken supporter of woman suffrage. She came to Michigan in 1856 and lived in Battle Creek where a strong Quaker community had been active in Underground Railroad work. "With an earnest manner, a rich and mellow voice, loud and distinct enough to be heard and comprehended by all in the room, for more than two hours she captivated her audience by a recital of her trials and tribulations during the rebellion and strongly showed up the degradation into which her own race had been plunged by the great curse of slavery. She was neatly and plainly dressed, wearing on her head the turban so commonly worn by the colored women of the South."[426]

She told them that Northern farmers had better hog pens than the shanties the freed slaves were living in. She told of her plan to bring the dependent black people out west where there was plenty of land to spare, giving them a chance to do something for their own support and teaching them to do for themselves. "There is an island near Washington where the colored people live like beasts in the field, with white men and women getting $100 a month to take care of them, when they ought to be taught to take care of themselves," Sojourner Truth told her listeners. "Then they would not be starving to death as they did last winter." At the end of the lecture the crowd donated liberally to fund a trip to Kansas so that she might find a suitable place for the people on the island to live.[427]

With the growth of factory smoke stacks along the banks of the Grand River came an increase in unlanded residents in Lansing and the associated health, housing, and food problems characteristic of factory workers in Detroit and Chicago. Marian and her family were supporters of the movement to help the poor, and, as the business enterprises of the family grew, her son Jim strived not to follow practices that exploited the laboring class. According to a friend, John Holbrook, during Jim's business career he employed thousands of workers in his many enterprises. In 1890 Holbrook said, "Go to the men who worked for him upon the railroad, for who he always had a jovial word, and to whose complaints he always turned a patient ear. Go to the hands upon his farm, where toil is sweetened by the kindest consideration. Go to the grimy miners of the north, who for twelve years have received the highest pay for the hardest service, who have never been asked to receive a store order, or any other substitute for honest dollars, who never once have been seduced by the pestilent agitator into a strike or a disturbance, but who eat wholesome food every day, and when they sleep lie down with their own roofs above their heads."[428] Those in Lansing would ascribe his employee practices to his "noble mother,"[429] to his father's example, and to his Methodist upbringing.

The national movement begun in the 1850's to aid the poor was developing Children's Aid Societies, but the people of Lansing chose to name their group The Industrial Aid Society. The volunteers of the Industrial Aid Society found heartbreaking conditions much different from those created by employers such as Marian's son. "From these kind-hearted women may be heard the sad story of homes visited where crime and misery hold full sway, of families without bedding or furniture, living for months with only a stove and a kettle. Go but once to one of these wretched abodes, where the ladies of the various committees must often go, and no words are necessary to impress upon your mind the good work they are doing," said one of its woman leaders, Franc Gardner.[430] It was time to find a solution suitable for townspeople who were no longer connected to farm life.

Franc Gardner explained the need, philosophy, and work of the Industrial Aid Society in an article from a local newspaper Marian saved. Gardner's article expressly explained the Society's attitude toward the poor and assured her readers they distinguished between the incompetent, shiftless and others they deemed unfortunates versus the worthy poor – lest the society be considered too compassionate and cause possible funders to be unsympathetic to their cause. Gardner wrote: "To study the questions and methods of wise giving has ever been the aim of the Industrial Aid Society, and its members have sought, in the exercise of charity, to prevent those receiving from becoming paupers. Each year's experience strengthens the belief that without organization, and an element of industry, charity may be a crime rather than the sweetest grace of a human heart. Ruskin says: To give alms is nothing unless thought is given also; not 'blessed is he that feedeth,' but 'he that considereth the poor.' ...Begging from door to door is both unlawful and unnecessary, and should be discountenanced by every right-thinking person. Unless the giving of food and clothing is a real necessity, it becomes rather an evil than a good."[431] Hard times had brought much necessity.

The society confronted the poverty in the community as best they could, finally concluding that they needed to build an industrial training school for women. Of course, the reformers themselves would likely be the employers if they could help poor women become well-trained housekeepers and do laundry and other needed chores in the houses of the growing middle class. The main factor in choosing these occupations was the limited range of occupations that were available to uneducated women. As the name of the society implies, industry would also benefit if poverty on the periphery of a sometimes misused workforce could be reduced and not at the expense of industrial manufacturers.

When the Society members considered their work, they knew a training center was needed, but they had no means to carry out the plan. Finally they decided to open the school on the theory that if they did, the funds would be forthcoming. The school moved about the town eight times before a permanent school was established in the 1890s. Adella Case and Esther Scott were greatly involved with this phase then and for years to come. Gardner wrote:

> Here all receive instruction in practical housekeeping, plain sewing, and such lessons of domestic economy as may be taught orally. The more advanced pupils are taught plain cooking and simple dishes for the sick.
>
> Weekly sessions are held from September to May. Many of the most influential ladies of the city, into whose hearts the seeds of kindness have fallen, willingly give two hours every Saturday afternoon; thus helping

to carry on the excellent work, but as yet, no one has volunteered to take charge of the laundry department and instruct in that industry. Daily we hear the cry of housekeepers for better service along this line. In no way can the excising of evils be better remedied than by teaching the girls (and mothers if need be) to do this work correctly... Thousands of garments made or repaired in the school, scores of quilts have gone into the homes of the destitute, still, owing to the free contributions of clothing, and material, from the charitable people of the city, the actual cost for the work of the school is very small indeed...

The initial effort involved a number of businessmen, but at the first annual meeting Mrs. N. B. (Irma) Jones was elected president and it was mainly women who carried on the work, although the support of "energetic men" continued to be sought. The society constantly needed to recruit new members because they wanted to provide more than temporary physical relief – they wanted to give individual on-going support and to teach self-help to ensure the needy could get back on their feet. They believed, "Many poor need more than all else a friend, one who will counsel and reprove in a manner that will not wound but tend to uplift the fallen victims."[432]

These women and the male supporters of the city, including several physicians, were developing its first welfare system, jobs training, and employment services. "In sickness and emergency it gladly extends aid, and at all times in every possible manner, it aims to encourage SELF-HELP. It has found employment for many, has furnished nurses for the sick, and buried the dead. It clothes children of very poor families, thus enabling them to attend school; but to do this easily requires the cooperation of many not personally identified with the society."[433]

One of the "energetic men" of Lansing's Industrial Aid Society, who helped them get a permanent industrial training school and home, was James Little, a freed slave who had settled in the area at the same time Marian and James came to what became Lansing. He was a friend of the Turners, a Methodist and, like the Turners, a supporter of temperance. Little was from eastern New York and was born about 1803. He died in 1884 at the home of Lloyd Nelson Turner, a friend and former slave, and also a member of the African Methodist Church they helped found. Little's story is found in a worn newspaper article preserved in Marian's family scrapbook. Little was greatly admired and respected by everyone in the community for his outstanding character and genius of mind. His funeral was held at the African Methodist Episcopal Church on Pine Street. The pastor of the Central Methodist Church gave the sermon, for Little was a member of both churches and James Turner and other members of the Central Methodist Church had helped him build the African Methodist Church. The choir was composed of members from all of the churches in the city. The service was under the direction of the Industrial Aid Society and the Central Methodist Church. It was the custom to include biographical material in memorials, and this article by Sabina Hasty, a Sunday school teacher at the Central Methodist Church, tells both about James Little and about the Lansing community he lived in:

> [James Little] said he was not a colored man but a black man. He was rather undersized, nearly bald, with a homely face, a slight stoop in his shoulders, and hands so thin and unshapely that they resembled bird's claws. His step was brisk and his whole physique betokened alertness, energy and native intelligence, but at first sight not a specially attractive figure
>
> No one who knew Father Little will fail to bestow upon his memory a loving, reverent thought, for no man ever walked the streets of Lansing who enjoyed the love and confidence of all classes more than he. He was a welcomed guest in the homes of many of the wealthiest, most cultured people. He was greeted lovingly in the humble homes of poverty, and no one, no matter how low or godless or profane, ever gave him taunt or insult or ill-treatment.
>
> He was born a slave in eastern New York, but was freed under the administration of [Governor] DeWitt Clinton. As a slave he several times changed hands, at one time being sold for $65. But his whole life long he did what so few, even with ample opportunities try to do, he constantly strove to make the most of himself. His greatest personal attraction was a piercing or rather a searching eye, and while, as a black man he always seemed to feel a shrinking from making himself just equal to white people (it was a habit of mind he could not overcome), yet in conversation he would look steadily at the speaker and literally drink in every word spoken.
>
> He was a student. I remember that in one of the many calls he made at our home he told me he was studying geography, and how intensely interesting he found it. He read history and biography, and was intelligent beyond many of those with whom he came in contact. But it was as a Christian that he excelled. Surely no one that ever heard him pray can forget it. He was not a fluent talker, sometimes finding it difficult to get words such as he wanted to use; but when he went on his knees in prayer, he seemed to forget every earthly presence and then his words would flow forth, until not infrequently he became oratorical, sublime even in his utterances.[434]

Father Little particularly ministered to the young men of the city who were frequenters of the saloons and billiard halls. He saw that many were brought down by alcohol.[435] Sometimes the devastation that he witnessed seemed to break his heart.

> The soul of Father Little was especially burdened for young men, and when he was possessed of the spirit led him to feel "Save the young men or I die." I remember him well coming into my home and as he came up the steps he threw himself down upon them and he burst into a

paroxysm of uncontrollable weeping as he talked about the young people of his race, and he said "The 6th verse of VI Psalm exactly expresses my feelings when I think of them." I found the verse and found it to read: I am weary with my groaning, all the night make I my bed to swim, I water my couch with my tears. His most familiar words of address to the Deity were: "Blessed Father," or "God of Israel," and many times as he uttered them it seemed as if he had direct audience with heaven.

Mr. Little did not know his exact age, but was probably about 81 years old at the time of his death. He came to Michigan when a young man about 1847, secured a small farm in Eaton County. About the same time he was married, by dint of thrift, industry and economy the couple accumulated some means

Rev. W. H. Thompson, who preached his funeral sermon, used these words, "For twenty years he tilled the soil on his farm. They were years during the whole of which the colored man was under the social ban, as were any disposed to befriend him. They were years during the whole of which the sum of all villainies struggled to capture the country and menaced, if it did not intimidate, the friends of the colored man."[436]

James Little and his wife moved to town from their farm when he was about 64 and lived in a home provided by a wealthy admirer until the friend no longer could do so. It seemed he would be homeless and set adrift, but the Littles had many friends throughout the whole city who came to his aid.

A purse sufficient was soon raised and a little house and lot in the western suburbs of the city was bought for them and here again they settled. It was not long before the little, new, uncultivated lot showed signs of improvement. Trees and shrubs planted, and growing flower and vegetable garden, showed the taste and public spirit of the new owner. His wife was a retiring, diffident woman, never in very good health, and she was seldom away from home. But she was an excellent housekeeper, and made a neat, pleasant home for them both. In this new home she died in April, 1881. They had no children.

As might have been expected, Mr. Little was in full sympathy with every good work, and so when the Woman's Christian Temperance Union was organized, he entered heart and soul into the spirit of the work, and for years was tract and literature distributor, having regular routes for such work. He could go into any vile place of any sort, and leave tracts or notices for meetings, always receiving kindly treatment, where almost anyone else would have been hooted. It was a tribute to his sterling integrity and manly Christian character.

When the Industrial Aid Society came into being, he recognized its worth, and after the death of his wife, he wished the little home to pass into possession of that excellent organization. And so, one lovely Sabbath afternoon, in presence of a large number of people, and with appropriate religious service, he "dedicated it to the use of the Lord's

poor," by formally presenting it to the society. This time his confidence
was not misplaced. The ladies of the society appointed one of their number to have especial charge of him, and until the day of his death, he was
kindly and carefully looked after each week. Owing to the remoteness of
this place from the central part of the city, it could not be utilized as an
industrial home, but it was sold and the proceeds made a payment on
the comfortable home which the society now occupies.

One other marked characteristic will be noted, his great love for
children. For many months he gathered numbers of them at his home,
to teach them any lessons which he thought would be helpful to them
and this work gave him intense enjoyment.

He died March 10, 1884. His funeral was held in the A. M. E. church,
and perhaps no funeral in the city was attended by a larger number of
representative people. The sermon was preached by Rev. W. H. Thompson, of the Central M. E. church, of which he was a member. "Mark the
perfect man, and the upright, for the end is peace." [The reference is to
King James Psalm 37:37] Mrs. Gilbert M. [Sabina] Hasty.437

To insure that James Little would not be forgotten, the sermon given
by Reverend Thompson, containing much of the biographical information
above, found its way into volume seven of a collection of papers and documents published annually by the Michigan Pioneer Society. James Little was
himself a member of the Society.[438]

The Pioneer Society

It is through the foresight and effort of Michigan's pioneer history preservation society that we know so much about these early days. "The object of the
Society shall be to collect and preserve in permanent form the recollections
and records of pioneer life and achievement in the region which is now Michigan, including such traditions as exist only in the memories of aged persons."
They went on to collect and preserve manuscripts, genealogies, books and
other printed publications, maps, plans, pictures, curiosities and antiquities
of every kind connected with the history of Michigan from the earliest times.
Beyond collecting, they would encourage historical study and antiquarian
investigations, and disseminate information. The State law establishing the
Pioneer History Society was enacted on April 5, 1873.[439]

Harriett Tenney, of Lansing, was the state librarian at the time and started
the collection by putting out a call for items to develop a collection for presentation to the State Library. Marian and her family were very supportive
and from the first meeting called in April of 1874, she regularly attended
meetings, which were held annually in Lansing. Marian and members of her
family helped gather pioneer accounts, and sometimes wrote and presented
them for the historical society's publications.[440] Musical programs usually
accompanied the events, and Marian often turned to her daughters to perform at these meetings for the pleasure of the older generation.

By the end of 1876 the society was already recognized for its work. A noted American historian, Benson J. Lossing, said that Michigan was "performing a noble task, in gathering accurate and voluminous information… [which] will give immense facilities to writers on the history of the Peninsula."[441] Harriet Tenney looked upon the group's progress and told them, "It is a potent agent designed to rescue from oblivion the history of the hardships, toils, trials and successes of those noble men and women who came here, labored early and late in the wilderness to lay the foundations of a State, that in enterprise, education, intelligence, humanitarianism, and all the elements of material wealth and greatness, to-day ranks as a peer with any of the states of the great American Union."[442] Tenney served as Recording Secretary, was a member of the committee of historians, and aided substantially in the publication of the *Pioneer Collections*. Without any compensation she took charge of all the papers, documents, books, and museum relics belonging to the society.

In later years when Marian and three of her sisters, Betsy, Adella and Harriet (Eliza wasn't present that day) attended the thirtieth state annual meeting together they were invited to be seated on the rostrum of the Senate Chambers. When they were introduced, it was as the Munroe girls.[443] The influence of these Munroe women through their contributions and achievements to the work of the society and beyond, and the impact of their goodhearted families drew abiding respect and love from their fellow pioneers. They seemed to embody the pioneer virtues of honesty, industry, and hospitality.

Local societies were encouraged to form. Marian's membership in the Pioneer Society of Ingham County may not have been formal as a listing of members from 1873 through 1880 listed only men who were settlers. Perhaps there were women members, but they simply were not listed, since any person who was forty years of age who had lived in Michigan for 25 years was eligible to become a member on payment of one dollar, and women did attend the meetings. Either way, Marian attended all the meetings to meet with old friends, share in their memories and enjoy the program of music and the reading of papers prepared by the members.[444] The family's circle yielded Frank N. Turner, a medical doctor by profession and an historian who contributed to preserving the history of Ingham County. At various times, Daniel served as the president of the Ingham County Society, and Hiram served as vice president. Ephraim was the treasurer of the State Society for many years.

The Year of the Great Fire

After the war there was a considerable amount of building in the capital city. About eighty buildings, costing from $300 upward, were erected in 1871, mostly wood frame and totaling $181,000 in value, with an additional $200,000 in expenditures by the State for State facilities.[445] Aside from that spurt, the improvements in the city were more or less steady and permanent, as they were around the state. The Legislature talked about plans for a new capitol building to break ground in 1872 which was very reassuring to the locals and beneficial to the business climate. It was proof the capitol was in Lansing to stay, and that made it a safe place to invest.[446]

In the early summer of 1871 Marian's Ladies Aid Society held a strawberry and ice cream festival in the Methodist church basement, and the Lansing Capitols baseball team beat the Agricultural College Clippers 50 to 37. The Odd Fellows were preparing to move to the former campus of the Lansing Female College. The Library and Literary Association was sponsoring an event with music and an address by the Michigan Agricultural College's second president, Abbot, followed by a play entitled, "The Spirit of 76 or the Coming Woman." The Lansing Woman's Suffrage Association was sponsoring lectures at Mead's Hall and so were temperance groups. The Warner Circus was coming to town. There was an excursion of prominent railroad men in stovepipe hats to the salt mining and lumbering region of Saginaw at the northern terminus of the Jackson, Lansing and Saginaw Railroad. Shiawassee County, to the north, reported late potato and apple crop failures due to the draught.

By the end of August smoky air marred the pleasant atmosphere in the city. Worrisome wildfires broke out intermittently on the east side of town until it finally rained on August 28. Three days later Lansing residents were reading of more disturbing news: "A correspondent of the Detroit Free Press, writing from Lakeport, St. Clair County, says that fire is raging in the vicinity, burning over fields and forests, consuming large quantities of hay and grain which has been stacked and even some buildings. In many places the inhabitants are moving away and leaving their property to be burned up as further resistance is futile. Vessels from Lake Huron report that for miles the shores are a line of fire and the smoke is so dense as to peril navigation. *The Sanilac Jefferson* says that fires continue to burn in the woods and all around, and the smoke is absolutely oppressive." [447]

On October 1, a row of wooden buildings on Michigan Avenue in Lansing caught fire. The fire bell had been fastened in a way that kept it from ringing so that the Fire Department was slow to arrive, and some grumbled that the crowd of men who lined the sidewalks refused the earnest calls for aid to the firemen. The *Lansing Republican* complained that a steam fire engine or the Holly Water Supply System should be installed to get water where it was needed. "It will be impossible much longer to save property by looking at the conflagrations, and guessing at the loss, and whether the loser makes money or not," wrote the local newspaper.[448] Other communities were not any better prepared for a major fire than Lansing was.

These localized flare-ups were a prelude to one of the most terrifying natural disasters in Michigan history. The fire affected the Upper Peninsula and the Lower Peninsula from Holland and Manistee on Lake Michigan to Port Huron on Lake Huron, demanding much resourcefulness and charity of those who came to the aid of the fire's stricken victims. For decades to come Michigan households of the descendants of those who lived through this period contained paintings of the flaming forests, but for those who had seen, the picture needed no painting. Henry Utley, a historian who lived through the disaster, wrote one of the most gripping accounts of this event. He explained what happened this way:

> The summer had been an unusually hot and dry one. From June there had been in the state only scattered and insignificant showers, and in some localities, it is said, not a drop of rain had fallen for several months. As a result all vegetation was parched, the earth was cracked from lack of moisture and everything was dry as tinder. The swamps were dried out, grass dried and withered, wells and cisterns exhausted and in some places no water for many miles from running streams. It will be borne in mind that at that time Michigan was enjoying its most prosperous days of pine lumbering. The forests were being felled, the severed branches of trees were piled upon the ground; the trunks, cut up into logs, were floated down the streams to near their mouths and there cut into lumber and piled, awaiting transportation to market. The sap and moisture had been thoroughly evaporated from all this wood by the merciless sun and wind. At this season of the year there were usually brush fires raging in the clearings.
>
> On Sunday, October 8, 1871, fire broke out in a wooden stable in the south side of Chicago, which on that night and the two following days and nights, literally wiped out the entire city. This was one of the great conflagrations of history. Many lives were lost, millions of dollars' worth of property was destroyed and thousands of persons were left homeless, without shelter or food. While our people were reading the startling news of this calamity and were planning to send relief to the sufferers, there came drifting to their ears the story of the horrible experiences of dwellers within our own borders. The wave of lurid flame swept across the entire state, wiping out, within a few hours, everything combustible in its path. The fire in Chicago and those in Michigan could have been controlled under ordinary circumstances, but the circumstances were very extraordinary. The atmospheric conditions were peculiar. A hot wave came up from the southwest with a gale which reached the proportions of a tornado. It was a gigantic blow-pipe which fed oxygen to the flames which withered and consumed every combustible thing in their path. On this same night of October 8, and on the following day and night, the fires crossed the entire state from Lake Michigan to Lake Huron
>
> The city of Holland in Ottawa county was entirely destroyed, and the city of Manistee in the county of that name, was nearly wiped out. From the latter city a zone of flame extended almost due eastward through the counties of Lake, Osceola, Isabella, Midland, Saginaw, Tuscola, Sanilac and Huron, where its further progress was stayed by the waters of the

lake. This entire region was one in which pine lumbering was then in active operation. Holland and Manistee were lumber towns, where the logs brought down from the interior were cut for the market. The numerous mills were surrounded by great quantities of highly inflammable material. Edgings and bark had accumulated in bulk; large piles of sawed lumber were stored in the yards, the streets were paved with sawdust and slabs. An eye-witness describing the destruction of Holland says that in the short space of two hours, between one and three o'clock on the morning of October 9th, the devastation was complete. No one, unless he had witnessed such a scene, could have any conception of its terror. The entire territory covered by the fire was mills and other manufacturing establishments, docks and warehouses. The estimated money loss was upwards of one million two hundred thousand dollars, a very large proportion of which was mill property and manufactured lumber. On account of the enormous destruction by fire at Chicago and elsewhere at that time, insurance policies had very little, if any, value. Fires also caused much damage in the surrounding vicinity, and by the destruction of bridges and telegraph poles practically cut off all communication for a time with the outside world.

As the fires raged in the belt extending entirely across the state, they swept everything in their path. The gathered crops of the season had been stored in the farm barns; the fall wheat had been sown, and the corn was ripening in the shock. All were destroyed, together with dwellings and their contents, farm buildings, in many instances, domestic animals, leaving nothing but ashes, blackened stumps and putrid carcasses. Orchards which had been the work of years to rear were wiped out in an hour. School houses, churches, bridges, disappeared, as if by magic. While this zone of flame stretched across the state, it seemed to work its greatest havoc as it approached Lake Huron. Huron and Sanilac counties, though largely devoted to lumbering, were nevertheless, quite well settled by an agricultural population and abounded in prosperous and well cultivated farms and orchards. Throughout this whole region, a tract at least forty miles square, scarcely a vestige of life was left.[449]

As early as 1867 the Legislature had been warned about the dangers of over-lumbering and the immense destruction it could cause by Robert Kedzie, Professor of Chemistry at the Michigan Agricultural College. It was at the time the big commercial lumbering companies were moving into full swing, largely unregulated. "Warning About Overlumbering," *The Lansing Journal* reported, "Hon. R. C. Kedzie has made a very able and very important report to the Legislature upon the subject of the means proper to be taken to avert the unfortunate results sure to follow, if not remedied by energetic measures. It should be in the hands of every farmer of the State. It is estimated that the loss to the wheat crop alone during the last four years resulting from the wanton destruction of forest trees is $20,000,000; an enormous sum. Bills were presented to encourage the leaving of forests standing and the planting of trees where they have been already destroyed. It is a subject eminently worthy of attention."[450] But for now, compassion overshadowed outrage within those fortunate enough to escape the environmental mayhem, and the citizens of Lansing organized to fight local fires and to help the misfortunate in the state.

Harriett Tenney, with her experience as former head of the Soldiers Relief Society, sprang into action. She chaired the first meeting of the Ladies' Relief Society, and women energetically threw themselves into the work of providing aid. Among the members of the organizing committee were Irma Jones, Mary Seager, Eliza Turner, and from the Agricultural College came Sarah Abbot and Harriett Tracy. They told the community, "Early gifts are very important, and those who can spare anything should give at once."[451] By the following week they had obtained work rooms and developed a work plan broken down by wards along the lines of the Soldiers' Aid Society organization during the war, expecting their efforts would be needed throughout the winter.[452] The State Relief Committee asked Lansing to become a center for nonperishable farm products, and James I. Mead was put in charge of asking the farmers of Central Michigan to bring in wheat, beans, potatoes, and all kinds of clothing and bedding. "The large harvest of this season ought to call out generous gifts from the thriving agricultural class," said Mead.[453]

The Ladies Relief Society worked to collect large amounts of clothing and cleaned and repaired it for the suffering and destitute. Eliza Turner was among the first to join in, asking for donations and gathering provisions.[454] With three donated sewing machines they quickly turned gifts of sheeting and flannel into bedding, underclothing, and children's' clothing. One box of bedding and eight boxes of collected clothing for men, women, and children were at once forwarded to Manistee, Menominee, and Holland.[455] It was in response to a plea from Manistee that a telegram from the Grand Rapids Relief Committee reached Lansing, "The people of Manistee are in immediate want of flour and meal,—something to eat. Their necessities are pressing and imperative. Ship to Grand Haven, care of Senator Ferry, where a Government vessel will be ready to take to Manistee. Manistee is in ashes! The people are houseless and without clothing." The *Lansing Republican* reported, "Through the exertions of Mayor Robson, C. W. Butler, N. B. Jones, S.D. Bingham, and others, a car-load of provisions and clothing was made up and started from Lansing … and was loaded with 72 barrels of flour, seven barrels of crackers, three barrels of pork, one box of ham and bacon, 255 pounds of cheese, a quantity of tea and coffee, and several bundles of clothing; the value outside of the clothing being about $650… This aid is timely and as Chicago is receiving help from the whole civilized world, this diversion of a portion of the funds for the aid of our own State will do no more good than if expended in any other way… The following telegram in relation to these supplies was received on Monday from Grand Haven: "Supplies for Manistee went forward yesterday. E. P. Ferry." [456] While the Lansing area was aiding the northwestern

Lower Peninsula, Detroit was helping on the eastern side and around Saginaw Bay. Other less affected towns were following their assignments.

Even as everyone organized, they continued to fight fires. Those in the way of fire fought back, but winning was not assured. On October 11, fire ignited the surroundings of the Agricultural College. Cut off as they were from Lansing by three and a half miles of rough road, they had to do for themselves as most rural dwellers did. *The Lansing Republican* reported local fires, fires at the college, and to the north:

> Destructive fires have been raging through the forests in this vicinity, causing not only a general loss of fences and cordwood, but in some instances dwellings, barns, and crops have been burned. Last Sunday the dwelling and out-buildings on the farm of C. Wolf, about three miles south of this city, were destroyed, and A. R. Burr had fences burned to the value of $500. The dwelling of Ezra Jones, about a mile south of the city limits, was in such imminent peril that the family packed their household goods ready to remove to a place of safety. On Monday the fire on the west side of the city became so alarming that a large force was kept at work to control the flames. The woods and marshes in the vicinity of the Agricultural College have been a sheet of flame, and the students ceased to prosecute their studies in order to keep the Fire Fiend at bay. By dividing the students into working parties of six hours each, the fire was held in subjection.
>
> On Tuesday a light rain fell, enough to prevent the fire from spreading, and the dense smoke that has enveloped the country for days has partially cleared away.
>
> Along the line of the Jackson, Lansing & Saginaw Railroad the conflagration has been general, consuming houses, portable mills, barns, lumber, and crops, and compelling families to leave their all and flee for their lives.
>
> We learn from the Saginaw *Enterprise* that near St. Charles a number of buildings have been burned, and at the village the mills were all closed and the men working faithfully to prevent the spreading of the flames. A portion of Carrollton is in ashes: Kawakawin is surrounded by fire, and Essexville is in danger. At South Saginaw the excitement is intense. The mills have shut down and ordered the men to the woods to fight fire. Chapin & Barber's loss will exceed $80,000. Lathrop, Insclio & Co's loss is $20,000. Two hundred people arrived in Saginaw on Monday, having been forced to abandon their homes…
>
> Along the shores of Lake Huron the fire has driven the people to the water's edge, destroying the villages of White Rock, Forestville, Cato, and Elm Creek. In the southwestern portion of the State, also, whole villages are reported to be in flames, viz: Wayland, Mattawan, Vicksburg, Holland, and Three Oaks. A devastating fire has also raged in the woods around Flint, Caro, Vassar, Bellevue, and many other places. It is certain

that the loss in this State will reach millions of dollars and impoverish thousands of people, at the verge of winter.[457]

Near the end of November Jim and his Uncle Daniel had a remarkable tale to tell about a heroic employee who saved their Turner and Case property to the northeast of Ingham County where Gratiot County had been overrun by fire for two or three weeks, destroying dwellings, fences, timber, saw mills and other property.

An old Englishman in their employ named Jacob Laird, saw that the mill was in the range of the fire, and that it was speedily coming upon him, and he made preparations to meet and fight it like an old soldier, for he had served the Union cause gallantly during the late rebellion. Taking all the movable property from the mill, blacksmith shop, and boardinghouse, he buried it where it would be safe from the devouring element. Then he dug a series of wells enclosing the mill and hundreds of thousands of feet of lumber, placing by the side of each well a barrel filled with water, a pail in each well and another in the barrel. These wells were dug as needed for the speedy protection of the property. One well he dug deeper than the others, that in case his efforts to save the property should be in vain and his own life in danger, he could jump in as a last resort.

The fire came down upon him like a tornado. With his force of hands he met it, and where it crossed the line here and there, setting fire to piles of lumber, the water ready at hand quenched the flames. At last, he came off victorious, for he saved the mill, lumber, and all the property with the loss of his own hair, eyebrows, whiskers, and even the woolen shirt from off his back. When rallied by his employers "as to whether he did not find it hot work," his reply was, "It was not much of a soldier who couldn't face the fire, after facing as many cannon as he had."

As a fitting reward, Laird's wages have been nearly doubled and he was furnished with a fine suit of clothes, and told that he could remain there as long as he chose.[458]

A large fund of money was raised in New York State, and the New England states and Ohio also began to contribute money when they realized the people of Wisconsin and Michigan had likely suffered greater loss in proportion to their valuation and population than Chicago. "When a people finds the wolf at the door, and is fighting him for life, it can spread a little money very thin. Our operations must continue a long time," William A. Howard, Chairman of the Western Branch of the Michigan Relief Committee, told the donors. Michigan's Legislature argued over whether to call a special session to provide relief. They argued over whether it would be unconstitutional to afford relief for such a purpose since all the moneys in the State Treasury were already appropriated. They argued over whether or not there were surplus funds to appropriate. The *State Republican* agreed with the Grand Rapids *Eagle* that it would be better for the great and wealthy

State of Michigan to provide for her own sufferers. "But as these surplus funds are mostly kept in Detroit banks, as they have been for the last twenty years, it might disturb the business of Detroit if they were distributed elsewhere instead of being deposited there to be loaned to wealthy businessmen, thus enabling them to meet their paper without protest," said the newspaper on November 2 with a dose of cynicism.[459]

It was over a month before all the fires were completely out. Thousands of people lost everything they had, and 1,200,000 acres were burned. Ten years later in the fall of 1881, the state was more populated, and a fire in the thumb area of the state caused even greater loss of life and destruction of property although it was in just five counties. Nevertheless, Michigan's first comprehensive forest fire law to protect lands outside of state forests wasn't enacted until 1903. The new government system of fire wardens included township supervisors, mayors, and village presidents as ex-officio fire wardens and authorized payment of temporary fire wardens. Fire wardens could press men into firefighting service and arrest fire law violators. The lesson from the Great Fire was that momentous wildfires often begin with small scattered fires that well up into uncontrollable destruction when conditions are right. Now a system was in place to begin an attack on fires before they get out of hand.

The Woman's Temperance Campaign

Not long after the fire of 1871, the organizational skills of the women of the relief effort were put to another good purpose. In 1874 Marian joined the Woman's Christian Temperance Union when it was organized in Lansing and became a lifelong follower of Francis Willard, of Chicago, who advocated for many progressive ideas. Willard told the W. C. T. U. members, "We know that indulgence in alcohol and opium, and in other vices which disgrace social life, makes misery for all the world, and most of all for us and for our children."[460] Marian's nephew John Munro Longyear described a not uncommon situation he came upon while inspecting lumber for his uncles at St. Charles in the Saginaw Valley in 1870:

> A great jam developed with saw logs and long-timber piled up twenty feet high in the roaring stream. Knowing that nothing could be done until the flood of water subsided, the long-timber drivers abandoned the river and came into town. It consisted of one street a half mile long with about a dozen saloons on each side. The long-timber men started at the first saloon on one side of the street, visiting each in turn and drinking steadily. Now, when the saw-log drivers reached the jam, they also had to wait for low water, and so they also came into town and started in on a tour of saloons on the opposite side of the street from that being visited by the long-timber men
>
> The last saloon on the street was a large billiard hall with a bar, and there the two gangs met head on. By that time all were fighting drunk

and ripe for battle. I heard the noise from the lumberyard where I was working, but had no idea what caused it until later. On my way to dinner, I passed the big saloon, which had been completely wrecked. One of the men in his efforts to get out of the fight, supposing he was running towards the door, smashed through a plate-glass window; they carried him home on a board, but nevertheless he recovered from the frightful cuts he had received. Not a whole piece of furniture, bottle, mirror, wall, or window remained, all being mixed up in one tremendous heap of wreckage. Such occurrences were common enough in the river towns of the lumber region. The inhabitants expected them as a matter of course, whenever the river-drivers reached town, or the men from the camps came in and received their pay after a winter in the woods.[461]

What John did not mention is that with saloons located near the lumber camps, or factories, or wherever men worked, came red light districts, brothels or houses of ill repute, and prostitution. This undesirable effect added to the reasons many women wanted to rid saloons from their towns.

The organization of women fighting to restrain the use of alcohol started in Hillsboro, Ohio, in 1873 and swept the country, touching every city and hamlet in Michigan. About thirty local groups had formed in Michigan before Lansing's group did, but Lansing was soon in the forefront of the movement. It wasn't until things finally got hot enough that the politicians began to move. After years of work by men's groups, the women's groups brought new organization, coalition building (unity, they called it), and energy to the movement. Their story is taken from *The History of Lansing Central Union Woman's Christian Temperance Union, 1874-1949*, originally written by Anna Hopkins in 1889. An updated Diamond Jubilee edition was given by the Lansing Central Union to the Lansing Library to preserve its history.

Under the leadership of Abigail B. Hasty, "a timid, godly woman," a group of Lansing friends prepared a notice which was read the following Sunday in every church in Lansing. This notice invited all the women who were interested in the suppression of the liquor traffic to meet in the Central Methodist Church on Tuesday, March 24, 1874. Sixty women responded to the call. Eunice Porter was chosen as chair of the meeting. A committee was appointed to prepare a plan of operation. The meeting was adjourned until 7:00 that evening when they met again and in a body attended a city council meeting held in Mead's Hall. The councilmen were in session to plan for the city election, and the women requested that they place only dry men on the spring ballot.

A group of twelve met daily for 11 days and then every other day as they planned for a mass meeting. On March 27, twelve ladies began to canvass the city and obtain commitments to attend the rally by getting people to sign the following pledge: "We the undersigned residents of Lansing do hereby pledge ourselves that when it shall be deemed expedient to call a public meeting in the interest of temperance, we will attend such meeting and assist to the extent of our ability." These women also requested all the ministers to preach on the subject of temperance the following Sunday or to hold a joint meeting, a union meeting as it was called, if they so desired. At this same meeting the constitution and pledge of the Lansing W. C. T. U. were approved, and seventy signatures secured. Fanny Mead addressed the group and offered the women the use of Mead's Hall for their mass meeting, as it had been made available to men's temperance groups in the past.

The next day, March 28, Lizzie A. Buck attended their meeting and offered the use of Buck's Opera House free, except for the expense of fuel and lights. The committee of twelve reported that the ministers would support a union meeting at Buck's Opera House with Rev. Isaac Taylor and Rev. George Duffield as speakers. The ministers did not want to take up a collection, so the ladies present took up a collection among themselves to help with the expenses and a goodly sum of $13.06 was received. Prayer meetings were arranged for every afternoon and evening of the following week. The next Sunday evening churches of Lansing held a joint meeting in Buck's Opera House, and the city mass meeting was held Tuesday evening, April 3, in Mead's Hall. Not just in Lansing but across the nation women's groups were having a lasting impact on religious groups in their communities by insisting they cooperate to fight the liquor traffic in ways they had not done before.

Three different pledges were written and adopted at one of the regular meetings, one for druggists, one for property owners of saloons and breweries, and one for liquor dealers. This was a strategy patterned after the one used by the first such organization in Hillsboro, Ohio, and others following. The women asked the clergymen to use only unfermented wine in the observance of the Holy Communion, to which they agreed. Every druggist in the city signed their pledge, and 32 property owners pledged that they would not allow any of the property under their control to be used for the manufacture or sale of intoxicating liquor after April 15, when their leases would expire.

The women also secured the name of every saloonkeeper in the city and names of the owners of the buildings. On April 6 another meeting was held and the following appeal was drafted and a voluntary committee formed to carry it to every citizen in Lansing and vicinity for their signature: "To every person engaged in the sale of intoxicating drinks as a beverage, we, the citizens of Lansing and vicinity, desiring the health, sobriety and purity of all and knowing from the highest medical authorities and from our own observations that the use of intoxicating drinks as a beverage is highly injurious to the health and morals of the community, do most kindly and earnestly request you to cease from the sale of the same and conform to the human and righteous law forbidding the traffic, thus removing the temptation to which all are exposed."

This appeal, with signatures, was printed, and a voluntary committee of three women sent to each saloon and seller of strong drink in the city and vicinity, advising them that if it was not complied with, a second committee would visit them with the appeal *and* the law. The second committee, which included Marian, had no success in getting saloonkeepers to sign such a pledge, and they reported they were not received very cordially. So the women went to the agents of law enforcement.

By April 14 1,700 signatures had been received in answer to the appeal for help in the mass meeting. Shortly after a call signed by leaders of thirteen unions from across the state was issued to all of the women's temperance societies in Michigan to send delegates to a convention to be held in Lansing, June 25, 1874, to plan a course of united action. They secured the Senate Chamber for the meeting and the Representative Hall for serving a light lunch.

This statewide meeting was called to order by Harriet Tracy, president of the Lansing Union, a former student of the Lansing Female College, a founder of the Fire Relief Society of 1871, and a member of the Industrial Aid Society. After singing the Temperance Union song, "Marching Along," a prayer was given by Miss Mary Manning, an organizer from Detroit. The record states that from the time that prayer was offered there could be no doubt the consensus was that the name of the state organization would be "The Woman's Christian Temperance Union." At the next convention held in Grand Rapids on September 10 of the same year, this name was formally adopted. (Some thought to Michigan belonged the honor of first giving the name to the National Woman's Christian Temperance Union in November of 1874 when it was organized, but a group in Fredonia, New York, first used the name in December of 1873.)[462] Harriet Tracy was named the first state president.

During the next few months, many mass meetings were held on the capitol grounds with noted speakers. In the fall the meetings were held in Mead Hall and Buck's Opera House, with audiences of 700 to 1,200. The women continued to be very active in raising money, prosecuting saloonkeepers who disobeyed the law, and attending court. According to Hopkins's history, when they commenced their work there were 46 saloons in the city, but by September 24, six months later, the number had been reduced to 28.[463]

At the height of this activity involvement by the Turners was brought to a halt. In the spring of 1875 a great sadness came again to the family. A newspaper article described the calamity in detail:

> On Wednesday afternoon, May 28, 1875, the two-horse team of Mrs. James Turner, attached to a small lumber wagon, took fright on Franklin Street East, near the North Lansing depot. Running towards home, the team caused the wagon to collide with a box-car that was standing partly in the street, and pitched the two occupants against the car, killing both.
>
> Anxious people soon collected around the dying persons, and recognized one as Mrs. Turner's son, Jesse, a bright and engaging boy about 11 years of age. The other was Mr. Thomas Langtry, who had been a faithful steward in the family for several years. He was about 57 years of age, a native of Ireland. If he had any relations, they were not known.

Jesse breathed only a few times, dying almost instantly. Mr. Langtry, though he had several broken bones, and was mangled and bleeding considerably, spoke a few words; he lived until about sundown, three hours after the accident.

It seemed there were no actual witnesses to the collision. A few seconds before the horses were seen acting unruly. It was conjectured that the wagon tongue dropped out of the ring in the neck-yoke and that both horses got on one side of the tongue, and as they ran straight forward, the tongue veered to the right and collided with the car; then the whiffletree broke and the horses became disengaged.

The box-car in question had been rolled into the street in order that wagons loaded with tile might be drawn up close by its side and the tile conveniently loaded onto the car directly from wagons. Had the car not been standing in the street, it is hardly probable both persons would have been killed. Looking at the matter in this light, several persons severely criticized the railroad company for occupying the street as a place for loading and unloading cars.[464]

For a time Marian pulled back from her public activities in mourning, as was the custom, but the W. C. T. U. was continuing to grow and was astonishingly effective. The Lansing W. C. T. U. kept up its engagement in local activities and agitation. In 1875, they got the State Fair to prohibit the sale of liquor. In February of that year the women attended in a body the hearing in the Legislature on the prohibition amendment. The state convention was held once again at Central Methodist Church in May 1876.

On February 4, 1877, a mass meeting was held featuring Dr. Henry Reynolds of the Red Ribbon Movement as speaker. (The women used the white ribbon as a temperance symbol. Reformed drinking men wore red ribbons.) A street parade and meals served to the crowds at several different churches made this one of the biggest events ever held in Lansing. Reynolds, a recovering alcoholic, had been brought from Bangor, Maine, and became an organizer in Michigan for the W. C. T. U. and the Red Ribbon Society, the latter being particularly focused on reforming patrons of saloons. His work was received with more enthusiasm in some areas of the state than others. It was said he was only moderately successful until he went to the lumbering region of the Saginaw Valley, where the Red Ribbon movement was welcomed with zeal.[465]

A year later *The New York Times* reported that the Lansing Red Ribbon Club had a membership of 1,200 abstinent men, in a city of about 1,850 voters. "The result is that the income of one saloon there fell off in a few days from $75 a week to less than $3, that several have closed, and that not one in the entire town is today paying expenses," said the *Times*. "At Saginaw the lumbermen engaged their men for the 'Spring drive' of logs wholly from the [Red Ribbon] club room." The *Times* said there was a considerable drop in tax revenue from saloons in the state and that the officers of the state reported a marked drop in arrests and police business.[466]

The women of the temperance movement had done much good to improve the lives of those who overindulged in alcohol (we now realize alcoholism is an addictive disease) and their families. They had also gained enemies to their larger cause whom they would encounter again because many women who were drawn to the woman's temperance movement also worked for woman's suffrage and many other reform causes in addition to the regulation of alcohol. The W. C. T. U. had taken a stand for woman's right to vote almost from its inception. The temperance leaders knew that without the vote they could not directly affect the regulation of alcohol, prison reform, education, aid to the poor, or any of the other reform issues they cared about.

Chapter 10

Politics and Progress in the 1870s

When the Fourteenth and Fifteenth Amendments were passed, the U.S. Constitution threw open its door to all men, instead of all people. This bolted the door against the possibility of voting by women because women could no longer be included in the constitutional definition of voters. The men and women in the Turner coterie understood the justice of giving everyone the right to vote. The problem was that most male voters, black and white, simply did not find any inconsistency in their failure to uphold a woman's voting rights or personhood while coveting these rights as their own. After this setback, for a few years there were only sporadic and unconnected efforts in the state to achieve the right to vote for women by the men and women known as suffragists (not suffragettes, a pejorative of British origin that American women found belittling). With the formation of the Michigan State Suffrage Society at its first convention, held in Battle Creek in 1870, the campaign for woman's voting rights resumed. The suffrage society stepped up efforts to educate and organize at the grassroots level by forming local societies, circulating tracts and petitions, securing hearings before the Legislature, and holding annual meetings in cities around the state.[467]

The First Drops of a Coming Shower

Local lobbying and agitation for woman's suffrage had been going on for several years. Nannette B. Gardner of Detroit and Mary Wilson of Kalamazoo were generally acknowledged as the first women to vote in Michigan in 1871, but an anonymous correspondent for the *Lansing Republican* insisted he had "read in a lecture delivered many years ago by Judge Walker the statement that women freeholders voted [in 1805] while Detroit was a town organization and he verified the fact by examining the record." Gardner said who voted first was not the main point, "Because the two of us have succeeded in getting ourselves recognized as really 'persons' under the constitution of our land the telegraph is startled into action, millions stand aghast, and an astute judge of our city has been digging up his charred and musty volumes to ascertain whether such a precedent had ever before been known. The general logic that women will soon universally vote, and their right to the ballot being only questioned by the same logic that slaves were denied their freedom, most rationally explains this phenomenon; and the few who begin to vote are [to be] regarded as the first drops of a coming shower."[468]

M. Adele Hazlett of Hillsdale County emerged as an able leader of the multi-state Northwestern Woman Suffrage Association. Victoria Woodhull became America's first woman presidential candidate in 1872. She was nominated by the Equal Rights party. Woodhull was against the government being composed only of men. It was said Hazlett took strong ground against Victoria Woodhull and her sister Tennessee Claflin because they held that equal rights included free love and they were considered the radical wing of the women's movement. Hazlett was against any and all side issues that would interfere with the work of the organization in securing suffrage for women.[469] Her October speech at Mead's Hall was covered by the newspaper.

Mrs. M. Adele Hazlett

Last Thursday evening Mrs. M. Adele Hazlett of Hillsdale, President of the Northwestern Woman Suffrage Association, lectured at Mead's Hall to a well filled house. Mrs. Hazlett has long been an earnest advocate of the right of woman to the ballot, and ranks as a champion of the cause with Mrs. Livermore, Anna Dickinson, and Mrs. Stanton. Her voice, though not loud, is forcible and could be distinctly heard in all parts of the room. She is a very rapid speaker, in person an attractive woman, and for nearly two hours the audience listened attentively. Her lecture throughout abounded in wit and sarcasm.

She received her education for the work from Lucy Stone and Mrs. Stanton, who she viewed as the Scylla and Charybdis of the Woman Suffrage Movement. The old and beaten roads were smooth with beautiful borders, but new paths are rough and uninviting and opposition is bitter and unrelenting... Never before in the history of the race has a man so needed an able champion as at the present time. A mania for rebellion seems to prevail among the women of the entire world, and everywhere they are crying. "Equal rights, equal representation, fair play, and fair wages," and men stand shocked as with a palsy.

She proposed to turn man's champion for the evening, and as Charles Reade would say, "Put myself in his place." She wished to be considered as belonging to the masculine side, and would make the best possible argument in favor of the men. To begin, she proposed to prove by the Constitution of the United States and Webster's Dictionary, two unimpeachable authorities, the woman is not a human being. The Fourteenth Amendment declares that all persons born in the United States and subject to the jurisdiction thereof are citizens of the same. It would seem from this, at first view, that women are persons, and therefore would come under the head of "human beings;" but Webster says that a person is one who has the privilege of exercising the elective franchise. Woman has not this right, therefore she is not a person nor is she a human being. Still further, Webster says that the people are the persons who compose the community of a State or nation. But women are not persons, therefore they cannot be considered people, and their status is definitely settled by the preamble of the Constitution, "We the People."

She would not say that women have no rights; but whatever their wrongs, they have a remedy in the law, and their chance to get justice in the courts is equal to men's—if they can afford to pay for it. Woman is perfectly free to go where she pleases, provided her father or husband can be prevailed upon to furnish the means. She is allowed to hold property by paying taxes upon it, but she cannot have a voice in voting the tax. She has a right to marry if she can get an opportunity, provided her father or guardian does not object, and every husband is obliged to support his wife, even though he be utterly incapable of supporting himself. Woman is relieved of all responsibility in this life, and she trusts implicitly in her husband although she may know that everything he utters be a falsehood; and under the law, if a man's wife go into a neighbor's pasture and steal a sheep, she is sent to jail, while if the man's dog kills a neighbor's sheep, the owner of the dog is compelled to pay for it.

Woman is neither mentally, physically, nor morally the equal of man. She is not fitted for the political arena, because physical strength is essential to the voter. These women cannot bear arms for their country's defense, although over 500 fought nobly in the Union army during the late war, and when their sex was discovered were turned out of camp without pay... Mentally woman cannot be compared with man; but it is the latter who shut Galileo in a dungeon, and ridiculed Columbus, while Isabella of Spain, weakly woman that she was, pawned her jewels to furnish means for the voyage. It was man's sagacity that located the soul in the stomach, then in the spleen, then in the heart... Man is the natural guardian of children, and dictates who shall be their teacher, what text-books they shall use, and what Sunday schools they shall attend; but he has never been found fault with for walking the floor all night with a sick baby...

Mrs. Hazlett was extremely bitter on Free Loveism and scathingly denounced the New York *Herald* and other papers whose great reverence for women leads them to indulge in the endearing terms of the "Shrieking sisterhoods," "American Amazons," "scratching hens."[470]

When the Ingham Woman Suffrage Association held its first annual meeting in April of 1872, it had a membership of about 120 women and men, but the committee appointed the previous summer had obtained the names of several hundred women who declared their intention to vote when all legal hurdles were removed. They held three lectures and two social gatherings. The first lecture was by Rev. Mr. Straub, for the second they brought back Adele Hazlett, and the third was by Sarah Van De Vort Emery of Lansing, a popular national and state lecturer on economics and women's rights. They met every two weeks for reading and discussion. The new officers were Alfred E. Cowles, President; Mrs. T. C. (Harriet) Abbot and Dr. S. W. Wright, Vice Presidents; Mrs. Ellene Westcott, Recording Secretary; and Miss Carrie W. Holmes, Corresponding Secretary; and Mrs. R. C. Dart, Treasurer. The Executive Committee was composed of many prominent citizens: Dr. I. H. Bartholomew, Mrs. J. W. Holmes, Mrs. Stephen D. (Charlotte) Bingham, Mrs. J. I. (Fanny) Mead, Mrs. J. W. Robinson, Mrs. J. J. Bush, Mrs. H. B. Armes, and Mr. W. L. Larned. Their plan was to circulate petitions during the coming summer to be presented to the Legislature the next winter.[471] Representing the capital city, Lansing's suffragists often hosted prominent leaders who came to Lansing to testify to the Legislature or to lobby. Among them were two famous western New Yorkers, Elizabeth Cady Stanton, who lived in Seneca Falls to the west of Cazenovia, and Susan B. Anthony of Rochester, to the east.

The Presidential Election of 1872

The election of 1872 pitted President Grant against former Republican Horace Greeley and split off a faction of the Radical Republicans in Lansing and across the country that joined the Democrats to support Greeley. However, Detroit's ex-mayor, William W. Wheaton, former head of Michigan's Democratic State Central Committee, said a Democratic party that nominated Greeley could not expect to command the loyalty of Democratic voters.[472] Among local defectors were liberal Republicans Austin Blair, Whitney Jones, Nelson B. Jones, George Sanford, and Dwight S. Smith (Hiram's son). Nationally leaders of the defection included many founders of the Republican party, such as Charles Sumner and Cassius Clay. They held a convention in Cincinnati and formed the short-lived Liberal Republican party that joined with the Democratic party in nominating Greeley. But other Radical Republicans took to the stump for Grant, certain that the election of Greeley on the Democratic ticket would restore rebel power throughout the Union, even though they were terribly disappointed by the process of Reconstruction in bringing economic assistance, education, and equal rights to freed slaves. They were put in the position of defending an administration facing many charges of corruption.

For the first time the Republican platform contained two planks in support of equal rights for all women, the work of Radical Republicans. Though faced with fighting a political battle from the outside, national suffragists urged women to advocate for Grant in their communities because Greeley was seen as an enemy of woman suffrage. Susan B. Anthony and Matilda Joslyn Gage wrote a letter on behalf of the National Woman Suffrage

Association which was widely publicized in the press (reproduced in full in the *State Republican*), stating that the Republicans' planks gave hope to women's rights advocates and that Horace Greeley had ridiculed woman's suffrage and suffragists. Women were active, even though they could not vote. They attended public political meetings, finding themselves cordially welcome at the meetings of such suffragist men as Daniel Case, Judge Jesse E. Tenney, and Stephen D. Bingham, all out stumping the state for Grant. At a meeting in Owosso, a huge crowd of over 1,000 women and at least 2,000 men turned out to hear Judge Tenney speak.[473] When suffragist and spiritualist Mrs. F. A. Logan of New York City came to speak at Mead's Hall lecture series, she attracted an attentive audience that was said to give the friends of temperance and woman suffrage fresh impetus with her eloquence. She also spoke at the reform school and in Mason, Jackson and Detroit.[474] Adele Hazlett traveled extensively for the GOP to re-elect Grant and barely mentioned woman's suffrage directly when she came to Lansing and Mason that fall, so intent was she on getting men to support Grant.[475]

Lansing's black voters sided with the anti-Greeley view: "A well-attended meeting of our colored citizens was held Tuesday night at the Baptist Church on Pine street, in this city, for the purpose of giving expression to their political sentiments. Mr. Niece was appointed chairman, and stated the object of the meeting. Mr. Salapaugh was appointed secretary. Mr. J. H. Hubbard addressed the meeting, giving reasons why he should support Grant for the Presidency and not follow the advice of Sumner, a faded 'flower' of Republicanism. Mr. S. D. Bingham gave a history of the Republican cause and reviewed the movements of the so-called 'Liberals.'" Other Republican party guests also made remarks that were enthusiastically received, and the invitation to join the Grant and [Henry] Wilson Club was accepted by all 27 of the group.[476] A week later the group grew to 39. "The colored citizens of this city met on Tuesday evening, at the Pine Street Church, and were addressed by Rev. Mr. Niece and J. H. Hubbard. There were 12 new voters joined the Grant and Wilson Club, which now includes every colored voter in the city. They resolved to turn out with the Tanners when notified and most have paid for their own uniforms. This is their last meeting as a separate organization. [The Tanners were a group of supporters of Grant who attended parades and rallies and carried torches – Grant helped his father in the tannery business as a boy.] This class of our citizens is all staunch Republicans, and are welcome to an honorable place in the party."[477] A couple of weeks earlier it was reported, "There are 80 colored votes in Mason, all of whom are for Grant and Wilson."[478] They were a step ahead of an open letter by Frederick Douglass reprinted August 22 in the *State Republican* urging black voters to steer clear of Horace Greeley followers and to vote for Grant.[479]

This was the first presidential election since the inception of the Republican party in which the Lansing Radical Republicans did not have their old friend James Turner with them, but they gave it their all. Daniel was true to form in his role of rallying supporters. Once a Democrat himself, albeit, a Northern Democrat, he knew well the failings of Reconstruction at the hands of Johnson and his former party and drove them home with fiery denunciation and a heavy serving of sarcasm:

The Republicans of Lansing assembled on a Monday evening at Representative Hall, to hear Hon. D. L. Case of this city speak upon the issues of the campaign.

Mr. Case in his argument took the ground that the rank and file of the Northern Democracy had been true and loyal men, but that the Southern wing had controlled the Democratic party in all its relations to the Government. This was in 1848, when a Democratic Legislature of Michigan voted unanimously for the Wilmot Proviso, but had to eat their own words at the will of the Southern members of Congress. It was true in 1854, when Franklin Pierce was President, his policy being dictated by the Southern slaveholders. And it had been true from that time to this...

Mr. Case went on to show that the Democratic party had not repented before the Rebellion, but, under the lead of the Southern wing, had done all that it could to extend the area of slavery. They had not repented at the beginning of the Rebellion, for every man who took up arms against the Government was a Southern Democrat; while the leaders of the Democratic party in the North sympathized with the rebel cause in a great degree.

That party had not repented at the close of the Rebellion, for when laws were proposed in Congress, giving all loyal men in the late rebel States the right to vote without regard to color or race, the Democrats in Congress unanimously opposed it. They had not repented when the Ku-Klux law was passed, restraining these mobs from committing outrages upon the lives and property of unoffending citizens of the South, for the Democrats opposed this law in a solid body. They had not repented at the time of the meeting of the Cincinnati Convention in 1872, which was controlled by the Democratic party; for the resolution offered by Congressman Hooper at that time, declaring that the 13th, 14th, and 15th Amendments were valid and binding, received only nine Democratic votes in the House. They had not repented up to the time of the meeting of the Philadelphia Convention, for another resolution, offered by a Republican member from Ohio, declaring the Constitutional Amendments valid and binding, and that they should be enforced by proper legislation, received not a vote from a Democratic member.

They did not talk repentance until the Baltimore Convention, when August Belmont, the Hebrew, came forward and declared that Horace Greeley was a great and good man, and that they should vote for and support him. It was then that the spirit of repentance pervaded the whole assemblage, and the Democratic leaders, North and South, responded to his call.

Mr. Case logically proved, from these premises, that the party which nominated Greeley in Baltimore had opposed every effort to extend civil and political liberty in the South, and was not a party to be trusted today.

He had nothing to say against Mr. Greeley as an editor or a citizen, but he was a passive opponent of the principle of Secession, as shown by his record during the Rebellion and by his late speech at Pittsburg. He was willing to allow the South or any other portion of the Union, if they should give a majority vote in favor of Secession, to secede without opposition from him. Such a man is not fit to fill the Presidential chair.

As a financial theorist he is also full of vagaries and unworthy the confidence of the business men of the country. The speaker read extracts from the New York World to prove that ever since the nomination of Horace Greeley at Baltimore it had expressed its want of confidence in his financial ability and a disinclination to trust him.

Mr. Case also took up the record of Austin Blair, showing how ardently he advocated the passage of the Ku-Klux bill but a few months ago, and how he sustained and supported the Administration of General Grant; reading from Austin Blair's own speech at Jackson to prove that he dared not trust the Democratic party with power in the country.

Mr. Case also adverted to the fact that no prominent Democrat in Michigan, of state reputation, has this year taken the stump. Such men as Lothrup, McClelland, Stuart, Hughes, and others, who have won a wide reputation in the Democratic party in Michigan, are silent and have not a word to say in advocacy of defense of Horace Greeley…

Mr. Case earnestly advocated Woman Suffrage, and said that the Republican party was the only one committed to this movement.

The speech occupied nearly two hours. It was well received and often interrupted by applause.[480]

Grant won reelection that fall, but the cause of woman suffrage remained elusive. Suffragist and reformer Elizabeth Cady Stanton spoke at the Lansing Equal Suffrage Association meeting held May 4-5, 1874. A bill had at last been submitted to the voters by the Michigan Legislature as an amendment to the constitution to permit woman suffrage. Michigan was the second state to introduce such an amendment, and everything that could be done was done by the friends of the amendment throughout the state. However, the liberal action of the Legislature in passing the bill, of Governor John Bagley in signing the bill, the appeals of women, and the votes of forty thousand of the best men of the state—all of this was not enough. The State Equal Suffrage Association continued its work although the resounding failure of the proposition at the ballot box dampened the spirits of the advocates of the movement for a time.[481] Elizabeth Cady Stanton later wrote:

> In 1874 Michigan was the point of interest to all those who had taken part in the woman-suffrage movement. The Legislature, by a very large majority, submitted to a vote of the electors an amendment of the Constitution, in favor of striking out the word "male" and thus securing civil and political rights to the women of the State. It was a very active

campaign. Crowded meetings were held in all the chief towns and cities. Professor Moses Coit Tyler [of the Michigan Agricultural College], and a large number of ministers preached, every Sunday, on the subject of woman's position. The Methodist conference passed a resolution in favor of the amendment by a unanimous vote. I was in the State during the intense heat of May and June, speaking every evening to large audiences; in the afternoon to women alone, and preaching every Sunday in some pulpit. The Methodists, Universalists, Unitarians, and Quakers all threw open their churches to the apostles of the new gospel of equality for women. We spoke in jails, prisons, asylums, depots, and the open air. Wherever there were ears to hear, we lifted up our voices, and, on the wings of the wind, the glad tidings were carried to the remote corners of the State, and the votes of forty thousand men, on election day, in favor of the amendment were so many testimonials to the value of the educational work accomplished.

I made many valuable acquaintances on that trip, with whom I have maintained lifelong friendships. One pleasant day I passed in the home of Governor Bagley and his wife [Frances], with a group of pretty children. I found the Governor deeply interested in prison reform. He had been instrumental in passing a law giving prisoners lights in their cells and pleasant reading matter until nine o'clock. His ideas of what prisons should be, as unfolded that day, have since been fully realized in the grand experiment now being successfully tried at Elmira, New York.

I visited the State prison at Jackson, and addressed seven hundred men and boys, ranging from seventy down to seventeen years of age. Seated on the dais with the chaplain, I saw them file in to dinner, and, while they were eating, I had an opportunity to study the sad, despairing faces before me. I shall never forget the hopeless expression of one young man, who had just been sentenced for twenty years, nor how ashamed I felt that one of my own sex, trifling with two lovers, had fanned the jealousy of one against the other, until the tragedy ended in the death of one and the almost lifelong imprisonment of the other. If girls should be truthful and transparent in any relations in life, surely it is in those of love, involving the strongest passions of which human nature is capable. As the chaplain told me the sad story, and I noticed the prisoner's refined face and well-shaped head, I felt that the young man was not under the right influences to learn the lesson he needed. Fear, coercion, punishment, are the masculine remedies for moral weakness, but statistics show their failure for centuries. Why not change the system and try the education of the moral and intellectual faculties, cheerful surroundings, inspiring influences? Everything in our present system tends to lower the physical vitality, the self-respect, the moral tone, and to harden instead of reforming the criminal.

My heart was so heavy I did not know what to say to such an assembly of the miserable. I asked the chaplain what I should say. "Just what you please," he replied. Thinking they had probably heard enough of their sins, their souls, and the plan of salvation, I thought I would give them the news of the day. So I told them about the woman suffrage amendment, what I was doing in the State, my amusing encounters with opponents, their arguments, my answers. I told them of the great changes that would be effected in prison life when the mothers of the nation had a voice in the buildings and discipline. I told them what Governor Bagley said, and of the good time coming when prisons would no longer be places of punishment but schools of reformation. To show them what women would do to realize this beautiful dream, I told them of Elizabeth Fry and Dorothea L. Dix, of Mrs. Farnham's experiment at Sing Sing, and Louise Michel's in New Caledonia, and, in closing, I said: "Now I want all of you who are in favor of the amendment to hold up your right hand." They gave a unanimous vote, and laughed heartily when I said, "I do wish you could all go to the polls in November and that we could lock our opponents up here until after the election."

I felt satisfied that they had had one happy hour and that I had said nothing to hurt the feelings of the most unfortunate. As they filed off to their respective workshops my faith and hope for brighter days went with them. Then I went all through the prison. Everything looked clean and comfortable on the surface, but I met a few days after a man, just set free, who had been there five years for forgery. He told me the true inwardness of the system; of the wretched, dreary life they suffered, and the brutality of the keepers. He said the prison was infested with mice and vermin, and that, during the five years he was there, he had never lain down one night to undisturbed slumber. The sufferings endured in summer for want of air, he said, were indescribable. In this prison the cells were in the center of the building, the corridors running all around by the windows, so the prisoners had no outlook and no direct contact with the air. Hence, if a careless keeper forgot to open the windows after a storm, the poor prisoners panted for air in their cells, like fish out of water. My informant worked in the mattress department, over the room where prisoners were punished. He said he could hear the lash and the screams of the victims from morning till night. "Hard as the work is all day," said he, "it is a blessed relief to get out of our cells to march across the yard and get one glimpse of the heavens above, and one breath of pure air, and to be in contact with other human souls in the workshops, for, although we could never speak to each other, yet there was a hidden current of sympathy conveyed by look that made us one in our misery."

Though the press of the State was largely in our favor, yet there were some editors who, having no arguments, exercised the little wit they did possess in low ridicule. It was in this campaign that an editor in a Kalamazoo journal said: "That ancient daughter of Methuselah, Susan B. Anthony, passed through our city yesterday, on her way to the Plainwell meeting, with a bonnet on her head looking as if it had recently descended from Noah's ark." Miss Anthony often referred to this description of herself, and said, "Had I represented twenty thousand voters in Michigan, that political editor would not have known nor cared whether I was the oldest or the youngest daughter of Methuselah, or whether my bonnet came from the ark or from Worth's."[482]

The Woman's Club Movement

Among the many organizational innovations happening in this period was the advent of the Woman's Club movement. One of the leaders was Lucinda Hinsdale Stone, who became known nationally as the "Mother of the Women's Club Movement." Having also attended the Lima Seminary that Abigail Rogers attended, she came to Grand Rapids where she met her future husband, Dr. James A. B. Stone. The two helped found Kalamazoo College where her husband became President, and Lucinda headed the innovative Female Department. By now she had acquired statewide recognition for her work in developing higher education for women and, after the death of Abigail Rogers, gained the admission of Madelon Stockwell as the first woman to attend the University of Michigan. When the Stones left Kalamazoo College, Lucinda continued the work of the Female Department by educating women in her own home. She advocated for woman's suffrage, for the development of literary clubs, and European travel as an important part of education for women. She led many study tours for young women to Europe and the Middle East and travelled about the state organizing women's clubs.[483] She worked tirelessly to raise the status of women. Her view point was well known: "Whatsoever things are true, and good, and holy, must be done by men and women working together, without jealousy or prejudice, without distinction to caste or sex."[484] Her movements were reported in the local newspapers.

While some members of Marian's family were involved with the Industrial Aid Society, the Woman's Christian Temperance Union, and the Pioneer Society, several also joined in the formation of the first Woman's Club of Lansing. Frances Smith Longyear (whose husband was Ephraim Longyear) helped found the Lansing Woman's Club and the first meetings were held at her home. We learn the story of the Lansing Woman's Club from Harriet Tenney. At a meeting of the club in 1890, Harriet Tenney recalled how "the few whose hearts desire it" created a society for mutual improvement by forming the Lansing Woman's Club. The city already had a successful Library and Literary Association that she helped found in 1871, but this was different. "Many were the words of discouragement met with, both sarcastic and of disapproval. By some it was thought incompatible for a good wife and mother to devote so much time from feminine duties to the pursuit of studies, either classical or modern," Harriet Tenney recalled. As she wrote in her account, the first attempt in the state library on the third floor of the capitol was rocky, but then she turned to her suffragist friends, Ellene Westcott, Fannie Cowles, Eliza Stebbins, and Frances Longyear:

During the fall and winter of the years 1871-1872 there were frequent notices in the daily papers of the literary work that Mrs. L. H. Stone was doing in this state; of the clubs she was interested in, and of the history classes she was conducting in various cities, and of the great interest taken by the members in their studies under her directions. It seemed to me that such a class might be formed in this city. Several of our ladies also expressed to me their desire to join such a class. I opened a correspondence with Mrs. Stone which resulted finally in her coming to Lansing and giving two conversations before the Library and Literary Association in its rooms on the evening of July first and second 1872. She gave in a conversational way some account of her travels abroad, one evening being devoted to an account of the Passion Play at Oberammergau witnessed by her. There was a good attendance and much interest manifested by both the ladies and gentlemen present. But it was evident that the time had not arrived for the organization of either a club, or a history class. Two mistakes had been made. First the meeting should have been held in the parlors of a private residence instead of in the Association rooms, and none but ladies should have been invited. Second instead of placing Mrs. Stone upon a high platform, with theatrical surroundings to give conversations, she should have been invited to a parlor, with the "Round Table" placed in the center, around which the guests could have sat in a magic circle and drunk in inspiration from the words that dropped from her lips. The undertaking was given up for the time being but not by any means forgotten.

On the morning of March 12, 1874 Mrs. John J. Bagley [Frances] visited the State Library as was her custom when in the city, and whilst turning over the leaves of some of the choice books that she was fond of examining, she entered into a conversation with me about woman's works; what women were doing in the field of literature etc., and of the History Classes and Clubs that had been organized not only in this State but in other States also. She gave me an interesting account of the Detroit Woman's Club of which she was at that time the President, as well as having been the prime mover in its organization.

Ah! Thought I, the very note has surely been struck, as, when I, having been intensely interested in her account, exclaimed, "Oh, Mrs. Bagley why can't the Lansing ladies form a Club, there surely are a good many who would be glad to unite in such an enterprise." She replied "There can be a Club organized here in Lansing, and I will assist all that I can. I go home to Detroit tomorrow evening I will bring with me our Constitution and By-Laws and I will also prepare a paper on Clubs for women and the best way to organize them. In the meantime you can see and talk with a few of the ladies of Lansing and appoint a meeting for Wednesday afternoon at some lady's house, and you must not invite more than twelve ladies to be present because if you invite more I cannot read my paper."

The promise that not more than twelve ladies should be present at the contemplated gathering had to be made, though reluctantly, before Mrs. Bagley left the Library. What initial steps to take, where to meet, and who to invite, were not easy matters to decide. Visions of the failure of 1872 rose before my eyes. Such a failure must not occur again. Early the next Saturday afternoon, Mrs. E. L. Westcott [recording secretary of the Ingham Women's Suffrage Association] as was her wont often to do, stopped into the Library on her way to the rooms of the Library and Literary Association which were always open on Saturday afternoons. I told her of the conversation with Mrs. Bagley and asked her advice in the matter. She replied "That was what she had long wanted to do, join a Woman's Club for study, and she would do all that she could to assist in the organization of one." Mrs. Westcott spoke that afternoon to Mrs. Fannie Cowles [her husband, Albert, was president of the Ingham Women's Suffrage Association] and Mrs. Eliza O. Stebbins who were both pleased with the plan. Mrs. Cowles called at the Library immediately, and after telling her of Mrs. Bagley's wishes, we both thought Mrs. E. Longyear would be pleased to unite with us, and that she would also be pleased to open her parlors for the occasion. Mrs. Cowles called upon Mrs. Longyear telling her of our aspirations, and she entered heartily into the spirit of this undertaking, and promised to do all that she could to aid in organizing such a Club.

On Monday the 16th of March Mrs. Longyear called at the Library to talk with me about the plan, and we decided that it was best for her to issue the invitations to some twelve or fifteen ladies to meet in her parlors on Wednesday afternoon the 18th instant for the purpose of taking steps to organize a Woman's Club and to listen to a paper by Mrs. Bagley. With beating hearts we anxiously awaited the result of this new undertaking, knowing well that "Every noble work is at first impossible." but that also "Whoever perseveres will be crowned."[485]

On March 18, 1874, fifteen women met at Frances Longyear's home, including young Marian, the daughter of Marian Turner. They decided the group should form to study Literature, Science, Art and "miscellaneous topics of mutual interest." Frances Bagley read the paper that she had promised, giving many valuable suggestions on how to form the club and what the work of the club should be. Frances Longyear offered her parlors as a meeting place for as long as they wished. The next meeting brought another eleven members, including young Marian's aunt, Adella Case.

Frances agreed to present the paper the group had agreed upon about the Honorable Charles Sumner, a national leader of the Radical Republicans who had died March 11. The club met weekly, receiving encouraging letters from clubs in other cities. At the sixth meeting, Charlotte Bingham gave an inspiring talk, followed by intense discussion, about Mary Somerville, a Scottish astronomer, mathematician, geographer, and scientist who became known as the "Queen of Nineteenth Century Science." The seventh week they heard a paper on Margaret Fuller Ossoli, journalist, critic, and woman's rights leader who wrote *Woman in the Nineteenth Century*, now considered to be the first major feminist work in the United States. There was also a paper given by Ellene Westcott and Lozie Paddack on current topics. At the eighth meeting they studied the Carey Sisters and decided to invite Lucinda Hinsdale Stone to meet with the group. Phoebe and Alice Carey were acclaimed contemporary American poets. Phoebe edited *The Revolution* for a time, the woman's rights newspaper published by Susan B. Anthony.

At the eleventh meeting a constitution and by-laws were adopted and the officers elected included Harriet Tenney as President and Frances Longyear, Helen Jenison and Sophie Knight as Vice Presidents. The twelfth meeting was devoted to their special guest, Lucinda Hinsdale Stone, who presented a paper on *The Merchant of Venice* for the twenty-five club members. Harriet Tenney recalled this meeting with fondest memories: "The Club was then adjourned, but many of those present were greatly mystified by the somewhat unusual activities of certain of our usually staid members who seemed possessed with a sudden desire to push the chairs, as well as the other members to one side. The solution of their mysterious ways was received with laughter, and many pleasant remarks of approval when it dawned upon their minds that the "Club" was to indulge in the first tea drinking and banquet. We can never forget that table nor those who surrounded it; Mrs. Stone whom we had already grown to love was seated at the south end of the table and when all were seated, asked that first blessing not only on the viands placed before us, but on the club, in such beautiful language, so affecting us all that the memory still lingers with us."

The following afternoon Lucinda Hinsdale Stone read a paper about her personal recollections of a trip to Rome, and she and Frances Bagley were voted honorary members. After Stone, twenty-five members signed the membership book and several others followed in future weeks. By this time the club began to feel that their high aims had truly entered into their organization. Harriet said, "It required but a glance at the group of faces aglow with interest and animation to convince one that the time had come when we could say of our effort, 'Hope was planted with it, Love is around it, and we have Faith that our Tree will live.'"[486]

Knowing they might meet with disapproval, they soon armed themselves with knowledge to refute their critics. They were suffragists, as were their husbands, and they took great joy in reading about suffragists and the ideas and accomplishments of women. Harriet said they could now refer their critics to women who had been good mothers and wives and also engaged in intellectual pursuits:

Mary Somerville, "the woman whose house was the happier; honored and loved by both husband and children. She who outstripped nearly all of the men of her time in Scientific studies."

Mary Carpenter, "that noted philanthropist, she also taught Homer and Virgil as her father's assistant in his school." [She was a celebrated educational and social reformer who advocated educational opportunities for poor children, abolition, and woman suffrage in England.]

Miss Sedgwick "of whom it is said, 'She graced domestic duties by the relief of study.'" [Catherine Sedgwick was a renowned American novelist of the first third of the nineteenth century, when American writers of neither gender were given much credit.]

Caroline Herschel, "Supplementing the cares of the household, with the gaze of the heavens." [She was a German astronomer acclaimed for discovering several comets.]

"Remember," said Harriet, "if you devote your time to study, you avoid all the irksomeness of this life, nor will you long for the approach of night being tired of the day, nor will you be a burden to yourselves."[487] The rigorous weekly study of world culture and the history of the human race required both reading assigned books on the topic and preparing papers for discussion. The Club soon launched into challenging yearlong study plans that spanned a decade.

Public Progress, Private Losses

This period from post-reconstruction to the end of the century was often looked upon as the flowering of the reform movement. All-women organizations were springing up in communities everywhere after the war and the spirit of reform did not end with the end of slavery. Women were growing in awareness of their political, economic, and social status and looking for reforms in religion and law. Woman's suffrage was a recognized goal by some, but the development of women's potential as individuals was also encouraged. Some argued for the separate sphere view that granted moral superiority to women and stressed woman's special responsibilities, while others challenged conservative thinking and advocated progressive views that insisted on equal rights as people and citizens under the law. So many women, so many ways of thinking. Once empowered during the Civil War, women became active on all fronts, a course that both strengthened and weakened their cause.

One new direction for women in Lansing that had been slowly growing was foreign missionary work by several denominations in the community. On a Saturday in March of 1867, Harriet Seymour, of the Presbyterian Church and an adventurer like her father James Seymour, left behind her position at the Female College and set sail from New York on Saturday, March 2, for Kharpont in Asiatic Turkey, where she would take charge of a Female Seminary. "It was a city of 150,000: it is situated 750 miles inland from Constantinople, in a southeasterly direction near the head of the Persian Gulf. The best wishes, and prayers, of numerous friends will follow Miss Seymour to her far off field of labor," said the local newspaper.[488]

Marian helped organize the Woman's Foreign Missionary Society of the Methodist Church in December of 1877, about eight years after the national organization was formed, and she became its first president. One of the founding principles of the Woman's Foreign Missionary Society was that women and girls around the world should be educated to be leaders within their countries to change the lives of women in general, as well as their families, and their societies. With total belief in the superiority of American education, medicine, and religion, the organization thought that what women were doing at home to improve their status needed to be spread beyond American shores. The local group decided to assist Gertrude Howe, once a member of their congregation, who had become a missionary to the "heathen Chinese," as they were called, because the Methodists felt women missionaries were needed to best help the women there. Gertrude Howe had attended the Lansing Female College and The University of Michigan. She became one to the best known Methodist missionaries. She matriculated January 1, 1873, as one of its first women students, along with Mary E. Baker, a very successful schoolteacher in Lansing and a clerk in the Auditor General's office.[489] Gertrude had been in China since 1872 and recruited her sister Dr. Delia Howe, a physician who graduated from the University of Michigan medical school, to work with her in China. One of the Foreign Missionary Society publications told of their work in establishing a boarding school in central China:

> The report of the official correspondent [of the Woman's Foreign Missionary Society] for the year 1879 said: "For nearly seven years the work of a female boarding-school has been carried on in Kiukiang with exceptional success. Our two faithful missionaries continued as heretofore until February, when Miss Howe was obliged to return to America to recruit her health. The school began with seven pupils, and a poor man of the literary class as teacher. Much difficulty was experienced in finding a native matron who could read, but after a month or more had elapsed a woman, with the very small Chinese feet and ladylike manner, engaged to come for a month, studying and reading; she has continued in the school up to the present time. This was Mrs. Tong, of whom a recent letter says, 'She is as faithful as ever, self possessed, dignified, gentle in her ways, with an unusual degree of tact in managing the school children.'
>
> "The year began with thirty-one pupils and the five orphans who have been adopted into the [Gertrude Howe] family; it closed with forty-seven scholars, and four who were yet too young to commence study." Besides this, the school has proved an effectual door to many of the women of Kiukiang... Desirous of improving every opportunity for good, Miss Howe, (who expects soon to return to her work in China,) has secured the services of her sister, Miss Delia Howe, who will sail with her to take charge of the work among these women...
>
> In addition to the care and labor of founding the boarding-school, and teaching and superintending its general interests, they erected a new building for school and home. This was completed in 1876.[490]

Her fellow missionaries sometimes disapproved of Howe because she declined to attend "Western only" resorts for vacations and preferred to save her money to help her adopted children by living as the Chinese did. When she and another Michigan missionary, Lucy Hoag, founded the Rulison Girls High School in 1873, she insisted that if girls were to attend,

The Lansing Woman's Club, CADL photo.

they must not have bound feet. When one of the first Chinese Methodist pastors asked her to help his daughter, Shi Meiyu, become a doctor, she agreed and arranged for Shi Meiyu and one of her own adopted daughters, Kang Cheng, to study English, Latin, and Western science in preparation. In 1892 they attended the University of Michigan with funds provided by state Woman's Foreign Missionary Society groups. After they returned to China, they eventually established a training school for nurses. When the Woman's Foreign Missionary Society was founded in 1869, the members felt their place in the church and the world granted them little freedom. Now they felt they could go to the ends of the earth.[491] Other women were also sensing change.

Change was reflected in the homes of the women of Lansing, in style, technology, and woman's role. Marian decorated her home with beautiful, elaborate, Victorian decor. Multi-patterned wallpapers of complimentary designs in purple, wine, and gold on both the walls and ceiling, presenting a dazzling dining room, entrance, and parlor to her many visitors. Women's organizations continued to grow, and conversation at the Turner house was often about the doings of the Methodist Church and the Woman's Christian Temperance Union, which continued to be a major force in the city.

The Michigan W. C. T. U. held its convention in May 1882 at Kalamazoo and Frances Willard, national president of the W. C. T. U., spoke. The following Sunday evening the Lansing Central Union brought Willard to Lansing as speaker, and all churches closed for her speech to a crowded mass meeting held at Buck's Opera House. The Union was lobbying for a law requiring that temperance education based on scientific knowledge be taught in public schools. An open-air meeting was held in August on juvenile education and during the summer months water barrels were placed in front of the stores with iced water for those who wished a drink. A year later Mary Hunt, of Detroit, who was now National Director of Scientific Temperance Instruction, spoke for the bill in Representative Hall and at Buck's Opera House. The state Prohibition Party convention was held on August 12, 1883. Members of the Central Union met with them and marched with the Prohibition Party to the opera house for their meeting.

In March of 1883, the Lansing Woman's Club met at the home of Frances Longyear to celebrate the tenth year of the club's formation. Since it was organized, 130 women had joined the club although active membership was at first limited to forty and then to sixty. They calculated they had held 420 sessions or the equivalent of 84 ten-hour days. Members were expected to devote at least thirty minutes a day in reading or study. Among the members of the first decade or so were a mix of generations that included both Lansing's pioneers and the next generation, such as Dr. Anna Ballard, Delia Rogers and her nephew's wife, Alice Seager, and Addie, Eva, and Marian Turner and their cousin Ida Longyear, niece of Frances Longyear. (Abby Turner, who was a young girl when this group began, had already turned her passion to music.)

Eliza Smith, Matilda Howard, and Irma Jones compiled a publication that reviewed their ten-year course of study since the club's founding; "any account of the club would be incomplete which failed to mention the modern and practical papers which have filled about one-half of our club-time." The group had studied developments on all fronts in the United States through "notes of travel" and considered the biographies of journalist, sociologist, feminist and philosopher Harriet Martineau; American educator and anti-suffragist, Catherine Beecher; novelist and sociologist of England, Charles Kingsley; and many others. They studied Guy Fawkes and the Gunpowder Plot in England. "To keep informed of the progress of industry and invention, we have had papers on many such topics as 'Bank Bills and Postal Cards,' 'American Pottery,' 'Wood-Carving,' and 'Oleomargarine'... But by far the larger number of our modern papers has aimed at the improvement of home and society, to learn the best methods of training and educating children, and to encourage public and private philanthropy. They have included practical hygiene, ventilation, and the discussion of questions of vital interest." They studied modern literature and maintained a strong interest in reforms of the day. Many members combined their interest in the Woman's Club with activism in other clubs such as the Woman's Christian Temperance Union, The Woman's Suffrage Association, and/or Industrial Aid Society. Their studies made them receptive to innovation and agents of change.[492]

In 1885 the group decided to build a club building which opened in 1890 in downtown Lansing at 118 W. Ottawa. It was the second privately owned woman's club building in the United States. Over the years the club built up a strong feeling of sisterhood, confidence, and, while striving to perfect their womanly role, they affirmed a belief in their own equality with men. They were well aware of how the experience had changed them: "It is altogether impossible to sum up the far-reaching results of work of this kind... we realize better than any others can the weakness and imperfection of our best work, we still rejoice in that which has come from it—was an ideal womanhood, not as a devotee of fashion, a household drudge or a literary pendant, but as the tender and loving housemother, the genial and courteous friend, the intelligent and self-poised teacher and companion of little children, the help-meet and equal of father, brother, or husband... In the joyful realization of such an ideal let us hope that our club may exist for many decades, till the glad bells of grander civilization [ring]."[493] Indeed, the Lansing Woman's Club has existed for many decades and meets to this day (but not in their original building). The 1890 Women's Club House, just east if the capitol on W. Ottawa Street, has a coffee shop on the first floor.

The growth of organizations such as this across the state built a growing understanding among women of the true status of woman. Later on, when various groups took up advocacy to improve the status of women and girls, these organization provided a foundation of support.

Home life, of course, did have a way of superseding one's interests outside the home, no matter how worthy the activity. Ten years after the death of his wife Harriet, Jesse Munroe came to live with Marian and his three grand-daughters, Adda, 24, Eva, 23, and Abby, 18, and over his remaining years, he also lived with his other daughters, Adella, Harriet, Betsey, and Eliza, who were all living in Lansing. His three sons were successful farmers on or near the family farm in Eagle. Having carried on for a decade on his own, the old Scotsman had the satisfaction of enjoying the hard-earned comforts of life with his family. He had become one of the most prosperous farmers in Clinton County. He had no enemies, for his daily life was marked by "strict integrity and that charity and love for all which springs spontaneously from a generous heart," said a Michigan Historical Society report of his death. He was widely known by all as "Uncle Jesse." He was 92 when he died of cancer in the dead of winter, December 29, 1883. The service was attended by the largest assembly of people ever gathered at a funeral in Clinton County. Harriet and Jesse's descendants numbered 92, of whom 86 were living, according to the book of Munroe genealogy in 1912.[494]

Not a month later, death came again to the Turner house, this time to take another Turner child. In 1884, Adda [Addie] Turner, the fourth daughter of James and Marian died. Her chronic painful disease, which may have had its onset while her father was still alive, is unidentified.

From *The Evening Telegraph* of January 30:
Died.

At ten o'clock this forenoon at the family residence, North Lansing, Addie Turner, aged 31 years.

Those few words record the passing away of one of the most beautiful spirits, who, for a time, abide the ills of earth. To all who know Addie Turner, eulogy of her character is needless. With mind naturally active and buoyant, it fell to her lot to undergo for nearly half her life the chastisement of pain. More as a benediction than a chastisement, though, it came, for through the weary years the beautiful character has shown itself only more and more beautiful, as the supreme moment approached, until the day we are permitted to think of her amid the great throng who have been made "perfect through suffering."

From *The Evening Telegraph* of February 1:
Laid to Rest.

The large circle of relatives and intimate friends who hold the memory of Miss Addie Turner dear, gathered at the family residence this afternoon to mingle the sympathetic tear and bid adieu to the last of earth of one whom to know was to love. Addie is the seventh member of this family who, one by one, have taken up their abode in the silent halls of death, and left the others to mourn their loss.

The casket lay in the north parlor and on it reposed a beautiful wreath and a large pillow of white primroses, on a bed of green with the word "Rest" in carnations. The sad exercises began with singing "Cast thy burden on the Lord" followed by the reading of the psalm "The Lord is my Shepherd" and prayer by Rev. Mr. Hamilton. A duet, "Whispering Hope," was followed by readings of scripture passages appropriate to the occasion by Rev. Mr. Valentine, with remarks of eulogy on the pure life, Christian graces and benediction of the memory of the departed.

A quartet – "He giveth His beloved sleep" - closed the exercises at the house, and sadly and slow the remains were borne to their last home in Mount Hope cemetery, there to await the morning of the resurrection.

About a year and a half later, Marian attended the thirteenth annual meeting of the Ingham County Pioneer Society at the Rayner Opera House in Mason. Four people in attendance had been in the county for 50 years, 45 had been there for 45 years. It was 49 years since Marian arrived in Clinton County. The long-anticipated guest was a Universalist minister who once attended the Lansing Female College. The reunion had by far the largest attendance ever. One hundred sixty pioneers from outside Mason had come to hear Rev. Augusta Chapin, whose family had come as pioneers to Ingham County when she was a girl. Rev. Chapin had been invited to speak several times but had always been unable to attend. Finally, on a beautiful day in June, she spoke for over an hour to a rapt audience. She told them that to know the future one must be able to judge from the principles established in the past, the laws in operation, the whole trend of nature, and the spirit of the times. However, she said, it is not easy to find out what the authentic history is.

The greatest name will perish from human history, the finest moment crumble into dust, and the time will come when our names will be lost and our places know us no more. Yet we shall survive in the memories of our friends as long as the remembrance will serve any good purpose, and then our work and thought and influence will mingle with the great ocean of human achievement, and the sum total of that will be something more, and something different from what it would have been without us...

It is also a sacred task to help preserve from oblivion the names of those who have gone before us, and to perpetuate the influence of the good they did. This is one of the chief reason for the existence of this pioneer society, to rescue from oblivion the names and heroic deeds of the early settlers of our county. This society, with others of similar purpose, is helping to make an authentic history.

Now is the time to correct the records and make them complete so that they may be of use hereafter. This county will not see the like again of this generation that is now passing away. There is no place now within the limits of the United States so wild and inaccessible as Ingham county was fifty years ago. The pioneers have penetrated every forest; their white covered wagons have been seen on every prairie: they have encamped at the foot of every mountain, on the banks of every river and the shores of every lake.

Then they bathed in dreamlike memories of pioneers in covered wagons, towering maples with trunks over five feet in diameter, and wolves howling in the night, as she spoke of her youth.[495]

Making it Difficult to Do Wrong

Marian knew Anna Ballard from the time she was a baby. Anna was born in 1848 not long after her parents had arrived to help settle the capital city. Anna went to school with two of Marian's children, Marian and Jim, and to Sunday school at the Methodist Church. Anna was an early beneficiary of the efforts to open higher education to women, attending the Michigan Female College herself. Her brother Henry also attended the college. Her father was active in the Republican party and was a class leader in their church with the elder James Turner. Mr. Ballard was a strong temperance advocate, some even said radical on the subject. Anna became a highly admired and respected doctor and joined the W. C. T. U. Here is her profile published in 1891 in *Portrait and Biographical Album Ingham & Livingston Counties*, a book that published biographical information for prominent people of the day but rarely included women:

> She is a woman of intellectual superiority, of pleasing presence and manners, yet of striking individuality. In the twelve years which she has devoted to her profession in this city she has earned an enviable reputation in the community and State and among the profession, as well as a profitable and extensive practice which calls her to all parts of the State for counsel among women. Her success in business has been such that at the death of her father the family made her their choice to administer the affairs of the estate...
>
> She opened an office as physician and surgeon in the central part of the city and with persistence won, and zealously maintained her position in the front rank of the profession in the city. She was one of the organizers of the Lansing Medical Society in 1882, at which time she was elected Secretary and was continued in the position for seven years, after which she was elected President, holding the chair for one year...Dr. Ballard has always taken an active part not only in all progressive movements relating to science and art but also in everything that promises to further

the advancement of womankind in every avenue of life. She identified herself with the work of the Lansing Industrial Aid Society in 1879 and for several years has been the First Vice-President and member of the Board of Trustees. She is associated in the Lansing Chapter of the Eastern Star. She is a promising member of the Lansing Woman's Club, an old literary society that has been a potent agent in the community for the elevation of literary tastes and in educating its members in business ventures, as it owns its building, a handsome edifice in the center of the city, erected in 1890, and in which property each member is a stockholder…

Dr. Ballard's church relations are with the Methodist Episcopal body, being a member of the Central Church of this city. Here too she has not hesitated to exert her influence in a progressive way, and with a logical paper took part in a public discussion on the admission of women to the Methodist General Conference.

The Young Woman's Christian Association finds in her an enthusiastic worker and liberal supporter, and with her religious tendencies she finds in this organization an ideal avenue for work of heart and brain. With the pen she is at home and is a fluent writer. The Transactions of the State Medical Society of 1886 contains a valuable paper presented by her to the society, recording original work and study. She is the author of some of the best literature circulated by the Woman's Christian Temperance Union. She takes the delight of an educated and cultivated woman in current literature, and being an advanced thinker with decision of character and opinions, but with modesty and deference of manner, she is an interesting conversationalist. Her life is characterized by simplicity and integrity, which with her earnestness of purpose is endearing her to a large circle of associates socially as well as professionally.[496]

Ballard was elected president of the Central Union in 1887 and served until 1900. In 1887, she also became State Superintendent of the Social Morality Department. The Woman's Christian Temperance Union was then working for laws to protect women and girls from male violence, for a law to raise the age of consent, and for a prohibition amendment to the constitution. On March 10, Dr. Ballard and Frances Willard spoke before the Legislature on the age of consent bill, establishing the age at which a girl is legally capable of consenting to sexual intercourse. Willard also went to Buck's Hall to speak on the prohibition bill. About half way through her address, someone cried "Fire." A panic was avoided when the pastor of the Free Will Baptist Church calmed everyone's fears over the hoax and Willard finished her address.

In April, the women served meals and helped at the polls when the amendment for prohibition was voted on. The amendment passed, but Michigan was under prohibition for only a few weeks because the liquor forces soon rallied and demanded a recount. The liquor interests in the state were ready to stoop to any level, and the recount was very suspect when it resulted in their favor. The amendment was lost.

About this time Buck's Opera House was sold and James Baird became its new owner. The policy of the Opera House was changed when Baird allowed obscene plays and displayed lewd pictures on the billboards. One picture of a nude woman was displayed on a billboard at the stairs that led to the Young Women's Christian Association rooms where the Lansing Central Union meetings were held. The women had him arrested and brought to trial with Mrs. H. C. Ward making the complaint. The women were allowed to choose their own jury and selected all church men. They expected the men to stand by them, but instead they returned a verdict of "No cause for action." When the women asked why they had done this, they replied, "Well you see, we are business men and Mr. Baird could hurt our business as he is interested in nearly every business in the city." James Baird confessed later that he was guilty and that he honored the women who wore the white ribbon and had the courage of their convictions.[497]

Stories about abuse of women and children, incest, and violence were not unknown to local newspapers, depending on the editors. The new editors—referring to themselves as Messrs. Thorp and Godfrey—of the new Republican newspaper in Lansing, the *State Republican*, could be very flippant and sometimes treated organizations such as the W. C. T. U. or the Knights of Labor (a union for workers founded in Philadelphia in 1869) in ways that were unfair. For the community they were vastly different from previous Republican editors who strived through their newspaper's policy to treat every group and everyone respectfully and with an eye to advancing understanding. A visit by Susan B. Anthony, which would have been reported in detail in previous newspapers, was given a few tart lines of humor at her expense: "Susan B. Anthony and another cold wave are advertised to strike Lansing simultaneously to-morrow. But then it cannot always be spring, you know."[498] Anthony and Francis Willard both came to Lansing to help lobby for a Municipal Suffrage bill taken up by the House and Senate, but the event was ignored. However, when they received a letter from Emily E. Riley that year, they noted, "The plaintive eloquence of a woman in trouble—she says it's lots worse than she has written, for she can't write what he has said." The capitalized phrases in the letter were undoubtedly the device of the editors:

MAN'S INHUMANITY TO MAN

MRS. RILEY SAYS THAT HER HUSBAND KICKED AND ABUSED HER WHEN SHE WAS SICK

A heart touching communication was brought to the STATE REPUBLICAN this morning by a slender woman, whose eyes appeared to be acquainted with weeping and whose tongue told with plaintive eloquence of "man's inhumanity to man." Her words are printed above her signature as follows:

DOMESTIC INFELICITY

Editor State Republican.

"Beneath the rule of men entirely great, the pen is mightier than the sword," but in all civilized countries, if a man strikes a defenseless woman he is immediately condemned by all respectable people. What then says public opinion if a man repeatedly strikes and even KICKS A SICK WOMAN, in the presence of their children, without other provocation than the fact that she is sick, so sick that it is utterly impossible for her to perform the usual household duties and, as she could prove had he not pleaded guilty, she had repeatedly tried to do, only to grow worse and suffer more pain. Then the gentle husband and father, to console and quiet her nerves, calls her vile and indecent names, threatens to kill the children, tells her she is bringing them up for immoral purposes, that she is teaching them all evil, that he works ten hours a day, and that he will do as he pleases. If she can't endure it, she can leave; that it is nobody's business what he does, as he supports himself; that if she can find a better place, she can "dig out;" that these things belong to him; that he can claim EVERY RAG OF CLOTHES she has by law, if he has a mind to; that she is only mad, because she can't be the vile object he insists in calling her—and all these things said with curses that fill every corner of the room.

He tells her continually that the children know more than she does, that she never did a thing decent, that he does all the house work, that she don't "KNOW ENOUGH TO DIE," tells her to go to _____ (a place of fire), as he can take care of himself, that women of ill repute are better than she, and that it is no worse for her to earn money than for him. No; the law does not tell a woman to endure this treatment, and I want it understood I took the only course there was left me to put a stop to it, and this man pleaded guilty to the charges, and, in consideration of his supporting his family his fine is only one dollar, one dollar to treat a woman this way for years. Verily justice is born crippled as well as blind! Yes; she is deformed and hunched backed, because this same man now says he will NOT EVEN FEED HIS CHILDREN, because he has his fine to pay. And my appeal to the law, for him to support his children, is of no avail! I am powerless! All efforts on my part fall to the ground! The more I do the more he condemns me! He says we must starve! I await the crisis with calm contentment!
EMILY E. RILEY [499]

There had been a number of notorious incidents of rape and sexual assault including a report of twenty or thirty young girls "ruined" by a lecherous teacher in Shelby County, Ohio, and other incidents closer to home. For almost a year the state newspapers covered the sensational story of a woman in Port Huron named Emma Moore. The "beautiful and unfortunate Emma" was charged with shooting and killing her divorced husband in March of 1886. Capt. Duncan McCaig was said to be drunk when he went to her father's house threatening and trying to gain an entrance. He was said to have previously persecuted her intolerably. It was a sensational trial that drew a great audience.. The story of McCraig's once happy home which by his habits of intemperance and brutal conduct was later made a place of torture for his wife and child caused all present, even the jury, to shed tears for the unhappy woman who was on trial for what seemed an accident. There was great satisfaction at her acquittal. [500]

In April a seven year old girl was assaulted by John Hill in Kalamazoo.[501] Messrs. Thorp and Godfrey editorialized after two attacks in June: "Brutal outrages upon little girls are becoming horribly frequent. And in nearly every case the same attempted excuse is made—that the man was drunk. The fiendish beast now in jail in Marquette for outraging a little baby girl of only four years of age says he was drunk. Another degraded brute was arrested in Kent county, on Sunday, charged with outraging a little girl in Ottawa county who is dangerously injured. He says he was drunk... Now as long ago as the time of ancient Greece, one of the wisest of her lawgivers, Pittacus, decreed he who should commit any violence when drunk should be punished double as much as though he were sober: because he was guilty of a double crime—the crime he did while drunk: and also because every man, when he drinks, intends to risk the consequences of his drinking. That was good common sense and good law two thousand years ago. If it were adopted and acted upon now, there would be less getting drunk, and less crime committed while drunk."[502]

Violence against women was never far from the minds of women. In response, the W. C. T. U. circulated a petition to urge legislators to raise the age of consent along with petitions for Municipal Suffrage and a new prohibition law. Many of the age of consent petitions used similar wording:

> The increasing and alarming frequency of assaults upon women, and the frightful indignities to which even little girls are subject, have become the shame of our boasted civilization. A study of the statutes has revealed their utter failure to meet the demand of that newly-awakened public sentiment which requires better legal protection for womanhood and girlhood.
>
> Therefore we, women of _city___, State of Michigan, do most earnestly appeal to you to enact such statues as shall provide for the adequate punishment of crimes against women and girls. We also urge that the age at which a girl can legally consent to her own ruin be raised at least to 18 years; and we call attention to the disgraceful fact that the protection of the person is not placed by our laws upon so high a plane as protection of the purse.[503]

For boys, there was no such thing as an age of consent protection. Boys were never "ruined," and it would be more than one hundred years before such things were brought to light. When men contributed to the ruin of women or girls by frequenting a brothel, they had little to fear, as this Ohio story carried in Michigan papers and dubbed "Worse than Ku Klux," shows:

"The 'Knights of the Switch' to the number of twenty, went into the house of a woman named Martin, in Jefferson township, Monday night and demanded admittance. Upon being refused they promptly battered down the door. Two men were inside who made some show of resistance, and several shots were exchanged without injury before the 'knights' overpowered the inmates. Mrs. Martin and her daughter Lily were then dragged from bed, stripped and tied to the door frame and whipped with hickory switches until they were unconscious and their bodies a shocking mass of bruised and bleeding flesh. The elder of the two women was the first to revive, and was told if she did not leave the county within twenty-four hours they would be killed. The men, who were married farmers living in the vicinity, were dismissed with the admonition that if again found in a house of ill-repute they would be killed. The knights then rode off."[504]

Representative Benjamin D. Ashton, M. D., from Grand Traverse District by no means defended such actions, nor did he defend the unfairness of damming the women and letting the men go free, but he thought the age of consent should be raised to thirteen, no more than fourteen. "These moral pest houses are all over the land, filled and overflowing with whom, by whom? Mostly the daughters of your neighbors and your friends. The result of one evil, unthoughtful, unguarded moment, only one, has doomed her to everlasting disgrace and infamy," he said. But a minute later he argued, "Now, gentlemen, the majority, and a very large majority, of all the sins are kept by this very class of abandoned women. The world to them is a mockery, Christian ministrations a myth, and charitable institutions a shadow. She turns her back upon the world, and cursing with revengeful oaths that echo from the lowest Hell, she forever severs herself from the moral world." Ashton concluded, "And now the women come, and with thousands of names to their petitions ask us to jeopardize the liberties and souls of our young men and older ones to the machinations of these kind of women, and ask us to offer bids in dollars for their ruin; yes more, the menace of imprisonment and disgrace."[505]

A petition from Manistee supported by both the W. C. T. U. and the Knights of Labor stated, "Fully realizing the injustice of our present laws relating to the rights and remedies of our unfortunate females, and its intolerable injustice in not meting out proper punishment to those by who their ruin is accomplished, we respectfully petition… raising the age of consent from the age of ten years to the age of eighteen." Those responsible for seeing that justice be done, however, advised the legislators in a different direction. They informed the legislators that at a meeting of their association, the prosecuting attorneys of the state "unanimously agreed that the statue in reference to rape be so amended that the 'age of consent' be fixed at fourteen."[506]

Those who supported the current age of consent law claimed young girls were capable of resisting the pressure put upon them for having sex and that they could fully realize the consequences of the situation and were empowered to control their situation. At issue was the continuation of the law enabling males to legally have sex with young girls, as young as age ten. Anna's speech on behalf of the W. C. T. U. was before the Judiciary Committee of the Michigan Legislature. This is the speech that so impressed one of the members of that august body that he had it printed and distributed in leaflet form:[507]

LEGAL PROTECTION FOR GIRLS,

A Plea by Dr. L. Anna Ballard, Lansing, Michigan, at the joint meeting of the Judiciary Committee of Michigan Legislature, 1887.

Gentlemen of the Senate and House of Representatives of the State of Michigan:

I come before you to-day representing the State Department for the Protection of Social Purity of the Woman's Christian Temperance Union. We are supported in the hearing of our petition for raising the age of consent to 18 years of age, by the highest moral interests of the State, by the highest educational interests of the State, and by the great home interests of the State.

Gentlemen, you may feel that we have been unduly importunate and distrustful of your action upon this bill. Let me say to you that we wish simply to assure you that the women of our State, as the women of every State in the nation, are intensely interested in this measure, and feel it their duty to use their influence to the uttermost to right this great wrong. Neither do I confine the interest upon this measure to the women, whom we have the honor to represent. All good and true men, we believe are equally as concerned in just legislation upon this question, and though we come petitioning and importuning we are confident that you gentlemen, as well as the majority of the honorable members of our Legislature, are not only willing but anxious that the law upon this question shall be adjusted upon a right basis.

We do not come as antagonists. We come as mothers, wives, sisters and daughters. We come to you as we go to our fathers and brothers, asking that our wishes and needs may be expressed and considered in those things in which our interests as well as yours, and yours equally as ours, are concerned, but over which you have exclusive power. We believe we are beings capable of intelligence and common sense, and I do not suppose any amount of ridicule would convince us that we are the sentimentalists we are reputed as being. We believe, also that equally with you we hold dear to us the good of our commonwealth, and of our race. The moral integrity of our country is alike sacred to us as to you, and we have no wish or intention to be one-sided in this or on any other subject under your consideration.

We believe it is our duty and our aim, as we trust it is yours, to so protect and hedge about the virtue and moral integrity of the people of our State that they may then more easily grow into virtuous men and women. Mr. Gladstone says, 'it is the provision of government to make it easy to do right and difficult to do wrong,' and when we ask that the age at which a girl can legally consent to her own ruin shall be placed at 18 years, we are asking that so far as law can effect it, you will make it more difficult than at present for licentious men to entice young girlhood from a path of virtue. We do not expect that all licentiousness can be expunged from our social fabric by means of legislation, but we do believe that crimes are lessened when there are adequate penalties for the violation of law relating to crimes. We believe there is less robbery because there is a penalty for stealing; and we believe there will be less licentiousness, there will be fewer girls enticed into lives of degradation if the law affixes a just penalty for such crimes.

When you remember the frequent outrages committed against defenseless girlhood, do you wonder that mothers want more stringent laws, laws by which the offender may in some degree be punished? It is a fact that there is seldom a girl who takes her first wayward step after 18 or 20 years of age. The ranks of that heart sickening procession of girlhood that has been ruined by persuasion, and is marching to that most infamous and relentless of all prisons, the brothel, is constantly being reinforced from the class of girls between the ages of 14 and 18 years.

Gentlemen, the mothers of this country have their eye upon the brothel. They regard it as an influence such as Washington Gladden characterizes as an unsocial force, a power that is menacing the happiness of the home life; and they are intently studying this problem: How best to "lend a hand" to the inmates of this institution and lead them to a respected and useful life, and also, how they may cut off the supply that fills it. They believe that the condition of civilization that tolerates such an institution is an unnatural, yes, and a monstrous one! The heart and brain of womanhood are peering out from the home nest to learn what influence is blighting the aspiration and the hopes of the home and nullifying its teaching among the boys. We enter this plea for this change in our laws as much to guard and hedge about the purity of the boys as to protect the girls from older offenders who under present statutes nearly always escape punishment. We have been taught that if women are not virtuous men will not be, but we have also learned another maxim, that if men are not virtuous women cannot be. If there is a laxity in the moral sentiment of one sex it will prey upon the other and drag it to its level.

We would aim both by home teaching and statute teaching to strengthen the moral sentiment of our people. We are told that the laws of a country reflect the opinions and feelings of the people. If this be so, if the law teaches that "the virtue of a girl is her own affair only, a fair prey to anyone who can win it, a treasure to be guarded at her peril, and its loss entailing a penalty upon her alone," if the law teaches this by laying the responsibility of her ruin upon her consent during her minority, then that sentiment will prevail among men and boys. It is this widespread sentiment that mothers are seeking to change and thus protect both sons and daughters alike.

The law reflects the sentiment of the people in regard to its sacredness of property. Is the property of a girl during her minority more sacred to the State than her person? Is wealth of more value to the State than virtue? Which should be the best guarded to secure the highest good of the race? A father dies and leaves to his daughter of 14 years a small property. Does the State presume that she is capable of taking care of that property and leave her to use it as her own feelings and judgments dictate. Not at all! It appoints a guardian, and it hedges about that guardian by penalties for misuse of this property. Do you suppose that fewer guardians misappropriate the moneys in their hands because of such laws? Why does the State thus hedge about and protect the property of your daughters? Because it holds that she is not capable of fully realizing consequences or of resisting influences, and therefore by its penalties it protects the guardian from temptation as well as the property from misuse. If your girl of 14 is not capable of realizing the consequences of the misuse of her property, is she capable of realizing the consequences of the misuse of her person? and is she capable of resisting unwise influences that may play upon her immature emotions? If it is wisdom to protect her property during what it pleases to call her minority, is it not greater wisdom to protect her virtue, by laying penalties upon the one who violates it?

But we will suppose your daughter is between 14 and 18 years of age. She is coming in contact with the outside world. She knows nothing of herself. The boy of 16 is far more wise in knowledge of himself and of the ways of the world than the girl of the same age. She is, however, confident in her trust in herself. She is equally trustful of others, and believes every fair word. Her physical organization is passing through that delicate process of development in which new energies and emotions are awaking. She knows not her power and is not liable to use it, but she is very susceptible of influence. There is much talk of fixing the "age of consent" at 14 years, because young people come into their development at this age. What a mistake. Rather the development begins then. No stage of physical development is abrupt. It is a gradual unfolding, and only in its maturity is it fully capable of discharging its functions. Any influence that forces development hastens decay. Has the State no responsibility in the development of her young people? We believe it should be the aim of the State to aid the home influence by protecting the young people until they develop into the strength and beauty of true manhood and womanhood.

This law upon the "age of consent" has rested unmolested upon the statute books of this State for fifty years. Three years ago Dr. DeCasta, rector of St. John's church, N.Y., sought to permeate the sentiment of public opinion with the belief that a change was needed for the sake of the morality of youths, as well as for protection for girls. About two months ago we circulated these petitions, asking that this Legislature should make the change to 18 years. We have had both the highest clerical and legal authority for this step. This bill that was introduced into the Senate on Friday last was framed by Hon. C. I. Walker, and in the hands of the judiciary committee of that body, or of the gentleman who introduced the bill, is a letter from Judge Walker endorsing this change. We have also the petition by signature of about 10,000 of the best men and women of our State. We who are equally interested with you in this measure do not understand the necessity for hasty action upon it. The public, and even the members of this Legislature, are just waking up to an understanding of it.[508]

Gentlemen of the judiciary committee, we would respectfully ask that you will amend the bill now in the House committee, making it read 18 years, and that both the judiciary committees of the Senate and of the House will recommend to your respective bodies that the law be so changed as to raise the age of consent to 18 years. We also ask that you do not hasten action upon this measure, but that you give opportunity for intelligent consideration of it by the members of the Legislature.

Queen Victoria's Prime Minister, William Gladstone, had said that it is the duty of government to make it difficult for people to do wrong, easy to do right, but this was not entirely the case in Michigan. Despite this eloquent plea and the logic of the women's arguments, the men of the Legislature only raised the age to 14. The *State Republican* later remarked, "Part of the sentence inflicted in Toronto upon a wretch who assaulted a girl of 12 years was fifty lashes upon the bare back. That sort of punishment for that sort of crime would be a reform in Michigan."[509] It wasn't until 1895 that the Legislature could again be pressured to raise the age of consent, or age of protection, as it was sometimes called. That year over 10,000 persons petitioned for raising the age to 18. The petitions were brought to the Legislature and women speakers and supporters from the Woman's Christian Temperance Union, the Equal Suffrage Association, and the Woman's Clubs came to Lansing to show their support. The legislation was passed in the House at age 18 but was amended in the Senate to age 17. After supporters went home, the bill was reconsidered the next day, and both houses amended the legislation to 16 years. The penalty was life imprisonment or for *any* such period as the court shall direct; however, to the dismay of many, no minimum penalty was stated. It wasn't until the year 2000 that the federal Trafficking Victims Protection Act covering labor trafficking and sexual trafficking was designed to protect all minors, girls and boys, 18 and under and provide a penalty of forty years for these particular forms of exploitation and slavery.

With much energy, the women's movement was underway. When the Woman's Christian Temperance Union was formed, it was called a crusade, an uprising, a revolt. It was just a segment of the wave of work undertaken by women in all parts of the country and all walks of life to gain the vote, help the poor and abused at home and in other countries, free themselves from violence and the burdens of unjust laws, and educate themselves. Just as these themes were interwoven into the work of any single organization, they were woven into the being of those individuals who joined these groups and enriched their lives in an ever-widening sphere.

Chapter 11

Jim in the Gilded Age

James Munroe Turner was once introduced to newspaper readers as "The humble lad who became a clerk, landlooker, real estate dealer, railroad builder, miner, and farmer and will be governor."[510] Just as the rise of the women's movement in the Victorian Era is part of the story of the second generation of pioneers in the capital, so, too, is the story of how Jim mastered great enterprises following his father's death. This was an expansive period of rapid growth and economic development in the state and nation, a Post-Reconstruction period dubbed the Gilded Age by Mark Twain who satirized the ostentatiousness, political corruption, and greed of the wealthy. Journalists said of Jim in 1890, "The story of his life and marked business successes reads almost like a romance, but through it all the sturdy worth and force of character which weaves valuable history from the commonplace web and woof of everyday life, are the prevailing characteristics. His successes are only those which are possible to all the young men of America who are true to themselves and the opportunities which are from time to time placed within their grasp"[511]

Jim grew up to be much like his father, a giant of a man, and nicknamed Jim as his father had been. His work as a clerk in his Uncle Daniel's general store for two years, with stock encompassing everything from silks and satins to salt pork and washtubs, helped prepare him. "This service," he recalled 40 years later, "was the best business schooling that I ever received. It taught me a great deal about the relative values of a wide variety of articles."[512] He was different from his father's circle—and many of his friends. He did not belong to the Masons or any other secret societies or fraternal organizations. His experience in the land office of the Jackson, Lansing, and Saginaw Railroad, where he was in charge of field notes and surveys, allowed him to closely observe his father as land commissioner for the railroad and at the same time, a leader of many other enterprises. When his father embarked on the actual building of the Jackson, Lansing, and Saginaw Railroad and the Ionia and Lansing railroads, young Jim was given charge of the construction of the latter railroad.[513]

John M. Longyear wrote a remembrance of Jim many years later that further illuminates his character:

James M. Turner portrait, CADL.

> Jim, as I have always called him, was my cousin. His mother and mine were sisters. I was born eight days before he was. We lived in the same town and were very intimate until I went to the Upper Peninsula in 1873. He was a thoughtful, jolly, resourceful boy and always companionable. His judgment on business matters was remarkable. My father once said of him that he never was a boy, that he always thought like a man. He was one of ten children, of which six grew to maturity though only three are now living. During vacations we were almost constantly together—I would spend days at his house and he would spend days at mine. Often without any intermission between the visits. In his 19th year his father died. Jim had already acted as paymaster on the Ionia and Lansing R. R. which his father built, and he died just in time to lose the results of his labors. Jim immediately engaged in active business and was very successful. He was always something of a "plunger," and fond of taking big chances in a business deal. The chances he usually turned to his advantage.[514]

In 1871, the year of the great forest fire, Jim was just 21 and beginning his life in business and public affairs. Already his generation of Turners, Smiths, Cases and Longyears were working together. Jim and his partner Dwight Smith were involved in real estate. They bought land in the local area, cleared the timber, sold it locally, or kept it to put in a crop of wheat or seed for meadow pasture. In their general land business, Dwight had charge of the office while Jim did landlooking and surveying, traveling by foot with an 80 pound backpack and a compass in hand in the Tawas area of Iosco County and later throughout northern Michigan. "To give you an idea of the privation of those land looking times," Jim once reminisced in an interview, "I remember coming out of the woods on the shore of Huron bay one bleak winter day with a fellow who was looking land with me. We discovered an old vessel that had been wrecked and driven on the beach, where it was frozen in as tight as a new barrel. We clambered, stiff with the cold, into the old hulk for shelter and found a galley stove. We built a fire, cooked supper and stayed there that night. Well, I cannot remember a time in my life before that day or since, when I so thoroughly enjoyed myself and felt so comfortably as I did that dreadful day within the shelter of that old wreck."[515]

The partners employed more landlookers, including John M. Longyear, and worked in the Upper Peninsula. Another son of a pioneer that they worked with was William Butler whose father was Charles W. Butler, a friend of their fathers and active in the real estate business in the Lansing area and northern Michigan since 1848.[516] Eventually it was Charles and Jim who formed a partnership in the Upper Peninsula. Jim and John took a contract with the state in 1872 to examine all vacant government lands in the northern counties and Upper Peninsula so that the state could provide compensatory school land where needed. Roughly square townships of 36 sections, 640 acres each, had been surveyed by the federal government during the Northwest Territory period and although section 16 of each township was set aside by the state to benefit education, the benefit was not the same for all townships. This was because not all the acreage of every section 16 was equally valuable if it had lakes, rivers, marshes, or other unusable topographical features. It was decided that once the lost acreage was identified, the state would select better agricultural and hardwood timbered acres from vacant land to make up for it. Of course the Great Fire required adjusting this plan, but land evaluations were greatly needed. This was a reform that John W. Longyear long supported both at the Constitutional Convention of 1867 and as a Congressman. And so it was that the state contracted with the sons of Lansing's pioneers to actually look at the lands.

In the fall, Jim and John went to Cheboygan County and "looked" timberlands around Mullet Lake. In 1873 John headed for the Upper Peninsula. It was in this capacity that they accumulated a vast fund of information and expertise regarding northern Michigan and its great natural resources. This set both cousins on a path that would lead them to great success in land sales, lumbering, and mining. John became an engineer and in time became a millionaire operating his own iron mine, the Great Norrie, starting in 1885. He took part in the development of the Gogebic, the Menominee, and the Mesabi iron ranges. He lent his expertise in later years to the development of coal regions in arctic Norway.[517] He acquired a reputation for many of the same things as Jim: honesty, kindness, generosity.[518]

Julian Case was about six year older than his two cousins. He came to the Upper Peninsula after his Lansing mercantile business which he had purchased from his father had failed during the depression of 1873. The stringent economic conditions forced him into bankruptcy in 1874. According to John Longyear, "He worked at various things until in November 1879 he and James M. Turner met in Chicago, at which time Case was out of employment and discouraged. He afterwards told me that if it had not been such a cowardly thing to do, to leave his wife and three children, he would have 'made a hole in the water.' As a result of this meeting Turner gave a letter to me, gave him a railroad ticket to Marquette, told him to go into my office, hang up his hat, and go to work whether I paid him or not. In the letter to me Turner said Case must have help, and that if I could not find profitable work enough for him to do, to set him at something to keep him busy and draw on him for living wages. I found profitable work for Case to do after he appeared at my office in December and was never obliged to call on Turner for money with which to pay him."[519]

After a year John and Julian made an arrangement for Julian to work at land deals as an outside man for the business and soon all three cousins were working together. John thought Julian a tremendous worker and a man of excellent ability. Julian found people who furnished money to buy tracts ranging from 80 acres up to 32,000 acres. On the larger tracts he was assisted by Jim and his Upper Peninsula land partner, Charles W. Butler. They split the profits.[520]

Jim's cousin Frank Turner was doing a two-year stint as principal in Essexville, but the U. P. bug got him, and he came up in August of 1883 by train to take a principalship at L'Anse in Baraga County, not far from Arvon, before beginning his medical training.[521] According to Frank, it was land-looking that took a toll on Jim's health. Although Jim was big and strong, he contracted rheumatism and pericarditis, a heart complication causing chest pains, fatigue, and coughing. Such illness was not an unusual occurrence among landlookers, said Frank. It eventually became necessary to send Jim to New York for convalescence at Clifton Springs Sanitarium. It was famed for the mineral waters of its sulfur springs and was a place where his cousins Amos Turner[522] and John Longyear[523] had each gone in search of better health. As fortune would have it, the family of Miss Sophie Scott's mother, Esther Kennedy Scott, lived in Clifton Springs. How Jim and Sophie met we do not know, but in 1876 they were happily married.

Sophie's father Ira Scott was a prominent Chicago attorney and Master of the Chancery of the Superior Court of Illinois for more than twenty-five years. The Scotts' home and Ira's offices had been destroyed by the Chicago Fire of 1871. In September of 1880, Jim's cousin Howard Longyear, now a Detroit physician, married Sophie's sister Abbie.[524] With both daughters in Michigan, Ira and Esther moved to Lansing in 1880, leaving an impressive mansion they had built near Lake Shore Drive after the fire and settling at 609 North Washington Avenue, not far from Sophie and Jim and across the Grand River from Marian's home on the bank above.[525]

It was said that the tender and affectionate side of Jim's character was always manifest in his relations with his family. "This," Jim was heard to say of the day he married, "was the most important event of my life. I have been a happy man ever since that eventful day. To my wife's influence and encouragement I owe a large measure of what success I may have achieved."[526] Later one journalist stated, "The well-mated couple are lovers still, and one does not need to be long in their society to discover that they will so remain to the end."[527] The same year Jim married Sophie, he was elected to the Legislature, one of the last sessions to be held in the old capitol building on Washington Street. Here he served on the Railroad Committee and the Rules and Joint Rules Committee where he won recognition for his thoughtfulness. When urged to run again, however, he stoutly professed that one term in office should be enough for anyone.

Their son James came along in 1878 and Scott in 1880. To his two sons he was a companion as well as a father. "The sight of Mr. Turner and his sons driving away to the farm with dog and gun for a day's hunting was familiar to many of the citizens, and it was at his fireside, surrounded by his family and friends, that the great large-hearted man was at his best," said a local newspaper.[528]

Family friend Francis Farrand, whose father Hart Farrand was a partner with Jim in the condensed milk business, remembered her preschool days when she and her sister played with the Turner boys: "Harriet and I were sometimes invited down to the Turners to spend the day with Scott and James. It was very exciting for we had no boys to play with as there were none in the neighborhood at the time of whom mother approved. Mrs. Turner would come for us with the coachman and carriage. The boys had ivory jack straws with which we played and Scott always won because the nurse would steady his hand. Then Mr. and Mrs. Turner with the boys would come with the three-seated carriage and we would go for picnics into the country or to Grand Ledge where we rented boats and went to see the high rocks. This was all before kindergarten days."[529] Francis later married Arthur Dodge, nephew of Frank and Abby. She became a famous artist with paintings, lithographs, and etchings in the Smithsonian and museums in numerous states—including exquisite works at the Turner-Dodge House and the Michigan Women's Historical Center and Hall of Fame in Lansing.

Years later Scott Turner recalled those days for a publication about modern American engineers by science writer Edna Yost: "At seven, his father took him inside a mine for the first time. On the walls of the Turner home in Lansing were cabinets filled with minerals to which Scott's father occasionally added new specimens. His remarks, as they examined minerals, often included, 'Now when you study mineralogy, son ...' or 'When you take up the study of metallurgy, you will discover that ...' So Scott never put much thought upon what he was going to do when he was grown. He moved naturally along toward mining engineering... At eight, he had another experience which left its imprint for life. He was presented with his first man-sized shotgun. Partridge, duck and rabbit were plentiful around Lansing. (They were good food on the family table too.) Summers in Michigan's Northern Peninsula brought new hunting and fishing experiences. Scott killed his first deer when he was thirteen."[530] As the boys reached their teens, Jim took time to read newspapers with the boys, such as the *Mining Journal*, the *State Republican*, and the *Detroit Tribune*.

It was said of their home, "There is an air so common-place that the most unsophisticated country lad would feel at home. Mr. and Mrs. Turner are the most pleasant common-place people imaginable, and if there was ever a gentleman and lady to whom the people could go for sympathy, council, and aid or friendship, they are Mr. and Mrs. James M. Turner, of Lansing."[531] However, they were far from commonplace, if "ordinary" were taken to be the meaning of the word.

Fighting the Grand Trunk

"Next to the war, the American people saw one of the greatest games afoot on this continent that has ever been enacted here, in the years when the railroad reached Lansing from the southwest and another from the northeast was built into Flint about the same time. This big game, which went its frenzied limit, in say from '69 to '80, was riding for a tremendous fall in 1871. It was in '73 that came 'Black Friday' and all the engulfing panic of that year. But the Vanderbilts and the Goulds rode out the storm. So did the English capital interest backing the Grand Trunk," wrote Glen K. Simpson, a railroad historian of the 1920s. He knew Jim Turner had a major role when he jumped into the game, but Simpson could not figure out what it was: "The more one hears of the fragmentary details, the more one is convinced there is a good story underneath it all."[532] And so there is.

For some years the newspapers covered the "frenzy" as the fate of land grant railroads in other states fell to the railroad giants' will, and Michigan changed the state constitution to try to protect its citizens from the big multi-state corporations. Stephen D. Bingham, editor of the *Lansing Republican*, seemed to have a deep and prescient understanding of these mighty financial forces and did his best to give warning. In 1871, he said the Michigan Supreme Court's ruling that railroads are private roads, not public transportation, prevented municipalities from taxing railroad corporations for use of the very railroads the communities had built. The ruling allowed the railroad corporations, as "public highways" in the matter of business, to "tax" the producers and manufacturers who were their customers by charging them double the freight rates necessary. Bingham also complained that railroad corporations falsely valued their stock. They watered their stock (as a dishonest farmer might water his stock before it is weighed in order to get a higher price) by not showing capital expenses in their statement of worth. This increased the profits of their stockholders at the expense of their customers.

Bingham wrote: "Our ablest political writers and essayists have for years discerned the coming conflict between railroad monopolies and the people. In the contests that arise between the various railroad corporations the weak uniformly 'go to the wall,' and are swallowed up by those having the largest capital." He lamented that while the attention of the people of the country had been called to the great struggle between the Erie and Central railroads of New York and the railroad barons' war that raged between Drew, Vanderbilt, Fisk, and Gould, there was a growing threat in Michigan. He said, "The people of Michigan, by the late constitutional amendments adopted in relation to railroads, wisely sought to check the power of great monopolies like the Michigan Central and Southern roads… [It is] now a part of the Constitution of the State… that parallel lines shall in no case be consolidated, and that no road shall consolidated without sixty days' notice being previously given to each and every stockholder in said road."[533]

But Bingham knew it would just be a matter of time before Lansing's railroads were swallowed up if something were not done. "The danger of these amendments becoming a dead letter lies in the fact that a large majority of those who subscribe for the building of railroads do it expecting that the stock thus taken and paid for will be to them individually worthless. The money thus raised is absorbed by the grading of roads now building. The capitalists controlling the great lines running East and West through the State contribute the money to furnish the rails and rolling stock for these lines."[534]

Monopolies have two objects in view, Bingham said. "First, to obtain feeders to swell the enormous business which they now control, and, second, to jealously guard against rival corporations controlling the freight and passenger business which they desire to make subsidiary to their own interests. Hence, when a new company is organized and has graded its line, and procured by the aid of these great monopolies its iron and rolling stock, it is glad to surrender its franchises and corporate rights to either of these monster corporations who will provide for the floating debt, and take the elephant off their hands."[535]

Powers that corporations could not get through laws voted upon by the citizens of the country were obtained by cadres of attorneys filing numerous law suits before obliging judges. Growing corporations spread into many states, while each state was left to cope with the financial power of the corporations alone because they could not regulate interstate commerce. Many foresaw the dangers of losing public control of transportation to corporations but were powerless to do what was needed to stop the process. Bingham saw the conflict between the public and corporations as the most important issue of the coming decade: "And the man or men who have courage to fearlessly grapple with this great evil which threatens to absorb the political and financial power of the State and nation will find rallying to their support the great body of the people. This of all other questions will be the issue ten years from the present time. And with our best men in the legislative halls it is a matter of surprise, and we may say wonder, that the power of corporations has not been checked long before this. Here must be a stop put to the consolidations of railroads which destroy the competition necessary to business success and growth of wealth in the interior," Bingham warned. "This question must be met at the threshold, and only such men elected to enact and enforce the laws as are not interested in, and cannot be controlled by the moneyed power of these great railroad corporations, the fungus growth of the nineteenth century."[536]

Nothing could touch the moneyed power of the Vanderbilts; it was almost beyond imagination. According to the calculations of his biographer, T. J. Stiles, when Cornelius Vanderbilt died in 1877 his estate was estimated to be worth the equivalent of about ten percent of the national economy.[537] He was the first of the corporate tycoons; however, throughout Post-Reconstruction and the Gilded Age, the ranks of the super wealthy were growing, while the ordinary citizen was being left behind. Cornelius Vanderbilt preserved his empire by leaving most of his estate to just one son, William H. Vanderbilt, instead of dividing it equally among his eleven children. William and his sons doubled the estate in just a few years through tactics even his father had shied away from, tactics that were increasingly emulated by the robber barons and corporate banditti of the age. As great power was ever more concentrated in the private hands of a few oligarchs, and "fungus" monopolies squeezed out both private and public competition, every person and every region in America was affected, including the people of Lansing.[538]

Bingham was proven right; it was only a matter of time before the patchwork of linked local railroads in Michigan became a target of the Vanderbilts. They wanted a trunk line of their own from their railroad lines in Chicago to the Canadian railroad systems in the east that linked to the New York Central and the east coast tidewater. Cornelius respected James F. Joy, renowned as a great legal mind and president of the Michigan Central, by now a formidable monopoly, but was content to cooperate with Joy. His son William did not leave things as they stood. The efforts of the next generation of Vanderbilts to expand their monopoly across Mid-Michigan and southern Canada increased after the death of Cornelius. They were in competition for this route with the Grand Trunk Railroad, the Canadian railroad owned and financed in London and headed by Joseph Hickson and Henry Tyler.

In a speech to the Pioneer Society in 1893, James Joy told the story of how the Michigan Central officials initiated the Great Western Railroad Company from Windsor to Niagara Falls because there was no road through Canada. "The travel and business was across Lake Erie on magnificent steamers, constituting the Michigan Central line between Detroit and Buffalo. A splendid line of boats, and constituting a most pleasant as well as magnificent mode and route for both pleasure and business... They enlisted with them the New York Central Company [Vanderbilt], and started into life the interest of Canada all along the line of the proposed road, and at Detroit. By the united strength of all, the required life was given to the enterprise, and the road was built, though with immense difficulty and effort. It was the first road built in Canada. It was injured by the alliance of the Michigan Central with the Canada Southern, and finally fell into the control of the Grand Trunk, of which system it is now a part, and is known only as Grand Trunk."[539]

Lansing was left out of this east-west route. It was Jim who organized the Chicago and Northeastern Railroad Company in 1874 and built the line from Lansing to Flint. When completed it was 53 miles long, had 10 stations, 19 wooded bridges, and 110 employees. It cost $2,250,000—$1,000,000 raised in stocks and $1,250,000 raised in bonds that were sold to the same investors. Jim was the majority stockholder and served as the president and general superintendent of the line through the depression years which meant taking on debt.[540] Establishing a northern route from Port Huron to Chicago that passed through Lansing was a long-time dream of the community. But if any local railroad got caught between William H. Vanderbilt and Jacob Hickson, toes were going to get stepped on.

William L. Bancroft, a railroad developer from Port Huron, subscribed to stock at the formation of Jim's Chicago and Northeastern Railroad because it would connect his two lines, which were on each end of the proposed Chicago and Northwestern railroad route. However, by the time the Chicago and Northeastern was completed, Bancroft was in debt and disposed of a large amount of his stocks and bonds to what was known as the "Flint Pool" of investors and to two other investors from Port Huron.[541] Once the Flint to Lansing link was completed, Bancroft began to run trains of Grand Trunk cars from Port Huron to Chicago. He paid to use the Chicago and Northeastern between his two lines and another company to get into Chicago. At the same time, Bancroft was maneuvering to get the Chicago and Northeastern sold to the Grand Trunk Railway.[542] By what authority is unclear.

According to Frank Turner, short for funds, Jim went to New York, forced his way into the presence of the Vanderbilts through sheer personality and succeeded in interesting them and other eastern capitalists in the enterprise. This was the stepping-stone to his future and assured his success. It was his delight in later years to recount his interview with the elder Vanderbilt and his refusal to be bluffed by anything which the millionaire might say.[543] Eastern capitalists had made money during the war and were eager to invest. "Many times after that first interview did Mr. Turner succeed in securing the attention and co-operation of these money kings of the east in his various big enterprises. The subsequent sale of his railroad to the Grand Trunk people also formed interesting state history," reported a local newspaper, but it didn't say what that interesting history was.[544]

On January 28, 1878, Jim, acting for himself, the Flint Pool, and others who constituted a majority ownership of the stocks and bonds, sold their interest in the Chicago and Northeastern Railroad Company to William H. Vanderbilt. The sale represented 5,525 shares (55.25 percent) of the capital stock of $1,000,000 at $100 per share and 720 first mortgage bonds at $555 each. Jim still owned 290 of the bonds and other stockholders such as the Cleveland Iron Company of Ohio also owned stocks and bonds that were not part of the transaction. From then on Vanderbilt was president and controlled the Chicago and Northeastern, with Jim managing the railroad in Vanderbilt's interest. A friend of John Longyear's recalled that Jim wanted to keep the Chicago and Northeastern out of the hands of the Grand Trunk, and the two cousins, still in their twenties, often discussed the matter. "On one occasion he gave at length with great particularity the 'inside' story of the struggle between James Turner of Lansing, a relative of his, and the Grand Trunk Railroad for the control of the line which Turner had built between Lansing and Flint. Unknown to the Grand Trunk, Turner had effected a junction of interest with the Vanderbilts and this gave him success."[545] However, the sale of the majority control to Vanderbilt turned out to be only a short-lived victory.

At this time other takeovers were happening as part of Vanderbilt's grand plan. The previous year the Michigan Central Railroad, managed by James

Joy and New York financier Samuel Sloan, had survived an attempted board takeover by Vanderbilt and Russell Sage. Although Joy and Sloan had been working with the Vanderbilts' lines for some years, they did not look forward to a closer relationship. The Michigan Central Railroad superintendent, H. E. Sargent, told Joy back in May of 1874, when they observed William Vanderbilt taking control of two other railroads' boards, that he found Vanderbilt ambitious, headstrong, and, to some extent, unreliable and unfair.[546] Nevertheless, Joy lost control of his own board on the Vanderbilts' second try. Six of the nine Michigan Central board members were replaced.

In the meantime, the Jackson, Lansing, and Saginaw Railroad was also falling under Vanderbilt control. The April 1878 annual report indicated the corporation was leasing the Jackson, Lansing, and Saginaw Railroad (under an arrangement made earlier by Joy, after Hiram Smith left its board) and working to gain control of it by buying up its bonds and taking its property in payment for services.[547] By December of the same year Sloan, too, was out. William Vanderbilt took over as Michigan Central's president, and his new Eastern board of directors included two of his sons. They immediately instituted the Vanderbilts' typical takeover strategies of cutting costs and reducing competition, standard practice for a corporate monopoly. In the next report the new president said, "Much careful attention has been given to the alliances and connections of the company, with a view to prevent unnecessary rivalry… and no small improvement in that direction has been effected."[548]

The *Boston Journal* said in September of 1878, "We expressed the opinion at the time Vanderbilt secured the control of the Michigan Central Railroad and the link from Flint to Lansing in the Grand Trunk's independent Chicago connection from Port Huron, that his victory would prove a barren one, inasmuch as it would be impossible for Vanderbilt to control for any length of time the Grand Trunk's Chicago connections. That the opinion was a sound one is verified by the facts as they now exist. We learn from one of our Western exchanges that the Grand Trunk is moving actively to secure connections independent of Vanderbilt's control."[549] Joseph Hickson's plan entailed purchasing the lines at each end of what was now Vanderbilts' Chicago and Northeastern road (Bancroft's two Northwestern lines that were bankrupted and in receivership were indeed sold to the Grand Trunk at auction) and threatening to build a parallel line in the middle. These tactics enabled Hickson to force Vanderbilt to sell the Chicago and Northeastern to the Grand Trunk in 1879.[550]

Jim later confirmed that William Vanderbilt purchased the Chicago and Northeastern to prevent its use as part of a Grand Trunk through-line, which would have competed with Vanderbilt's Michigan Central line. Jim said it was under Vanderbilt's direction that through-traffic business was discouraged, and the Grand Trunk made no profit.[551] Vanderbilt, with the assistance of Jim, acquired about seven-tenths of all stock of the Chicago Northeastern and was also acquiring more bonds because their coupons required the railroad to pay seven percent interest payments and they were falling due. He was concerned about paying all coupons that came due on bonds he didn't own to make sure none were defaulted upon and to prevent any chance of a declaration of bankruptcy and control by an outside receiver. In fact, in 1879 he paid out $84,000 in interest payments. In May of 1879, Vanderbilt asked Jim to resign a month before the end of his contract because, under pressure, Vanderbilt was now ready to make the sale to Hickson and the Grand Trunk in August.[552]

Jim left the employ of the Chicago and Northeastern after less than two years under Vanderbilt. He did not stop the monopolies' growth, but at least his efforts had helped assure that the northern route from Port Huron to Chicago went through Lansing and did not bypass it. He had gained the lifelong friendship of James Joy, Christian Buhl, and Henry P. Baldwin of the Michigan Central and the goodwill of William H. Vanderbilt and his New York financier friends. On the other hand, he gained the undying animosity of Joseph Hickson and the Grand Trunk Railroad. It was not until 1887 that Congress passed an Interstate Commerce Act to regulate railroad monopolies, the first federal law to regulate private industry. It was too little, too late for Michigan.

There is one more aspect to this story. Perhaps it fits in where Jim said that "under Vanderbilt's direction through-traffic business was discouraged." It was not a part of the story that was widely known at the time. Many years later Jim's cousin John wrote what he remembered of the Chicago and Northeastern business in a private manuscript for his family:

> He built it on some kind of understanding with the managers of the Grand Trunk Ry., which at that time was trying to get into Chicago through some connecting lines, which was afterwards accomplished by the consolidation of several small roads from Port Huron, Michigan, and the Chicago and Northwestern [He means Northeastern.] was one of the roads. Jim and two or three of his friends loaded themselves very heavily with debt and built the road. The Grand Trunk people learning that they were financially embarrassed drew back from the deal and it was reported to Turner that Hickson, manager of the Grand Trunk, had been heard to remark that Turner was so loaded that he would soon go to pieces and they could pick up the pieces cheaper than to buy the road. Turner had a consultation with some friends and attorneys and they saw no help for him. He remarked that Hickson thought he was sitting on a country boy, but that he would find he was sitting on a volcano.
>
> He went to Detroit and had a consultation with his father's old friend, James F. Joy, president of the Michigan Central Road. Joy said he could not help him but that he could get Turner and interview with someone who could, and he arranged an interview between Turner and William H. Vanderbilt, at that time at the head of the N. Y. Central system. Turner showed Vanderbilt that he controlled these 40 miles of road absolutely and he had the stock and bonds with him. As the Grand

Trunk was a rival road Vanderbilt saw an opportunity for a business deal and asked Turner what he wanted. Turner said that, in consideration of the money to take care of the debts and $100,000.00 for himself and his friends, he would turn the road over to Vanderbilt. Vanderbilt accepted at once, stating that he would close the deal as soon as Turner gave him possession of the road.

At that time the Grand Trunk was operating the road with the other connecting links to Chicago, under contract leases. In order to get his possession Turner was obliged to find a time when there was no Grand Trunk train between Flint and Lansing. The Vanderbilt roads, the Michigan Central, and Lake Shore & Michigan Southern had branches running into Flint and into Lansing. A telegraph operator tapped the wires and ran them to an instrument in a house near the track, so that he could keep track of the movements of all trains. At Flint a Michigan Central train and crew, with steam up, stood by the junction of the east end of Turner's road, and a Lake Shore and Michigan Southern train and crew, with steam up, stood at the Lansing Junction at the west end. The conductors of these trains were under instructions to be ready at any moment to act under orders from Mr. Turner. It was two weeks before the Chicago & Northeastern was free from Grand Trunk trains.

At about 2 o'clock one morning Turner received a telephone message from his operator that the road was clear and he immediately telegraphed to his men to run their trains on to the lines of the Chicago & Northeastern and leave them there until further orders. He then called up the manager of the Grand Trunk at Port Huron, told him that he was dissatisfied with the lease arrangements and had taken possession of his road. This started a long litigation between the Grand Trunk and Vanderbilt. Vanderbilt holding the Grand Trunk out of Chicago for three years, when the Grand Trunk surveyed a line alongside of the Chicago & Northeastern and began construction. Then Vanderbilt sold them the road, as it was of itself of no value.

Vanderbilt is said to have made a large amount of money for the Michigan Central and Lake Shore by keeping the Grand Trunk out of Chicago and he obtained a good price for the Chicago and Northeastern. Turner was helped out of his financial difficulty and made a good profit. I often told him afterwards that it would have been better for him if he had failed at that time, for he was young enough to recover and it would have taught him caution, which he seemed to need. His success in this venture encouraged him to take other chances in business ventures, in which he was successful for several years.[553]

A Large-Hearted Thoroughbred

During the period of March 1872 through November 1889, Jim acquired large mining, quarrying, timber, and other interests in the Upper Peninsula and was soon classed as a wealthy man and millionaire. His letterhead in 1882 read, "James M. Turner, Dealer in Lands" with offices in Marquette, Lansing, and Cheboygan, listing Charles Butler as his agent in Ontonagon in the Upper Peninsula. It also listed 15 nationally known millionaires as references, including Russell Sage and Moses Taylor, among the richest men in the United States, then or since. Also included were millionaires from the boards of the Michigan Central—William H. Vanderbilt, Baldwin, and Joy, long-time family friend Horatio Seymour, and his cousin John M. Longyear. He invested for others and for himself. In land grant lands alone, Jim bought 1,653 acres of land in the lumber and ore-rich counties of Iron, Gogebic, Ontonagon, and Baraga in the western Upper Peninsula. His presence in the Upper Peninsula was welcomed. "There is scarcely a county on this peninsula but that J. M. Turner hasn't landed interests in, and his large hearted business methods are daily felt," said the *Ontonagon Herald*.[554] At the northern tip of the Lower Peninsula, he owned 11,124 acres for lumbering in Cheboygan County and 3,096 in Emmet County. He also owned smaller parcels of 40 to 120 acres in Isabella, Oceana, Newaygo and Calhoun Counties.[555]

At home Jim and Daniel consolidated their two stores into one as Turner and Case.[556] He did more investing in several local businesses, starting two local corporations toward the end of the 1880s. The first was the Michigan Condensed Milk Company, incorporated in 1887 with $1,000,000 capital. Jim was president and treasurer, and Hart A. Farrand was secretary. The plant was located east of the bridge on Shiawassee Street.[557] It served the entire region and was made possible because of the market access Lansing's railroads gave to farm products. In three years it handled 40,000 pounds of milk per day and manufactured its own cans. Production was expected to double during the next year. A train car load left Lansing every other day, some bound for the West, but most headed to Eastern coastal cities.[558] The second new Lansing business was the Riverside Brick and Tile Company incorporated May 1888 with $50,000. Jim was president and treasurer, C. P. Ten Eyck secretary, and William Appleton manager and superintendent. The plant was located on Elm Street on the bank of the Cedar River.[559]

Jim was very well thought of: "In political matters he was a progressive and leading spirit, and fearlessly stood by his convictions. As a citizen and businessman he was always approachable and accommodating, never disdaining a man on account of poverty or position. His charity frequently excited admiration but was never accompanied with ostentation."[560] During the winter in 1886 an article in the *Lansing Republican* entitled "Sidewalk Glimpses" gave this remarkable description of Jim:

> When the late James Turner started the present James and the Ionia & Lansing railroad he accomplished the two principal achievements of a useful life. The railroad is now part of the Detroit, Lansing & Northern line. James and the railroad were planned on the broad-curve, easy grade, well tied and ballasted main through line principle, and both have proved

among Lansing's notable successes. When the man on the sidewalk runs against a tall, massive gentleman with a large, pleasant face, cheerful voice, brown mustache and dark hair, steady brown eyes, clad in the knobbiest and most peculiar overcoat in the State, it being made from the hide (soft tanned with the hair on) of a favorite black horse, he knows who it is every time. There isn't any other of exactly the same sort in the vicinity. Although large in his movements James always gets there a long way ahead of the crowd. In temperance principles he is a shorthorn, in massive business energy a Percheron, in staying power a thorough-bred. He suits his manners to his companions, greeting grangers with the genuine hundred-acre-blooded-stock-big-barn-with a slate-roof-agri-cultural-fair-grin, or saluting a committee of railroad magnates in the regulation palace-car-special-train-millionaire style. Everybody knows James and is proud of him. He is the representative Lansing business man, a terror to lazy people, a man of magnificent distances like the city. When he looms up on the street like the dome of the capitol, the man on the side-walk steps respectfully to one side, stops whistling Them Golden Slippers, gazes after him, and thinks to himself that if he possessed half a slice of Jim Turner's business judgment he wouldn't be loafing along the sidewalks taking in the world by mere glimpses.[561]

Other new millionaires of the period were building huge, elaborate, and very expensive castle houses with steep pitched roofs in the Queen Ann style. The Italianate house of Jim and Sophie on Franklin Street, to the east of the former Michigan Female College, was a lovely and spacious two-story with a low-pitched hip roof, a wide bracketed cornice, shutters on either side of the windows, and arched molded window The interior woodwork was oak and the house was eclectically furnished in oak. In the late 1880s a two-story wing was added to the east, enlarging the dining room downstairs and the bedroom upstairs, and there was a summer room on the east side with vine-covered wirework walls that offered a cool and serene place to relax in the warm months.[562]

According to Scott Turner, "At the time of my birth there was no public gas, electricity, water or sewer system available. Our water was carried by hand from an artesian well about 75 feet northeast of the northeast corner of the house, and later was pumped from there by an early version of a gas-oline engine. Eventually a system of lighting with gasoline was installed in the house, the main storage tank being on the Walnut Street side. The gas-oline was run by gravity into the cellar, and there vaporized and distributed through small pipes in the house by means of pressure produced by a heavy weight in the basement. This weight had to be wound to the ceiling daily by means of a geared hand-windlass. There was no plumbing in the house and no city sewers were installed outside. The house was heated with six-foot-long wood logs fed into a homemade furnace in the basement. There were three or four fireplaces on the ground floor. All cooking was by wood fire."[563]

The town had but two parks at the time, both privately owned—one by the Davis Family and the other by the Turners. Scott recalled dirt roads and plank sidewalks bordered their corner lot to the south and west. Weinman's Creek, a "nice little stream," flowed toward the Grand River and passed through a small park-like area across the street to the south where the Turner family kept Shetland ponies, deer, and elk.[564]

The Battle Continues

After Jim arranged the sale of the Chicago and Northeastern Railroad in January of 1878, he and C.C. Moody created excitement in the city when they purchased a portion of a vacant lot downtown on the northeast corner of Washington Avenue and Ottawa Street and announced that they planned to build a brick block on that site. "The building will have 44 feet front on the avenue and 100 feet on Ottawa street, and will contain three stories and a basement. The first story will be finished for stores, with fronts on each street. The upper stories will be finished for first-class offices, with all modern conveniences, and will be accessible by wide hallways from either street. The entire block will be heated by steam, furnished with an ample water supply in each story, and proper sewage. A flag walk will be laid around both fronts. We understand that Watkins & Arnold are the architects. If the proposed plan is carried out, Lansing may soon boast of another of the finest business blocks in the state."[565]

For the next year, the newspapers were full of little snippets describing the progress of this new structure, especially when it became known that the U. S. Post Office would be in the building. "The brick work on the new post office building was completed last week, and a full force of workmen are now at work on the inside of the building, pushing things along as fast as possible," the *Lansing Journal* reported. The post office had moved around in previous years from one small rented room to another so the citizens of Lansing delighted in their new post office, very respectable and commodious, with 1,650 boxes.[566]

One of the occupants of the first class office space in the new building was the law firm of Crane and Dodge. Isaac M. Crane, the attorney for the Michigan Central Railroad, was a politically active Democrat. Frank Luke Dodge was a young attorney from Eaton Rapids who had studied law under Crane before becoming his partner in 1876.[567] "Soon after his admission to the bar, he was taken into a partnership with Mr. Crain [sic], whose ability as an advocate and orator was of State renown. This at once introduced him to a wide practice. The partnership was continued until about the time of Mr. Crain's decease in 1881. While he was one of the firm, the well-known work entitled, 'The Railroad Laws of the State of Michigan, with a Digest of Decisions of the Supreme Court relative to Railroad Corporations,' was published. This work was chiefly from the researches of Mr. Dodge. It attained a wide circulation and is considered a valuable authority upon these important matters."[568] Frank Dodge would put his railroad knowledge to work to help Jim, who was sued in 1889 by attorneys for the Grand Trunk Railroad, after Jim had successfully sued the Grand Trunk.

The dispute began after the Grand Trunk bought the Chicago and Northeastern from William H. Vanderbilt in 1879. A few days after the sale, employees of Hickson found that the package, wrapped in newspaper and containing 7,000 shares of stocks, bonds with coupons, and detached coupons that Vanderbilt had given them, was short 290 coupons they were expecting. The Grand Trunk was acquiring all stocks and bonds because it could not get the mortgage on the Chicago Northeastern discharged until all were accounted for, so they contacted Vanderbilt. Vanderbilt contacted Jim, but Jim said he thought they would find the books of the company would provide the answers to any questions.[569]

Jim had disposed of his bonds in March by selling 250 of them to Russell Sage, Vanderbilt's business associate on the Michigan Central takeover, for $1,000 each under an option provided for in the contract with Vanderbilt. The sales agreement to Sage still gave Vanderbilt the privilege of buying the 250 bonds by January 1879. Attached to the bonds were coupons for an interest payment due in March 1878. The coupons were all cut off on March 30, 1878, for the sale to Sage, most likely because Jim had not received the interest yet. Subsequently, Vanderbilt exercised the privilege under his contract with Jim and bought the bonds from Sage in 1879.[570]

The remaining 40 bonds were sold to a Mr. Bingham of the Cincinnati Iron Company in August of 1878. Before handing them over, Jim asked Sophie to cut the coupons off the 40 bonds and after she did, she simply put them in her desk because Jim had said they were a gift to her. When the Chicago and Northeastern Railroad owners and bondholders were the same people, the coupons were not considered to be worth much since paying interest on the bonds would be like paying themselves from their own fund, perhaps explaining why neither gave them another thought until two years later. Now they were worth something. When Sophie overheard Jim talking about the missing coupons with Schuyler Seager, who had been legal counsel for the Chicago and Northeastern Railroad when Jim was president, she gave them to Jim and Schuyler. He was an astute attorney and family friend who had studied corporate law with John W. Longyear and was his partner until Longyear became a judge. It was decided to hand the 40 coupons over to Russell Sage to present to the Grand Trunk agents.

The problem arose at this point because Jim expected to be paid the worth of all the coupons, i.e., the interest that was due. Hickson maintained that they were part of the Vanderbilt deal, saying that he already owned them, and he refused to pay. Jim maintained they had never been owned by Vanderbilt and therefore could not be already owned by Hickson when he made the purchase of Vanderbilt's bonds.

Schuyler Seager died in November of 1883. "The suit was advised and begun by Messrs. Huntington and Henderson. Upon Judge Huntington's death and removal of Judge Henderson to Utah, Mr. Dodge took charge of the case." After these delays Jim and Frank Dodge decided to file a suit against the Grand Trunk Railway Company at the circuit court in Ingham County on February 25, 1885, for the payment to Sophie of interest represented by the coupons in question. He and Cy Black represented Sophie. As expected, the court found in her favor.[571]

However, the Grand Trunk attorneys then appealed to the state Supreme Court in a suit against Jim and Sophie, accusing them of fraud and asking the court to enjoin Sophie from pursuing payment and to surrender the coupons to the Grand Trunk. The Grand Trunk pretty much got its way in the Supreme Court decision, which held on December 28, 1889, "the wife not being a *bona fide* purchaser, the coupons must be regarded as canceled, and the complainant was entitled to an injunction restraining collection thereof by her, and requiring them to be delivered up.[572] Unquestionably it hurt Jim's defense that William H. Vanderbilt died December 8, 1885, and could not give testimony as to his understanding of the sale to Hickson. Furthermore, Vanderbilt's previous testimony was apparently lost.[573] And so, while the court found no cause of action for fraud, it reversed the circuit court decision and "a decree will be entered here in conformity to the prayer of the complainant's bill, with costs of both courts against the defendants Turner."[574] The argument of a decade was over. The Grand Trunk got the coupons for free. Jim was unsuccessful in fighting against the power of the Grand Trunk, even in this comparatively small matter.

The School for the Blind Incident

In 1880, Governor Croswell appointed Jim to the Board of Control of the newly established Michigan School for the Blind. "My first knowledge of the appointment was the receipt of a telegram from him, announcing my selection. I promptly wrote a telegraphic reply declining the appointment; but such pressure was brought upon me by Mr. S. D. Bingham and other citizens of Lansing, that I very reluctantly consented to serve on the board, and lend what aid I could toward the permanent location of the institution and the construction and establishment of the school," Jim recalled a decade later.[575] Jim, working with the Odd Fellows, a benevolent fraternal organization, became an instrumental figure in bringing the School for the Blind to Lansing and nurturing its development. In 1871, the Michigan Female College grounds and buildings were sold to the Grand Lodge of Odd Fellows of the State of Michigan for an Odd Fellows Institute, which was to be operated for its members' use. The Odd Fellows made many alterations to the facility for its new purpose, but it never took off as a successful operation for them. When the Legislature decided in 1879 that it was time to provide a separate school for the blind, which had been part of the Institute for the Deaf, Dumb and Blind of Flint until this time, many communities made proposals to have the new school built in their location, but none suited the state commission.

The Odd Fellows then made an offer to the state commission, and the state took them up on it in August of 1881, after leasing the premises for about eight months.

Once the School for the Blind was settled in Lansing, Jim intended to end his relationship with the school as his business interests were expanding, but his friends would not hear of it. "The services of Mr. Turner on the board were secured by the late Gov. Croswell, after great effort, and he continued on the board to the detriment of his private business at the earnest solicitation of the friends of the institution," said Tom Applegate, a member of the School for the Blind Commission.[576]

After the purchase was completed, as Albert Cowels, a Lansing historian, recalled in 1905, "The commission immediately set about making necessary improvements, erecting a building for an engine house and laundry and one for shops and additional dormitory accommodations, besides fitting up the building purchased, placing a good system of steam and water supply throughout all the buildings, constructing a sewer to the river, thoroughly underdraining and grading the grounds and walks."[577] In 1883 north and south wings to the main building, a residence for the superintendent, and a barn were added. The next year an electric lighting plant was built. Because Jim was the only local member of the board, he spent many hours overseeing the building and activities of the institution. In addition he freely advanced loans to the board from his private funds when necessary because of the embryonic condition of the school. When he resigned, the school was in his debt.[578]

The school admitted all blind persons between the ages of 10 and 21 (later changed to age 7 to 17). All blind children in the poor houses were transferred from Flint. Until the establishment of the school, all scholars were sent home during the annual vacation, even if their only home was the poor house. Now, according to the annual report, "Once rescued from the poor house, the child has never been allowed to return to it. We have endeavored to obtain all possible information in regard to the antecedents of the child, and in cases where its natural home did not seem to be a fit place, we have taken the responsibility of providing suitable accommodations elsewhere during the recess of school."[579]

The School for the Blind Board of Control wanted to equip their students to become useful and self-supporting members of society who thought of the school as a place of study and work, not an asylum. According to the 1881-1882 bi-annual report, "The children frequently come to us with deformed and diseased bodies, showing a lack of intelligent care, and with minds in which fixed habits of thought or application have never existed. Our system has aimed to educate and strengthen both body and mind."[580] The school provided these guidelines for parents and guardians of blind children:

1.Blind children, unless under the most favorable circumstances at home, should be in the institution at eight years of age, or before.

2.Teach them to take plenty of exercise in the open air, to run on little errands, to be as active and helpful as possible.

3. Do not permit the fact of blindness to make you less strict in securing obedience, cleanliness and respectfulness on the part of the child, otherwise you do him a gross wrong by permitting him to form unseemly habits and manners which require years of teaching to efface. Especially should their physical growth be guarded so that they may possess healthy, symmetrical bodies and be free from any peculiarity of movement, such as the nervous twitching of arms and fingers, and turning of head.

4. Permit the blind child to enjoy all the privileges granted other children. Let him attend the public school, the Sunday-school and church, and places of amusement.

5. Teach him the names, forms and uses of the common objects around him. Teach him to count, to add, to subtract, multiply, divide, etc.

6. When pupils enter the school, health permitting, they should attend punctually and regularly until the course is completed.

7. Forbid the use of tobacco in any forms, or of strong drink.

8. Do not dwell upon the blind child's misfortune in his presence nor permit others to do so. Encourage him to be cheerful, hopeful and industrious.[581]

The school curriculum was akin to common schools and included vocal and instrumental music, physical activities and exercise, several trades and occupations for boys, and cooking, sewing, knitting, and fancy work for girls. The girls became very proficient with sewing machines. For boys, "The trades taught are broom and brush making, piano tuning, hammock making, carpet weaving, fly net making, rug making and book making with the Braille raised point system of stereotype plates, which are also made in the institution. The broom shop is equipped with six broom and one brush tying machine, five sewing presses for brooms and one for brushes. Young men leave the shop able to take broom corn from the bales, prepare it and make it into brooms of all kinds, also brushes, both plain and fancy." The school's orchestra and choirs performed for the school and often participated in celebrations and entertainments in the Lansing community.[582]

The clerk of the board of state auditors, T. M. Wilson, handled the funds of the School for the Blind. Wilson recalled that, after several years of work, Jim had never submitted any bills for travel or service. "I asked him one day why he had never presented one. Mr. Turner replied that he would look it up, and finally, in 1886, he presented a bill. "According to Wilson's ledger, "The bill was for the following years: 1881, 3 days; 1882, 5 days; 1883, 6 days; 1884, 7 days; 1885, 17 days; 1886, 8 days—amounting to $141." Wilson thought that, considering the many months spent on those buildings and grounds, if Jim had charged for his time as he had an undoubted right to do, "as was customary, his bill would have been from $1,200 to $1,500, or even more."[583]

During Jim's service as treasurer he requisitioned over $300,000 from the Auditor General for money appropriated by the Legislature. Each requisition and receipt was certified by the school superintendent and approved by the president.[584]

Not long after Jim stepped down from the board of control, Governor Luce appointed Daniel Case to the board in 1887. Daniel became treasurer. At the time there was a brouhaha at the school engendered by its soon-to-be former superintendent, Professor James F. McElroy. It was a ruckus confined mainly to the circle closest to the school, but McElroy had a reputation for being prickly.[585] He was active in Lansing community social organizations, a chemist and engineer, and organized the Capital Wagon Company with five others while with the School for the Blind.[586]

The board had found McElroy's services unsatisfactory for some time and cut back his fiscal responsibilities because of misuse of funds. Tom Applegate recalled, "I cannot remember the date exactly, but it was the year before McElroy was superseded as superintendent, Mr. Turner was confined to his house by illness, and the meeting was held there. The board unanimously decided to curtail McElroy's powers, and cut down his emoluments, such as supplying his private table at the cottage, paying his servants, etc., and a steward was hired to purchase supplies, keep the books, etc., and McElroy was barred from the proud privilege of summarily discharging a scrub woman if it so happened she had fallen under his displeasure. Then it occurred to McElroy that even his head might be in jeopardy through the action of this iconoclastic board and he began to take measures accordingly. Mr. Turner was the first member of the board whose term of office expired and at once McElroy took measures which he thought would bar Mr. Turner from re-nomination to a place on the board and he hoped to secure a subservient substitute. It was doubtless part of his plan to attack the other members of the board, seriation, if they could not be controlled by him, and he hoped to secure the dictatorship of the institution and run it as he pleased."[587] What McElroy did not know was that it was highly unlikely Jim would have served another term anyway since he considered himself philosophically in the one-termer tradition.

"It was McElroy's extravagance that secured his decisive dismissal from the charge of the school," according to Daniel, "The resolution to this effect contained several whereases which condemned him and censured him in no small degree. I was then entering upon my duties, and as a new man refused to vote for the condemnation clauses, and only the part which asked him to quit was left in… McElroy presented me with his bundle of trash when I first went into office. The maliciousness of the charges [aimed at Jim] was such as to cause suspicion, and when I examined them I found they contradicted themselves. They were not consistent with themselves, and were glaringly false."[588] Daniel was further taken aback after he examined the books; he found McElroy "was compelled to indorse all of Mr. Turner's vouchers, and if Mr. Turner was doing wrong at all, then McElroy was indorsing him…

There was no deficiency of $8000 or any other amount, but the school actually owed Mr. Turner a balance and I made the order which balanced the accounts."[589] McElroy attempted to get Governor Luce to take action against Jim and to get the Detroit *Sun* to print his charges but failed. McElroy moved to Albany, New York, where he organized the successful McElroy Car Heating Company, formed to manufacture several of his inventions relating to the railroad car building industry.[590]

It seemed to everyone involved that that was the end of it.

Work in the Upper Peninsula

At about the time the School for the Blind was moved to Lansing, Jim formed the Michigan Slate Company in the Upper Peninsula, with an extensive quarry at Arvon in Baraga County on Huron Bay, after receiving geological reports showing the high quality of the slate and finding out that the lack of success of the previous owners could be attributed to poor management. Black, purple, green, and all varieties of slate were produced, and it was regarded as the finest roofing slate on the continent.[591] He formed a board of investors from friends in Lansing and Jackson, employed competent engineers, upgraded the existing site operation, and used the contacts of the board to jumpstart orders.[592] The State's Mining Commissioner, Charles E. Wright, saw rosy prospects for the new company on Lake Superior's Keweenaw Bay. Wright's report stated:

> The officers are: James M. Turner, President, Lansing, Mich.; W. K. Prudden, Secretary and Treasurer; J. M. Turner, S. F. Seager, S. L. Smith, Lansing, Mich.; C. K. Knickerbocker [related to the Longyears], W. D. Thompson, Jackson, Mich., Board of Directors. [Thompson was the President of the Jackson City Bank. Schuyler Seager and Samuel Smith were brothers-in-law.]
>
> The new company began work at the quarry in the fall of 1881, and have thus far built a new stone engine house, and placed in it a 75-horse power engine, for hoisting and pumping; have built a small saw mill to obtain, for immediate use, the timber and lumber required for repairing the buildings and erecting new ones, etc... The company claims to have orders from New Orleans to the Pacific for this slate, to be used in covering public buildings where first-class slate is required. The new State capitol building of Texas is to be covered with it, and several other important edifices, including the new University Library building at Ann Arbor...
>
> The company is said to be composed of gentlemen who possess unlimited capital, and who are likewise thoroughgoing, practical business men, who are nearly certain to carry on the business successfully, and in the not distant future to make the Huron Bay Slate product one of the chief industries in the Upper Peninsula.[593]

Wright's report proved correct. The quarry became one of the most valuable industries of Baraga County for two decades. Michigan's Huron Bay slate was likely used to cover the Texas state capitol roof because its architect Elijah E. Myers also designed Michigan's new capitol building and knew its worth. Success meant Jim traveled to the Upper Peninsula many times to provide personal supervision of the work of his enterprises and to place Lake Superior slate on the national market. The trip was made much easier with the advent of trains with palace sleeping and parlor cars, and dining cars serving "sumptuous meals." He put a large amount of money into the development of the resources there and studied the needs of the people, demonstrating to them his faith in them and his willingness to do something toward promoting the region's advancement.[594]

Charles W. Turner came north and established a grocery store at Arvon. When the economy caused him to close the store, Jim made him superintendent of the quarry and dock.[595] Just as his father had developed the pearl ash factory and pursued transportation for the local community, Jim Turner seemed to be guided in part by his conscience when it came to some business decisions. The Turners were about to gain another such individual to their family.

Chapter 12

Abby and Frank

Abby's life growing up in Lansing was very different from Jim's who was 11 years older. Michigan was 25 years old when Abby (or Abbie, as it was spelled in her early life) was born to Marian and James in January of 1862. The capital had been located in Lansing for fifteen years. She never lived in a tent or the little white frame house on Turner Street. She grew up in the Victorian Era, in the period after the Civil War, when bell-shaped hoop skirts were replaced by the "rump" or bustle and the movement of society was increasingly away from the agrarian and rural life style. By the time she was born, her parents were free from many of the hardships of their early years and could place more emphasis on the arts and culture. Indeed, Abby's family was distinguished for their civic influence and their contributions to the cultural development of the community.

The Education of Abby

Marian was among the wealthiest women in the city, based on the cash value of her property. When the city assessor reported on the top 184 persons, firms, and corporations in the city with property valuations for tax purposes of $4,000 or more, there were fourteen women listed. Only Mrs. Frank M. Cowels was listed with assessment higher than Marian's, $15,600 as opposed to $14,000. This was not a measure of total worth; however, no one in the city had property values near the six figure dollar amount of O. M. Barns at $109,850. James Turner's old friends all owned property in the city: Daniel Case, $17,850; James F. Joy, $4,050; Longyear and Sons, $42,700; Horatio Seymour, $6,900, Hiram Smith, $25,000. The Turner and Seymour property was valued at $6,000; Jim was valued at $9,550, and the Turner and Moody block at $18,000.[596]

With the Michigan Female College no longer in operation, Marian sought a fine education for her two youngest children elsewhere. Eva elected to attend the Cazenovia Seminary as her older brother Jim had done, but Abby's passion for music led her to choose the Lasell Female Seminary in

Massachusetts. Lasell was established at Auburndale near Boston in 1851
and acquired by ten men of the Methodist Episcopal Church in 1873.[597] Its
innovative approach to women's education was considered radical by some. A
brochure published after the years Abby attended gives the general thrust of
the school: "The Lasell idea of a girl's education is that a cultural mind avails
but little in a weak body, and it is a poor companion for impractical hands.
The study and practical applications of Domestic Science is not incompatible
with the highest order of Literary training."[598] The school had a reputation
for both literary instruction and unique opportunities to study music and
art. Abby loved the concerts that were offered, as she tells her mother and
sister in this letter, which also reveals their close and affable relationship:

Lasell Sem.
Auburndale, Feb. 26, 1879

My Darling Mamma and Sister,

I received the newsy letter Eva penned last night and it would be just
impossible to tell you [how] delighted I was to hear from you all again.
The document was handed to me in the library by our... preceptress
and it was nearly time to go to the concert, in the chapel, one of the girls
said, "Abbie T. you can't keep from reading that letter two minutes." Well
I thought I would, so told the young lady I could keep the letter until I
went to the concert. Well in spite of all of my good resolutions the letter
was opened about two minutes after received and I was laughed at furi-
ously but none of the girls seemed to blame me a particle.

I attended the first concert, given by Prof. Hill, last night, (as you
will see from the beginning of this epistle) and was again carried off into
another world, everything was so beautiful.

"O would I were a bird"— well, if I was I would soar away and the
first place I would stop at, would be at my dearly beloved home and I
would arrive just in time to attend the party. What a gorgeous time you
will have. I am just crazy to come home, but no more of this...

How I would like to come home during the spring vacation and see
you all. Home is really the loveliest place on the globe. The furniture
in our house was always so old fashioned and horrid but I think it's all
beautiful now. We girls had such a lovely time here on the 2nd and best
of all we were allowed to do as we pleased all day long. In the evening we
had a sort of Martha Washington Tea party. Nearly all the girls dressed
in fancy costumes, some were hideous while others quite...

With a <u>huge</u> lot of love,
Lovingly,
Abbie[599]

As part of her Lasell education, Abby attended the Boston School
of Cooking, a school established by the Woman's Education Association
of Boston, and one of the most renowned of the first American cooking
schools. That same winter her letter was written, the cooking school took

on an instructor who became one of the most famous cooks in the world, Mary Lincoln. Lincoln's students learned innovative scientific cooking. She required that her young cooks understand systematic measurement, nutrition, digestion, and the chemistry of cooking. They also learned intricacies of how to keep an orderly kitchen and be a gracious hostess. Lincoln's *Fannie Farmer's Boston Cooking School Cookbook* was published in 1896, the first of several editions and many printings. Abby loved to cook and entertain, and wore out several copies of the cookbook during her lifetime.[600]

It was not at all unusual in the Victorian Era for those who could afford it to send their children abroad for travel and to complete their education. Lucinda Hinsdale Stone advocated it, and the Turner girls' cousin Howard Longyear and uncle Charles Turner, both doctors, had studied in Berlin. Abby and her sister Eva, who was also very talented musically, were both sent by their mother to the Alvord School in Berlin to study music in 1882-83. Abby studied piano and Eva studied voice. They also sharpened their German language skills. They attended many concerts, individual performances, social functions, and dances, and when Eva thought far too much attention was being paid to Abby by a certain Prussian Prince, she wrote home to tell her mother. But by the time they received a reply by ship from their mother saying they should come home, it was time to go home anyway.[601] Here Abby writes home about Alvord students, summertime in Berlin, and her plans to tour during the summer:

Zummer Thasee 97
Berlin, Germany.

June 11. '83
My Dear Mamma and Sisters,

This is a beautiful warm summer evening and I am seated with Miss Tucker on the balcony at "Pension Kahon" with the intention of penning a few thoughts to you. Berlin is getting too warm to be pleasant and for the past few weeks I have been baking in my old blue silk and pink gingham, so you can imagine how excessively warm it has been. For sweet fresh air now, we ramble in the Their-Garten, (which is beautiful at this season.) toward the close of the evening, and before coming home we stop at these out-door restaurants and refresh ourselves with coffee or the famous German beer. It really seems as if the Germans spent the greater part of their time, during the warm months, in their own and public gardens eating and drinking. It looks too jolly for anything, and even passing through the most elegant streets we see whole familys taking their meals on their balconys. They seem to take solid comfort and I have decided when I come home to introduce the same custom at "The Bluffs." We have made our plans to leave this dear old city on the twentieth. Mrs. Pope, her mother, and sister, go with us. We expect to spend from five days first in Dresden, then we shall go to the country on Lacheen Lech Switzerland, and enjoy a few days quiet among the mountains. I can't help but wish daily that you were with us to make our pleasure complete…

Eva went to be photographed the other day, and if the photos are good will forward you one immediately. She is just as well as can be and is looking very nicely at present in a blue cloth dress. Don't blame me for not writing oftener, it is not because you are not in my heart constantly, and that I do not want to talk to you all, but you know letter-writing was always the hardest thing in the world for me and the most dreaded. I wish nature had made it otherwise, but my big sister makes up so beautifully for my shortcomings that if my friends are content I should be quite happy.

In leaving Berlin I think I feel the worst about taking leave of my Music teacher Mr. Raif. He has done wonders for me and made me feel very independent, but yet I can't help wishing for another year. Don't think me ungrateful, but one more year you know would be so lovely and then at the end of that time to play to Liszt would be gorgeous. My instructor told Mr. Mills last week, that I was as talented a pupil he had and if I was to keep on studying I could make a gorgeous player. He was very sorry I was going home, when I was doing so finely, but even if I did, if I practiced well I could make improvement by myself. So there is a bright side to it all, and the compliment delighted me and at the same time made me very ambitious to go on.

We were all up to Aunt Emma Mill's last night to hear a Mr. Howell play the violin. He has studied here three years and the last two years have been spent with Joachim, who is considered the finest violinist in the world. This young man's father has recently given him a three thousand dollar violin (a Guesnerie I believe) which he displays with a great deal of pride and which sends so far the charming music. He intends studying two more years in Europe and then goes to America as a concert player. No doubt at some future time you will also have the pleasure of hearing him play and seeing the beautiful violin. Mrs. Mills is going to Weimar with a young lady who intends playing to Liszt before departing for the States. You can tell Mrs. M's friends that she is very well, in fact I never saw her looking better in my life.

How I wish that some of you were going to join us this summer. James and Sophie at least might spare three months to see Germany and Switzerland with us. We would like above all things to see the little nephews. It has become quite dark so I may draw this missive to a close. With a great deal of love to you all.

Lovingly, Abbie R. Turner[602]

Conscience as Hereditary as Intelligence

It was while Abby was still in Germany and after his term in the Legislature that Representative Frank L. Dodge settled down in private practice in the

Turner-Moody block over the post office.[603] How and when he and Abby became close we do not know, but the Turners and the Dodges frequently crossed paths after he came to Eaton Rapids at the age of 17. Frank and his brother William were part of a wave of settlers who came to the area from Oberlin, Ohio, following Oberlin College's founder, Rev. John Shipherd who settled 30 miles southwest of Lansing in 1844 in order to establish a similar institution, Olivet College. Frank's background bore similarities to Abby's own family as shown in this biographical sketch written for publication after his first term in office. The portrait, as it was called, went back to his Puritan roots and, with gusto, to the Revolutionary War. (In those day, this wasn't unusual.) It touched on the role of his abolitionist ancestors, Nathan Dane, who ensured the Northwest Territory would be free of slavery, and Thaddeus Stevens, a leader of the Radical Republicans in Congress with Charles Sumner and Zachariah Chandler during the Civil War years.

Frank L. Dodge, Representative from the First District of Ingham County, was born at Oberlin, Lorain Co., O., on October 22, 1854, and is the youngest member of the present Legislature.

The Dodges are of New England extraction and are descended from those Puritan fathers of our Republic who exerted, in so signal a manner, their wisdom and energy in planting the seeds of freedom, piety and learning, the fruits of which are so richly enjoyed, from the Atlantic to the Pacific. It is a true remark, because so obvious and just, that no people on earth owe more to their ancestors than the descendants of these early New England families.

The courage and devotion manifested by these zealous and freedom-seeking people generally, throughout all the American Colonies, during the opening scenes of the Revolution and the long-continued trials of war, is entitled to the profound respect and admiration of us all. Against pressures of social influence in the large colonial towns, where bribes and offers were freely made by the emissaries of the crown, and where predictions of anarchy and ruin were constantly poured forth by the timid and mercenary; against the temptation held out by the wealthy and ruling classes, and threats hurled at them by the most powerful of the royalists, these New England born men and those noble women were proof.

Mr. Dodge comes from this New England stock in which conscience seems to have been as hereditary as intelligence, and in which the fine cumulative results of the moral struggles and triumphs of many generations of honest lives appear to have been transmitted; in which originality as well as practicability of conception are combined with an ambitious and energetic support of action. These qualities, which have been noticed in Mr. Dodge's individuality, are thus easily traced. He was the son of Hervey Dodge, a native of Essex Co., Mass., and a grandson of Samuel Dodge, (whose father Andrew Dodge married Elizabeth, a sister of Nathan Dane.) His mother was Angeline (Stevens) Dodge, a daughter of Bradstreet Stevens, a family name well known in the annals of early New Hampshire, especially in and about Grafton County, where he resided. He was one of the pioneers of Lorain County, Ohio; a man who possessed advanced views, and an astonishing foresight. He took great interest in educational enterprises, and was one of the charter members, in 1834, of Oberlin College. Its originality of scheme, providing a liberal education for both sexes and all colors and in which students might assist to defray their expenses by manual labor, shows the founders to have been men far advanced in thought and most liberal in their views. Its influence has been in the highest sense religious and practical.

Mr. Dodge is also from the same stock on the maternal side as was Nathan Dane, framer of the remarkable ordinance, "The Northwest Territory," and of whom the immortal Webster gave great praise for the master foresight he displayed in incorporating into its measures a clause prohibiting slavery. Thaddeus Stevens, the eminent Pennsylvania Legislator, and also distinguished as an opponent of slavery, was of this same line.

Mr. Dodge received the educational advantages of Oberlin until his fourteenth year when he engaged in railroading and traveling, making Cleveland his headquarters. In 1871 he came to Eaton Rapids where he engaged with his [brother] Wm. H. Dodge in the hotel business for about two years. In 1876 he took up the study of law under the preceptorship of the late Hon. Isaac M. Crain [Crane]. Possessing a remarkably retentive memory, by close application, in two years he mastered facts, doctrines and principles that are usually prescribed for a three years' course, so that when he passed examination before the Judge of the Fifth Judicial Circuit court of Michigan he was highly complimented by him for the thoroughness of his readings and the correctness of his views. The press of Eaton County also complimented him and prophesied high honors should health permit of his carrying out the desires of his ambition, which, thus far, as gleaned from friends conversant with his professional labors, prove their predictions well drawn… Of Mr. Dodge's career in the Legislature the Lansing *Republican*, the leading Republican organ of that city, makes the following comment in its issue of June 16, 1883:

While the *Republican* has ever been from principle, consistent in its defense and advocacy of the doctrines of the Republican party, and has always exhausted all honorable means at its command to secure the election of candidates for office who were exponents of those principles over those of all other parties, it has never been tardy in its recognition of a public officer who performed his official duties promptly, faithfully, wisely, nor niggardly in its commendations of such a course, regardless of political party bias. It is in this spirit that we review the legislative record of our Representative from this district, Frank L. Dodge, and commend it as worthy of the man and of the district which he was elected to represent.

During the session just closed, Mr. Dodge introduced 41 bills and resolutions. Each of these, in its turn, received his personal care and attention, and he was absent from his place, during the entire session but one and a-half days. Some of the bills introduced by Mr. Dodge were among the most important legislation of the session, as regards their direct influence for the correction of abuses in the execution of the laws.[604]

In the newspaper article mentioned, *The Republican* gave the title of many of his bills with reference to each one in most complimentary terms and concluded as follows: "The above are by no means all the acts of which Mr. Dodge has secured the passage, but they are 'specimen bricks,' and indicate that in the performance of his duties he has been singly successful and remarkably free from petty partisan practices."[605]

Frank L. Dodge, Turner-Dodge House photo.

By 1882 Frank's brother Charles had arrived in Lansing. He and his wife Arta had a pleasant home at 117 North Larch Street. Charles was four years older than Frank and in 1885 became the engineer of the city's new water works under the Board of Water Works. He was a pioneer in the development of Lansing's publically owned utility. Like Frank, he worked for Ohio railroads from the age of 14 and had ten years' experience as a railroad engineer before coming to Lansing. He was an ardent Democrat, as were his three brothers (William, Ezra, and Frank), and a member of the Fifth Ward Committee. He was a frequent delegate to both County and State conventions.[606]

Frank served two terms in the Legislature as a Democrat. When he was re-elected, he was also endorsed by the Greenback convention.[607] True to his family legacy, he quickly distinguished himself as a man of conscience, fairness, and legal skill by acting on behalf of the House to uncover a scandal in the Department of Education. In his second term he served as chair of the Investigating Committee of State Expenditures, looking at misuse of state funds for personal use, using staff for campaign purposes, and campaigning on state time. He found the director of the public education department had raised the pay of several of his employees but forced them to pay him the equivalent of the raise as a condition of employment. The shady practice was termed "division of salary." In the course of the investigation Frank also inquired into the difference in pay for male and female clerks.[608] At the end of his second term in 1885, he was appointed United States Commissioner for the Eastern District of Michigan and served for ten years. As an attorney he was connected with several celebrated cases early in his career, among them the conspiracy suits growing out of the great mill strike at Saginaw and a sensational impeachment trial. His involvement related to the friendships he had established in the House of Representatives through the labor caucus composed of Democrats, Greenbacks, and a fusion ticket of the two parties.

In 1885 they passed a law that manufacturers who employ women must furnish them with seats. However, of all the things Frank was involved in, Act 137 of 1885, The Legal Day's Work Law, proved to have the most immediate repercussions and led to his early involvement in the rights of the laboring class. The story began when the Legislature passed a law that in all factories, workshops, salt blocks, saw-mills, logging or lumber camps, booms or drives, mines or other places used for mechanical, manufacturing, or other purposes where men or women are employed, ten hours per day shall constitute a legal day's work. The idea was that if workers worked more than ten hours per day, they would be paid for all overtime at the regular per diem rate, unless there was an agreement to the contrary. The sponsor of the bill was Thomas B. Barry, a State Representative from Tuscola County elected on the Fusion party ticket which included the Knights of Labor in his area.

Frank Defends the Knights

As a member of the Knights of Labor, Thomas Barry hoped to address hardships of workers in the Saginaw Valley who worked eleven, sometimes twelve, hours per day, six days a week, for salaries in the range of $1.25 per day. Beginning when only a child of eight, Barry had worked in a cotton mill in Albany, New York, fourteen and sixteen hours a day, until he was sixteen.[609] When he moved to Cleveland and engaged in union organizing activities, he was banned from his burnishing job as a journeymen in the axe-making industry, and his family was impoverished. Because the Ohio factory owners blacklisted him, Thomas and Maggie Barry[610] moved to Michigan where he found an employer in East Saginaw who was not part of the axe manufacturers blacklisting consortium. He held his job until the factory owner joined the Michigan Manufacturers Association and fired him. In 1884, Barry rode a Democratic/Greenback fusion ticket to the House of Representatives and that is how he met Frank Dodge, who was in his second term.[611] This friendship led to one of Frank's most famous court cases and was the beginning of his reputation as a friend of workers.

Times were tough and employers nationwide seemed to have no plan other than to respond by cutting wages and putting masses of people out of work. The local newspapers were full of stories of strikes from Texas to

Maine. Fledgling unions were trying to organize to protect the workers, both men and women. The *State Republican* covered Knights of Labor conventions and meetings on the state and local level. When the Knights met for their annual conference in October of 1885, in Canada, it reported, "among the questions to be considered are life insurance, strikes, child labor, the organization of unions for women, and the adoption of an eight-hour law. At the present meeting an earnest effort will be made to prohibit a resort to strikes by members or local assemblies of the order, and the advocates of arbitration will point to the fact that while the number of labor difficulties during the present year has been larger than in any proceeding one, eight-tenths of the disputes have been ended by arbitration, while in every such case the workmen have come out on the winning side."[612]

There were strikes around the state and there had been a strike at the Muskegon saw mills a few years before. By far the most famous of the sawmill strikes began on July 6, 1885, in Bay City. According to the *Lansing Republican*: "Strikers at Bay City on Wednesday morning took forcible possession of Carrier, Heath & Co.'s salt block. [Salt blocks, which processed salt brine, were associated with sawmills because both needed to be located near a steam.] Sherriff Brennan ordered them to disperse at which they yelled and hooted at him. He then attempted to arrest a man whom he thought was a ringleader, and a riot began. Clubs and edgings were used on the officers and they in turn pulled revolvers. The sheriff's forehead was grazed by a pistol ball fired by an unknown man and also received a blow on the side of the head. Several strikers were badly injured. Nine of the strikers have been arrested and are now in jail."[613] A dispatch from Detroit to the *New York Times* said, "July 6.—Scarcely a mill or salt-block in the Saginaw Valley are running today. The strikers held a meeting at Bay City today which was attended by upward of 1,000 men, and it was resolved to hold out for a reduction in the hours of work. The mill-owners were equally determined to accede to nothing. No riotous disposition is shown by the workmen, and no trouble is apprehended, but the mills are generally well guarded."[614]

The strike quickly spread to Saginaw when workers attempted to get owners to implement the Ten Hour Work Day Law, as it was called, and to bargain with the mill owners over announced pay cuts. The Knights of Labor did not initiate this rather disorganized and spontaneous strike spanning two counties, but Thomas Barry soon found himself the elected leader of it. In the next few days he was arrested five times under the Baker Conspiracy Law and then on a trespassing charge. Each time he was required to post $6,000 in bail. The workers raised a defense fund and assembled an imposing array of counsel. Frank Dodge became his lead defender. Associated with him were Judge Lawson C. Holden, of East Saginaw; Hon. Jerome Turner, of Owosso; and Hon. W. D. Fuller of Newaygo.[615]

The case attracted statewide and national attention because of the prominence of Barry in the Knights of Labor, whose fast-growing membership was striking in many states. In Lansing, it was of special interest because their state representative was involved. He offered his usual confident face: "Representative Frank Dodge went to Saginaw Tuesday night to take part in the defense of Representative Barry, whose trial for conspiracy under the Baker act begins to-day. A total of five cases hang over Mr. Barry's head and his bail foots up to $30,000. Mr. Dodge is confident he will be acquitted, and it may not be inappropriate to add that when Frank talks that way the goddess of justice usually takes the bandage off her eyes and balances the scale with careful delicacy," wrote the *State Republican* on September 6.[616] Three months later the *Republican* quoted the *Saginaw Evening News* saying: "The examination of witnesses for the defense in the Barry case is being conducted by Frank L. Dodge of Lansing in an exceedingly able manner. He is laying the corner stone for the general summing up, and has a happy faculty of bringing out the information needed speedily and to the point." The *Republican* commented, "Our own Frank has carried a peculiarly confiding atmosphere from his youth that somehow impels a witness to hold up both hands and tell everything he has ever heard about the case from the beginning, and it is worth a mint of wealth to the genial representative."[617]

JUSTICE HAS TRIUMPHED,
Barry is Acquitted of the Charge of Conspiracy
    The Jury Wrestles 23 Hours with the Case—The One Wise Man was There—Enthusiastic Workingmen—Other Cases to be Dropped
    East Saginaw, Jan. 23. – The long trial of Thos. B. Barry, charged with conspiracy for leading the striking mill men last summer, ended this morning by the jury returning a verdict of not guilty after being out 23 hours. The jury retired at 10 A. M. yesterday and a large crowd hung about the court house expecting an early verdict. But as the hours dragged on the crowd gradually diminished and at midnight it was learned that there was no prospect of an immediate agreement. At that hour the jury stood 9 for acquittal to 3 for conviction. From that time till 7 A. M. they stood 11 to 1 for acquittal. At 9 A. M. they came in with a verdict of acquittal.
    Immediately after the jurors were discharged Barry shook hands with them and gave each one a cabinet photograph of himself. This being the principal case against Barry it is said that the other cases will be dropped, as it would be impossible to convict with this precedent. The workingmen are enthusiastic and the general cry is, I told you so. A demonstration will probably be made tonight.[618]

However, mill owners in Saginaw wanted a conviction. After all, they had hired Pinkertons from Chicago to break up the strike, each armed with a Winchester rifle and two revolvers.[619] They called in Governor Alger, a fellow lumberman, and requested Michigan Troops—although the troops didn't stay long in the face of so little by the way of violence. One of the Saginaw group of mill owners was Hon. William L. Webber, owner of the Wickes Mill and Salt Block which employed sixty or seventy men manufacturing lumber and salt. Webber was well known by many in the Valley as a former mayor of East Saginaw. He was an attorney and for the last fifteen years he was land commissioner of the Flint and Pere Marquette Railroad. He sold over two-thirds of the 500,000-acre land grant the railroad had received along the line at an average of $11.53 an acre for a profit of over $4 million for investors. He was a former Democratic Senator who was remembered for putting together a deal with six Republican Senators to deny Radical Republican Zachariah Chandler re-election to the U. S. Senate in favor of Isaac Christiancy (also a Republican). He was also involved with other railroading, salt, and lumbering development activities in the region.[620]

Some owners had gone along with the ten hour work day and improved wages; some kept the eleven hour day and paid for the eleventh hour; others reduced hours but, as the workers feared, reduced wages too. A meeting of the workers still out decided to accept ten hours and reduced pay where such terms were offered by the mill owners to get back to work. "The upmost good feeling prevailed," said the *Lansing Republican*.[621] Some owners in the group from Saginaw made sure as much as possible that none of the strikes resulted in either better wages or better hours, taking advantage of a weakening feature of the Legal Day's Work Law that allowed an employer to set wages however he wanted if an employee signed a contract agreeing to his terms. Webber pursued a civil suit in circuit court against Barry and three others, claiming trespassing and inflated damages for harm done to his premises and business during the strike. Although strikes in the Valley were over, state and national interest in the suit remained high. Frank had his work cut out for him.

Webber claimed damages he suffered to the premises in the amount of $5,000. He said he was unable to continue manufacturing lumber and salt for six weeks resulting in a loss and damages of $10,000 and was otherwise greatly hindered and obstructed in the conduct of his business, from which he suffered great loss and damages of $10,000. A total of $25,000. Webber brought a second complaint, charging combination and conspiracy to commit unlawful acts, claiming: "the four defendants on July 11, 1885, did, with 200 persons, unlawfully and maliciously combine and conspire together to obstruct and impede operation of the Wickes Mill and salt-block and grounds and with force and arms, broke and entered the property where there was a large amount of machinery run by steam-engines and 60 employees at work who were necessary for the full and proper conduct and operation of the plaintiff's manufacturing business." As plaintiff, Webber further said that it was in pursuance of the combination and conspiracy that the defendants caused the mill to be set on fire and damage done.[622]

The case was tried in Circuit Court before Judge Chauncey Gage, who studied law under Webber from 1859 through 1862,[623] though Frank and the Knights of Labor and the press were most likely unaware of this. The proceedings were conducted before a jury and resulted in a verdict on June 9, 1887, for Webber. However, the damages awarded were for only one day, the sum of $290.18. But Frank maintained there was no conspiracy to injure property and that the Knights were not allowed to provide witness testimony to verify the facts about what they intended to do there. Furthermore, to their way of thinking, it was unfair and illegal that the attorney for Webber in the trespassing case, James H. Davitt, had been the assistant county prosecutor in the previous Baker Conspiracy Law cases. Davitt had been employed by the county board of supervisors to assist in prosecuting these cases. For the Knights, Frank said the judge was in error in his statement to the jury, that it biased the jury toward giving a guilty verdict. Because of these errors, the defense team appealed the verdict despite the considerable reduction in damages the Knights would pay compared to what Webber had claimed.

The case was argued on January 11, 1887, and decided on June 9, 1887. All but one of the Supreme Court judges concurred with the lower court. Judge Sherwood dissented in a very lengthy opinion that laid out in great detail the particulars of the incident itself and the facts of the case as he saw them. Sherwood was alone in saying the errors in the proceedings allowed for the judgment to be reversed and a new trial should have been granted. The story below of what happened is taken from his opinion in William L. Webber, Trustee, v. Thomas B. Barry et. al.

Judge Sherwood began his dissenting opinion by describing the particulars of the case. The plaintiff was in possession of a steam saw-mill and salt-block on the Saginaw River known as "Wickes Mill and Block." It consisted of a saw-mill, gang and circular saws, with a capacity of 100,000 feet per day, and the salt-block, with a capacity of 125 to 130 barrels per day. On July 11, 1885, the mills and salt-block were in full operation and in good running order. Then Judge Sherwood stated his objections to the finding of the Michigan Supreme Court's majority. He said regarding the assistant prosecutor acting as attorney for Webber, the first assignment of error raised a preliminary question in the case, which by itself would render a reversal necessary. Other key points he made concerned establishing intent:

> Upon the trial of the cause it appeared that Charles Sherwood [not related to the judge] was one of the leaders of the crowd who visited the plaintiff's mill on the occasion of the alleged trespass. He testifies that he was paid to march and carry the banner; that on their way to the plaintiff's mill, they stopped at Patterson's mill. Counsel for plaintiff then asked the witness: "Didn't you go there for the purpose of inducing the men at Patterson's mill to stop work?" And also asked the further question: "Did you hear any of the people in the procession say what their object was in going to that mill, or did you hear the crowd who went to the mill, who was in the procession, say what their object was in going to Patterson's mill?..."
>
> To the first question the witness answered, "No." This, of course, could not have harmed the defendants. To the second question the answer was—"I heard them say they were going to consult the men in the mills about the ten-hour system."

I think the questions were proper… It was competent to inquire how long the mill and salt works remained still. The loss of the use of the mill and works was part of the damages claimed by the plaintiff as the direct and natural consequence of the trespass alleged against defendants, and whether those acts were committed by the defendants, or under their direction or sanction, was a fact to be passed upon by the jury. Moreover, the appearance of the defendants, and all that they said and did, as well as what was done and said by those with them, within their presence or to their knowledge, bearing upon the question, was entirely competent to be put in evidence. Of course, the defendants could not be made liable for the use of the mill any longer than their wrongful acts were the necessary cause of the stoppage.

Davitt, as counsel for plaintiff, had been permitted to give evidence tending to show that, on the day before the alleged trespass, defendants had been out with the crowd visiting mills, and shutting them down, and what defendant Barry did and said on that day, evidently for the purpose of showing unlawful intentions and acts of said defendants. Upon the cross examination, counsel for Mr. Barry asked witness, after he had testified that he heard Barry's remarks to the crowd in the morning,—"Do you remember what he said to the men that day about observing the law, if anything?"

This was objected to as immaterial, and the objection was sustained by the court. I think this ruling was error … and, whether it would be sufficient to repel the charge of trespass or not, it would have a bearing as to the amount of recovery, and as to the conspiracy to injure property. [624]

In his minority opinion Judge Sherwood also objected to the instructions given to the jury by Judge Gage for two reasons. First, he said, the amount of damages was solely for the jury in this case to determine and the instruction of the court to them that they should find for the plaintiff $78 for damage to the boiler and $62 for loss of the use of the mill ought not to have been given. The second was in advising the jury on its verdict by telling them the defendants were indeed liable both for trespassing and for the action of others. The prejudicial portion of the charge by Judge Gage that had been objected to by Frank was presented by Judge Sherwood, followed by his own objections. Judge Sherwood wrote that Judge Gage had told the jury:

"Now, if those parties,—Mr. Barry, for instance,—who was with those men, if the circumstances were such when they arrived at the Wickes mill, before he entered upon these premises, that he, as an ordinarily prudent man, had reason to apprehend that they might, some of them, commit acts of violence, he would be responsible for taking the men onto the premises without the consent of the proprietors, under such circumstances. That he had such an apprehension is evidenced by the fact that before they commenced their journey at all he advised them to refrain from any acts of violence; that he had such apprehension is evidenced by the fact that while they were on the premises he himself says that he requested them to remain at some distance from the mill, until he went into the mill personally. They, as he states it, disobeyed his request and followed him into the mill. Now, taking them onto the premises without the permission of the owners of the property, under such circumstances, would render a party who was with them liable for their acts. I might remark that there is evidence tending to show that, after these acts were committed, he went away and took these men to another mill, notwithstanding they had committed these acts of violence. All these circumstances satisfy the court, the evidence not being disputed, as a matter of law that these defendants are not only liable for the trespass, but are liable for the wrongful acts that others committed there at that time. One is liable for all, although he personally might not have taken any part in it."

In this instruction, [wrote Sherwood] I think the learned circuit judge went too far. The defendant Barry states that he went with the crowd on the occasion mentioned in the declaration within 200 feet of the mill; that he there halted the men, and told them to remain there until he could see the foreman in the mill, and ask permission to see the men, and learn from them whether the men were satisfied with their present system of working 11 or 11 ½ hours per day, or whether they desired to join the movement for 10 hours; that they consented to remain; that he had no other business there; that there was no understanding that the crowd should come into the mill after he left them and went in, and he did not know of their going into the mill until he saw them in the fire room; neither was there any understanding that the Wickes mill should be closed down; that he did not go there for that purpose, and had no intention of closing down the mill; that he was in the mill about 10 or 15 minutes, looking for the foreman, before the crowd came in; that he believed he had some influence with the men; that they came to the mill against his understanding with them that they would not; and that when they came in he got them out as soon as he could, which took from three to five minutes, and that he did not see them put out the fire.

The testimony, and what it proved, was for the jury. If Barry's statement of his connection with the transaction is true, it would go far to exculpate him; especially is this true when there was testimony showing that the object of taking the crowd with him was for a lawful purpose, and that he urged them to obey the law, and to commit no acts of violence to persons or property.[625]

Judge Sherwood disagreed with the directions to the jury because he said the Circuit Court Judge directed the verdict against the defendants and prejudiced the jury. "I have now noticed the principal points argued and urged upon our attention by counsel at the hearing, and for the errors mentioned I think the judgment should be reversed, and a new trial granted."[626]

Even though Judge Sherwood's opinion did not prevail, it was reported that when Frank arrived by train with Saginaw Senator Chauncey Wisner that evening in Saginaw, they were met at the depot by 10,000 citizens who desired to pay homage to their champion. "It is safe to say that the two gentlemen's visit will be one of unalloyed pleasure," said the *State Republican*.[627]

The sawmill workers' dissatisfaction subsided only when the lumbermen eventually left Michigan for Canada after stripping the state of its pine. The Saginaw Valley strike has been judged by some historians to be the most important strike of the nineteenth century in Michigan. It was an important early battle against the injustices the workers suffered and that individual workers were powerless against. "Protection against unfair working conditions for which the Saginaw lumber workers went on strike did not become a reality until the next century, when the laws regulating hours, wages, and working conditions we take for granted were adopted," concludes the Legal Milestone historical marker which was placed at the downtown Morley Plaza in Saginaw in 1988 by the State and Saginaw County Bar Associations to commemorate the "Ten Hours or No Sawdust" strike.

Better working conditions was an idea taking hold. In Lansing even the bustling shop owners in North Lansing tried many times to band together to reduce their weekly hours by agreeing to be closed earlier. Their pact never seemed to work because somebody was always staying open, seeking an advantage and breaking the agreement, until June 13, 1887. One anonymous shopkeeper who had been in the trade since 1849 explained why he favored early closing: "For all these years I have never had one week day evening to myself. My time has been from 6:30 a. m. to 9 p. m. and 10 p.m. Much of the time without dinner. My help come at 6:30 and 7:30 and stay till 9 p. m. Most laboring men kick at 10 hours with one hour for dinner. The lady help in my store only take from 30 to 40 minutes for dinner. I don't think there is a farmer within forty miles who can not come in during the hours and do all the shopping he wants to, and the laboring men in the city trust most of their shopping to their wives. I don't think anyone will be discommoded by the early closing not near as much as the 500 or 600 clerks, two-thirds of whom are ladies, will be benefited."[628] That evening the people of Lansing celebrated the inauguration of the early closing hour in the city. They joined together in music, fireworks, a procession headed by a band, and an address.[629]

The Impeachment of Milo H. Dakin

The Saginaw mill workers were not entirely powerless. They had the power of the vote. In 1885 they elected not just one of four House Representatives from Saginaw County but two. The City of Saginaw representative was Milo H. Dakin. Dakin was a local official of the Knights of Labor and had been their state treasurer. He was a member of the Grand Army of the Republic and had marched with Sherman from Atlanta to the sea. He was in every major battle at the end of the war. The Knights were also shaking things up by electing aldermen to the Saginaw city council. In 1886, businessmen and officials of the Saginaws—the City of Saginaw and the smaller City of East Saginaw—began to push legislation to approve consolidation of the two warring cities that, they emphasized, would create one harmonious metropolis of 60,000. However, East Saginaw and Carrolton, another small town up the river, opposed conditions of the bill promoted by Saginaw because they said it would decrease their communities' valuation and give nothing in return.[630]

The trouble began when Representative Milo Dakin did not introduce legislation proposed by businessmen and politicians of the twelve-man governing clique of Saginaw but instead introduced consolidation legislation designed from the workers' perspective by the Knights of Labor and drafted by Judge Lawson Holden who had so ably served with Frank as a defense lawyer for Barry. The Saginaw clique's version was drawn up by Frederic Eaton, a former attorney of the city. A major difference between the two bills concerned a strip of land along the coast of the Saginaw River called Florence. This was a strip of land of particular interest to David Jerome, the former governor of Michigan (1881-1883). Jerome owned the only street car line between the two cities and wanted control of that land in order to control access to the bridge which led to a newly built driving park (race course). Monopoly of the bridge would be worth thousands of dollars to him in future profits, and he wanted to block a movement to build a free public bridge.[631] Dakin opposed Eaton's run for alderman five or six years earlier and, along with a fellow Knight of Labor and alderman, Giles Fuller, prevented Eaton from being reappointed as city attorney, with its annual salary of $500, leaving the appointment to be made by John Schakelton who was an aldermen but about to take office as mayor.

Using various delaying tactics, Dakin allowed the representative of East Saginaw and the mayor of Saginaw to get together and work out a compromise. The trouble escalated when the City of Saginaw sent lobbyists to Lansing to work for passage of the bill. In the process alderman Fuller and Dakin met attorney Eaton at the Winston Hotel on April 19, 1887, to discuss how things were going. After several weeks of lobbying on the bill, Dakin, a shingle inspector and packer in the mills, and Fuller, a streetcar conductor, could not afford the expense of following the custom of buying cigars and drinks for legislators they wished to speak with or, as Dakin put it, "to use some money" with them. Eaton asked Dakin to mark a roll call of Legislators to indicate who and how many he thought he would contact, and Dakin did. Then Eaton asked Dakin to write down next to each how much money it would take, and Dakin, unfortunately, did. It was about $5 or $10 per legislator, for a total of $125. The list could be used to make charges that Dakin intended to bribe legislators. Eaton took the list and immediately wrote a letter to the Speaker of the House. A few days later Dakin found himself in a public trial by the House, including fifteen legislators whose names had appeared checked on the list. Every detail of this sad tale was preserved in the 253 page transcript of the trial, published in Volume II of the *Journal of the House of Representatives* for 1887.[632]

Again Frank found himself in the center of a brouhaha of statewide interest that pitted the interests of businessmen against union members. The day before the trial Frank, as part of Dakin's defense team, spoke to the press. "Mr. Dodge states that Mr. Dakin's absence has been occasioned by the advice of his counsel and that he will be on hand for the trial. The respondent's answer denies the specific charges made in the articles, vindicates the gentleman named in connection with purchase money, denounces the charge that his object in soliciting funds was for private use as 'utterly and absolutely false and without any possible foundation' and discloses the fact that, if the proof sustains it, he has been made the victim of a conspiracy and unjustly and wickedly accused."[633]

By April 26, most people in the state seemed to have decided Dakin was guilty. "Will they kick him out tenderly? Will they bounce him with care? Will they paint the Hall red, or Confiscate Dakin's chair?" tooted the *State Republican* on April 21, four days before the trial.[634] His three defenders for the trial before the Legislature likely felt there was about to be a true miscarriage of justice —the smell of it was in the air. "The Dakin trial was the one excitement of Lansing today. The galleries of the House, where the proceedings were conducted, were literally jammed full of outsiders, mostly women, and only such as were fortunate gained admittance to the 'floor,' for the rules were stringently enforced...The committee appointed to investigate the case, augmented by Representatives [Gerrit J.] Diekema and Herrington, conducted the prosecution, and Commissioner Dodge, Judge Holden of East Saginaw, and Judge Van Zyle, of Charlotte, appeared for Dakin. Representative Goodrich opened the prosecution. He called Fred I. Eaton, the author of the paper exposing Dakin, to the stand. His testimony was merely a repetition of his sworn statement already printed."[635]

Dakin was accused of misfeasance, malfeasance, or venal and corrupt conduct in office on four charges. First, he was charged with taking money from Mayor Schakelton for the purpose of corruptly influencing votes for passage of a bill to amend the Saginaw charter. Second, he was accused of trying to procure money from Schakelton, Eaton, and others ostensibly to corrupt Legislators as stated but in fact to keep for himself. Third, he was accused of making a list of fifteen Legislators together with the amount of money necessary to procure their vote, thereby bringing the good name and character of said members into ill repute. Finally, he was accused specifically of trying to corrupt the committees on labor interests and municipal corporations jointly. If found guilty he might be charged with a misdemeanor, or he could be expelled.[636]

"Evidently Mr. Dakin is going to make the best defense tomorrow that his attorneys are capable of fixing for him. In substance it will probably be that he is more a fool than a knave, so that a wicked conspiracy was played upon his innocent and confiding nature. But no wicked conspiracy theory can explain away that fatal list in his own handwriting of members of the Legislature with Saginaw ward bummer prices marked opposite their names; and the question will still remain whether either a knave or a fool is fit to represent people of Michigan in the Legislature," said the *State Republican*.[637]

When the defense's turn came, Frank revealed a most peculiar custom of the House and particularly the labor interests and municipal corporations committee. It provided context for why Dakin believed they needed money to get things done before these legislators and certainly could not have been news to citizens of Lansing, who had observed the social practices of the Legislature for nearly forty years. Frank brought out through testimony that there was at the capitol a Third House, composed mainly of Legislators. There was an elected Third House Speaker, a speaker *pro tem*, and a treasurer who was the mistress of the House post office. The unofficial Third House assessed those doing business before the Legislature (the word lobbyist was never used during the trial) and even posted a sign in some committee rooms saying something like, "We smoke, if you don't, up goes your bill."[638] When Frank endeavored to show the relevancy of testimony of a former speaker of the Third House, he said:

> We want to show that it is not only the general custom in the Legislature, but in the city of Lansing to entertain members by treating them to cigars, oranges, confectionery, and things of that kind, in a perfectly legitimate manner, and further, that entertainments have been given, we desire to show, at the Eichle House, at the Lansing House, and been given by the members of the Legislature of the present session without any evil intent or anything of that kind ever having been imputed to them by anyone. This is simply to show the general custom of the manner and the methods of conducting affairs here at Lansing.[639]

The testimony even revealed that when Third House members recently observed that they had failed to give a customary gratuity of $100 to "a reverend gentleman who came here every morning and offered prayers," they voted to assess all candidates for the U. S. Senate. The candidates were sent letters requesting them to "contribute such sums as this body may deem just, in aid of the long neglected workers in the vineyard of the Lord." When the current speaker of the House, Daniel P. Markey, remarked that the custom of the Third House should have been abolished long ago, Frank replied, "I do not doubt that there is a member of the House but that regrets that there has ever been such a practice, but they have gotten into the habit thoughtlessly and unconsciously without any intention of doing wrong, or allowing themselves in any way to become influenced by these things."[640] However, none of this aspect of the defense was reported in the newspapers.

The motives of the accuser, Frederic Eaton, the lobbyist from Saginaw, were brought to light by testimony of Jerome V. Shank, a journalist for the *Lansing Sentinel* with an office on Michigan Avenue near the capitol. He said Eaton and three other gentlemen came into the office two or three weeks before the trial to see the editor. When Eaton found the editor was not there, he left, but not before inquiring if Shank knew where Dakin was and remarking that Milo H. Dakin is raising the devil with the charter. He testified Eaton said, "We are down here to knock him out." And he told Shank they were "after his scalp, and meant to have it." They referred to Dakin as a damned traitor. After discussing this with his brother, Dr. Rush Shank, Jerome Shank offered to testify for the defense. He was then subjected to cross-examination that intimated he was not fit to testify because eleven years before he had been unable to take care of his children the year following the death of their mother, his wife—he was in a deranged state of mind for about a year, and his relatives cared for his children. It was also intimated that he could not see, although he wore glasses and could see well enough to write for a newspaper and to see things nearby. Eaton simply said he was never in the *Sentinel* office.[641]

Eaton did admit that he was passing notes to the prosecutors with questions for the witnesses, consulting with the prosecutors, and offering suggestions. All of this elicited a feeling of contempt within Frank that he said he could not conceal. Frank attempted to show the legislators that Dakin had no motive, and no motive had been proven other than Eaton's conjecture that Dakin might be planning to keep some of the money. Eaton, however, did have a motive, and Frank tried to get the legislators to admit to themselves that they didn't believe Eaton did what he did without malice. He pointed out that Dakin had always had an excellent reputation and committed no criminal act, that the legislators themselves had removed those words from the articles of impeachment. Of Eaton, Frank said, "I despised that man from the day he took the witness stand, with every drop of blood in my body, and it is hardly possible for me to look him in the face or speak kindly of him. I cannot do it with any consciousness that I am doing my duty, because I believe that that man, in his bitterness of heart, because of his being defeated for the renomination as city attorney, or some bad and wicked reason, is pursuing Milo H. Dakin today, and this poor man Fellows who has lived so long in Saginaw valley, and borne a most excellent reputation, that they are being pursued not as criminals, but being hunted down as victims of a horrible conspiracy." What he wanted to know was, "the 15 have had their feelings hurt and wounded and injured no doubt... Will you visit your spite and animosity upon Milo H. Dakin?"[642]

On the final day, the *State Republican* described events:

> When the hour arrived the blazing lights of the House glared down on a vast assemblage. The galleries were literally packed with men, women and children drawn there to witness the closing scene in the first expulsion trial which has disgraced the Michigan Legislature. Then on the floor below besides the members, 94 of them were present, were many men not belonging there and women, in all a sufficient number to fill up the side aisles and to sprinkle the interstices between the desks with high hats and low hats and brown black, red, white, and bald heads.

Promptly at 7 o'clock Speaker Markey's gavel struck the granite block and all was order in the House. U. S. Commissioner F. L. Dodge opened the argument for the defense in a half hour speech. He declared that the State press had taken up the case and judged upon its merits prematurely and so had many of the people of Michigan, and asked if it were fair to judge a man before he had been tried. He affirmed strongly that he believed the respondent Dakin to be innocent of evil intent in the matter, or he would not be on the floor of the House defending him. Judge Holden, of Saginaw, picked up the slender thread of defense upon which Mr. Dakin was dangling and argued strongly and well that he believed the unfortunate man to be the victim of Eaton's wiles. He thoroughly exonerated the 15 men drawn into the unpleasant matter from any complicity in the disgraceful proceedings.

Representative Goodrich spoke next. His argument was tempered with kindness, but it was firm, and he made his auditors laugh when he declared that the defense had brought "a blind man" up to prove that he saw Eaton under circumstances which indicated an ill feeling in the latter's heart against Dakin. He said that a stigma had been cast upon the 15 honorable and upright members of the House and that only one thing could be done to right the wrong as far as it ever could be righted.

Judge Van Zile, of Charlotte, closed the defense with a vigorous speech. He began by saying that it was against legal procedure for accusers to act as judges, and, since such was the case in this trial, he wished to urge most earnestly that any personal feeling, if such existed, be placed aside and that the case be adjudicated upon the facts in it. He declared that not one single point had been proved against Dakin, and defied the prosecution to show where any one of them had. In short Dakin ought to be acquitted at once.

Representative Diekema's was the last voice to sound in argument. He recited damaging testimony and made the deduction that, as the testimony proved the points conclusively in spite of ingenious defensive argument, Dakin aught to be expelled from the House as an act of Justice. He reaffirmed it even though no one could feel more "sorry for Dakin" than himself.[643]

The prosecuting committee dropped the first charge because they agreed it was not proven. The vote for the second charge, that Dakin tried to get money ostensibly for the purpose of passing the Saginaw bill, but really it was going to be for himself, was 83 to 11. The vote that he was guilty of the other two charges was unanimous. Speaker Markey at once pronounced Dakin expelled from the House of Representatives. Dakin was not present. "Mr. Dakin was seen by a reporter for the STATE REPUBLICAN to-day. He said that he rested his case in the hands of his attorneys and had no idea how it was coming out; that the counts against him were not proved; that he was innocent; and that he was going home to-night to resume his work at milling."[644]

It fell to Senator Chauncey Wisner of Saginaw County to see the process through and vindicate Dakin. On June 9, 1887, he delivered an eleven-page speech to the Senate Chamber for consolidation of the two cities that included remarks about the Dakin trial. Wisner said that it was because Dakin's actions for consolidation were against the wishes and hopes of the dozen men who in the past had ruled the Saginaw people with a rod of iron, that they decided Dakin must go and put a legal blood hound upon his track, who entrapped him in a snare deliberately set for him by these men in a saloon. "And as long as Milo Dakin's ghost walks these corridors and his blood stains that map, so long as the sobs of his wife and the tears of his disgraced children cry to heaven for justice, so long will this spirit of consolidation march on. It is equally true the blood of Dakin is the seed of this consolidation, and poor Schakelton, your mayor, unsophisticated but honest, working side by side with Dakin for consolidation, is now being investigated by these men with a view to consign him to the same disgraceful political oblivion into which they have sent their representative."[645]

Wisner's speech in the Senate Chamber met with such decided approval that it was ordered to be printed verbatim in the *Senate Journal*. It was said that it was printed word for word, including the accusations against former Governor Jerome and the twelve Saginaw businessmen, in every newspaper in the state.[646] On June 2, 1889, a bill for consolidation was passed which provided for election of officers for the consolidated city of Saginaw the following March.

That summer it was reported that Frank was off for a well-earned vacation, "Messrs. Frank L. Dodge and Isaac Lederer are spending a few days in rustication at Pine Lake."[647] A few days later Frank, Isaac, and a number of other gentlemen headed for the Lake Superior region.[648] Doubtlessly the trip would include stops at the various Upper Peninsula enterprises of his future brother-in-law.

The Wedding of Abby and Frank

Somewhere between her teens and adulthood Abby changed the spelling of her name from Abbie to Abby, and on November 20, 1888, she became the third of Marian's children to marry. Abby's oldest sister, Marian, had married Nelson Reasoner, a Methodist minister, in June of 1875, and had three sons. Jim had married Sophie in 1876, and they had two sons. The guest list for Abby and Frank's wedding was long and the preparations for the wedding day of this well matched and talented couple were meticulous. The guest Presbyterian minister was Louise Seymour's husband. The newspaper, which more and more seemed to set aside space for "society," covered everything in detail:

A BRILLIANT WEDDING
The Marriage of ex-Representative Frank L. Dodge and Miss Abby
Turner.

NEARLY 200 GUESTS WERE PRESENT
The Ceremony at the home of the Bride's Mother
Mr. and Mrs. Dodge Depart on an Eastern Trip.

One hundred and seventy-five invited guests witnessed the wedding of ex-Representative Frank L. Dodge and Miss Abby Turner last evening in the parlors of Mrs. Marian Turner on North street, The guests from out of town included friends from Cleveland, Toledo, Detroit, Marquette. Port Austin and several other Michigan cities, and the pleasant home was crowded with those present, the effect of the brilliantly lighted rooms and the large assemblage being still further heightened by numberless baskets of dainty flowers scattered about the parlor where the ceremony was performed. The wedding occurred at 5:30, Rev. Dr. C. S. Armstrong of Jackson officiating. O. F. Barnes served as master of ceremonies, while the bride's sister Miss Eva Turner, Miss Ida Longyear and Miss Mattie Stebbins of Toledo formed a charming trio of bridesmaids. The best men were A. W. Osborn, manager of the Cleveland Press, Fred B. Dodge of Cleveland and Harry Dodge of Newport, Mass

The bride—one of the most prominent and attractive members of capital city society—was attired in an unusually effective costume, even for these days of masterpieces of art in wedding garbs. It was a white faille Françoise silk made en train and with rich trimmings. She held a bouquet of white roses and carnations, and wore ornaments of diamonds, including diamond earrings, the gift of the bridegroom. Like Miss Turner, the bridesmaids were attired in evening dress. Miss Eva Turner wore a cream China silk costume trimmed with dotted tulle. Miss Ida Longyear was garbed in a cream Surratt silk, with white trimmings of moirés silk and pearl ornaments. Miss Mattie Stebbins wore a charming costume of light blue surah with white moiré silk trimmings. All carried bouquets. A reception followed the ceremony and refreshments bewildering in variety were served. The reception continued until 8 o'clock when Mr. and Mrs. Dodge departed for Detroit. From there they will go East spending the next three weeks in Washington, Boston and New York. Among the innumerable wedding gifts was a superb standing lamp from the Ingham county b bar, of which the bridegroom is a member.

Music and dancing held full sway until the bridal party left, and it was 10 o'clock before the guests departed. Among those present from out of the city were District Attorney C. P. Black and Major Anderson of Detroit, Congressman M. S. Brewer of Pontiac, Mr. and Mrs. Dwight Smith and Mrs. H. H. Smith of Jackson. Mrs. Osborn, a sister of the groom, and Miss Lucy Heller of Cleveland, Mrs. C. N. Turner of L'Anse, Mrs. Chas. A. Towne of Marquette, Mr. and Mrs. Richard Wisner of Port Austin, Mrs. Richard Wisner, Jr. of White Rock, James Monroe and wife of Portland and Mrs. Chas. Scott of Alma.[649]

The couple moved into the Turner family home on the Grand River with Marian, and Abby's older sister Eva or, rather, Frank moved in. Abby had lived there all her life. Among the gifts they received was an exquisite set of plates with gold-painted rims, each featuring a different beautiful white flower on a background of gleaming white porcelain. All were hand-painted by Abby's very accomplished artist cousin and bridesmaid, Ida Longyear.

When Frank became a member of the family he easily fit in, albeit he was a Democrat. His values were very similar, and he had long been a colleague of Jim's. A local newspaper reporter approached Frank the following May while the couple was staying at the Russell House in Detroit, and he gave this amusing interview:

> He is an ex-member of the Legislature, a rising young lawyer and universally popular. His Democracy is of the brand which defies the exigencies of time and circumstances and rises serenely to the surface of current events after every political storm. It is floating serenely on the aforesaid current of the present time.
>
> A few months ago he added to his popularity—and insured his own happiness for life—by wedding the accomplished sister of the Hon. James M. Turner, the well-known Lansing millionaire and intrepid Republican politician. It was the social event of the year, both parties to the alliance being universally popular and just as universally respected. Since that event the happy couple has spent several weeks in the east, visiting friends and relatives in the principal cities.
>
> "Anything to do with politics at present?" Mr. Dodge was asked, "Politics?" he repeated, still swallowing resolutely at the quinine for his cold. "Well, I should say not. It seems to me that I have heard the word somewhere, but, for the life of me, I cannot exactly place it. Is politics the game where two fellows run for the same something or other, and all the rest of the world proceeds to go crazy over the fact? Where one fellow ruins himself for life by running for something and getting defeated, and the other fellow ruins himself for life by running for the same thing and getting elected? Is that what you mean when you ask me about politics? I have a faint recollection that in my young and callow days—before I knew much about the world and its wickedness— I did take an occasional hand in some such game of chance. I also remember that whether I won or lost I was worsted every time. But now," straightening his form to its most imposing height, "now I have something else to live for. I am a married man now, sir—married so happily that the hours of my enjoyment and contentment are only remembered by the hours that I live. Politics, indeed! What have I to do with politics or politics to do with me? I am leading an honest and straightforward life."
>
> Yet you are living in a city that is founded upon politics. "I presume that is true—but it doesn't bother me nowadays. I have settled down to the practice of law and the enjoyment of home, and Legislatures may

come and Legislatures go, but my peace and contentment will go on forever. Seriously, I am aware of nothing potential that would be of public interest. I aim to avoid all things political, and, so far, I have very nearly succeeded. They talk about a great many things out there at Lansing, but when it is generally understood that one prefers to be left to his own enjoyments, as a private citizen, he is seldom molested. I am thoroughly honest in my desire to have nothing to do with politics. When I was single and my time was all my own, it did not so much matter. But it is all very different now."[650]

Of course everyone knew all along that having three older brothers involved in politics and being married into a family equally full of passion for public issues and politics would make avoiding "all things political" an impossibility. Even if they were to believe for one minute that Frank didn't love it that way, he would have much to do with politics, and so would Jim.

Chapter 13

Farmer and Party Reformer

When Jim ran for mayor of Lansing in 1889, Democratic as well as Republican newspapers as far as Detroit took note of it: "Hon. James M. Turner swore by all the gods that he wouldn't take the nomination for mayor of Lansing, but the republicans dragged him out, stuck his mangled remains at the head of the ticket and expect him to carry the day," said *The Evening News*.[651] Lansing Democrats were skeptical: "This is not the first time that the Republicans have set out to accomplish great moral reforms in this city through the elevation of one of the adherents of the g.o.p. to the mayoralty."[652] Nonetheless, he was soon credited with securing both law and order, and economy in government. "Hon. James M. Turner was the great expansionist. While in office the city limits were extended, new brick pavements laid to replace the old cedar blocks, and the present city hall was built. The new United States post office was erected. He was a friend of labor, and gave all classes a chance to work and earn something through city employment. He declined a salary for services except a dollar which he placed in a frame and hung in his office."[653] He raised revenue by $4,000, paid off the debt, and balanced the budget, teaching the alderman the wisdom of not paying interest when avoidable.[654]

Everyone seemed delighted with the new mayor of Lansing. The editor of *The News* wrote:

> The Hon. James M. Turner, the present mayor of the city of Lansing is one of the most enterprising men it has ever been my good fortune to meet anywhere. Mr. Turner is not only the leader of the coterie of progressive men to whom Lansing may be said to owe its present enviable position among the cities of the state, but he possesses those attractive and attracting traits of character which invite to them the masses everywhere.
>
> He possesses a marvelous faculty for remembering names and faces of persons he meets. He is already a very rich man. His stock farm itself represents the investment of a fortune, and he is also the owner of a fine residence and considerable business property in the city. His business

pluck and enterprise are shown by the investment of his money and the moral support he gives to one or more of the banks, to the Michigan condensed milk company and to half dozen more business enterprises in Lansing in which he holds stock and in many of which he figures as an executive officer. Mr. Turner is also part owner of very valuable iron mines and stone quarries in the northern peninsula and has a multiplicity of business interests in other parts of the state. His manner is affable and every-day-like in the extreme, and his personal popularity, not only in Lansing, but in the upper peninsula and wherever he is known in other parts of the state, is immense.[655]

The Mayor and the Fair

According to the Editor of the State Agricultural Society's Journal, *The Michigan Agriculturalist*: "Mr. James M. Turner is the surviving son of Hon. James Turner, so well known in Lansing business circles a score of years ago. The son partakes of the characteristics of his father to a remarkable degree; the same raven locks, keen black eye, and robust physique. Constantly associated with his father in his immense railroad, real estate and other enterprises under his father's tutelage, he readily acquired the habit of thought, caution, accuracy, vigilance, and attention to detail, which achieves success."[656]

He and Ephraim Longyear were both strong supporters of the Michigan Agricultural College. Ephraim served as college treasurer from 1871 to 1885.[657] Jim's exemplary stock farm contiguous to the Agricultural College was by now transformed from the wilds of the Michigan forests into a model of great interest to all. He studied every aspect of his farm and farming, and was respected for his work. He willingly traveled to meetings to provide information for the college's Agricultural Experimental Station on such topics as the farm's practices regarding silage. Jim had a roll top desk with his nameplate on it at the school.[658] He collaborated on scientific studies with the Veterinary Department at the college when others would not because they thought experimentation was too risky. [659]

> An interesting feature of Mr. Turner's economic stock farming is his corn ensilage, of which over 3,000 tons is annually fed to horses, cattle, and sheep. He knows every animal on the farm, as well as how it is bred. As a rule, only men with families are employed, and each is provided with a comfortable house, garden and cow. Every employee of the farm has for the past fifteen years been paid his wages in full every Saturday night. Can any man be more of a friend to his employees than is shown by this record?
>
> Mr. Turner is also president of the Michigan Condensed Milk company, a Lansing enterprise, which uses 60,000 pounds of milk per diem the year round, and ships its goods all over the world. This milk is purchased from surrounding farmers, and requires a daily expenditure of from $600 to $800.[660]

Giving an inkling of things to come, the European Edition of the *New York Herald* in Paris said, "James M. Turner, Mayor of Lansing, Mich., wishes to be Governor of his state. He makes the best butter in Michigan, but can he fry the fat?"[661]

Laura Barnes, whose husband George was the owner of *The Livingston Republican*, visited the farm in the fall of 1890, hosted by Sophie, who was doubtlessly engaging in a bit of soft-sell politicking. Barnes filed this story for the newspaper describing her visit:

> Springdale stock farm owned by Hon. James M. Turner, of Lansing and containing between 1800 and 1900 acres was visited by Mrs. George Barnes, son, and daughter last Saturday, Mrs. Turner being the escort with her simple three-seated canopy-top spring wagon, colored driver, and two spirited bay roadsters. We made the four mile trip from Lansing to the stock farm in half an hour. The farm is situated southeast of Lansing coming up to the city limits on the east side toward the Agricultural College and extending south and east over hill and dale for a distance of three or four miles. The farm is a model of its kind, being fully equipped with all needed machinery and conveniences of every kind. As we entered the first barn we were greeted with the barking, yelping and whining of six large mastiffs. We were somewhat terrified at first but Mrs. Turner informed us that they meant no harm but were simply begging to be let loose as they knew the family was on the grounds. This barn contains the office and is headquarters of the farm manager, Mr. Hurd. A telephone runs from the office to Mr. Turner's office in Lansing, so he can be called up at any moment if needed. The office is also supplied with a great variety of farm papers and agricultural reading matter of all kinds. The barn is 280 ft. long with a row of box stalls on either side of the main alley. The barn contains forty stalls and is for the use of the

Springdale Farm, CADL.

Clydesdale horses. Each stall is provided with running water and a little yard at the back where the horses can get exercise during the day.

The next visited was a large barn for the short horn cattle and attached to this was an immense silo. The next was a sheep barn with all the necessary racks, etc. In the main part was a little room at one side with a stove in it used as a sort of nursery for the young lambs until strong enough to go with the flock.

The next was the barn where the 300 cows are kept. A silo is also attached to this and we had the pleasure of seeing the cutting and filling process. The farm proposes to store 3,000 tons of ensilage this year. The milk room was next visited which contains two large vats filled with water and the cans turned up to dry. Mrs. Turner said it was a very pretty sight to see the cows coming in to be milked. The milk is strained in cans and then put into the water to cool as soon as the required temperature is reached it is carried to the condensed milk factory at Lansing. One other barn one and a half miles away we were unable to visit on account of lack of time. Six car loads of stock were away to the fairs and most of the rest at pasture, but we were informed that every stall was full when all there. Some fifteen or more cozy and comfortable cottages dot the premises, here and there, the homes of the employees on the farm. We counted eight or ten in the immediate vicinity of the barns. Each cottager has a garden spot and cow kept. Help and the manager's children have a Shetland pony to go to school with. Each department has a chief manager who is responsible for the charge. Mrs. Turner said they all knew their respective work and they had no trouble in keeping responsible and efficient help. She also said the farm was a source of profit as well as pleasure.

Mr. Turner makes it a point to visit the farm every day and see that everything is in proper order. Shetland ponies direct from the Shetland Islands, can be seen. Clydesdale horses, American trotters, herds of shorthorns and Herefords with records mile long; besides the 500 Shropshires and 300 dairy cows. The day was cold and windy and the time short, but we shall ever remember our visit to Springdale farm with pleasure.

> Happy the man who tills his field,
> Content with rustic labor;
> Earth does to him her fullness yield,
> Hap what may to his neighbor.
> Well days, sound nights; Oh, can there be
> A life more rational and free?[662]
> [P. H. Stoddard]

The newspapers in Lansing and across the state often reported the goings on at Springdale Farm, what new stock had come in, prizes won at the fair, e.g., "Springdale farm received an addition to its live stock this morning, in the shape of a handsome bay colt by Sphinx, he by Electioneer, dam by

Ethan Allen. The owners are as much pleased as though they had received a check for $5,000 from some good friend."[663] They loved their mastiffs, too, an English breed which seemed to suit the personality of their owners. An adult could weigh 175 to 190 pounds, yet they were as good with children as with sheep or livestock and have a good-natured, calm, easygoing, and surprisingly gentle disposition. "What the lion is to the cat—the mastiff is to the dog, the noblest of the family; he stands alone, and all others sink before him. His courage does not exceed his temper and generosity, and in attachment he equals the kindest of his race," said an old 1800 *Cynographia Britannica*.[664]

Jim had always had a great interest in the state fair. He shipped his prize-winning stock to fairs all over the state. The state fair had started out in Detroit in 1849 but had been moving around the state. One of the issues for several years was the desire on the part of the state fair's sponsor, the Michigan Agriculture Society, to locate their fair in some permanent place. Jim was on the executive committee of the Michigan Agricultural Society in 1886[665] when he was asked for his views on the matter:

> "No, I do not believe that Lansing will be able to secure the State fair permanently this year," said Mr. James M. Turner to the STATE REPUBLICAN reporter to-day.
> "Why not?"
> "Because," replied Mr. Turner, his pleasant smile breaking off into a tinge of regret, "it will be just like locating a State capital. Every member of the society wants it dropped down in his own town… It was important for the Central Michigan Society to place itself in a position to take advantage of any move towards locating that the State organization may make, but I am not sanguine that the fair will come here or anywhere else permanently."[666]

The opportunity came for Lansing while Jim was serving on the executive committee of the Michigan Agricultural Society and as mayor. By then the finances of the state fair were in poor shape, and interest had declined by other communities in bringing the fair to their locale. The last two years of the fair had been bad ones and left only $854 in the treasury as compared to $20,000 to $54,000 carry-over in previous years. After forty years of state fairs, they worried whether they would be able to mount another. At the May 13 meeting in Lansing, proposals were made for a location. A representative from Grand Rapids presented a proposition and invited the Society to locate permanently in Grand Rapids. The other invitation was made by a group of citizens from Lansing which included the president of the Central Michigan Agricultural Society who offered the Society's sixty-two acres[667] of grounds, buildings, etc. The representatives of the Lansing Board of Trade agreed to pay all indebtedness of the Central Society so the gift would be free and clear. The city would run a water line and the electric company would run a line and provide twenty lights. By June 25 the State Society was building a new grand stand and second carriage house and making other preparations for a fair in Lansing. On September 11, Jim was elected president of the Society.[668] Jim enlisted all the necessary resources and backing, and set upon a path. He felt the Michigan State Fair should be as good as any state fair and a little bit better.

One of Jim's plans was to get the Lansing street railroad to extend its line to the fairgrounds so visitors could come by train and take the trolley to the fair. The route was a big issue, but finally it was negotiated to everyone's satisfaction, ending at Pine Street, two blocks south of Main Street, and the required ordinances were passed. A platform and waiting room were erected at the northeast corner of the grounds, and every convenience furnished passengers. After the fair it would make the trip once a day, year around. The concessions on the part of the street railway were considerable, and Mayor Turner was heartily congratulated.[669] Some people said the grand stand could not safely accommodate all the people it claimed to be built for, but Jim calmed their fears, reminding people that he had built many railroads and could vouch for it.[670]

The Michigan Agricultural College produced an impressive exhibit aimed at updating citizens of the state on agriculture's present advancement. "The superior vegetables in great variety; the fruit; the farm products; the stock; the tools, machines and steam engines made by the students in their regular shop-work; the beautiful display of hot-house plants; the few very attractive cases of insects that were shown from the McMillan collection, so rich in rare specimens; the suggestive exhibit of skeletons and models of animals from the Veterinary department; the singular appearance of the apparatus from the chemical and physical laboratory; and the instructive specimens from the botanical department drew a constant and curious crowd," the college reported to the Agricultural Society. "The College is indebted to Senator James McMillan, of Detroit, for the most generous gift of a large collection of butterflies and beetles. The butterflies include 8,000 species and 12,000 specimens. The beetles include 8,000 species and 40,000 specimens." Afterwards the exhibit headed for the State Exhibition in Detroit."[671]

On the fourth day of the fair that September of 1889, all the regular trains were overloaded and special runs were jammed. The grounds were packed with happy humanity, an estimated 30,000. The fair management was jubilant. The weather was great, and so were the receipts. "Everything is running with precision of clock-work today. The exhibit is as bright fresh and attractive as it was on Monday morning and the people are attesting to their approbations in a decidedly satisfactory manner... In the afternoon the [horse] races took their attention and when the day closed a tired crowd of sight-seers wended its way to the city and claimed it for their own." The Michigan Equal Suffrage Association passed out over 2,000 pieces of literature. Congressman Mark S. Brewer of Pontiac said it was the best state fair he had ever seen and the grandest display to promote the cause of agriculture and the mechanic arts that Michigan had ever had.[672]

When all was accomplished, Jim made a final speech to the Society. At the Society's annual meeting he again put before the members an uplifting vision and purpose:

> Our exhibitors gather together from year to year bringing the products of their farms and shops, such models of excellence in their respective branches of industry as will awaken a new interest and desire for improvement in those who visit us, and who are less enterprising and less skillful, and point out to them new avenues for success. We annually gather in all classes of our people, to promote more friendly intercourse and lead to mutual respect and intelligent cooperation. The week of our annual fair furnishes an occasion for needful relaxation to our toiling masses, who but for some such opportunity of combining instruction and entertainment, would rarely be relieved of the everlasting grind to which they have become but too well accustomed ... the wonderful strides being made in the development of the various natural resources of the great State of Michigan, the improvement of her fields, the upbuilding of her industrial interests, the fabulous development of her mines, and in fact the wonderful growth and increase on all sides of us.[673]

The fair was judged a great success, of incalculable benefit to the state. Nevertheless, while it covered expenses, it did not bring in enough to cover unforeseen expenses such as the debt payments from improvements and the replacement of several rows of horse stalls that were destroyed by fire after the fair. Jim solicited contributions to offset the debts, and the Society worked to again have a balance to begin a new fair season. However, Jim urged the society not to be penny wise and pound foolish and to continue to fulfill its educational mission with outstanding and advanced exhibits.[674]

The 1890 fair reported more visitors and fewer expenses. The number of entries in stock and horticulture was 3,778. When the other departments of machinery, implements, vehicles, and farm and dairy product were added in, the total was 7,976.[675] Under different management the fair eventually moved back to Detroit; however, Lansing's improved fairgrounds facility regularly attracted large groups that held overnight meetings of several days, such as the Grand Army of the Republic, church conferences, the Maccabees and Ladies of the Maccabees, and membership insurance organizations. For nearly 120 years the Michigan State Fair was part of Michigan's history. At the turn of the twenty-first century the fair experienced declining attendance and was increasingly dependent on state financial support. When this support ended in 2008 due to a period of economic hard times, the state fair ended.

The job of mayor was a whirlwind of accomplishments, and Jim did it as a Republican in a Democratic city with a Democratic Council. When his year was up in May of 1890, a plot was discovered among the aldermen that culminated in a presentation that reportedly dazed the mayor. At his last meeting, "An ebonized object with a beautifully chased gold mounting at one end was reverently inspected by the members of the Common Council. They were very cautious and secretive in their inspection of the object, too, and at the entrance of Mayor Turner it was hurriedly hidden from the admiring gaze of the aldermen. At the first lull in the Council proceedings Ald. Baird arose and said sweetly: 'I understand that this is a special meeting called to settle with the outgoing officials. I suppose the clerk has already drawn his order for the mayor's $1 salary, but that does not entirely straighten things out.' Then Ald. Baird launched out into a clever and eloquent little address while the mayor stared at him in helpless surprise." [676]

Mayor Turner wonderingly stared at him, and grew more and more astonished every minute until Ald. Baird reached that part of his speech where he remarked: "Even enemies, after becoming better acquainted, oft times become attached to each other, and can appreciate the good points in their opponents...

I expect , your honor, that you have received your share of adverse criticism from the public, but I wish, on behalf of the members of the council, who have been here and watched your administration, and who appreciate its many excellent qualities, to present you with this present. It comes entirely from your opponents in political faith, and is given for just worth."

As he presented the handsome gold-headed cane, the alderman remarked: "I trust that I may see that cane, someday, enter the capitol, if it must be a republican that enters." A perfect storm of applause greeted the close of the speech.[677]

Down in Detroit, the *Free Press* translated all of that into three sentences, "Turner has a cane. The common Council egged on the gubernatorial boom of James M. Turner, the retiring Mayor, by presenting him with a gold-headed cane last night. The presentation was made by Ald. Bair, leader of the Democratic side of the council."[678]

Politics Were Changing

The old liberal Radical Republican leaders of Jim's father's generation were dying off. Kingsley Bingham died in 1861, Theodore Foster in 1865, Jim's father in 1869, Jacob Howard in 1871, John W. Longyear in 1875, and Zachariah Chandler in 1879. Others were elderly and taking less part in public affairs. Michigan was still the citadel of Republicanism, but now the party was controlled by a more conservative group of lumber and mining barons, and railroad and shipping magnates who had taken part in the tremendous concentration of wealth that happened at the end of the war and with the rise of corporations. This was the day of the money king, the coal king, the cattle king, the telegraph monopolist, and as well as the railroad and lumber barons. Now the spoils and plunder were of a different kind.[679] These changes resounded throughout the halls of justice, Legislatures, and all political machinations.

During this period in Michigan's history, the state was dominated by the Republican party's "Big Four:" former U. S. Senator Thomas Palmer (term of 1883-1889) a lumber merchant and mill owner, and a champion of woman's suffrage who wanted a cabinet appointment from President Benjamin Harrison and/or to be governor; U. S. Senator Francis Stockbridge (term of 1887-1894) who was involved in lumbering, mining, and shipping, and a former rival of Senator Palmer; former Governor Russell Alger (1885-1886) a brilliant Civil War general and lumberman who wanted to be a senator; and U. S. Senator James McMillan, chairman of the Republican State Central Committee and a U.S. Senator who wanted to control the governorship.[680]

Relations between Alger, McMillan, and Palmer were suffering from a recent fray in which McMillan and Alger had deprived Palmer of an appointment to President Harrison's cabinet, even though Palmer and President Harrison were friends. According to the *New York Times*, "A report had been made to the President that Michigan Republicans were divided against themselves, and McMillan's highly qualified denial of this fact, together with Alger's faint endorsement of Palmer, induced Harrison to ignore Michigan just as he did New York because her 'Big Four' were pulling and hauling with reckless disregard for the party's welfare."[681] Into this increasingly embittered factional warfare stepped Jim. His public persona was far different from theirs; as the *Mining Journal*, on March 6, 1890, put it, "He is a man of business and a man of the people."[682]

While mayor, his friends in the sixth congressional district tried to convince him to run for Congress, but Jim refused because he said his business concerns did not allow him to be out of state. "Then his friends said that he should allow his name to be used as a candidate for governor, and to this he finally consented."[683] When he decided to run for governor in February, the other contenders in his party who were thought likely candidates were former Senator Palmer who was the U. S. Ambassador to Spain (because he didn't get the cabinet post) and Major Milton C. Watkins of Kent County. However, in the end the only opposition came from John T. Rich of Lapeer County who was Speaker of the House when Jim served in the Legislature. Rich had been State Railroad Commissioner since 1887 and had held several elected offices. He was a farmer when he didn't have an office to fill. Rich had been seeking the nomination for governor since the 1880 convention and was part of the McMillan faction that dominated the party.

McMillan, a Detroiter, owed his great fortune to railroads, lumber, manufacturing, and shipping. In the 1880s he became involved in politics, succeeding Zachariah Chandler in 1879 as Republican State Central Committee chairman, serving again as chair in 1886-87, stepping down for a time during the first term of the Democratic administration of President Grover Cleveland and again holding the position from 1890 to 1896. McMillan built his influence upon federal patronage he controlled during the Republican national administrations and to his personal financing of legislative candidates. He was known to openly pay expenses of legislative candidates and convention delegates so he could manipulate Michigan politics to the advantage of his own political career and prevent legislation counter to his railroad and shipping interests.[684] During his final term, he was both the powerful Republican state chair and U.S. Senator. Eventually, when he could not prevent the nomination for governor of reformer Hazen Pingree and did not want to manage Pingree's state campaign, he stepped down. It might have been much better for Jim if McMillan had not headed the party during his election campaign either.

In this period of much reform activity, civil service reform produced a major change in how politics were to be conducted. No more "to the victors go the spoils." Civil service was a challenge to the "powers that be" and an attack upon the patronage system that McMillan headed. This was made no clearer than in 1889 in the seventh congressional district. Here was a district on the eastern side of the state composed of five counties—Huron, Sanilac, Lapeer, St. Clair, and Macomb. The seventh district was the home of a very fractured local Republican party with a history of squabbling factions. The McElroy faction, led by the Scotch-Irish McElroy families in Lapeer and St. Clair Counties, had elected Crockett McElroy to the Senate and his son Frank McElroy to the House of Representatives. They were most likely related to James F. McElroy, formerly of the Lansing School for the Blind, since they claimed all McElroys were in their clan.[685]

The McElroy faction included Railroad Commissioner John Rich and Harrison Geer. Geer was a McMillan political operative, a long-time friend and political aide of Rich, and an attorney for the Grand Trunk Railway. Another faction was the so-called Howard followers, and the third faction was made up of those not belonging to the other two factions or holding allegiance to geographic factions. Things heated up in February. The *Imlay City Optic*, a Lapeer County newspaper, explained, "We have refrained from saying anything about the struggle going on lately for the collectorship at Port Huron, as we have always supposed that no one outside Port Huron would stand any show at all for the office…We predict that there is not a man in the seventh district, who can lead under the incoming administration, more successfully than Harrison Geer. While he can neither whistle nor sing the funeral dirge, he can mark time and comprehend the difference between a chronic office seeker and an aspirant of political merit and qualification. Let the Democrat papers pipe their foghorns, Geer will get there just the same."[686]

In April of 1889 McMillan, whose railroad involvement included connections to the Grand Trunk Railway Company, chose Harrison Geer to replace the current Democratic district collector of the port authority at Port Huron. Geer then appointed Frank Mills of Lapeer as his chief deputy.[687] Mills kept a scrapbook of all articles concerning the port authority from the time he was appointed. This documentation of political strife, factional dissention, and mudslinging seems to be the very scrapbook that is now part of the Bentley archives at the University of Michigan.[688] This raucous seventh district exhibition of politics at the end of the century was portrayed in the scrapbook as a school for scoundrels, a picture of politics at dissentious heights as was seldom seen in Ingham County.

McMillan's appointment seemed to enrage everyone not from Lapeer County, especially Democrats. It was a job with far-reaching power over patronage jobs for the port authority and its stations along the coast, post offices, government printing contracts, shippers, and railroads. People who lived in Port Huron thought the appointment should have been a Port Huron man. Democrats were mad because they feared Geer would put all the current employees out of a job. He might have intended to, as would have been the flat-out case in the past when any out-of-office party came in. Now the new Pemberton Civil Service Act tended to slow him down. "The collector becomes the dispenser of patronage after May 1st," said the *Sunday Herald*. It worried, "McMillan and the Grand Trunk have put the railway attorney in office and the attorney will in turn do his level best to boost the railway director (Rich) into a seat in congress."[689]

After that, the Democratic newspapers never let up. The barrage of criticism must have been instructive to Geer who was moving into state-wide politics. Some comments were humorous: "The Herald is authorized to state that no young man who has fallen in with the prevailing craze and shaved off his mustache need apply for office under Collector Geer. The absence of a mustache will be deemed to be sufficient evidence of the lack of that sound judgment and nice discrimination which should always distinguish a United States custom official."[690] The newspapers referred to him as the Lapeer Man, the Italian, the spoilsman. The Republican *Port Huron Times* didn't help much by reporting on June 4 that the Republican *Mt. Clemens Monitor* said of a man from Armada, "a good citizen and Republican, who is likely to be appointed marine clerk, with a salary of $1400. But he will have to go through the ceremony of a civil service examination."[691] The *Sanilac Republican* complained all the best positions were going to other counties. "The recent experience of collector Geer in his efforts to adjudicate and determine who were the next of kin and lawful heirs to all the Custom House Estate positions and perquisites would naturally put him in the frame of mind to regard our allusion to the matter as indicative of the existence of factional divisions in the County," but that "whatever opposing views, wishes, or ambitions, will be adjusted among ourselves, without the aid of interposition of outside agencies."[692] After further consideration the newspaper, editorializing, said that when people in Sanilac County were disappointed about Geer's appointment, he should in no way take it to mean they were dissatisfied.[693]

There were fake Geer interviews and quotations, and phony telephone conversations printed in various newspapers. Evasion of the Civil Service Act was the most serious charge. The Democratic Detroit *Free Press* said Geer circumvented the Civil Service Act by cutting salaries that were formerly higher to under $900 so they would not fall subject to the Civil Service requirements.[694] Once positions were filled, salaries could be raised.[695] The battle went on all summer as they fought about the Civil Service exam requirements, about how the exams were scored, and about the results. The *Sunday Herald*, by now one of Geer's strongest critics, accused Geer of coaching his favorites.[696]

It was up to the port authority collector to determine how custom fees were calculated and regulations were carried out. The *Sunday Herald* spelled out the issue by accusing Geer, as an attorney for a foreign corporation, of a conflict of interest between his two jobs. Conflict of interest was one of the practices the Civil Service reform was designed to curb. "A large proportion of the work of Mr. Geer's office is to protect the government in its dealings with the C. & G. T... If the United States Senate were not made up of railway attorneys and the hirelings and tools of corporations it would when the opportunity occurs vindicate the purity of the public service by refusing to confirm the Chicago & Grand Trunk railway as collector of customs at this port through one of its attorneys."[697]

The biggest to-do came over an interview in the *Detroit Free Press* that was soon carried in other newspapers:

CIVIL SERVICE REFORM – Collector Geer is Emphatically Opposed to the Whole Measure. HE TELLS WHY IT DOES NOT WORK

"Judging from my observations so far, I am not an advocate of civil service reform or a believer in the political principles which it sets forth," said Hon. Harrison Geer, Collector of Customs at Port Huron, as he tarried for a brief period in the Russell House lobby, en route to Lansing, last evening. "As the rule largely prevails in the office to which I have been appointed, I have excellent opportunities for judging of its efficiency and desirability. It is only natural that a man who is placed in a responsible position should desire those who are more agreeable to him, politically as well as in a business sense, about him. As it is, I have practically no voice in the matter. When an applicant comes in, no matter how much I should desire to give him a favorable answer, all that I can do is refer him to the Civil Service Examiner and await the result. That result, according to the very nature of things, is apt to be anything but satisfactory. There are already no less than ninety such applications on file in my office awaiting action. The questions that are put to applicants are almost wholly of an educational character and have little, if any, bearing upon the duties which an attaché of a customs office is expected to perform. They are theoretical rather than practical. There can be but one result. The man or woman who has recently left school, or passes the examination with flying colors whether I want him or not, while the sound-headed business man and man of affairs who has forgotten a few of the theories taught him at schools and colleges, but who is nevertheless the man of all others who would do me the most good, is unmercifully plucked and sent forth in disgrace... This is why I do not believe in civil service reform, as at present applied to applicants for minor political positions. Had Mr. Cleveland less to do with it, he would have fared much better at the hands of his party in the recent campaign. The old adage, 'To the victors belong the spoils,' may sound harsh and grasping, but to the man who is familiar with political exigencies it forms about the only safe and satisfactory rule for guidance in partisan matters."[698]

These anti-civil service remarks were so widely reported that they reached the ears of the President Harrison's newly appointed Civil Service Commissioner, Theodore Roosevelt. "Commissioner Roosevelt's views upon the civil service law can hardly afford pleasant reading to those Republicans of Port Huron who have picked out comfortable jobs in the custom house. If they are to have no better show than a Democratic applicant, the victory of last fall will turn to the deadest of Dead Sea fruit in their hungry maws," opined the *Sunday Herald*. [699] The New York *Evening Post* reported that Roosevelt said of Geer, "The Commission has, of course, no control over the expression of any public officer... They will tolerate no violation and no evasion of the statute."[700] Contrary to the expectations of some, the Republican administration was going to enforce the new reform law. Geer said the Detroit *Free Press* interview never happened, but that ninety percent of all Democrats and Republicans agreed with the sentiments at the end of the article.[701] Armed with this experience, Geer entered into the Michigan gubernatorial campaign working for McMillan and John Rich.

The Worst Republican Primary Ever

Many Republican newspapers in the state were quick to endorse Jim. "He is popular everywhere, because he is a generous, whole-souled, genial gentleman, whose record as a citizen of Michigan and as a stalwart Republican is without a blemish," said the editor of Saginaw's *Courier-Herald*.[702] It would be very difficult to beat anyone if such a reputation were allowed to stand.

The state election of 1890 was filled with turmoil few people of the era would likely forget, even though it was not a presidential year. Campaigns were vicious, and Jim must have known what to expect and felt ready for it. But the viciousness of this campaign was felt in the primary, soon after Jim announced he would run and John Rich became his opponent. While there were many more newspapers back then, they were often very partisan and reckless. Some newspapers could be relied upon for support, such as *The Detroit Tribune* and *The Detroit News* which were both published by James E. Scripps and once inscribed on their mastheads, "No more street railway franchises on any terms. Restoration of government by the people and not by private corporations."[703] Jim's friend Thomas Applegate, the editor of the *Adrian Times and Expositor*, was active in Republican party politics from the party's founding. Democratic newspapers such as *The Lansing Journal*, *The Detroit Free Press*, and *The Detroit Journal* were more than willing to stir things up in the Republican party and print any sort of muck.

In those days the convention system prevailed. A party's statewide candidates were not selected by all voters in a party primary election but by delegates to a state convention held for that purpose. The first step was to elect delegates to the nominating convention at the local level. Jim's primary campaign for delegates started off quite well, and Sophie was there to help. "Mrs. Turner is the constant companion of her husband during the arduous labors connected with the present campaign, cheering and sustaining him with her comforting presence and influence. Two fine lads, ten and twelve years of age, have resulted from this union of hearts and of hands, and the Turner home in Lansing is an ideal paradise of domestic happiness and love," wrote the local newspaper.[704]

As the convention approached, Sidney Corbett, Jr., Publisher of *The Critic*, a magazine covering arts, culture, and politics, wrote from Detroit on August 23, 1890:

> They have 2 boys, James and Scott, aged 12 and 10 years respectively, bright little fellows whom you may see any pleasant day flying about the streets of Lansing on their fleet Shetland ponies.
>
> The state convention to be held here next week promises not to be a kid glove affair but a bear dance, and a bear dance in a Republican Convention in Michigan is such an anomaly that an inquiry into the causes of the condition of the affairs that produces such a result is pertinent.
>
> The great contest will be for governor... Both men are strong physically and mentally. Mr. Rich is a man of dollars only in his name. Both are farmers. These two men have taken dramatically different attitudes during pre-convention days.
>
> Mr. Rich seemingly has made no effort to secure the plum, while Mr. Turner, through his friends, has made a thorough, systematic and vigorous campaign. There has been a degree of boldness in it that has excited much admiration. So far as official endorsement is concerned, Mr. Turner hasn't had any. But Mr. Rich, on the other hand, in addition to aid from the Grand Trunk railroad, is said through Counselor Geer of Port Huron, to have been working the machine for all there is in it, and Senator Stockbridge's secretary, "Sky" Olds, and Senator McMillan's W.R. Bates, are using all the potent means in their command to crush out the young aspirant to gubernatorial honors and elevate Mr. Rich to a throne where he can aid the august autocrats, perhaps in seeking re-election to the United States Senate. And Governor Cyrus G. Luce has been guilty of stooping from his "high chair" to work against his Lansing neighbor, it is said, for personal reasons akin to those animating the present United States Senators. This is the situation today.[705]

The district delegate selection practices brought accusations of unfairness from the Turner supporters. The *Detroit Free Press* reported on August 24, 1890, that Geer's machine in the seventh district was faltering, "Mt. Clemens County Republicans who were not for Rich protested and denounced the proceedings of the county convention held in the city August 16, 1890."[706] Other difficulties loomed when three small factional parties announced their primary selection conventions for choosing their own gubernatorial candidates.

It had been thought that the Patrons of Industry Party, founded the year before and composed of many members of the Grange, would endorse Jim. They wanted someone who was a genuine farmer and would curtail public expenses, lower taxes, and refuse to issue special charters of all kinds, especially to syndicates.[707] However, when the Patrons' state convention was held at Lansing July 29, they chose to run their own candidate, a move they hoped would strengthen their own party rather than the Republican party. They nominated Eugene A. Beldon, which would most certainly cut into the Republican vote. The Prohibition and Labor parties were not interested in fusing with the Patrons and went ahead with organizing to field candidates of their own.

> *The Republican*, Livingston County, June 26, 1890
> The candidates most prominently mentioned at present are James M. Turner of Lansing, and John T. Rich, of Lapeer, with the first named gentleman much in the lead. Mr. Turner is well and favorably known in all parts of the state and is a staunch republican from way back. He is never found napping when there is work to be done. As a candidate for governor he is said to have many followers in the north part of the state and certainly has many friends in the lower peninsula. There is probably no one in the state who knows the agricultural needs and who is more closely identified with farming interests than James Turner. The Michigan Farmer last week devoted several columns of its space to a description of Mr. Turner's Springdale stock farm of 2000 acres just east of Lansing.[708]

National issues were a big part of the state campaign that year. *The Detroit Free Press* on August 7 reported, "Democrats proposed to beat Turner on the issues of tariff reforms, free coinage of silver and national currency."[709] The Democrats argued silver coinage would put more money in the hands of ordinary people and ease the credit pinch. It was widely perceived that the McKinley Tariff Act put tariffs so high they favored the large industries at the expense of the consumer. *The Sunday News*, August 17, said "The failures of the Republican Congress to give the people free silver are strong arguments before the people." But in the Michigan Republican party primary, it was politics, not issues, that were the driving force. The *State Republican* stepped up to lay out the story when it perceived disharmony could threaten the success of the party in the general election:

> We refer to the intensely personal attacks sprung within the past three weeks upon James M. Turner, one of the candidates for the gubernatorial nomination… John T. Rich of Elba, Lapeer county, and James M. Turner of Lansing … are warm personal friends, and each has a large following in the state. The masses of the party felt that in the nomination of either of the candidates would make no serious mistake, and were prepared to accept the winner with all the old-time enthusiasm. For about five months the canvas progressed quietly and amicably. Not a

word of personalities was injected into the matter until within about four weeks of the nominating convention, when a strongly personal article, relative to a railroad suit of Mr. Turner's appeared in a Chicago paper. This was followed by another, appearing under the head of Lansing correspondence in the Detroit Journal and even more offensively personal than the first. The Grand Rapids Leader then led with lying interviews. It is fair to say, right here, that none of Mr. Turner's friends charge Mr. Rich with any complicity in this despicable business, nor will the public.

With the truth or falsity of the charges preferred against Mr. Turner the Republican has nothing to do. The parties making the stab at Turner claim to be republicans, and are active in republican councils. But it is certain that his opponents now bring the matter into the state convention, their inconsiderate action in seeking to crush Mr. Turner through the public press, at this late day, will have aroused a feeling which may require careful action to avoid disaster.[710]

From then on the attacks on Jim were endless. Every facet of his life brought orchestrated, trumped-up charges. One of the characteristics most universally known about Jim was his honesty. Like his father, he was called "Honest Jim." The charges seemed designed to paint him as dishonest. Among the claims were that he had given away free over 6,000 state fair passes to cheat the State Agricultural Society in order to get votes;[711] he was a land shark, a crooked businessman; the Grand Trunk coupon case was proof he was a thief; he lobbied for a sixty day suspension in the sugar duties to circumvent the sugar trusts and benefit the Michigan Condensed Milk Company; and he wasn't really a farmer. It was claimed Luce's men said he was unfit and a very poor apology as mayor of Lansing; he catered to the liquor and "bagnio" interests;[712] he had made his fortune from brothels and saloons in Lansing; he went on benders in saloons in Detroit; and Governor Luce was against him.

One thing that was not debated or even discussed publically was Jim's support for a plank in the platform calling for more equal assessment and taxation of all property—because that intended to include hitherto untaxed railroads.

Fake interviews, false documents, and false information abounded and received plenty of coverage in the Democratic press. Each accusation had to be responded to in not just the Democratic press but in the Republican and independent presses as well. Sometimes the newspapers would print the Turner response, but then go right on with the same accusations.[713] The average citizen would have a difficult time discerning the truth without first considering the source. This continued unrelentingly through the election season, and always in the background, was thought to be Harrison Geer, attorney for the Grand Trunk Railway and campaign manager for Rich.

Sylvester Kinney of the *L'Anse Sentinel* thought all the mudslinging would boomerang: "The Detroit Journal is pouring its vials of venom upon the head of James M. Turner, which will have the effect (unintentioned of course) of putting Turner several notches ahead in the race for the governor's chair. The Journal would be honest and have far more influence if it would come out flat footed for the prohibition party."[714] The Grand Trunk Railroad Corporation, fearing regulations Jim might institute, provoked Democratic newspapers, but the Lansing *State Democrat* thought the attacks were so far from the truth regarding Jim's character that they would backfire. "The State Democrat is politically just what its name implies. But we are at liberty to say, and we are morally bound to say, that when James M. Turner's character as an honest, upright, public-spirited citizen is assailed, the vermin who do it are gnawing at a file. As a businessman, as a citizen, as a man, no truthful word of disparagement can be whispered against James M. Turner. He is in every way the equal of any citizen of Lansing, or of Michigan. And any and all attempts to assail his character are sure to react in his favor … said attacks on Turner are being generated by an employee of the Grand Trunk Railroad."[715] The *State Republican* commented on phony news stories planted in some newspapers: "Smears—attributed to the banking commissioner, Mr. T. C. Sherwood, that there was material in the capitol that is alleged to defeat Turner, and that the Ingham Co. delegation was split between Rich and Turner because of it, were all denied by Sherwood—a negative campaign."[716]

The rebuttals included testimonials for Jim's character such as this one:

Mr. Turner's Generosity

Peter Mortonson of Edmore, a native of Denmark, is a man who can remember a good deed, and furnishes another testimonial to the generosity of James M. Turner similar to the many already published in the Republican. The following was sent to the Detroit Tribune:

As Mr. James M. Turner is a candidate on the republican ticket for governor, I think it nothing but just to state one of the good acts performed by Mr. Turner. About seven years ago I was engaged in building a railroad fence for the Detroit, Lansing, & Northern railroad through the farm of Mr. Turner. I had the job nearly completed when Mr. Turner happened along. He remarked: "Boy, you have done a good job, and when you get through call at my office up town." When the fence was completed and I called at the office as requested and without any further words Mr. Turner gave me $15, saying as he handed me the money, "I think you deserve it."

At that time I was a poor hard-working man and the money was very acceptable, and I shall always remember his generosity. The railroad company paid me for the work as agreed upon, and Mr. Turner was a stranger to me and under no obligation to pay a cent, and it was not solicited by me. I have not seen Mr. Turner since, and as he did not ask my name I presume he has forgotten the transaction. I think Mr. Turner a good kind of a man for governor. [717]

According to Gratiot County's *Republican Leader*, Jim was a rising new light: "Mr. Turner frankly admits the truth of the Journal's statement that the federal office-holders of the state and nearly all of Governor Luce's appointees are arrayed solidly against him. This of course, means a decided strengthening of Mr. Rich's hand, but in the agricultural counties, where it was expected that Rich would show his greatest strength, Farmer Turner has captured delegation after delegation, and has written pledges to show for it, despite the desperate and unscrupulous attempts made to defeat him in certain localities."[718] On the eve of the convention, *The Lansing Journal* told its readers in an article entitled "A Hustling Candidate:"

> We congratulate our hustling fellow townsman, James M. Turner, on the gamey fight he is making for the Republican nomination for Governor.
>
> He is opposed by great odds—not only has the influence of the state administration been thrown against him, but the powerful aid of the federal office-holding set in Michigan has been successfully involved to defeat him. It appears that he has also incurred the disfavor of the two United States Senators from this State, and their great personal influence is being openly exerted against him. This opposition is the penalty which Mr. Turner is compelled to pay for his daring to start out in politics on his own hook and the divvle take the hindmost. But he is a pretty lively young man, and he may yet triumph over the big combine. Stranger things than that have happened when the rare combination of brains, stand, and unlimited self-confidence has been the propulsive power.
>
> It was called "one of the most exciting and altogether intense struggles for a gubernatorial nomination ever carried on in Michigan" ... ex-Senator John Holbrook shall present the Lansing candidate's name to the convention, and that Roswell G. Horr of Saginaw and ex-Governor of Jackson shall make the chief seconding speeches.[719]

Stanley W. Turner was Jim's campaign manager. (They were not related—Stanley was from Ohio.) They came to know each other when they both served in the House of Representatives in 1877. It was the same session for which Rich was Speaker of the House. Stanley Turner had even endorsed Rich for governor during one of Rich's earlier campaigns, but now he sided with party reform. Austin Blair and Dwight Smith, both back in the Republican fold, and Daniel Case were at the convention to help, and John Longyear came down as a delegate from Marquette. The Turner camp said Rich had used his position as Railroad Commissioner to favor the railroads over the good of the people.[720] The end of that kind of favoritism was at stake, and the McMillan faction knew it. Jim's reform practices as mayor demonstrated his support for the Pendleton Civil Service Reform Act of 1883, and he opposed the special treatment of the railroads. At the convention the tension was building. The *Evening News* described the two camps on August 23:

> Stanley W. Turner, with his soft hat crushed out of shape and an unruly necktie crawling over the top of his collar, rushed from point

to point, receiving all comers and keeping the Turner lines intact and adding recruits whenever susceptible subjects were encountered.

"Pay no attention to these outside newspaper correspondents," is one of the young manager's stock pieces of advice. "Their reports are incorrect and misleading. They claim Shiawassee, for instance, yet we have four-fifths of the delegation. They quote Van Buren for Rich, yet we have the county too dead to skin. They grow jubilant over the third district, yet two-thirds of its delegates will stay by Turner till the cows come home. We've got them on the run, and nobody can stop 'em."

Harrison Geer, collector of customs at Port Huron, is chief pilot for Rich. His tactics are the direct opposite of those adopted by Turner's lieutenant. Geer is as non-committal as a sphinx and has a self-possessed air of confidence and mystery that puzzles and produces uneasiness in the opposition. He ... conveys the impression that he has a masked battery all along the political route laid out by Turner as the way to the gubernatorial chair. He is content with saying that Rich will succeed Luce.[721]

Frank Mills, for many years chairman of the Lapeer county Republican committee and Geer's chief deputy at the port authority, said to the *Tribune*: "We believe the people of Michigan want Mr. Rich. He embodies all the necessary qualifications to lead the party to victory. He is a man of character, ability and availability. His record is clean and honorable, and with him as our standard-bearer the Republicans will have nothing to apologize for or defend so far as his private record is concerned."[722]

The headquarters of the two candidates were stocked with the best brands of cigars and a copious supply of badges for delegates to wear. On August 27 the two candidates arrived in Detroit on the same train; however, Jim's arrival was much more spectacular. "Farmer Turner" rode to town on top of one of the nine box car loaded with his stock for the exposition in town, all headed for ribbons.[723]

As the *Detroit Tribune* reported it, "While the nominating speeches were being made for Governor, Mr. Turner sat in his rooms at the Russell house talking with Mr. W. Bates [secretary to Senator McMillan.] In a pause of the conversation, Mr. Turner's eager son said: 'Papa, after they get through speeches and balloting, then what will they do?' 'Then, my son,' said the imperturbable candidate, 'they will appoint a committee to come over and get me to go and make a little speech accepting the nomination, and you shall go with me.' And it was even so."[724]

Former Senator John Holbrook took to the platform to give his nominating speech, offering a candidate who was dedicated to serving the needs of all of the people, a reformer: "I offer you a strong, stalwart man, whose physical proportions culminate in a massive head chock full of brains. (applause), one in the full blush of manhood, brave, courageous, who stands upon an eminence made up of difficulties which he has conquered and put under his feet. I offer you a man of genial good-fellowship, companionable, approachable, one who makes friends wherever he goes and keeps them. I offer him to you, not as the representative of any class or interest. My candidate stands for all that is best and most inspiring in American life, and he is broad enough to comprehend the needs and sympathize with the feelings of every interest in this great state."[725] Blair pleaded the case for not forgetting that the goals of the Civil War for Negroes were not yet fully realized. He strongly endorsed and applauded the nomination of Jim. W. S. Linton was nominated as lieutenant governor. He was a prominent manufacturer and businessman from Saginaw. He was the well-known State Representative from East Saginaw who had helped broker a deal with Mayor Schakelburg during the Saginaw consolidation fight.

In his acceptance speech, Jim acknowledged the history of the great city of Detroit and its great men in the Republican party: "that mild-mannered, grand gentleman, Henry P. Baldwin;" James F. Joy a "level-headed broad-minded, aggressive man" who pushed ahead and gridironed this state with railroads… "made the waste places blossom as a rose, now over 80 years of age(cheers);" "the big-headed, large-hearted, genial Thomas Palmer;" the wheel-horse of the Republican party, Zachariah Chandler." (loud applause) "Then again," Jim said, "the city of Detroit gave us that man of splendid brain, magnificent fellow, who has done so much to develop the industries of the city and the state, and has led us so often to victory and will lead us again, James McMillan. (cheers)" He reached out with praise for the recognition of Alger, Luce, and Austin by the convention. He concluded by saying that should he win he would use his abilities "for the next two years in the interest of all the people of the two peninsulas."[726]

The welcome home in Lansing the next day at the Michigan Central depot began earlier in the evening on the capitol lawn where a band played, and cheer after cheer went up.

> At 8:30 the crowd began moving towards the depot where they crowded around the place and long platform and filled the streets adjoining and cheered the expected nominee. When the train pulled in and Mr. and Mrs. Turner and two sons made their appearance the din was simply deafening, and it was with difficulty that President Nesen of the Turner club and President Clute of the Agricultural college, who had been chosen to welcome the party, could make a way through the crowd to the wagon that was to convey them home, so eager were all to grasp Mr. Turner's hand and congratulate him on his convention victory.
>
> Once seated, the procession formed in line, headed by the band and to the inspiring music of "Hail to the Chief" and amidst the blaze of torches and fireworks and cheers from thousands of throats, marched to the capitol square where another ovation was in waiting. When the cheers had somewhat subsided, Dr. Wellings introduced President Clute … who addressed the crowd. ("A Royal Welcome") Then Jim spoke:
>
> Fellow citizens, kind neighbors and friends, this ovation completely overwhelms me. I have been away from home many times in my life, but

never before has the return seemed so good, and never has the old city of Lansing, the place of my childhood, the place of my manhood, and the place where I expect to spend my old age, looked so sweet as at the present time. I left home on Monday and since then I have had less than six hours sleep, and the fact of the matter is what little time I have slept has been with one eye open (laughter), so I know you realize how tired I am, and will not expect much of a speech. Lansing, somehow, has a way of getting what she goes after, as a general thing, and I know that she wanted the gubernatorial nomination and it was expected when myself and friends returned we would bring it with us. (Tremendous cheers

Now, my friends, just a few words more. Have no fears about the result of the election in November, we will make satisfactory arrangements for that. It's pretty late in the evening, and early in the season to open the campaign, but never mind, we will get a-going pretty quick. Good night.

At the close of Mr. Turner's remarks the crowd formed in line again and escorted Mr. Turner and family to their pleasant home on Franklin street, where an informal reception was held and light refreshments served; where, after giving three loud cheers and a tiger for the next governor of Michigan, the crowd dispersed.[727]

The Election of 1890

That fall Jim got some excellent endorsements, including testimonials of praise from the Upper Peninsula. *The Miner's* editors said, "In this sense he is a millionaire, as he represents millions of capital invested by himself and friends in these great industrial industries, which to-day are giving employment to thousands of men. Every man that is employed by him is treated as a *man*, no strikes have ever occurred among his men; they all know him as Jim Turner, and will vote for him. That's the kind of a millionaire he is, and would to God Ontonagon county had a few more of his kind here just now, instead of men that send away every dollar earned here to invest in banks, lands or real estate in distant towns, counties or states. Of one thing Mr. Turner can be justly proud, and that is the fact that he does not own nor is he the possessor of a mortgage on any man's farm or home in the state of Michigan. He is in every sense the poor man's friend."[728] Ironwood's *Interstate News-Record* said, "He is a joyful gentleman and is possessed of a magnetism that wins him hosts of friends, excellent adjuncts to a leader of clear perception and rare executive ability. The upper peninsula will give Mr. Turner a rousing majority. He has extensive interests in all sections of this country, extending from Gogebic county at the west to Chippewa at the east, and he is thoroughly conversant with the U. P.'s peculiar industries and requirements. Mr. Turner is a staunch friend of the mining school and believes it one of the state's best institutions."[729]

The St. Louis newspaper quoted a Saginaw paper saying, "We had been informed that he was a railroad magnate. So this point received attention and we discovered that he and his father had used their own money, their influence, their muscle and brains to secure to Lansing a system of railroads that the capitol might be reached by every citizen in the broad territory. They were builders of the Jackson, Lansing & Saginaw and the Chicago & Northeastern, now operated by the Michigan Central and Grand Trunk corporations. Hence Mr. Turner's railroad interest was identical with every citizen in the state."[730]

On October 2 Battle Creek's *Daily Journal* reported, "They spent an hour in pleasant handshaking with our citizens last evening," after a visit to the Calhoun County Fair at Marshall. The Republican city committee hosted a public reception in the parlors of the Williams House which was appropriately decorated for the occasion. Guests, including many ladies, were introduced to the candidate and his wife. "Everyone feels that he will not permit the dignity of the gubernatorial office to make him less accessible to the people than he has hitherto been as plain 'Jim,' the familiar title by which he has always been addressed by his friends throughout the state… Mrs. Turner, by her easy grace, unaffected manners, and superior womanly sense, won the esteem and admiration of all who met her and demonstrated that her husband has an efficient ally in his home and public career and will be ably seconded in the social duties of his administration."[731] They headed home that Wednesday on the 8:45 train and then were on their way to Bay City and Alpena. Jim expected to campaign in eighty counties in forty days, mostly by train. "Of course, this means life on the wing and hard work for a few weeks, but it is in a good cause and I am happy in it," quoted the editor of the *Alpena Pioneer*.

As often happens when there is a bloody primary battle, the mud then sticks because it is now in the interest of the opposition to keep bringing it up—but more was coming. The lawsuit by the Grand Trunk Railroad was used to claim Jim lost a case that charged fraud. In an article about the attack, Cy Black, William P. Wells, and Henry F. Henderson, all attorneys in the case, detailed the charges and the facts of the case. They said they believed that when Jim cut the coupons from the bonds he sold, he did not intend to cancel them but to claim payment that was due before the sale. They said Sage knew the coupons were missing, and Vanderbilt could not have supposed to buy what Sage did not have. They pointed out that William Vanderbilt died in 1885, and his testimony was lost so it couldn't be used to support their case. There was no evidence that he ever laid claim to the coupons. They said: "If, upon the points set forth the Supreme court, as we think, disregarded the weight of the testimony given, it is certain that their conclusions must be unfairly strained to support any charge of fraud." They said the attorneys and Judge Peck were all Democrats and friends of Judge Winans, and they were confident "Judge Winans would willingly join in their protest against a method of political warfare which involves an assault upon the personal integrity of an antagonist like this."[732] They undoubtedly felt certain of this, since Frank was a warm personal and political friend of Edwin B. Winans, Jim's Democratic opponent.[733]

In early October, James F. McElroy came back into the state from Albany, New York, where he had been working in the railroad car manufacturing industry, serving all the major railroad companies by providing couplings, brakes, and heating devices for thousands of train cars, an industry in which Senator McMillan held a near monopoly. He came for vengeance and made the same old charges he had attempted to peddle three years before when he was fired from the School for the Blind, but this time they were printed in a six-column article on Sunday in *The Detroit Free Press* (which was a far cry from the newspaper it is today). To be sure, the article did not mention that he was tied to the passenger and freight car industry or that McElroy had been fired, much less why.[734] McElroy took the case to court, and the Democratic papers covered it widely, including the *New York Times*.

These charges were successfully and promptly refuted by Thomas S. Applegate and many other friends, but the attacks contributed in no small degree to Jim's defeat. McElroy's charges were filed with Gov. Luce, and some said that although frequently appealed to, the ex-governor did not do enough toward silencing the tongue of slander. This action on the part of Gov. Luce was hard for some Turner supporters to forgive.[735]

The *Kalamazoo Telegraph* said, "'Jim' Turner's reply to the sensational 'charges' made by the Free Press will be a 15,000 majority next November." In Bay City they advised Jim not to respond: "If candidates are expected to refute each and every libel uttered by such party organs as the Detroit Free Press, they may as well be relieved from all other duties relating to the campaign. It is shameful commentary upon the state of Michigan that one of her leading papers, in point of circulation and general news, should bear the reputation of being the rankest cesspool in the journalistic field." And old wounds surfaced with the comment, "No party need look for popular

The School for the Blind, postcard. E.A. Homer collection.

support in loyal Michigan so long as they recognize leadership in a news-paper whose columns still reverberate with echoes of the old rebel yell and whose campaign tactics consist in defamation of character and promulgation of the vilest and most obvious falsehood."[736]

Jim made a great effort to disprove each charge with affidavits and sworn statements of those involved, and Applegate and Daniel Case did all they could. Jim found himself saying right up to the last week of the campaign, "I state positively, unequivocally and absolutely that I never derived in the way of profits $8,000 or 8 cents, or 1 cent, or any other sum, at any time, from or through a sale of any materials to the school for the blind, during, before or since my connection with that institutions, and I challenge the world on this proposition"[737]

However, all of this may not have made any difference. Whatever the turbulence of the primary process and the McElroy scandal had cost Jim, it was a Democratic year across the nation, bringing Democrats to the polls and to power in Congress and in many Republican stronghold states. "We are Downed," said the headline of one newspaper; "A Cyclone Struck the Republicans Tuesday. The slaughter seems to be quite general."[738] No one seemed to blame Edwin Winans: "If we must have a democratic governor we do not know of any better man than Hon. E. B. Winans of Livingston county," said Livingston County's *Republican*.[739] "Mr. Turner always claimed, after his defeat by Gov. Winans, that the disastrous result chiefly owed to lack of enthusiasm on the part of Senator McMillan and his state central committee," said the *Telegram*.[740]

In the vote for governor, Winans received 183,725 votes with Jim getting 172,205. Azariah S. Partridge of the Labor party won 28,681,and the Patrons of Industry did very well with two seats in the Senate and six seats in the House, although Eugene A. Beldon got only 13,198. The two minor parties undoubtedly pulled votes from Jim. An analysis of the votes further down the ticket, where there were no third party candidates, showed there was only a base Republican vote of about 178,000 voters out of the 398,655 who voted. Jim lost by 11,520 votes. He did carry the Upper Peninsula.[741] The disastrous primary, scurrilous attacks in the general election, lack of support by some of his party's leaders, the competition of the two minor parties, and national issues had all cut into his vote.

John Longyear had his own take on the election, "In 1890 I was a delegate to the Republican State Convention at Detroit when Jim was nominated for Governor. It is said that the Grand Trunk Railway spent many thousand dol-lars in that campaign. Anyhow Jim ran behind the ticket… It was doubtless the old fight with the Grand Trunk that defeated him. There was no other reason why he should not have been elected."[742]

After the election people were still angry months later, and there were repercussions for many years. This letter, written with ferocity and insight, gives a full airing to the feelings of many about the election. Jim never threw gasoline on the flames; he tried to discourage people from continuing to battle, but the *Lansing Journal* coverage apparently did not want to take this route when Robert Montgomery, an attorney and party activist from Eaton Rapids, was seeking the Republican nomination to the Supreme Court.

The State Republican, May 12, 1891

A FEW PLAIN FACTS, James M. Turner and the Montgomery Soap Bubble

To the Editor of the Republican:

Many of the friends of James M. Turner labored earnestly for the nomination of Judge Montgomery, and all of them are working zealously for his election. As I understand it, Mr. Turner himself took no part in the matter before the nomination, because all of the candidates had been friendly to him in the last campaign. But neither Mr. Turner nor his friends are like Achilles, "sulking in their tents" in this present conflict. Whenever they oppose a candidate the objection will be politely but properly made in convention. There will be no "guerilla" or "bushwhacking" warfare. They are neither "dagos" nor "greasers [a slur directed at Geer]," and do not stab opponents in the back. In this connection a retrospective view of the last political battle in this state may not be inappropriate.

James M. Turner made a magnificent campaign. He fought black-guardism with blood. He met, face to face, charges born of avarice, jealously and malice, and, where shame was not effective, policy has driven them into their rat holes. The figures on the result break the proverb: they lie.

James M. Turner was slandered, maligned, vilified and lied about. All the devious devices of ingenious deceit were directed against him. He was the target of treachery. Republican inanition deadened his campaign. Men who should have been true were merely trifling. Men who should have exercised their best energies exercised their worst. Many whose feet had been quick to hunt for the honors of the party were slow to walk towards their duties. From the start to the string, from the bell to the judge's stand, Jim Turner ran his race alone. The glory of it belongs to him. Against odds that would have appalled a person of more than ordinary daring he struggled with placid courage. Against defamation, against indecency, against all the resources of ready falsehood, against all the obstacles of doubtful loyalty, he picked his way through to the result. He accepted that result with religious fortitude and in the spirit of Christian resignation. What he has done for the republican party of the state deserves its reward. The contest was one of straight republicanism. It was made for straight republicanism. The effect is for straight republicanism. Defeat on such an issue would be better than a gorgeous display of complicating extravaganzas on any other. Better a telescope than a kaleidoscope. This was a crazy quilt of treachery. It may be worthwhile to study every pattern and know the pieces.

If James M. Turner had only a hundred votes it would have been a triumph of sense over sensation. He reached but one hand above the froth, and the falsity and the folly of the ugly nastiness of the water through which he waded, and honest men recognized the signal. But he led an army of wooden soldiers. There were more knives in the rear than guns in the front, and in that great struggle of crime against creed, it is the disgrace of some of our leading republicans that they forgot their party catechism, and only remembered their personal ambitions. It is as well to be plain in the declaration, as they were plain in their motives.

John N. Lucas[743]

The *State Republican*, interviewed Jim on the hornets' nest that *The Lansing Journal* had tried to stir up about Jim's support for the local judge's candidacy for the Supreme Court:

DENIES THE STATEMENT
James M. Turner Says the Statement in Saturday's Journal Was False.

On Saturday the Lansing Journal published a characteristic article in which it conveyed to its readers the startling information that James M. Turner and his political friends were "on the warpath" for the scalp of Judge Montgomery, and that the cause of this uprising was Judge Montgomery's expressed preference for John T. Rich in the state convention last summer. The Journal was so circumstantial in its details that some members of its staff must hold close and confidential relations with Mr. Turner, or possessed an imagination that would make H. Rider Haggard turn sky blue. The following relation of an interview held with Mr. Turner by the Republican will enable our readers to decide between the theories of truth and imagination:

"Mr. Turner, Have you read the article in the Journal defining your position towards Judge Montgomery?"

"Yes," said Mr. Turner, "and have replied to it. When I was a candidate I suppose the newspapers were licensed to tell every infernal lie about me that their ingenuity could devise, and I accepted the situation; but I am now a private citizen; trying to mind my own business; and it is about time the newspapers stopped lying. It seems however, that the Journal has grown so accustomed to abusing me that it can't break short off."

"But about Judge Montgomery?"

"Not a word of truth in it of course. I am a republican. Judge Montgomery is a man for whom I have a high personal admiration. He is clean. He has ability. I think the state convention did well in nominating him and I hope and expect to exercise my rights as a vote in favor of Judge Montgomery this spring. If I have any friends who feel differently, I don't know it. I have notified the Journal of my feelings on the matter."

It may please the Journal to make such unauthorized use of the names of private citizens for political ends, but it certainly gains nothing by such a course but contempt.[744]

Robert M. Montgomery won the nomination to the Supreme Court in 1891 and was elected by a 25,000 vote majority.[745] Eventually the heat generated by the 1890 election died down. Whenever it was necessary to refer to that election, people simply said things such as, "and no more need be said" or "we are all familiar with the details." By 1904 when the history of the Republican party, *Under the Oaks*, was written, only a page was devoted to this election. Internal party conflicts were ignored; it blamed the loss on unnamed scandals, and the fact that the Party's temperance plank in the platform was weak, merely saying that it reaffirmed previous positions of 1886 and 1888 and that Turner was not a strong temperance candidate. It said some Republican voters just stayed home. Voters do stay home when they are sufficiently turned off by an ugly campaign; however, about 17,000 more votes were cast than in the previous off-year election. By and large, the facts of the election were forgotten as the participants died away.

The unseemly power struggle over the Republican party nomination in 1890 was just one of the battles in a war to usurp the lumber, shipping, and railroad barons who controlled the state to their own financial benefit. Jim was in the forefront of a Republican progressive movement reflected in other parts of the state and the nation as well, so his candidacy was all the more threatening to the powers that be who seemed disposed to let Jim lose rather than see him and his reformers take over the party. In doing so, they created something of a folk hero for many.

The machine had erred in another way when it recruited Hazen Pingree to break through the Democrats' hold on Detroit politics the previous year. Pingree was a successful shoe manufacturer and was recruited in 1889 by the Republican party for mayor because he was well regarded and well known in the city. It was not clear at that point that Pingree would side with the liberal Turner reformers of the party, but Pingree was soon in the thick of it and observed one result of Winans' election: "A president of one of Michigan's railroads, a Vanderbilt corporationist and an alleged Democrat; the grandson of one of Michigan's illustrious generals, long since dead, a general who got his honors and his money through the Democratic party; he, the grandson, furnished money to support the candidacy of a *Republican* for Governor of Michigan. When a *Democrat* [Winans] was elected Governor [a seemingly Democratic] railroad president got the attorney for one of Michigan's railroads appointed railroad commissioner for Michigan [Charles R. Whitman], thus controlling that important office in the interest of railroads. These incidents are only related to illustrate a condition now patent to nearly all men, and that is, that corporations do not care a straw for the furtherance of the principles of any party, but worm themselves into the conventions of all of them for the express purpose of gaining their own private ends."[746] In 1891 an issue before state railroad commissioners and the railroad industry was the regulations and requirements regarding brakes and couplings of railroad cars, an issue of great interest to James F. McElroy and his partner George Westinghouse who both held patents that would be greatly affected by the decisions of Congress and state Legislatures—and the Railroad Commission.

Jim and Pingree, or Ping as he was called, were the most visible leaders of reform in the state when Jim set out to boom Pingree's move toward statewide politics. As a popular leader, Jim's opinions were sought by newspapers and they reported his every move. They knew Jim and Pingree were spending a lot of time together.

Chapter 14

The Not So Gay Nineties

People did not foresee the economic downturn that was coming. Jim was dealing with financial problems precipitated by a slump in the iron market, but he was getting a handle on them, and things seemed to be getting better and better for most people at the beginning of the last decade of the century. "We were living in prospect of better times, and we have lived to receive everything that we hoped for," Governor Josiah Begole told the Michigan Pioneer Society in 1889.[747]

Marian did not save many articles about the campaign of 1890 in her scrapbook—perhaps they were too much to bear or perhaps she knew her son's clipping service would take care of it. She saved an article from the Livingston County *Republican* about a special exhibit at the Detroit International Fair: "How Art and Science Have Elevated and Softened the Lives of Women—The Luxuries, Elegancies and Comforts of Modern Life." It was the same fair to which Jim sent nine carloads of stock for exhibition during the convention. At age 72, her lifetime experience traversed the wonders of the exhibit.[748] The whole idea was to encourage parents to take their children to the fair so that present day children could learn to appreciate the comforts and luxuries of modern homes and life. A lesson in gratitude and Marian saved it. Marian had six grandchildren now, Marian and Nelson's two boys, Jim and Sophie's two boys, Abby and Frank's little daughter Sophie, born in November of 1888, and their new baby boy, Franklin L. Dodge, Jr. Only through her stories could they imagine the lives of their grandparents here in what was once the city in the forest.

On January 28, 1891, Eva married Cy Black, long-time law partner of Frank. Their offices were in the Moody-Turner Block, which eventually became the Dodge Block. He had served with Frank in the Legislature, representing Tuscola County from 1883 to 1885. Cy was appointed U. S. Attorney for the Eastern District Court of Michigan by the district judge at the same time Frank was appointed U. S. Commissioner. Cy had been widowed in 1889. He was a western New Yorker who came to Tuscola County in 1866, at the age of 23, to begin his law career. He then went to Marquette to practice law with D. H. Ball from 1873 until 1877 and was elected prosecuting attorney of Marquette County. The firm of Ball and Black was interested and successful in many important mining law suits.[749]

The wedding notice read, "Turner-Black, A Swell Society Wedding at the Turner Bluffs, North Lansing." They were married "at the home of the bride's mother, Mrs. Marian Turner ... at 6 o'clock last evening by Rev. H. S. Jordan. The ceremony was simple and impressive and the bride looked unusually handsome in a becoming traveling dress. The bridal pair left on the 8:50 train for the west and sought to be at home at Detroit after two weeks. The home was charmingly decorated with flowers and plants, and music from the orchestra led to dancing after the ceremony and wedding supper. About sixty-five guests were present, among whom were: Mr. and Mrs. T. F. Stepard and Mr. and Mrs. C. F. Carrington of Bay City; Hon. Ezra Rost of Saginaw; Hon. Charles Butler [partner of Jim in northern real estate] and wife; C. T. Wilkes, Frank Marlette and ex-Rep. Gardner of Niles; Mrs. Dwight Smith and Mrs. H. H. Smith of Jackson, and Miss Rena Black of Detroit."[750]

The Panic of 1893

The *Adrian Telegram* summed it up: "The campaign entailed heavy expenses, which his then financial condition ill fitted him to bear, added to which was the fact that certain party leaders gave him little encouragement or support. After his defeat, Mr. Turner's financial difficulties rapidly increased although, when he entered upon the campaign, he was generally regarded as a prospective millionaire. He had immense property interests, but they were in such shape that little ready money could be realized upon them. Finally, as a last resort, he was obliged to file trust deeds covering all his property."[751]

Among his many other enterprises, Jim was president of the Land, Tax, and Loan Agency. (The letterhead said "Money to loan on improved farms. Pine and farming lands bought and sold."[752]) The agency held hundreds of thousands of acres of land in much the same way the Bank of Rochester had done in the Lower Peninsula when things were slowing down. On the brink of the financial crash of 1893, he found himself holding even more land than intended. Charles Butler, co-owner of much of their property holdings, had died, and Jim must have borrowed a lot of money to acquire Butler's share. Jim, Julian Case, and John Longyear owned similar businesses in real estate, and they also all owned shares in multiple mines. When Julian died suddenly on a business trip to London in 1890, John and Jim acquired Julian's shares in the process of helping to settle his estate.

Julian's death was unexpected despite health problems. John recalled, "Case built a good house in Marquette and for the winter of 1887-1888 Case was taken violently ill with a serious illness. In the spring, when able to travel, he returned to Marquette. He did not recover his strength readily, and his attending physician administered alcoholic stimulants, with the view of building up his strength. But Case would work on the artificial strength, and when that waned he would take more stimulant, and so, before he or his

Marian, Abby, and baby Sophie, Turner-Dodge House photo.

friends realized it, he was drinking hard. I saw but little of him during the year of 1889 but heard of him occasionally." Julian had gone to England to negotiate a deal for serpentine marble property in Marquette County. He had borrowed heavily from John and put up land for the loans.[753]

Changing federal iron import policies benefited the railroad corporations who lobbied for them by making the manufacture of railroad rails cheaper. However, the Great Western Mine at Crystal Falls in the Menominee Iron Range and many other iron mines across the Upper Peninsula and Wisconsin were hurt. The Great Western was owned by Jim's Iron Star Mining Company and was sometimes referred to as the Iron Star Mine. This property, opened in 1882, was the area's leading mine and was at the time the deepest mine in the area at a depth of 700 feet. It employed about 130 men.[754] A statement of estimated Assets and Liabilities as of March 1, 1892, for Jim's Iron Star Company showed liabilities of $181,006 and assets of $226,306. However, the assets included "Ore on Hand:" 13,071 tons at Lake Erie ports, 37,626 stock-piled at the mine, and 1,530 at Escanaba – valued at $101,755.[755] Loss of a market plunged the iron ranges into a depression and left Jim short of ready cash and other Turner enterprises endangered. He owned varying amounts of stock in 39 mines. John Longyear remembered the situation and the way he came to Jim's aid:

> A month or so after his defeat at the polls Jim met me in Chicago and told me that while in politics he had neglected his own affairs until he was in bad financial shape, and that he must have endorsement on $100,000 of notes. I discussed his affairs with him somewhat and made a suggestion that he had better get his creditors together, explain the situation to them, offer them his property if they wanted it, but state that he could make much more out of it than they could, and if they would carry him until he could turn the property into money that he could not only pay them but have sufficient left to go on with his own affairs. He was unable to consider this, and he seemed to be in a very

excited and nervous state. The labors of the campaign and the financial stress seemed to have exhausted his vitality. He went to Marquette with me and I realized the condition he was in. Within a few more weeks it became necessary to endorse $20,000 more of his notes.

In February 1891 I was in California for several weeks, and in April, in Denver, on my way home, I received a telegram to the effect that Turner had given up the financial fight which made it necessary for me to pay the endorsed paper. The banks which held the paper were very decent about it. In fact, as one of the bank officials said, they were very much pleased to have the paper in the shape it was and that I could take any reasonable time in which to pay it. I paid the paper off during the next three or four years, though it upset my own affairs a good deal to do it. Jim had always managed to work himself out of tight places and I supposed he would do so in this case."[756]

The problems soon became public. On May 12, 1891, *The State Republican* attempted to calm the fears of Lansing citizens concerning the rumors that had been flying about Jim's financial condition, and Marian saved the article. The editor knew Jim's extensive involvement in the local and state economy meant his economic failure would have far-reaching effects. James acted quickly to address the problem in a very public way. The lead headline read "Embarrassed. James M. Turner's Creditors Are Crowding Him," with subheadings, "The Depression in the Iron Market causes Temporary Embarrassment" and "At the Insistence of His Friends He Files Deeds of Trust to Secure His Creditors – No Serious Trouble Apprehended."

The citizens of Lansing and the whole state of Michigan for that matter were greatly shocked and surprised this morning at the article that appeared in the Detroit Tribune stating that Hon. James M. Turner of this city was financially embarrassed and had made a trust deed of his vast property interest to Christian H. Buhl and James F. Joy of Detroit, his life-long friends and backers.

The Republican is in position to say today, however, that while it is true that Mr. Turner has made certain trust deeds to these gentleman there is no cause for alarm and his embarrassment will be only temporary. Credible information is received that the whole cause of the trouble is the present depression of the iron market, Mr. Turner being largely interested in upper peninsula mines.

The creditors, who have been willing to carry Mr. Turner's paper heretofore, with the present depression, demanded a liquidation of such sums that could not be hastily complied with, and at the earnest solicitation of some of his friends who are several times millionaires, Mr. Turner placed his affairs temporarily in their hands, thereby preventing any possible sacrifice of his property interests, and thus Mr. Turner late yesterday afternoon filed a bill of sale with Clerk Hinman of this city, covering all his personal property of every kind, save such as is exempted by law, to Joy and Buhl in trust for themselves and the Lansing banks, the district national bank and Stephen Baldwin of Detroit, to secure $110,000 worth of indebtedness, consisting of drafts and checks made on bank and promissory notes.

To get needed cash, the trust deed agreement would allow his assets to remain in the Detroit bank's possession for six months. This action would afford time for him to pay off the loans and then if all went as planned the title to the properties would revert back to Jim. Frank Dodge and others also came to his aid. The *State Republican* went on to say:

> The statement that his connection with the new Iron Range & Huron Bay railway, now building in the upper peninsula, had been the cause of his embarrassment is in no sense true. Mr. Turner never invested a single dollar in that enterprise and is simply a constructor, backed by capitalists of unlimited means and is but a co-partner of these gentlemen.
>
> No figures of Mr. Turner's liabilities and assets have been made public, and his creditors have made no demand for such a statement. They realize that Mr. Turner is perfectly able to meet all demands if given a reasonable length of time to straighten things out, which will be done as speedily as possible.
>
> Mr. Turner is about his office as usual today, while he is of course annoyed at the disastrous turn his affairs have taken, is cheerful, and expresses himself as confident he will be able to pull through without more serious difficulty.

That night Howard wrote to his brother, enclosing clippings from the *Detroit Tribune.* "Jim is very badly cut up and blames himself all the time for getting you into this mess. He was almost crazy at first—but he is better now and is figuring things up with those interested… At first he was inclined to throw everything into the heap," but Howard said he held Jim in check until he got his breath. Howard went with Jim to a meeting with Christian Buhl and James Joy. "They told him they would do anything that he would say—even to putting up more for him." Buhl and Joy spoke to the press, and James Joy was quoted as saying it was his opinion that Mr. Turner would be able to pay all of his debts at an early date and still have a comfortable fortune left. "But you can't always tell with these things… Mr. Turner's affairs in my opinion depend entirely upon his creditors."[757]

The failure of the Iron Range and Huron Bay Railway added to Jim's trouble even though he was not an investor. The company owed the Michigan Slate Company at Arvon for the work it had completed for the railway company at the port. The chief engineer was a man from Detroit named Milo H. Davis whose miscalculations of slopes for the track made it unusable, but that wasn't found out until all work was completed and a train was actually trying to climb a grade at the grand opening of the track. Interestingly, Davis was among four city school board commissioners arrested in Detroit by Pingree on corruption charges. The *State Republican* reported in August of 1894, "It is now asserted that Inspector Milo H. Davis, one of the alleged boodlers, has dropped out of sight with a suddenness that is absolutely painful to contemplate."[758] Christian Buhl, was president of the company and Frank L. Dodge was secretary. The actual construction was subcontracted, and the builder was way over budget in October of 1891 when the board of the railroad doubled their investment from $500,000 to $1,000,000 in a document drawn up by Frank, thinking they would have to complete the railroad to get their initial investment back.[759] But Frank, who was not a major investor, soon got out of the company, and eventually it failed completely.

Jim worked continuously over the next few years to sell his properties and pay off his debts. Howard and Jim wrote to John frequently to tell him how he was being secured. By December of 1891 Jim had cancelled three of Longyear's notes to the Detroit National Bank totaling $55,000, and he made a deed to John covering all lands of interest in the Upper Peninsula counties, including the Gogebic and Ontonagon Land Company. By March 1892 over $90,000 in notes were cancelled, and he had wiped out the remainder of the debt with the Detroit National Bank in exchange for assets. Jim wrote, "the bank [is] accepting a full payment of 80 acres of land which belonged to my wife in Sec. 5 in Lansing Township and $14,000 in stock in the Michigan Condensed Milk Company... This wipes out my Detroit debt, except $7,000 to S. Baldwin, $7,000 to James McMillan (collateral loans), and the C. H. Buhl debt for which he holds the Iron Star Company stock." He told John he had plans for further reductions of the amount he owed and that he would finally be able to extricate himself from all the difficulties. In the summer of 1892 he found time to double the capacity of the Michigan Condensed Milk Company by building a factory in Howell. In December of 1892 he sold stock from the Springdale Farm at a loss to a C. C. Church in Watertown, Pennsylvania, and they were shipped off in a special train of ten palace stock cars.[760] Prices were starting to fall.

Sophie put up more of her investments to help. She sold the pine on a 2,000-acre tract for $4,000 and put the land up for sale. In December of 1892 she sold a mill site at the Straits of Mackinaw for $81,000. They turned to John for help in selling her other lands. Marian secured some of Jim's debt at the Lansing Banks for $22,000, and he sold stores and property in Lansing for another $70,000. He was also being advised and helped by General Alger, as ex-governor Russell Alger was called. A year later he wrote to John, "I am sure that General Alger is acting from the kindliest of motives, and that he only wants what would be for my interest, and he always knows that my only ambition in life is to pay my debts at one hundred cents on a dollar with interest."[761] Alger was now trustee of his affairs in the place of Joy.

In January of 1893 he told John of problems beginning to crop up with the sales—lands sold on time were surrendered back to Jim by people who could not make good on what they owed, leases for lumbering were being defaulted on, and taxes owed on the land according to the lease agreements had not been paid.[762] John and Jim were still working to settle Julian Case's affairs including bills in and about Marquette, and Jim had taken on debt in order to do so. When John came down for a visit in 1893 to help, he took time for riding about the streets of Lansing in one of the earliest automobiles, constructed by Ransom E. Olds.[763] (Frank Dennison Longyear, the grandson of Franc and Ephraim, worked for the Olds Company for eight years and then as a division superintendent for the Reo Motor Car Company.[764]) It was a moment of fun in an otherwise grim situation.

The decline that escalated into a panic in the spring of 1893 was the worst economic crisis the country had experienced to this point. Once again, it was the failure of banking management brought on by American financial policies and ineffective banking regulations, precipitated in part by a run on the gold supply. The crash began with two major national banks in Chicago. Their inability to cover combined assets of two million dollars led to the collapse of private and state banks and associated business firms and corporations, making it impossible to get loans and bringing the country to the verge of a crisis. It was thought this American crash was a repercussion of the crash which began in 1890 in Europe and Australia. The boom in the economy of America had attracted European capital as never before. People had not fully realized the magnitude of these loans and investments by foreigners because they put the American money paid to them in interest and dividends back into investments in the United States.[765]

According to historian Henry Utley, "when this process was suspended and when foreign capital was withdrawn from municipal obligations and industrial investments there followed at once heavy shipments of gold to Europe without any compensating return in kind or equivalent. It was computed that at this time the principle of America's debt to Europe was not less than two billion dollars. The interest alone upon this vast debt was sufficient to turn the balance of trade against us when demand was made for its payment in gold. The Sherman law of 1890 for the compulsory purchase by the government of silver by the issue of new treasury notes had been a part of the effort of bi-metalists to preserve the equality of the two metals." Attempts to negotiate with European countries to preserve the two metals failed. "In the meantime gold was flowing out of the treasury in an uninterrupted stream, until the net reserve had fallen far below the one hundred million fixed by the law. Thus a combination of influences worked together to produce an unhealthy condition of finance."[766] Bank failures continued throughout 1893 in Lansing and across the country. The squeeze on the currency supply was disastrous for many factories, forcing them to shut down for lack of money to pay their employees. In Michigan, four banks closed between April and July in Crystal Falls, Big Rapids, Greenville, and Lansing; however, all had enough assets to wind down their affairs without much damage to their depositors.[767]

In 1894 Jim hired a representative to help him with his creditors by getting them to accept land for what was owed, but land values were falling. It became apparent to John that Jim would not be able to buy back his deeds.

John later recalled: "I then took up the active management of the property, which I found in a very tangled shape. Owing to his financial difficulties Turner had not paid his taxes for several years and thus there were seven or eight years accumulated taxes against the property. Much of the property consisted of more or less defective titles, which his Upper Peninsula manager, Charles W. Butler, had accumulated under his management. Butler was now dead and Turner had bought his interest from his heirs." Longyear said he hired an assistant to get the land matters straightened out. It took over twelve years.[768]

The Upper Peninsula was hard hit. The *Mining Journal* reported from Lansing on December 3, 1893, that a committee sent by Governor Rich to the mining regions to investigate the conditions of the idle miners wired a report to Lansing that the situation was distressing and alarming. It was ten degrees below zero and there were two feet of snow, yet women and children had no covering for their feet. The committee appealed to manufacturers of knit goods and everyone in the state to send aid. "There are 5,000 persons at Ironwood, 2,000 at Bessemer, and 500 at Wakefield that must be cared for during the entire winter," and more at other points not visited by the committee. Typhoid fever had devastated the Gogebic range. "Notwithstanding the great destitution prevailing it is only by a house to house inspection that it can be discovered and the committee says that they have never seen so great unwillingness to acknowledge poverty and accept aid." The people of the state were aroused and relief committees organized. General Alger went to Cleveland for several days to consult with some of the heaviest stockholders in the Michigan iron mines. He tried to induce them to resume operations so that the starving miners could find work. The *Mining Journal* reported, "General Alger says that if the men can be given employment only a part of the time the state of Michigan will appropriate money to help them through the winter. He was met with little encouragement here, however, the mine owners seeing no immediate prospect of a market for their ore."[769]

The panic and depression that followed brought changes to the Lansing Industrial Aid Society. In the years after the height of the panic, the real estate market for both farms and cities was depressed, and conditions for industry and business declined as well. At a monthly meeting in October of 1892 the minutes stated, "The Matron, Mrs. Andrews, reported the work done at the 'Home' during the summer vacation: there had been but little call for relief, and a small quantity of clothing distributed."[770] By February 11, 1893, "The committees reported several families had been sent here from other towns, and will therefore be dependent upon the city for support. A large number of calls for help had been granted and bills allowed."[771] By March 14, 1893, Nancy Andrews reported to the trustees, "The clothing given out was unusually large." The Society reached out to groups to help raise funds—the North Lansing Literary Society held an entertainment for the benefit of the society and raised $30.60. School children took collections to aid families at Thanksgiving. The trustees organized seven ministers to ask for a collection at their churches for the Society. An entertainment by teachers and young people of North Lansing raised $50.[772]

In the early fall of 1893 the calls for relief seemed to lighten for a time, and the Society decided to sell their old building and the James Little property, and move to a building near the river on the northwest corner of Shiawassee and Grand to improve their services.[773] In April they moved into their new building and decided to name the school The Andrews Industrial Home "in accordance with the expressed wish of the children of the school and the workers—this was carried by a standing vote."[774] Mrs. Nancy Andrews was a kind and resourceful woman whose reports bristled with wit and clarity. She had excellent executive ability.[775] Through her reports the trustees, headed by Mrs. N. B. (Irma) Jones with Dr. Anna Ballard as Vice President, could track the demand for their services and identify the community's needs. Nancy Andrews was the mother of Irma Jones.[776]

The trustees met at the new building, and sometimes at Dr. Ballard's office, and monitored all services closely. They voted to postpone improvements to their new location and not to increase administrative expenses because of "the stringency of the times." They lowered dues for members to 25 cents (for ladies) annually. They followed a policy of providing "assistance given as the cases demanded." In one case, "A motion prevailed that the society purchase two quilts of a poor woman in need of help, paying therefore $5 as she did not want to become a public charge." In another case, they voted to pay Mrs. Schofanski $1.00 per week to care for a sick woman. Sometimes they made small loans such as $10 to Mrs. Davidson, a black woman, for a new stove which would be paid back at fifty cents a week or an $8 loan to a widow whose house had a mortgage. They paid expenses for the ill, for crutches and similar needs, and $2 for transportation for a family that needed to move. They did a great deal with a budget that was usually about $900 per year. At the November 14, 1893 meeting, the treasurer reported for the year to date: receipts $634.85, disbursements $592.43, balance $72.92.[777] When a case was more than they could handle, it was referred to the County Poor House, which they felt was well managed and provided good care for the unfortunate.[778]

By October 10, 1893, "Mrs. Andrews gave an account of a woman who came to her destitute, weary, and exhausted. Several cases of begging were reported. One family in the 5th ward, mentioned in the daily paper had been assisted and were desirous of work."[779] The numbers of students at the Society's school was growing with average attendance 57; the total number was 75.[780]

The winter of 1894 found the Society's volunteer ward committees were serving 32 families, and in January, 131 persons, half caused from lack of employment. Work was found for only seven persons. Andrews reported, "A much larger amount of clothing had been distributed than any time before." And in February the ward committees served 86 families, 348 persons, and found employment for four persons. Four-hundred-seventy garments had been distributed besides shoes, bedding, furniture and a large quantity of flour and groceries. The treasury of the society was fast being depleted, and at times when cases could not be referred to the County Poor House, they asked a church to help a specific person. In October of 1894 they found employment for ten people and added a new category of service: "Four women tramps had been lodged and fed." The annual report for 1895 by Andrews "shows that there were 2309 articles of women's and children's clothing distributed during the year besides bedding, fruits, vegetables, and delicacies for the sick. Forty-five families have been aided from the rooms [of the Andrews Home] and fifteen tramps." Every month seemed to bring a new phase of want before the society.[781] At the same time, Jim was struggling to keep his enterprises going and his employees working because each business failure had a ripple effect that added to the load of the community in providing for the poor.

People knew how attached Jim was to his farm, especially the horses, how Sophie loved the Shetlands, and Frank was also particularly interested in raising trotting horses. To strengthen the financial standing of the Springdale Farm, Frank became co-proprietor, thus protecting the farm from creditors. The 1892 Springdale Fame catalog described the stallions and dams available for producing standard bred light harness or trotting bred horses just as usual but now much of the stock was gone.[782] It was also necessary to sell off part of the land. By 1894, the farm was still extensive by most standards but reduced to only 830 acres. In that year the stock was cut back to 35 horses and the number of milch cows was cut by half, to 150. Hay and corn silage production and the number of sheep remained the same.[783] In 1892 the Michigan Condensed Milk company had been organized with General Alger as president. Its main offices were in Detroit but the factories remained in Lansing and Howell.[784] When John inquired about some Springdale farm assets not listed in their agreements, Jim explained they were not listed because Frank owned half. He wrote, "I am willing, however, that you should have anything on earth belonging to me which you want."[785]

On a Still Hunt

By the end of 1893, Jim was on his financial feet enough to get back in the political fray, but he was willing to take his time to plan and build a political organization. Jim's friends said, "Turner is on a still hunt."[786] On a still hunt, the hunter isn't sitting in a duck blind or in some other fixed position waiting for his game to come by. The hunter stalks his prey through the thick undergrowth in woods, overgrown fields, river bottoms and marshes. He walks slowly, uses the wind to his advantage, and blends into the environment. It is slow and deliberate. Each step is precise. A still hunt requires focus. The biggest mistake is to move too fast.[787] They might have said he was after delegates. They might have said he was after the soul of the Republican party.

"He is one of the brainiest, biggest hearted men in the state, and in spite of the political disaster that befell him he has a personal following that would be a source of pride to any man," observed the *Detroit Tribune*.[788] Jim set about organizing the progressive faction of the Republican party to again challenge the ruling clique. He formed "The One Term Republican Club," a low-key approach, at least at first, to getting enough delegates to control the 1894 convention. He traveled across the state under the pretext of the club, talking up the challenge to Republican party bossism. Party activists who might be hesitant about the wisdom of taking on powerful incumbents were more comfortable in saying it wasn't that they were against the incumbents, it is just that they believed officials should hold office for only one term, and, anyway, they thought it was time for a candidate with a military record. It just so happened that Ping was a military man.

Ping hadn't put in enough planning prior to the 1892 convention, but Jim and Pingree were becoming close friends and confidants, so this time would be different. Ping had met with a similar assault from the McMillan faction in his efforts as mayor of Detroit as Jim had in his campaign for governor. Ping was elected mayor on a platform of exposing and ending corruption in city paving and sewer contracts, and on the school board. He fought the city's privately owned utility monopolies and beat them at their own game by establishing municipally owned competitors to the electric and gas monopolies. The Detroit City Railways Company fought him over lowering streetcar fares to three cents, drawing on the combined power of street railways throughout the United States. Ping attempted to create a municipally owned streetcar company but was barred from doing so by the state constitution, a provision included by the railroads. One of Ping's Detroit supporters sent a letter to the *State Republican* which printed it saying the letter was sharply critical of those who opposed Pingree but also "bears marked evidences of truth in every line." The *Detroiter* wrote:

If the true story could ever be written of how the mayor of this city, Mr. Pingree, has for three years heroically battled for the right, against powerful combinations of capital, and of their wrong doings, people would stand aghast. As is well known, the city of Detroit, until Mr. Pingree became mayor, had been bound hand and foot and delivered over to the spoiler. Those few, who owned every franchise, such as the city railway, the gas company, the electric lighting company, etc., had in order to more readily carry on their nefarious deals, corrupted the council for years. The council and the city officials had been of their own making and did their bidding. In this manner they have become rich at the expense of the people. Nor were the people who did this thieves or robbers. To the contrary, they sat and still sit, in the front benches of churches. One by one, the mayor who is an honest, but a stubborn man, has closed for a death struggle with these bribing and corrupting combinations. In doing so, they have, by fair means and foul, arrayed against him nearly all the wealth and influence in Detroit. Because of his struggles for the right, every artifice that Satan could think of has been used to injure him. Detroit banks have refused him credit; his pew in church has been taken from him; he has been maligned and traduced by every newspaper in the city.

Some of these papers can be bought like so many cattle if one has money enough. He has fought the fight in the interest of the city—of its great middle class—of its poor; but in doing so he has arrayed against him, almost solidly, the rich. The power of money to do wrong is something over which people who love our common country may well ponder."[789]

Ping brought the Wayne County delegates to vote for him at the nominating convention of 1892. He got into the race too late, and the convention was already wired for John Rich, so his supporters voted a blank ticket. After the conservatives' temporary loss of control of the party in 1890 and the win of the Democrats statewide, the party oligarchs moved to regain their power. However, Jim's former campaign manager Stanley Turner won the 1892 nomination for auditor general. Rich was elected governor but under him the state was said to be run from the offices of McMillan who had been easily re-elected to the U.S. Senate by the Michigan Senate.[790]

According to Pingree, "Money is first in consideration in the republic to-day, and the corporations and their brothers, the banks, control the money. Trusts and combines rule the Congress, and the corporations are represented in the administration. The Canadian Pacific [The Canadian Pacific had an interest in the Duluth, South Shore and Atlantic Railroad whose president was Senator James McMillan through July1890 and the president of the C. P. was vice president of the Duluth road.] is the real government of Canada, just as the Pennsylvania Railroad is the government in the State of Pennsylvania. In Michigan the Michigan Central rules the Legislature... The corporations run the conventions, and the people think they run the polls. Corporations do not care what party is in control so long as the men of either party are on their side, and they usually are... Conventions block candidates from the people. Conventions are controlled by a few men, and these few men are largely in the hands of the corporations—either directly belonging to the corporations or indirectly connected through business channels."[791] For the convention of 1894, Jim Turner had another design.

The newspapers got their first clue that something was up when a reporter from the *Evening News* spied Jim dropping in at Mayor Pingree's office on May 28, 1894. Many state leaders were there, including a well-known leader of the farmers' Grange, H. D. Pratt, who is said to have been interviewed by a reporter. He was claimed to have said, "The people who are counting on the nomination of Hon. John T. Rich for governor have an amount of disappointment in store for them that will surprise you. While Mr. Rich's services as governor has been eminently satisfactory, as was his long term of service in the capacity of railroad commissioner, congressman, legislator, county treasurer, supervisor, etc.—covering in all, a period of more than 20 years—I very much mistake the temper of the people if he is accorded a renomination this year."[792] Since the report was by the *Evening News*, just what he said or how satisfactory Pratt said Rich was is hard to say, if he said anything about Rich at all. Pratt did declare for one-termism. The upshot was that on June 19 a larger meeting was held at the Wayne Hotel in Detroit for about seventy leaders.

They were Republican reformers and Silverites. They recalled Jim's pledge in 1890 to be a one-termer, and they thought Rich had gone along with the pledge then, too.[793] "Some of the leaders of the movement, notably James M. Turner of Lansing, John B. Corliss and other friends in Detroit of Mayor Pingree, ex-Senator Wesselius of Grand Rapids, as well as friends of ex-Congressman Bliss of Saginaw, took it upon themselves to issue invitations, and accordingly, about seventy gentleman from various parts of the state gathered in the parlors of the Wayne last evening and devoted several hours to an exchange of views and to the perfection of the organization."[794] Both Aaron T. Bliss and Pingree were former soldiers; both had been prisoners of war and incarcerated at Andersonville prison. Bliss had also been moved around for six months. Both had escaped. The assembly said they wanted to support a soldier but didn't say who.

The result of the One Term Club of Michigan conference was a platform endorsing one term for governor and president and a soldier candidate in 1894.[795] The One Termers did not anticipate much challenge from the Democratic party because factionalism had dashed Winans' plans for re-election in 1892, and they remained split. Whoever could gain the Republican convention's nomination would likely win if the Republicans had learned from 1890. The *Grand Rapids Democrat* reported the One Termers were "In a rosy glow."[796]

The executive committee of the One Term Republican Club met and elected Jim president. Ex-governor Luce was at his side, along with L. M. Sellers, editor of the *Cedar Springs Clipper*, Charles Sligh, a furniture manufacturer and leading Silverite from Grand Rapids, and many other well-known party activists and office holders. A letter of principles from Pingree was read. Its theme was "Equal rights to all and special privileges to none." He wrote: "That is a good old-time Republican doctrine: the doctrine of the party of Abraham Lincoln; the doctrine of the great Republican party when it stood for the principles of right and justice; when it was a party of the people, for the people and by the people. I am a Republican of that stripe. I was born such a Republican, and my father and grandfather before me stood for that great, broad principle of the greatest good for the greatest number, not a role for the few which crushed out the life and independence of the many. I fought for that principle on many a battle field. I stand today where the great Republican party stood when it was the party of the people, and I expect to stand there as long as my life exists."[797]

The *Grand Rapids Democrat* was one of the newspapers that reported the contents of Pingree's letter:

> The power of money in securing political preferment must cease or the republic is in danger. Every official, high and low, should be brought so closely in touch with the people that he would not dare to enter into

a combination against their interests. He advocates the election of senator by direct vote of the people, and in the meantime nominates them in convention. "Elected as he is today, to whom does a senator owe his allegiance?" he asks, and gives the answer, "To his pocketbook and nothing else."

On corporations he says: "If the state cannot own the telephone and telegraph it should at least regulate the tolls charged for their use. Corporations should not be allowed to do business on one dollar more of stock or bonded capital than is actually paid in and kept in the business. They should not be permitted to capitalize their supposed earning capacity in the shape of watered stock and bonds. Whenever and wherever this is done it means that a fraud is being perpetrated upon unsuspecting persons who invest their money in good faith."

Differences between capital and labor should be adjusted by arbitration and a state arbitration board should be established. He believes in regulating railroads with a stiff hand.

On the financial situation he thinks the contraction of the currency is one of the causes of the hard times. The approach to a single gold standard is threatening the industrial interests. "Silver as well as gold should be coined and used as money. I am satisfied with the declaration of the Republican platform of 1892 on that subject."

In conclusion Mr. Pingree remarks: "The Republican party has been the party of progress. It has been the party to which the people have looked to meet the exigencies of the times. It must now meet the question of the enormous concentration of wealth in the hands of a few, by the means of robber trusts and watered stock. It must wage a war of extermination against these trusts and monopolies, if it hopes to regain and retain the confidence of the people."[798]

The One Term group had already been canvasing for delegates before they went public. Their chances were good. The stakes were high. In July Ping and his campaign manager visited Jim in Lansing at his home on a weekend, and then they went over to his office where other state organizers joined them. In turn, Jim made trips down to Detroit for meetings.[799] They divided up their lists and wrote to supporters, including former governor Luce, asking them to make contacts with certain prospects to get more supporters on board for district conventions. "Father Jim," as some called him, organized a tremendous effort. When the One Term Republican Committee came to consult with him and report their progress, he would tell them, "Get your skates on."[800] Jim's aide wrote to Charles Sligh, their manager in Kent County, from Ping's office on the Detroit Mayor's stationery, "We went into St. Clair and in the face of Harrison Geer and Rich's own lieutenants, right in his own district, we beat him out."[801]

At about this time the *Detroit Tribune* assessed Ping's chances. "There is not the slightest doubt he could be elected if nominated, but there are many grave doubts as to the latter. Rich has with him the officeholders, the old-timers, and Senator James McMillan, the Chairman of the Republican State committee, a millionaire and a most astute politician, who well knows when to spend money. The political machinery of the State moves when he moves, and neither Pingree nor Bliss can make any serious impression on it. Pingree, in his role of defender of the common people, never failed to plant a dart in the skin of the chief monopolist and millionaire of the city. McMillan was a heavy stockholder in the gas companies, the street railways, the car shops, and a score or more of other well-known enterprises, and Pingree not only injured his bank account, but repeatedly wounded the feelings of Mr. McMillan by bitter personal attacks. The Senator has been busy in Washington, and has not, apparently, taken any notice of the attacks, but the reckoning is yet to come, with little room for doubt that it will be of a kind to suit Mr. McMillan."[802]

A few days after the win in St. Clair and just before the state convention, things started to take a turn: "The Scripps newspapers in Detroit have charged Mayor Pingree, directly or indirectly, with about every offense excepting arson, horse-stealing, and rape, and they still have a full week in which to cover that deviancy, before the state convention meets. They have charged that he was a populist, but as that did not seem to be doing the work expected of it, the Detroit News of Saturday gave Mr. Pingree a 'shot-gun dose.' It charged that he had become a confidant of Don M. Dickinson [chair of the Democratic party]."[803]

The One Termers' delegate contenders were being hit hard at the county conventions. A cartoon the *Detroit Evening News* ran August 2 was labeled "Wayne's Tin Idol." It showed a statue of Pingree on a pedestal with a leg and arm labeled Saginaw and Grand Rapids fallen off. James Turner was shown behind Pingree propping him up and Pingree's supporters were at his feet as worshipers.[804]

Even in Ingham County, Jim had trouble getting elected. Jim told the Lansing *State Republican*, "with the good-natured laugh for which he is so famous, that it might be a little lonesome for him up at Grand Rapids as a representative of the one term club, 'but we haven't laid down the battle axe,' said he, 'and we expect to have some fun yet. The one term club may be a little run down at the heel, but its mission is not yet ended. Talk about your fishing and hunting clubs and your Michigan Club [made up of Republican leaders and businessmen], none of them have had any more fun this summer than the one termers.'"[805]

When Jim met with the organizing committee in Grand Rapids for the convention, they met behind closed doors. The evidence they were accumulating from across the state was shocking, but Jim did not disclose it to the press and said they had no idea of retreating.[806] The group compiled a systematic report of the methods used by the Rich campaign. When Ping arrived, there were more meetings. Finally, at 4:00 p. m., Ping made the statement that he had withdrawn from the gubernatorial race. The announcement was accompanied by a letter because he said the methods used by Rich could not be endured without protest. In the letter Ping told his followers, "If you have ever questioned my republicanism it has been by reason of the misrepresentation, the vilification, the subsidizing of republican newspapers." He wanted to stop the current conduct of the officers and the convention of the party, saying, "in no other way can the government of the people, by the people, and for the people, be maintained."[807] The letter went on:

> I am credibly informed, and I state the fact without fear of contradiction, that the chief political manager employed by Candidate John T. Rich is one Harrison Geer, the paid attorney of the Chicago & Grand Trunk railway company, and that the campaign was planned and executed in every detail under the management of said railroad attorney.
>
> I am informed also by some of the most reputable citizens and active republicans of St. Clair county that this railroad attorney attended the republican county convention and demanded that employees of that company vote a ballot favorable to Mr. Rich or be discharged from the company's employ. The republican party insists on a free and untrammeled ballot and complains bitterly of the intimidation of the voters of the south, and now in line with their police enter a solemn protest against any section of any party adopting the slave-driving methods in the north.[808]

Delegates were shut out in Kent County despite being selected in party caucuses. Similar tactics were used in Calhoun, Eaton, Gratiot, Grand Traverse, Ionia, Montcalm, Mason and Cheboygan Counties, wrote Ping. "In Luce county, especially in the village of Newberry, the employees of corporations were intimidated by their bosses and instructed to vote a Rich ticket at the caucuses or be discharged from their employment... It has become well understood that a portion of the vote can be got, intimidated or hired and subsidized, for the purpose, not only of opposing by fair methods any candidate who seeks a nomination at the party's hands, but in like manner can be procured for the purpose of slandering, vilifying and misrepresenting men in the ranks of the party whose party fealty has never before been questioned... Under no circumstances could I permit my name to go before a convention constituted under influences so disastrous to good government. H. S. Pingree"[809]

After the One Term Campaign

Ping was no longer the candidate for governor, but his campaign for the ear of the voter continued four days later at a political barbeque in Webberville, not far from Lansing. The event was most likely organized by Jim, but for some reason he was not present. Ping was the guest of Kate and Dr. Frank Turner, Jim's cousin. Frank and his brother Ezra Dodge were there. Families were invited too. The Democratic party's candidate, former congressman

Spencer O. Fisher, attended the event with Cy and spent the night with Eva and Cy before boarding the train for Saginaw the morning after the event.[810] Good humor seemed to be the order of the day.

Everybody is out and the political pot is boiling on every corner. The shouts of the people are heard on all sides, and the savory smell of the roasted ox give an appetizing effect to the whole scene. The village is crowded with politicians from the cities and surrounding country and the success of the gathering is much greater than was anticipated.

True to his promise Mayor Pingree of Detroit is here and will speak this afternoon. Dr. A. W. Nichols, candidate for governor on the people's party ticket, is also here and will address the crowd. There are present politicians of all grades and sizes and complexions of faith. There are Pingreeites, Richites, Fisherites, Nicholites, labor men and prohibitionists, all here to see what will be done and get posted as much as possible on the unknown quantities.

Upon entering the village from the train one is rather amused by the display of opposition. There are stretched across the main street two banners, each some sixty feet long. One was raised in honor of Dr. Nichols [of the People's Party] and bears the following declaration: "Dr. Nichols, welcome to our home;" while the other, immediately opposite, has the following declaration: "Oh, but we only vote for Mayor Pingree."… Frank L. Dodge of Lansing came to Webberville this morning in company with Ezra Dodge and some other well-known capital city democrats, and was made master of ceremonies… The greatest interest hangs on Mayor Pingree's words, as 'tis said he has prepared a regular corker of a talk.[811]

The crowd at Webberville met the trains and cheered the candidates who rode in a parade of carriages to town. The big guns were escorted to the homes of prominent citizens, the band played, and the people devoted the rest of an hour or two to sampling ox, the Lansing commonwealers having front seats. After dinner a procession was formed and everybody waded through the dust to a grove half a mile east of town, where the speeches were held. Cy urged the populist and the Pingree Republicans to unite around Fisher: "They all stood on the platform of free silver and together they could accomplish something."[812]

Because Frank Dodge was asked to officiate at the last moment, one can only speculate that the original master of ceremonies was Jim. It appears Jim and Sophie did not attend the

Frank and Abby, Turner-Dodge House photo.

picnic with the rest of his family members, nor was he mentioned as being in Jackson, by newspaper accounts, at an event he most certainly would have attended unless he were ill or too far away to get back in time. For even as picnickers gathered in the Webberville grove, the relatives of Austin Blair were summoned to his bedside in Jackson. He was not expected to last the day. Soon Michigan would be mourning the loss of their "war governor." He was among the last of the founders of the Republican party, had served it as a state senator, governor, congressman, and prosecuting attorney in Jackson County, and finished a seven year term as regent of the University of Michigan four years earlier.[813] "Two of nature's priceless gifts contributed generously to make Austin Blair a leader of young men in those formative days when the country was new and political forces were organizing for the greatest conflict of the century. He was endowed with the gift of eloquence in speech and that tremendous earnestness which sways multitudes and inspires unfaltering confidence," said his obituary.[814] The Michigan Equal Rights Association offered a resolution to Blair's wife Sarah and four sons, which said, in part:

Before and during the great civil war, to say nothing of what was accomplished by him during the reconstruction acts of congress, he always being found on the side of liberty for humanity.

Resolved, That an all wise and just God has seen fit to end the earthly life: by his death the colored people of the entire American republic has sustained the loss of a true and faithful friend and a wise counselor, one whose voice and acts were always vigorous in the just cause of the black man when in oppression, and for his elevation; his demise is an irreparable wound to the colored people.

Resolved, We who well remember his kindly acts toward us as a race when our children were so abruptly turned out of the public schools of this city. And how willingly he assisted in reinstating them, carrying our cause to the supreme court and winning the case as he did without recompense.

Resolved, That we, in special meeting assembled, do thus take means to express our esteem, and offer our sincere sympathy to the bereaved family of the late ex-Governor Austin Blair.

And that a memorial of these resolutions be appropriately prepared and presented to the family of the distinguished dead.

(Signed) W. Wendell Gaskin, President

Frank M. Thurman, Secretary, Jackson Auxiliary M. E. R. A.[815]

The Unitarians sent a floral tribute which was placed at the head of the casket, and flowers were also sent by many others. The hearse making its way to Mount Evergreen Cemetery in Jackson was followed by a long parade of dignitaries, and the honorary pall bearers were General Russell A. Alger, Detroit; General Byron M. Cutcheon, Grand Rapids; Hon. James F. Joy, Detroit; Governor John T. Rich, Lapeer; Hon. E. A. Grosvenor, Jonesville;

Hon. O. M. Barnes, Lansing; ex-Governor Cyrus G. Luce, Coldwater; Hon. H. A. Hayden, Colonels C. V. DeLand, and W. L. Seaton, Jackson. The parade included suffragists from the Michigan Equal Suffrage Association and many military and other marching bodies. The Grand Army of the Republic and other veterans met in Grand Rapids and prepared this resolution:

> A nation as well as the state of Michigan mourns the loss of one of her bravest, most patriotic and true citizens, a man of exalted character whose many virtues were but the reflex of a well spent life, devoted to the best interests of his country... He is one of the grandest and most historic figures among the prominent men of Michigan, having been identified with its legislation, government, and political history for half a century. We, the soldiers of Grand Rapids, knew him best as our 'war governor.'... He was always welcomed in the camp and in the field with great pride and loud huzzas when he came to the front, as he often did, to look after the interests of his 'Michigan boys.' How well we remember his classic face. How well his cordial greeting to privates as well as commissioned officers. He realized that 'The boys who did the fighting were the privates in our army.'
>
> And every Michigan soldier respected and loved him. The state of Michigan owes him a debt of gratitude which is beyond computation... We desire therefore to place on record our appreciation of his high character. He was a brilliant executive, an honest man and a true friend. He was loved by those who knew him best.[816]

Only two years earlier the great reformer and party founder had rallied to the side of Jim and had sought to remind his party of their ideals, the ideals Jim and Ping now demanded of their party on behalf of the reformers of the party's first generation. Less than a week later a fusion meeting held at Mead's Hall tried to get Ping to run on an independent ticket. They tried to draft Jim into the leadership, although he wasn't present. Frank Fogg, editor of the *State Democrat,* a new newspaper in town published on Thursdays, said he was born a Republican and always was a Republican, until driven out by ring rule. He said the election of Governor Winans happened because so many Republicans had been driven from the ranks of their party by the party machine and that he opposed Rich for the same reasons Pingree did. The next morning, when Jim heard of his recruitment, he said, "Of course I will act with the committee if Mr. Pingree will run." However, he was in touch with Ping and undoubtedly was sure Ping would not run. "This is a very poor year to bolt," Mr. Turner continued. "The people are disgusted with the present congress and are all ready to vote the republican ticket, so that I don't think Mr. Pingree will be likely to run against Rich this fall."[817] And so he would wait for another day. The still hunter is slow and deliberate. The biggest mistake is to move too fast. This was not the year for the reformers.

In these harsh times, the city needed reassurance and hope. Frank was invited to be speaker for the city's July 4, 1894, celebration and, for the time being, politics were set aside. Both he and Jim knew the comfort of reminding people that government is in the service of the people and for the benefit of all. One dreary year into the depression, Frank took the time to remind those in the vast crowd that day of their heritage and the pioneering spirit that had overcome so many hardships in the past. His speech was reported in the newspaper and saved by Marian. In the course of his address he said:

> Those who founded this state knew no baseness; cowed to no danger; they were fearless, generous and humane. Their corner-stone was based on the right of the individual, and society was formed for the protection of him, and that the states and governments were formed for the preservation of society, thus giving the broadest scope to individual liberty with a safety on which states and governments may be founded for the benefit of all… I sometimes fear that we are in danger of forgetting those virtues, but when this day comes the story of what our race accomplished on this continent springs into vivid freshness; the old flag flashed its glory to the sky and all hearts beat true and proud. I conjure you then, my fellow citizens, to encourage the remembrance of this day.[818]

Another newspaper account reported: "For forty minutes Mr. Dodge gave our people one of the best addresses they have listened to for years. Mr. Dodge surely did himself justice in that attempt and his patriotic points were very clearly brought out."[819] Jefferson or perhaps the Federalist Papers would doubtlessly have been incorporated into Frank's talk on the "characteristics essential to the preservation and enlargement of liberty," but, unfortunately, the newspaper did not print that part of the speech and thus preserve Frank's ideas on this subject that day. Perhaps they would have paralleled the principles of the Democratic party: "those great essential principles of justice and liberty upon which our institutions are founded, and which the Democratic party has advocated from Jefferson's time to our own—freedom of speech, freedom of the press, freedom of conscience, the separation of personal rights, the equality of all citizens before the law, and the faithful observance of constitutional limitations."[820] Frank's view that government must work for the benefit of everyone was shared by Jim, who kept up his push on the Republican party.

Soon after, another special celebration took place in Jackson. The first day of August was Emancipation Day and people from Lansing joined in. The black people of Jackson planned the event which included the city officials in the parade.[821] They too were celebrating the preservation and enlargement of liberty. It was the sixtieth anniversary of the emancipation of the slave in the British West Indian Islands:

> Sixty years ago today human slavery was abolished in the British West Indies. The emancipation of the slaves is today being celebrated by the colored people of Jackson, assisted by many friends from the surrounding towns. Thirty years after the liberation of slaves of the West In-

dies, Abraham Lincoln, by a few strokes of the pen, unloosed the chains which bound in hopeless bondage four millions of human beings. In view of these great historic facts, colored people have every reason to dress in their finest array, and to joyously celebrate their emancipation.

The local committee have worked hard to accomplish a successful celebration and succeeded admirably. At each of the morning trains was the reception committee, who at once welcomed the visitors… It was 12 o'clock when the procession left the depot. It was composed of the marshal, Boos' band, the speakers and committees in carriages, a chariot filled with children bearing American flags, and a large number of hacks and citizens in carriages.

The column marched up Main to Jackson street, down the latter thoroughfare to the fair ground, where the parade disbanded. Refreshment booths were numerous, and all were well patronized, though a large proportion of the people carried large lunch baskets. About 1:30 p.m. the assemblage was called to order in the beautiful grove. The speakers were Frederick Merchant, of Ypsilanti, George Balley of Battle Creek; and Rev. Catman.[822]

At the conclusion of the addresses, the sports events began and the grandstand was taken over by spectators for the athletic contests. With segregation becoming law as well as practice across the South, the events were open to all amateurs with but one exception, a one mile bicycle race open to black men only. There was the 100-yard dash; half-mile bicycle dash; hop, step and jump; quarter-mile bicycle dash; standing broad jump; half-mile foot race; and another one mile bicycle race open to all. There were first, second, and third prize winners and a baseball game as the final sports event. The day ended with a band concert followed by dancing until midnight at one of Jackson's large halls.[823]

The committee gave consideration to everyone, and so on August 3, black convicts at the prison celebrated emancipation day with a musical and literary program at the chapel.[824] Perhaps this aspect of the emancipation celebration was to raise awareness of the rise of laws to oppress blacks in the old confederate states, particularly in the use of the convict lease programs that leased out convicts to work as cheap labor to railroad and mining corporations and tobacco plantations.

As a W. C. T. U. activist in the black community of Jackson and a suffragist, Lucy Thurman was called to action by the worsening situation in the South. Through her inspiration, she had already organized the black women of Jackson. Her husband was the secretary of the Michigan Equal Rights Association. She persuaded the National W. C. T. U. to appoint her the head of the first Superintendent of the Department of Colored Work. At 44 years of age, Thurman headed south to organize W. C. T. U. groups among black women, "for it will be to them just what it has been to our white sisters, the greatest training school for the development of women." It was said that there was scarcely a hamlet anywhere in the South that did not remember her for years to come.[825] These were not the times to let up on the work of the W. C. T. U. In Lansing, under the auspices of the African Methodist Episcopal Church, the Sojourner Truth W. C. T. U. was formed.[826]

Wets and Dries

During this time Lansing's Central Methodist Church moved to their new church building one block to the west on Ottawa Street. The vacant corner of the former church was used to display hardware and implements, and the W. C. T. U. used this corner on Saturday nights for ice cream socials. Jim answered the solicitation for contributions for stained glass windows by donating $250 for a window on the east wall of the sanctuary in honor of his father who had been a lay leader and the Sunday School Superintendent for so many years.[827] Marian helped found the Central Methodist Church, and the Turners were also founders of the First Methodist Church, which began in North Lansing in 1868, where Marian had been president of the Ladies' Aid Society and Woman's Foreign Ministry. When the church building was erected on Franklin Avenue a stained glass window on the south side of the sanctuary was dedicated to her.

Marian was a follower of Francis Willard, the leader of the W. C. T. U., but it is not clear whether Marian was for prohibition of alcohol, its manufacture, sale and transportation, or mainly for temperance in its use and the regulation of alcohol. Jim never said it outright, but his position seemed to be for temperance. This would have satisfied many, but not the prohibitionists. The liquor question was always a factor in politics in Michigan at both the state and local level. When the National Prohibition Party formed in 1869, the first chairman was from Michigan. The intensity of the struggle began to heat up with the organization of a prohibition society at the local level and the organization of saloonists and brewers fighting back.

The liquor dealers in Jackson, Detroit, Grand Rapids, and other towns were organizing and nearly half the counties in the state were members of the state Saloon Keepers Society. The first day of February 1893, Lansing's thirty-two saloonists held a secret meeting in the parlors over the Senate saloon to incorporate an organization and join the state society. No one but those with the grip and password were admitted. The local society planned to aggressively lobby to repeal the current liquor law providing for a local county option of dry or wet and to establish a uniform tax of $300, with the privilege of keeping open on all legal holidays except Sundays and religious days. They also wanted to be open after the polls were closed on election days. If the Lansing group joined the state organization, they would get the saloonkeepers' life insurance and mutual benefit company assistance available through the society. Locally, at the next election, they were intent on defeating the present city officers, especially Mayor Arthur O. Bement and Marshall Sanford. The group complained that the two had waged an unceasing war against them. The *State Republican* said the liquor dealers persisted in disobeying state law and city ordinances and were angry because all bars were closed promptly, and no liquor was sold during the times forbidden by law.[828]

The *State Republican* had a decidedly prohibitionist tone. However, it managed to offend several of its constituencies, especially the W. C. T. U., perhaps due to changes in its ownership to W. S. George and Darius D. Thorp or "Messrs. George & Thorp," as they referred to themselves. Fortunately for the prohibitionists, the paper soon came under the sole proprietorship of Thorp, who seemed to be a Republican of the sort more in the tradition of the paper's previous editors and owners. The thorough coverage of organized labor resumed. Gone was the elaborate ladies' fashion page. The Industrial Aid Society and the Women's Christian Temperance Union both had weekly columns written by their members. There were some improvements in coverage of women in the state and locally, but nothing like the days when suffragist Stephen Bingham had been editor. Women's activities in the Legislature didn't receive much attention by Thorp, even when May Stockings Knaggs, a woman of rare gifts and national reputation,[829] dropped by *the State Republican* office as a *Tribune* staff member from Bay City and the leader of the Michigan Suffrage Association. Her visit was mentioned, but her mission in the city to lobby for Municipal Suffrage was not.[830]

While the lobbyists for the saloonkeepers were zeroing in on their priorities, the Lansing W. C. T. U. members embraced a growing number of interrelated interests. Hopkins wrote: "Many new departments of work were instituted, such as prison work, co-operation with the prohibition party, mother's meetings, work with lumbermen and miners, etc. Mary T. Lathrop, an ardent prohibitionist, was the state president and the Woman's Christian Temperance Unions were working toward state and national prohibition."[831] The position of the W. C. T. U. was now completely for prohibition, not temperance.

The July newspaper column of the Lansing W. C. T. U. was written by Blanch H. Mason who told about a disappointing speech at the Methodist church by Judge Person; "He gave no remedy beyond a better enforcement of existing laws. We thought the judge, from his large experience, would have learned before this, that the saloon is too cyclonic a thing to 'regulate,' and the only proper way to deal with this colossal and insolent evil is to exterminate it root and branch."[832] Their remedy was to remove the temptation, but they also knew they must equip men to resist temptations. In the same column, Mason also published "The White Cross Pledge." The Pledge was aimed at changing the character of adult and young men and was an attack on the double standard. "I promise by the help of God—First. To treat all women with respect and endeavor to protect them from wrong and degradation. Second. To endeavor to put down all indecent language and coarse jests. Third. To maintain the law of purity as equally binding upon men and women. Fourth. To endeavor to spread these principles among my companions, and try to help my younger brothers. Fifth, to use all possible means to fulfill the command, "Keep thyself pure."[833] They saw a relationship between drinking, saloons, prostitution and the treatment of women. But there were early clues that complete prohibition might not work.

Eaton County was one of the five counties (Van Buren, Allegan, Antrim, Hillsdale, and Eaton) that had voted to be dry. The W. C. T. U. didn't think the "Local Option" legislation was working well and reports from nearby Grand Ledge underscored that opinion:

> The story of the failure of local option in this county, and the flagrant violation of all law and order as a consequence, has oft been told by your correspondent, but the conditions grow steadily worse instead of better, and were never worse than at the present time. "Commercial" pharmacies, "lunch rooms," and "soft drink" bars administer to those who are athirst. Some of these places are now connected also with disreputable resorts, and vice stalks openly and defiantly in the light of open day.

> A spurt of virtue resulted two weeks ago in the edict to the "lunch counters" to let up on Sunday sales; the order has been partly enforced, and there has been less drunkenness on the weekly gala-day. But the fraternity has a suspicion that all are not treated alike, and the result of this feeling, it is feared, will be a relapse of executive myopia in the police department.

> The wives, mothers and sisters of Grand Ledge are moving again. They got up a petition to the aldermen as follows: "We, the undersigned, citizens of Grand Ledge, respectfully petition you to enforce our city laws against vice and crime; especially we ask you to enforce against the proprietors and inmates of the houses of prostitution now present and open in this city, those state and municipal laws which provide for the suppression of such places; and we hereby pledge our support to you in all measures you may take for breaking up the places aforementioned."[834]

Though the long-sought-after county Local Option legislation had been won by the prohibitionists in 1890, the liquor question was always an underlying issue in Michigan elections, whether it was about enforcement or who the prohibitionists would support or who the liquor interests would fight or a myriad of other facets of the problem. There was just such a furtive undertow in the 1895 election for Lansing's mayor.

Chapter 15

The Progressives

$\mathbf{S}$arah Elizabeth Van De Vort Emery was a leading progressive of the era. She was noted for her ability to meld together the issues of bimetallists, farmers, labor reform, the ballot for women, and temperance in a way that helped people to understand the relationships of the progressive issues. "She handled her theme with great skill and made a strong impression in favor of woman suffrage as necessary not only to the cause of temperance and other vital reforms, but the perpetuation of republican government."[835] The work for which she was most famous had to do with her economic explanations about how the availability of currency affected the daily lives of the nation.

She grew up in Phelps, New York, in the Finger Lakes region, where her family was Universalist and her father a farmer interested in reform politics. She came to a Michigan lumbering settlement called Midland at the age of 28, taught and superintended school, and at 31, in 1869, she married Wesley Emery, also a teacher. They settled in Lansing in 1870. She joined the Ingham County Equal Suffrage Association in 1872, the state organization in 1874, and the Michigan Equal Suffrage Association when it formed in 1884. She held state offices for many years. Her husband, Wesley, had been a student of the Genesee College at Lima, as had so many others in the Lansing area. He opened a bookstore in Lansing in 1873. Sarah joined the Lansing Women's Club and the W. C. T. U. She rose to national prominence in the 70s and 80s as an economist, suffragist, and temperance leader, and traveled throughout Michigan as well as nationally.[836] The Emerys were progressives, prohibitionists, and populists who believed government was failing to address social and economic problems in society. They fought greed and the rise of corporate power, corruption, and the widening gap between the rich and the poor.

In 1893, at age 55, she was profiled in *The Literary Century* as a member of the Michigan Woman's Press Association. The new organization, formed in 1890, had numerous prominent members in journalism and publishing. Many of them were also prominent suffragists and reformers:

MRS. S. E. V. EMERY.

There are women who seem fitted by nature for certain lines of work; who, under the pressure of unexpected circumstances have displayed unusual energies, which have brought them into prominence and public service. One of the tireless workers, a busy woman doing the work which has echoed her name throughout the land, is Mrs. S. E. V. Emery, of Lansing, Mich. As early as 1868, when reform movements were in their infancy, and when woman's sphere was still supposed to be limited to her home and family, Mrs. Emery began writing upon the questions of suffrage and temperance. In 1871 she made her first public speech on these subjects. In 1880 she became interested in the subject of finance reform and immediately entered the campaign in the interest of the Greenback party. From her first effort Mrs. Emery met with marked success. In 1881 she was elected delegate-at-large to the Greenback state convention, which was held in Lansing. Since that time she has been a delegate to nearly every state and national convention of reformers.

In 1887 she wrote and published the little book entitled "*Seven Financial Conspiracies which have Enslaved the American People*," which attracted immediate attention in political circles, it being so unlike any work of the kind ever published. The book had a most gratifying sale and in 1888 fifty thousand copies were distributed in Kansas alone and in 1890 several thousand more.[837]

Emery had a fine presence, a clear and powerful voice, and an easy, often eloquent, style. Her success upon the rostrum met with great praise and enthusiastic crowds, none more so than in Kansas. Local accounts reported:

At 2 p.m. the people gathered in Lafayette park, and listened to a long and interesting address by Mrs. Emery. The gathering was so large that not more than one-third of the people were able to hear the address. There were no newspaper men on the stand and a full report of the speech cannot be given. It is said to be one of the finest talks on the vital questions of the day made in Kansas this year. Mrs. Emery is a forcible writer and understands the history of our country as well as anyone that is on the public stage now. The talk was well received from first to last and made a good impression on the hearers. —The Beacon, Great Bend, Kansas.

One of the largest audiences ever assembled in the court house greeted the lady speaker last evening. Mrs. Emery, besides being an orator, proved herself to be a master of her subject, and her command of language was somewhat amazing to those at least who think that a lady is not capable of delivering an address in public, more especially when the subject chosen deals with the great political questions of the day. —Abilene (Kansas) Gazette.[838]

According to the Michigan Woman's Press Association profile the populists of Kansas attributed their recent political success largely to the book's influence. Three hundred thousand copies were sold, and the demand was constantly increasing. In 1892 Emery wrote another book entitled *Imperialism in America*. This work also had phenomenal sales, furthering the interests of reform. *Conspiracies* was translated into German and sold over 400,000 copies in all.

> In January, 1893, Mrs. Emery commenced the publication of The Cornerstone, an eight page monthly, which already has a circulation in nearly every state and territory.
>
> She was one of the early members of the Knights of Labor, the [Farmers] Alliance and the W. C. T. U. In November 1892, she delivered an address before the National W. C. T. U. in Denver, Col., and was elected national superintendent of the department, "Relation of Temperance to Labor and Capital."
>
> Generous, benevolent, kind, liberal in her religious views, firm in her convictions, yet solicitous and considerate, her highest enjoyment is to uplift the fallen and oppressed, and she has ever labored with an earnestness of purpose in the reform movements of which she is a most thorough and convincing advocate.[839]

Jim and Emery held similar views on bimetallism and shared a compassion for working people. Jim continued to work within the Republican party for reform but increasingly reached out to form coalitions. Emery worked within populist third parties—the Greenbacks, the People's Party, the Prohibitionists—perhaps because these parties welcomed her both as a woman and a thinker whose economic analysis fortified their complaints. The issues were not abstract. The people of Lansing were dealing with them every day.

Lansing's First Labor Day

For working families, everything was made worse by the depression. As workers struggled to improve their condition, strikes were reported across the country, not just by big city papers but by the daily small town newspapers as well. In May of 1894 the railroad workers at the Pullman Palace Car Company in Pullman, Illinois, went on strike against George Pullman. It was a strike that eventually spread to all of the American Railway Union, led by Eugene V. Debs. It was first of the industry-wide unions. There was some violence; federal troops were called in by President Cleveland who said the strikes interfered with delivering mail. The investigation and trials of Debs were intensely covered by the *State Republican*. Debs and the other leaders ended up with a six months minimum security jail term in Indiana for conspiracy. The strike had involved 250,000 workers in twenty-seven states.

In an attempt to appease organized labor, Labor Day was established by Congress six days after the trial ended. Workers were organized in the

Lansing area. They had held Labor Day marches before this, but this time when trade unionist Charles McMahon was appointed Grand Marshal of Lansing's parade, he put the parade in a new context. The sentiments of progressive leaders were not lost on him. McMahon invested great meaning in the first-ever national Labor Day parade as "a death struggle for the rights of organized labor on the one hand and organized labor and thieving politicians on the other:"

As labor day (September 3) this year will be the first occasion on which may be termed a national affair, congress having passed an act making it a legal holiday. It should be the duty of every labor organization to participate in the grand street parade and demonstration on that date, not alone to impress upon the public the importance of organized labor as a factor in the industrial and social questions of this country, but also to show its solidity and unity of purpose. There are several other important reasons why organized labor should show its full strength in 1894, not the least of which is that the industrial crises through which we have passed and are yet passing have given the enemies of organized labor the opportunity to spread the false rumor that many unions have felt its evil effect in loss of influence, and you should turn out in the labor day parade, if possible, your full membership, to show that the trade unions of Lansing are standing steady along the line.

Events pass quickly, the world moves and with it must move the great labor organizations of the country. We must admit that at present every tendency points to the fact that we are in the midst of times in which rapid changes will take place, politically and industrially, the ultimate result of which no one can foretell. The most interested in the change are the working people, and it behooves them to be ever on the alert, to fraternize and show their strength, and labor day affords the best occasion.

Working men of Lansing, show your strength. Unite on labor day, September 3, in one solid phalanx. Never was there a more critical time to prove your courage and manhood by marching under the banner of true unionism. The time is rapidly approaching when it will be necessary to throw your whole united strength against the organized monopolies and political thieves of this country, in a death struggle for the rights of man, his right to a footing on God's earth, his right to toil and his right to the full fruits of his toil. Before this great battle between organized labor on the one hand and organized monopolies and thieving politicians on the other, the great strikes of the last few years will be in comparison but mere skirmishes. One side or the other must go down in utter defeat and woe to the vanquished. Workingmen, show that you are prepared for this great battle by turning out in full force on labor day. Prove that organized labor stands ready to meet the issue in whatever field of action the battle may be fought. Charles McMahon, Grand Marshal, 727 Saginaw street west.[840]

The Labor Day celebration was a huge success. "It was early morning when the people began to arrive from surrounding country in buggies, carriages and wagons. Later the special trains began to unload their human freights, and gradually the crowd began to take on proportions of immensity, until at 10 o'clock the line of march was a solid mass of people. The crowd was of the usual kind and well assorted, each one striving with the other for the most advantageous places from which to see the parade. They crowded out into the street until the policemen had much pushing to do to keep a little space clear for the parade; they pushed their way with little ceremony into offices, and found even the roofs of buildings an advantageous spot from which to view the passing show. The crowd was everywhere." The parade included four bands from Jackson, Owosso, Ovid, and Lansing. The paint-ers and decorators in immaculate white pants and coats provided the only variety in the column of marchers. The sports began at 2 o'clock with races, followed by a twelve-mile bicycle race. There were three baseball games."[841]

Grand Marshall McMahon raised an alarm when he called for the Labor Day parade, yet the day ended quietly and serenely. However, the lesson of the Pullman strike and its brutality toward the workers was not to be forgotten. On August 23, 1894, less than two weeks before the parade, it was reported that John P. Altged, the governor of Illinois sent out an appeal to the citizens of the state to relieve the starving strikers at Pullman and turned to Illinois county commissioners, calling attention to the suffering in Pullman and urging them to furnish the immediate assistance—but only after he had satisfied himself, he said, that the Pullman Company would do nothing to relieve the distress.[842] He begged George Pullman to "cancel all rents due Oct. 1, and work some of the men half time, so they can get something to feed their families." Pullman said the workers brought it upon themselves and Altged replied, "It seems to me you would prefer to relieve the situation yourself, especially as it has cost the state upwards of $50,000 to protect your property."[843] For McMahon it felt like a war, and he feared the worker's defeat.

A few months later Hazen Pingree wrote his account of a little known aspect of the strike, the objection by Army officers to their troops being drawn into the dispute against citizens on behalf of corporations. This kind of educating endeared Ping to the common man and woman, and infuriated the moneyed class in Detroit who were working against his re-election as mayor:

There is a secret connected with the Chicago riots, which were brought about by Pullman who refused to arbitrate the case of his distressed working-men. The secret is that the officers of the regular or United State troops, who were brought to Chicago by the order of President Cleveland, who foolishly took the advice of Olney, the corporation lawyer who was attorney-general in Cleveland's cabinet, met at one of the hotels and denounced the policy of using the army to perpetuate wrongs and by so doing degrade it in the eyes of the people.

The swindling, highway robbery, and general dishonesty in the man-agement and manipulation of most roads has been such that the people have no sympathy with them, and self-respecting men felt aggrieved that the army should be used in their behalf against the laboring classes. Whatever the excuse may have been, the army was there to over-awe employees and the laboring classes generally, for the Chicago police were at all times fully able to handle the criminal classes, and everybody in authority in the State of Illinois knew this… It will be a sorry day for this Republic of ours when it becomes the rule to settle disputes about wages and coerce workingmen by bullets and bayonets. No settlements of this kind can be lasting.[844]

Mayor During Hard Times

As the depression deepened, citizens of Lansing turned once again to Jim for leadership. In accepting the nomination for mayor in March of 1895, he made a speech about the state of politics in the city. It expressed his view of political parties, government reform, and politics—as threatening as ever to the political powers in the state. The *State Republican* headline read, "Lansing's Next Mayor Clearly Defines His Position, On National as Well as Local Issues—He will See to it that the Taxpayer's Money is Wisely and Judiciously Expended." Jim's speech pledged to his fellow Republicans that unlike his earlier term, there would be no new projects. He told them they could expect no spoils system favoritism, more bipartisanship, and advised them that he did not support the party position on the gold standard. He said, in part:

> I was never foolish enough to want office but once in my life, and, as you all know, I did not get that one. If I consulted my personal feeling tonight, I should naturally shrink from any added responsibilities; but to my mind one of the most sacred things in the world is American citizenship and… that the citizen should obey the command of the community…
>
> As you all know, I was born and bred in Lansing, where my parents were among the sturdy pioneers, and in common with you I have a pride in our native land. It seems to me that Lansing has reached a critical point in her development. She has discarded the swaddling clothes of the country village, and it seems to have been decreed that we shall build here a splendid city, which shall be a pride not only to us but to those who are to come after us…
>
> There is nothing in the administration of a municipal government that could possibly justify a partisan spirit, and I wish it distinctly understood that I could not become your candidate except with the understanding that, if chosen as the mayor at the coming election, you would each and every one help me to be the representative of all the people without party distinction, our interests being a community of interests without reference to political creed.
>
> In these times of great depression and business disaster, the burdens of taxation should be made as light as possible and the municipal government administered as carefully as any private business. The people's money should never be spent for the purpose of advancing the interest of any man or combination of men, or to build up or sustain any political

party. "Equal rights to all and special privileges to none," should be our guiding principle.[845]

Jim reiterated his passionate support for silver, and then his populism came through. He told them what he thought of a party that did not meet the people's needs in a time of depression:

> If this position is in conflict with any political platform, I refuse to be bound by such a platform, as I believe the question of restoring silver to its former position as a money metal transcends all other questions in this nation. We all know that the great mass of the people in this country have been oppressed and driven almost to despair through the financial policies adopted by the government under the leadership of John Sherman and Grover Cleveland, and the party that fails in its duty to the downtrodden and the oppressed is, in my judgment, not worthy of perpetuation.
>
> Ill fares the land to hastening ills a prey
> Where wealth accumulates and men decay;
> Princes and lords may flourish or may fade,
> A breath can make them as a breath has made,
> But a bold peasantry, their country's pride,
> When once destroyed can never by supplied.
> [From "The Deserted Village" by Oliver Goldsmith]
>
> Again thanking you for the mark of high esteem which you have tonight extended to me, I assure you that if your selection shall be ratified at the polls I will use whatever energies and ability God may have given me to serve faithfully, not sect or clique, but all the people.[846]

When Jim said "Equal rights to all and special privileges to none," they all knew he was quoting Thomas Jefferson. It was a favorite call to action of Susan B. Anthony and many other reformers in this period, including Ping, Jim and his Democratic brothers-in-law, Cy and Frank. Frank went so far at the turn of the century as to join the Patrons of the Jeffersonian Cyclopedia, a group of admirers of Thomas Jefferson who supported the creation of a manual of Jeffersonian doctrine. The Cyclopedia organization believed Jefferson was the foremost expounder of the rights of man, of the inalienable right of every human being to life, liberty, and the pursuit of happiness, and belief that this is the object of government. The book took as its leading Jeffersonian quotation, "I have sworn upon the altar of God eternal hostility against every form of tyranny over the mind of man." The Jeffersonian Cyclopedia was published in 1900 as a comprehensive collection of the views of Jefferson.[847] The quotation in Jim's speech from Oliver Goldsmith (1730-1774) shows he was well aware of similarities in the helpless plight of ordinary people under the oligarchs of Europe to the situation of his listeners.

When the Democrats met to nominate their choice for mayor in March of 1895, Frank and his brother Ezra and Cy Black were on hand. The Democrats were said by the *State Republican* to have had a hard time finding an opponent for Jim. Finally, they drafted a reluctant A. A. Nichols.[848] Their position on the liquor question also brought difficulties, at least as reported in the *State Republican*:

> The committee on resolutions and orders of business met at the secretary's desk. C. P. Black drew the resolutions. They consisted of an endorsement of the free silver platform of the democratic state convention, and two paragraphs favoring an honest, economical and law enforcing administration. Mr. Black read the resolutions to the committee. When he came to the third paragraph he read: "We are in favor of the rigid enforcement of all laws and ordinances for the maintenance of order and morality in the city."
>
> "Don't say 'rigid." said Mr. Smith.
>
> "Why not?" said Black.
>
> "Well it sounds too strong," said Secretary Rikerd.
>
> When the resolutions reached the reporter's table the word "rigid" was still there, but two black pencil lines were drawn through it. Thus did the committee steer between the rocks of the federate council and the whirlpool of saloon interest. The reports of the two committees were adopted without objection.[849]

This did not stop the *Lansing Journal* from claiming liquor dealers were all supporting Jim. "It is not necessary for the observing citizen to spend much time on the streets or about the saloons of the city these times in order to discover that the saloonkeepers of the city, practically without a single exception, have during the past week banded themselves together in a common cause, and to a man are shouting and working for the election of James M. Turner as Mayor of this city." The *Journal* was sure there was some sort of payback deal for their support. "This condition of things will not be viewed with complacency by the law abiding citizens of Lansing. As is well known, the Democratic candidate for Mayor is pledged simply to the enforcement of the laws."[850] The next day *the State Republican* said, "SLANDEROUS AND FALSE, was the Lansing Journal's 'Saloon' article yesterday so far as it relates to Mr. Turner."[851] And so it went.

But the election of Jim had a different significance for others. All the way up north, *The Ontonagon Miner* editor, Alfred Meads, said, "Mr. Turner is an outspoken free silver man and, in accepting the nomination made one of his electrifying speeches in favor of this government coining its silver at the ration of 16 to 1, without waiting the dictation or acquiescence of any foreign government. Mr. Turner never minces his words on any question and gives his reason for the faith that is in him in no misunderstood terms. Jim will win."[852] Silver was thought to exist in the world at a quantity sixteen times greater than gold, so that ratio would bring parity between the two metals.

The Sunday following the successful election of Jim as mayor and re-election of Frank as alderman, Rev. C. F. Swift of the Plymouth Congregational Church assured his flock of Jim's stand on the liquor question by endorsing the part of his nominating speech that said, "Certain laws and regulations deemed necessary to the promotion of the best interests of the community and society have been established, which it will be the solemn duty of the incoming administration to see fairly and impartially executed."[853] This support must have been of some gratification to Abby and Frank as members of the Plymouth Congregational Church, though the election meant Frank was now one of only three Democrats on the city council. Swift told his congregation:

> Thomas Jefferson said that the enforcement of law is as important as the making of law. The community does not ask Mr. Turner to make or unmake laws, nor to enforce laws that are not in existence, but to see to the execution of the laws that have been made.
>
> Few laws can be enforced with absolute exactness. But the same vigor and interest that clears the sidewalks of bicycles in the forbidden district, applies to the discovery and punishment of various other violations of the law, will keep the saloons closed on Sunday and holidays and after 11 o'clock p. m., and will rid the city, very largely, of houses of ill-fame and gambling resorts…
>
> There are some who claim to see in the last clause of Mr. Turner's address, 'not sect or clique, but all the people' a covert fling at the Federation of Churches. I have more confidence in the good sense of our Mayor-elect than to accept the charge that in the same breath with which he said 'all the people,' he should, even covertly, make an exception of one group of "the people," a group which stands for the identical municipal principles laid down in his own address."[854]

When Jim won handily over Nichols in April, the statewide view was that it was a victory for the Silverites. *The Mining News* was happy that their long-time subscriber had won by a majority of 900 votes. The *Mining Journal* chortled that "The Democrats of Lansing elected just one of their candidates Thursday." It said *The Lansing Journal* said, on commenting on the outcome of the election there, that "Hon. James M. Turner, who was chosen mayor as the Republican nominee, but who in his speech of acceptance put himself before the voters as a free silver candidate, will be in the race for congress in that district in 1896 as a candidate of the silver men. Good enough. Mr. Turner showed the courage of his convictions by stating where he stood on the silver issue when he was put up for mayor, and such men as he are going to be much needed in congress until we get the currency legislation that the country requires to bring back its former prosperity."[855]

Municipal Suffrage Meets its Waterloo

Progressives found the path to total suffrage for women full of crushing set-backs, and the status of women's voting rights seemed always in flux. Because they were denied, progress had to be made step by tiny step. Constant legal challenges meant few got to vote, even in school elections. In 1881 Michigan's school law was amended to include parents or guardians of children of school age. Tax-paying women could also vote on bonds and appropriations for school purposes. However, women could not vote for the state or county school superintendents because these offices were established by the state constitution and required a change in the state constitution to fix it.

The story of Municipal Suffrage in Michigan began in 1884, which happened to be just before a major issue on a local expenditure of a large sum of Lansing taxpayers' money was to take place. In 1885 the male voters of Lansing voted to establish a municipal utility to provide drinking water and fire protection by approving a $100,000 bond.[856] Lansing women had no say in it. Even if their vote would likely have not changed the outcome, many were painfully reminded that they had no say. Lansing equal suffrage groups continually helped to lobby, educate, and host the state organization.

Both nationally and in Michigan, municipal suffrage became the new goal for suffragists. Municipal Suffrage would allow women to vote at town meetings on local measures. The national suffrage association wisely set this as a goal for all states. It was seen as a step toward Universal Suffrage which required an amendment to the federal constitution. Sarah E. V. Emery took up this goal in earnest. With twenty years of suffrage work behind her, according to the *Lansing Journal*, she "was ever aggressive in working for equal suffrage, and was instrumental in causing several suffrage bills to be framed and introduced into the Legislature."[857]

To the progressive women and men who worked for Municipal Suffrage, victory often seemed just beyond reach. The Michigan story told here is gleaned from volume four of *The History of Woman Suffrage: 1883-1900*, by Elizabeth Cady Stanton, Susan B. Anthony, and other members, including May Knaggs and Mary L. Doe, both former presidents of the Michigan Equal Suffrage Association. In 1886 the suffragists approached the conventions of the four political parties in the state to include a plank endorsing a Municipal Suffrage bill. "Sarah E. V. Emery appeared before the Prohibition convention, which adopted the plank. She also attended the Democratic, where she was invited to the platform and made a vigorous speech, which was received with applause, but the suffrage resolution was not adopted. Emily B. Ketcham, of Grand Rapids, attended the Republican convention but was refused a hearing before the Committee on Resolutions. After its report had been accepted, friends obtained an opportunity for her to address the meeting, but she was received with considerable discourtesy. Mrs. Fowler secured the adoption of the plank by the Greenback convention."[858]

In 1888 school law was used to test the right of the Legislature to confer *any* form of suffrage upon women. Mrs. Eva R. Belles made the test through a lawsuit against the Flint inspectors of election. Belles, 31, was a suffragist. She was a landowner and mother of a 7½ year old attending the Flint schools. Her vote was refused at a school election because the inspectors said Belles was not a qualified voter under the state law. Belles won her case, which was then appealed to the Supreme Court, which sustained the law.[859] The State Bar of Michigan and the Genesee County Bar Association placed a Legal Milestone Marker on the courthouse lawn in downtown Flint in 1990, commemorating the Eva Belles' decision as a legal milestone for woman suffrage in Michigan. When Eva Belles moved to Grand Rapids, she continued her work with the Grand Rapids Equal Suffrage Association.

In 1889 a hearing was to be held on a Municipal Suffrage bill before the entire Legislature during the annual convention of the Michigan Equal Suffrage Association. "A letter was received from Senator Palmer, enclosing a draft for $100 and saying: 'Equal suffrage in municipal affairs means better statutes, better ordinances, better officers, better administration, lower taxation, happier homes and a better race.' This generous gift enabled the association to keep a committee—Helen Philleo Jenkins, Harriet A. Cook, Mrs. Ketcham and Mrs. Knaggs—at the capital for several weeks, where they worked systematically to convert members and to secure victory." Only women of Michigan would be allowed to speak; however, material from outsiders was permitted. "Just before this hearing, the bevy of officers and speakers passing through the corridor on their way to the House were warned by Joseph Greusel, a friendly journalist, that a circular of protest had been placed upon the desk of each member. This was headed: 'Massachusetts Remonstrates against Woman Suffrage, to the Members of Michigan Legislature;' and contained the familiar array of misrepresentations. With the cooperation of Lucy Stone [leader of the American Equal Suffrage Association], a reply was printed immediately after the convention and likewise distributed in the Legislature."[860]

Emery's close friends in Kansas, the governor, attorney-general, ex-attorney-general, and Laura M. Johns of the Kansas Equal Suffrage Association, provided expertise to Michigan suffragists on how Municipal Suffrage worked in Kansas which was presented to the Legislature by May Knaggs. She then submitted an exhaustive legal opinion by Judge Charles B. Waite of Chicago. The Judiciary Committee was unanimously in favor of the bill. Senator Palmer, who was leaving for his appointment as Minister to Spain, went to Lansing on the very eve of leaving the United States and made a strong plea for the measure. However, the opposition quietly arranged to have an address delivered in Representative Hall by a Mrs. Mary Livermore, who had been holding parlor meetings in Detroit for pay and speaking against woman suffrage. They claimed this was the great suffragist of like name who had discarded her lifelong convictions and gone over to the enemy.[861]

The bill was considered on May 15, 1889. By the courtesy of the Detroit, Lansing and Northern Railroad, a special train carried a large delegation of women from Detroit. Onlookers came from other parts of the state, and the equal suffrage societies of Lansing were well represented. The galleries were filled, and the floor of the House was lined with interested women. After a largely favorable discussion, the vote was taken, resulting in 58 ayes, 34 noes. The Senate lost no time in bringing the measure under consideration and, after a brief discussion, it was defeated by one vote—11 ayes, 12 noes.

That evening the Mary Livermore impersonator gave her belated dissertation and, upon a motion, was followed by Adele Hazlitt, who, "with great courtesy slew her weak arguments." At this session the charters of East Saginaw and Detroit were amended to give women of those cities the school ballot. The Detroit women also obtained the change in their law just before the spring election. They made a house-to-house canvass to secure registration and polled a vote of 2,700 women, electing Sophronia O. C. Parsons to the school board.[862]

In 1891 Sarah A. C. Plummer of Lansing put out a press release for the call to the seventh annual convention of the Michigan Equal Suffrage Association February 10-12 at the capitol. It read: "All who believe that 'governments derive their powers from the consent of the governed,' are invited to meet with the association."[863] The Municipal Suffrage bill was again presented to the Legislature while the state suffrage convention was in session. Again a joint hearing was held in Representative Hall for its speakers. Only Michigan women were allowed. Sarah E. V. Emery and Belle M. Perry, of Eaton County, both members of the Woman Press Association, were among those speaking. The senate bill was taken up March 25, discussed and lost by a close vote. It was taken up again May 13 and lost again, receiving 14 ayes, 15 noes. They found the suffrage petitions had been ignored. "After the quick defeat in the Senate it was found that the chairman of the committee to which these had been referred had on file the names of 8,502 petitioners (4,469 men, 3,033 women) out of twenty-one senatorial districts. These were in addition to many thousands sent in previous sessions, when petitioning had been a method of work."[864]

This discussion was the most trying of all during the ten years of effort to secure Municipal Suffrage, owing to the character of the chief opponent, Senator Frank Smith, who represented the basest elements of Detroit. Knowing his illiteracy, the reporters had expected much sport by sending his speech to the papers in full, but in the interests of decency they refrained from publishing it. Women came down from the galleries white with anger and disgust, and avowed that if they never had wanted the ballot before, they wanted it now. The suffrage committee received many friendly courtesies from Lt. Gov. John Strong, besides a substantial gift of money. When asked for the use of the Senate Chamber for one evening of the convention he said: "Certainly; your money helped to build the State House. You have as much right to it as any of us."[865]

Belle Perry published an account of the convention in her column in the *Charlotte Tribune* called "The Women's Department." It was actually two or three columns long and usually in some way related to women's rights. On February 19 she told her readers: "At the 7th Annual Conference of the Michigan Equal Suffrage Association, besides the hearing before the Legislature asking for Municipal Suffrage, resolutions were passed … that Mrs. Tenney's successor as state librarian be a woman, that a woman be placed on the board of managers of the state school at Coldwater, that the commissioner of labor be required to complete statistics of women's labor in the state, as well as of men's labor." They appointed committees to work on these things. Her husband was the publisher of the paper and besides the "Women's Department," they included women in the regular news sections.

Although Municipal Suffrage legislation had been blocked by the Senate, in August of 1891 Mrs. Helen P. Jenkins of Detroit, president of the Michigan Equal Suffrage Association after Mary Doe, urged the women of the state to participate in the election for members of the school board, which was to occur in all <u>townships</u> of the state on September 7.[866] In 1889 Belle Perry was the first woman to be elected to the Charlotte School Board in neighboring Eaton County. In an article entitled "Women and School Affairs" in the Women's Department, Belle Perry reported receiving a Letter to the Editor about a janitor who was disgruntled because a woman on the school board wanted to see the school's basement. He was disgusted because "nobody never asked to see the basement but now," and in fact, "the basement ain't fit to be inspected." She often used a "Letter to the Editor" format with her own comments to follow. On August 30 she signed this one "The Gold Pen:"

> I am glad that Charlotte is in the advance guard of the movement for engaging in the cooperation of women in public matters upon the welfare of the home and the family. "What is a home without a mother?" A man wouldn't undertake raising a family without the help of a female assistant… But that is about what the average school board is doing as a result of which many matters relating to health and morals and beyond the teacher are practically ignored.
>
> The advance thought of Michigan, molding her laws, have put in the hands of every woman who is the parent or guardian of every child of school age, the right to a vote at the election of members of the school board. It also gives the responsibility to all women liable to pay taxes and adds to their care the right to vote on the expenditure to pay taxes… Let your presence and power be known at school at school meetings. Elect, with the liberal-minded men amongst you, some good women to share the labors of the busy men, now bearing their share of public burdens.[867]

Perhaps Belle Perry's article was inspired by what was going on in Jackson. The *Lansing Journal* reported "that Jackson citizens are considerably excited over the approaching school election in which the ladies are expected to figure prominently. The *Patriot* pats the fair ones on the back and urges them to go in and win… The women's agitation, relative to their right and title to serve as members of a city school board, is occasioning no little comment upon the street, and there is a general disposition to acknowledge their claims to especial fitness. The law makes them clearly eligible and as to their average intelligence, as compared with that of the opposite sex, no man in his right mind dares question. Then their duties and vocations are such as to give them ample time to consider and investigate matters pertaining to the office and what is of more importance, they would enter into the work with a zest, stimulated by that love of children that no man can ever know. The women have entered upon a campaign that will only end with victory, and they deserve the support and admiration of every right thinking voter."[868] The *Lansing Journal* was foursquare for woman suffrage. The day after the Jackson election, the *Journal* reported, "Mrs. C. C. Bloomfield and Mrs. A. L. Ford, two estimable ladies of Jackson, were last night elected members of the school board of that city. One hundred and twenty votes were cast, of which eighty-three were for the ladies."[869]

Despite the fact that women were voting, what women could vote for and where was still a controversy and not fully agreed upon by the courts, despite the Eva Belles school election decision by the State Supreme Court. In Lansing, which was under a city charter, the school board elections did not take place until March 1893, another six months away. A lot could happen in six months.

After the election of 1892, when Edwin Winans was voted out of office, the climate in the Legislature seemed more favorable to Municipal Suffrage for women. In January of 1893 the Lansing Equal Suffrage Association prepared for the Ninth Annual Convention, which would be held at the capitol in the Pioneer Room, February 1-3. They made a chart for one wall showing the number of women tax payers in Michigan, as obtained from the assessment rolls; the amount of property for which women were assessed; the amount of taxes paid by women; and the proportion of taxes paid by women in Michigan.[870] In below zero temperatures, the Michigan Equal Suffrage Association leaders held an executive board meeting on January 31, 1893. They were well aware that the new state of Wyoming was now the first state to have Universal Suffrage, yet it was nearly ten years since the campaign for woman's right to vote in municipal elections in Michigan began. The board planned to introduce legislation once again.

"The Women of Tomorrow" was the topic of a main speaker from Grand Rapids and another was a talk on reform institutions. The notion that the nineteenth century would be "The Year of the Woman" was beginning to catch on. Twentieth Century Clubs were beginning to form around the state. Nationally known speakers from Michigan, Reverend Caroline J. Bartlett of Kalamazoo and Reverend Anna Howard Shaw of Ferris, currently of Washington, D.C., came to speak on the last day of the conference.

A few weeks later they found gains for school suffrage had been snatched away. On March 22, the *State Republican* reported, "An Unusual Amount of Interest Shown in the Selection of Men for This Important Board—The Ladies did not Attempt at Representation."[871] Now women could not vote in school board elections. The situation was absurd. "In response to numerous inquiries Attorney General Ellis has filed an opinion to the effect that while women can legally be candidates for and hold the office of county commissioner, of school inspectors, and members of city boards of education, they are not qualified to vote for candidates for these offices."[872]

Octavia Williams Bates, of Detroit, studied the Municipal Suffrage campaign that year. She was a brilliant young attorney with a L. L. B. in International Law from the University of Michigan.[873] In October of 1893 she was a Michigan delegate to the Congress of Women held in the elegant Woman's Building at the Columbian Exhibition in Chicago. She presented a paper entitled, "Municipal Suffrage for Women in Michigan." She remembered that day following the state convention when the municipal amendment was voted down once again:

> The measure had been made the special order for 2:30 P. M. the next day. The House assembled at 2 o'clock… At this time a member in the rear, at a sufficient distance from the Speaker's desk to give impressiveness to what would follow, rose and presented "A petition from the people of Chippewa County in favor of the Municipal Woman Suffrage Bill." A page sprang forward and taking the document, which was prepared upon paper of an extra size and ornamented with long streamers of red and green ribbons, ran with it to the clerk's desk, and that officer proceeded to read it at length, including a long list of signatures which comprised Patrick O'Shea, Annie Rooney, Spotted Tail, etc. This petition was followed by two others of similar character, bearing phony *Indian names* of such significance as the wit of the opposition could invent. After this undignified prelude the House discussed the measure at length, and defeated it by a vote of 38 ayes, 39 noes. A reconsideration was moved and the bill tabled.
>
> This Municipal Suffrage Bill was taken up again in May and passed the House on the 19th with an *educational amendment*: "Women who are able to read the constitution of Michigan in the English language." The vote was 57 yeas, 25 noes. On May 25 it was considered in the Senate and, after a vigorous battle, was carried by a vote of 18 ayes, 11 noes. Gov. John T. Rich affixed his signature May 27, an *apparent victory was won after ten years* of effort. Representative Newkirk and Senator Hopkins [the two sponsors] received the heartfelt gratitude of those for whom they had given their ardent labors, and local societies held jubilee meetings. The newspapers of the State were unanimous in expressing welcome to the new class of voters…

Mayor Pingree of Detroit recognizing the new law, ordered a sufficient additional number of registration books, but Edward H. Kennedy and Henry S. Potter, who were opposed to it, *filed an injunction* against

Hazen S. Pingree and the Common Council to restrain them from this extra purchase. Mary Stuart Coffin and Mary E. Burnett "countered" by filing a mandamus [request that a judge order the law be followed] September 30, to compel the election commissioners to provide means for carrying out the law. As these were cases for testing the constitutionality of the law they were taken directly to the Supreme Court. They were set for argument October 10, at 2 p. m., but a case of local interest was allowed to usurp the time till 4 o'clock, one hour only being left for the arguments with three advocates on each side. Two of the women's lawyers, John B. Corliss and Henry A. Haigh, therefore filed briefs and gave their time to the first attorney, Col. John Atkinson. A decision was rendered October 24, the *mandamus denied* and the injunction granted, all the judges concurring, on the ground that the Legislature had no authority to create a new class of voters.

In spite of this Waterloo, the names of those men who, through the ten years' struggle in the various sessions of the Legislature, stood as champions of the political rights of women, are cherished in memory… In both Houses, session after session, there were many eloquent advocates of woman's equality.[874]

In July of 1894 the League of Republican Clubs meeting in Denver advised its members to study up on female suffrage. "Verily the day of enlightenment dawneth," said the *State Republican*.[875] Indeed, not long after, in 1895, woman's suffrage again came within one vote of success when Representative George H. Waldo, without first consulting with the Michigan Equal Suffrage Association as to timing, introduced a joint resolution to amend the constitution by striking out the word "male." He was fulfilling a promise to his mother and his wife. Although ill-timed, the officers of the State Association could not withhold a friendly hand from so ardent and sincere a champion. The resolution was lost by one vote. This Legislature passed The Blanket Charter Act, which substituted an "and" for an "or" that seemed to affect the right of women to the school ballot in cities of the fourth class, cities of less than 10,000 residents. The action created a general ruckus resulting in an appeal to the Attorney General who rendered an opinion sustaining the suffrage of women in those cities.[876]

With school suffrage reestablished in cities of less than 10,000, Municipal Suffrage hopeless, and the failure to initiate an amendment to the state constitution by one vote, Olivia Bates foretold more trouble ahead because the Municipal Suffrage campaign in Michigan, as elsewhere, had made enemies. Just six months after formation of the Lansing Saloon Keepers' Society, Bates told the Congress of Women there were men with purely selfish reasons organizing against woman's right to vote: The "Michigan Liquor Dealers' Association met in delegate convention two hundred and fifty strong, at Arbeiter Hall, Grand Rapids, August 23, and resolved to oppose the law giving women Municipal Suffrage. In a preliminary circular sent out to the trade some weeks ago, the association says: 'The last session of the Legislature in this state, by giving to the women a franchise with an educational restriction, struck a blow directly at our interests and rights. It is only a question of time as to what the inevitable result will be to us, unless we promptly get under one banner and fight shoulder to shoulder for our interests.'[877]

To put the best face on this latest blow to their suffrage work, Michigan suffragists maintained that it had not all been in vain. School suffrage would pave the way to Municipal Suffrage, leading to a state women's suffrage amendment. And then federal suffrage, or Universal Suffrage, would be "only a matter of time." They would educate and urge women to exercise their right to vote, no matter how limited, to make way for full political enfranchisement. Their subsequent legislative goal was to improve the condition of women.

According to the only account of Michigan woman suffrage history published by the Michigan Historical Commission (and not until 1918 when Michigan passed universal suffrage), in 1895 the women's movement lobbied for and succeeded in winning the passage of protective labor laws regulating hours of labor for girls and women, the age at which girls might be employed, and improving the sanitary and moral conditions of places of labor. In the same year the age of consent was raised from fourteen to sixteen. In 1896, after a good deal of lobbying, Governor Rich appointed Mrs. Jane M. Kinney to the Board of the Eastern Asylum for the Insane for a term of six years and police matrons were employed in cities of more than 10,000. Saloonkeepers were prohibited from employing women as barkeepers, liquor servers, dancers or musicians in saloons or any place where liquor was sold. Laws were enacted to prohibit the use of indecent, immoral, obscene or insulting language in the presence of any woman or child in the state.[878] By the end of the twentieth century this protective legislation was overturned on the grounds that it denied women opportunities or that it was no longer needed.

After the 1895 election year, the women of Lansing did not give up on the many issues that affected women and children's rights. However, they did turn part of their attention to other things. Cultural pursuits that allowed them to use their musical talents had always been important for many of Marian's family. Eva and Abby joined a new organization in the city to advance music performance by offering concerts and strengthening both individual talent and music appreciation in Lansing. It was in March of 1894 that a group of ten women came together to form a chorus at the home of Kate Kedzie, wife of Michigan Agricultural College President Frank Kedzie, at 420 W. Ottawa Street. This meeting included Eva, and, soon after Abby and their cousin Ida Longyear joined the group as charter members. Their Aunt Eliza Turner was voted in as an honorary or associate member two years later. The group adopted the name "Matinee Musical Society" in 1899 while Eva was President of the group. Later it became just "Matinee Musicale." The members voted in a one dollar annual membership fee. If a member missed a chorus rehearsal they were fined ten cents. A librarian was soon appointed to take care of choral music, and their performances often included music by early nineteenth century German composers such as Felix Mendelssohn and Robert Schumann. Kate, as well as Eva and Abby, had musical training in Berlin and they united to encourage several of their young members to go to Europe to obtain training as well. Abby accompanied the chorus for some performances and sometimes performed as a piano soloist.[879]

The group included many of the most prominent women of Lansing, and audiences for their performances included their influential friends and families. The *State Republican* noted that during the group's first public concert, held in 1896, many well-known luminaries in business and social circles, including Mrs. Frank L. Dodge, turned out for the event. [880] Abby also performed professionally, giving performances across the state, according to her decedents.[881] Such programs and organizations offered welcome relief from the tumult of the times. This was not to say that Abby wasn't interested in politics.

The Silver Movement

It is much easier to complain about wrongs that members see in their party when it is out of power. When it is in power the criticizers are often attacked for trying to weaken the party. With the exception of Josiah Begole and Governor Winans, Michigan Republicans were always in power. Under such circumstances, to demand change is inherently to criticize and requires a considerable degree of fearlessness. At the beginning of the movement, the Republican Silverites could work within their party. It wasn't easy, but they knew where levers of power lay, and they had a measure of access to them.

"We should think that even such a doughty fighter as Jim Turner would give up after a while trying to remove the grip of the railroad corporation on the management of the Republican party of the state," observed the *Lansing Journal* in February of 1895. "This is about the steenth time that Jim has fought against the nomination of a stalking-horse for the McMillian-Rich corporation combine, and he has got it in the neck every time. It would seem that after the failure of his efforts to get the judgeship for his friend Cahill he would see the futility of running a 'gravel train' line in competition with the palace car routes of the big Republican magnates."[882]

Jim was 45 years old when he embarked on the Silverite campaign in full force. In February of 1895 Jim, Governor Cyrus Luce, and Judge Jonathan Ramsdell of Traverse City—who were both well-known leaders of the Grange—made an unsuccessful attempt to strengthen the silver plank of the state Republican platform against opposition from party boss Senator McMillan. O. C. Wright of the *Ionia Express* characterized it as a gallant fight and said, "Republicans will show themselves wise just in proportion as they elect men of such views to legislative and executive offices. Certainly, 'Jim's' head is level and heart right to the extent so declared. And the masses of Republicans, as well as of all other political parties in this state, are heartily and decidedly with him."[883]

In March, Cy and Jim, working with a bipartisan coalition of about fifty supporters, began to establish Free Silver Clubs to strengthen the movement's grass roots. They began with the Lansing Free Silver Bi-metallic Club which had 200 members at its formation. Jim became the chair. The object was to restore coinage of silver and gold at the ratio of 16 to 1. They would work for laws to guarantee the free and unlimited use of both metals as money. If they could not succeed by working within their respective parties, only then would they consider establishing a new party.[884]

Jim prepared a manifesto explaining how John Sherman's Silver Purchasing Act established the gold standard that was contributing to deflation and calling upon people of the state to organize. It said, in part: "If the friends of silver will join on this plan and perfect an organization in each locality and courageously declare their principles, we will have a band of minute men as did our forefathers at Concord, who can come together at the tap of the bell whenever it seems necessary to protect our liberties. We find that the price of wheat, wool, cotton, iron ore and other staples, agricultural lands, labor and so on through the list, have followed the bullion price of silver in its downward course, since it was degraded and discredited by the act of congress. This leads to the conviction that all values would increase in the same ratio with silver if congress would undo the mischief. The club urges each citizen to earnest effort within the ranks of the party to which he is attached. If present political parties fail to stand for the people on this burning question, then that strongest law of nature, the law of self-preservation, will dictate our course."[885]

The club gained over 500 members in a few days, and the manifesto was sent across the state to a carefully constructed network of supporters—legislators, judges, farmers, workers, and businessmen of all parties. Also, in short order came this assessment from the *Chicago Herald*: "Michigan Men for Silver—Growth of the White Metal Sentiment in Republican Ranks: Grand Rapids, Mich., March 22.—The Republican party managers are becoming alarmed at the growth of silver sentiment in the state and their lack of foresight in not falling into line early in the day. They count on the shortness of the spring campaign and the big victory of last fall to pull them through, and when it is over there will be a careful studying of the signs of the times preliminary to a speedy drop into the procession next year if the circumstances warrant it and the popular demand seems to call for it. The republican platform last year simply straddled the silver issue, and the platform adopted at the recent state convention in Detroit reiterated the straddle. The democratic campaign last fall was conducted on free silver lines and the platform adopted this spring contains but a single plank and that an unqualified free silver declaration. The platform and previous record of the republicans and the well-known attitude of Senator McMillan and other party leaders will make an open avowal of the silver faith exceedingly difficult, but no fears are entertained that next year, if the circumstances seem to warrant it, the party will be able to say almost anything that will gain it votes."[886] The rapid success of silver clubs showed politicos everywhere that it was relatively easy to organize the silver vote, and Jim's win for mayor in 1895 demonstrated they would vote for a silver man.

Jim attended the Free Silver Party National Committee meeting in Chicago that April, and noted bimetallists winds were sweeping Michigan.[887] At home he was frequently asked if he were still a Republican, and he would answer: "If a firm belief in the principles taught by Lincoln and Blaine constitutes a good republican, then I am one. But if it is necessary to endorse the financial policy of John Sherman and Grover Cleveland in order to be a good republican then most emphatically I am not."[888]

Sarah E. V. Emery also targeted John Sherman's policies. In his public career Sherman was a banker, U. S. Senator, and Federal Secretary of the Treasury, and Secretary of State. A Republican, he had mounted several campaigns to run for president. He most recently had authored the Sherman Antitrust Act and the Sherman Silver Purchase Act, both in 1890. The Silver Purchase Act required government purchases of increasing amounts of silver, expecting to stop deflation and cause inflation by allowing debtors to pay back their debts in cheaper dollars. However the government paid for silver in Silver Certificates and Treasury Notes, to be redeemable in silver *or* gold—and investors chose gold. That raised the value of gold, which the Sherman detractors found to be harmful to ordinary people. The charges in Emery's book, *The Seven Financial Conspiracies which have Enslaved the American People,* so challenged Sherman, particularly in his role of contracting currency and causing deflation, that he could not ignore the attack and published a rebuttal. Emery printed Sherman's rebuttal in the next of many, many re-printings of her book, along with her reply.

The nonpartisan Silverites leagues were forming around the state and the *Port Huron News* noted "men are joining them regardless of past political differences."[889] Jim was making the rounds of Free Silver Clubs where he was greeted with generous applause. He could hold the attention of his audience for two hours from beginning to end and generated speculation that he would be the next congressman from the Capital City district. In Owosso it was reported that "according to Mr. Turner's theory, to the present generation belongs the task of correcting the wrong that was done by demonetizing silver in '73, and he is full of confidence and hope that the year '96 will see the correction made. But he does not expect to see the change brought about by either of the old parties. The members of the Owosso Club were highly pleased with Mr. Turner's talk and only regret that it was not heard by every voter in the City."[890]

Between speaking to clubs in Fremont, Lapeer, and Brighton, he was arguing with the Common Council about enforcement of city contracts, insisting that agreements must be fulfilled as written and the previous practice of constantly modifying them be ended. A vote in the Senate to modify a railroad charter to reduce fares for customers led to his public criticism of Lansing's Senator who voted against it. He continued on his still hunt, building toward control of the local nominating conventions and reform of the Republican party.

That fall the city lost a highly regarded citizen, and the Progressives lost one of its great advocates. Sarah V. D. Emery died of cancer at 58 after almost two years of decline. "Mrs. Emery's career as agitator and reformer was both unique and brilliant," said the *Lansing Journal*. "From the time she first began to speak on the Greenback rostrum until disease incapacitated her for further work, she was constantly in the harness, campaigning in all sections of Michigan and in many other States."[891] Her obituary remembered her worth: "Few Michigan women succeeded in attracting more attention or took a more active part in the agitation of political and social questions than has Mrs. Emery during the 25 years she has resided here," said the *Lansing Journal* weekly edition, "When the People's party was formed she immediately set out to preach Populism in Michigan and was recognized as one of its ablest champions… Mrs. Emery's religious affiliations were with the Universalists, and her devotion to church work was constant until failing health rendered further work impossible. For several years she was superintendent of the Sunday school of the Universalist church and almost her last thoughts were concerning the church. Last spring she presented the valuable site at the intersection of Capitol avenue and Ottawa street to the church."[892]

The funeral services were conducted by Rev. Charles Legal of the Universalist Church, and addresses were made by leading activists and suffragists Mrs. May S. Knaggs of Bay City, Mrs. Mary D. Doe, Bay City, Mrs. Carrie Cole, Lansing, and Mrs. Marian Marsh Todd from Eaton Rapids.[893] The silver cause had lost an advocate among suffragists, populists and the Farmer's Alliance, but as a movement it continued to build.

Ping was re-elected mayor of Detroit despite the usual savage opposition, and the two mayors continued to organize for Progressive ideals. As Progressives, they worked on politics and economic issues, particularly on how the depression was affecting their cities. Ping expanded the public welfare programs in Detroit, initiated public works for the unemployed, and built new schools. Upon the behest of the women's clubs of the city led by Clara Arthur, he built parks for children and public baths. He also fought for lower streetcar and railroad fares. When Ping and Jim got together he sought Jim's advice on his plan to help Detroit establish gardens for taking care of the poor.[894] Ping gained national recognition through his "potato patch plan," a systematic use of vacant city land voluntarily provided by land holders for gardens to produce food for the city's poor. He started with what amounted to about 1,000 acres of farming land which was then platted for gardens, and he funded the project with money collected with the help of churches for seeds and farming materials. The goal was 4,000 to 5,000 idle acres of land bearing crops for the poor. A commission was set up to devise a method of work, which was documented. The acclaimed program design was distributed later by the U.S. Department of Agriculture for use in other states.[895] The two mayors continued to work toward the fall election. Jim kept up the push on the silver issue at the state and national level.

Chapter 16

The Great Contest

A great political battle was building in both Michigan and the United States, a battle between those for the gold standard (The Gold Bugs) and those for a bimetal standard (The Silverites). It was understood as a battle for power between the rich and the common people. Jim, Ping, Cy, and Frank took the side of the Silverites. Under bimetallism the monetary standard established for each basic unit of currency would be two metals, with values set at a ratio of 16 to 1, silver to gold. It amounted to a battle between powers that could buy what they wanted and those who could vote for what they wanted, if they only understood their own power.

With the coming election in mind, Jim invited Ping to attend a meeting of political importance in Lansing with the Knights of the Grip. It was to be held on the last day of 1895. The Knights was a business organization of traveling salesmen in the late 1800's and early 1900's known for their ever-present suitcases (grips) containing their samples. The salesmen banded together to rate the best and worst hotels, rooming houses, restaurants, bars, and so forth. They passed along stories of experiences going from city to city by train and, most importantly, they used their numbers to bargain for better train ticket fares than were available to the general public by allowing members to buy discounted mileage coupon books.

Organized Greed in the Saddle

In Jim's New Year's Eve welcoming speech to the Knights' first convention, he urged them to use their combined bargaining power as railroad patrons to help everyone. The women of the Plymouth Congregational Church had served the dinner and the 700 members finished eating, but Ping had not arrived. The acquiescent guests nibbled on food that had not been cleared from the tables and waited for the speaker and for the New Year to come in. Other speakers helped pass the time. The Lansing mayor's speech became a highlight of the evening. Before he could introduce Ping, Jim brightened the evening as he talked of their roots as salesmen and his father as a traveling salesman and pioneer merchant. He spoke of deflation and the business at hand, the fight over taxing railroads and regulation of railroad fare rates—issues also championed by Ping, and finally he pointedly urged his listeners to make changes for the better by working to elect people who would work for the interest of all:

> I cannot refrain from congratulating this organization upon their efforts to secure for the people of Michigan concessions from the railroads of the state in keeping with the constantly dropping prices of all our commodities. The adoption of the interchangeable mileage book and 2 cents a mile on all railroads would have been a step in the right direction; but you should go further in your next step, and direct your efforts toward securing a uniform fare of 2 cents per mile to all travelers in this state, even to the poor washerwoman who never at any one time had accumulation of funds sufficient to purchase a 1,000 mile book. The fare should be made uniformly 2 cents per mile without any mileage book.
>
> When I began farming, you could ride a hundred miles on any railroad in Michigan on the avails of one bushel of wheat or three pounds of wool or three bushels of potatoes. Now the farmer must exchange for such a ride six times as much wheat, eight times as much wool and ten times as many potatoes. Certainly if low prices are a good thing, they should be applied to the rich and the poor alike. Under present conditions Mrs. Vanderbilt is enabled to spend $10,000,000 cash for the purchase of the Duke of Marlborough for Miss Consuelo, but the poor farmer must give up three hundred bushels of potatoes for the purchase of a $21 overcoat and thirty pounds of his best wool for a hundred-mile ride on the Vanderbilt railroad. This injustice can be wiped out by the united efforts of this organization, and coupled with it you should urge the repeal of all laws that provide different methods of taxation for the railroads than for the plain people. You can readily make these sentiments a part of the creed of the various political parties to which you belong. Make it your business to see that no man is nominated or elected to the Legislature who is not thoroughly patriotic and interested in the plain, common, every-day folks. Also see that they have a reputation for integrity and honor, that they may not be seduced either by the influences of a free pass or the paid lobby that swarms the capitol during every session.
>
> While many of you have heretofore expected your representatives in the Legislature unbidden to lead off in this matter, you have as often been disappointed and discovered when too late that the stream would not rise above its source. Hereafter you must make your demands so emphatic that they will not go unheeded... It is right you should have this legislation, but you must go after it yourselves and go after it hard. Then and then only will your efforts be crowned with success, and the people will rise up and call you blessed.
>
> Then, as a cap-sheaf to insure success, interest yourselves in the question of a gubernatorial candidate. Two cents a mile on railroads would be made easy by the right kind of Legislature and a man in the

executive office pledged to carry out these reforms, and certainly from the large number of able and patriotic men who will be submitted by each of the great political parties in 1896 as gubernatorial candidates, you can readily make a selection of one who would loyally serve the people in this important matter.[896]

When Ping arrived and was introduced by Jim, he was met with a storm of applause. "It was a splendid testimonial to the popularity of the potato man," said a local journalist. Perhaps it was the late hour for the reporter did not much care for the speech Ping read – too many dry statistics and quotations, he did not seem quite as spicy as usual. The reporter made it a point to cover another of the after-dinner speakers: "He closed with a numerous description of the new woman's most characteristic garment—bloomers. He said they were made quite full at the pistol pocket and very full where you scratch a match. 'You can tell where the front is, ladies,' he said 'by the buttons where it buttons at the neck.'" It was 2:30 a. m. when they all went home, after seven hours of bringing in the New Year.[897]

The day after New Year's Day, Jim wrote to Charles Sligh, planning a state-wide silver conference and giving him a list of Democrats from Cy and a few more names of his own, including Hazen Pingree's. He told Sligh: "I have talked to prominent republicans who were here at the annual meeting of the Knights of the Grip. Some of them thought we ought to call a conference exclusively of republicans, but I doubt the wisdom of making it thus exclusive. Our republican newspapers almost unanimously are insisting that the silver issue is dead. The metropolitan press generally is taking this position, so it would only weaken our cause to confine it to either party. My idea is that the time has arrived when we should come together simply as patriotic men and discuss the subject and see if there is anything we can do to relieve the stress of the present situation." Jim was on the board of the National Bimetallic League and received a list for invitations from them as well. He wrote to Sligh from the Mayor's Office, the Michigan Slate Company, and Springdale Farm as he went about his mayoral and business activities.[898]

Six days before the meeting, Jim wrote to Sligh with names of people he had heard from and assured Sligh it was shaping up to be a bi-partisan meeting. Jim was still looking for an evening speaker "to give the silver cause a big sendoff throughout the state. We want to emphasize our criticism of present conditions and financial system in every way possible. Our producers are groaning throughout the land, notwithstanding the granaries and barns are bursting with God's bounties. The whole trouble seems to be with the price, and the low price is made unavoidable by the ever-lasting purchasing power of the standard of value [gold]. Each year more products will be offered for the unit, thus each year decreasing the purchasing power of the people. I find the masses know little of the cause of this blighting depression. Between now and the campaign of 1896 is a very short time in which to educate them, especially as nearly all the newspapers are against us. Possibly the meeting here can speak out in such a way that the newspapers will give it to the public as a matter of news."[899] In addition to this meeting, the reformers worked on preparations for their fourth run at the nominating convention.

The Knights of the Grip dinner served as a good mid-Michigan launch for Ping's gubernatorial campaign, and now Ping was trying to recruit Albert Pack, a businessman who helped Ping accomplish his street railway plan, to put up his name for chair of the Republican State Central Committee. Ping asked Charles Sligh to help. However, although Pack could "see the great necessity, in the interest of better politics, that Senator McMillan should be allowed to retire at this time," Pack wrote back saying his business was too great a burden and his health too poor to take it on.[900] As early as February, Ping's shoe manufacturing stationery from the Pingree and Smith block on Jefferson Avenue in Detroit bore a political message in small red print: "If you are for <u>Pingree</u>, or for any other candidate for governor, <u>attend the caucuses</u> and suggest to others the propriety of attending."[901] Pingree shoe advertisements were widely placed in local papers. Jim continued to direct his educational campaign against the "Gold Bugs." Those for the gold standard wore gold pins that looked like something between a fly and a bee. Jim arranged to circulate 20,000 copies of a silver speech by the Minnesota Congressman Charles A. Towne, formerly of Pontiac. He also arranged a speaking tour. He told Sligh: "As Mr. Towne is a young man and new as a member of congress, the people may not understand that he is probably the greatest orator on the floor today, and his speech on the silver question attracted more attention than any speech ever delivered on that subject."[902] Jim made plans to attend the executive committee meeting of the nonpartisan American Bimetallic Union in Chicago prior to the Bimetallist convention in June to work out more ways to promote a public sentiment favorable to silver.[903]

On March 16, 1896, Jim published this letter in the *Lansing Journal*, which was printed with the headline "Bonds and Lights, Mayor Turner Talks About the Railroads." He was throwing logs on a fire that would rage over the next four years until Michigan corporate property was assessed fairly and railroads were taxed. He showed how railroad corporations manipulated their reported income to reduce their income taxes. He explained his actions as mayor and how railroad corporations cheat the public and their stockholders by creating sweetheart deals with companies they own in order to bleed them of profits, just as foreseen by the *Lansing Republican* a decade earlier. Jim was not intimidated by his opponent's attack. He exposed once again the corrupt practices of the Grand Trunk Railroad, the long-standing nemesis that he had fought for two decades, and he did it in his usual good humored way:

> To The Editor of The Lansing Journal:
>   In the issue of the State Republican of March 14th appeared an article headed, "Handling Live Coals," from which it becomes apparent that the "bogie man" is again at large frightening that prominent busi-

ness man, and he argues that the city administration is likely to drive the railroads centering here to boycott the town if the Council "continues to wage warfare" against them. From the tone of the communication one is led to believe that "prominent business man" is a recent arrival in the capital city and without much knowledge of the real facts of the case. For his benefit a brief resume of the oppression that has been practiced on the poor railroads entering Lansing may be of benefit.

The first road entered here from Owosso about 1861 or 1862. The citizens of Lansing oppressed this road with a contribution of about $30,000, and the road has paid nothing into the city treasury in the way of taxes from that day to this. Next came the Jackson & Lansing road (now Michigan Central). To this Lansing issued $22,800 of 10 percent municipal bonds and paid more than $25,000 of interest in addition to the principal. Added to this our citizens raised a fund of about $25,000 which went into the road in aid of its construction. The road has since paid nothing into the hands of the local tax gatherer. The city of Lansing has also furnished this road, free of charge, with right of way through the city for more than thirty years

Next came the Ionia & Lansing (now Detroit, Lansing & Northern.) In aid of this enterprise $32,600 of municipal bonds were issued drawing ten percent interest, the property owners here contributed more than $63,000 before the debt was liquidated. Our citizens put into this project more than $50,000 in addition to the road. This corporation has, during the 27 years it has been here, contributed nothing to the fund held by the local tax gatherer.

Next came the Peninsular Railroad (now Chicago & Grand Trunk). In aid of this $22,000 more ten per cent bonds were issued, and the property owners in Lansing have paid on this issue more than $50,000 in principal and interest, in addition to which about $25,000 was contributed by our citizens in cash and donations of right of way. This road has in the meantime, paid no taxes into the city treasury. The next road to enter Lansing was the Lake Shore, to which $15,000 was donated.

Added to the above acts of oppression and repression on the part of our citizens and municipal government of which "Prominent Citizen" complains, the city of Lansing, out of funds provided by her taxpayers, has for the past thirty years enumerated police protections as well as the protection to the railroad properties furnished free by our fire department.

The present administration discovered that the law provided that the railroads might be required by the Council to furnish such lights at their crossings with streets as might be demanded by reference to the public safety. A further examination developed the fact that lights had been provided at many of the most dangerous crossings, but that they were being maintained at the expense of our taxpayers instead of by the Vanderbilts and other roads, as provided by law. The mayor recommended that this manifest injustice to our property owners be corrected, and an ordinance was drawn requiring those railroads to maintain those lights at their own expense

About half the street crossings in the city (the most dangerous ones), about twenty in all, were embraced in this ordinance, but the ordinance was not drawn until after two persons had been struck by trains and killed at May street and one on Mt. Hope avenue, making three deaths in all which it was thought would not have occurred if crossings had been properly lighted. Then come the "bogie man" and frightens "Prominent Business Man" and some of the Aldermen. I confess the proposition to shift the burden from the backs of the people who pay the taxes onto poor Vanderbilt, Sir Joseph Hickson and other interests as provided by law is a little severe, coming just at the breaking-up of a hard winter, and the figures furnished by the Railroad Commissioner showing what a hard time the poor railroads are having would bring tears to the eyes of a crocodile.

The references made to the earning of the Chicago & Grand Trunk road were particularly touching, four-tenths of one percent being given as the net earnings left for stockholders. When the Commissioner submitted these figures he must have been impressed with the idea that they were to be perused by a nice, verdant, juicy constituency of ignoramuses. This road is operated in connection with the Grand Trunk road of Canada. On page 30 of the Railroad Commissioner's report for 1895 is given the cost of this road in Michigan, represented by the stock and debt to be $63,507.66 per mile. I know of my own personal knowledge that portions of this road were built for $10,000 per mile. Is it strange, then that it fails to earn a revenue on six times its cost, especially when it is considered that the gang which has had charge of the operation of the road and the manipulation of its stock and bonds and the stock and bonds of the Grand Trunk in Canada, own within themselves the St. Clair tunnel [The railway tunnel under the river between Sarnia and Port Huron was built by and for the Great Western Railway, a subsidiary of The Grand Trunk Railroad, under the purview of Harrison Geer, who was still head of the port authority.], the International bridge at Buffalo and the Victoria bridge at Montreal and make contracts with themselves for enormous tolls at each crossing and also similar contracts with car loan and trust companies owned by themselves for equipment of the lines, and in this way have filched most of the earnings of the road for the past twenty years.

The terminals of this road in Chicago and at other points are conveniently owned by companies organized by themselves so that favorable contracts can be made with the railroad company for entrances into points where the business originates. These facts may in a measure account for the wail of English stockholders and the recent changes in the management of the road; but it would be hardly fair to charge the Common Council of the city of Lansing with the effects of the various flimflams in the manipulations of the stocks and bonds, and wheels within wheels which have absorbed the legitimate earnings of the road.

These vested rights should, of course, be looked after, but I am not retained to take care of that interest. I should suggest that Judge Jenkins or Judge Cox might be called in and asked to issue one of their world-renowned injunctions; for, take it all around, government by injunction for railroad purposes has many advantages over the kind of government prescribed by the constitution.

In the meantime, Eli Bidleman [director of the city poor[904]] ought to be instructed to see that no man suffers. If Vanderbilt is out of provisions or needs any old clothes or a soup bone, it should be furnished unhesitatingly at public expense; and Mr. Billing's "figgers" should be framed and hung in the Council chamber as a warning to future administrations.

What a monstrous proposition! Think of it, taxpayers! That your own Common Council should, after thirty years of "innocuous desuetude," at this late date dare to rise up and ask Vanderbilt to pay for his own lights! You always have and therefore you always should pay the freight. What are you here for, anyway.

"Prominent Business Man" may see a gleam of light ahead, however, in the fact that the spring campaign will soon open, when with his assistance, the railroad interests may select a local administration "that will right the great wrongs" to which they have in the past been subjected.

James M. Turner[905]

The Vanderbilts and "Prominent Business Man" were faced with a brilliant and fearless antagonist and champion of the common people. His 1890 campaign was one of the earliest head-on confrontations with corporate power by the new progressive reform movement. By 1896 Jim was working harder than ever to change the course of his party; however, a few weeks before the expiration of his term as mayor, Jim was taken ill. The trouble was thought to be nothing more serious than a cold or perhaps the grip. The cold settled upon his lungs and kidneys and confined him to his home. His condition grew steadily worse. With each meeting of the common council his friends expected to see him once more in the mayor's chair, but he was unable to attend the inauguration of Mayor Ostrander. When he did not improve, he was moved to Alma Sanitarium, a large and up-to-date medical institution for the scientific treatment of chronic diseases, fifty-four miles north of Lansing. His cousin Howard Longyear was brought in for consultation.[906] He returned home somewhat improved in health on May 30 and spent a part of his time in his office transacting business.

In mid-June the Republican Convention met in Saint Louis, Missouri, on June 16, 17, and 18. All Jim could do was read about it. He was angered when the convention repudiated former Republican positions on tariff protectionism and bimetallism, and rebuked bimetallist leaders. "It only goes to show," he wrote to the *Detroit Tribune*, "that organized selfishness and greed are in the saddle, and with the aid of foreign syndicates expect to run the country as it has been run for the past four years, only the troubles and distress of the common people will, of course, be intensified."[907]

U. S. Senator Henry M. Teller of Colorado made an argument to the convention assembly against the changes proposed for the financial platform similar to the arguments Jim so often made. He demonstrated very clearly that the fight over the gold standard was really about something much deeper. Teller said, "If you have love of country, patriotic fervor and independence, you must have your citizens comfortably fed and comfortably clothed. That is what made me a Republican in 1853: that is what made me a Republican all these years, because I believed that the Republican party was good for the great masses of men, that its legislation was intended to lift up and elevate and hold up and sustain the unfortunate and the distressed and give all American citizens equal opportunities before the law. (Applause) I do not believe that it can be had with the gold standard." Teller most painfully said that if the gold standard plank should succeed, he would sever his connection from the party. This was followed by cries of "No! No!" Within Michigan's delegation, Teller's words were unheeded and the vote was twenty-five to three for the proposed platform. Indeed, Teller joined the Silver Party and in 1902 became a Democrat.[908]

On the final day the candidates' names were put in place for nomination for president, mostly "favorite son" nominations—and the Silverites were mocked by a corporate attorney, Chauncey Depew, who represented Vanderbilt railroad interests.

> By direction of the Chairman, the Secretary continued to call the roll of States, no response being made until the State of New York was reached, when Mr. Sutherland of that delegation arose and said:
>
> "The claims of the State of New York and her favorite son will be presented by her other favorite son—that citizen of all the States of the Union—Chauncey M. Depew."
>
> The appearance of Mr. Depew was the signal for a great ovation, in which the whole body of delegates took part. Before Mr. Depew was able to address the Chair a delegate inquired: "What about the erring sisters who walked out of here a while ago?"
>
> Mr. Depew: They have deserted a Republican convention, composed of representatives of the party from all sections of the Union, and they walked out because they objected to the gold standard. I wonder how they will feel when they arrive at the gate of the Celestial City where they will find that it is run under a Republican government.
>
> (Laughter). I wonder how they will feel when they find that, as we are told by the old Apostle, the streets are paved with gold. (Laughter and cheers).[909]

Jim's comment for the newspapers may have left some wondering how long he would remain a Republican. Despite his illness, he wrote, "When Vanderbilt sent his hired man, Depew, up to Detroit to the late state convention of the republican party to instruct the party in Michigan how Vanderbilt and his plutocratic friends desired the party platform to be formed, it boded not good to the plain people, and I noticed that when it came to the selection of delegates to the St. Louis convention, with the exception of one colored man, no one but gentlemen interested in banks were permitted to go as delegates. Although in the past perhaps one-half have come from the farmers or a representative of producers of Michigan not one was permitted to go upon the delegation."[910]

A Real Public Calamity

The newspapers were always eager to inform their readers of Jim's assessments, but now there was sad news. "The kidney disease which finally carried him off slowly tightened its grip and with the exception of the one brief interval, when he seemed to rally a little, his health slowly broke down. His rugged constitution, fostered by a life of activity and out-door exercise, was slow to give way to the ravages of his illness, but at last the awful truth dawned upon his friends and family that the end was surely coming. The immediate cause of his death was heart failure, the result of Bright's disease."[911]

On June 26 the disease had made such inroads that Jim returned to Alma but without benefit. He sank rapidly and was unable to keep any food on his stomach for some time before the end came.[912] The lengthy headline told the story: "The City Mourns Ex-Mayor Turner, Passed Away This Morning, Was at Alma Sanitarium Where He was Receiving Treatment When the Death Summons Came, The News a Great Shock to His Fellow Citizens." His mother saved this article:

> At an early hour this morning a dispatch was received by relatives in this city of the death at Alma sanitarium, shortly after 4 o'clock, of ex-Mayor James M. Turner. The news was such a surprise and such a shock, so few of his friends knowing of his serious condition, that it was at first discredited, but the sad news was soon confirmed by later dispatches announcing that the remains would arrive here on the Grand Trunk train at 10:40 o'clock. Mrs. Turner, his two sons, Scott and James, and his cousin and physician, Dr. Longyear of Detroit, were at his bedside when death came.
>
> The remains arrived at 10:40 and were met at the depot by Gov. Rich, Mayor Ostrander, and other state and city officials and citizens, and escorted to the family residence on Franklin street west. The exact time of the funeral has not been decided upon but it will probably be held Friday and will be from the late residence.

His friend, the Reverend Charles Legal of the Universalist Church, presided at the funeral: "He said he did not know what faith he accepted, I do not care. I know that he was a loyal citizen, good friend and the kindest of fathers in the home... Rev. Legal said, 'Two incidents occurred to my own personal acquaintance with him which have revealed his essential character. The first meeting with him and the grasp of the hand seemed to reveal the characteristics of a man who a friend could trust, and a foe fear. The other was at a funeral of a mutual friend where the soul was touched with grief, and tears coursed down his cheeks. Seldom do we see these two qualities combined in one man. In the face of opposition and adversity he knew no fear, but before sorrow and poverty, and under the genial rays of the home he was the personification of charity and gentleness.' The funeral services were held at his home on Franklin Street and were said to be simple, impressive and beautiful." [913]

The obituary of the *Lansing State Republican* reviewed his life as the people of Lansing knew it:

> His political career embraced one term in the Michigan Legislature, the term of 1876; two terms as mayor, one in 1889 and again in 1895, and a term as a member of the board of education. He was a candidate for the office of governor in 1890 and the history of that memorable campaign is too well known to need comment. His great popularity with his own townspeople was best demonstrated by the very large majority accorded him when he was last elected mayor.
>
> James M. Turner as a business man was enterprising, sagacious and energetic. He possessed both breadth of view and mastery of detail which enabled him to conceive great enterprises and carry them to successful issue. In politics he was aggressive and his personal qualities were such that he possessed a host of friends always ready to work and sacrifice for him... Mr. Turner leaves, beside his immediate family already mentioned, three sisters, Mrs. Marian Reasoner, Mrs. C. P. Black and Mrs. F. L. Dodge, all of this city. His mother, Mrs. Marian Turner, who resides with her daughter, Mrs. Dodge, also survives him.
>
> Besides his large property interests he carried $120,000 life insurance, divided between the Equitable of New York, New York Life, Mutual Benefit of New Jersey, Michigan Mutual and the Union Central." [914]

The State Republican said, on Wednesday, July 8, 1896: "Stalwart and massive in his physical proportions, his mental powers were not less remarkable, and each were dominated by a spirit which knew no rest, acknowledged no defeat... from many a humble home in Lansing whose occupants have been the recipients of his spontaneous and unheralded bounty, arises today the voice of sorrow for a friend departed. But the bereavement is not of these alone. The city and the state have suffered a common loss in the death of one strong for usefulness." [915]

There were many tributes. The board of the Michigan School for the Blind adopted a resolution: "This institution loses a warm friend, to whom is largely due the fact of the establishment of the school in this city, and who in its earlier years gave thoughtful care and serious consideration to the problems connected with its control and management… In our opinion, those traits of generosity and sympathy which characterized his life, and were the occasion of his earnest efforts on behalf of the blind of this state should be borne in mind and kindly remembrance."[916] The board of the Michigan Fair Association said, "Agriculture was his hobby, and this fact led this society to place him at the helm, and to seek his advice and counsel in all that pertained to the advancement of the interests of the laborer, the mechanic and the tiller of the soil."[917]

The Michigan Board of Agriculture and Michigan Agricultural College in connection with the Michigan Association of Breeders recognized his scientific contributions to the field of agriculture: "We are untimely deprived of the able counsel and energetic activity of one of our most efficient members, whose earnest and intelligent interest in advancing the live stock industry of our State has been of vast and enduring benefit to his fellow breeders: that the success achieved by him will leave such an impress upon the flocks and herds of the great state he loved so well, as will remain an enduring monument to his memory."[918]

Just as Jim once quoted from a poem, "There are billows far out on the ocean that never will break on the beach; there are waves of human emotion that can find no expression in speech," people struggled to express what this sudden loss meant, a work incomplete. *The Battle Creek Moon* said he should be regarded as one of Michigan's foremost men. *The Bay City Tribune* said, "His death will be regretted by friends and foes, for he was a loyal friend and a manly opponent." *The Detroit Journal* said, "Those who knew him best recognized in him a man of marked ability, capable of much greater things than he had yet accomplished, having only arrived at the age of man's best judgment and discretion when stricken down by the hand of death." *The Detroit Tribune* summed up the feelings of many in an editorial: "His death just upon the eve of what promises to be the hottest campaign in 30 years, cannot fail to be a great loss to the cause of good government, no matter what good government may prove to be. We are all of us looking for the truth, and to such a purpose one like James M. Turner, upon whatever side of the controversy, is a great help. No cause that is honest would have anything to fear from the straightforward, manly discussion that was habitual with Mr. Turner. It is greatly to be regretted that he could not be spared to fill the allotted span of life. His death is a real public calamity."[919]

In 1912, John Longyear wrote in his reminiscences:

> Turner died in July 1896, leaving a wife and two boys, James and Scott. The boys were then about nineteen [eighteen] and eighteen [sixteen] years of age. Among other property assigned to me at the time I made the endorsements was about one hundred thousand dollars of life insurance, which, of course, became due when he died. Knowing that

Mrs. Turner would be unable to live or educate the boys without help I turned over fifty thousand dollars of this insurance to her. This enabled her to educate the boys, and they both became fine men. An account, of course, was kept with the Turner property—all expenses being charged to it, all receipts credited, etc. In 1910 Mrs. Turner's father died and she inherited one half of his estate. In 1911 her son James asked me for a statement of the Turner account and I had it prepared. This showed about fifteen thousand dollars still due me. This they paid and at the request of the Turner heirs I conveyed all the remaining property to Mrs. Turner. At their request I am still managing the property for them.

What I did for Turner and his heirs seems by some of my friends to have been thought unusual, but I was glad to do it for him and them, as Jim was like a brother and our feelings for each other were more like that of brothers than that of the more remote relationship of cousins and the outcome of the business has afforded me great satisfaction.[920]

About a week after Jim's death, the Silver Party held its convention under the leadership of Charles Sligh. The first resolution they passed said, "Whereas, death has lately called from our midst our fellow citizen and co-laborer, Hon. James M. Turner, who has been amongst the foremost in this state in the great contest to restore to the people the constitutional money of our fathers, and whose untiring labors and patriotic devotion to the cause of free silver coinage was the cause of his untimely death."[921] They expressed deep sorrow and sympathy to Jim's family that this truly great man was gone from among them. That afternoon they committed to unite Democrats, Republicans, Prohibitionists and Populists in a movement for the common people.

William Jennings Bryan Visits Lansing

When the delegation at the Democratic Convention was chosen in Detroit in April, all were supporters of the gold standard, not unlike the banker Gold Bug delegates attending the Republican Convention. However, at the July Democratic national convention in Chicago, the Silverites did battle and managed to replace all eight of the delegates with Silverites. The *State Republican* enjoyed reporting on the Democratic uproar: "Michigan's Gold Delegation thrown out at Chicago. C. P. Black Gets Seat in the Convention— The Vote Was 558 to 368—Was no Hitch in the Program—Gold Men Talk Ugly."[922]

Cy worked throughout the summer and fall alongside Frank and his brothers. Over several weeks, Lansing held a Chautauqua series in a tent downtown at Allegan and Washington. This popular phenomenon was patterned after an educational and cultural entertainment program of lectures, concerts, and plays, originating in western New York. The tent was full, and people were turned away the night Judge Black and Dr. J. A. Marvin debated tariff and currency matters. Marvin blamed the Democratic administration for the hard times and said the rapid decline in manufacturing was due to apprehension that the Republican policy of protectionism would be abandoned. Cy said he was there simply to speak upon the money question, although he also talked about what he called the principles of a new democracy. He denounced President Grover Cleveland's adherence to the gold standard. He was frequently interrupted with cheers and applause from silver people, while gold men were conspicuously silent. The next week Mrs. Blanch H. Mason, a staunch prohibitionist, spoke on governmental reform and provided a display of stereopticon views each night. The lively discussion on the money question was continued on Wednesday. The Salvation Army Band gave a performance following the Chautauqua series.[923]

As Jim had predicted, when William Jennings Bryan came to Lansing, local papers did not acknowledge the Silverite's visit. The *State Republican* did a short story a few days before Bryan's planned appearance, and the Gold Bugs at the *Lansing Journal* said nothing. The visit itself was not covered by any local paper. This must have been exasperating to Frank because he was both campaign chairman for the Democrats and secretary of the Michigan Democratic State Central Committee.[924] Cy and the Dodges sided with the radical Democrats led by D. J. Campau, chair of the State Central Committee and of course a friend and supporter of Bryan. Long-time party chair Don Dickerson bolted the party to work for McKinley, but Frank would have none of that. "When the Bryan wing of the national Democratic organization gained control in 1896, Mr. Dodge was as aggressively loyal to the new leader as he had been to Cleveland. His action in this regard was in accord with his entire political career. Democratic principles were fundamental with him," *the Detroit News* said later.[925] The Democratic party principles were laid out in the platform thrashed out in Chicago. However, the platform and candidate were repudiated by prominent Democratic newspapers, including the *Lansing Journal*.

The undertaking of a national presidential campaign was expensive, and state campaign chairmen, such as Frank, had an important role in the campaign. The *State Republican* explains the process to readers: "Estimating its length of ninety days, which is a fair average, the actual running expenses of the national committee will foot up about $5,500,000. This is at the rate of $12,500 per day, and that does not include that which is spent with a view of influencing results. The principal items of expense are printing, which calls for a large force of expert writers, the translators, for documents are printed in all languages, and the canvass of the close states, which is practically a census of voters and requires hundreds of canvassers, most of whom are liberally paid. Oratory and hotel bills involve no inconsiderable outlay. This really only includes the expense of a national committee. In addition there are state, county and town committees, all of which are compelled to expend large sums of money."[926] In Michigan, Campau was credited with running a well-organized canvass.[927]

After the election, "The Great Commoner," as Bryan was called, published an account of the campaign for his followers, *The First Battle: A Story of the Campaign of 1896.* The country's oligarchs were pouring money into McKinley's campaign. To try to counter it, Bryan traveled the country by train. His trip began from his home in Lincoln, Nebraska. He spent four days in Michigan, taking the train across the Upper Peninsula from Duluth with major stops at Iron Mountain, Ishpeming, and Marquette, and shorter stops at smaller towns. The third day he departed from Muskegon. He made twenty-five speeches along the train route, including two in Jackson and six in Lansing, his last stop of the day. He made two speeches to all-women audiences, one in Grand Rapids and one in Lansing. He likely spent his rest time with Frank and Abby at their home.[928] It was a long day and did not end until almost midnight. Bryan held that society was divided based on the money question with capitalist classes on one side, "the idle holders of idle capital" on the one hand, and the "struggling masses" on the other. Reports don't tell us if he spoke to the women about suffrage or women's rights. Women were being fed a constant stream of talk about the disaster the silver standard would bring to their ability to afford everyday necessities, but the issue, he said, was whose interests were really being served by the gold standard. Bryan's speech was typical of his Silverite speeches along the way:

> In a great contest like this, we must be on one side or the other—there is no middle ground. If the gold standard is right we ought to be for it; if the gold standard is wrong we ought to be against it. But, my friends, you need not hope that everybody will think the same way upon the money question even after investigation. There is a valid reason for these differences of opinion; they spring largely from difference of interest. I do not want you to think that I am putting politics on a low plane when I tell you that a person's interests will affect that person's judgment on any political question. Let me illustrate: I used to live at Jacksonville, Ill., and while I lived there, there was an election and the question to be determined was whether cows should run at large. It was an exciting election. People would gather upon the streets and discuss the subject and you would frequently hear an argument like this: One person would say, "The cows ought to be allowed to run at large. The grass is going to waste in the streets; it is better for the city to have the cows run at large and eat the grass up." You would find that he had a cow. Then another would say, "The cows ought to be shut up. You cannot leave your gate open at night without danger that the cows will get in and ruin your garden. It is better for the city to have the cows shut up." And you would find that he did not have any cow. When the vote was counted it was found that each voter was largely influenced by the question, whether he kept a cow or not. Now if you have ever passed through an election where that question was submitted to the people you will recognize what I say to be true, that the cost of keeping a cow will largely determine the vote of a person upon the question. If that is true in small things it is also true in large things; some people want the gold standard because they,

so to speak, have cows running at large. It is bad enough to have them feeding their cows upon the public domain, but they are not satisfied with that. They want to feed their cows upon private pastures as well.

When a person takes a position upon any question you have a right to examine and see what that person's business is and what his interests are.[929]

Again and again Bryan told his listeners, if the laws are made by people who want tight money, they will make money scarcer by adopting the gold standard. If people want sufficient money supply to do business with and to stop deflation, they will become Silverites. In Flint, he illustrated the idea this way:

Let me call your attention to a local interest. This is a great city for the manufacture of wagons, carriages and buggies. I want to ask those who make carriages to think for a moment and see whether they sell their wagons to financiers or to farmers; and if they sell their wagons to farmers, I want them to figure out how a farmer can buy more wagons when he gets less for his products. I want those who sell wagons to farmers to realize that their prosperity depends upon the prosperity of the farmer who buys wagons, and not upon the prosperity of a financier who charges interest on the money loaned to the wagon maker. If you sell buggies, I want to ask you whether you are interested in selling more buggies than you are selling now. If you are, remember that you can only sell more buggies when more people are able to buy buggies. When you lessen the number of people who can buy buggies, you lessen the product of your buggy factories, and when you lessen the product of your buggy factories you lessen the number of men employed in making buggies, and when less men are employed in making buggies, your storekeepers have less people to sell goods to.

My friends, we are able to meet the arguments of our opponents, and the best evidence that they have lost faith in their cause, in the logic of their arguments and the justice of the gold standard, is to be found in the fact that instead of submitting their case to the judgment of the people, they have resorted to coercion and intimidation in order to secure by force that which they cannot secure by reason.[930]

In Bloomington, Indiana, Bryan spoke to the Republicans exactly to the sentiments that had engaged Jim and driven many Michigan Republican Silverites to support Bryan: "Are you surprised when you find that the policy inaugurated at St. Louis and reiterated by the Republican candidate is driving out those in the Republican party who still believe in a government of the people, by the people and for the people?"[931]

In Michigan that year the vote for President was 293,582 for McKinley and 236,714 for Bryan. [932] McKinley was undoubtedly helped in Michigan by Ping who ran 26,000 votes ahead of President McKinley. Many attributed Ping's win to his strong stand against the party's "monopolistic tendencies," i.e., the control of his party by one group. The depression was waning. Silver was not much of an issue. Discoveries of gold in Alaska and worldwide meant a greater supply would be available to back currency, the Sherman Silver Purchase Act was repealed, and the country went on the gold standard.

Frank and the County Supervisors

Frank was not only a city alderman, he was a member of the county board of supervisors. He believed sincerely that in a democracy all power should be derived from the consent of the people and that corporate lobbyists undermine this.[933] While Ping was out speaking at every turn about corporate power and lobbyists in order to alert the public about what was going on in the Legislature, Frank was working to establish an organization to help provide a counterbalance to corporate lobbyists by providing a voice for the needs of common people living in the counties throughout the state. It would be a step closer to the notion of government by the people and for the people. Township and city officials met in the capitol to found the State Association of Supervisors of Michigan on Tuesday, February 1, 1898. The group would serve as a liaison between the Legislature and county government, and work for statewide rather than local interests.[934] Twenty-seven supervisors representing fourteen counties responded to the call from the Ingham County Board for a two-day meeting. Frank gaveled the meeting to order at 2 o'clock. The *State Republican* said the men who attended the session were an earnest lot: "It is expected that great good will result from this meeting."[935] The Legislature regulated both how the counties raised money and how they could spend it, and the supervisors had plenty of ideas about how county business and services could be improved.

On Wednesday the supervisors met in the senate chamber. In the morning they discussed resolutions. "The great burden of the supervisors' song is taxation. They have a long sharp knife out for the railroads and corporations, who, they claim, do not pay their fair share of taxation burden," said the *State Republican*. Some argued "all property" should include church property, but finally "they all agreed that all railroads and corporations in the state shall be taxed on their cash value instead of their earnings." As to all the items referred to the legislative committee, Frank reported that there was not a committee of a dozen men who could draft a bill to correct all the issues before them. He suggested the group set up a legislative committee as a standing committee and submit their ideas. He said the time of the convention was too short to correct all the evils discussed that morning. The committee could work up a bill or see if a bill such as they favored had already been introduced. Then in October or January if the individual county boards in the state approved, it could be sent to the Legislature. At 4:30 the meeting adjourned so they could visit the Agricultural College at President Jonathan L. Snyder's invitation and resume the meeting at 7 o'clock.[936]

They elected officers and Frank became secretary—a position he held all of his life, until he accepted the presidency in 1929 just before he died.[937] J.

W. Ewing from Grand Ledge in Eaton County was elected president. Ewing had been a candidate for lieutenant governor for the People's Party in 1893 and now served on the Democratic State Central Campaign Committee with Frank. Nonetheless, when Frank was chosen as legislative committee chairman, the group agreed to be as nonpolitical as possible in taking positions, which they sustained for many years. They voted on selected legislative proposals for changes in the laws or new regulations. Sometimes a favorite of one or more supervisors was soundly voted down. However, "The best of feeling prevailed at the meeting and the supervisors went home feeling that a good start had been made," said the *State Republican*.[938] Frank always served as the legislative committee chair and as its member lobbyist. Many times he assisted the program planning committee for future meetings.

By their second annual meeting, Frank could report that several bills of interest to them had been introduced during the new legislative session. There were quite a few new bills on railroad legislation introduced but little progress on the tax issue. The committee invited Governor Pingree to speak on February 8 for a lesson in the present day legislative process. It was an eye opener for many. Every word of his speech was reproduced in the *State Republican,* and it was later reproduced by Ping as a pamphlet. He told his listeners in part:

> Many years ago our fathers created the corporation and gave it a personality. It has an office to perform and was needed. It has been the means of accomplishing much in public improvement.
>
> It has its proper place and function now. It is not the corporation in its legitimate sphere that we criticize, but rather the corporation as a corruptionist that we denounce.
>
> The days have been within your memory when legislation in city councils, Legislatures and congress was not corrupted. Today, no measure affecting the great corporations of the country, or smaller ones allied into trusts, can be reached by the most just legislation.
>
> It is necessary that the taint of bribery should soil but few in any legislative body in order to defeat the will of the people.
>
> A committee can hold a bill in its possession with all sorts of excuses. It can change and modify it until it is without force or effect. Members can offer amendments, substitutes or other bills that look fair, and refuse to vote for the main bill because their suggestions have not been adopted… It is always the business of the corruptionist to furnish an excuse or a cover, that a member may not lose caste with his constituency. Our legislative halls are infected with these smooth, well-dressed gentlemen, who ply their trade with unfailing success. Some of them have no other business. Some of them secure places and positions by appointment, and are thus in easier touch with members… While the people are at home, behind the plows and counters, in the shops and factories, the great corporate interests, the trusts and combinations, are busy with their

lobbyists, buying up the people's representatives in councils, legislative halls and congress.

The one who dares raise his voice against them is denounced as an anarchist, socialist and demagogue. That these influences are controlling factors in legislation, no man can deny.[939]

Ping told them about bills before the Legislature, the great struggles going on over taxation that would affect every individual within their county and in the state. He said: "There is but one way in which the passage of a measure of consequence to the people, and affecting corporate capital, can be influenced or brought about, and that is by arousing the public sentiment to such an extent that legislators shall feel that they are instructed, and watched, and held accountable to their constituents. In no other way can it be done, and no state or party can furnish a different record within the last ten years." As they listened, the outsiders became insiders in the behind-the-scenes maneuvers. He spelled out how they should go about the task before them:

The committees before whom corporation bills must come are scrambled for as valuable treasures, for these committees are the first ones whose acquaintance is sought by the lobbyist... If perchance a committee can be induced to bury a bill, or hold it back, to change or to report against the measure, a great advantage has been gained.

The first attention of the people should always be directed to the committee that has a bill in its charge, and then to the acts of its individual members.

You gentlemen are here representing the taxpayers of the state, honestly seeking legislation in their interest. The farms, the merchants' and working men's home, the factories, the stores and stocks of goods, are placed upon your tax rolls, while a third, if not half of the wealth of the state, a wealth that knows not the pinching of want, escapes with little or no burden... Perhaps you can fathom the motives that inspire the introduction of many bills along the same line, with side questions that ought to be reached by independent bills.

Can it be that the introducers of such bills are not aware that every railroad and corporation lobbyist is planning, preparing and securing the introduction of such measure for the purpose of creating confusion? ... The cunning and shrewd devices of the skilled railroad and corporation lobbyists are evident in their every move, and the fruits of their work are already manifest in the desire which is beginning to be expressed for a compromise measure, even among those who are sincere and earnest in their efforts to make the railroad, telegraph, telephone and express companies pay their just share of taxes.[940]

Frank toiled for this organization for the rest of his life. Much later, in 1969, the group adopted the name Michigan Association of Counties.[941] Shortly after the State Association of Supervisors of Michigan formed, the

Michigan Municipal League formed for much the same purpose but to represent more urban needs, and it exists today.

Initially, the League came together to "come to grips with the state and, more specifically, the state Legislature." At the time, all cities were chartered directly by the Legislature. In the words of Harold D. Smith, the first director of the League, "they were at the mercy of a body composed of members who had little or no experience in municipal affairs." Their initial efforts were focused on securing home rule for cities and villages, or as Smith put it, "bringing impressively to the attention of a rural Legislature the problems of growing cities in the state."[942]

Frank Turner had great admiration for Frank Dodge for all of his contributions to the city and state: "Even in a democracy where there is every opportunity for self-expression, mass thinking is largely conditioned upon and directed by individual leadership. And so there has for many years been in Lansing and vicinity an outstanding character, a pillar of strength, a tower of community leadership in the person of Hon. Frank L. Dodge, distinguished in the law, in official public service and in commonwealth development. The outstanding features of Mr. Dodge's brilliant career are not only of rare interest but also a source of great pride to Lansingtonians."[943]

Frank's support for Ping as a reformer never evolved into anything more. Perhaps because of what Ping had to say about his party's politics: "Mr. Cleveland disrupted his party in doing the biddings of a money syndicate which made enormous profits out of a scandalous bond deal. Today all the trusts, all the monopolies, every agency which is bleeding the country, has taken refuge under the wing of the Republican party because they fear the Democratic party which has kicked them out. To them party is a means to an end, and that end is to get rich at everybody's expense, right or wrong."[944] Albeit a minority party in the birthplace of the Republican party, Frank remained an earnest Democrat and frequent party standard bearer in the Sixth Congressional District and a loyal supporter of Bryan.

Lessons from Ping

Ping was reelected to a second term in 1898. Though he won handily, it was not an easy campaign. Ping said the tax issue brought out the worst obstruction because railroad corporations fought against it: "an attempt in the last Legislature to ask them to pay more is denounced by them, their hired newspapers and paid politicians, as revolutionary and unrepublican... every railroad attorney and railroad doctor, every little country newspaper editor who has a pass, every politician who hopes for financial favors to help re-elect him, is out of breath crying 'Pingree is not a republican.'"[945]

During his tenure, the controversial party primary nominating system was under attack. Reformers were working to do away with the corrupted state convention delegate system. Ping was also working to get the Michigan Legislature to support a resolution requesting a federal constitutional amendment providing for the direct election of U.S. Senators. He sought an eight-hour workday, municipal ownership of public utilities, and above all else he continued to fight for repeal of special railroad charters so they could be brought under Michigan's general tax law.[946] Taxing railroads had been a plank in the Turner platform of 1890, a goal since the beginning of Ping's campaign at the Knights of the Grip banquet, and for years before that in Detroit. Now public opinion was informed, only enough votes in the Senate were lacking. He made a last ditch attempt to get some of these things accomplished by calling a special session at the end of his term. Conservative Republicans resisted their party leader's proposals. They even called for investigation of expenditures of the governor's office, but no evidence of wrong-doing could be produced. One can only speculate about whether his friend Jim Turner could have helped the Pingree administration accomplish more in the face of such opposition. Some said the old guard McMillan Republicans in the party deliberately blocked many of Ping's attempts at popular reforms in the state until after he left office. McMillanites wanted to deprive Ping of a future name, said the *State Republican*. "It is doubtful, however, if the McMillan supporters will be able to rob Pingree of his glory."[947]

Ping could be blunt, and truth ruffled the feathers of his fellow politicians not infrequently. On the subject of bribery, Ping minced no words: "Bribery, by the payment of money, or by promise of office, or by gifts of money for campaign expenses of members of the Legislature is such a common practice that the public conscience has become hardened and calloused to it. Investigations of such bribery have always been farces and 'whitewashing' processes. Experience has shown that grand juries and committees of investigation have been easily influenced by powerful and wealthy interests." He said corruption in the U.S. Senator selection process "inevitably taints legislation throughout the session of the state Legislatures which elect the Senators" and we end up with "fighting, scheming, and intriguing" that delays legislation and "creates feeling and evil effect throughout the sessions."[948]

In his last year as governor Ping was invited by the Republican party's Michigan Club to speak at a banquet in Detroit on February 22, 1899. Ping was a founder and had served a four-year term on its board and as its President in 1890. The founding officers in 1884 were Christian H. Buhl, President, and James McMillan, Vice President. It was a group of party leaders and anyone else who could afford the two dollar fee for membership and admission to the annual banquet in Detroit. The formally stated purpose was for study of political and social science, and civil and political institutions. An informally acknowledged purpose was to help rehabilitate and reinstate the party to power after the gubernatorial defeat of 1882.[949] They invited as their guests state officials and office holders from other states, especially New York, and party heroes such as the beloved James Blaine and General John Logan from the presidential defeat of 1884.[950]

Ping knew most of those present, and he reminded them that they knew when they invited him what his views were on public matters, so he wanted to speak to them without reservation. What he planned was to sound the alarm against the direction the party was going. His topic was "The Duty of the Republican party in the Present Hour."[951] He knew, he said, there were people in the audience who had attacked him ever since he began to introduce public reforms in the government of Detroit by saying he was against the wealthy or powerful. He said he saw his duty neither to oppose any man because he was rich and powerful nor to refrain from attack because he was rich and powerful. "It is high time that claims to respectability in this republic rested upon something more substantial than money or political cunning," he added. He judged people by their deeds. As Jim had so frequently done, Ping began by assessing where they were and reminding them of their history and the founding principles of the party. He said:

> I remind those of you who are familiar with the facts, of the street railway and street paving fights, and the board of education and other scandals in Detroit while I was Mayor. Work of that kind, gentlemen, cannot be done without some sharp and rough handling of men. The public officer whose duty compels him to interfere with the schemes of shrewd politicians and public contractors, will soon learn that, however honest his intentions, he must expect abuse in every form that cunning men can invent. I care nothing for all that. I recognize no class among citizens when it comes to matters of public duty.
>
> My republicanism has occasionally been called in question, because I have declined to promote the interests of certain men and of certain measures on the ground of party expediency.
>
> The Republican party came into power as the party of the common people. The welfare of an enslaved race was the chief cause of its organization. The principle of equal rights for all found its fullest expression in the greatest of all Americans—Abraham Lincoln.
>
> The Republican party was formed to make men free and equal. Its votes came from the farmer and his sons; from the villages and the country districts of the various states. They did not come from the overcrowded portions of our great cities where the voters were controlled by bosses. Republican majorities came from the States that afterwards furnished patriotic soldiers. So long as the great questions growing out of the civil war remained unsettled, the Republican party was controlled by men chosen to represent the people.
>
> But in time these questions disappeared and other questions demanded attention. Problems of trade and finance, and questions of administration came up. Meantime wealth increased and capital and labor drifted into conflict. Gradually the men of wealth dropped into the Republican party. Corporations found their interests well cared for by the men who were chosen to the legislative bodies as Republicans.
>
> Now this has been going on so long and so steadily that it has become notorious. Old Republicans have been held in line because they

could do nothing else. Some leaders of the Democratic party have made it almost impossible by their acts for prudent and thoughtful business men to join it.

All the men who had schemes, and all the corporations who wanted privileges joined the Republican party, expecting that party to bear their burdens and to serve them. This has been going on for years, but it cannot last forever, gentlemen.

I deem it a valuable service to the party to speak a word of warning at this time. For it is time that corporations, combines, trusts and multi-millionaires were requested to leave the front seats, at least, and let the men who can speak for the great body of voters, the men who believe in the republicanism of Abraham Lincoln, have room and part in the conduct of public affairs. I do not even suggest that men be ignored and humiliated simply because they are rich, but the legislative and executive offices of this nation cannot much longer be filled with men whose claims are based solely upon their devotion to corporate interests.[952]

Ping wanted his listeners to choose party leaders from those who were like Lincoln and to hold in check the influences controlling the party. He went on to talk to the audience of wealthy business men and politicians about how the concentration of wealth due to corporate monopoly influences was cutting off the opportunities of the young men who were not wealthy, particularly opportunities to create their own businesses:

Already the enormous business of this nation has passed into the control of gigantic trade and transportation combinations. I need not submit any proof it this. You have only to look around you. The men in this room know that this is true. But what is to come of it all?

The problem has been partially solved by the man who carries a dinner pail. He has entered another kind of a combination, one which relies upon physical strength and skill. The combination of money is answered by the combination of muscle.

The power to start in business to make a career, has been taken away from our educated young men. The boy comes from the district school, the high school, or the university, quick-witted, able, competent, and seeks employment. What does he find? This. That he must choose between farming, a trade, a profession, or a clerkship in some corporation.

The mercantile world, as it was organized thirty years ago, no longer exists. Ability does not count except as corporations can use it. When they are supplied, the boys must go to farming or go into politics, and maybe turn "political strikers." Or perhaps they may lose their self-respect through idleness and drop into vice and maybe fall into criminal practices—possibly become lobbyists.

The corporation jobs, professional, mechanical, and clerical, are given, first to the sons of favorites of the stockholders and directors. Any small jobs left over are given with more or less show of generosity to young men who are permitted to do the work for which some of the favorites preferred to get the pay.

Brains, ability, power, in the young man without capital, will eventually bring, if his life is spared to maturity, a fair living salary—no more —unless, as sometimes happens, an unusually bright man comes to know too much to be put off with only a salary.

These young men I have been speaking of, and their fathers, too, are beginning to ask: Why are these things so? Business, as you all know, is at present in the control of very few men. The growth of corporate power has been rapid. It is now well nigh complete.

But this is a republic and a republic of intelligent men, and they cannot be deceived much longer. The ballot is mightier than money and an aroused public sentiment will make short work with every combination that stands in the way of justice and fair play.

I believe that the Republican party of Michigan can be depended upon to do its duty in the matter in such a way that it can hold the allegiance of the working man, by which I mean not only the man who carries the dinner pail, but all who are dependent for their living upon their work. If it fails in this, history will simply repeat itself, and some other party will be found to administer the government.[953]

Ping's criticism of the party brought invitations to speak in other states. His speeches were printed in the local paper and carried in other newspapers. In Buffalo, New York, in a speech entitled "What Constitutes Party Loyalty," he told them much the same message he had given to the Michigan Club and said, "It is the party leadership which is most always at fault when things go wrong. The average man who has belonged to a party for a great many years, will stand a great deal before he leaves it. This fact has often been taken advantage of by those who control a party, directly or indirectly, and people submit to what they know is wrong and to policies and platforms with which in their inmost heart they do not agree, for party's sake. If those men are of the type of Mr. Lincoln, we have government for the people. If they are of other types which I might mention, we have government for bondholders and plunder. These two kinds of government are not at all alike; the former will perpetuate, the latter destroy a republic."[954]

After completing his term as governor, Ping left office and retired from public service. He told the press: "I have quit politics for good. The one aim of my official life, bringing the Michigan railroads under the general tax laws of the state, is now about to be accomplished. I am satisfied and want no more of public life."[955] He died less than a year later on June 18, 1901, and was buried in the Woodlawn Cemetery in Detroit, Michigan. Shortly after his death, a statue was placed in Grand Circus Park, near Woodward in Detroit. The inscription that shows his admirers thought he was the first to warn against private corporations: "The citizens of Michigan erect this monument to the cherished memory of Hazen S. Pingree. A gallant soldier, an enterprising and successful citizen, four times elected mayor of Detroit, twice governor of Michigan. He was the first to warn the people of the great danger threatened by powerful private corporations. And the first to awake to the great inequalities in taxation and to initiate steps for reform. The idol of the people." Today the statue marks a stop on the People Mover's route.

The Progressive Movement continued to gather steam on several fronts, and then something unpredictable happened. In September of the year Pingree died, President William McKinley was assassinated at the Pan-American Exposition in Buffalo, New York, and McKinley's Vice President, Theodore Roosevelt, was sworn in as President soon after.

Roosevelt proved to be just the sort of progressive, trust-busting, champion of the people and the regulation of business and corporations that Pingree was calling for and that Jim and so many Lansing reformers had been organizing and agitating to elect for over a decade. Roosevelt was re-elected in a landslide of over 54 percent in 1904, 69.5 percent in Michigan, winning every region but the solid South. When he came to Lansing by train on the occasion of the Michigan Agricultural College's 50th anniversary on May 31, 1907, he spoke to the State Legislature and thanked them for their efforts to break monopolies and trusts. He road out to the campus in a REO driven by R. E. Olds. He gave the commencement address to a crowd of 20,000 and returned to the Lake Shore depot in an Oldsmobile.[956]

The imprint of the pioneers was giving way to the next generation. Pioneer times seemed long ago.

Chapter 17

Passing from Time

The first generation pioneers were passing away. In 1898, Marian lost her brother-in-law, Daniel Case who was 87 and her long-time family friend from pioneer days, Hiram H. Smith, age 89. Hiram had moved back to Jackson in 1864 and engaged in a successful railroading career building and managing several lines that extended the reach of the railroads passing through Lansing and to the south and west of Jackson. The city's first mayor maintained property in Lansing and kept his interest in the town. His death was felt deeply in Lansing and in Jackson. He was buried in the Evergreen Cemetery in Jackson.[957] Marian's sister Adella died in 1887, and her sister Harriet's brother-in-law Ephraim Longyear died in 1889. By 1901 all remaining Munroe sisters, Marian, Betsy, Harriet, and Eliza, were widows and still living in north Lansing. Of the four Munroe brothers, William Munroe and their youngest brother, James Turner Munroe, were also living in Lansing. Josiah was still on the farm in Eagle, and Horace Munroe had moved to La Mesa, California.

On a slope on the west side of the Mt. Hope Cemetery is a tall Case Family obelisk. On the west side of the base is the name of Daniel L. Case. On the north side is the name of his first wife, Miranda Brown, mother of his children, and on the east side is Adella's name. Nearby is a flush gravestone for his son Daniel Case with a small metal Civil War marker near it. Further down-slope are the simple grave markers of the Turners, characteristic of Methodists. Some slabs are about two inches from the ground; some are flush markers and a bit grown over. The lofty Longyear family monument and markers are nearby on the slope and eastward on the top of the hill is the prominent Scottish and American granite monument for the James M. Turners and a similar family monument for the Scotts.[958]

The W. C. T. U. Honors Willard, Invites the Smasher

The death of Frances Willard on February 17, 1898, was mourned throughout the United States. She was one of the nation's most important reformers whose supporters far outnumbered the membership of the Women's Christian Temperance Union. She was known and admired around the world and known to Lansing because of her visits to the Legislature on behalf of temperance and women's rights. Marian clipped this March 4 article on the ideas of Frances Willard as presented at a memorial service held at the Baptist Church in Lansing. Willard worked all of her life to empower women through education and organization, and to improve the lot of all common working class people. She defended the eight-hour day and the right to strike. In the article below, Louis W. Rogers, director and editor of *The Railway Times*, came as a representative of the American Railway Union. He was among those jailed with Eugene Debs as a result of the Pullman Strike of 1894. Rogers came to speak of the importance of Frances Willard:

HER RELATION TO THE LABOR PROBLEM REVIEWED
Sunday afternoon at the Lansing Baptist church an audience that crowded both the main auditorium and galleries listened to ten-minute talks on the life and work of Frances E. Willard. L. W. Rogers had been invited to represent union labor at the meeting and as this part of the program specially interests our readers we reproduce his address from the many excellent ones on the program. Mr. Rogers spoke as follows:

I am conscious of the impossibility of reviewing Miss Willard's relation to the labor problem in ten minutes. Double the time would not suffice to even lightly touch upon her noble words for those who toil and rightly estimate her work for the cause of labor.

It is unfortunate that we do not better appreciate the living, that we do not grasp the true import of great thoughts from great souls until the curtain of death has fallen and hidden them forever. Frances Willard uttered truths about the labor problem that should have startled the people into attention and now that she can speak no more let us hope that her past words of wisdom will be heeded...

POVERTY THE CAUSE This thoughtful woman was a philosopher. She clearly saw that poverty is largely responsible for intemperance and believed that the cause rather than the effect must be dealt with. Instead of assuming the self-righteous attitude of those who excuse their indifference with the assertion that poverty comes from faults that must not be condoned, she said that wretched fare, miserable quarters and wearying hours of toil lead to drink and degradation, and told her followers that they must do something to improve labor's financial condition "or stop preaching Christianity to the toilers" if they would escape the just charge of hypocrisy.

THE CRUELEST INJUSTICE This gentle woman felt the blows that fell upon others. She declared the unequal distribution of wealth to be the cruelest injustice of our times. She insisted that all alike should share the advantages of education and refinement, that the labor movement would "put into everyday life the ethics of the gospel of Christ" and that our present industrial condition is "a relic of barbarism." Some of us have thought her reform narrow but we should remember that she was but entering upon the broader field that comprehends all human rights and wrongs, when death cut short her work... If there be any one thing in all the attributes of the human heart that deserves to be enthroned in this world it is sympathy. Let no one who is devoid of it attempt the uplifting of the people. They will never be raised by "the cold hand of ambition." Sympathy is the sunshine that fosters hope in the soul of the lowly. Ambition is the frost that blights it. Miss Willard was sympathy...

AS BAD AS THIEVES AND BEGGARS Frances Willard was as brave as she was noble. In the midst of a wealth worshiping people she declared that the humblest labor is holy. She knew, and she said, that her labor sentiments would be laughed at and she would be cursed; but she boldly spoke the truth. Standing in a city where multi-millionaires reared palaces upon bleeding human hearts, surrounded by a country gone mad in the ferocious struggle for gold, speaking to a generation that has produced the richest aristocracy this world has seen, she declared that "an idler is as bad as a thief, as disgraceful as a beggar," and that the only real aristocracy is that of honest toil.

Frances Willard was a typical American gentlewoman whose life was a factor of progress and whose death has taken another ray from the star of the reformer's hope. Her memory will live far into the future. She needs no monument, for in unconscious modesty she erected one in the hearts of the people. If there is any immortality more certain than another it is the immortality of good words and noble deeds. In the material world she erected a temple for the society of which she was president, but in the realm of justice she built a sanctuary where the labor principles she declared will live when the temple stones are dust, when the rights she demanded for labor have come and the wrongs she denounced are gone and forgotten.[959]

The death of Frances Willard did not signal the end of the W. C. T. U. It seemed there was more work to do than ever because the opposition was growing. The breweries were growing in strength in Lansing. The Lansing Brewery Company on Turner Street in north Lansing, employing twenty men, was incorporated in 1898 by Lawrence Price and had a capacity of 15,000 barrels in a year. Price was president and general manager, and active in the Business Men's Association. He was a Democrat on the City Council.[960] In the spring of 1902 the Michigan brewers were contesting the state liquor law by supporting a law suit that they hoped would make it to the federal courts. Wholesalers of brewed and malt liquors paid $500 for a license (manufacturers in general paid $65). The state attorney general held that agents of brewing companies in other state were wholesalers subject to Michigan's $500 fee. At Gladstone, 75 miles north of Lansing, one agent of a Minneapolis brewer was arrested and convicted for refusal to pay the

$500 fee. The brewer's attorney argued his client was simply a manufacturer who shouldn't be categorized as a wholesaler and held that Michigan had no right to discriminate by charging a Minnesota manufacturer more than a Michigan manufacturer. Seeing an advantage for themselves, the Michigan brewers were on the side of the Minnesota brewer's fight.[961]

Yet their attention was divided since Lansing's Anti-Saloon League was on the warpath because bonds for saloon operation were up for renewal, and the League didn't trust city officials to properly enforce regulation requirements. Furthermore, Michigan was being attacked by a notorious enemy of the liquor business, known for using a hatchet to smash up saloons. It was said that the saloonists were afraid of her. "The Smasher," as she was called by the press, was coming to town at the invitation of the Lansing W. C. T. U. She would stay at the home of the Central Union President, Anna Hopkins.

Carrie Nation began her ten-year campaign in 1899 in her home state of Kansas. She was a striking figure at nearly six feet tall and traveled in the somber garb of a Methodist deaconess. Lansing residents knew about Carrie Nation's trip to Michigan that spring well before she arrived on Wednesday, May 7, 1902, for a program on Thursday. The *Lansing Republican* reported on her visit in Detroit: "Nation, the hatchetur, invaded Detroit Sunday. Though she did no smashing with her hatchet, she pursued her usual course of attacking several persons in her familiar manner on various scores of smoking, etc. At 3 o'clock she lectured at the Grand River Avenue Baptist church. The edifice was crowded and many were unable to gain admittance. Nearly 2,000 people heard Mrs. Nation speak. In introducing her, Mrs. Andrus referred to Carrie as a mother-hearted, whole-souled woman, fighting the fictitiously legalized saloon. Carrie waded in, without any preliminary frills. For an hour or so she entertained her audience with assaults, a few stabs at the political parties after her usual manner, then departed on the electric road for Ann Arbor."[962]

News of her visit to Ann Arbor to lecture students and townsmen on the subject, "For God and my neighbor" also preceded her: "The university students are anxious to set Carrie a-going and are busily at work hatching schemes. 'Doc' Rose, the saloon keeper-prohibition lecturer, is, of course, the one aimed at by the boys. One of the Main street saloonists has a big sign out representing Carrie with her hatchet, and reading: 'All Nations but Carrie are Welcome.' Other drinker bosses have held counsel and there is talk of injunctions to stop Carrie from breaking anything."[963] It turned out saloonkeeper Rose closed his doors and quietly headed for the hills.

Carrie Nation had offered $25 to Doc Rose to debate, and in the afternoon, before starting for the Rose house, she raised it to $50. "With the wad of bills in her fist, ready to give to Rose in case he accepted her offer, Mrs. Nation arrived in front of the famous 'respectable' saloon." But Rose had headed out of town. "'The doctor should be criticized as to his methods of business,' shouted Carrie on the sidewalk. 'I'm Carrie Nation, come to pay him a visit, and I'm sorry he's away. 'Then Mrs. Nation gave Mrs. Rose some good advice in how to run a husband and closed by telling her to go after 'Doc' with a hatchet," or so it was reported.[964]

The *Scripps-McRae Telegram* recounted a mean trick played on Nation: "While Carrie Nation was addressing 1,000 students on the campus this morning a whisky labeled bottle, containing some dark fluid, to all appearance genuine booze, was passed up to her. She held it aloft. 'Smash it!' demanded the crowd. Carrie broke the bottle upon a hack wheel upon which arose a fearful stench of rotten eggs. The crowd held their noses and backed away, but Carrie kept on talking."[965]

That sort of reporting was typical of coverage on her speaking tours, but the people of Lansing were treated to such a description of her visit that they could see it all before their eyes, even if they stayed home the whole time:

MRS. NATION IS IN TOWN

With a Brand New Hatchet and a Line of Talk, WANTED TO SEE BLISS, But the Governor is Out of Town—May Visit the Saloons

Carrie Nation is in town. She arrived at 10:40 o'clock this morning from Flint, and is the guest of Mrs. Edward Hopkins, 401 River st. This evening she will lecture under the auspices of the W. C. T. U., at the First Presbyterian church instead of the Baptist church, as announced.

A State Republican reporter was the only 'reception committee' to meet Mrs. Nation at the Grand Trunk depot. She carried two big telescopes and had checked several other pieces of baggage. The crowd about the station eyed the saloon smasher curiously, but Mrs. Nation is used to that. After reaching the home of Mrs. Hopkins, she was perfectly willing to talk.

"I'm going to see the governor this afternoon," she said. "I am going to ask him if he don't think Michigan needs reforming. I want to ask him why it is that houses of prostitution are allowed to run on $25 government licenses. We never had anything like that in Kansas. I want to know what he thinks about licenses anyway, and I'm going to ask him a lot of questions to put him on record, and if he ain't one of these sneaking kind of men he'll answer 'em."

When Mrs. Nation was informed that Mayor Hammell is a cigar manufacturer she shook her head hopelessly. "You can't expect anything of such people," she remarked. "Why, they're pretty near as bad as folks that sell whisky. I'll have to call on him, too. So the city council extended the hours of saloons, did they? Do you think I ought to speak to the governor about that? Wouldn't do anything, eh? Couldn't? Well, he could remove a mayor that don't do his duty, couldn't he? I'll ask him, anyway."

"I don't know whether I'll do any smashing or not," Mrs. Nation continued. "Oh, I'll take my hatchet along with me. I'm lost without it, I've got a new one, too, with a lot of red paint on it. Mr. Earl gave it to me in Detroit." And she brought out a shiny new weapon with a long handle.

"I don't know just what I will do after I see the governor and the mayor. Maybe I'll visit a few saloons, I want to see the toughest places you have. Got any dance halls? No, and not what you'd call a regular house of prostitution? Lansing's better than I thought it was. Thirty saloons? Well, that's bad. I'll see what I can do."

"I don't feel very lively today, because I was out slumming at Flint last night and didn't get in till most 12. There were five or six reporters with me, and we had two hacks. Flint's got eight or nine houses, and we got into some of 'em. Ain't they awful! And they come after saloons. You never see one until after the saloons come. We don't have 'em in my state.

"You heard about Ann Arbor, didn't you, and that old Doc Rose? He didn't dare argue with me, though I offered him $50 to meet me. Their bonds weren't good.

"Politics? Mine? I'm prohibitionist. I don't believe in licenses and I'm going to tell your governor and mayor what I think about 'em. I'll see you at his office at 2, and then I want you newspaper men to go, with me. You won't print what you see, but you're all willing to print what I see and publicity is what I want to give these hell holes.

"Want one of my souvenir hatchets? Let me pin it on. There? Now you belong to my hatchetation. See, they've got my name on—Carrie A. Nation. Carry a nation—isn't that name appropriate and my initials are C. A. N.—can, not can't. Good bye, I'll see you at the governor's."

Mrs. Nation is a shrewd, kindly-faced woman, with hair almost white. She wears glasses, dresses plainly in black and is cheery and chipper in manner as a proverbial cricket.

Gov. Bliss went to Saginaw at noon, and Mayor Hammell is also out of the city. When Mrs. Nation learned this she decided to rest this afternoon, and do her 'slumming' after her lecture tonight.[966]

YELLING MOB FOLLOWED HER, CARRIE NATION STIRRED THINGS UP IN THE SALOON CIRCLES, TALKED ALL THE WHILE AND GAVE THE SALOON MEN SOME OF HER RATHER ROUGH TALK

Mrs. Carrie Nation was abroad last night. The only hatchet she carried was one of gold finish, worn on the front of a gray shawl which encompassed her shoulders, but her tongue was so sharp and her wit so nimble that several saloon men winced under verbal volleys in a ringing nasal accent, which were hurled at them over their bars. Some of them looked worried, but others were masked in an air of sangfroid, in which there was a suggestion of bravado.

Mrs. Nation started out from the Presbyterian Church, where she delivered her lecture, shortly after 10 o'clock. W. C. T. U. women, numbering perhaps a dozen, who had been inspired by her ringing edicts and appeals, and a score or more of boys and young men, formed her body-guard. Carrie reminded one forcibly of a huge rubber ball, when, with her bonnet set well back on her grey head, and a shawl gathered tightly around her substantial and slightly stooping figure, she bounded along at the head of the crusading party. So rapid was her progress, that her following found it difficult to keep pace with her. She fairly radiated animation, and in the mellow glow of the street lights the firm lines of her face seemed stronger than usual and signified determination as plainly as it could have been expressed in vivid capital letters.

"Where is this Congress saloon that I have heard tell of?" asked the smasher briskly. Several small boys, who fairly hugged themselves in delightful expectation and bubbled over in a vain effort to repress their glee fairly tumbled over each other to furnish the desired information.

By the time that Carrie reached the 'Congress' her following had been materially augmented by a large number of men and boys who had loitered about all the evening on the strength of the intimation in the newspapers that there would be something doing. Carrie led the way under the glass dome and through the saloon portals, and almost instantly the door was clogged up by a struggling, eager mass of attendant curiosity seekers in which the W. C. T. U. women were buffeted about with no more consideration than was received by others whose motives were less heroic.

Several of the women pushed their way through the crush by exercise of sheer determination, which was almost desperation to a position where observation of the tactics of the prime mover was possible.

Carrie first faced the light-haired barkeeper of the place and waded to that worthy. She wanted to see the proprietor of that devil's retreat, she said. Her prayer was shortly answered by the appearance of the rotund figure of 'Tug' Wilson, who declared himself for what he was. He faced Mrs. Nation and received a heavy broadside of condemning words full in the face. Unswervingly to the point were the words of the smasher. She had entered the hell gate, she said, to warn its keeper that he was swamping wagon loads of precious souls. Tears of blood would be wept in the day of judgment if said keeper did not deviate from the path leading down to the ignoble grave and onward to a flaming perdition, etc., etc.

The proprietor of the Congress told her she was a nice, old lady, but was not justified by that in her tirade. He urged her gently, but with determination, to leave, but Carrie gave no heed to his admonitions and continued to express herself forcibly in a remarkable flow of denunciatory words.

Finally Wilson demanded that the way be cleared and taking the smasher by both arms from behind pushed her gently through the crowd and out onto the sidewalk. The W. C. T. U. women murmured their indignation. Mrs. Nation bounced away with unmitigated zeal, and talking incessantly made her way to the 'Fashion' saloon, followed by a steadily increasing and hooting crowd. In the 'Fashion' she read the riot act to Dan Bowers, who calmly faced the music and pointed out the fact between volleys that she had brought in with her a large number of minors who had never before been allowed in the place. "A glimpse of hell may save some of them," was Mrs. Nation's ready response.

When finally she had had her say, Mrs. Nation visited the "Senate" saloon. In following her, the crowd caused the partitions of the place to creak, so heavy was the pressure exerted.

In the "Senate" Mrs. Nation threw the hooks into Eddy Grove, who refused to lend her an attentive ear, but continued to wait on his customers, after having commanded the other women to leave his place. They obeyed, but waited outside for the smasher to reappear. Carrie's following had now resolved itself into a jeering, hooting mob, in which there was a sprinkling of women of ill repute. Her remarks were almost drowned in challenges and taunts, and an occasional hoarse and concerted rendition of a popular air, entitled "Good Morning Carrie."

Mrs. Nation visited Louis Ehlinger's place and the Eichele house before abandoning her crusade… Her protectors prevailed upon her to give up the chase in the Eichele and, making a way for her to the back door, hurried her through the alley and put her into a carriage. She was then taken to the home of Mrs. Edward Hopkins [Anna] on River st.

"Do you know," she said to a newspaper man, "I like a hooting, howling mob such as the one I have just escaped. When the young men in that crowd think this all over in solitude it will set them to thinking and analyzing. That is just what I want. My treatment tonight is not a marker to the abuse I have received in other places," and Mrs. Nation smiled benignly.

Before retiring in the house she kissed several young men who had followed her as best they could to her home, and gave them her blessing.

Mrs. Nation appeared this morning looking robust and happy and referred lightly to her experiences of last night.

The first Presbyterian church was packed to the doors when the smasher was introduced last evening by Rev. R. C. Dodds.

The audience was struck by the firmness of her face, and her energetic and easy manner. She wore a black dress and a huge white necktie tied in a bow.

One of her preliminary movements was a physical exercise in which she arose from her seat and swung several chairs out of the choir box with athletic ease, placing them at the foot of the rostrum and saying, with a slight nasal twang, "Come forward now and sit down some of you who are standing. I can't be comfortable until you are."

In response a number of people came forward, and in answer to another invitation a number of small boys seated themselves about her feet on the rostrum.

"That's right," said Carrie, "I like youngsters, and don't care if they are so thick that I have to stand in my tracks continuously."

The smasher said she is not a temperance lecturer, but a prohibitionist.

"That word temperance covers a multitude of sins" she said briskly. "It means intemperance is wrong doing. Evil doers are always glad to get into temperance organizations, but they avoid prohibitionists societies as a timid woman avoids a snake show. The devil insinuates himself into temperance movements and tricks those who think they are accomplishing good through the Anti-Saloon league, and other similar organizations."

Mrs. Nation gave an extended account of her experiences in Kansas jails, throwing denunciation at judges, lawyers and other authorities of that state, as well as the prosecuting attorney of her county...

"Hells are licensed in Michigan. We don't license them in Kansas...A man pays a $500 license to the state and $25 to the government in a year to drug American manhood, murder precious lives and send souls to hell..."

After conducting a mothers' and fathers' meeting at the First Presbyterian church this morning, Mrs. Nation left on the Lake Shore road for Albion, where she will lecture tonight. After filling several other engagements she will leave for her home in Kansas, where she intends on establishing a home for drunkards' wives.[967]

The next big event for the W. C. T. U. was held in December. Though women rarely take up erecting statues and monuents in public places to honor their own gender, after Willard's death the Central W. C. T. U. decided to join the movement to create public memorials to Willard by erecting a public drinking fountain. Carrie Nation contributed $25 to the Lansing memorial fundraising campaign while in Lansing.[968] This fountain would provide drinking water for both humans and animals. It was made of Vermont granite and placed at the busy downtown northwest corner of Washington and Michigan Avenue. After the fountain was unveilled at the dedication ceremony by pulling away the flag that hid it from the crowd, local union president Anna Hopkins said, "We trust that this fountain sending forth pure, cold water, which Abraham Lincoln declared to be the best beverage ever brewed, may be the means of helping many a soul to resist the temptations of the open saloons in our midst." Several others spoke and then the main speaker, who was state organizer of the W. C. T. U., Mrs. E. C. Calkins from Kalamazoo, spoke for an hour about the history and growth of reform movements, particularly the temperance movement. "Nations," said Mrs. Calkins, "do not die of tariff or lack of it; of a double money standard or a single. A man may not believe in fair trade or even in government ownership of railways, yet he may be a good man. It is not such things that destroy men or nations. It is immorality. The history of a nation is the history of moral reform."[969] She closed with an earnest plea for all to work harder than ever for reform.

Marian enjoyed good health and continued to take an active part in the Lansing Central Union and in church work at the North Lansing First Methodist Church. In 1902 the Lansing W. C. T. U. was able to secure a curfew ordinance in the city. The Union kept up a steady flow of educational activities and lobbying. From 1906 on until 1919, Anna Hopkins served as president of Lansing Central. Hopkins wrote in the history of the Lansing W. C. T. U.: "In June 1907, the Lansing Unions entertained five hundred delegates for the state W. C. T. U. convention. At this convention a petition was prepared for a prohibition amendment to the Michigan constitution, which was being revised." The president of the National Union, the president of Albion College, and the state Sunday School Superintendent of the Methodist Church all spoke for the amendment before the committee for revision of the constitution, but it was voted down. "That was the year when one of Lansing's leading hotel proprietors was arrested for selling liquor on New Year's Day and Judge Weist sentenced him to the Mason jail," Hopkins recalled.[970]

Under Hopkins' leadership, a bill for an anti-cigarette law was drafted in 1908 and quickly passed in the Senate under the direction of Senator Luren Dickinson (Governor in 1939-40, Republican). According to Hopkins it was a different story in the House. Since all petitions were called for and read each session, she placed one or two each day on the Representatives' desks. "The day the bill came up for final reading and the clerk called for a reading of petitions, every man was on his feet and the Speaker was surprised to know that every man had petitions. He ordered the page boys to get the baskets and gather them. They had three large clothes baskets of petitions, 34,347 in all. The representatives decided it was wise to recognize the request of their constituents at home and the bill was passed in the spring of 1909," wrote Hopkins. They worked on three Local Option campaigns with the Anti-Saloon League in 1910, 1912, and 1914. They secured petitions, raised money, worked in the office addressing envelopes and sending out literature. Anna Hopkins also chaired the county W. C. T. U. and coordinated the county effort. In 1911 the state W. C. T. U. opened headquarters in the Prudden building to work on a state prohibition law. But it wasn't until 1916 that Michigan adopted the amendment with a majority of 68,624 votes. The 18th Amendment to the United States Constitution was ratified on January 16, 1919, and Anna Hopkins stepped down as Lansing's chairman. "Michigan was under prohibition until 1933 when Governor Comstock and his party worked to make Michigan the first state to vote for repeal after the democrats took office," wrote Hopkins in her history of the Union.[971]

The City at some point moved the fountain to the Potter Park Zoo. In the 1980s, it was inexplicably found in cement being used for land fill to the southwest of the Dodge Mansion, as it was called, where work was being done to fill in the bank. It was rescued and moved to a mini-park at the corner of Turner Street and Grand River Avenue (once Franklin Street) until it was conserved and put in working order by Lansing Board of Water and Light workers and moved to the heritage garden of the Turner-Dodge House in 2001 to the delight of the local Baltimore orioles.

Lansing enters the 20ᵗʰ Century

By the turn of the century, the long years of depression were over. Lansing made great leaps in business and manufacturing, starting about 1897. Frank Turner said of the tremendous changes that were happening: "It has been observed that no decade so marked the end of the primitive and the beginning of maturity in this section of Michigan as the decade from 1880 to 1890. So sharp was the break with the past in this decade that when the twentieth century dawned the past was speedily forgotten in the new glamour...Comparing activities in Lansing in 1890 with those in 1900, one may realize that an entirely new era has dawned."⁹⁷² There was a major shift from lumbering to manufacturing: "One of the reasons why Michigan lumbermen are having great difficulty in securing men for their camps, even though the wages offered are 40 per cent higher than two years ago, may be found in the fact that since Jan. 1, 1897, a total of 1,005 new factories have been established in Michigan. These factories, which were not in existence in 1896, are today giving employment to 23,000 hands. The average wage rate in Michigan being $1.40 per day."⁹⁷³

In 1901, when the Lansing Business Men's Association was organized with about 200 members, Frank joined. The group planned to secure manufacturing enterprises for Lansing as quickly as possible by offering every reasonable inducement to create favorable conditions. The first year was phenomenal, with twelve new companies. By 1902 there were no vacant houses or stores, and nearly 200 dwellings were built that year.⁹⁷⁴

Credit was given directly to the Lansing Business Men's Association for enticing Ransom E. Olds to come back to Lansing after his new Detroit automobile factory burned to the ground in 1902. Lawrence Price, an active Democratic colleague of Frank's who served on the city council four years and on the Ingham County Board of Supervisors, became head of the Business Men's Association. Some say Price, not just Ransom E. Olds, was responsible for turning Lansing into the "Auto City," although Price is little known today.⁹⁷⁵

All traces of the enterprises of the pioneers on the northwest corner of Turner and Franklin Streets disappeared in 1901 when the Auto Body Works, as it was called, was built by Price to manufacture auto bodies. Down the street was Price's Lansing Brewing Company and later on Price organized the Acme Motor Company and became president. Next to the Auto Body Works on Turner Street, Price built the Peerless Motor Company in 1903, a small engine manufacturing plant. Peerless' motto was "There are others, but none so good." Price was an original investor in the REO Motor Car Company and was also a director and stockholder in the City National Bank of Lansing, the Novo Engine Company, and the Auto Wheel Company, a reorganization of the Lansing Spoke Co.⁹⁷⁶ Price had become one of Lansing's leading industrialists and financiers. He continued his interest in politics and served on the Democratic State Central Committee. He also took a turn with Frank, in running for Congress in the predominantly Republican district. REO Motor

The Turner-Dodge House just after the renovation. Turner-Dodge House photo.

Car Company was purchased by General Motors Company in 1908. Today, on the south side of downtown is a huge Cadillac manufacturing plant called Lansing Grand River Assembly and to its east is REO Town, a small business district working on restoration of its community.

The Lansing women had taken on many community building works that were thriving, among them were the library and hospital. After years of nurturing libraries by the Library and Literary Societies in the city, there was now a handsome new Carnegie library. It was obtained through an application to Andrew Carnegie by Mary Spencer, the state librarian and a club member. They received $35,000 in 1902 and became one of 61 Carnegie libraries in the state.[977] The building is now part of the Lansing Community College campus. The Women's Hospital Association formed in 1896 with 114 members. They initiated the City Hospital which then evolved into the Edward W. Sparrow Hospital in 1912, with a donation of land on Michigan Avenue and $100,000 by E. W. Sparrow. The Women's Board of Managers, as it came to be called, still exists and is represented on the Sparrow Health System board.[978]

For years Frank walked to Turner Street every day and took the city's horse-drawn trolley downtown to his office. He might sit near the window and read the newspaper or peruse his red leather pocket diary to check the calendar or make notes about business, the children, or the weather. But with the manufacture of automobiles in North Lansing, it wasn't long before the

Dodges owned an automobile. Rod McLean remembered that his grandfather drove the car to work but not in the wintertime. In the winter he had the car placed on blocks in the garage. That kept the tires from getting a permanent flat spot while not in use.[979] Frank resumed taking the trolley to work; however, a horse-drawn trolley seemed very out of date.

For many years the businessmen of St. Johns had been agitating for a St. Johns-Lansing Railroad. At the time the only railroad route from St. Johns was by way of Owosso, and then, there was a long tedious wait at the junction for the ride to Lansing. Their attempts always seemed to end in failure. In April 1893 they went so far as to pledge $50,000 for a trolley line.[980] At last, in May the *State Republican* reported: "The proposed electric railroad to St. Louis is a certainty. Secretary Frank L. Dodge said yesterday that it was safe to announce this fact, remarking that, the Lansing, St. Johns and St. Louis' Railway is beyond preadventure a reality... Mr. Dodge has been heart and soul in the project of building the line for the past two years. He has given hours and hours and days of toil, and the hardest kind of toil, too, to the promotion of the line, and when the road is finally constructed, a liberal amount of the credit, must be given to him."[981]

There were still many sticking points. In the fall of 1896 Dwight Smith was called upon to come to Lansing to talk about the Jackson Street Railway. He was one of the proprietors of the Jackson electric streetcar line. He told the *Lansing Journal*, "The city does all the paving in Jackson, collects no specific tax, does not require employment of conductors, and is well satisfied with the arrangement. Mr. Smith thinks the provision in the ordinance passed by the Lansing Council this week, which placed the power in the hands of the Council to revoke the street railway franchise is one which no company would think of accepting."[982] Dwight headed the electric car company for fifteen years. His career was cut short a year later when he died in Jackson, preceding his father by six months.

By the turn of the century, Lansing and St. Johns still didn't have an electric trolley line between them. The interurbans were in demand because they were bigger and faster than the older model trolleys. On April 10, 1900, The Lansing, St. Johns, and St. Louis Railway Company was launched, subscriptions taken, and an innovative contractor chosen. But nothing happened right away. Fights over right-of-way descended into law suits. The existing steam railroads wanted to cause as much trouble and delay as possible. The Pere Marquette Railway resisted allowing the electric railway to build an overpass in St. Johns.[983] The Agricultural College finally got a trolley out to the campus and a post office/trolley depot combination in 1902, but they wanted to be included in the electric trolley plans.[984] There were also fights among the investors that Frank had to deal with.[985]

And then there was a breakthrough. As the *State Republican* told it, "On Saturday night the law office of Ald. Dodge was the scene of one of the most important business transactions ever consummated in this city, so far as the material interests are concerned. This was the execution of a contract for building the Lansing, St. Johns and St. Louis Electric Railway." The battles for right-of-way were almost over. The electric trolley line was going to be first-class in all aspects and carry both passengers and freight. "It is about 16 years since the idea of building the road was first started in this city. Among the original projectors were F. L. Dodge and Jacob Stahl. These gentlemen subsequently enlisted Fred Thoman in the enterprise," said the *State Republican*. "They have never lost faith in the ultimate result and deserve great credit for their perseverance and indomitable pluck. To them is largely due the present bright prospects for Lansing's first interurban railway."[986] A few months later, it was predicted that the electric trolley line would bring a substantial business boom. Some calculated the increased wealth to the city could support one or two first-class grocery houses and more manufactories.[987] The interurban was expected to reach St. Johns by the fall and 65 miles to the north by the end of 1901.[988]

The first trip from St. Johns to Lansing was on March 26, 1901, temporarily run by steam.[989] After the electric trolleys were in place, there were still a number of years when the changes in transportation were in flux. On a trip down Washington Avenue in Lansing a shopper might see horses and buggies, a few automobiles, and the electric trolley mingling on the streets. The technology of the electric railroad was soon overtaken by the automobile, however, and by 1929 the trolleys ceased to be, supplanted by buses.

Frank was also busy providing legal help on a project for the City of Mason. One of the pieces of legislation that Frank had sponsored as a Legislator required two terms of the Ingham County circuit court be held in Lansing each year. This did not sit very well with the people of the city of Mason, who didn't want the loss of visitors to Mason that a reduction in circuit court traffic would bring and worried that the county seat might someday be moved to Lansing. When the necessity for building a new county courthouse came up, Frank pitched in on the court house committee and volunteered all the legal services that were needed. According to the *Ingham County Press* a gold-headed cane was in the offing. "There is no doubt but that Mr. Dodge has been very instrumental in getting this magnificent structure where it is and our citizens did no more than right in this slight token of remembrance."[990]

His work as the promoter, incorporator and secretary of the St. Johns and St. Louis Railway Company was another of the projects that gained Frank the esteem of the community. It was considered such a public service to Lansing that almost two decades later it was saluted in a wacky poem printed in the newspaper as a tribute and saved in the Turner family scrapbook:

Lansing Hall of Fame
    How many of the actions of the famous human race are guided by the wise work from a politician's face! And when he is a lawyer and a counselor as well, how many more if he should roar, are smitten by his spell. He weaves the English language in a wondrous web of words and voters follow after him in large and loving herds.

To know the facts and set them forth in words that last and lodge, such is the art and proper part of Lawyer Frank L. Dodge. He wares the issues of the hour in terms that zoom and zip, he spellbinds voters in his power and holds them in his grip: and when he has a jury where they cannot get excused, the lever of his eloquence is violently used.

The Lansing - St. Johns trolley line he helped to found and build, the only one by which the Clinton county folk are thrilled. He's rescued many dollars in an ownership dispute where dust was flying freely and the tension was acute, and nothing speaks more truly of his talents and his rank than his Colonial mansion sitting in the river bank.[991]

Marian continued to live in the house on Grand River even after she sold it to Abby and Frank on June 20, 1899. When the property in the estate was divided among the three daughters, Abby received the land surrounding the house. Marian (Reasoner) received the acreage northwest of the house (now the Reasoner Park area). Eva (Black) received acreage to the west which later became the site of the Michigan Sugar Company. Marian retained the Turner home.[992]

The transformation of the house began with the aid of Lansing pioneer and well-known local architect, Darius Moon. The changes were made in stages over about three years. By 1903, the home was among the most comfortable and luxurious in Lansing. The two-story flat-topped Greek revival house evolved into a stately 8,600 square foot three-story house in the popular Georgian Revival style, which they referred to as Colonial. There is an etching of a Southern Colonial house in the music room which may have been the inspiration for their house. There are massive two-story tall Ionic columns in the front, brackets similar to the picture, and a porte-cochère in the back offering a grand secondary entrance. Horses and buggies drove up to the porte-cochère to discharge their passengers. Dodge River Drive was created from Turner Street to the southwest of the house and out to East North Street.

A carriage house almost as big as the house itself was built on the west side. The family enjoyed horseback riding, especially their daughter Josephine. They often took the horses out for a ride to Springdale Farm and back. Frank and Abby could take the carriage to the near-by train station where they boarded their palace car for a trip to Chicago or New York. According to their great-grandson, John (Jody) Pemberton, the train took them right up to their hotel where they attended elegant social events.[993] Eventually the carriage house was made into a three family apartment house when horse-drawn carriages were replaced with automobiles, and a garage was built next to the river bank.

The warm and welcoming interior of the house reflected the interests of the family. The two first floor bedrooms on the east side of the house were now the music room where Abby's 1898 grand piano was placed under a rectangular, leaded "piano window" for the best natural light. Her

Grand-Rapids-made sheet music cabinet was nearby. The former dining room on the south side of the house was now Frank's library. There were beer steins from their many trips to Germany displayed on the top book shelves. The front room was the entry hall and parlor where an upright piano was placed – the one that went to Washington D.C. when Abby played for the President. The two bedrooms on the west side became the dining room. The oak wainscoting included a plate rail to display the beautiful hand-painted plates that Ida Longyear had given them over ten years before. On the north wall was a small three-tone chime that was used to call the family from all parts of the house at dinnertime. Jody Pemberton remembered that dinners were formal, and children had to be on time and properly dressed.[994] The dining table could seat twenty-two.

The kitchen was a far cry from the old kitchen in the basement. To accommodate Abby's enthusiasm for cooking, a new wing was added to the house on the west end, and on the first floor it provided a spacious kitchen and butler's pantry. The house was heated with steam radiators. The kerosene lamps were now electric. There was open electric wiring in some places which ran on narrow grooved wood molding. The telephone was placed on a small table at the back entrance.

Marian's room became a favorite place for the Dodge grandchildren to spend the afternoon sipping tea and listening to exciting tales of pioneer days. They remembered it as a happy house. There were stories about old Chief Okemos who camped on the riverbank nearby, and stories of blazing the way through rugged wood. In 1905 the Dodge family consisted of Sophie, 15, Frank, 13, Wyllis, 12, Josephine, 5, and baby Marian was ones, fording rivers, making paths that later became the streets of the city.

The ballroom was used for dancing and hosting events, whether friends and family, cultural or political. On the right was a billiard room and on the left was a large trunk room used to store the steamer trunks used for traveling abroad. They loved entertaining and the *Fannie Farmer Cookbook* was in constant use. Abby and Frank's daughter Marian once recalled, "My father was a delightful man and very convivial. He invited guests home for dinner so often that my mother was accustomed to keeping supplies for an extra half dozen on hand… The Christmas parties in the ballroom were the most exciting parties of all. All the family came and my uncle played Santa Claus in a red suit, whiskers and all. He distributed presents to the children and then we'd all sing Christmas carols and dance old-style cotillions and the Virginia Reel."[995]

While the Dodges were making all of these changes, Marian's nephew John and his wife Mary Longyear were making some rather astounding changes of their own. In 1892, they built a sixty-five room mansion overlooking Lake Superior. Despite their protests and offers to negotiate for alternatives, a railroad commandeered a swath of land across their property and built a railroad track. Efforts to sell the house, valued at $500,000, failed. They decided to move from Marquette to Brookline, Massachusetts, near

Boston[996] to be close to Mary Baker Eddy, the founder and leader of Christian Science and Mary's friend. The Longyears then added some twenty rooms to the original house. Moving the mansion was recognized by "Ripley's Believe It or Not," a newspaper article series that featured the strange and unusual. It said the Longyear house in Marquette was dismantled, numbered stone by stone, and moved the 1,300 miles by train in 172 freight and flat cars. Marian saved the article.[997]

One of the outstanding events at the Dodge House was in the fall of 1908 when Abby and Frank hosted a Farmer's Club meeting. The Ingham County Farmers' Club was established in 1872, and for 27 years it existed as a men's club, holding its meeting in a public hall. Perhaps in reaction to the policy of equality of the Grange, it reorganized to admit women, "in accordance with the trend of the times," and began holding its meetings at the homes of its members. Its meetings were always open to the public, unlike the Grange, which was modeled after the Masons and Odd Fellows, and it did not bar discussion of politics or religion. Abby and Frank were among the sixty prosperous farm families that composed its membership.[998]

Another red letter day has passed into the history of the Ingham County Farmer's Club, and those who availed themselves of the opportunity of attending the meeting held Saturday, Oct. 10, 1908, with Hon. And Mrs. F. L. Dodge of North Lansing will always be glad that they were... It surely is an ideal location for a home and good judgment was shown when this was selected in the wilderness and Mr. and Mrs. Turner erected the first frame house, where now the modern dwelling, remodeled in the 20th century, stands, and Mrs. Turner still lives to enjoy the home and surroundings. Of the original farm of 60 acres, 12 are retained to make the spacious grounds, and as one went out to the point and looked up and down the river and saw the busy city with its many manufacturing interests then turned and looked at the forest primeval, no wonder one of the company said "no need to go far from home to see fine scenery."

The Mason members went on the 12:18 train most of them going directly to the place of meeting and after being warmly welcomed by Mrs. Dodge and daughter and given the liberty of the place and surroundings, each felt at home. A few went to the sugar factory, others to the Blind School, and still others just visited, and wandering around visited the ponies and the puppies.

Everything was in readiness for the contents of the baskets and volunteer committee helped to get things ready for the table, and just at the commencement of twilight the large company were seated and Mrs. Dodge, with able corps of assistants, attended to all the wants of the inner man, and probably some were no more comfortable afterwards than before. Our host welcomed all in a few well chosen words and after no one could eat more, each one took his chair and repaired to the third story where all were comfortably seated in one room… All went merry with joke and laughter and common sense. Judge C. P. Black was given the subject. "What I know about farming, the farmer," and Rev. Ward, "Some observations on farm gaits, not omitting the gate of the electric car between Mason and Lansing." Mrs. Black gave another solo and responded to an encore and Judge Weist told some things he knew of the hydraulic ram. Mrs. Hildreth pleasingly recited "Christmas Baby" by Will Carleton, and responded to an encore by reading from Ben King, "If I Should Die Tonight."

Judge Ostrander's subject was "Fishing in the Grand fifty years ago," and, in part, said it was very fitting this meeting should be held here, one of the first homes in the city, and this house never sheltered anything but kind hearts, and the roof was raised a little higher only for the purpose of sheltering more heads. Judge O. came to Lansing 50 years ago, when it was still under township rule and the assessed valuation was $3,000,000. Last year, exclusive of the city of Lansing, the assessed valuation was $15,000,000, and that the non-taxable property had increased more than the taxable [Russell Ostrander was elected to the Supreme Court in 1904

Joe Warner came to Lansing in 1850 and gave in his own peculiar style a brief biography of his early life.

After singing one verse of "God be With You Till we Meet Again," the club adjourned, feeling Mr. Dodge and family were royal entertainers… Mrs. Tanswell, Cor. Sec'y.[999]

The Turner-Dodge House is now a heritage center owned by the City of Lansing. In 2012, the descendants of Abby and Frank made a loan of much of the original furnishings of the house at the turn of the century. It is now on display at Turner-Dodge House through the efforts of Jody Pemberton, grandson of Josephine Dodge McLean. It is called the Pemberton Family Collection. North Lansing with Turner Street as its main north and south street, is revitalized as an arts and cultural community in Lansing and is called Old Town. It was a Main Street Project of the National Trust for Historic Preservation.

The Suffrage Campaign of 1908

Frank once said: "The civic unit of America is not the dollar but the individual man. All that goes to make better, happier and freer men and women is Progress: all else is reaction."[1000] It was anticipated that the twentieth century would bring great progress for women and so it was with enthusiasm that Michigan women prepared for the Constitutional Convention of 1907-08. After ten years of struggle they had won Municipal Suffrage and then were told they could only achieve the universal right to vote through an amendment to the constitution. For fourteen years they tried to get such an amendment on the ballot, and now, at last, revision of the constitution was expected. From the moment the Legislature provided for the convention, they made their plans and built their coalition. To give women full enfranchisement simply required that the word "male," as a qualification for voting, be omitted from the voting qualifications section of the revised constitution.

The convention began on October 22. Only a few subjects received prolonged attention,[1001] and when the request of the suffragists was made on the twelfth day, the suffragists were there to present a memorial enumerating their arguments for it in writing. "An appeal through the state press and by hundreds of letters was made to influential citizens to write in behalf of the memorial to members of the Convention … and many so received were read in the general sessions" reported Clara Arthur, a member of the Michigan Federation of Women's Clubs and the Michigan Women's Suffrage Association.[1002] Arthur wrote in the Women's Club journal: "Daily, from the presentation of the memorial in November, until the vote was taken on the measure in March, the suffragists presented petitions from societies, or lists of individuals asking favorable action by the Convention. Two hundred and twenty-five thousand citizens sent their names endorsing the suffrage proposal. Of these one hundred and seventy-five thousand were women. Twelve times at discreet intervals suffrage literature was mailed to or placed upon the desks of the Convention members. Ex-Senator Palmer contributed copies of his celebrated speech made in the [United States] Senate in 1887, in which the principles of equal suffrage are so ably enunciated. This speech was the first ever made in behalf of woman suffrage in any parliament of the world, and its delivery created much discussion in many countries for several years. Of the intensive statewide campaign to rally all favoring sentiment to support the suffrage effort, there is not space to tell."[1003]

The press gave a great deal of attention to the hearing held by the Committee on Elective Franchise in Representative Hall, January 8, 1908. An immense audience of men and women from Lansing and all over the state filled the hall and galleries. The day's event was moderated by the president of the Michigan Equal Suffrage Association who introduced the panel of women speakers. She said that they had been told that when women wanted the right to vote, the men would give it to them. She then presented the speakers who took on the economic, financial, business, educational, moral, and ethical interests of women, in terse and forceful terms. The speakers represented the following groups:

The Michigan Federation of Labor was represented by the first president of the Michigan Women's Suffrage Association, Mrs. Mary Doe of Bay City

The Michigan State Association of Farmers' Clubs, Dr. Gertrude Banks of Detroit

The State Grange, Rev. Olivia J. Woodman of Paw Paw

The M E.S.A. and the Women's Clubs, Mrs. Clara B. Arthur of Detroit

Ladies of the Modern Maccabees, Mrs. Rachel A. Bailey of Grand Rapids

Ladies of the Maccabees of the World, Dr. Blanche Haines of Three Rivers

Detroit Garment Workers Union, Mrs. Alecia Nangle of Detroit

The Women's Christian Temperance Union, Mrs. May S. Knaggs of Bay City

The Michigan Press Association, Mrs. Jennie Law Hardy of Tecumseh[1004]

In addition, Mrs. Carrie Oostdyk, representing the Women's Independent Voter's Association of Detroit, reviewed the use which Michigan women had made of suffrage since obtaining it, and Mrs. Catherine Waugh McCulloch, an attorney from Chicago, discussed the Constitution of Michigan as it directly affected women, and the changed conditions since the first state constitution expressly excluded duelists and women from voting. Clara Arthur described what came next:

Rev. Anna Howard Shaw, National Suffrage President, followed, and in a matchless flow of eloquence made a plea for the citizenship of women which her admirers claim to be the crowning triumph of her life. To the undying regret of the writer that plea was not recorded.

The favorable effect of the hearing upon the Franchise Committee and the audience was plainly evident. As speaker after speaker presented unanswerable arguments and pressed home fact after fact the attention of the entire house became increasingly absorbed. Miss Shaw dwelt on the justice of full citizenship for women, on the wrong inflicted *on the State by the State* through the disabilities of one-half its people: on the efforts and sufferings of the pioneer women of which she was one, in the development of Michigan; and on the present needs of society for the expressed interests of its women, her hearers were profoundly affected and many were in tears. She spoke for over an hour and scarcely a person moved.

After the adjournment, the audience stormed the platform, applauding the hearing and congratulating the suffragists. Chairman Watson declared that the suffrage cause had been presented in the most concise and effective manner of any subject introduced into the Convention and that his Committee would report favorably. This it subsequently did, bringing the subject before the Convention."[1005]

Based on this successful reception, what happened next could not have been anticipated and the ordinary citizen of Michigan would never have guessed at the effort that had been put into persuading the delegates. "Wives Defeated the Suffragists" said the *State Republican*. The convention killed the proposal to allow women to vote, 34 in favor and 47 against. The excuse of several of the delegates was a claim that their better halves told them they need not come home if it passed. "There were several set speeches in favor of the proposal and no one said a word in opposition. A bevy of women suffragists was present to witness the debate and contest, and apparently they expected another result than the one reached by the convention... Again, it was stated that by refusing to give women the right to vote the men were classing them with lunatics, infants and slaves," said the newspaper.[1006]

For some delegates full suffrage was denied because they thought the constitution might not be approved if it was included. Finally, two changes by way of compromise were made in the constitution regarding whether women could vote: women taxpayers could vote on any question involving the direct expenditure of money or an issuance of bonds, and women taxpayers could vote on the grant of a franchise or the acquisition of a public utility in cities or villages.[1007] With the adoption of the constitution by the male voters, Marian, as a taxpaying woman, had the right to vote in some elections, but could not vote for those who would represent her in government or other matters. All of Marian's sisters, her daughters, and her daughter-in-law Sophie would be able to vote in the specified elections, but there were many women who did not own property. A proposal to prohibit the sale of liquor and cigarettes was lobbied for by prohibitionists, including Anna Hopkins of the W. C. T. U., and failed. It was said by some a more restrictive liquor law might have been approved, but the prohibitionists wanted complete prohibition or nothing.[1008]

A proposal to move the capitol back to Detroit never went anywhere, but such talk was always somewhat disturbing to the people of Lansing. They blamed Pingree for calling the move the "crime of 1847" when he was mayor and believed such talk was the reason the capitol facility was slow to expand.[1009] But that was not enough to slow the growth it was experiencing from the mills and the wheat industry, manufacturing, and the auto industry. The report of the Lansing Women's Club for its centennial observance, entitled "The Middle Years 1910-1940," described the City:

> In 1910 Lansing had 31,000 inhabitants, and there were just a few automobiles seen bumping along the brick paved avenue —and every new one was duly noted... By 1912 Lansing was a busy place with a population of 45,000. There were 14 miles of paved streets, 17 public schools, 8,500 homes, 1,500 businesses. There were four steam rail roads and 35 passenger trains daily. There were three interurbans and 31 miles of city car tracks. Steamers went up and down the Grand river. Michigan Agricultural College had 1,568 students and 120 instructors. There were five hotels, seven theaters and five banks. Pine Lake, now Lake Lansing, had 150 cottages and the Reo Motor Car Company's slogan was "You Can Do It With a Reo." The average daily wage was $2.22, but Mr. Ford changed all that for he paid a minimum of $5.00 a day by 1914.[1010]

The report, which was presented to the club in 1974, did not mention the remarkable campaigns for women's suffrage that occurred in Michigan after 1908, in 1912, 1913, and 1918, nor the many small conquests their antecedents won for them along the way. It wasn't until 1916 that two Lansing wards elected the first women school board members after more than two decades of sporadic failed attempts. They were Ella Aldinger and Bertha M. Redfern.[1011] Aldinger was a former president of the Lansing Women's Club, an ardent follower of militant suffragist Alice Paul, and the wife of a minister. Both were teachers. They out-organized the male opposition. Progress was facilitated nationally when the Prohibition Amendment was won without the votes of women and that took away the impetus by the liquor industry for fighting to keep women from voting. Michigan women attained Universal Suffrage in 1918, and Michigan was the second state to ratify the national suffrage amendment, the 19th amendment. At long last, justice.

The Oldest Resident Died Last Night

Marian attended a program in celebration of the 50th anniversary of the City of Lansing on March 15, 1909. She had long held the affectionate, unofficial title of "Lansing's Grand Old Lady," so naturally she took a prominent part in the celebration.[1012] "When I look out over this beautiful city, see the smoke from the chimneys of its manufacturing establishments and its growth, it seems to me I am living in a dream, and this is not the Lansing I once knew as a mere dot in a wilderness," Marian told the audience. After her brief remarks she turned to her daughter Marian Reasoner who read from her mother's manuscript. This was the story of her arrival in Michigan, a paper she and her sisters had shared in slightly different versions whenever they were called upon to tell their story.[1013] In her later years she required a wicker wheelchair to go any distance, and her daughters Marian or Abby, or another member of the family helped see she could attend the meetings of the organization she so enjoyed. She enjoyed honorable distinction in the community for her early, able, and efficient contributions in the founding and building of Lansing.

Marian and her family members had long supported the Pioneer Historical Society, which was fast evolving into the Historical Society of Michigan (the name given to the state's original historical group in 1828 by Territorial Governor Lewis Cass) because so many of the pioneers were gone. In future years, Sophie built a house in the style of Mount Vernon on Capitol Avenue across the street just north of the capitol. She donated it to the Historical Commission in 1927, and it became the state historical museum. When the museum was moved to a larger facility in 1980, it was sold to Lansing Community College. In 2003 it was torn down to make way for a new campus building because it was riddled with termites and could not be saved. It was said that down deep the ground was peppered with old rotten wood that was probably thrown into a swampy depression in that area and filled in.

At one of the last meetings she attended, the Society members thought about how and why they had endeavored to preserve their story. The Introduction to Volume 35 of their series on Michigan Pioneer history stated: "To perpetuate the story of the pioneers, the real makers of Michigan; to rescue from oblivion their struggles, trials and sacrifices when opening this beautiful peninsula to the light of civilization; to place on permanent record the political, industrial and social progress of the past for future generations, and have at hand for the coming historian the most trustworthy material for his pen."[1014]

They believed that history deals with the acts and purposes of women and men and communities but existing in a continuum of time; "everything in the present is a sequence of life and conduct in the past. We, today, are molding the future." They hoped the historians of the future would capture the ethical principles and philosophy underlying their governance of society and convey them to generations to come. To them, true historians would include the evolution of domestic, economic, and industrial arts; the evolution of the growth and development of public and private morals and conduct; the evolution of the various complex forces that constitute an imperfect civilization." They would catch the spirit of the times. "The governing law in all these movements is that as men and nations sow, so also must they reap."[1015]

Michigan was celebrating 75 years of statehood, and Marian had lived through them all. Her family scrapbook and her many activities indicate that she was engaged with the challenges of her times and the pioneer's obligation to molding the future. But now all of that would be set aside. The *State Journal* announced the death of Marian on Thursday evening, July 11, 1912:

OLDEST RESIDENT DIED LAST NIGHT
Mrs. Marian M. Turner Passed Away at Home of Daughter, Mrs. Dodge. WAS 93 YEARS OF AGE
Beloved Pioneer Came to Michigan in 1836--Funeral Services Will Be Held Saturday Afternoon at 2 o'clock. Mrs. Marian M. Turner, one of the oldest and most beloved residents of the city, died Wednesday night shortly after midnight, in her ninety-fourth year, at the home of her daughter, Mrs. Frank L. Dodge, North St., where she had lived for the past 22 [54] years. Mrs. Turner was one of the earliest if not the earliest pioneer of Lansing and Michigan living in this day.
Came to Michigan in 1836.
Mrs. Turner was a wonderful woman and a member of an extraordinary family. Born in Amhurst, Erie county, N. Y., December 8, 1818, she came to Michigan with her father, Jesse Munroe, in 1836 and settled in Eagle, Clinton county. She was the oldest of 11 children and, up to three weeks ago, she was one of seven of these children still living and each past three score years and ten. Late in June her brother, Josiah Turner, aged 89 years, died in Eagle. She is survived by three sisters, Mrs. Betsey Webber, aged 91 years, Mrs. John W. Longyear, aged 87 years, and Mrs. Liza Turner, aged 80 years, and a brother, William Munroe, aged 75 years, of this city, and Horace Munroe, who is past 70 years of age, of California.
Mrs. Turner had been in perfect health until recently, taking active part in family, social, philanthropic and church work, and even during the past few months when she was failing in strength she has attend-

ed frequent social functions and has been active in her home life. Her faculties were all keen and perfect to the last. In June last she attended the graduation exercises of the high school when her grandson, Willis [Wyllis] Dodge, was a member of the class, and June 5 she attended the wedding of her grandson, James M. Reasoner and Miss Bessie Davis. She possessed a character of wonderful sweetness and goodness, kindness and gentleness, which endeared her to all who knew her.

During the past few months when her health has been failing she has been patient and uncomplaining.
Married to James Turner.

In 1843 Mrs. Turner, who was Miss Marian Munroe before her marriage, was married to James Turner, who was then a merchant of Mason, and in 1847 they came to Lansing. Mrs. Turner taught school in Ingham and Clinton counties before her marriage, in the early forties... Mr. and Mrs. Turner were both active in church and philanthropic work and were among the founders of First M. E. church at North Lansing. Mrs. Turner was a member of both the state and county pioneer societies and until the last year attended all the meetings of these societies.

They are Mrs. Marian T. Reasoner, Mrs. C. P. Black and Mrs. F. L. Dodge. The 11 grandchildren surviving her are Sophia, Franklin, Willlis O. [Wyllis], Josephine, and Marian Dodge, children of Mr. and Mrs. F. L. Dodge; Allen Black, son of Judge and Mrs. C. P. Black; James and Scott Turner, of Detroit, son of the late James M. Turner; James T. Reasoner of this city, Rev. Arthur T. Reasoner of Detroit, and Fiske Reasoner of Chicago, sons of Mrs. Marian T. Reasoner. Also two great-grandchildren survive her, children of James Turner of Detroit.

In his *Pioneer Recollections* Dan Mevis mentioned that one of the locust trees planted by Marian could still be seen at their first home on Turner Street, just one door north of the Lansing Brewing Company. He observed that even as she reached the end of her journey, Marian was "in possession of all her faculties apparently and all her remarkable grace and womanly beauty, of body and mind, notwithstanding all these long years of pioneer life with its varied experiences, not excepting the successful raising of one of the grandest families a Christian mother was ever blessed with. Surely she has her reward."[1016]

It cannot help but be supposed that her generation's achievements and those of the Turner's made something more for this world and something better than it would have been without them.

Discussion Themes

1. What were the distinguishing characteristics of the Turner and Dodge families?
2. Discuss the enduring values of the Turner family. Discuss the way you noticed the values of these families passed from generation to generation.
3. Discuss the way Marian Munroe Turner's role as a woman changed in society over the years of her life. Did the women of the family meet their potential?
4. Do you think human nature has changed over the years since the founding of Michigan? For better or for worse? In what ways?
5. Pick one individual in the book whom you admire, discuss the person's character and values and why you admire him or her.
6. How did the industrial revolution impact the people of Lansing over the years?
7. In what ways did economics in the state and country affect the people of Lansing?
8. How did being a capital city make Lansing different from other cities?
9. What are some of the things that Jim Turner might have gone on to do if he had not died at such a young age?
10. What are the ways you have been shaped by the spirit of your time?
11. What are the most important political, social, and economic lessons to be learned from this historical narrative?
12. How does the use of primary source material affect your view of history? Which story based on primary source material did you like best and why?
13. What makes for a meaningful life?
14. What are some of your favorite quotations and why do you like them?
15. How have we evolved on some of the 19th century issues?

Bibliography

Manuscripts, Papers, Abbreviations

AFC Allcott Family Correspondence, 1835-50. East Lansing: Michigan State University Archives and Historical Collections.

BHL Michigan Historical Collections, Bentley Historical Library, University of Michigan

JMT James Munroe Turner: Ann Arbor: BHL.

Mrs James Munroe Turner Collection, photographs: State Archives of Michigan, Department of Natural Resources.

John Tredway Rich Papers. Ann Arbor: BHL.

JWL John W. Longyear Papers. Ann Arbor: BHL.

James Seymour Papers. Ann Arbor: BHL.

HGC Harrison Geer Collection: Ann Arbor: BHL.

Iron Range & Huron Bay: Marquette Regional History Center, J. M. Longyear Research Library.

MHC Michigan Historical Commission. and Michigan Pioneer and Historical Society, Michigan historical collections.

Richard Butler Papers: State Archives of Michigan, Department of Natural Resources.

Quarry and Stone Quarrying folder: Marquette Regional History Center, J. M. Longyear Research Library.

TFS Turner Family Scrapbooks, Lansing: Turner-Dodge House, City of Lansing.

Books and Publications

"Abstracts of Early Probate Records of Ingham County, Michigan, 1838-1839". In Occasional Paper No. 10: Mid-MI Genealogical Society, Lansing, MI.

Adams, Franc L., and Ingham County Pioneer and Historical Society. *Pioneer History of Ingham County*. Lansing, Mich.,: Wynkoop Hallenbeck Crawford company, 1923.

Adams, Pauline, and Emma S. Thornton. *A Populist Assault: Sarah E. Van De Vort Emery on American Democracy, 1862-1895*. Bowling Green, Ohio: Bowling Green State University Popular Press, 1982.

Arthur, Clara. "When the "Gay Nineties" Saw Women in Sober Earnest." *Michigan Women's Club Journal*: Michigan Women's Historical Center and Hall of Fame, 1908.

Author's discussion with Val Berryman, Curator of the Michigan State University Museum, 2004.

Bakerville, Peter. "Sir Joseph Hickson." Dictionary of Canadian Biography Online, 1891-1900.

Ballard, M. D., L. Anna. "Legal Protection for Girls." In Speech to the Michigan Legislature on Age of Consent edited by Women's Christian Temperance Union, 5-10. Chicago: Woman's Temperance Publication Association.

Barber, John Warner, and Henry Howe. Our Whole Country; or, the Past and Present of the United States, Historical and Descriptive. 2 Vols. Cincinnati,: H. Howe, 1861.

Barnard, F. A. American Biographical History of Eminent and Self-Made Men ... Michigan Volume. Cincinnati,: Western biographical publishing co., 1878.

Bates, Octavia William. Municipal Suffrage for Women in Michigan. *The Congress of Women Held in the Woman's Building, World's Columbian Exposition, Chicago, U. S. A., 1893.* edited by Mary Kavanaugh Oldham Eagle. Official ed. 2 Vols. Chicago,: W. B. Conkey company., 1894.

Beal, William James. History of the Michigan Agricultural College : And Biographical Sketches of Trustees and Professors. East Lansing, Mich.: Agricultural college, 1915.

Beale, Joseph Henry, and William Gay. Photos and Picturesque Sketches of American Progress: Comprising Official Descriptions of Great American Cities. The Empire Co-operative Assoc., 1889.

Bingham, S. D. Early History of Michigan, with Biographies of State Officers, Members of Congress, Judges and Legislators. Lansing: Thorp & Godfrey, state printers, 1888. http://name.umdl.umich.edu/BAD6021.

Bordin, Ruth Birgitta Anderson. *Women at Michigan: The "Dangerous Experiment," 1870s to the Present.* Ann Arbor: University of Michigan Press, 1999.

Brintnall, Jan. "Turner-Dodge Estate Site Analysis and Historical Evaluation." Lansing: City of Lansing, 1985.

Bryan, William Jennings. *The First Battle. A Story of the Campaign of 1896.* Chicago,: W. B. Conkey company, 1896.

Campbell, James V. *Outlines of the Political History of Michigan.* Detroit, Mi.: Schober & Co., 1876.

Canada, Dictionary of Canadian Biography/Dictionnaire biographique du. "Sir Joseph Hickson." In Dictionary of Canadian Biography Online, 1891-1900.

Carleton, Will. *Farm Ballads.* New York,: Harper & Brothers, 1874.

Case, Daniel L. "Address to the Democracy of Ingham County." In The Morris Collection, 15. Lansing: CADL, 1856.

Ceasar, Ford Stevens. *The Bicentennial History of Ingham County,* Michigan. s.l.: s.n., 1976.

"Chandler, Zachariah, National Statuary Hall Plaque, 1913-2011." Washington, DC.

Chapman bros. Chicago pub. [from old catalog]. *Portrait and Biographical Album of Ingham and Livingston Counties, Michigan.* Chicago,: Chapman bros., 1891.

"Christmas in an Early Day, Recollections of Two Well Known Lansingites." reprinted in "The History Explorer," Greater Lansing Historical Society, Nov. 2006, Dec. 19, 1896.

Clarke, Lewis. Narrative of Lewis Clarke: Electronic Division. Charlottesville: Stephen Railton; Institute for Advanced Technology in the Humanities: Electronic Text Center, 1998. http://utc.iath. virginia.edu/abolitn/abaulcbt.html.

Clinton County Historical Society (Mich.). *The History of Clinton County, Michigan.* St. Johns, Mich.: Clinton County Historical Society, 1980.

Commission., Michigan Historical. *The State of Michigan Biographies.* Vol. III L-Z, Lansing1924.

Contributors, Wikipedia. "Lansing Board of Water & Light, Http://En.Wikipedia.Org/W/Index. Php?Title=Lansing_Board_of_Water_%26_Light&Oldid=547452857 ": Wikipedia, The Free Encyclopedia accessed May 5, 2013.

"Corr. Abbie Turner to Marian Turner." In Pemberton Family Collection. Berlin: Turner-Dodge House, June 11, 1883.

"Corr. Abbie Turner to Marian Turner." In Pemberton Family Collection. Auburndale: Turner-Dodge House, Feb. 26, 1879.

Cowles, Albert Eugene, and Michigan historical publishing association Lansing Mich. *Past and Present of the City of Lansing and Ingham County, Michigan.* Lansing, Mich.: The Michigan historical publishing association, 1905. http://name.umdl.umich.edu/BAD0934.

Current Literature. edited by Edward Jewitt Wheeler. Vol. 37, Issue 2, NY: Current Literature Publishing Co., 1904.

Cyclopedia of Michigan: Historical and Biographical. New York and Detroit: Western biographical publishing co., 1890.

Daboll, Sherman B., and Dean W. Kelley. *Past and Present of Clinton County, Michigan.* Chicago,: The S. J. Clarke publishing co., 1906.

Darling, Birt, *City in the Forest, the Story of Lansing,* New York, Stratford House, 1950.

DeLand, Charles V. Deland's History of Jackson County, Michigan: Embracing a Concise Review of Its Early Settlement, Industrial Development and Present Conditions. Logansport: B. F. Bowen, 1903.

The Detroit Journal Year-Book for Vol. 1-3. Detroit, Mich.: Detroit Journal Co., 1888.

Detroit Journal. *The Detroit Journal Year-Book.* v. Detroit, Mich.: Detroit Journal Company, 1889.

"'Did You Know?, Lansing State Journal, Date Unknown." edited by "The Gatekeeper Newsletter:" Friends of Historic Meridian, Winter 2007.

"'Do You Remember' Lansing Home-Coming Interview of J. H. Gunnison." reprinted in "The History Explorer," Greater Lansing Historical Society, May 2006, Aug. 25, 1913.

"Do You Remember" and "Homecoming Interviews." reprinted in "The History Explorer," Greater Lansing Historical Society, Mar. 2005, Aug. 15, 1913.

Dodge, Frances Farrand, Bell Farrand Rahn, et. al. "Childhood Memoirs by the Four Farrand Girls." Lansing: State of Michigan Library, c. 1962.

Dunbar, Willis Frederick, and George S. May. *Michigan: A History of the Wolverine State.* 3rd rev. ed. Grand Rapids, Mich.: W.B. Eerdmans Pub. Co., 1995.

Durant, Samuel W. *History of Allegheny Co., Pennsylvania/* Philadelphia: L .H. Everts & co., 1876.

———. *History of Ingham and Eaton Counties,* Michigan, with Illustrations and Biographical Sketches. Philadelphia,: D. W. Ensign & co., 1880.

Eagle, Mary Kavanaugh Oldham. *The Congress of Women Held in the Woman's Building, World's Columbian Exposition,* Chicago, U.S.A., 1893...With Portraits, Biographies and Addresses. Official ed. Philadelphia,: International publishing co., 1895.

Edmonds, J. P. *Early Lansing History.* Lansing: Franklin DeKleine Company, 1944.

Electrical World and Engineer, Vol. 45 New York: Electrical World and Engineer, Inc., April 1, 1905.

Ellis, Franklin. *History of Genesee County,* Michigan with Illustrations and Biographical Sketches. Philadelphia: Everts and Abbott, 1879.

Emery, Sarah E. Van de Vort. *Seven Financial Conspiracies Which Have Enslaved the American People.* American Series. [Rev. ed. Lansing, Mich.: R. Smith & Co., 1894.

Fairle, John Archibald. *The Michigan Constitutional Convention,* Reprinted from Michigan Law Review, Vol. Vi No 7, . May 1908.

"The Farm Journal Illustrated Rural Directory of Ingham County," Michigan. Philadelphia: Wilmer Atkinson Company, 1916.

"Feeding America: The Historic American Cookbook Project." Michigan State University Digital Library, In., http://digital.lib.msu.edu/projects/cookbooks/html/authors/author_lincoln.html.

Foley, John P. *The Jeffersonian Cyclopedia,* a Comprehensive Collection of the Views of Thomas Jefferson. New York & London: Funk & Wagnalls Co., 1900.

Forty-Ninth Annual Report of the Woman's Foreign Missionary Society of the Methodist Episcopal Church. Boston, MA: 581 Boylston Street, Boston, MA, 1918.

Foster, Lille. "Foster/Capper Family Genealogy, Correspondence, August 16, 1857, Theodore Foster to His Sister Lydia Comstock in Wisconsin." http://familytreemaker.genealogy.com/users/k/o/s/ Lille-Koski-CA/(

Fox, Karolena M. "History of the Equal Suffrage Movement in Michigan," *Michigan History Magazine,* 1918.

Frazier, Richard, and David Thomas. *Let the Record Show : A Legal History of Ingham County.* East Lansing, MI: Michigan State University Press, 1997.

Fred. E. Farnsworth, compiled by *Proceedings of the Fourth Annual Meeting of the Michigan Club.* Detroit: Winn & Hammond, 1890.

Fuller, George N., Michigan Pioneer and Historical Society., and Michigan Historical Commission. *Historic Michigan, Land of the Great Lakes.* [Dayton, Ohio]: National Historical Association, 1924.

Fuller, William D., Reporter,. Michigan Reports, Cases Decided in the Supreme Court of Michigan from March 18 to May 20, 1892. Vol. 9, Chicago: Callaghan & Co., 1892.

Gombach Group. "Clarkson Corners Historic District." Cazenovia Library, New York, 2009.

Gordon, Elizabeth Putnam. *Women Torch-Bearers.* Evanston: NWCTU Publishing House, 1924.

Haigh, Henry A. "The Michigan Club." *Michigan History Magazine,* Vol. 4, 1922.

Hecker, Eugene A. A Short History of Women's Rights from the Days of Augustus to the Present Time. 2d ed. Westport, Conn.,: Greenwood Press, 1971.

Hemans, Lawton T., William Lee Jenks, and Michigan Historical Commission. *Life and Times of Stevens Thomson Mason, the Boy Governor of Michigan.* Michigan Historical Publications. Lansing: Michigan Historical Commission, 1920.

Holmden, Floyd. "The Matinee Musicale, 100 Years of Culture." *Lansing Metropolitan,* Spring, 1994.

Homer, Elizabeth Giese, ed. *Michigan Women's Suffrage, a Political History.* Lansing: MI Political History Society and MI Women's Studies Association, Inc., 1995.

Hopkins, Anna. "The History of Lansing Central Union Woman's Christian Temperance Union, 1874-1949, Updated by Mrs. C. C. Ludwig in 1944, and Updated for the Diamond Jubilee Edition by Mrs. H. H. Beeman": CADL, 1889.

Howery, Tim. "Index to Civil War Veterans of Ingham County, MI in Records of Service " MIGenweb, www.migenweb.net/ingham/cwvets.pdf.

Hurd, D. Hamilton. History of Middlesex County, Massachusetts, with Biographical Sketches. Philadelphia,: J. W. Lewis & co., 1890.

Interview by Author with Roderick Mclean, grandson of Abby and Frank Dodge, 2006. Lansing: Turner-Dodge House.

Interview by Author with John Pemberton, great grandson of Abby and Frank Dodge. 2006. Turner-Dodge House.

James, Edward T., Janet Wilson James, Paul S. Boyer, and Radcliffe College. *Notable American Women, 1607-1950; a Biographical Dictionary*. 3 Vols. Vol. 2, Cambridge, Mass.,: Belknap Press of Harvard University Press, 1971.

James Francis Burke, Recorder. *Official Proceeding of the Eleventh Republican National Convention*, St. Louis, 1896. Minneapolis: C. W. Johnson.

Jenks, William Lee. St. Clair County, Michigan, Its History and Its People; a Narrative Account of Its Historical Progress and Its Principal Interests. Chicago and New York,: The Lewis publishing company, 1912.

"John M. Longyear, Landlooker." *In Men of Progress: Embracing Representative Men in Michigan*. Detroit: Evening News Association, 1900.

Johnson, Charles J. "In Memory (of John M. Longyear)." *Michigan Historical Magazine*, 1922.

Jones, Carolyn. "White Oaks (Mount Pleasant) Cemetery, Dansville, Ingham County, Michigan." MiGenWeb Archives, http://files.usgwarchives.net/mi/ingham/dansville/cemetery/m53101.txt.

"Lansing Census 1850." MIGenweb, http://ingham.migenweb.net/.

Lansing Improvement Association. "Capital of Michigan: Advantages, Natural and Acquired, a Center of Trade and Manufacturing." Lansing: W. S. George & Co., Printers and Binders, 1873.

Lansing State Journal. *Lansing and Its Yesterdays*. Lansing 1930.

Lawler, Jerry. "James M. Turner Land Purchases - U. S. Patent Lands, 1872-1899." in unpublished research. Lansing: Turner-Dodge House, 2007.

Lewis, Helen F., Compiler. Pioneer Families of Southeastern Michigan, Especially Ingham Co. And N.Y. Origin. Rhinebeck, N.Y.: Kinship.

Lewis, Kenneth E. *West to Far Michigan: Settling the Lower Peninsula, 1815-1860*. East Lansing: Michigan State University Press, 2001.

Livingstone, William. Livingstone's History of the Republican Party. A History of the Republican Party from Its Foundation to the Close of the Campaign of 1900, Including Incidents of Michigan Campaigns and Biographical Sketches. 2 Vols. Detroit, Mich.,: W. Livingstone, 1900.

Longyear, (M. Dash), John Munro. "A History of the City of Lansing, from the Foundation Thereof Down to the Present Time." Lansing: W. S. George & Co., 1870.

Longyear, Howard. In Corr., 1891: Marquette Regional History Center, J. M. Longyear Research Library.

Longyear, John M. *Landlooker in the Upper Peninsula of Michigan*. edited by Marquette County Historical Society of Michigan Helen Longyear Paul. Second ed. Marquette: John M. Longyear Research Library, 1983.

Longyear, John Munro. "Reminiscences," an unpublished manuscript: Marquette Regional History Center, J. M. Longyear Research Library, 1912.

———. "James M. Turner." In "Reminiscences," unpublished. Marquette: Marquette Regional History Center, J. M. Longyear Research Library, 1912.

"Lucinda Hinsdale Stone." *The Literary Century*, Vol. II May, 1893, No. 13 Ann Arbor.

"March 13, 1879." In Bentley 235-U, Rich, John Tredway, 1841-1926: Michigan Historical Collection, Bentley Historical Library.

"Mastiff, Cynographia Britannica, 1800." In, Mastiff Club of American, http://mastiff.org/, accessed Jan. 27, 2012.

May, Charles S. "Equal Suffrage--New Constitution--Duty of Republican." American Memory, http://memory.loc.gov/rbc/rbpe/rbpe08/rbpe084/0840060c/003r.jpg.

"May Stocking Knaggs." The Literary Century, Vol. II May, 1893, No. 13 Ann Arbor.

McCracken, Stephen Bromley. *State of Michigan: Embracing Sketches of Its History*. Lansing: W. S. George & Co., 1876.

McDan, Mrs. George. "History of the Matinee Musicale, 1894-1919." Lansing: Capitol Area District Library.

Mevis, Daniel S. Pioneer Recollections, Semi-Historic Side Lights on the Early Days of Lansing. Lansing: Robert Smith Printing Company, 1911.

Michigan Framer, "42nd Annual Fair!". *Michigan Farmer*, Sept. 13, 1890.

Michigan Pioneer and Historical Society, Michigan Historical Collection, MPHS:
"Driving the First Stake for the Capitol at Lansing," Rev. F. A. Blades. MPHS Vol. 33, Lansing [etc.]: Michigan Historical Comm. [etc.], 1904.

———. 'James Little,' MPHS. Vol. 7, Lansing [etc.]: Michigan Historical Comm. [etc.], 1886.

———. MPHS. "The Story of Emancipation". Vol. 29, Lansing [etc,] Michigan Historical Comm. [etc.], 1891.

———. MPHS. Vol. 2, Lansing [etc.]: Michigan Historical Comm., 1880.

———. MPHS. Vol. 3, Lansing [etc.]: Michigan Historical Comm., 1881.

———. MPHS. Vol. 4, Lansing [etc.]: Michigan Historical Comm., 1883.

———. MPHS. Vol. 6, Lansing [etc.]: Michigan Historical Comm., 1884.

———. MPHS. Vol. 7, Lansing [etc.]: Michigan Historical Comm., 1886.

———. MPHS. Vol. 13, Lansing [etc.]: Michigan Historical Comm., 1889.

———. MPHS. Vol. 14, Lansing [etc.]: Michigan Historical Comm., 1890

———. MPHS. Vol. 16, Lansing [etc.]: Michigan Historical Comm., 1890.

———. MPHS. Vol. 17, Lansing [etc.]: Michigan Historical Comm., 1892.

———. MPHS. Vol. 22, Lansing [etc.]: Michigan Historical Comm., 1894.

———. MPHS. Vol. 29, Lansing [etc.]: Michigan Historical Comm., 1901.

———. MPHS. Vol. 33, Lansing [etc.]: Michigan Historical Comm., 1904.

———. MPHS. Vol. 34, Lansing [etc.]: Michigan Historical Comm., 1905.

———. MPHS. Vol. 35, Lansing [etc.]: Michigan Historical Comm., 1907.

———. MPHS. Vol. 39, Lansing [etc.]: Michigan Historical Comm., 1915.

Michigan Historical Magazine, Vol. 60: Michigan Historical Comm., 1976.

Michigan Historical Magazine, Vol. 6: Michigan Historical Comm., 1922.

Michigan Legislature. "Joint Documents of the Senate and House of Representatives." Lansing: Thorp & Godfrey, State Printers and Binders, 1887.

Michigan Municipal League. "About the League: History." http://www.mml.org/newsroom/about_history.html.

Michigan, State of. "12th Annual Report of the Secretary of the State Board of Health for Fy Ending Sept. 30,1884." Lansing: W. S. George & Co. State Printers, 1885.

———. "13th Annual Report of the State Board of Agriculture, July 1, 1890-June 1, 1891." Lansing, 1891.

———. "25th Annual Report of the State Board of Agriculture, Oct 1, 1885-Sept. 30,1886." Lansing: Thorp & Godfrey, Printers, 1886.

———. "28th Annual Report of the State Board of Agriculture, July 1, 1888-Jun 30, 1889." Lansing: Thorp & Godfrey, Printers, 1889.

———. "30st Annual Report of the Secretary of the State Board of Agriculture from July 1, 1890 to June 30, 1891." Lansing: Robert Smith and Co., 1891.

———. "31st Annual Report of the Superintendent of Public Instruction." Lansing: John S. Kerr & Co., 1867.

———. "32nd Annual Report of the Superintendent of Public Instruction." Lansing: John S. Kerr & Co., 1868.

———. "Acts of the Legislature of the State of Michigan Passed at the Annual Session of 1843." Detroit, 1843.

———. "Acts of the Legislature of the State of Michigan Passed at the Annual Session of 1849." Lansing: Munger & Patterson, Printers to the State, 1849.

———. "Annual Report of the Auditor General, Dec. 20, 1840, Joint Documents, No. 2." Lansing, 1841.

———. "Annual Report of the Board of State Auditors for the Year 1863." 1863.

———. "Annual Report of the Jackson, Lansing and Saginaw Railroad Company, 1868." In Compilation by the Auditor General of the Annual Reports of the Railroad Corporations in the State of Michigan, for the Year 1868, edited by Auditor General, 67-71. Lansing: State of Michigan.

———. "Annual Report of the Jackson, Lansing and Saginaw Railroad Company, 1869." In Joint Documents of the State of Michigan, for the Year 1870, edited by Auditor General, 90-94. Lansing: State of Michigan, 1869.

———. "Michigan State Agricultural College, Report of the President" In Joint Documents of the State of Michigan, for the Year 1870, edited by Auditor General, Lansing: State of Michigan.

———. "Annual Report of the State Bd of Agriculture, Oct 1 1883 to Sept 30 1884." Lansing: W. S. George & Co. Printers 1884.

———. "Fifth Annual Report of the Commissioner of Railroads for Year Ending Dec. 31, 1876." Lansing: W. S. George & Co. Printers 1877.

———. "First Annual Report of the Board of Control of the House of Correction for Juvenile Offenders, for Fiscal Year Ending November 18,1857." State of Michigan, 1857.

———. "Joint Documents for Annual Session of 1842, Nov. 25, 1842, Nov. 30, 1842, Dec. 7, 1842." Lansing, 1842.

———. "Joint Documents of the State of Michigan for the Year 1879 in Three Volumes." edited by Report of the Chicago and Northeastern Railroad Company. Lansing: W. S. George and Co., 1880.

———. "Journal of the House of Representatives ". Lansing: W. S. George, 1885.

———. "Journal of the House of Representatives, 1887 ". Lansing: Thorp and Godfry, 1887.

———. "Journal of the Senate, 1887." Lansing: Thorp and Godfrey, 1887.

———. "Journal, Constitutional Convention, 1867." Lansing: John A. Kerr and Co., 1867.

———. "Michigan Annual Report of the Commissioner of Mineral Statistics of the State of Michigan for 1881." Lansing: W. S. George, 1882.

———. "Official Directory and Legislative Manual, 1885-86." Lansing: Robert Smith & Co., 1885-86.

———. "Official Directory and Legislative Manual, 1891-92." Lansing: Robert Smith & Co., 1891.

———. "Report of Investigation 8, Geology and Magnetic Data for the Northern Crystal Falls Area." Lansing: State of Michigan Department of Natural Resources, Geological Survey Division, 1970.

———. "The Report of the Superintendent of Public Instruction of the State of Michigan, 1858."Department of Public Instruction, 1859.

———."The Report of the Superintendent of Public Instruction of the State of Michigan, 1859 "Department of Public Instruction,1860.

———. "The Report of the Superintendent of Public Instruction of the State of Michigan, 1889." Department of Public Instruction, 1889.

———. "Report of the Secretary of the State Board of Agriculture, July 1, 1898." Lansing: Robert Smith Printing Co., State Printers and Binders, 1899.

———. "Senate Doc. 30 of 1865, State Treasurer Communication, Giving the Names, Salaries, Etc. Of the Clerks Employed in His Office." 1865.

———. "Journal of the Senate of the State of Michigan, 1867."

———. "Special Schedule of Agriculture of the State of Michigan Census." Lansing, 1894.

Michigan Supreme Court. "William L. Webber, Trustee V. Thomas B. Barry Et Al." In 66 Mich. 127; 33 N. Q. 289; 1887.

Michigan. Governor (1897-1900), Hazen S. Pingree. "Ex-Augural Message of Governor Hazen S. Pingree to the Forty-First Legislature of Michigan January, 1901." Lansing, MI: Wynkoop Hallenbeck Crawford Co., 1900.

MichMarker.com. Michigan Historic Markers Registered Site S0625, Erected 1991 935 North Washington, Lansing, Ingham County.

Millspauh, Arthur Chester. *Party Organization and Machinery in Michigan since 1890.* Baltimore: John Hopkins Press, 1917.

"Minute Book, Nov. 12, 1889-Feb. 18, 1901, B1, F1." In Lansing Industrial Aid Society: State Archives of Michigan, Department of Natural Resources.

Moore, J. Geoffrey. "The Memorial Windows". Lansing: Central United Methodist Church.

"Mrs. S. E. V. Emery." *The Literary Century*, Vol. II May, 1893, No. 13 Ann Arbor.

Meyer, Douglas K. "The Changing Negro Residential Patterns in Lansing, Michigan, 1850-1969." Michigan State University, 1970.

Northrup, Guilford Smith. *Genealogy of Josiah Munroe, Revolutionary Solider.* St. Johns, Mich.,: G. S. Northrup, 1912.

Northwestern Reporter, Jan. 25 – April 26, 1890 Vol. 44: St. Paul West Publishing, 1890.

O'Reilly, Henry. Settlement in the West. Sketches of Rochester; with Incidental Notices of Western New-York. Rochester,: W. Alling, 1838.

Peck, William F. History of Rochester and Monroe County, New York, from the Earliest Historic Times to the Beginning of 1907. 2 Vols. New York and Chicago,: The Pioneer publishing company, 1908.

Piatt, Harriet, "The Middle Years —1910-1940, Lansing's Woman's Club Centennial Observance, Paper Given by Harriet Piatt at the Clubhouse." Lansing Woman's Club, March 29, 1974.

Pierce, Frederick Clifton. Foster Genealogy, Being the Record of the Posterity of Reginald Foster. Chicago: F. C. Pierce, 1899.

Pierson, Arthur. T. Zachariah Chandler: An Outline Sketch of His Life and Public Services. New York: The Post and Tribune Company, 1880.

Pingree, Hazen S. Address of Welcome of Governor H. S. Pingree Delivered at Michigan Club Banquet, Detroit, Michigan, February 22, 1899. "The Duty of the Republican Party in the Present Hour.". Lansing,: R. Smith printing co., state printers and binders, 1899.

———. Facts and Opinions; or, Dangers That Beset Us. Detroit, Mich.,: F. B. Dickerson Co., 1895.

"Pioneers Recall Early Days When City Was Young". reprinted in "The History Explorer," Greater Lansing Historical Society, Jan. 2007, Apr. 16, 1909.

Portrait and Biographical Album of Members of the Legislature, Michigan. Chicago,: Chapman bros., 1883.

Putnam, Daniel. A History of the MI State Normal School at Ypsilanti, MI, 1849-1899. Ypsilanti: The Sharp Tag, Label, & Box Co., 1899.

Reddy, D. D., William First Fifty Years of Cazenovia Seminary 1825-1875, Cazenovia, New York: Nelson & Phillips, 1877.

Reed, George Irving. Bench and Bar of Michigan. Chicago: The Century Publishing and Engraving Co., 1897.

"Report of the President and Directors of the Michigan Central Railroad Company for the Year Ending December 31, 1877." Detroit: Daily Post Book and Tribune Book and Job Printing Establishment, 1878.

"Report of the President and Directors of the Michigan Central Railroad Company for the Year Ending December 31, 1878." Detroit: Daily Post Book and Tribune Book and Job Printing Establishment, 1879.

Reynolds, Cuyler. Hudson-Mohawk Genealogical and Family Memoirs. Vol. 2: Lewis Historical Company, 1911.

Robertson, John. Michigan in the War. Revised Edition ed. Lansing: W. S. George & Co., State Printers and Binders, 1882.

Sarasohn, Vera H., and Stephen B. Sarasohn. Political Party Patterns in Michigan. Detroit: Wayne State University Press, 1957.

Sargent, H. E. In James F. Joy Papers, Box 9. Ann Arbor: Michigan Historical Collection, University of Michigan, May 24, 1874.

Schenck, John S., and Earl De La Vergne. History of Ionia and Montcalm Counties, Michigan. Philadelphia: D. W. Ensign & Co., 1881.

Signor, Isaac Smith, and H. P. Smith. Landmarks of Orleans County, New York. Syracuse,: D. Mason & Company, 1894.

Smith, Mrs. E. C., Mrs. M. W. Howard, and Mrs. N. B. Jones. "Our First Decade, Lansing Woman's Club. Lansing: The Lansing Woman's Club, March 28, 1884."

Smith, William Locke. Historical Sketches of Education in Michigan. Lansing,: W. S. George and Co., state printers and binders, 1881.

———. "Michigan State Reform School." In Historical Sketches of Education in Michigan. iv, Lansing,: W. S. George and Co., state printers and binders, 1881.

Soper, Steve. The "Glorious Old Third" a History of the Third Michigan Infantry, 1855-1927. Old Third Publishing, www.oldthirdpublishing.com). online book.

Sparrow Health System. "Sparrow Women's Association." In http://www.sparrow.org/sparrow-womens-association.

Stanton, Elizabeth Cady, Susan B. Anthony, and Matilda Joslyn Gage. History of Woman Suffrage. 3 Vols. Rochester, N.Y.: Susan B. Anthony, 1887.

Stanton, Elizabeth Cady, Susan B. Anthony, Matilda Joslyn Gage, and Ida Husted Harper. History of Woman Suffrage, 1883-1900, Vol. 4. Vol. 4, Rochester, N. Y.: Susan B. Anthony : Charles Mann.

Stanton, Elizabeth Cady, Theodore Stanton, Harriet Stanton Blatch, Carrie Chapman Catt, and National American Woman Suffrage Association Collection (Library of Congress). *Elizabeth Cady Stanton as Revealed in Her Letters, Diary and Reminiscences.* 2 Vols. New York and London,: Harper & brothers, 1922.

Stein, Stephen J. *The Cambridge History of Religions in America.* New York: Cambridge University Press, 2012. http://dx.doi.org/10.1017/CHOL9780521871105.

Stevens, ed., Albert C. *Cyclopedia of Fraternities.* 2nd ed. New York: E. B. Treat and Company, 1907.

Stiles, T. J. *The First Tycoon : The Epic Life of Cornelius Vanderbilt.* 1st ed. New York: Alfred A. Knopf, 2009.

Stimson, Glen K. "Rail Growth of Michigan's Capital City," *Michigan History Magazine*, Vol. 5, July-Oct., 1921. 461-491.

Stocking, William. *Under the Oaks.* Detroit: The Detroit Tribune, 1904.

Streeter, Floyd Benjamin. Political Parties in Michigan, 1837-1860. An Historical Study of Political Issues and Parties in Michigan from the Admission of the State to the Civil War. Lansing,: Michigan historical commission, 1918.

"Talk Hunting Community." http://www.talkhuntin.com/index.php?topic=32495.0.

Tenney, Harriet A. "The Lansing Woman's Club, the Club's Beginning." The Lansing Woman's Club, April 25, 1890.

Theobald, Mark. "Auto Body Co., 1901-1927," http://auto_body/auto_body.htm, accessed April 18, 2013.

Troester, Rosalie Riegle. "Lucinda Hinsdale Stone: Champion of Women's Education." In *Historic Women of Michigan: A Sesquicentennial Celebration.* Lansing, Mich.: Michigan Women's Studies Association, 1987.

Turner, Frank N., George N. Fuller, and Michigan Pioneer and Historical Society. *An Account of Ingham County from Its Organization. Historic Michigan, Land of the Great Lakes,* George N Fuller. [Dayton, Ohio]: National Historical Association, Inc., 1924.

Turner, James M. In Box, "Turner Lands Corr., 1863 -1906": Marquette Regional History Center, J. M. Longyear Research Library.

———. In Corr. Box T-Z, Dec. 1, 189? to Oct. 1893: Marquette Regional History Center, J. M. Longyear Research Library.

"U. S. Department of Interior Land Office Records." U. S. Department of Land Management, www.glorecords.blm.gov/.

Utley, Henry M., Byron M. Cutcheon, and Clarence Monroe Burton. Michigan as a Province, Territory and State, the Twenty-Sixth Member of the Federal Union. From the Close of the Civil War to the End of the Nineteenth Century. 4 Vols. Vol. 4, New York: The Publishing society of Michigan, 1906.

Weir, Robert E. Unhorse, *Internal Conflict in a Gilded Age Social Movement.* Detroit: Wayne State University Press, 2000.

Wheeler, Mary Sparks. Women's Foreign Missionary Society of the Methodist Episcopal Church with Sketches of the Missionaries. Phillips & Hunt, Cincinnati: Walden & Stowe., 1881.

"When the Everett House Was Erected, Recollections of Theodore E. Potter." reprinted in "The History Explorer," , Greater Lansing Historical Society, Summer 2006, October 4, 1902.

Whitney, Luna M. Hammond. *History of Madison County, State of New York.* Syracuse N.Y.: Truair, Smith & co., printers, 1872.

Wisner, G. Franklin. *The Wisners in America.* Baltimore1878.

Wright, Charles E. "First Annual Report of the Commissioner of Mineral Statistics of the State of Michigan, for 1877-8," Mining Journal Steam Printing House, 1879.

Yost, Edna. *Modern American Engineers.* Philadelphia,: Lippincott, 1952.

Endnotes

Chapter 1

1 Arthur T. Pierson, *Zachariah Chandler: an outline sketch of his life and public services* (New York: The Post and Tribune Company, 1880). 66.

2 2 Harriet Munroe Longyear, State Republican, in TFS, (Lansing: Turner-Dodge House).

3 Ibid.

4 Ibid.

5 Guilford Smith Northrup, Genealogy of Josiah Munroe, revolutionary solider (St. Johns, Mich.,: G. S. Northrup, 1912). 221.

6 Harriet Munroe Longyear, "The Settlement of Clinton County," MHC, 40 vols., vol. 39 (Lansing [etc.]: Michigan Historical Commission [etc.], 1915). 360-64.

7 Kenneth E. Lewis, West to far Michigan : settling the Lower Peninsula, 1815-1860 (East Lansing: Michigan State University Press, 2001). 69.

8 Frank N. Turner, George N.Fuller, and Michigan Pioneer and Historical Society., An Account of Ingham County from its organization, Historic Michigan,Land of the Great Lakes / George N Fuller ([Dayton, Ohio]: National Historical Association, Inc., 1924). 38.

9 MHC, vol. 7 (Lansing [etc.]: Michigan Historical Commission [etc.], 1886). 437.

10 The Inflation Calculator, http://www.westegg.com/inflation/infl.cgi

11 MHC, 39: 360-64; Longyear. TFS.

12 Clinton County Historical Society (Mich.), The History of Clinton County, Michigan (St. Johns, Mich.: Clinton County Historical Society, 1980). 29.

13 MHC, 39: 360-64.

14 Clinton County Historical Society (Mich.), The History of Clinton County, Michigan: 486.

15 Harriet Munro Longyear, MHC, 39: 360-64.

16 Longyear.

17 Harriet Munro Longyear, MHC, 39: 364.

18 Longyear.

19 Harriet Munro Longyear, 39: 364.

20 Clinton County Historical Society (Mich.), The History of Clinton County, Michigan: 474.

21 Ibid., 28.

22 Harriet Longyear, SR 1899. TFS.

23 Harriet Munro Longyear, MHC, 39: 360-64.

24 Sherman B. Daboll and Dean W. Kelley, Past and present of Clinton County, Michigan (Chicago,: The S.J. Clarke publishing co., 1906); Clinton County Historical Society (Mich.), The History of Clinton County, Michigan: 438.

25 State of Michigan, "Special Schedule of Agriculture of the State of Michigan Census," (Lansing1894), 306.

26 Longyear.

27 Betsy Munroe Webber, "Pioneer Life (Munroes in Clinton County)," State Republican, TFS.

28 Samuel W. Durant, History of Ingham and Eaton counties, Michigan (Philadelphia,: D.W. Ensign & co., 1880). 307.

29 Charles V. DeLand, DeLand's History of Jackson County, Michigan: embracing a concise review of its early settlement, industrial development and present conditions, together with interesting reminiscences (Logansport: B. F. Bowen, 1903). 337.

30 Durant, History of Ingham and Eaton counties, Michigan: 308.

31 Ibid.

32 (M. Dash) Longyear, John Munro, A History of the City of Lansing, from the foundation thereof down to the present time (Lansing: W. S. George & Co., 1870). 14-15.

33 Durant, History of Ingham and Eaton counties, Michigan: 308.

34 Ibid., 127.

35 Eugene A. Hecker, A Short History of Women's Rghts from the days of Augustus to the present time. With special reference to England and the United States, 2d ed. (Westport, Conn.,: Greenwood Press, 1971). 174.

36 "Marion M. Turner Passed Away at the Home of Daughter, Mrs. Dodge, Was 93 Years of Age," The State Journal, 1912. TFS.

37 MHC, vol. 16 (Lansing [etc.]: Michigan Historical Commission [etc.], 1890). 429-30.

38 Franc L. Adams and Ingham County Pioneer and Historical Society., Pioneer history of Ingham County (Lansing, Mich.,: Wynkoop Hallenbeck Crawford company, 1923). 780.

39 Ibid., 780-81.

40 James M. Turner, "Inghams' Pioneers, Brave Hearts and Strong Arms Hewed a Capital from a Forest, June 4, 1895," 1985, in TFS.

41 MHC, vol. 6 (Lansing [etc.]: Michigan Historical Commission [etc.], 1884). 293; F. A. Barnard, American biographical history of eminent and self-made men ... Michigan volume (Cincinnati,: Western biographical publishing co., 1878). 77.

42 ———, American biographical history of eminent and self-made men ... Michigan volume: 77.

43 "U. S. Department of Interior Land Office Records," U. S. Department of Land Management, www.glorecords.blm.gov/.

44 Turner, N.Fuller, and Society., An Account of Ingham County: 69-70, 691.

45 Barnard, American biographical history of eminent and self-made men ... Michigan volume: 77.

46 D. D. Reddy, William First Fifty Years of Cazenovia seminary 1825-1875, Cazenovia, New York (New York: Nelson & Phillips, 1877). 48, 84-85.

47 Adams and Ingham County Pioneer and Historical Society., Pioneer history of Ingham County: 5.

48 Ibid., 176.

49 "For Seven Hours the Knights and Their Friends Listened, January 2, 1895 ", in TFS (Lansing: Turner-Dodge House).

50 ———, Pioneer history of Ingham County: 189.

51 Samuel W. Durant, History of Allegheny Co., Pennsylvania (Philadelphia: L.H. Everts & co., 1876). 127.

Chapter 2

52 Luna M. Hammond Whitney, History of Madison County, State of New York (Syracuse N.Y.: Truair, Smith & co., printers, 1872). 229.

53 William F. Peck, History of Rochester and Monroe County, New York, 2 vols. (New York and Chicago,: The Pioneer publishing company, 1908). 738; Isaac Smith Signor and H. P. Smith, Landmarks of Orleans County, New York (Syracuse,: D. Mason & Company, 1894).

54 The Gombach Group, "Clarkson Corners Historic District," (Cazenovia Library, 2009).

55 Henry O'Reilly, Settlement in the West. Sketches of Rochester; with incidental notices of western New-York (Rochester,: W. Alling, 1838).

56 S. D. Bingham, Early History of Michigan, with biographies of state officers, members of Congress, judges and legislators, (Lansing: Thorp & Godfrey, state printers, 1888), http://name.umdl.umich.edu/BAD6021. 578.

57 Peck, History of Rochester and Monroe County, New York, from the earliest historic times to the beginning of 1907: 203, 793.

58 Franklin Ellis, History of Genesee County, Michigan (Philadelphia: Everts and Abbott, 1879). 273.

59 Ibid.

60 Allcott Family Correspondence, 1835-50, (East Lansing: Michigan State University Archives and Historical Collections).

61 Ibid. December 12, 1836, Folder 1

62 Turner, N.Fuller, and Society., An Account of Ingham County: 64.

63 Ibid., 60.

64 Allcott Family Correspondence, 1835-50. April 5, 1837, Folder 1.

65 Lawton T. Hemans, William Lee Jenks, and Michigan Historical Commission., Life and times of Stevens Thomson Mason, (Lansing: Michigan Historical commission, 1920). 317-18.

66 Ibid., 271-90.

67 Ibid., 2710290.

68 , *Rochester Daily Democrat 1837.* June 6, 1837, 2-7.

69 Allcott Family Correspondence, 1835-50, Oct. 31, 1837.

70 Turner, 60.

71 Ibid., 65.

72 Allcott Family Correspondence, 1835-50, Folder 5.

73 Ibid., Folder 6.

74 Ibid.

75 J. E. S., "The Story of a Decade, The Day of Great Enterprises in Michigan, Reminiscences of the WIldcat Banking of the Early Days," in TFS.

76 MHC, 6: 295.

77 Turner, 68.

78 Richard Frazier and David Thomas, Let the record show : a legal history of Ingham County (East Lansing, MI: Michigan State University Press, 1997). 19-21; Samuel W. Durant, History of Ingham and Eaton Counties, Michigan, (Philadelphia,: D. W. Ensign & co., 1880). 110, 24.

79 ———, History of Ingham and Eaton Counties: 122-24.

80 Turner, 68.

81 Durant, History of Ingham and Eaton Counties: 125.

82 State of Michigan, "Acts of the Legislature of the State of Michigan passed at the Annual Session of 1843," (Detroit1843), 213.

83 Durant, History of Ingham and Eaton Counties: 197.

84 Albert Eugene Cowles and Michigan historical publishing association Lansing Mich., Past and present of the city of Lansing and Ingham county, Michigan, (Lansing, Mich.: The Michigan historical publishing association, 1905), http://name.umdl.umich.edu/BAD0934. 54-55; Durant, History of Ingham and Eaton Counties: 122-25.

85 ———, History of Ingham and Eaton Counties: 124.

86 Ibid.

87 Ibid., 127.

88 Ibid., 123.

89 Ibid., 125-26.

90 Adams, 13-14.

91 Durant, 125-26; Turner, 85.

92 ———, An Account of Ingham County: 70.

93 George N. Fuller, Michigan Pioneer and Historical Society., and Michigan Historical Commission., Historic Michigan, Land of the Great Lakes ([Dayton, Ohio]: National Historical Association, 1924). vi, 258.

94 Durant, 122.

95 Ibid., 128.

96 Turner, 66.

97 , The Ingham County Herald 1846., June 25, 1845.

98 Ibid., January 23, 1846.

99 Ibid., June 17, 1846.

100 Peck, History of Rochester and Monroe County, New York, 1907: 203.

101 Daniel S. Mevis, Pioneer Recollections, Semi-Historic Side Lights on the Early Days of Lansing (Lansing: Robert Smith Prining Company, 1911). 177.

102 Durant, 75-76.

103 Ibid., 122.

104 Michigan Historical Commission. and Michigan Pioneer and Historical Society., Driving the First Stake for the Capitol at Lansing, Rev. F. A. Blades, vol. 33, 1904. 17-19.

105 State of Michigan, "The Report of the Superintendent of Public Instruction of the State of Michigan, 1859 " (Department of Public Instruction 1860).

106 Ibid.

107 Turner, 83-84; Michigan, "The Report of the Superintendent of Public Instruction of the State of Michigan, 1859."

108 MHC, 7: 418-19.

109 John Warner Barber and Henry Howe, Our Whole Country; or, The Past and Present of the United States, historical and descriptive., 2 vols. (Cincinnati,: H. Howe, 1861). 1128.

110 Turner, 84.

111 MHC, vol. 29, 1901. 17-19.

112 Durant, 127.

113 Turner, 85.

Chapter 3

114 MHC, 7: 418-19.

115 Turner, 368.

116 Ibid.

117 "The State Journal," (Lansing, Mich.: Robert Smith Print. Co.). April 16, 1909.

118 MHC, 7: 418-19.

119 Turner, 319.

120 Ibid., 89.

121 Cowles, Past and present of the city of Lansing and Ingham county, Michigan.

122 "The State Republican," (Lansing, Mich.: Thorp and Godfrey). Lansing Pioneers column, May 18, 1901, reprinted in History Explorer newsletters of the Greater Lansing Historical Society, January 2008, 4

123 SR, Lansing Pioneers column, May 18, 1901, reprinted in History Explorer newsletters of the Greater Lansing Historical Society, January 2008, 4.

124 "The Lansing Journal," (Lansing, Mich.: George P. Sanford)., October 4, 1909.

125 Barber and Howe, Our Whole Country; or, The Past and Present of the United States: 1129.

126 Durant, History of Ingham and Eaton Counties: ; Cowles and Michigan historical publishing association Lansing Mich., Past and present of the city of Lansing and Ingham county, Michigan. 115.

127 "Commemorative Newspaper Article," 1869, in TFS.

128 Turner., 180-81.

129 Adams. 78.

130 Ibid., 471.

131 Turner, 180-81.

132 Ibid., 180-81.

133 Adams, 591.

134 Durant, 128.

135 Chapman bros., Portrait and Biographical Album of Ingham and Livingston Counties, Michigan (Chicago,: Chapman bros., 1891). 361.

136 Carolyn Jones, "White Oaks (Mount Pleasant) Cemetary, Dansville, Ingham County, Michigan," MiGenWeb Archives, http://files.usgwarchives.net/mi/ingham/dansville/cemetery/m53101.txt.

137 "U. S. Department of Interior Land Office Records".

138 Durant, 329.

139 "Abstracts of Early Probate Records of Ingham County, Michigan, 1838-1839, " in Occasional Paper No. 10 (Mid-MI Genealogical Society, Lansing, MI).

140 Turner, 290.

141 Cowles, 429.

142 "Christmas in an Early Day, Recollections of two well known Lansingites," reprinted in The History Explorer, Greater Lansing Historical Society, Nov. 2006, Dec. 19, 1896.

143 Durant, 126-27.

144 Turner, 73.

145 Ibid., 94.

146 "Lansing Early History: The First Show," Lansing Journal, May 12, 1906.

147 ———, An Account of Ingham County: 86.

148 Ibid.

149 MHC, 7: 419.

150 Joel Warner, "Pioneer Times at the North End," The State Journal, May 9, 1905.

151 Durant, 128; Cowles, 55.

152 Turner, 31.

153 Adams, 28.

154 Ibid., 726.

155 MHC, vol. 34, 1905. 405.

156 Cowles, 88-89.

157 Willis Frederick Dunbar and George S. May, Michigan: a history of the Wolverine State, 3rd rev. ed. (Grand Rapids, Mich.: W.B. Eerdmans Pub. Co., 1995). 134.

158 Adams. 438.

159 Ibid.

160 Dunbar and May, 134.

161 Durant, 210.

162 Adamsl. 438.

163 "'Did You Know,' Lansing State Journal, date unknown," ed. The Gatekeeper Newsletter (Friends of Historic Meridian, Winter 2007).

164 Chapman bros., 775.

165 MHC, 7: 419.

166 Adams. 68.

167 MHC, vol. 3, 1881. 433.

168 Adams. 70.

Chapter 4

169 Turner. 91.

170 Ibid.

171 Harriet Longyear, SR 1899. TFS.

172 MHC, "Driving the First Stake for the Capitol at Lansing," Rev. F. A. Blades, 33. 40-41

173 Ibid., 40-41.

174 Turner. 91.

175 MHC, vol. 2], 1880). 133.

176 "Do you Remember" and "Homecoming Interviews," reprinted in The History Explorer, Greater Lansing Historical Society, Mar. 2005, Aug. 15, 1913.

177 Longyear.

178 Northrup, Genealogy of Josiah Munroe: 354.

179 Pierson, Zachariah Chandler: 73.

180 Floyd Benjamin Streeter, Political Parties in Michigan, 1837-1860. An historical study of political issues and parties in Michigan from the admission of the state to the civil war (Lansing,: Michigan historical commission, 1918). 24.

181 Ibid., 16-17.

182 Ibid.

183 Ibid., 151.

184 Daniel L. Case, "Address to the Democracy of Ingham County," in The Morris Collection (Lansing: CADL, 1856), 10-12.

185 Ibid.

186 Elizabeth Cady Stanton, Susan B. Anthony, and Matilda Joslyn Gage, History of Woman Suffrage, 3 vols. (Rochester, N.Y.: Susan B. Anthony, 1887). 514.

187 Mary Kavanaugh Oldham Eagle, The Congress of Women held in the Woman's building, World's Columbian exposition, Chicago, U.S.A., 1893 ... With portraits, biographies and addresses, Official ed. (Philadelphia,: International publishing co., 1895). 665.

188 Edmonds, Early Lansing History (Lansing: Franklin DeKleine Company, 1944).

189 "Oldest Resident (Daniel L. Case)," in TFS, ed. State Repubican (Lansing: Turner-Dodge House).

190 Michigan Historical Commission. and Michigan Pioneer and Historical Society., vol. 13 (1889). 125.

191 "Oldest Resident (Daniel L. Case)." State of Michigan, "Official Directory and Legislative manual, 1891-92 " (Lansing: Robert Smith & Co., 1891), 185.

192 Durant, 111.
193 Turner, 91.
194 Longyear.
195 James V. Campbell, Outlines of the political history of Michigan (Detroit, Mi.: Schober & Co., 1876). 486.
196 Turner, 101.
197 Longyear, A History of the City of Lansing, 16.
198 Turner, 101.
199 Ibid., 101-04.
200 Ibid., 104.
201 Durant, 126.
202 Chapman bros., 5-46.
203 Durant, 95.
204 "'Do you Remember' Lansing Home-Coming Interview of J. H. Gunnison," reprinted in The History Explorer, Greater Lansing Historical Society, May 2006, Aug. 25, 1913, 95.
205 Durant, 95
206 Dunbar and May, Michigan, 460.
207 MHC, vol. 35, 1907. 489.
208 "Lansing Census 1850," MIGenweb, http://ingham.migenweb.net/.: Chapman bros., 1891. 162
209 Turner, 80.
210 MHC, vol. 14. 194-95.
211 , in John W. Longyear Papers, file correspondence 1850-1854 (Ann Arbor: BHL).
212 Durant, History of Ingham and Eaton Counties: 126.
213 Turner, 69.
214 MHC, 6: 292-95.
215 Durant, History of Ingham and Eaton Counties: 122.
216 "Our Republican Leader, Biographical Sketch of Hon. James M. Turner," 1890, in TFS.
217 Ibid.
218 Turner,175-76.
219 Ibid., 176.
220 Longyear, A History of the City of Lansing, 11-12.
221 Longyear, Reminiscences,1912).
222 MHC, 6: 293.
223 Turner, 176-77.
224 LR, Dec. 15, 1855.
225 Durant, 63.
226 Clinton County Historical Society (Mich.), The History of Clinton County, Michigan: 28.

Chapter 5

227 Michigan, "The Report of the Superintendent of Public Instruction of the State of Michigan, 1859 " 6.
228 Turner, 113.
229 Chapman bros., Portrait and Biographical Album: 384.
230 The Lansing State Journal, Lansing and Its Yesterdays (Lansing1930). 60.
231 "Lansing Pioneers (John N. Bush)," in TFS 1 (Lansing: Turner-Dodge House).
232 "When the Everett House was Erected, Recollections of Theodore E. Potter," reprinted in The History Explorer, Greater Lansing Historical Society, Summer 2006, October 4, 1902.
233 Durant, 111.
234 MHC, 7: 421.
235 Michigan, "The Report of the Superintendent of Public Instruction of the State of Michigan, 1859 " 4-6.
236 ———, "Annual Report of the Auditor General, Dec. 20, 1840, Joint Documents, No. 2," (Lansing1841), 139, 41; ———, "Joint Documents for Annual Session of 1842, Nov. 25, 1842, Nov. 30, 1842, Dec. 7, 1842," (Lansing1842).

237 ———, "Official Directory and Legislative manual, 1891-92 " 525; Turner, 52; "The State Reform School, First Annual Report of the Board of Control," ed. The Lansing State Republican (Lansing, Mich.: Hosmer & Fitch, 1867).

238 State of Michigan, "First Annual Report of the Board of Control of the House of Correction for Juvenile Offenders, for fiscal year ending November 18,1857," Joint Documents of the State of Michigan for the year (State of Michgan, 1857), 39.

239 Lille Foster, "Foster/Capper Family Genealogy, Correspondence, August 16, 1857, Theodore Foster to his sister Lydia Comstock in Wisconsin," http://familytreemaker.genealogy.com/users/k/o/s/ Lille-Koski-CA/(

240 Ibid.

241 Frederick Clifton Pierce, Foster Genealogy, Being the Recor of the Posterity of Reginald Foster (Chicago: F. C. Pierce, 1899). 307-08.

242 Ibid.; LSR, Jan. 3, 1866

243 Adams, 28

244 Michigan, "First Annual Report of the Board of Control of the House of Correction for Juvenile Offenders, for fiscal year ending November 18,1857," 316-17.

245 Ibid., 317.

246 William Locke Smith, "Michigan State Reform School," in Historical sketches of education in Michigan (Lansing,: W. S. George and Co., state printers and binders, 1881), 114-18.

247 Durant, 83; Pierce, Foster Genealogy, Being the Recor of the Posterity of Reginald Foster: 307-08.

248 Michigan, "First Annual Report of the Board of Control of the House of Correction for Juvenile Offenders, for fiscal year ending November 18,1857," 317-18.

249 Smith, "Michigan State Reform School," 119-20.

250 Michigan, "First Annual Report of the Board of Control of the House of Correction for Juvenile Offenders, for fiscal year ending November 18,1857."334-35

251 Ibid., 334-35.

252 Ibid., 241.

253 Daniel Putnam, A History of the MI State Normal School at Ypsilanti, MI, 1849-1899 (Ypsilanti: The Sharp Tag, Label, & Box Co., 1899). 161.

254 William Locke Smith, Historical sketches of education in Michigan.140.

255 Turner, 133-34.

256 Ruth Birgitta Anderson Bordin, Women at Michigan: the "Dangerous Experiment," 1870s to the present (Ann Arbor: University of Michigan Press, 1999). 1-6.

257 Michigan, "The Report of the Superintendent of Public Instruction of the State of Michigan, 1859." 419.

258 Ibid., 96.

259 ———, "The Report of the Superintendent of Public Instruction of the State of Michigan, 1858," (Department of Public Instruction

1859), 420.

260 Durant, 95.

261 Brintnall, "Turner-Dodge Estate Site Analysis and Historical Evaluation," (Lansing: City of Lansing, 1985).

262 MHC, 6: 286.

263 Michigan, "The Report of the Superintendent of Public Instruction of the State of Michigan, 1858."

264 MHC, 6: 286.

265 Michigan, "The Report of the Superintendent of Public Instruction of the State of Michigan, 1858," 123.

266 William James Beal, History of the Michigan Agricultural College. 28.

267 Ibid.

268 Ibid., 29.

269 William Lee Jenks, St. Clair County, Michigan, its history and its people; a narrative account of its historical progress and its principal interests (Chicago and New York,: The Lewis publishing company, 1912). 208-09.

270 Beal, History of the Michigan Agricultural College: 31.

271 Smith, Historical sketches of education in Michigan: 79-80.

272 Michigan, "The Report of the Superintendent of Public Instruction of the State of Michigan, 1859 " 154-55.

273 Ibid., 125-26, 53-60.

274 Ibid., 84.

275 Ibid., 124.

276 Pierson, Zachariah Chandler: 363-64.

277 Beal, History of the Michigan Agricultural College: 398.

278 Ibid., 30.

279 Ibid., 31.

280 Michigan, "The Report of the Superintendent of Public Instruction of the State of Michigan, 1859." 2.

Chapter 6

281 Cowles, 68.

282 "Lansing--A Bit of History," The Lansing State Republican Nov. 7, 1866.

283 SR, Apr. 4, 1909.

284 Turner, 164.

285 Cowles,68.

286 Frazier and Thomas, Let the record show: a legal history of Ingham County: 60.

287 Longyear, A History of the City of Lansing, 23-24.

288 "Farmer's Club, October 1908," in TFS.

289 "'Mother' Clark Helped Many Slaves to Freedom," News Tribune, Detroit, 1890, TFS.

290 Lewis Clarke, Narrative of Lewis Clarke: Electronic Division, (Charlottesville: Stephen Railton; Institute for Advanced Technology in the Humanities: Electronic Text Center, 1998), http://utc.iath.virginia.edu/abolitn/abaulcbt.html. 17-21.

291 Douglas K. Myer. Changing Negro Residential Patterns in Lansing, Michigan, 1850-1859. 51.

292 Streeter, Political Parties in Michigan: 52-53.

293 Ibid., 59-60.

294 Turner,190.

295 Streeter, Political Parties in Michigan: 191.

296 William Stocking, Under the Oaks (Detroit: The Detroit Tribune, 1904). 44.

297 John Rich Scrapbook, JTR. BHL

298 Stocking, Under the Oaks: 49.

299 Ibid.

300 Ibid., 50.

301 MHC, 13: 128.

302 Case, "Address to the Democracy of Ingham County," 8-9.

303 Ibid., 14-15.

304 Streeter, Political Parties in Michigan: 5-6.

305 Case, "Address to the Democracy of Ingham County."

306 SR, April 16, 1909.

307 Campbell, Outlines of the political history of Michigan: 564-65.

308 Ibid.

309 Robson, John, Box 1, file 1, Corr, 11.14.1946 by Robson to James Turner, son of James M. Turner

310 Campbell, Outlines of the political history of Michigan: 565.

311 Pierson, Zachariah Chandler: 51-52.

312 U.S. House of Representatives, Eulogies on the Late Hon. Zachariah Chandler, 1880, 8.

313 SR, Apr. 16, 1909.

314 McCracken, 20-21.

315 "Ex-Gov. Blair Death," Jackson Citizen Patriot,August 8, 1894.

316 Campbell, Outlines of the political history of Michigan: 565-66.

317 Livingstone, 258.

318 Adams, 179.

319 Longyear,13.

320 Ibid. 40.

321 Ibid., 259.

322 MHC, "The Story of Emancipation", vol. 29, 1891. 599.

323 Darling, City in the Forest, 48.

324 Box 1, Corr. Jan. 2, 1864. JWL.

325 Tim Howery, "Index to Civil War Veterans of Ingham County, MI in Records of Service " MIGen-web, www.migenweb.net/ingham/cwvets.pdf.

326 Longyear.18-19.

327 "Oldest Resident (Daniel L. Case)."

328 Box 1, Corr. Feb. 7, 1865. JWL.

329 MHC, 13: 127.

330 "Dwight S. Smith," in TFS.

331 SR, Apr. 16, 1909.

332 "The State Republican."

333 Barnard, American biographical history of eminent and self-made men ... Michigan volume. 75.

334 SR, Oct. 10, 1866.

335 State of Michigan, "Senate Doc. 30 of 1865, State Treasurer communication, giving the names, salaries, etc. of the clerks employed in his office," (1865).

336 ———, "Annual Report of the Board of State Auditors for the year 1863," (1863).

337 Adams, 155.

Chapter 7

338 Turner, 368.

339 John Robertson, Michigan In the War, Revised Edition ed. (Lansing: W. S. George & Co., State Printers and Binders, 1882). 119.

340 Ibid., 74.

341 McCracken, 22

342 "Highly Important! The President Shot! Secretary Seward Attacked," 1865, in TFS.

343 LSR , Oct. 10, 1866

344 "Appeal to the Women of America," Lansing State Republican, Aug. 15, 1872; MHC, 35: 506-07.

345 George Sanford, "Mr. Horatio Seymour," Lansing State Republican, Oct. 31, 1866.

346 "Appeal to the Women of America."

347 "The State Republican." Feb. 20, 1867

348 Edward T. James et al., Notable American women, 1607-1950; a biographical dictionary, 3 vols., vol. 2 (Cambridge, Mass.,: Belknap Press of Harvard University Press, 1971). 421.

349 ed. Stevens, Albert C., Cyclopedia of Fraternities, 2nd ed. (New York: E. B. Treat and Company). 367.

350 Pierson, Zachariah Chandler. 381-382.

351 Turner, 135.

352 "Generic," Lansing Republican. Jan. 1, 1856.

353 DeLand, History of Jackson County: 307-08.

354 Turner, 135-36.

355 Ibid.

356 MHC, 2: 133. "Address of O.A. Jenison, on the Occasion of his Presenting Certain Articles to the Society" Read Feb. 7, 1878.

357 Adams, 155.

358 Lewis, West to far Michigan : settling the Lower Peninsula, 1815-1860: 298-300.

359 Barnard, American biographical history of eminent and self-made men ... Michigan volume: 77.

360 "Oldest Resident (Daniel L. Case)."

361 Turner, 421.

362 MHC, 7: 421.

363 State of Michigan, "Annual Report of the Jackson, Lansing and Saginaw Railroad Company, 1868," in Compilaion by the Auditor General of the Annual Reports of the Railroad Corporations in the State of Michigan, for the Year 1868.

364 "The Nominee for Senator," The Lansing State Republican, Oct. 10, 1866.

365 Livingstone, Livingstone's History of the Republican Party: 259.

366 "Appeal to the Women of America." 0ct.10, 1866

367 Ibid. Jan. 14, 67.

368 State of Michigan, "Journal, Constitutional Convention, 1867," (Lansing: John A. Kerr and Co., 1867), 378.

369 Ibid., 471.

370 "The State Republican." Apr. 1, 1869.

371 Charles S. May, "Equal Suffrage--New Constitution--Duty of Republican," American Memory, http://memory.loc.gov/rbc/rbpe/rbpe08/rbpe084/0840060c/003r.jpg.

372 "Appeal to the Women of America." Feb.23, 1868.

373 "Oldest Resident (Daniel L. Case)."

374 Barnard, American biographical history of eminent and self-made men ... Michigan volume: 77.

375 "Appeal to the Women of America." Feb. 6, 1867.

376 State of Michigan, "31st Annual Report of the Superintendent of Public Instruction," (Lansing: John S. Kerr & Co., 1867), 55.

377 Ibid.; ———, " 32nd Annual Report of the Superintendent of Public Instruction," (Lansing: John S. Kerr & Co., 1868), 78-79.

378 "Appeal to the Women of America." LSR Feb. 20, 1867.

379 ———, "Journal, Constitutional Convention, 1867," 105-06.

380 ———, "31st Annual Report of the Superintendent of Public Instruction," 226.

381 Ibid., 225-26.

382 Ibid., 225-29.

383 Ibid., 181.

384 Ibid., 191.

385 ———, "32nd Annual Report of the Superintendent of Publi ciety.c Instruction," 191-92.

386 MHC, vol. 17,1892. 101.

387 MHC———, Michigan historical collections, 6: 288.

388 Turner, 134.

389 Ibid.

390 "Michigan State Agricultural College, Report of the President" In Joint Documents of the State of Michigan, for the Year 1870. 278.

391 Ibid., 277-79.

392 Ibid. 279.

393 Beal, History of the Michigan Agricultural College: 151.

394 "Men and Women," Lansing State Republican July 18, 1972.

395 Longyear, 22.

Chapter 8

396 "The Nominee for Senator." LSR, Oct. 10, 1866.

397 State of Michigan, "Senate Journal, 1867," MI Joint Documents.

398 "Ionia and Lansing Railroad," The Lansing State Republican, Oct. 17, 1866.

399 Barnard, American biographical history of eminent and self-made men ... Michigan volume: 14-15; John S. Schenck and Earl De La Vergne, History of Ionia and Montcalm Counties, Michigan (Philadelphia: D. W. Ensign & Co., 1881).

400 Dunbar and May, Michigan: a history of the Wolverine State: 13.

401 Bingham, Early History of Michigan, with biographies of state officers, members of Congress, judges and legislators. 646; Durant, 126-27.

402 ———, History of Ingham and Eaton Counties: 97.

403 Bingham, Stephen D., "The Vanderbilt Monopoly," The Lansing State Republican, April 16, 1868.

404 Ibid.

405 Ibid.

406 State of Michigan, "Annual Report of the Jackson, Lansing and Saginaw Railroad Company, 1869," in Joint Documents of the State of Michigan, for the Year 1870, ed. Auditor General (Lansing: State of Michigan, 1869).

407 "Obituary of James Turner," The Ingham County News, 1869, TFS.

408 "His Last Long Sleep," 1896. TFS.

409 "Appeal to the Women of America."

410 Inflation Calculator, http://www.westegg.com/inflation/

411 Bingham, Stephen D., "Ingham County Income," The Lansing State Republican, April 16, 1868.

412 Bingham, Early History of Michigan, with biographies of state officers, members of Congress, judges and legislators. 595.

413 "Mark Twain, His Open Letter to Com. Vanderbilt," Lansing State Republican, Mar. 11, 1869.

414 "Lansing State Republican," Sept. 24, 1868.

415 Ibid.

416 "North Lansing Items," Lansing State Republican, Dec. 31, 1868.

417 Ibid.

418 Interview by author of Patty Pemberton, TD

419 , The Ingham County News Oct. 14 1869; ibid.

420 Barnard, American biographical history of eminent and self-made men ... Michigan volume: 77.

Chapter 9

421 Geneva Wiskeman, "Draft Report, Turner-Dodge Master Plan - Phase I."

422 Dunbar and May, 460.

423 "Oldest Resident Died Last Night, Mrs. Marion Turner," 1912, in TFS.

424 Turner, 316.

425 "Death of Isaac M. Crane," Lansing Republican, June 4. 1881.

426 "Sojourner Truth," Lansing State Republican, July 2, 1877.

427 Ibid.

428 "An Eloquent Nominating Speech and a Good Second," in TFS.

429 "Oldest Resident Died Last Night, Mrs. Marion Turner."TFS, 1912.

430 Franc Gardner, "Our Cause (Lansing Industrial Aid Society)," in TFS.

431 Ibid.

432 Ibid.

433 Ibid.

434 "Father Little," Lansing State Republican, in TFS.

435 MHC, 'James Little,' vol. 7, 1886. 438-444.

436 "Father Little."

437 ibid.

438 ———, 'James Little,' Michigan historical collections, 7: 438-44.

439 ———, Michigan historical collections, 39: 7.

440 Durant, History of Ingham and Eaton Counties.

441 MHC, 2: 7.

442 Ibid.

443 ———, Michigan historical collections, 34: 1.

444 Durant, History of Ingham and Eaton Counties.

445 Dunbar and May, Michigan: a history of the Wolverine State: 141.

446 Lansing Improvement Association, "Capital of Michigan: Advantages, Natural and Acquired, A Center of Trade and Manufacturing," 5.

447 "Drought and FIres," Lansing State Republican, Aug. 31, 1871.

448 "A Midnight FIre," Lansing State Republican, Oct. 5, 1871.

449 Utley, Michigan as a Province, Territory and State, vol. 4, From the Close of the Civil War to the End of the Nineteenth Century, 77-80.

450 "The Lansing Journal," Feb. 20, 1867 Warning About Over-lumbering.

451 "Forest Fires," Lansing State Republican, Oct. 12, 1871.

452 "Help Our Own," Lansing State Republican, Oct. 19, 1871.

453 "Lansing Republican," Oct. 16, 1871.

454 "Ladies Relief Society," Lansing Republican, Oct. 19, 1871.

455 "One box of bedding," Lansing Republican 1871.

456 "Aid for Manistee," Lansing State Republican, Oct. 19, 1871.

457 "Forest Fires." LSR, Oct. 12, 1871.

458 "Saved by Heroism," Lansing State Republican, Nov. 26, 1871.

459 "An Extra Session," Lansing State Republican, Nov. 2, 1871.

460 Elizabeth Putnam Gordon, Women Torch-Bearers (Evanston: NWCTU Publishing House, 1924). 70.

461 Longyear, "James M. Turner," in Reminiscences, 4.

462 Gordon, Women Torch-Bearers: 13.

463 Anna Hopkins, "The History of Lansing Central Union Woman's Christian Temperance Union, 1874-1949, updated by Mrs. C. C. Ludwig in 1944, and updated for the Diamond Jubilee Edition by Mrs. H. H. Beeman " (CADL, 1889).

464 Ford Stevens Ceasar, The Bicentennial history of Ingham County, Michigan (s.l.: s.n., 1976). 280-81.

465 "Temperance in Michigan," The New York Times, May 20, 1877.

466 Ibid.

Chapter 10

467 Eagle, The Congress of Women: 664.

468 "The First Woman Voter," Lansing State Republican, June 15. 1871.

469 "Mrs. M. Adele Hazlett," Lansing State Republican, Nov. 30, 1871.

470 "Mrs. Hazlett Speech," Lansing State Republican, Sept. 19, 1872.

471 "Lansing State Journal title unknown," (Lansing, Mich).

472 "Repudiates Greeley," The State Republican, Aug. 2, 1872.

473 "Appeal to the Women of America."

474 Ibid.

475 "Mrs. Hazlett Speech."

476 "Unanimously Against Sumner," Lansing Republican, Aug. 3, 1872.

477 "Colored Men Vote," Lansing Republican, Aug. 15, 1872.

478 "Brevities," Lansing Republican, Oct. 10, 1872.

479 "Fred Douglass' Urgent Appeal," Lansing State Republican, Aug. 22, 1872.

480 "Speech of Hon. D. L. Case," Lansing State Republican, Oc. 3, 1872.

481 ———, The Congress of Women: 664-65.

482 Elizabeth Cady Stanton et al., Elizabeth Cady Stanton as revealed in her letters, diary and reminiscences, 2 vols. (New York and London,: Harper & brothers, 1922). 155.

483 Rosalie Riegle Troester, "Lucinda Hinsdale Stone: Champion of Women's Education," in Historic women of Michigan : a sesquicentennial celebration (Lansing, Mich.: Michigan Women's Studies Association, 1987), 41-58.

484 "Lucinda Hinsdale Stone," The Literary Century, Vol. II May, 1893, No. 13 Ann Arbor. 387.

485 Harriet A. Tenney, "The Lansing Woman's Club, The Club's Beginning," (The Lansing Woman's Club, April 25, 1890).

486 Ibid.

487 Ibid.

488 "Hattie Seymour," Lansing March 1867.

489 "Brevities." SR

490 Mary Sparks Wheeler, Women's Foreign Missionary Society of the Methodist Episcopal Church with Sketches of the Missionaries (Phillips & Hunt, Cincinnati: Walden & Stowe., 1881). 128-31.

491 Forty- ninth Annual Report of the Woman's Foreign Missionary Society of the Methodist Episcopal Church, (Boston, MA: 581 Boylston Street, Boston, MA, 1918). 6.

492 Mrs. E. C. Smith, Mrs. M. W. Howard, and Mrs. N. B. Jones, Our First Decade, Lansing Woman's Club (Lansing: The Lansing Woman's Club, March 28, 1884). 22-26.

493 Tenney, "The Lansing Woman's Club, The Club's Beginning."

494 "Eagle News," Clinton County Independent, Jan. 10, 1884.

495 Adams,62-69.

496 Chapman bros.. 677-87.

497 Hopkins, "The History of Lansing Central Union Woman's Christian Temperance Union."

498 "blurb," State Republican, Sept. 6, 1886.

499 "Man's Inhumanity to Man," State Republican, June 11, 1887.

500 "The State," State Republican, April 22, 1887.

501 "Young girls 'ruiined, Ohio," State Republican, January 23, 1886; ibid.

502 "Brutal outraegeous," State Republican, June 29, 1887.

503 State of Michigan, "Journal of the House of Representatives, 1887 " (Lansing: Thorp and Godfry, 1887). 444.

504 "Worse than the Klu Klux Klan," State Republican, June 29, 1887.

505 ———, "Journal of the House of Representatives, 1887". 1086-87.

506 Ibid. 261.

507 Chapman bros., Portrait and Biographical Album. 677-687.

508 M. D. Ballard, , L. Anna, "Legal Protection for Girls," in Speech by Ann Ballard to the Michigan Legislature on Age of Consent ed. Women's Christian Temperance Union (Chicago: Woman's Temperance Publication Association).

509 "The State Republican," (Lansing, Mich.: Thorp and Godfrey, July 7, 1887).

Chapter 11

510 "Our Republican Leader, Biographical Sketch of Hon. James M. Turner."

511 Ibid.

512 Ibid.

513 Turner, 324-325.

514 Longyear, 85.

515 Jr. Sidney Corbett, Editor and Publisher, "The Critic, Aug 23 1890," in JMT BHL..

516 Turner, 324-325.

517 Longyear, Landlooker in the Upper Peninsula of Michigan, 168.

518 Charles J. Johnson, "In Memory (of John M. Longyear)," Michigan Historical Magazine 1922.

519 Longyear; ibid., 199.

520 Ibid.

521 ,in Quarry and Stone Quarrying folder (Marquette Regional History Center, J. M. Longyear Research Library).

522 Frank, 60.

523 Longyear, 40.

524 Northrup, Genealogy of Josiah Munroe. 228.

525 "untitled," Lansing Journal, Feb. 21, 1902.

526 "Our Republican Leader, Biographical Sketch of Hon. James M. Turner."

527 Ibid.

528 Ibid.

529 Frances Farrand Dodge, , Bell Farrand Rahn, et. al., "Childhood Memoirs by the Four Farrand Girls," (Lansing: State of Michigan Library, c. 1962).

530 Edna Yost, Modern American Engineers (Philadelphia,: Lippincott, 1952). 61-62.

531 "The Republican Leader, Sept. 18, 1890, J. N. Foster, Proprietor, St. Louis, MI," in JWL BHL.

532 "Railroad Monopolies," Lansing Republican, June 22, 1871.

533 Ibid.

534 Ibid.

535 Ibid.

536 Ibid.

537 T. J. Stiles, The first tycoon : the epic life of Cornelius Vanderbilt, 1st ed. (New York: Alfred A. Knopf, 2009). 568-569.

538 Ibid.

539 MHC,.,vol. 22, 1894. 295-296.

540 State of Michigan, "Fifth Annual Report of the Commissioner of Railroads for year ending Dec. 31, 1876," (Lansing: W.S. George & Co. Printers 1877). 509-512.

541 William D. Fuller, Reporter,, Michigan Reports, Cases Decided in the Supreme Court of Michigan from March 18 to May 20, 1892, vol. 9 (Chicago: Callaghan & Co., 1892). 230.

542 Ibid. 174-175.

543 Glen K. Stimpson. "Rail Growth of Michigan's Capital City," Michigan History Magazine, Vol. 5, July-Oct., 1921. 481.

544 "Was Sudden! James M. Turner of Lansing Dies at Alma, Lansing, Mich. Special Telegram, July 1896," in TFS.

545 Michigan Historical Magazine, Vol., vol. 6 (Michigan Historical Commission, 1922). 253.

546 H. E. Sargent, in James F. Joy Papers, Box 9 (Ann Arbor: Michigan Historical Collection, University of Michigan, May 24, 1874). BHL

547 Report of the President and Directors of the Michigan Central Railroad Company for the Year Ending December 31, 1877, (Detroit: Daily Post Book and Tribune Book and Job Printing Establishment, 1878).

548 Report of the President and Directors of the Michigan Central Railroad Company for the Year Ending December 31, 1878, (Detroit: Daily Post Book and Tribune Book and Job Printing Establishment, 1879). 7.

549 "The Grand Trunk Railroad and Vanderbilt," Boston Journal, Sept. 27, 1878, Reprinted in the Montreal Gazette Oct. 2 , 1878.

550 Peter Bakerville, "Sir Joseph Hickson," (Dictionary of Canadian Biography Online, 1891-1900).

551 Northwestern Reporter, Jan. 25 – April 26, 1890 vol. 44 (St. Paul West Publishing, 1890).

552 ———, "Sir Joseph Hickson." 175-78.

553 Northwestern Reporter, Jan. 25 – April 26, 1890 44. 178.

554 "Governor Turner, The Appellation by Which Hon. James M. Turner will be Known, Sept. 27, 1890," in JMT BHL.

555 Jerry Lawler, "James M. Turner Land Purchases - U. S. Patent Lands, 1872-1899," in Unpublished Research (Lansing: Turner-Dodge House, 2007).

556 "Consolidation of Turner and Case," Lansing Republican, March 1, 1878.

557 Turner, 338.

558 "Michigan Condensed Milk Company, Lansing Republican, March 27,1889," in JMT BHL.

559 Turner, 338.

560 "In political matters," in TFS.

561 "Sidewalk Glimpses, Lansing Republican, September 17, 1886," in JMT BHL.

562 , in Mrs James Munroe Turner Collection, photographs (State Archives of Michigan, Department of Natural Resources).

563 "Conservatory Building Laden With City History," Lansing State Journal, June 5, 1959

564 Ibid.

565 "blurb, The building will have 44 feet front," Lansing Republican November 15, 1878.

566 Cowles, 87.

567 "Death of Isaac M. Crane."

568 Chapan bros., 267-68.

569 Northwestern Reporter, Jan. 25 – April 26, 1890 44. 174-175.

570 "Supplement," Charlotte Tribune Sept. 27, 1890.

571 Ibid.

572 Northwestern Reporter, Jan. 25 – April 26, 1890 44. 174.

573 "Supplement." Charlotte Tribune Sept. 27, 1890.

574 Northwestern Reporter, Jan. 25 – April 26, 1890 44. 180.

575 "Every Fabrication Torn to Tatters, Times and Expositor, Oct. 6, 1890," in JMT BHL.

576 Tom Applegate, "The services of Mr. Turner, Times and Expositor, Adrian, Oct. 3, 1890," in JMT BHL.

577 Cowles, 108.

578 Tom Applegate, "McElroy's Misstatements, Times and Expositor, Oct. 2, 1890," in JMT (Adrian: BHL); "Gov; Luce Talks, The Telegram-Hearld, Oct. 5, 1890 ", JMT BHL.

579 Cowles, 110.

580 Ibid.

581 Ibid.

582 Ibid. 111.

583 "A Significant Straw," in JMT, ed. State Republican (Lansing: an, Oct. 6, 1890). JMT BHL.

584 Tom Applegate, "Truth Tells, James M.Turner's Manly Answer to McElroy, Times and Expositor, Adrian, Oct. 7, 1890," in JMT BHL.

585 State of Michigan, "12th Annual Report of the Secretary of the State Board of Health for FY ending Sept. 30,1884," (Lansing: W. S. George & Co. State Printers, 1885). 265.

586 "Another Big Enterprise for the Capital City," State Republican, Jan. 25, 1886.

587 Tom Applegate, "Applegate, I cannot remember the date, The Sunday News," Oct. 5, 1890. JMT BHL.

588 "The resolution to this effect, Daniel Case," Oct. 3 1890, ed. Detroit Journal. JMT BHL.

589 "McElroy endorsed Mr. Turner's vouchers," ed. Telegram-Herald , Oct. 5, 1890). JMT BHL.

590 "Time to Speak Up, A Terrific Attack Upon Candidate Turner by a Fellow Republican," Lansing Journal, Oct. 3, 1890 Oct. 3 1890.; Cuyler Reynolds, Hudson-Mohawk Genealogical and Family Memoirs, vol. 2 (Lewis Historical Company, 1911). 567-568.

591 McCracken, 72.

592 State of Michigan, "Michigan Annual Report of the Commissioner of Mineral Statistics of the State of Michigan for 1881," (Lansing: W. S. George, 1882). 157-158.

593 Ibid.

594 "Corr. from James M. Turner to Chas. M. Sligh, July 21, 1894," in Sligh Family Papers, Box 2, JMT BHL.

595 James M. Turner, in Corr. Box T-Z, Dec. 1, 189? to Oct. 1893 (Marquette Regional History Center, J. M. Longyear Research Library).

Chapter 12
596 Durant, History of Ingham and Eaton Counties.142.

597 D. Hamilton Hurd, History of Middlesex County, Massachusetts, with biographical sketches of many of its pioneers and prominent men (Philadelphia,: J. W. Lewis & co., 1890).232.

598 Current Literature, ed. Edward Jewitt Wheeler, vol. 37, Issue 2 (NY: Current Literature Publishing Co., 1904).

599 "Corr. Abbie Turner to Marian Turner," in Pemberton Family Collection (Auburndale: Turner-Dodge House, Feb. 26, 1879).

600 "Feeding America: The Historic American Cookbook Project," http://digital.lib.msu.edu/projects/cookbooks/html/authors/author_lincoln.html.

601 "Interview by author with Patty Pemberton, 2000," in TFS.

602 "Corr. Abbie Turner to Marian Turner," in Pemberton Family Collection (Berlin: Turner-Dodge House, June 11, 1883).

603 "blurb," Lansing Republican, June 12, 1883 June 12, 1883.

604 ; Chapman bros., 322-23.

605 "Lansing's Pride" SR, TFS.

606 Chapman bros., 322-23.

607 State of Michigan, "Official Directory and Legislative manual, 1885-86," (Lansing: Robert Smith & Co., 1885-86). 572.

608 Ibid.

609 Beale and Gay, Photos and Picturesque sketches of American progress: comprising official descriptions of Great American Cities (The Empire Co-operative Assoc., 1889). 444.

610 Bingham, Early History of Michigan, with biographies of state officers, members of Congress, judges and legislators. 444.

611 Robert E. Weir, Unhorse, Internal Conflict in a Gilded Age Social Movement (Detroit: Wayne State University Press, 2000). 47-50.

612 "Knights of Labor, the Annual Convention Being Held at Hamilton, Canada, ST," State Republican, Oct. 7, 1885.

613 "Criminal," Lansing Republican, Aug. 19, 1885.

614 "Strike of Workmen Throughout the Saginaw Valley," New York Times, July 7,1885.

615 Beale and Gay, Photos and Picturesque sketches of American progress. 444.

616 "blurb." LR, June 12, 1883.

617 "Personal, Column," State Republican, Jan. 19, 1886.

618 "Justice has Triumphed," State Republican, Jan. 23, 1886.

619 "Pinkertons," Lansing Republican, July 15, 1885.

620 George Irving Reed, Bench and Bar of Michigan (Chicago: The Century Publishing and Engraving Co., 1897). 115-17.

621 "Miscellaneous," Lansing Republican, Aug. 19, 1885.

622 Michigan Supreme Court, "William L. Webber, Trustee v. Thomas B. Barry et al," in 66 Michi. 127; 33 N. Q. 289; (1887).

623 Reed, Bench and Bar of Michigan. 475.

624 Michigan Supreme Court, "William L. Webber, Trustee v. Thomas B. Barry et al."

625 Ibid.

626 Ibid.

627 blurb, "It is safe to say," State Republican, June 11, 1887.

628 "Pulse of the People," State Republican, June 13, 1887.

629 "That evening the people of Lansing celebrated," Times and Expositor, June 13, 1887.

630 State of Michigan, "Journal of the Senate, 1887," (Lansing: Thorp and Godfrey, 1887).1850-1853.

631 Ibid. 1854.

632 ———, "Journal of the House of Representatives, 1887". 1565-1817.

633 "blurb, Dakin," State Republican, April 25, 1887; ibid.

634 Ibid.

635 "Dakin Dangling, In Suspense as to the Outcome of His Trial," (Lansing, Mich.: Thorp and Godfrey).

636 ———, "Journal of the House of Representatives, 1887". 1565-66.

637 "blurb, Dakin." SR, April 26, 1887.

638 ———, "Journal of the House of Representatives, 1887". 1726.

639 Ibid.

640 Ibid. 1727-1734, 1770-71.

641 Ibid. 1770-71.

642 Ibid. 1786-87.

643 "Don't Want Him Anymore," SR, April 29, 1887.

644 Ibid.

645 Michigan, "Journal of the Senate, 1887." 1860.

646 G. Franklin Wisner, The Wisners in America (Baltimore1878). 169.

647 "blurb, Messrs. Frank L. Dodge and Isaac Lederer," State Republican, July 13, 1887.

648 "blurb, Messrs. Frank L. Dodge and Isaac Lederer, et. al. to Lake Superior," State Republican, July 16, 1887.

649 "A Brilliant Wedding," Nov. 20, 1888, in TFS (Turner-Dodge House.

650 "He is an ex-member of the Legislature," in TFS (Turner-Dodge House).

Chapter 13

651 "blurb, Hon. James M. Turner swore by all the gods, Evening News, March 29, 1889," in JMT BHL.

652 "blurb, This is not the first time, Lansing Journal, March 29, 1889," in JMT BHL

653 Turner, 165.

654 "The Record," State Republican, March 24, 1890.

655 "Sprindale Stock Farm, The News, c March 1890," in JMT BHL.

656 State of Michigan, "13th Annual Report of the State Board of Agriculture, July 1, 1890-June 1, 1891," (Lansing1891). 407.

657 Beal, History of the Michigan Agricultural College. 49.

658 "Author's discussion with Val Berryman, curator of the Michigan State Univeristy Museum, 2004".

659 State of Michigan, "Annual Report of the State Bd of Agriculture, Oct 1 1883 to Sept 30 1884," (Lansing: W.S. George & Co. Pringers 1884). 337.

660 "Our Republican Leader, Biographical Sketch of Hon. James M. Turner."

661 "New York Herald, European Edition, Paris, March 1, 1890," in JMT BHL.

662 Laura Barnes, "Springdale Farm, Ingham County Republican, September 18, 1890," in TFS (Turner-Dodge House)..

663 "blurb, Springdale farm received an addition ", State Republican, April 21, 1891.

664 "Mastiff, Cynographia Britannica, 1800," Mastiff Club of American, http://mastiff.org/, accessed Jan. 27, 2012.

665 State of Michigan, "25th Annual Report of the State Board of Agriculture, Oct 1, 1885-Sept. 30,1886," (Lansing: Thorp & Godfrey, Printers, 1886). 286.

666 "Mr. Turner is Not Sanguine," State Republican, Jan. 30, 1886.

667 "In Excellent Shape, Times and Expositor, Oct. 9, 1889," in JMT BHL.

668 ———, "28th Annual Report of the State Board of Agriculture, July 1, 1888-Jun 30, 1889," (Lansing: Thorp & Godfrey, Printers, 1889). 558-66

669 "A New Route," State Republican, Aug. 3. 1889.

670 "State Fair Grand Stand," State Republican, Aug. 29, 1889.

671 ———, "28th Annual Report of the State Board of Agriculture, July 1, 1888-Jun 30, 1889." 26.

672 "State Fair, State Republican, Sept. 12, 1889," in JMT BHL.

673 ———, "30st Annual Report of the Secretary of the State Board of Agriculture from July 1, 1890 to June 30, 1891," (Lansing: Robert Smith and Co. , 1891). 407-10.

674 Ibid.

675 "42nd Annual Fair!," Michigan Farmer, Sept. 13, 1890.

676 "Exit the Mayor," Lansing Journal, May 9, 1890.

677 Ibid.

678 "Turner Has a Cane, The Detroit Free Press, May 4, 1890," in JMT BHL.

679 Sarah E. Van de Vort Emery, Seven Financial Conspiracies which have Enslaved the American People, [Rev. ed., American series (Lansing, Mich.: R. Smith & Co., 1894). 6.

680 "Big Four," The New York Times, April 24, 1892.

681 Ibid.

682 "He is a man of business, The Mining Journal, March 6, 1890," in JMT BHL.

683 Tom Applegate, "Then his friends said, Times and Expositor, Feb. 25, 1890," in JMT BHL.

684 Vera H. Sarasohn and Stephen B. Sarasohn, Political Party Patterns in Michigan (Detroit: Wayne State University Press, 1957). 9-10.

685 Reynolds, Hudson-Mohawk Genealogical and Family Memoirs, 2.

686 "Harrison Geer, Imlay City Optic," c. Feb. 1889, in HGC BHL.

687 "Corr. From J. S. Smith to Chas. M. Sligh, July 9, 1894," in Sligh Family Papers, Box 2. BHL.

688 "Mills kept a scrapbook," Port Huron Times, Oct. 28, 1889, in HGC BHL.

689 "The collector becomes the dispenser," Sun Herald, April 27, 1889, in HGC BHL.

690 Ibid.

691 "a good citizen and Republican," Port Huron Herald, April 27, 1889, in HGC BHL.

692 "The recent experience," Sanilac County Republican, May 2, 1889, in HGC BHL.

693 "dissapointed but not dissatisfied," Sanilac County Republican, May 9, 1889, in HGC BHL.

694 "Geer circumvented Civil Service," Detroit Free Press, July 19, 1889, in HGC BHL.

695 "Geer coaching his favorites," Sun Harold, Aug. 1, 1889, in HGC BHL.

696 "A Disgraceful Condition," Sun Herald, July 7, 1889, in HGC BHL.

697 Ibid.

698 "Civil Service Reform," Detroit Free Press, June 19, 1889, in HGC BHL.

699 "Commissioner Roosevelt's views, Sunday Herald, June 23, 1889," in HGC BHL.

700 "The Commission has no control over, New York Evening Post, June 29, 1998," in HGC BHL.

701 "interview never happened," Port Huron Times, July 1, 1889, in HGC BHL.

702 "He is popular everywhere," Courier-Herald, Saginaw, July 22, 1890, in JMT BHL.

703 Sarasohn and Sarasohn, Political Party Patterns in Michigan.

704 "Our Republican Leader, Biographical Sketch of Hon. James M. Turner." TFS.

705 Sidney Corbett, "The Critic, Aug 23 1890." JMT BHL.

706 "Mt. Clemens County Republicans," Detroit Free Press, August 16, 1890, in JMT BHL.

707 "Patrons of Industry," The Evening News, Detroit, Feb 28, 1890, in JMT BHL.

708 "They nominated Eugene A. Beldon," The Republican, Livingston County, and June 26, 1890, in JMT BHL.

709 "Democrats proposed to beat Turner," Detroit Free Press, August 7, 1890," in JMT BHL.

710 "The General Outlook," State Republican, Lansing, Aug. 26, 1890, in JMT BHL.

711 "state fair passes, Detroit Free Press, Sept. 19, 1890," in JMT BHL.

712 "more charges against Turner," Detroit Journal, Aug. 24, 1890, in JMT BHL.

713 "Turner and the Press," Livingston County Republican, Oct. 23, 1890, in JMT BHL.

714 Sylvester Kinney, "The Detroit Journal is pouring its vials of venom," L'Anse Sentinel, Aug. 12, 1890, in JMT BHL..

715 The State Democrat,Lansing, Aug. 21, 1890, in JMT BHL.

716 "Smears," State Republican, Lansing, Aug. 23, 1890,in JMT BHL.

717 "Mr. Turner's Generocity," State Republican, TFS.

718 "Mr. Turner frankly admits the truth," Gratiot County Republican Leader, Sept. 1890, in JMT BHL.

719 "A Hustling Candidate," Lansing Journal, L. E. Rowley, ed., Aug. 25, 1890, in JMT BHL.

720 "The Turner Camp," New York World, Aug. 26, 1890, in JMT BHL.

721 "All ready for the Fray," The Evening News, Aug. 23, 90, in JMT BHL.

722 "We believe the people," Detroit Tribune, Aug. 26, 1890, in JMT BHL.

723 "Farmer Turner," Detroit Tribune, Aug. 26, 1890, in JMT BHL.

724 "While the nominating speecher," Detroit Tribune, Aug. 29, 1890, in JMT BHL.

725 "Eloquent Nominating Speech," Aug. 29, 1890, in TFS.

726 "Turner is the man," Aug. 28, 1890, in TFS.

727 "A Royal Welcome," State Republican, Lansing, c Aug. 29, 1890, in TFS.

728 "In this sense he is a millionaire," The Miner, Sept. 13, 1890, in JMT BHL.

729 "He is a joyful gentleman," News-Record, Ironwood, Sept. 28, 1890, in JMT BHL.

730 "We had been informed,' Republican Leader, St. Louis, Sept. 18, 1890, in JMT BHL.

731 "Our Next Govenor," Daily Journal, Battle Creek, Oct. 2, 1890, in JMT BHL.

732 "The Charlotte Tribune Supplement," Oct. 1890, in JMT BHL.

733 "Frank L. Dodge taken by Death," Detroit News, Dec. 25, 1829, in TFS.

734 ""Grand Rapids Leader," Lansing Journal, Oct. 3, 1890, in JMT BHL.

735 "To add to his troubles," Telegram, July 7, 1896, in JMT BHL.

736 "Politics in Michigan," Bay City, c.Oct 6, 1890, in JMT BHL.

737 "I state positively," Howard Record, Oct. 23, 1890, in JMT BHL.

738 "We are Downed," Livingston County Republican, Nov. 11, 1890, in JMT BHL.

739 Ibid.

740 Telegran, July 7, 1896.

741 Michigan, "Official Directory and Legislative manual, 1891-92 ".

742 Longyear. 87.

743 "A Few Plain Facts," State Republican, May 12, 1891.

744 "Denies the Statement," State Republican, c May 1890.

745 Stephen Bromley McCracken, State of Michigan: Embracing Sketches of its History (Lansing: W.S. George & Co., 1876). 117.

746 Hazen S. Pingree, Facts and opinions; or, Dangers that beset us (Detroit, Mich.,: F. B. Dickerson Co.,, 1895). 16

Chapter 14

747 MHC, 13. 21.

748 "Grandmother's Kitchen," Ingham County Republican, July 10, 1890, in TFS.

749 Portrait and Biographical Album of Members of the Legislature, Michigan.

750 "Turner-Black, Jan. 29, 1891," in TFS. 252-252

751 "The campaign entailed heavy expenses," Telegran, July 7, 1896, in JMT BHL.

752 Richard Butler Papers (State Archives of Michigan, Department of Natural Resources).

753 Longyear. Reminiscenes. 200

754 . Doc. of Iron Star

755 Ibid; State of Michigan, "Report of Investigation 8, Geology and Magnetic Data for the Northern Crystal Falls Area," (Lansing: State of Michigan Department of Natural Resources, Gelolgical Survey Division, 1970). 12

756 Longyear. 87-88.

757 Howard Longyear, in Corr., 1891 (Marquette Regional History Center, J. M. Longyear Research Library).

758 "blurb, Mayor Pingree's arrests," The State Republican, Aug. 22, 1894.

759 Iron Range & Huron Bay folder (Marquette Regional History Center, J. M. Longyear Research Library).

760 Turner.

761 Ibid.

762 Ibid.

763 Johnson, "In Memory (of John M. Longyear)." 353.

764 Turner, 554.

765 Utley, Michigan as a Province, Territory and State, 4. 209-210

766 Ibid.

767 Ibid., 213.

768 Longyear, Reminiscenses. 88.

769 "Thousands are Suffering," The Mining Journal, Marquette, Dec. 4, 1893.

770 "Minute Book, Nov. 12, 1889-Feb. 18, 1901, B1, F1," in Lansing Industrial Aid Society, (State Archives of Michigan, Department of Natural Resources)., 39

771 Ibid., 48.

772 Ibid., 49-50.

773 Ibid., 52.

774 Ibid., 67.

775 "May Stocking Knaggs," The Literary Century, Vol. II May, 1893, No. 13 Ann Arbor., 411

776 Ibid., 411

777 "Minute Book, Nov. 12, 1889-Feb. 18, 1901, B1, F1." Industrial Aide Society, Lansing, Archives, State of Mich.

778 Ibid., 63-67.

779 Ibid., 10.

780 Ibid., 65.

781 Ibid., 67-79.

782 "Sprindale Farm catalog," 1892, in TFS.

783 State of Michigan, Special Schedule of Agriculture of Michigan Census (1894).

784 E. A. Holden, National Grange in Michigan Souvenir, November 12-22, 1902 (R. Smith Co.).

785 James M. Turner, in Box, "Turner Lands Corr., 1863 -1906" (Marquette Regional History Center, J. M. Longyear Research Library).

786 "Corr. From J. S. Smith to Chas. M. Sligh, July 9, 1894." BHL.

787 "Talk Hunting Community," (http://www.talkhuntin.com/index.php?topic=32495.0).

788 "He is one of the brainiest," Detroit Tribune, April 21, 1894, in JMT BHL.

789 "Pingree," State Republican, Lansing, July 21, 1894, in JMT BHL.

790 Michigan Historical Magazine, Vol., vol. 60 (Michigan Historical Commission, 1976). 44-45; Stocking, Under the Oaks. 108-112

791 Pingree, Facts and opinions; or, Dangers that beset us., 15-17.

792 "An Assault," The Evening News, May 29, 1894, in JMT BHL.

793 "Bliss Out," The Evening News, June, 6, 1894, in JMT BHL.

794 "No Second Term," Cedar Springs, June, 20, 1894, in JMT BHL.

795 Ibid.

796 "In a Rosy Glow," Grand Rapids Democrat, June 18, 1894, in JMT BHL.

797 Ibid.

798 Ibid.

799 "His Honor the Mayor," Lansing Journal, July 16, 1894, in JMT BHL.

800 "For a Soldier," State RepublicaN, Lansing, July 25, 1894, in JMT BHL.

801 "Corr. from James M. Turner to Chas. M. Sligh, July 21, 1894." Sligh Family Papers BHL.

802 "Is a Unique Fight," Detroit Tribune, July 21, 1894, in JMT BHL.

803 "Contemptible Tactics," Lansing State Republican, July 24, 1894, in JMT BHL.

804 "Wayne's Tin Idol," Detroit Evening News, Aug. 2, 1894, in JMT BHL.

805 "The Convention," Lansing State Republican, July 28, 1894, in JMT BHL.

806 "The Convention," Lansing State Republican, July 30, 1894, in JMT BHL.

807 "Pingree Withdraws from the Gubernatorial Race, July 30, 1894," in JMT BHL.

808 Ibid.

809 Ibid.

810 "Political Oratory," State Republican, Aug. 8, 1894, in JMT.

811 "Rah for Everybody," State Republican, Aug. 3, 1894, in JMT BHL.

812 "Political Oratory," State Republican, Aug. 8, 1894.

813 "Gov. Blair Dying," Lansing State Republican, Aug. 4, 1894, in JMT BHL.

814 "Ex-Gov. Blair Death." Jackson Citizen Patriot, August 8, 1894.

815 "Blair funeral," Jackson Citizen Patriot, August 10, 1894.

816 Ibid.

817 "Cal Smith's Bantling," Lansing State Republican, Aug. 11, 1894, in JMT BHL.

818 "Mr. Dodge was warmly greeted," July 5, 1894, in TFS.

819 "Blurb Mr. Dodge speech," July 7, 1894, in TFS.

820 "Democratic Party Platform. Adopted at Chicago," July 9, 1896, in JMT BHL.

821 "Emancipation Day," Jack Daily Citizen July 31, 1894.

822 Ibid.

823 "A Liberated Race", Jackson Citizen Daily, Aug. 1, 94.

824 "blurb on Emancipation Day," Jack Daily Citizen July 28, 1894.

825 Elizabeth Giese Homer, ed. Michigan Women's Suffrage, A Political History (Lansing: MI Political History Society and MI Women's Studies Association, Inc., 1995). 23.

826 "blurb Sojournor Truth W. C. T. U. formed," State Republican, May 13, 1896.

827 J. Geoffrey Moore, "The Memorial Windows" (Lansing: Central United Methodist Church).

828 "They're After Him," State Republican, Feb. 1, 1893.

829 "May Stocking Knaggs." 420.

830 "blurb May Stocking Knagg," State Republican, Jan. 29, 1891.

831 Hopkins,"The History of Lansing Central Union Woman's Christian Temperance Union."

832 "W. C. T. U. Column," State Republican, July 18, 1894.

833 Ibid.

834 "Local Option," State Republican, Aug. 16, 1894.

Chapter 15

835 Emery, Seven Financial Conspiracies which have Enslaved the American People. Quote from Emporia Daily Gazette, no pagination.

836 Pauline Adams and Emma S. Thornton, A populist assault: Sarah E. Van De Vort Emery on American democracy, 1862-1895 (Bowling Green, Ohio: Bowling Green State University Popular Press, 1982). 7-10

837 "Mrs. S. E. V. Emery," The Literary Century, Vol. II May, 1893, No. 13 Ann Arbor. 418.

838 Emery, Seven Financial Conspiracies which have Enslaved the American People.

839 "Mrs. S. E. V. Emery." 418.

840 "Organized Labor," The State Republican, Aug. 11. 1894.

841 "Drew a Big Crowd," The State Republican, Sept. 3, 1894.

842 "Plea for the Poor," The State Republican, Aug. 23, 1894.

843 Ibid.

844 Pingree, Facts and opinions; or, Dangers that beset us. 5-14

845 "Lansing's Next Mayor Clearly Defines His Position", Lansing Republican, Maatch 24, 1895, in TFS.

846 Ibid.

847 John P. Foley, The Jeffersonian Cyclopedia, A Comprehensive Collection of the Views of Thomas Jefferson (New York & London: Funk & Wagnalls Co., 1900).

848 "Nichols Will Run, Lansing Journal," March 29, 1895, in JMT BHL.

849 Ibid.

850 "Without a Bread," Lansing Journal, Mar. 29, 1895.

851 "Slanderous and False," The State Republican, March 30, 1895.

852 "Jas. M. Turner, The Ontonagon Miner, March 30, 1895," in JMT BHL.

853 "Hold Up His Hands," Lansing Journal, April 8, 1895, in JMT BHL.

854 Ibid.

855 The Mining Journal, April 6, 1895, in JMT BHL.

856 Wikipedia contributors, "Lansing Board of Water & Light," http://en.wikipedia.org/w/index.php?title=Lansing_Board_of_Water_%26_Light&oldid=547452857 (Wikipedia, The Free Encyclopedia. , accessed May 5, 2013).

857 "A Busy Life Closed," Lansing Journal, weekly edition,, Oct. 18, 1895.

858 Elizabeth Cady Stanton et al., History of woman suffrage, 1883-1900, Vol 4, vol. 4 (Rochester, N. Y.: Susan B. Anthony : Charles Mann). 756.

859 State of Michigan, "The Report of the Superintendent of Public Instruction of the State of Michigan, 1889," (Department of Public Instruction 1889). 293-305.

860 Bates, Municipal Suffrage for Women in Michigan.

861 Ibid., 763.

862 Stanton et al., History of woman suffrage, 1883-1900, Vol 4, 4. 756.

863 Belle Perry, "Suffrage notice," Charlotte Tribune, March 1891.

864 Bates, Municipal Suffrage for Women in Michigan.

865 Stanton et al., History of woman suffrage, 1883-1900, Vol 4, 4. 762-764.

866 "Blurb Helen P. Jenkins urging women to vote ", The State Republican, Aug. 28, 1991.

867 Belle Perry, "Women's Department Column," Charlotte Tribune, Aug. 30, 1891.

868 "Jackson citizens are considerably excited", Lansing Journal, Aug. 29, 1891.

869 "blurb Mrs. C. C. Bloomfield and Mrs. A. L. Ford," Lansing Journal, Sept. 8, 1891.

870 "Zealous Women," The State Republican, Jan. 23, 1893.

871 "The New Members," The State Republican, March 22, 1893.

872 "Women Cannot Vote," The State Republican, March 22, 1893.

873 "A Detroit Portia," Aurora Daily Express, June 19, 1899

874 Bates, Municipal Suffrage for Women in Michigan. 664-67.

875 "Verily the day of enlightenment dawneth," The State Republican, July 27, 1894.

876 Stanton et al., History of woman suffrage, 1883-1900, Vol 4, 4. 766.

877 Bates, Municipal Suffrage for Women in Michigan. 664.

878 Karolena M. Fox, "History of the Equal Suffrage Movement in Michigan " Michigan History Magazine 1918. 96.

879 Mrs. George McDan, "History of the Mantinee Musicale," 1894-1919, (Lansing: Capitol Area District Library).

880 Floyd Holmden, "The Matinee Musicale, 100 Years of Culture," Lansing Metropolitan, Spring, 1994. 20-23.

881 "Interview by author with John (Jody) Pemberton, May 2004," in TF (Lansing: Turner-Dodge House).

882 "We should think that even such a doughty fighter," Lansing Journal, Feb. 22, 1895.

883 "Hon. James M. Turner," Ionia Express, Feb. 28, 1895, in JMT BHL.

884 Oren Fogg, "A Good Beginning, The State Democrat, Lansing, March 14, 1895," in JMT BHL.

885 "Over 500 voters have signed their Constitution, The Free Press, Detroit, March 20, 1895," in JMT BHL.

886 "Michigan Men for Silver," Chicago Herald, March 23, 1895, in JMT BHL.

887 "Silverites in Town," Chicago Mail, April 13, 1895, in JMT BHL.

888 "The Silver Speech," Owosso Argus, April 24, 1895, in JMT BHL.

889 "Free Silver Clubs," Port Huron News, March 12, 1895, in JMT BHL.

890 "The Silver Speech," Owosso Argus, April 24, 1895.

891 "A Busy Life Closed." LJ, weekly edition, Oct. 18, 1895.

892 Ibid.

893 Ibid.

894 "Pingree depression activites," Detroit Tribune, c1895, in JMT BHL.

895 "Land for the Poor," June 20, 1894, in JMT BHL.

Chapter 16

896 "For Seven Hours the Knights and Their Friends Listened," January 2, 1895.

897 Ibid.

898 "Corr. from James M. Turner to Chas. M. Sligh, January 1896," in Sligh Family Papers, Box 2 BHL.

899 Ibid.

900 "Corr. from Hazen Pingree to Chas. M. Sligh, February 1896," in Sligh Family Papers, Box 2 BHL.

901 Ibid.

902 "Corr. from James M. Turner to Chas. M. Sligh, March 24, 1896," in Sligh Family Papers, Box 2 BHL.

903 "Silver Men are Active," New York Times, June 27,1896, in JMT BHL.

904 "Aid to the Needy," State Republican, Feb. 26, 1896, in TFS.

905 James M. Turner, "Bonds and Lights, Mayor Turner Talks About the Railroads, Lansing Journal, Mar. 16, 1896," in TFS (Lansing1896).

906 "In political matters."

907 James M. Turner, "Letter to the Editor," Detroit Tribune, c June 18, 1896, in TFS.

908 Recorder James Francis Burke, Official Proceeding of the Eleventh Republican National Convention, St. Louis, 1896 (Minneapolis: C. W. Johnson). 96.

909 Ibid., 112-113.

910 "Last Appeal," July 1896,in TFS.

911 "Kidney disease," July 1896, in TFS.

912 "The City Mourns," State Repubican, July 10, 1896, in TFS.

913 Ibid.

914 "Was Sudden! James M. Turner of Lansing Dies at Alma, Lansing, Mich." Special Telegram, July 1896.

915 State Republican, July 8, 1896, in TFS.

916 "Was Sudden! James M. Turner of Lansing Dies at Alma, Lansing, Mich." Special Telegram, July 1896.

917 "Resolutions were Passed, State Republican", in TFS.

918 State of Michigan, "Report of the Secretary of the State Board of Agriculture, July 1, 1898," (Lansing: Robert Smith Printing Co., State Printers and Binders, 1899).

919 "Was Sudden! James M. Turner of Lansing Dies at Alma, Lansing, Mich." Special Telegram, July 1896.

920 Longyear., Reminisences, "James M. Turner."

921 "Union Silver Party," SR, July 16, 1896.

922 "Michigan's Gold Delegation," The State Republican, July 9, 1896.

923 "blurb Chatauqua," The State Republican, July 13, 18, 1896.

924 "Dodge is Chairman," The State Republican, Feb. 27, 1897.

925 "Frank L. Dodge taken by Death," Detroit News, Dec. 25, 1829.

926 "Cost of a campaign," State Republican, July 11, 1896, in TFS.

927 Arthur Chester Millspauh, Party Organization and Machinery in Michigan since 1890 (Baltimore: John Hopkins Press, 1917). 454-455.

928 Ella Lee Rich, "Abby Turner," in Daughters of the American Revolution (Lansing: CADL, 1947).: Frank N. Turner, 452.

929 William Jennings Bryan, The first battle. A story of the campaign of 1896 (Chicago,: W. B. Conkey company, 1896). 556.

930 Ibid., 562.

931 Ibid., 578.

932 Ibid., 610.

933 "Hon. Frank L. Dodge, The Democratic Candidate of the Sixth Congressional District of Michigan," in TFS 1 (Lansing: Turner-Dodge House).

934 MichMarker.com, Michigan Historic Markers Registered Site S0625, Erected 1991 (935 North Washington, Lansing, Ingham County).

935 "The Supervisors," The State Republican, Feb.1, 1898.

936 "Tax System Unjust," The State Republican, Feb. 2, 1898.

937 "Frank L. Dodge taken by Death," Detroit News, Dec. 25, 1829.

938 "Very Modest," The State Republican, Feb. 3, 1898.

939 "Speech to the Supervisors, by Hazen Pingree," The State Republican, Feb. 8, 1898.

940 Ibid.

941 ———, Michigan Historic Markers Registered Site S0625, Erected 1991

942 The Michigan Municipal League, "About the League: History," in http://www.mml.org/newsroom/about_history.html.

943 Turner, N.Fuller, and Society., An Account of Ingham County. 450.

944 "Party Loyalty," State Republican, Jan.19, 1898.

945 Ibid.

946 Michigan. Governor (1897-1900 : Pingree) and Hazen S. Pingree, Ex-augural message of Governor Hazen S. Pingree to the forty-first Legislature of Michigan January, 1901(Lansing, MI: Wynkoop Hallenbeck Crawford Co., 1900).

947 "It Means Fame," The State Republican, Oct.10,1900.

948 ———, Ex-augural message of Governor Hazen S. Pingree to the forty-first Legislature of Michigan January, 1901. 16-17.

949 Henry A. Haigh, "The Michigan Club," Michigan History Magazine, Vol. 4 1922. 546.

950 compiled by Fred. E. Farnsworth, Proceedings of The Fourth Annual Meeting of the Michigan Club (Detroit: Winn & Hammond, 1890). 4.

951 Hazen S. Pingree, Address of welcome of Governor H.S. Pingree delivered at Michigan club banquet, Detroit, Michigan, February 22, 1899. "The duty of the Republican party in the present hour." (Lansing,: R. Smith printing co., state printers and binders, 1899).3-6.

952 Ibid.

953 Ibid., 6-8.

954 "Party Loyalty."

955 "Out of Politics," The State Republican, Jan. 19, 1898.

956 Garrett , Nicole, Theodore Roosevelt visits Lansing, Michigan. Department of Resources, http://www.michigan.gov/dnr/0,4570,7-153-54463_19313_20652_19271_19357-167386--,00.html

Chapter 17

957 "H. H. Smith Obituary," The Saturday Evening Star, May 21, 1898.

958 Durant, 180.

959 "Miss Willard's Ideas, May 4, 1898," in TFS.

960 Holden, National Grange in Michigan Souvenir, November 12-22, 1902.

961 "Brewers are Contesting the State Liquor Law," The State Republican, May 9, 1902.

962 "Mrs. Nation invades Detroit," The State Republican, May 5, 1902.

963 "Saloonists Afraid of Carrie," The State Republican, May 2, 1902.

964 "Saloonkeeper Rose of Ann Arbor Closed His Doors," The State Republican, May 3, 1902.

965 "Mean trick played on Carrie Nation," The State Republican, May 2, 1902.

966 "Mrs. Nation is in Town," The State Republican, May 8, 1902.

967 "Yelling Mob Followed Her," The State Republican, May 8, 1902.

968 "Mrs. Nation Gift to the W.C.T.U.," The State Republican, May 8, 1902.

969 "The Republican," The State Republican, Dec. 5, 1902.

970 Hopkins,"The History of Lansing Central Union Woman's Christian Temperance Union." 8.

971 Ibid.

972 Turner, 336-337.

973 , Lansing State Republican

974 Holden, National Grange in Michigan Souvenir, November 12-22, 1902. 2.

975 Mark Theobald, "Auto Body Co., 1901-1927, " http://www.coachbuilt.com/bui/a/auto_body/auto_body.htm , accessed April 18, 2013.

976 Ibid.

977 Turner, 542-543.

978 Sparrow Health System, "Sparrow Women's Association," in http://www.sparrow.org/sparrow-womens-association.

979 "Interview by author with Roderick McLean, May 2004," in TF (Lansing: Turner-Dodge House).

980 "Whereupon Many Rejoice," State Republican, May 1893, in TFS.

981 Ibid.

982 "How Jackson Does It," Lansing Journal, Oct. 1, 1896.

983 Daboll and Kelley, Past and present of Clinton County, Michigan. 466.

984 Beal, History of the Michigan Agricultural College. 277.

985 "Are Enjoined from Proceeding," State Republican, May 5, 1902.

986 "Lansing, St. Johns and St. Louis Electric R.R.," in TFS.

987 "Highly Important for Lansing, June 4, 1900," in TFS.

988 "Lansing, St. Johns and St. Louis Electric R.R." TFS.

989 Daboll, 467.

990 "Presented with Gold Headed Cane, 1905," in TFS.

991 "Lansing Hall of Fame, 1917," in TFS.

992 Brintnall,"Turner-Dodge Estate Site Analysis and Historical Evaluation."

993 Interview by author with John (Jody) Pemberton, May 2004.

994 Ibid.

995 Virginia Redfern, "Dodge Mansion Once a Happy House, State Journal, Feb. 24, 1974," in TFS.

996 Longyear. 161.

997 "Ripley's Believe it of Not," in TFS.

998 The Farm Journal Illustrated Rural Directory of Ingham County, Michigan, (Philadelphia: Wilmer Atkinson Company, 1916).

999 "Another red letter day, October 1908, Farm Club," in TF (Lansing: Turner-Dodge House).

1000 "Vote for Frank L. Dodge, Democratic Nominee for Congress, pamphlet," in TFS (Lansing: Turner-Dodge House, c1920).

1001 John Archibald Fairle, The Michigan Constitutional Convention, Reprinted from Michigan Law Review, Vol. VI No 7, (May 1908). 5.

1002 Clara Arthur, "When the "Gay Nineties" Saw Women in Sober Earnest."

1003 Ibid., 8-10.

1004 Ibid.

1005 Ibid., 12.

1006 "Wives Defeated the Suffragists," State Republican, Jan. 29, 1902.

1007 Fairle, Michigan Constituional Convention, 1908. 15.

1008 Ibid.,18.

1009 "Detroit as the State Capitol," State Republican, Nov. 2, 1907.

1010 "The Middle Years —1910-1940, Lansing's Woman's Club Centennial Observance, Paper given by Harriet Piatt at the Clubhouse," (Lansing Woman's Club, March 29, 1974).

1011 "Lansing Women Who Win at Polls," Detroit Journal, April 15, 1916.

1012 Darling, City in the Forest. 40

1013 "Marian Turner (Mrs. James Turner) at age 90," in TFS.

1014 Michigan Historical Commission and Michigan Pioneer and Historical Society., Michigan historical collections, 35. iv-v.

1015 ———, Michigan historical collections, 6.

1016 Mevis, Pioneer Recollections, 117.

Index

Dodge, Charles (brother) and Arta, 225

Dodge, Ezra (brother), 225, 286

Dodge, Frank L.: 4th of July 1894 speech, 290; and the County Board of Supervisors, 332-34; as state Democratic Party officer, 329; as co-owner of Springdale Farm, 280; as Legislator, 226; as United States Commissioner, 226; Crane and Dodge law firm, 211; early life of, 225. *See also* electric railroad, Milo K. Dakin, Saginaw mill labor strike

Dodge, William (brother), 225

dogs: deerhound, 17; mastiffs, 247

Douglass, Frederick, 171; in Cazenovia, NY, 16; Lansing visit of, 112

Durant, Samuel, 11, 12, 32

E

Eaton, Frederic. *See* Milo K. Dakin

economy: barter, 44; battle between rich and common people, 317; competition between cities, 32; education as driver of, 73-75; income inequality, 133; Michigan growth in 1870, 143. *See also* Frances Willard on labor and the

education, 121-28, complaints about, 74; log schoolhouse, 10, 15, 73–74; machine shop, 48; Michigan Education Association, 80; Primary School Fund, 117; public local, 73–75, 122; purpose, 73–75; union schools, 74. *See also* Agricultural College (MSU), Boys Reform School, Michigan Female College, Michigan School for the Blind

electric railroad, 353–55

Emancipation Day Celebration: Jackson, 292

Emery, Sarah E., 170, 295, 296-7, 304, 314, and Kansas Equal Suffrage Association, 305; and municipal suffrage, 304, 306; character of, 297; death of, 314–15; Lansing Woman's Club member, 295; *Seven Financial Conspiracies*, 296, 314

Environment: land drainage, 85-86; swamp lands, 116, 200. *See also* trees

F

Farm Club, 358

Farrand, Francis (Dodge), 201

Federal Bank, 25

Felch, Alpheus: and speculators, 39

fire: building of, 6; no matches, 7; smokey fall of 1856, 69; smokey fall of 1871, 154; stick chimney for, 6. *See also* forest fire of 1871

Flint and Pere Marquette Railroad, 229

Flushing: James and Mira Seymour, 22, 31

food: Case gristmill, 49; Frank Blades 36; Seymour Hotel, 45; gristmill, 18; hog and hominy, 19; pancakes, 48; pioneer women cooks, 30; pioneers, 10; price of pioneer's, 9; peculators and, 121; sugar, 138; Turner kitchen, 41

forest fire of 1871, 149; cause of, 146; State Relief Committee, 146; Turner & Case property saved from, 148–49

Foster,Theodore: Boys Reform School, 76-79

Free Silver Clubs, 313

Free Soil Party, 54

Looking Glass River, 5, 7, 10

Lower Town. 34, 38-40, 44, 48, 64, 89. *See also* North Lansing

Luce, Cyrus G., 256, 283, 312

M

Malaria, 4, 84, 86, 117

manufactories, 46–50

Mason, 12, 18, 20, 28, 27–32, 82, 122; Cassius Clay, 99; county seat, 13; travel to Lansing, 36; influence on Lansing, 136; Ingham Co. Democratic Convention at, 97; Jackson and Turner store at, 31; Literary Society, 118; locals first travel to Lansing site, 37; Whig Party convention at, 54

Mason, Stevens T., 25, 27, 55, 116

Matinee Musical Society, 311-312

May, Charles, 119-121

McClelland, Robert, 82

McElroy, James F., 216, 252; and School for the Blind scandal, 265–66; railroad car brakes and couplings, 270

McKinney, John, 99-100, 106

McMillan, James, 251-52, 266, 277, 284; Agricultural College gift by, 248; corporate connections of, 282, 285; machine of, 256, 260, 281, 285; McMillanites, 336; Michigan Club founder, 336; silver issue, 312-313

mechanic. *See* Joab Page

Merchant Princes: Hiram H. Smith and James Turner, 18

Meridian Township, 14, 49, 66

Methodist.; Albion College, 80; anti-slavery policy, 93-94; E. O. Haven, 125; first minister at Lansing site, 34–36; Genesee Wesleyan Conference, NY.; John Kilbourne organizer of, 49; Lansing Christmas Eve, 133, Lansing Ladies Aid Society, 143; role or James Turner as, 42; Turner windows, 292; visits to Turners by ministers of, 42; WCTU, 161; Woman's Foreign Missionary Society, 182. See also L. Anna Ballard, African Methodist Church, Cazenovia Seminary, James Little, Lima Seminary

Mevis, Daniel S.: on founding of Lansing, 32; on Marian Turner, 364

Michigan: 1850 population of, 62,102; Michigan Agricultural Society, 86, 246-47, 260, state fair, 249-51

Michigan Association of Breeders, 327

Michigan Central Railroad, 130, 204; Vanderbilt takeover of, 205

Michigan Club, 336-39

Michigan Condensed Milk Co., 209, 244, 280

Michigan Education Association, 80

Michigan Equal Rights Association: on Austin Blair, 288

Michigan Equal Suffrage Association, 195, 248, 289, 304, 308, 310. *See also* woman's suffrage

Michigan Female College, 75–79, 122–27, 154, 213, Board of Trustees, 81; Gertrude Howe, 181; Harriet Seymour, 180. See L. Anna Ballard, Abigail Rogers

Michigan Historical Commission, 311

Michigan Liquor Dealers Association: oppose woman's suffrage, 310

Michigan Municipal League, 335

Michigan Slate Company, 217–18

The Turner-Dodge House

City of Lansing, Parks & Recreation, Leisure Division
100 E. North Street in Old Town
http://www.lansingmi.gov/tdodge